Beauty Therapy Fact File

4th Edition

Susan Cressy

Beauty Therapy Fact File by
Cressy, Susan

www.heinemann.co.uk

✓ Free online support
✓ Useful weblinks
✓ 24 hour online ordering

01865 888058

Heinemann
Inspiring generations

Heinemann Educational Publishers
Halley Court, Jordan Hill, Oxford OX2 8EJ
Part of Harcourt Education

Heinemann is the registered trademark of
Harcourt Education Limited

First published 2004

09 08 07 06 05 04
10 9 8 7 6 5 4 3 2 1

British Library Cataloguing in Publication Data is available
from the British Library on request.

ISBN 0 435 45142 1

Cover design by Wooden Ark Studio

Designed by Hardlines

Produced by AMR Ltd

Original illustrations © Harcourt Education Limited, 2004

Illustrated by Art Construction, Chartwell Illustrators, David Woodroffe

Printed in the UK by Bath Press Ltd

Cover photo: © Getty

Picture research by Sally Smith

Websites
Please note that the examples of websites suggested in this book were up to
date at the time of writing. It is essential for tutors to preview each site before
using it to ensure that the URL is still accurate and the content is appropriate.
We suggest that tutors bookmark useful sites and consider enabling students to
access them through the school or college intranet.

Contents

Dedication

I would like to dedicate this book to my Father for his inspiration, advice and encouragement.

Acknowledgements

I would like to thank the following people.

My husband Richard and my children Hannah, Sarah and Thomas for their constant support and encouragement.

All my students, past and present, who provide me with the inspiration to continue writing.

My friends and colleagues, Emma Fairfield and her student Lauren Rathbone for hair and make-up, Sara Greenfield, for the step-by-step bridal make-up, models, Suki Kaur, Sinead Murray and Christina Ashman. Debbie Pennington, for helping with the false nail techniques. For their valuable contributions to the photo shoot, Faye Ramjaun, Jois O'Kell, Jayne Salt, Martine Cale, Judith Provan, Gill Broughton, Judith Hughes, Kathleen Fitzgerald and Fiona Rogers, my children Sarah and Thomas and my wonderful students Michelle Maxey, Sam Davies, Michelle Rose, Jenny Wong, April Harrison, Bridget Qashoua, Sophia Yiannoukalis, Louise Slaney and Michaela Manley.

South Trafford College Beauty Therapy and Holistic Department for providing the venue for professional photographs.

Daniel Lee, South Trafford College Marketing Department, for his never ending patience and great photographs.

Jane Martin, proprietor of be ..., and Janine Corciulo of Lido's Altrincham for supplying illustrations and photographs; Tracey and Marianne of KI Day Spa, Altrincham, Cheshire for their case study and photograph; Sharon Sweetham for a photograph.

For supplying photographs, Elemis Ltd, Pevonia UK Ltd, Finders International Ltd and Spa Illuminata.

Gareth Boden and Tony Poole for professional photographs.

Pen Gresford, Gillian Burrell, the team at Heinemann and Susan Ross for their enthusiasm and essential contributions.

Susan Cressy

The author and publisher would like to thank the following individuals and organisations for permission to reproduce photographs:

Gareth Boden – all other photos, Corbis – pages ii, 65 (middle), 69, 81, 83, 98, 114 (bottom), 193, 199, 201(left), 280, 439 (right); Depilex – pages 39; Elemis – pages 209 (middle), 229; Frevila – pages 194; Getty Images - pages iii (left); Getty Images UK/Darren England – pages 65 (right), 99; Getty Images UK/Imagebank – pages 189; Getty Images UK/PhotoDisc – pages 68; Getty Images UK/Stone – pages 103 (right), 196, 277; Getty Images UK/Taxi – pages 191 (left); Getty Images UK/Thinkstock – pages 112; Daniel Lee – pages iv, 45, 92, 127 (middle), 147, 150, 151, 152, 261, 265, 268, 269, 291 (middle), 314, 321, 430, 451, 452; Derek Murray – page 418; HBEC Ltd/Gary Pudy – page 263; Lidos – pages 417 (right), 452 (top); Mediscan – pages 110 (top left), 111 (top left, middle left, bottom left), 113, 114 (top left); Red Frost/be..healthy and beautiful – pages 417 (left), 423, 427, 439 (left); Science Photo Library – pages 22, 23, 24, 25, 26, 109, 110 (middle left, bottom left, top right, middle right, bottom right), 111 (middle left, top right, bottom right), 115, 123, 279, 282; Sharon Sweetman – pages 419; Spa Illuminata – pages 8, 442, 449; Totally UK – page 203; Wellcome Medical Photo Library – page 302

Every effort has been made to contact copyright holders of material reproduced in this book. Any omissions will be rectified in subsequent printings if notice is given to the publishers.

Preface

Having been in the beauty therapy industry for more than 25 years, I have become aware of the need for a book which includes the subjects covered in the syllabus of every awarding body and also provides additional material in order to enhance the therapist's knowledge.

It is important for the student to become commercially competent and familiar with the constantly changing trends in beauty therapy, so this fourth edition includes material for the new beauty therapy standards to be implemented in 2004. Also included is a comprehensive list of professional bodies and associations who provide an essential service to all in the beauty therapy profession.

Beauty therapists have to acquire a great deal of knowledge when undertaking any course. Whether you are studying on a full-time programme in beauty therapy or part time, learning one of the individual skills which form part of a beauty therapy qualification, this book will provide you with the essential underpinning knowledge you require to help you achieve your objective.

Once qualified, it is essential to continue with your professional development. This may involve embarking on further courses to achieve your chosen qualification, post-graduate training, management training or starting your own business, and it is important to have a source of reference to help you on the way. This book will provide that reference. It is an invaluable guide to the principles and practices of beauty therapy covering all aspects of the subject important to both the student and practitioner.

It has been my intention to produce a book which will appeal to all ages and levels of ability, providing a comprehensive and factual source of reference for teachers, students and practising beauty and holistic therapists. In fact, anyone who has an interest in the world of health and beauty.

This book is the only one of its kind to cover all levels of S/NVQs and to include the critical additional material to expand and reinforce knowledge. Written in easy-to-read sections, it will assist students in their studies, aid in revision for assessment and provide an easy source of reference for those returning to the profession or refreshing their technical knowledge.

Students studying for the following qualifications will find the *Beauty Therapy Fact File* especially useful:

* City and Guilds of London Institute (CGLI)
* VTCT who also offer international awards on behalf of VAI:
* Vocational Awards International (VAI)
* International Health and Beauty Council (IHBC)
* International Institute of Health and Holistic Therapies (IIHHT)
* International Therapy Examination Council (ITEC)
* Confederation of International Beauty Therapy and Cosmetology (CIBTAC)
* Comité International d'Esthétique et de Cosmétologie (CIDESCO)
* BTEC.

Susan Cressy
January 2004

'Beauty therapy', the very words conjure up many wonderful images:

* A sun soaked beach in the Maldives, under the setting sun, a massage therapist provides a relaxing aromatherapy treatment on a canopied couch in the shade, the scent of exotic flowers floating on the cooling breeze.
* A glamorous nail clinic in Los Angeles, catering for movie stars, models, politicians and tourists alike, all of whom have come to experience the best manicure and pedicure in the world.
* The luxury spa in a five-star hotel, offering a tranquil haven in a bustling city centre, with an intimate maze of treatment rooms providing head-to-toe beauty in a modern and stylish setting.
* The old country house now bustling with activity, young and old, all with a mission to reshape their bodies and change their lives.
* The beauty therapist on a cruise ship sailing to Alaska, round the Caribbean, Africa or the Mediterranean, providing therapies for holiday makers.

A therapist providing aromatherapy massage

If any of these scenarios appeal to you, all of them experienced first hand by some of my many former students, then beauty therapy is definitely the career for you!

The opportunities for employment are considerable compared with those available when I began my career in beauty some 30 years ago! Beauty therapy training will provide you with the many skills that are required to enable you to work in one of the fastest growing and diverse of industries, to travel the world working in the most exotic locations providing wonderful treatments and meeting many interesting people.

There are also many opportunities for those who would like to establish a career while looking after a young family as it will provide the flexibility of working part time or being self-employed. You can specialise in particular therapies, work with the medical profession or even open your own business.

There are many specialist areas in beauty therapy training and there are different educational paths that you may choose to take depending on your particular interest. You may become:

* a beauty therapist
* a spa therapist
* a massage therapist
* a nail specialist
* a make-up specialist
* a holistic therapist.

Career opportunities

Beauty salons

Therapists will practise all facial and body treatments in a professional beauty salon providing a sound base for progressing to other more specialised jobs and even to consider starting your own business. Working for a large organisation will have the benefits of a regular income, working with other professionals and learning from other members of the team. It also provides the opportunity for promotion and progression to a more senior or management level. It is possible to start at ground level working as a therapist, proving yourself competent in practical skills and showing your ability to work as part of a successful team, then taking on a supervisory role before becoming a manager. The next stage is area manager when you could find yourself responsible for several salons or spas and this could lead to an operational management position when you could play a part in setting up new ventures.

The experience you gain will be varied and you will learn how to sell products, keep records, supervise other members of staff, manage a salon and most importantly, please the client and promote the business.

Health farms

The type of work on a health farm is similar to that of a beauty salon, but the hours can be much longer and there is more emphasis on body treatments and weight reduction. The therapist will also work closely with dieticians and fitness instructors and, if qualified to do so, take exercise classes, which may include yoga, aerobics, aqua aerobics and jogging.

Spas offer a combination of beauty therapies

Spas

The treatments offered in spas are a combination of holistic massage therapies, water therapies, often using products that are derived from elements of the sea and other natural ingredients, as well as beauty treatments for both body and skin care. Spas abroad are a favourite holiday destination and urban spas are now becoming popular as day retreats in city centres.

Health and leisure centres

Many leisure clubs now offer the services of a beauty salon or spa providing a wide variety of treatments, often to complement the fitness aspect of a health club.

Cruise liners

All treatments are now available on cruise liners, but therapists are normally required to gain at least two years' experience before they are accepted. The hours are long and it is essential that therapists are experts in their field, flexible, able to use initiative and have excellent selling skills. It provides an ideal opportunity to travel and work with other therapists from around the world.

Airlines

Some relaxing treatments are available on some airlines and there are many salons located at major airports around the world.

Make-up artist

The make-up artist can work in a salon, with a professional photographer, in a model agency or freelance. Television or film work is highly competitive and quite often the therapist will be required to serve a long apprenticeship, but the work is interesting even though the hours are long. Theatres may employ make-up artists but probably on a part-time basis or in a self-employed capacity. The job itself involves a great deal of travelling, so a car is an essential. Set-up costs will include a make-up and hair kit, insurance to cover loss or damage of the kit and personal indemnity insurance, business cards and a working wardrobe. A computer is also an important resource as many photographers provide images on disk and having a website would be a good means of promotion. The drawback to being a self-employed make-up artist is finding a good agent and then giving the agent 20 per cent of your earnings for the service you provide. It is, however, an essential business resource for a freelance make-up artist hoping to work for the larger more prestigious companies.

A make-up artist at work

Make-up and skin care consultant

Cosmetics companies like to employ beauty therapists selling cosmetics in a retail environment, as their background knowledge is an asset when selling make-up and skin care ranges within a store. There is also the opportunity for promotion and to become an area representative for the company, responsible for many retail outlets.

Remedial make-up practitioner

This involves working in conjunction with a dermatologist or in a hospital, teaching people how to apply camouflage make-up skilfully to conceal scars and blemishes, skin care maintenance and make-up application after plastic surgery.

Dermatology/cosmetic surgery clinic

There are now many treatments offered in cosmetic surgery clinics, which do not require surgery. Because of the extensive knowledge therapists have concerning skin and beauty requirements, they are ideal people to present the services available in the clinics to other therapists and to the general public. They may also help with skin care and post-operative advice to clients who may never have worn or shown an interest in make-up before because of a problem that has now been corrected.

Beauty journalism

Writing articles or columns for magazines and newspapers requires a thorough, up-to-the minute knowledge of the industry. With this knowledge and the ability to write informative and interesting articles, you could also help to produce information booklets and brochures for manufacturers.

Teaching

It is important to gain as much industrial experience as possible before going on a teacher-training course. Teaching can then be full time or part time while still pursuing other interests within the beauty field.

It requires commitment, enthusiasm, good organisation skills and the ability to work as part of a team, communicating effectively with people of all ages and abilities.

A training session

Franchising

Taking out a franchise to sell products such as skin care, or offer a specialist service such as laser hair removal, provides therapists with a well-known name to trade under, training, the continuing guidance of a large organisation and the advantage of independence and self-employment. The risks are not quite as great when selling a tried and tested product and the franchise operator provides technical help and marketing support.

Technical representative

There are many companies producing beauty therapy equipment, professional skin and body care ranges as well as make-up. They employ qualified beauty therapists to demonstrate all their products to colleges and potential buyers. They also provide a follow-up service presenting new equipment and products and giving specialist training when necessary. Essential qualities are enthusiasm, knowledge, excellent communication and interpersonal skills.

Mobile therapist

This is an ideal way of providing beauty therapy services without the overheads of business premises and many people prefer treatments in the comfort of their home. The largest capital outlay would be a car, but there are limitations to the services you may offer as it would be difficult to carry a great deal of equipment. It is important to gain experience first in an established business and choose carefully the treatments you will offer, sometimes specialising in a particular treatment, such as aromatherapy, as it entails carrying only a minimum amount of equipment – a portable couch, towels and oils.

Nail technician

This is a specialist service which has grown in popularity in recent years. The nail technician can work in all types of salon, in sales, in the fashion and media industry, as a mobile or home-based business or in training.

For more information, visit www.susan-cressy.com. Whatever your career choice, I do hope that this book will contribute in some small way to your professional development and assist you in providing the best treatments possible to the many clients you will treat in the coming years. I hope that you enjoy using this book as much as I have enjoyed developing and writing it and I wish you every success in your future career.

Susan Cressy
January 2004

Professional practice

* The therapist and reception

* Client consultation

* Contraindications

* Health and safety

* Electrical science

Introduction

Clients are becoming far more discerning when it comes to choosing a salon or spa. When clients visit a salon they will have specific hopes and expectations. They may be looking for a peaceful oasis of calm to recharge their batteries, or they may be making a flying visit in their lunch hour for a short treatment. Whatever the reason and however long clients stay, their visit must be the best it possibly can be.

Beauty therapists are professionals and professional practice is an important aspect of the service you are providing whether you are part of a large team in a multinational company, a partner in a small business or a self-employed sole trader. The most successful salons with a reputation for excellence provide a professional service of the highest standards.

Quality must be evident in all aspects of the business. You will be expected to present a professional appearance and to provide high quality treatments. You must treat the client with courtesy and respect, provide a relaxing environment that is clean and safe while making the client feel comfortable and welcome.

The beauty industry is growing rapidly and there are more opportunities open to the therapist than ever before. The types of business vary greatly, from small suburban salons catering for the needs of a community or niche market, to large multinational companies offering their service nationally or worldwide. The key to any business's success is a quality service provided in a highly professional environment.

Professionalism must be maintained in all aspects of the business and includes:

* the staff employed
* the treatments offered
* the working environment
* the care of the client.

The therapist

Qualities

A beauty therapist has the opportunity to develop a close, personal relationship with clients that may go on for many years. In some cases, you may become the therapist to several generations in one family. Initially, to help in establishing this relationship it is important to have the following qualities:

* **The ability to communicate** – your communication skills are important as you will be dealing with people of all ages, both sexes, many different temperaments and personalities. You must learn when to remain quiet, for example during a relaxing facial or aromatherapy massage, when the client expects you to chat and when he or she just wants you to listen.
* **Friendliness** – to make people feel welcome and at ease.
* **Sincerity** – always put the best interests of the client first.
* **Honesty** – never mislead clients or give them unrealistic expectations.
* **Cheerfulness** – to relax the client and promote a pleasant atmosphere.
* **Politeness** – treat all clients with respect no matter how difficult they may be.

* **Discretion** – the client must feel secure in the knowledge that any personal information or anything that has been said in confidence will not be passed on.
* **Approachable** – helps to put clients at ease, particularly when they are new, and this allows them to communicate their requirements and feel able to confide in you.
* **A good listener** – your listening skills are important as clients often like to talk about their lives and problems. Unburdening themselves in this way is often as therapeutic as the treatment you are providing. Learn to listen and sympathise and clients will appreciate this.
* **Highly skilled** – achieving a qualification is important, but changes in the beauty industry will require you to continue to develop your professional skills to keep pace with current trends and innovations.

Appearance

It is important to present a professional, courteous and warm image to your clients, to inspire confidence, provide reassurance and make them feel welcome. Your initial contact with clients may help them to decide whether to become loyal and regular clients or to take their business elsewhere. The salon's management will

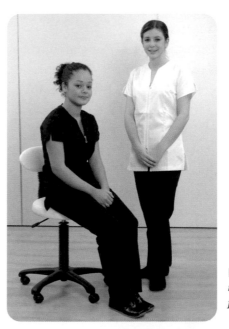

Figure 1.1 *A beauty therapist should dress professionally*

set standards in appearance, hygiene and conduct and it is the duty of the employee to maintain these standards.

As a therapist, your appearance must be professional at all times. Many salons have a particular image that they wish to portray and this is often reflected in the uniform that the therapist will wear. Uniform should always be clean and well pressed.

Comfortable low-heeled shoes, preferably with a covered toe to prevent injury to the foot, will help to maintain the correct posture during treatment.

The minimum amount of jewellery should be worn. Small stud earrings and a wedding ring are acceptable, but watches should be removed during treatment. Some salon owners supply staff with fob watches that may be attached to their uniform.

It is important to look neat and tidy with clean, well-groomed hair. If your hair is below chin length, it should be tied back so that it does not fall into the eyes or touch the client during treatment.

Make-up should be well applied and discreet so that it looks good even in warm working conditions. There are many types of false tan available and this, if applied well, will give you a healthy glow without the need for foundation. However, it is advisable to use a false tan only on a clear skin as blemishes will require camouflage.

Perfume if worn should not be over powering. If the salon has a retail fragrance line, it is a good idea to wear one as it could help to make a sale.

Therapists should have short, well-manicured nails, which allow treatments to be performed effectively and hygienically. Nail enamel should not be worn as it may become chipped during treatment and the client may be allergic to it. The exception to this would be the nail technician as the appearance of her nails is an important part of selling the treatment.

Your personal hygiene is also most important as you are working in close proximity to your clients. Bathe or shower daily, use an antiperspirant, wash hair regularly, clean teeth morning and night and after eating and use a breath freshener when required. Avoid smoking during working hours as cigarette smoke leaves an odour on your clothing.

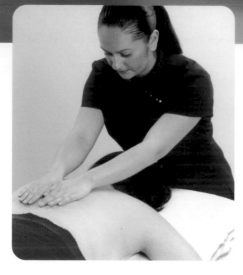

Figure 1.2
Personal hygiene is important when working in close proximity to the client.

Behaviour

The therapist must act in a professional manner towards clients, colleagues, suppliers and competitors. When treating clients always give them your full attention and ensure the treatment provided is appropriate. Do not discuss your personal problems, avoid controversial topics of conversation and do not gossip about other clients or colleagues.

It is essential to cooperate with colleagues, provide support and work as a reliable and effective member of the team. You will need to be hard working and conscientious and be able to use your initiative in all aspects of work. You should be open and honest in communication with management and show a willingness to learn, improve skills and continue professional development.

Remember, always be ethical in your behaviour by respecting other therapists and following the code of conduct laid down by the professional association to which you are affiliated (see below). (For a list of professional associations, see Glossary of professional associations and organisations at the end of this book.)

Code of ethics

Many professional associations and organisations will have their own code of ethics. This is a set of guidelines that the association's members are expected to follow to ensure that clients or consumers are protected from improper practice. The code consists of rules and regulations, which set out the conduct that the association expects of its members and establishes acceptable practices.

The code also sets out professional standards of behaviour for its members towards:

* other members of the organisation
* members of the public and clients
* other professional therapists
* members of other professional organisations
* colleagues within the industry.

In general, all professional therapists should:

* comply with statute law and local bylaws
* apply treatments for which they are qualified
* not treat a client who may be contraindicated
* consult with the client's medical practitioner when necessary
* maintain client confidentiality
* treat colleagues with respect
* not criticise other businesses
* not deliberately poach clients or staff from a competitor.

The reception

This is a very important part of the business because the client has to enter through the reception or make an enquiry over the telephone, which is normally situated in the reception. Clients' first impressions are lasting ones, so these must be good to ensure that they feel comfortable and at ease when arriving for treatment.

The decor should be attractive, relaxing and inviting so that it:

* reflects the image of the salon
* makes the new client feel at ease
* helps an existing client to feel at home
* encourages potential clients passing the salon to come in and try the treatments on offer.

Example of a code of practice for the beauty therapist

The beauty therapist should:

* be proficient in the practice of beauty therapy for the benefit of the client, working in a competent manner and within the limits of the training received
* not carry out any medical treatment or give injections
* ensure the comfort and welfare of the client at all times
* develop a professional client-therapist relationship, ensure client confidentiality, except where disclosure is required by law, and never discuss one client with another
* respect all the religious, political and social views of the client
* maintain accurate and up-to-date client records
* provide accurate details of salon treatments

* report infectious disease to the appropriate authority and advise clients to seek medical advice when necessary
* cooperate with medical practitioners, health care professionals and other complementary therapists
* not discredit other therapists or attract business unfairly in an unprofessional manner
* constantly update the skills required and continue their professional development in all areas
* provide insurance against public liability and malpractice
* adhere to the local by-laws in relation to the business.

Professional practice

Role of the receptionist

The receptionist should be:

* welcoming to all clients, both regular and first time
* helpful – she will need to attend to the client's needs, at the same time ensuring that she books appointments that will also suit the therapists
* patient – she will probably have to deal with awkward clients, overworked therapists and at the same time carry out the day-to-day duties and responsibilities of the reception
* pleasant and courteous – she will set the tone for the rest of the salon
* knowledgeable and able to answer any questions clients may have concerning treatments, prices, timings, special requirements, offers available, retail products, salon procedures and policies
* flexible and able to cope with problems as they occur or refer them to the appropriate member of staff when it may be outside the limits of her own authority
* a good team player liaising with all members of staff and the management
* organised – there are many different tasks that will require attention throughout the day
* a good time manager, both her own and others.

Figure 1.3 *The reception area should provide a good first impresssion*

Duties of the receptionist

The receptionist's duties include:

* answering the telephone
* booking appointments
* maintaining salon records
* using the till and processing payments
* welcoming clients
* dealing with problems when clients arrive late and appointments have to be re-arranged
* selling retail products.

Answering the telephone

The receptionist must have a thorough knowledge of all the treatments on offer and the prices charged. This will allow her to answer any queries made over the telephone, which should be situated in a quiet place so that full attention may be given to the caller. The receptionist should speak clearly so that there is no misunderstanding and the caller must always be referred to by his or her name.

When answering the telephone greet the caller in a friendly and courteous way, at the same time telling the caller the name of the business or person he or she is speaking to, for example, 'Good morning, Beauty Retreat, Sarah speaking, how may I help you?'.

The enquiry should be dealt with in an interested and helpful way making sure that all the information the caller requires is given. If the caller's query cannot be answered immediately, then he or she should be asked politely to hold while another member of staff who may be able to help is found. If this is not possible, a written record of the call must be made so that someone can ring back with the relevant information later in the day. The information to record includes:

* the name and telephone number of the caller
* the name of the person the message is for
* the date and time of the message
* brief details of the enquiry or message
* the name of the person taking the call.

There are clients who have a habit of cancelling appointments at short notice or just not turning up. It is a good idea to confirm their appointment by telephone the day before and the client will either cancel then, giving the opportunity to re-book the appointment, or he or she will feel obliged to attend.

There should be an up-to-date telephone book close to the phone and the clients' record cards with their telephone numbers clearly marked if computer records are not available.

Figure 1.4 *The reception is an important part of the business*

Booking appointments

An efficient booking system will make good use of the therapist's time. Each therapist will have her own column or page and a certain length of time will be booked according to the treatment the client is having. An appointment book with 15-minute or half-hour blocks is essential and it is advisable to book appointments in a regular order from the beginning of the day to the end. If a therapist is busy all morning and a client rings for an appointment, then it is more efficient to book the appointment in the first available slot after lunch rather than later in the afternoon.

Make sure that regular clients' appointments are put in the appointment book as the new pages for each month are put in. This will avoid any problems that will occur if their appointment slot is given away, particularly if they are having a course of treatments such as slimming or special facials. Staff holidays should also be

entered as soon as they are confirmed so the client can be told immediately if the therapist he or she has asked for will be available.

Take the telephone number of new clients when booking an appointment in case you need to contact them for any reason, as there will not be an existing record card available. It is advisable to use a pencil when completing the appointment sheet so that changes can be made easily. Write legibly, confirm the details with the client and, if the booking is being made when the client is at the salon, provide him or her with an appointment card containing all the relevant details.

A computer is now becoming an essential part of good business practice. It will help in the day-to-day running of the business, saving valuable time for the staff to use elsewhere. The reception is the centre of the business and it should have an up-to-date system with the most appropriate software package. Such a system can improve the efficiency of all business practice from booking appointments to maintaining stock levels. A computerised appointment system will indicate which members of staff are available to provide treatments and also show room availability. This will allow each therapist's time to be used efficiently and ensure the most appropriate treatment room is used.

Maintaining salon records

In a small business with no computer the receptionist should coordinate the storage and retrieval of record cards for other staff members and ensure that they are kept safely in accordance with the Data Protection Act. Having a computer eliminates the need to keep boxes and files full of client record cards. Maintaining detailed records is useful for any organisation as it provides instant access to a bank of information and helps a business to monitor its activities regularly.

Detailed records of products used for treatments may be kept on a client database, and this will allow all members of staff to have instant access to the information without having to hunt through hundreds of well-worn cards. This makes for a more efficient service and as long as details are regularly updated, useful information will not be mislaid.

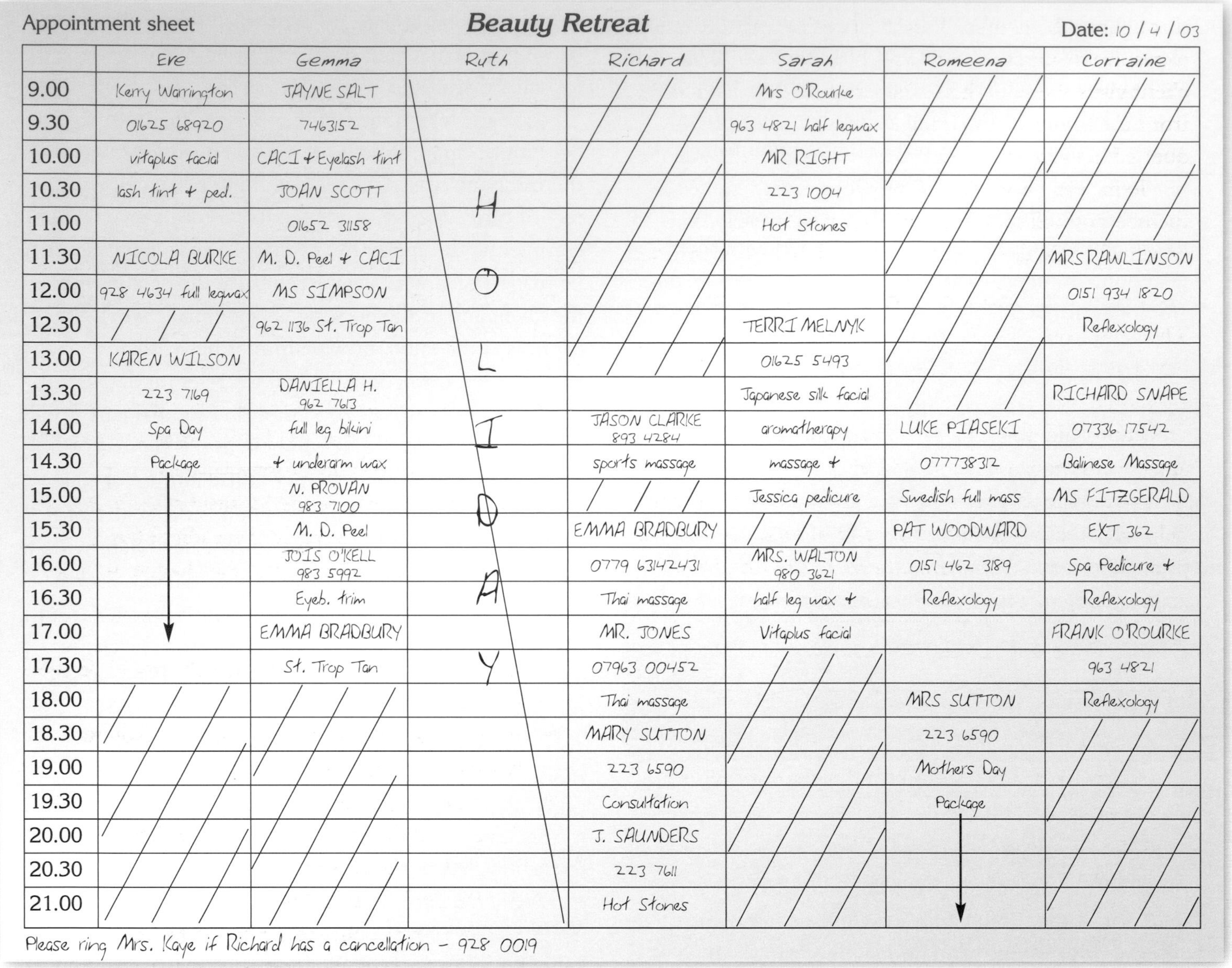

	Eve	Gemma	Ruth	Richard	Sarah	Romeena	Corraine
Appointment sheet				**Beauty Retreat**		Date: 10 / 4 / 03	
9.00	Kerry Warrington	JAYNE SALT			Mrs O'Rourke		
9.30	01625 68920	7463152			963 4821 half legwax		
10.00	vitaplus facial	CACI + Eyelash tint			MR RIGHT		
10.30	lash tint + ped.	JOAN SCOTT	H		223 1004		
11.00		01652 31158			Hot Stones		
11.30	NICOLA BURKE	M. D. Peel + CACI	O				MRS RAWLINSON
12.00	928 4634 full legwax	MS SIMPSON					0151 934 1820
12.30		962 1136 St. Trop Tan			TERRI MELNYK		Reflexology
13.00	KAREN WILSON		L		01625 5493		
13.30	223 7169	DANIELLA H. 962 7613			Japanese silk facial		RICHARD SNAPE
14.00	Spa Day	full leg bikini	I	JASON CLARKE 893 4284	aromatherapy	LUKE PIASEKI	07336 17542
14.30	Package	+ underarm wax		sports massage	massage +	077738312	Balinese Massage
15.00		N. PROVAN 983 7100	D		Jessica pedicure	Swedish full mass	MS FITZGERALD
15.30		M. D. Peel		EMMA BRADBURY		PAT WOODWARD	EXT 362
16.00		JOIS O'KELL 983 5992	A	0779 63142431	MRS. WALTON 980 3621	0151 462 3189	Spa Pedicure +
16.30		Eyeb. trim		Thai massage	half leg wax +	Reflexology	Reflexology
17.00	↓	EMMA BRADBURY	Y	MR. JONES	Vitaplus facial		FRANK O'ROURKE
17.30		St. Trop Tan		07963 00452			963 4821
18.00				Thai massage		MRS SUTTON	Reflexology
18.30				MARY SUTTON		223 6590	
19.00				223 6590		Mothers Day	
19.30				Consultation		Package	
20.00				J. SAUNDERS			
20.30				223 7611		↓	
21.00				Hot Stones			

Please ring Mrs. Kaye if Richard has a cancellation - 928 0019

Figure 1.5 *An appointment sheet*

It will be evident from computer records if regular clients have not been in for some time and the receptionist can then contact them and encourage them to return. There will also be a record of what home care products clients are using and when they require new supplies. Clients are always pleased when you show a personal interest and inform them of special offers on products that they use.

Analysis of the data recorded by the computer will allow the salon to see at a glance the most popular treatments and seasonal trends, allowing the business to plan for change. Computer records will also highlight your busiest periods and may indicate a need for flexibility in opening times. An efficient computer system will collate information about clients each time they attend for treatment or make a purchase. It will provide a history of individual clients, their personal details, the treatments they have, the purchases they make, the frequency of attendance and appointment times. This information although confidential can be used to good effect.

Software programmes can also be used to analyse client information and evaluate their motivation and suitability for treatment and then track their progress throughout the course. This information may also help to resolve disputes over courses of treatments. When the client visits the salon his or her treatment is deducted from the number remaining on the course. If this is queried, a list of treatment dates can be printed out.

To increase protection of the data recorded individual members of staff should be given their own password, which will only allow access to certain levels of information.

Using the till and processing payments

The receptionist will normally be responsible for taking payment from clients, but each individual therapist should be familiar with all methods of payment. A procedure laid down by the management should prevent any confusion or misunderstanding.

Processing payments using a computerised till will help with the cashing up at the end of each day and will provide immediate information about the number of clients, daily turnover, product sales and retail sales.

Procedure for processing payment

1   Make a record. The use of a computerised or electronic till provides an efficient method of taking money and recording sales. Numbered bills are an alternative and should include the following:
    * the name of the therapist
    * the date
    * all treatments
    * all retail sales
    * sundries, e.g. tea, coffee, lunch
    * other details, e.g. discount
    * total amount.
2   Inform the client. State clearly the total amount and show the client the itemised bill.
3   Accept payment. This may be cash, cheque, credit card, debit card or gift voucher.
4   Finalise the process. If the client is paying cash, count out the change, hand it to the client and place any notes in the till. If payment is made by another method, follow the correct procedure (see below).

Methods of payment

Cash

Make sure that notes are not forgeries by checking the water-marked picture of the Queen's head, the metallic strip running through the note, or by using an ultraviolet detector machine. Always count the change into the client's hand before placing notes into the till; this prevents any confusion about the denomination of note the client has given you and the client can check that he or she is receiving the correct change.

Cheque

A cheque is simply a written instruction signed by the account holder (drawer) to the bank telling it to pay a specified sum of money to a particular person or business (payee). It may be used instead of cash. A cheque should only be accepted if the client has a cheque guarantee card. Make sure the cheque includes the following:
* the date
* the correct written amount, which should be the same as the figures
* the payee's name – the business or person to whom the cheque is payable
* signature of the client.

If there are any alterations, make sure they have been initialled by the person writing the cheque.

A cheque guarantee card is issued as a safeguard to anyone who accepts a cheque for goods or services supplied and will guarantee payment up to a certain amount. When presented with a cheque guarantee card the receptionist must:
* check that the specimen signature on the card corresponds with the signature on the cheque
* ensure the cheque has been signed in the receptionist's presence
* write the card number on the reverse side of the cheque
* ensure the value on the cheque does not exceed the limit on the card
* ensure the sort code on the card matches the sort code on the cheque.
* ensure the expiry date on the card is valid.

Figure 1.6 *When accepting payment by cheque the receptionist must always check the client's cheque guarantee card*

Clients will normally present a crossed cheque. This is the most commonly used as it is safer than an open cheque. There are several types of crossing on a cheque:

* 'A/C payee only' may be written in the crossing to ensure that the money is paid into the account named on the cheque. It may not be endorsed and signed over to another account.

* The name and address of a specific branch of a bank may be written in the crossing to ensure the money may only be paid into that particular branch.

An open cheque has no crossing at all so the person to whom the cheque is payable could either pay the cheque into an account or take it into the bank and obtain the cash. If the cheque was stolen, it could be cashed by anybody posing as the payee.

Debit card

This method of payment eliminates the need for cash or cheques. Any business that provides this service will require a special terminal through which the card will be swiped. Duplicated receipts are signed and one copy is give to the client and the other copy retained by the salon. As long as there are sufficient funds in the client's account, payment will be authorised by the bank via this computerised system. This card may also be used as a cheque guarantee card.

Credit card

This is a popular method of paying for goods or services without using cash, as it is a form of credit given to a person by the credit card company. Accounts will be sent out monthly and may either be paid in full, thus incurring no interest payments or paid in instalments, thus incurring interest on the balance outstanding. To accept credit cards as a means of payment, the business must enter into an agreement with the credit card company who will set limits on payment. A sign should be displayed prominently in the salon to inform clients that payment can be made with a credit card and indicating clearly those that are accepted. Always check the expiry date is valid and the cardholder's signature matches that on the card.

If a computerised terminal is used, the receptionist simply swipes the client's card. The details are read and a duplicate receipt is produced, one for the client and one for the salon's records.

A manual credit card machine used by many small salons, uses triplicate receipts and is worked by placing the credit card in the correct position with the triplicate receipt on top. You must then push the handle across the receipt and back, firmly, to ensure that details are clearly recorded on all three copies. The client receives the top copy, the salon retains one and the third is sent to the credit card company. There are several types of credit card, each with their own stationery, and they should be filled in using a ballpoint pen. The client must be asked to check the details before signing and the receptionist must check the client's signature is the same as that on the card.

The disadvantage of accepting credit cards is the charge made by the credit card company, but it is a convenience to many clients who prefer this method of payment.

Gift voucher

An ideal method of increasing turnover and reaching potential new clients is to offer a gift voucher scheme. Vouchers can be for a particular treatment or a specific amount. When accepting a gift voucher as payment a record must be kept of the amount and serial number for accounting purposes.

Figure 1.7 *A beauty salon gift voucher*

Welcoming clients

As soon as clients enter the salon it is important to acknowledge them even if you are busy with another client or task. You could say 'Good morning', ask them to take a seat and inform them that you will attend to them as soon as you complete the task in hand. It is very off putting for clients, particularly if they have never been to the salon before, to be left standing waiting with no communication.

Check the client's appointment and inform the therapist that her client has arrived. Then take the client's coat, show him or her to the appropriate location, relaxation or changing area or treatment room. The client may need to wait in reception. If for any reason a client is to be kept waiting, always offer a drink and magazines to read.

Dealing with problems

It is important that the receptionist recognises potential problems and resolves any issues before they affect the therapists and the working day. The day should begin by checking the appointment book, taking messages from the answer phone and rearranging client appointments if necessary. If a therapist has not arrived or is unexpectedly absent for the day, it is essential that the receptionist reallocates her appointments to other therapists and contacts clients who cannot be accommodated and makes new appointments for them.

During the day it is the responsibility of the receptionist to solve problems caused by clients arriving late. Diplomacy and tact will be required where clients may not be able to have the treatment requested or their preferred therapist.

Selling retail products

The reception area is the point of sale for retail products. Even though the therapists may have made the sale, the receptionist is often the person responsible for processing payments. A thorough knowledge of the products, their features and benefits and recommended retail price is essential because clients may ask questions once the therapist has left to deal with her next client. There will also be times when members of the public or clients come in simply to make a purchase.

This is an important process as it allows you time to discuss issues relating to treatments with your client and record the outcomes. The initial consultation is particularly important, as it is the first step in establishing a professional and beneficial working relationship with the client. It will allow you to establish a rapport with your clients and make them feel comfortable and at ease and wanting to come back to you.

Benefits of consultation

The initial consultation will require time. However, consultation does occur naturally to a lesser degree on each occasion before and after treatment. Consultation is necessary as it:

* provides the client with the opportunity to talk to the therapist and explain his or her reasons for having treatment
* allows the therapist to cstablish the needs of the client and desired outcomes from the treatment
* provides the opportunity to explain the treatment and benefits to the client, offer further advice and suggest a treatment plan
* highlights contraindications that may prevent treatment or require the treatment to be adapted
* monitors the results of treatment.

Consultation techniques

During the consultation different methods will be used in assessing the client and providing information. These include:

* observation
* questioning and listening
* reference to client records
* use of visual aids.

Observation

As soon as the client enters the room, general observations may be made by looking at the client's body language and approach. Non-verbal communication is often as informative as the questions you ask as a client will express him/herself through body language. If the client is shy and hesitant, try to put him

or her at ease; if the client is stressed or agitated, be calm and reassuring. Always greet the client immediately, even if you are busy with something else. A simple acknowledgement is often all that is required such as 'Good morning, Mrs Graham, I will be with you in a minute, please take a seat'. Clients do not like to be ignored or kept waiting without explanation.

How relaxed the client is should be noted. For example, if the client appears ill at ease or uncomfortable, this may indicate a general nervousness, particularly if this is the first visit. However, it could indicate that the client is under stress, feeling generally low or suffering from a physical pain or discomfort. With further questioning your initial observations may be reinforced or changed altogether.

A client's physical appearance may also indicate their physical and emotional condition. If he or she appears clear skinned with glossy hair and bright eyes, well groomed and walking with a light step, this will indicate a person in general good health. However, if the client has a blemished skin with a greyish pallor, lank, lifeless hair and dull eyes, this could be symptomatic of depression, lethargy or other problems.

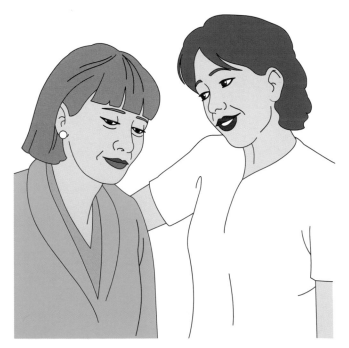

Figure 2.1 *The beauty therapist should observe the client's body language very carefully*

A much closer observation will be required to check the client for contraindications and to make observations relating specifically to each individual treatment.

Questioning and listening

This is an essential part of the consultation process and different types of questions may be used.

Open questions

These allow a free response from clients giving them the opportunity to express their wishes and provide the therapist with all the information required to put together an appropriate treatment plan. Open questions always start with 'How', 'What', 'Why', 'When', 'Where'.

The answers to open questions will provide detail,

Examples of open questions

How often can you come in for your course of body treatments?

What results do you hope to achieve?

Why do you need to change your appointment times?

When are you going away?

Where do you work now?

an insight into the clients' lifestyle and something about their personality. Open questions allow clients to respond beyond a simple 'yes' or 'no' answer. To build up goodwill it is a good idea to start the questions with one that will put the client into a relaxed frame of mind. This question does not need to be related to the treatment process. It could be about the weather, the client's general well-being or even where he or she lives.

Closed questions

These questions call for responses which are strictly limited and are used to obtain specific information from the client or when a 'yes' or 'no' answer is sufficient. They may include essential information such as name, address, telephone number, medical history, and so on.

Examples of closed questions

Do you smoke?

Do you take vitamin supplements?

How many glasses of water do you drink a day?

Have you had a facial treatment before?

Have you had an operation in the last six months?

Probing questions

Probing questions are useful when you need to find out a little more information than the client is offering, to clarify a point or to expand on a relevant issue. Often clients do not provide information because they think it is not relevant but you know will help to plan the right treatments for them.

Examples of probing questions

Probing questions were required when a client, who was anxious to delay the effects of ageing in her face, had booked a course of micro current treatments. During the consultation the therapist asked the client whether she had recently had Botox or collagen injections. When the client denied having either, the therapist went on to ask more probing questions as it was obvious to her trained eye that both of these treatments had been applied recently and it was too soon to provide micro current treatment.

The therapist asked the following questions:
* Do you suffer from any medical condition that has caused the slight swelling around the lips?
* Are you allergic to any cosmetic products?
* Have you had any recent medical treatment?
* Would you like to try a lymphatic drainage facial massage?

It is also very important to listen to your clients and summarise what they have said to show you have understood or to clarify a point. Good communication with clients requires active listening. This will help you to receive and understand the true message being conveyed. Because we think much more quickly than we speak, it often means that we are putting together our response before the client has delivered the whole message and we may only remember certain parts of the information and might have ignored something of importance. To actively listen, therefore, you should:

* concentrate on the speaker
* maintain eye contact
* ignore external influences
* look interested – do not fidget
* not interrupt
* be encouraging and empathetic
* reflect and summarise what the client has said.

Figure 2.2 *A client consultation*

Reference to client records

As a result of the consultation, all relevant information will be recorded in detail on a record card. This information provides the foundation for treatment and records relevant details for all those involved in providing the client with a quality service and will include:

* personal details
* medical history

* client's objectives and expectations
* client's lifestyle
* products bought.

Personal details

Personal details include name, date of birth, address and telephone number enabling you to communicate with the client when necessary. For those clients with a busy lifestyle and to make it easier for you to contact them, it is advisable to record mobile phone numbers, fax numbers and email addresses. In some cases, clients may not be keen to tell you their date of birth. However, this information may be significant if the client's age does not reflect his or her physical appearance, for example the client may appear older than he or she actually is and this may indicate a problem that should be taken into account.

Medical history

Medical history should include the name, address and telephone number of the client's doctor and any medication the client is taking, his or her height and weight, any health problems and any current medical treatment.

Past medical history is also important as this may contribute to any current problems. The family medical history may also provide useful information. There are certain general areas which need to be noted:

* general state of health
* past/present illness
* emotional trauma
* operations
* accidents or injuries sustained
* muscular/skeletal problems
* digestive problems
* circulatory problems
* gynaecological problems
* nervous system problems
* immune system disorders/problems
* allergies
* skin problems
* medication
* current medical treatment.

This information will also highlight any reason why the treatment may be contraindicated or need to be adapted to suit the client.

Aims, objectives and expectations

It is important to know why the client requires treatment. The client's objectives may be relaxation, to improve appearance, as an antidote to stress or to ease aches and pains. However, the majority of clients will be asking for your advice and recommendations as they may have tried other forms of therapy or have been recommended to you by a friend or colleague.

Providing as much information as possible will help clients enjoy their treatment and discuss the results that you hope to achieve. Clients should never have unrealistic expectations if you explain what the treatment involves and the benefits.

Treatment record

This should include the dates the client attends for treatment and, at the end of each session, an evaluation of the treatment and any comments you may think useful to record or the client wishes to make. The treatment record enables the therapist to adapt or change the treatment plan when necessary. A note must also be made of the date of any referral to a medical practitioner, the response and the date it was received. If you carry out any skin sensitivity or predisposition tests, record the date and outcome for future reference. Record details of all retail sales made so that you can remind your client when he or she will require more.

Clients are the most important part of the business and detailed records must be kept to ensure you have the correct information to hand at all times. It is impossible for anyone to be able to remember all the information required about each client all the time. Having up-to-date records creates a good professional image and will ensure that you can anticipate the needs of clients.

Use of visual aids

Using visual aids reinforces verbal information given to the client during consultation. You may show the client sample products, or the piece of equipment you will be using. Leaflets providing information about products and services and aftercare are useful for the client to have and will help him or her to follow up treatment at home.

The consultation

Choose an appropriate location

Greet the client warmly

Ensure the necessary records are available

Ask all the relevant questions

Listen to what the client says

Never assume what the client's requirements are

Clarify information when required

Provide literature or relevant information

Provide information about cost, timing and duration of treatment

Record information

Fill in all the necessary record and appointment cards

Confirm all decisions made

Figure 2.3 *The consultation process*

A full treatment will normally accompany your initial consultation, so extra time should be allocated when booking a client's first appointment to allow for the consultation process.

A short consultation will occur naturally at each subsequent treatment. This will provide the feedback required from the last treatment and allow discussion about any new issues, which may affect the treatment plan. Treatment may then be adapted if necessary.

Always ask the client to sign the record card when you have completed it together, as it provides evidence that the client agrees with the information which has been recorded. Your signature on the record card is useful if any other therapist has to treat the client in future and needs to clarify information. It also shows agreement between yourself and the client that the information is accurate.

Beauty Retreat – Spa Therapy

Lifestyle Consultation ☐ Confidential

Name: _____

Address: _____

Home Telephone: _____ Work: _____

Email address: _____

Today's date: _____

Doctor's Name/Telephone Number: _____

Date of birth: _____

Therapist's name: _____

LIFESTYLE – Please tick or circle **Y/N**

What is your general stress level?	☐ Low	☐ Medium	☐ High
What is your quality of sleep?	☐ Deep	☐ Light	☐ Disturbed
How many hours sleep on average?	☐ 4–6	☐ 6–8	☐ 8–10
What is your current status?	☐ Working	☐ Home based	☐ Retired
What is your activity level?	☐ Sedentary	☐ Average	☐ High
What hours do you work?	☐ Part-time	☐ Shift-work	☐ Full-time
How do you travel to work?	☐ Walk	☐ Public transport	☐ Car
How often do you take exercise?	☐ Never	☐ Daily	☐ Weekly
What level of exercise?	☐ Low impact	☐ Moderate	☐ High impact
Do you smoke?	☐ Never	☐ 1–20 per day	☐ 20+

DIET

Are the following part of your diet?	☐ Protein	☐ Carbohydrates	☐ Vitamins	☐ Roughage	☐ Fat
How is most of the food cooked?	☐ Roasted	☐ Grilled	☐ Boiled	☐ Fried	
Do you drink the following?	☐ Water	☐ Fresh juices	☐ Alcohol	☐ Coffee	☐ Tea
Do you eat the following meals?	☐ Breakfast	☐ Lunch	☐ Dinner		

Do you eat between meals? **Y/N** Are you a vegetarian? **Y/N** Are your meals disturbed? **Y/N**

FACE AND BODY ASSESSEMENT

Cellulite	☐ None	☐ Average	☐ Above average	
Water retention	☐ None	☐ Average	☐ Above average	
Weight	☐ Under	☐ Normal	☐ Over	
Circulation	☐ Poor	☐ Normal		
Facial skin type	☐ Oily	☐ Dry	☐ Combination	☐ Sensitive
Body Skin Condition	☐ Oily	☐ Dry	☐ Combination	☐ Sensitive
Muscle tone	☐ Poor	☐ Average	☐ Good	

MEDICAL HISTORY. If yes, please detail.

Are you on any medication or under medical supervision?

Y/N _____

Have you experienced any gynaecological problems?

Y/N _____

Is ther any history of any family illnesses?

Y/N _____

Do you suffer from any of the following?

☐ Allergies ☐ Arthritis ☐ Eczema ☐ Psoriasis ☐ Constipation

☐ Depression ☐ Varicose veins ☐ Headaches ☐ Asthma ☐ Rheumatism

☐ Epilepsy ☐ Claustrophobia ☐ Heart condition ☐ Hyperthyroid

☐ High/Low blood pressure ☐ Iodine (Seaweed) allergy

Have you suffered from any recent shock?

Y/N _____

Have you had any recent surgery or accidents?

Y/N _____

Are you pregnant or planning a pregnancy?

Y/N _____

What is the main purpose of your visit?

_____

GENERAL HEALTH

☐ Excellent ☐ Good ☐ Bad ☐ Average

Additional comments _____

_____

Client signature _____

Figure 2.4 *A client record card*

The treatment plan

The most important outcome of consultation is the treatment plan. It is a working document that you will have put together in agreement with your client detailing the most appropriate treatments. It will include:

* the treatment(s) recommended
* the length of treatment or course of treatments
* over what period of time
* the dates and times of treatment
* the cost of treatment
* home care advice
* retail products required to complement treatment.

Case study: Mrs Walker

Mrs Walker is in her mid-fifties and concerned about the lines around her eyes and mouth. She also has drooping eyelids. She has been using soap and water to cleanse her face and a light moisturiser when she remembers. She works three days a week, 9 am–5 pm, and looks after her granddaughter two mornings a week. She enjoys walking and is a member of a rambling club that meets on Saturday afternoon, but she has recently found she is aching more than usual after a long walk.

Treatment plan

Treatment(s) recommended: Microcurrent anti-ageing facials to improve the muscle tone and skin texture and relaxing aromatherapy massage.

Length of treatment or course of treatments: Course of ten microcurrent treatments and then a maintenance programme. Aromatherapy massage every two weeks on a Monday before her facial.

Over what period of time? Weeks 1 and 2 – three treatments; weeks 2 and 3 – two treatments. Monthly maintenance treatment as required.

Dates and times of treatment: Monday and Wednesday afternoon and Saturday morning to fit in with work, child-minding and the rambling club.

Cost of treatment: £360 includes a 10 per cent reduction on a course of ten microcurrent treatments and £35 for each aromatherapy massage.

Home care advice: Use an eye cream containing alpha hydroxy acids to help reduce fine lines around the eyes in addition to a rich antioxidant moisturiser to hydrate the skin and protect against free radical damage, and a cleansing cream instead of soap.

Retail products required to complement treatment: Vitace antioxidant cleanser and cream, Vita plus eye cream, blend of warming essential oils to use in the bath after walking.

Data Protection Act (1998)

Whatever the system used to store records and client details, this Act requires you to register with the Data Protection Registrar. Once registered, you must comply with the principles of good information handling practice, set out in the Data Protection Act. These are to:

* obtain and process data fairly and lawfully
* hold information only for the purposes specified in your register entry
* use information only for those purposes and disclose it only to the people listed in your register entry
* only hold data which is adequate and relevant
* ensure that data is accurate and kept up to date
* hold information for no longer than is necessary
* allow individuals access to information held about them
* take security measures to prevent unauthorised or accidental access to, alteration, disclosure or loss and destruction of information.

Different methods of consultation

In general, the consultation process is the same for all clients, whatever the treatment. However, there may be different questions to be asked for different treatments. For example, a client who is attending for epilation because she has superfluous hair growth caused by a medical condition will provide more information about her medical history than a client who wants an eyelash tint.

The location you choose to provide a consultation may also differ. If the client wants a course of weight reducing treatments, then you will need to ensure his or her privacy, while a client who wants to buy a new set of skin care products could have her consultation in reception where you can show her the products in stock.

Your detailed observations will differ depending on the type of treatments the client has asked for and the issues relating to the particular treatment.

There may be individual record cards that you can fill in for different treatments. These are often provided by the companies who supply you with the products, as they often customise their records to suit the treatment offered. These treatment specific records should be kept in addition to your general salon records.

Examples of detailed observations

* **Facial treatments** will require a detailed skin analysis and you may need to use a magnifying lamp for a closer inspection of the client's skin.
* **Body treatments** may require you to measure or weigh the client and you will also assess the client's body type and condition. Some therapists take photographs so that the client can see the results achieved after the course of treatments.
* **Hand, foot and nail treatments** will require a close inspection of the feet and hands to check the condition of the nails and skin.
* **Epilation** will require you to inspect closely the areas requiring treatment, to assess skin type and hair growth pattern, to make decisions about needle size, current strength and type of current to be used.

A contraindication is any reason why the therapist may not treat the client. During consultation, while questioning and observing the client, he or she may inform you of a possible contraindication he or she has, or you may notice a contraindication to treatment that the client may be unaware of. It is essential, therefore, that the therapist is able to recognise these contraindications in order to prevent treatment or to limit or adapt it in some way.

A contraindication exists when:

* an infectious disease is present
* a disorder or medical condition may prevent treatment
* a condition is present, for which medical approval must be sought before treating.

Contraindications may be defined as:

* general – would contraindicate most treatments and affect the whole body
* specific – would contraindicate a particular treatment or prevent treatment on a specific area of the body
* temporary – would prevent treatment only for a short period of time.

Under no circumstances must a therapist diagnose any medical condition, but there are some occasions when medical permission is required before treatment may be carried out. It is the responsibility of the client to obtain permission for treatment from his or her GP or specialist, preferably in the form of a letter, which may then be kept with the client's records.

When you suspect there is a medical condition that may contraindicate treatment, you will need to be tactful when discussing this with the client. Try not to alarm the client, but explain that it would be in his or her best interest if he or she sought medical approval.

The most important consideration for you as a professional therapist is to prevent cross-infection occurring in the salon. For this reason, clients with an infectious disorder or disease must not be treated. Once you have a clear understanding of what each treatment entails and a thorough knowledge of all possible contraindications, then you will know when treatment may be carried out and the circumstances when it has to be adapted in some way or restrictions made. The therapist is also under an obligation to clients not to contribute in any way to cross-infection. It is important, therefore, to ensure that you are strict in your own personal hygiene and presentation. Always make sure that you wash your hands immediately before treating a client and during treatment if you have to stop for any reason, for example if you need to blow your nose, or you change from a foot to a facial treatment or come into contact with something that may be infectious.

Contraindications fall into four categories:

* viral
* bacterial
* systemic
* fungal.

Some examples of each type of contraindication are shown in Table 3.1.

Viral	Bacterial	Systemic	Fungal
Herpes simplex	Impetigo	Diabetes	Ringworm
Chickenpox	Paronychia	Multiple sclerosis	Athlete's foot
HIV	Stye	Osteoporosis	
Warts	Boil	Asthma	
Rubella		Bronchitis	
Verruca		Bells palsy	

Table 3.1 *Classification of contraindications*

The following diseases, disorders and conditions are a broad selection of those that you may encounter in your work as a beauty therapist.

Skin disease

A skin disease is an infection of the skin with characteristics that can be seen. An infectious disease must not be treated, to avoid the spread of infection from one person to another. The presence of pus is a sign of infection, and staphylococci are the most common pus-forming bacteria.

Bacteria are harmful when they are **pathogenic** (disease producing). They invade the body by way of:

* a break in the skin
* breathing
* dirt in the eyes and ears
* the mouth through transferring germs from the hands.

Types of infection

Boils

A boil is an infection of a hair follicle by staphylococci bacteria. It begins as a small red nodule gradually increasing in size and becoming inflamed. It is sometimes called a **furuncle**, and when several adjacent follicles are infected the boil is known as a **carbuncle**.

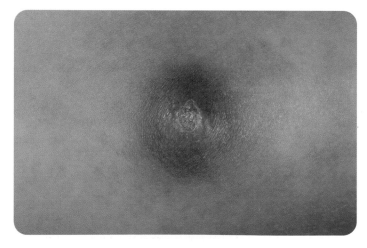

Figure 3.1 *A boil or furuncle*

Impetigo

This is bacterial infection of the epidermis. A pus-filled blister is the first sign. When this ruptures the infection spreads and the weeping blisters form a crust. This is more common in children and is highly contagious. It must be medically treated.

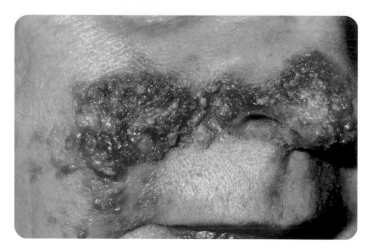

Figure 3.2 *Impetigo*

Herpes simplex

This is a viral infection, which occurs around the nose and mouth. Its characteristics are a group of blisters on a red area of skin. A tingling or burning sensation precedes the appearance of the blisters. The condition may occur repeatedly and usually at the same site each time.

This infection can be brought on by an illness with a high fever, exposure to the sun or when a person is generally run down. Its common name is a cold sore.

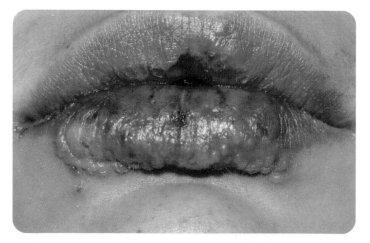

Figure 3.3 *Herpes simplex*

Ringworm

The common term for fungal infections is ringworm. The fungi causing this skin disease generally live in keratin (the protein from which skin is made). The disease affects the skin on different parts of the body and the disorders the fungi cause are known as **tineas**. The different types of tinea are:

* **tinea pedis** – ringworm of the feet (see Chapter 23 Hand and foot treatments, page 345)
* **tinea corporis** – ringworm of the body
* **tinea capitis** – ringworm of the scalp
* **tinea unguium** – ringworm of the nails (see Chapter 23 Hand and foot treatments, page 338)
* **tinea versicolor** – ringworm of the upper trunk and sometimes the neck and upper arms.

The fungus produces enzymes, which break down the keratin. Ringworm may appear as single- or multiple-ringed lesions in the skin varying in severity from mild scaling to inflamed itchy areas. The primary lesion is a small red macule, which spreads outwards.

Tinea pedis, or athlete's foot, affects the spaces between the toes causing a sodden, white appearance, often with deep splits at the base of the tissue. The foot is a common site for fungal infections because fungi grow better in moist conditions and the feet being enclosed in shoes provide ideal conditions. It is an extremely infectious condition and is usually spread by contact with objects which have been in contact with the disease. Communal areas such as swimming pools and sports changing rooms are common sources of the infection.

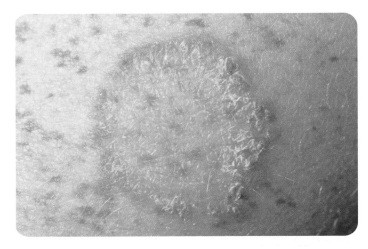

Figure 3.4 *Ringworm*

Verruca vulgaris

Verruca vulgaris, the common wart, is due to a viral infection and is very contagious. Verrucas occur frequently on the hands, sometimes in groups and often around the nail. There are treatments available from the pharmacist, but they can disappear spontaneously.

Verruca plantaris

Verruca plantaris is a viral infection that causes warts on the soles of the feet, which become flattened with pressure. The most common sites are the ball or heel of the foot. They can become painful, so to avoid discomfort, advise the client to seek advice from a chiropodist.

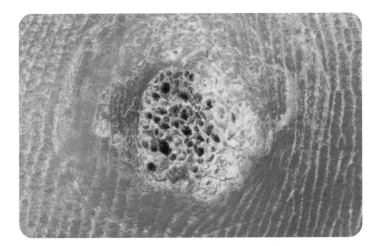

Figure 3.5 *Verruca plantaris*

Infestation

Scabies

This is a microscopic itch mite that can barely be seen by the human eye. The mite, an eight-legged creature with a round body, burrows under the skin. Within several weeks the affected person develops an allergic reaction. This results in severe itching, often intense enough to keep sufferers awake at night. Human scabies is almost always caught from another person by close contact.

Attracted to warmth and odour, the female mite burrows into the skin, lays eggs and produces secretions that cause the allergic reaction. Larvae, or newly hatched mites, travel to the skin surface, lying in shallow pockets where they will develop into adult mites. If the mite is scratched off the skin, it can live in bedding up to 24 hours. It may be up to a month before a newly infested person will notice the itching, especially in people with good hygiene and who bathe regularly.

Skin cancer

Basal cell carcinoma

Also known as a rodent ulcer, basal cell carcinoma arises from cells in the lowest layer of the epidermis and is a slow growing cancer. The most common place to find it is below the eyes or at the side of the nose. The condition is much more common in countries like South Africa and Australia, probably caused by over-exposure to ultraviolet light. It occurs more frequently in fair-skinned people and rarely on black skin, therefore the degree of pigmentation is a contributory factor. It is usually a condition of middle-aged and elderly people and is normally slow to grow, so if a doctor is consulted soon enough, it is possible to cure this cancer. However, if left untreated for many years, it may prove fatal.

Basal cell carcinoma comes in several forms:

* **Ulcer** – this begins as a small papule (pimple) and spreads outwards leaving a central ulcer.
* **Cyst** – this begins as a papule, which enlarges to form a cystic pearl-shaped lesion (wound) with an irregular surface.
* **Pigmented** – sometimes an ulcer or a cyst becomes pigmented and it then becomes difficult to distinguish it from a malignant melanoma (see below).

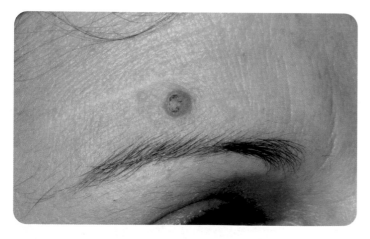

Figure 3.6 *Basal cell carcinoma*

Squamous cell carcinoma

This arises from cells within the upper layers of the epidermis. It grows more rapidly than basal cell carcinoma. Squamous cell cancers may occur on all areas of the body including the mucous membranes, but are most common in areas exposed to the sun. Although squamous cell carcinomas usually remain confined to the epidermis for some time, if not treated they may eventually penetrate the underlying tissues.

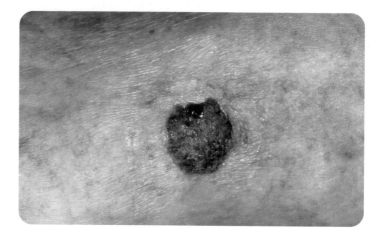

Figure 3.7 *Squamous cell carcinoma*

Malignant melanoma

This is a type of skin cancer that occurs due to cancerous changes in melanocytes (pigment cells). Sometimes melanocytes and surrounding tissue form benign (non-cancerous) growths called moles (naevi). A melanoma may arise from clear skin or from an existing mole and it may appear nodular or flat. The appearance of malignant melanoma has increased considerably in the last 15 years. This is thought to be due to the increased exposure to ultraviolet radiation from the sun's rays. Melanoma may occur anywhere on the skin's surface, but the legs have a higher incidence than other parts of the body.

Signs of malignant melanoma include:

A – asymmetry, when the shape of one half of the pigmented lesion does not match the other

B – border of the pigmented lesion is usually irregular with notches and prominences around the edge and the pigment may spread into the surrounding skin

C – colour of the lesion is uneven with mixed shades of black, brown, tan, blue or red

D – diameter, when there is an increase in size of the lesion; melanomas are usually larger than the eraser on the end of a pencil.

If the following should occur, it is advisable to seek medical help:

* An increase in size of a pigmented lesion.
* Alteration in pigmentation of the lesion.
* Ulceration or bleeding of a pigmented or non-pigmented lesion.

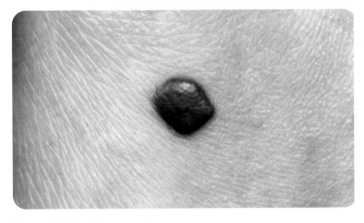

Figure 3.8 *Malignant melanoma*

Skin cancer fact

Skin cancer is the most common cancer in the UK – 60,000 people were diagnosed with this condition in 2003. More people now die of skin cancer in the UK than in Australia where the public has a greater awareness of safety in the sun.

Temporary skin disorders

* **Sunburn** – the skin becomes itchy, red and inflamed and in extreme cases it may blister.
* **Cuts and abrasions** – these may be covered before treatment or avoided altogether.
* **Recent scar tissue** – this must be avoided to ensure that the area has time to heal and there is

no discomfort caused to the client. After an operation medical approval must be given before treatment.

* **Bruising** – as this may be painful, always avoid the area. If it is widespread, do not treat. Recurring bruises for no reason may indicate a medical condition and should be referred to a doctor.
* **Severe acne vulgaris** – if the skin is very sore and inflamed, suggest the client seeks medical advice.
* **Allergic reaction** – this sensitises the skin.
* **Urticaria** – this is an acute allergic reaction causing red wheals of varying sizes on the surface of the skin. The attack may be local or widespread and lesions can disappear after several hours.

Eye disorders

Blepharitis

This is an allergic inflammation of the eyelid caused by allergy to dandruff or cosmetics used on the eye.

Conjunctivitis (pink eye)

This is an inflammation of the conjunctiva or membrane inside the eyelid and covering the cornea. The characteristics are redness, swelling and discomfort. The eye may have a watery or pus-containing discharge.

The causes are allergy (for example to pollen, dust, cosmetics, spores and animal fur, hair or feathers), physical or chemical irritation, and bacterial or viral infection. If an infection is present, the sufferer may require antibiotic eye drops.

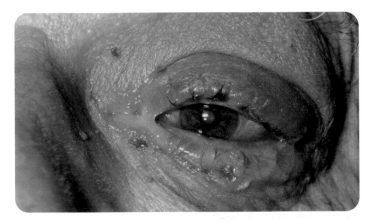

Figure 3.9 *Conjunctivitis*

Watery eye – epyphora

The function of the tear duct is to bathe and wash the eye with tears, which then drain away into the nasal cavity. When some irritation occurs preventing this happening, the over secretion of tears overflows on to the face.

Cataract

This is a cloudiness in the lens of the eye that results in blurred vision. It may be congenital or as a result of metabolic disease such as diabetes, through injury or prolonged exposure to infrared rays.

Stye – hordeolum

This is an infection in the hair follicle of an eyelash. The eye becomes red and sore and blinking is painful. A small papule forms, swelling occurs and pus is present. The stye may become itchy, but rubbing or scratching will increase the irritation and spread the infection. It sometimes occurs when the client is run down and it must only be treated by a doctor.

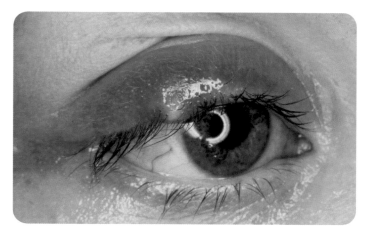

Figure 3.10 *A stye*

Black eye

This is bruising, normally caused by a blow, which breaks the blood capillaries under the skin. The area will be painful and swollen, but if steps are taken to reduce the temperature in the area with a cold compress, the result may not be quite so bad.

Nail disorders

Onychomycosis

This condition is also known as ringworm of the nails. It is a highly infectious disease caused by a vegetable parasite, which enters the nail at the free edge and spreads towards the matrix, causing the nail to become thickened and discoloured. The degree of the disease can vary from negligible to almost complete disintegration of the nail plate.

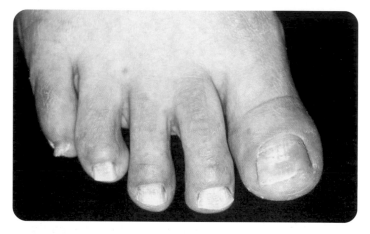

Figure 3.11 *Onychomycosis*

Paronychia

This is a bacterial infection of the skin surrounding the nail, which looks red and inflamed and is sometimes swollen. It may occur when the skin is broken, through incorrect manicure techniques, rough handling or picking of the skin around the nail or exposure to harsh chemicals.

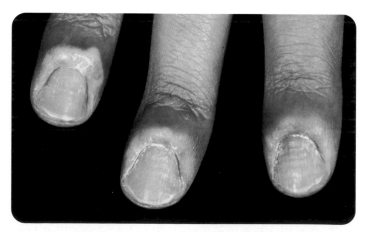

Figure 3.12 *Paronychia*

Disorders of the skeletal system

Osteoporosis

Osteoporosis (literally 'porous bones') is a condition which generally affects older people, especially women. It affects the whole of the skeletal system, particularly the spine, legs and feet. It occurs as a result of removal of more minerals from bone tissue than are deposited. By the age of 70, most people's bone density will have fallen by a third. Women are particularly vulnerable because of the hormonal changes that accompany the menopause, particularly the reduction in oestrogen that affects mineral deposit. Osteoporosis can be slowed down by a healthy diet containing adequate amounts of calcium and vitamin D and taking regular load bearing exercise.

Ankylosing spondylitis

This condition causes inflammation of the joints of the spine, resulting in pain and stiffness in the neck and back. It is thought to be an autoimmune disease in which the immune system attacks the body, and is often inherited.

Rickets

This is caused by a deficiency of vitamin D which results in an inability of the body to transport calcium and phosphorous from the digestive tract into the blood to be used by the bones. Calcification does not occur, which results in bones staying soft, and the weight of the body causes the bones in the leg to bow. The condition may be cured with large doses of calcium, phosphorous and vitamin D in the diet and ultraviolet light, which assists the body in manufacturing vitamin D.

Arthritis

This is the term used to describe painful and swollen joints. There are two types of arthritis with very different causes:

* **Osteoarthritis** is a degenerative disease of the joints. It affects the hips, spine and the hands. It causes swollen joints and pain and stiffness around the affected area, and may be as a result of ageing, wear and tear on the joints or irritation.

* **Rheumatoid arthritis** is in part an autoimmune disease, where the body attacks its own tissues. The inflammation begins in the synovial membrane, the lining of the sac enclosing a freely moveable joint. This swells up and then starts to break down. The cartilage at the ends of the bone then begin to wear away leaving the joints stiff and very painful.

Osteomyelitis

Osteomyelitis is inflammation of the bone due to infection. Infections reach the bone via the bloodstream, through an injury such as a fracture or an abscess, and may destroy bones and nearby joints.

Dislocation

This is when the bone is displaced from the joint and the ligaments, tendons and articular capsules are torn in the process. It causes pain, loss of movement and swelling.

Sprain

This occurs when a joint is twisted or wrenched and its attachments are injured. Blood vessels, ligaments, tendons and nerves can be affected. It causes swelling, pain and bruising, and the most common location is the ankle.

Disorders of the muscular system

Fibrositis

This condition is an inflammation of fibrous tissue causing pain and stiffness, in particular in the muscle covering. This may often follow an injury, repeated strain of a muscle or prolonged muscular tension.

Fibromyalgia

Fibromyalgia, or muscular rheumatism, affects the muscles, tendons, ligaments and joints of the body. The most common symptoms are aches and pains, particularly in the neck and upper back, fatigue, stiffness in the morning and numbness in the hands or tingling in the fingers.

Muscular dystrophy

This is a muscle destroying disease characterised by degeneration of muscle cells, which in turn results in wasting of the muscle. The causes are genetic, faulty metabolism of potassium, protein deficiency or the inability of the body to utilise creatine (a product of protein metabolism found in muscle).

Lumbago

A very common condition, lumbago is low backache caused by inflammation and pain in the muscles in the lumbar region of the spine. It may be a result of incorrect lifting or bending, a slipped disc or strained muscle or ligament.

Repetitive strain injury (RSI)

This is becoming increasingly common, in particular among computer keyboard users. It is the overuse or over stretching of muscles or ligaments resulting in injury or damage to a particular muscle or group of muscles.

Tendinitis

Inflammation of a tendon often occurs after excessive overuse. Achilles tendinitis (inflamation of the achilles tendon, which is situated at the back of the ankle and attached to the heel bone) is common among sports men and women as a result of incorrect footwear or insufficient preparation when competing.

Tennis elbow

This is inflammation around the elbow joint caused by overworking the muscles through sport or RSI.

Sports injuries

Common areas affected are the ankle and knee joints, back and shoulder. Injury may be due to muscle fatigue, not warming up sufficiently, excessive stretching or overworking the muscles.

Disorders of the cardiovascular system

Angina pectoris

Angina pectoris literally means 'chest pain'. It occurs when coronary (heart) circulation is reduced for some reason. It weakens the heart muscle but does not produce a full-scale heart attack. A common cause of this condition is stress, which produces constriction of the blood vessel walls, and also strenuous exercise after a heavy meal.

Atherosclerosis

This condition is also known as hardening of the arteries. It is caused by fatty substances such as cholesterol, cellular waste, calcium and fibrin (clotting material) being deposited in the walls of the arteries. This build up, called plaque, may partially or totally block the blood flow through the artery and it can cause a heart attack or stroke. It is a slow progressive disease which may progress rapidly for some people in their thirties, but for others not until their fifties or sixties.

Deep vein thrombosis (DVT)

This is a blood clot within a deep vein, most commonly in the calf or thigh, and it may partially or completely block the flow of blood in the vein. It occurs when the flow of blood is restricted in a vein and a clot forms. It can be caused by poor circulation because of other problems such as a recent heart attack or stroke, varicose veins, inactivity or it may develop during a long-haul plane flight.

The symptoms include tenderness in the area, a reddening of the skin, pain, swelling, fever, rapid heartbeat, joint pain and soreness.

DVT may also be caused by an injury to the vein, following surgery, during pregnancy, or as a result of severe infection, liver disease and some cancers.

Hypertension

This is a condition where the person's blood pressure is consistently higher than normal even when relaxing. It puts extra strain on the heart and the circulatory system and increases the risk of coronary artery disease, heart attack, stroke and kidney disease. It can be a natural consequence of getting older and there is some evidence that it may be genetic.

As the arteries harden and become narrower through age or a high-fat diet, the body's circulation is restricted and this puts added pressure on the heart as it works harder to keep the blood flowing. There are a number of factors which contribute to this condition including lack of exercise, smoking, obesity, stress and excessive alcohol consumption.

There can be specific causes, which can occur at any time, and these include kidney problems, complications during pregnancy, certain hormone imbalances, some heart conditions and side effects of drugs such as steroids. Symptoms of severe hypertension are breathlessness, headaches and dizziness.

When suffering from hypertension it is advisable to adopt a healthy lifestyle, give up smoking, lose weight if necessary, increase exercise, follow a healthy diet, cut down on fatty foods, learn to relax and avoid stress. Relaxing therapies may be recommended and yoga, tai chi or other complementary therapies will also help to produce a sense of well-being, thus reducing stress, which exacerbates high blood pressure.

Pulse

This is a wave of pressure passing along the arteries indicating the pumping action of the heart. The pulse is normally taken at the wrist just under the thumb on the palmar surface of the hand and is called the **radial** pulse. The fingertips should be placed into the hollow at the base of the metacarpal of the thumb and pressed lightly over the artery. The number of beats in a minute should be counted, using a watch with a second-hand count. The average pulse rate in an adult is 72 beats per minute, but varies between 60 and 80 beats. The pulse rate may increase due to stress, exercise, illness, as a result of injury and while consuming alcohol. A normal pulse will feel regular and strong.

Blood pressure

Blood pressure is the force exerted by the blood on the walls of any blood vessels, in particular arteries. The factors which affect blood pressure are:

* the force of the heartbeat
* the volume of blood in the cardiovascular system
* the resistance to the flow of blood in the arteries.

A decrease in blood volume due to blood loss causes blood pressure to drop. An increase in blood volume, for example excessive salt intake leading to water retention, will cause blood pressure to increase. Blood pressure also varies depending on the activity of the body.

Blood pressure is measured using a **sphygmomanometer**.

* **Systolic blood pressure** is the force exerted by the blood on the arterial walls during ventricular contraction. It is the highest pressure measured in the arteries.
* **Diastolic blood pressure** is the force exerted on the arterial walls during ventricular relaxation. It is the lowest blood pressure measured in the arteries.

The difference between the systolic and diastolic pressure is called **pulse pressure** (see below).

The average healthy adult male will have a blood pressure of 120 over 80. This would be a systolic pressure of 120 mm Hg (millimetres of mercury) and a diastolic pressure of 80 mm Hg.

Hypotension

A condition in which the arterial blood pressure is abnormally low. It may occur after excessive fluid loss, or blood loss. Other causes include pulmonary embolism (see page 31), severe infection, allergic reactions, Addison's disease and drugs. Some people suffer temporary hypotension when they faint.

Stroke

This is damage to part of the brain caused by a reduced blood supply as a result of blockage in a blood vessel or a blood vessel rupturing. People most at risk from a stroke are those who suffer with high blood pressure, heart disease or diabetes, who smoke, drink excessive amounts of alcohol or are obese. The results of a stroke can vary depending on which part of the brain is affected. Paralysis and loss of sensation may occur in varying degrees.

Haemophilia

Haemophilia is an inherited bleeding disorder in which the blood fails to clot normally. It is passed through the female line of a family to their sons. People with haemophilia lack the normal levels of 'clotting factors' which are particular proteins that are necessary to the blood clotting mechanism. This causes bleeding into the joints, muscles and other soft tissues, sometimes spontaneously. It is a common misconception that people with haemophilia may bleed to death from a simple prick of the finger. In fact, it is internal bleeding that is the problem.

Disorders of the lymphatic system

The lymphatic system is discussed in detail in Chapter 29. The normal antigen antibody response, which provides immunity, sometimes goes wrong. This leads to three problems:

* allergy
* autoimmunity
* tissue rejection.

Allergy

Allergic reaction to a substance can occur at any time even when the body has been exposed to it for some time. The antigens which cause an allergic reaction are called **allergens**. Some common causes of allergic reaction are milk, eggs, strawberries, nuts, penicillin, cosmetics, plants and house dust. Immediate reactions may be localised reddening of the skin, oedema, watery eyes, runny nose, bronchial asthma, dermatitis or hives. The most severe reaction is **anaphylactic shock**, which may produce life threatening effects such as asphyxia.

There is a huge increase in the number of people suffering from allergies. It is becoming a very common disorder as people are being constantly exposed to pollutants and irritants in the environment and chemicals in their food. Many clients complain of conditions such as eczema, asthma and allergy to metals, make-up, certain foods, animals and dust.

Autoimmune disease

Occasionally, the immune response of the body breaks down and an abnormal immune response occurs against the body's own tissues which are seen as foreign. Autoimmune diseases include rheumatoid arthritis, lupus, rheumatic fever, pernicious anaemia and multiple sclerosis.

AIDS

Acquired Immune Deficiency Syndrome (AIDS) is essentially a sexually transmitted disease, which lowers the body's immune system. It is caused by the Human Immunodeficiency Virus (HIV).

It is possible to remain healthy and live with HIV (HIV positive) for many years, but the virus attacks the immune system, the natural defence mechanism of the body and it is prevented from fighting disease, leaving a person open to infection. Those suffering from this disease are then susceptible to many different illnesses such as general malaise, fever, cough, sore throat, shortness of breath, muscular aches, weight loss, skin cancer and pneumonia.

For this virus to be transmitted, there has to be a mixing of body fluids and this does not happen through normal day-to-day contact. If infected blood or tissue fluid enters a break in the skin of an uninfected person, it can prove fatal. It is also transmitted through infected hypodermic needles. It is advisable for all therapists to be aware of precautions to take when using needles or dealing with an injured person (see Chapter 4 Health and safety).

Tissue rejection

After an organ transplant, the body recognises the new tissues as foreign and produces antibodies against them. This is often treated with immunosuppressive drugs.

Lymphatic disease

Some common illnesses and diseases such as cancer and heart, digestive and kidney diseases are directly affected by the proper health and functioning of the lymphatic system. When this system malfunctions, a number of diseases and related conditions may occur.

Disorders of the respiratory system

Asthma

A condition affecting the lungs which causes the walls of the bronchioles to swell and produce mucus, resulting in wheezing and difficulty with breathing. The bands of muscle around the outside of the bronchioles tighten, further blocking the flow of air. The cause is often an allergic reaction to pollens, house dust, animal hair, fur or feathers, tobacco smoke, pollutants, a change in the weather and respiratory infections.

Allergic rhinitis

An inflammation of the nasal passages resulting in a runny, itchy and inflamed nose. Caused by an allergy, the most common being hay fever, it is common in families with eczema and asthma as there is probably an inherited factor that affects the way the immune system reacts to allergens.

Emphysema

This condition occurs when the alveolar walls lose their elasticity and remain filled with air when the person breathes out. Damage occurs, which then reduces the surface area for normal exchange of oxygen and carbon dioxide. In severe cases, there is extreme breathlessness and, in most cases, it is caused by long-term irritation.

Pulmonary embolism

This is a condition where a blood clot sticks in the lungs and restricts blood flow, which prevents adequate amounts of oxygen being absorbed into the lungs. Symptoms may be shortness of breath, a cough, which may bring up blood, chest pain when breathing, raised heart rate and sweating.

Disorders of the digestive system

Constipation

A condition when bowel evacuation occurs infrequently or when the passage of faeces causes pain or difficulty.

Diarrhoea

A condition in which there is frequent bowel evacuation or the passage of abnormally soft or liquid faeces. This may be caused by intestinal infection or inflammation, irritable bowel syndrome (IBS, see below) or anxiety.

Appendicitis

This is an inflammation of the appendix causing abdominal pain and tenderness. Vomiting and diarrhoea sometimes occur.

Peritonitis

This is the acute inflammation of the membrane lining the abdominal cavity caused by bacteria spread as a result of an accident, surgical wounds or rupture of the appendix.

Hernia

This is a protrusion of an organ or tissue from the body cavity in which it lies.

Diverticulitis

This is inflammation of the diverticula (small pouches formed at weak points) in the colon. It is caused by infection and results in abdominal pain, constipation and diarrhoea.

Gallstones

These are solid lumps or 'stones' that collect in the bile ducts or gall bladder, causing pain, nausea and vomiting. They develop when the chemical composition of bile is upset.

Ulcerative colitis and Crohn's disease

These are both conditions in which there is a long-term inflammation of the digestive tract. Crohn's disease may affect any part of the digestive tract from the mouth to the anus while ulcerative colitis affects only the colon and rectum. These conditions are sometimes classified as autoimmune disease and often run in families.

Hepatitis

This is an inflammation of the liver which may be acute (a sudden crisis) or chronic (a prolonged illness). Both types are most commonly caused by hepatitis viruses, or excessive intake of alcohol.

The three most common hepatitis viruses are known as hepatitis A, B and C. Hepatitis A is caused by ingesting (taking in through the mouth) the virus through contaminated food and water or using contaminated cutlery and it does not usually cause permanent damage to the liver. Hepatitis B is more serious and often causes extensive liver damage. It is spread through body fluids and the most common methods of cross-infection are sexual contact with an infected person and contaminated needles. Much less frequently, it may be contracted through needles used for tattooing, acupuncture or ear piercing. Hepatitis C spreads in the same way as the B virus; it almost always leads to chronic hepatitis and liver damage, although initially the effects are less severe than those of the A and B viruses.

Hepatitis caused by excessive alcohol can be acute or chronic and contribute to cirrhosis of the liver. Hepatitis may also occur as a result of some rare genetic disorders or autoimmune diseases. There are a range of symptoms including fatigue, headaches, loss of appetite, nausea, vomiting and fever. As the disease progresses, other symptoms include jaundice, brown urine and abdominal pain.

Irritable bowel syndrome (IBS)

Recurring abdominal pain is caused by abnormal muscular contractions in the intestine with either diarrhoea or constipation. The cause is unknown but is often stress related and may follow a severe infection of the intestine. It may also be aggravated by certain foods.

Disorders of the urinary system

Gout

This is a hereditary condition associated with an excessively high level of uric acid in the bloodstream and joints. The condition results in attacks of acute 'gouty arthritis' and chronic destruction of the joints and is caused by an over production of uric acid or trouble excreting normal amounts through the kidneys. The excess uric acid may damage the kidneys, in which kidney stones may form.

Kidney stones

These may be small or large and form in the kidneys or bladder. Kidney stones can pass straight out of the body through the urine or increase in size causing an obstruction to the flow of urine. They can be extremely painful when passing through and blockage may occur causing infection and, in extreme cases, kidney damage.

Glomerulonephritis

This is an inflammation of the kidney, which may result in damage to the glomeruli, the network of blood capillaries. It may be caused by an allergic reaction to a streptococcal infection of the throat. There are many forms of this disease and it will affect each individual in a different way.

Cystitis

This is an inflammation of the urinary bladder often caused by infection. Characteristics are a desire to pass urine frequently and a burning sensation and is sometimes accompanied by a cramp-like pain in the abdomen.

Disorders of the endocrine system

Diabetes

There are two types of diabetes:

* **Diabetes insipidus** is caused by a lack of the antidiuretic hormone (ADH) and is characterised by the excretion of large amounts of urine and extreme thirst.

* **Diabetes mellitus** is caused by a lack of insulin and is characterised by hyperglycaemia (high blood sugar level), increased urine production, excessive thirst and eating. There are two major types:
  - **Maturity onset diabetes** often occurs in people who are overweight and over 50, when the level of insulin can be just above or just below the normal level and it may be controlled by diet alone. However, with increasing obesity in society, this condition is becoming more common in younger age groups. It is referred to as non-insulin dependent diabetes.
  - **Insulin dependent diabetes** develops in children and young adults. It is a more severe condition caused by a marked decline of islet cells in the pancreas, which causes insufficient insulin production and increase in the glucose level in the blood. This condition is controlled by insulin injections.

Diabetics are vulnerable to infection. They suffer from poor skin sensitivity and slow skin healing. Infection may lead to complications in areas affected by changes in blood vessels, for example the feet.

Because of the varied complications caused by diabetes, the condition may contraindicate some forms of beauty treatment and it will be necessary to seek permission from the client's doctor before proceeding with any treatment.

Thyroid disease

* **Hypothyroidism** is under activity of the thyroid gland. It is more common in women than men. It can cause lethargy, memory loss, heavy periods, hoarse voice, increased weight and intolerance to cold. The eyes may become swollen, the skin dry and the hair dull and lifeless.

* **Hyperthyroidism** is over activity of the thyroid gland. It can cause a racing pulse, tremor in the hands, weight loss in spite of increased appetite, diarrhoea and an intolerance of heat. The sufferer requires less sleep, may become emotional and

suffer anxiety attacks and the most striking feature is protrusion of the eyes.

Cushing's syndrome

This condition is a combination of symptoms caused by adrenal over activity as a response to excessive cell development of the adrenal cortex, a tumour of the adrenal cortex or anterior pituitary gland, use of steroids, cortisone or hydrocortisone.

The effects of this condition may include:

* obesity of the face, neck and trunk
* muscle weakness and wasting of the legs
* osteoporosis resulting in fractures
* a fall in protein synthesis, thinning of the skin with stretch marks particularly in the abdominal and thigh areas
* the ceasing of menstruation and hair growth on the face.

Seasonal Affective Disorder (SAD)

This is a type of depression that occurs at certain times of the year. Symptoms get worse in the autumn and winter when days are shorter and the amount of natural daylight is greatly reduced. In addition to depression, there is a slowing of mind and body, excessive sleeping and over eating. Some medical professionals believe that it is caused by abnormal levels of chemicals, such as serotonin and dopamine, in the brain. These chemicals play an important role in controlling sleep patterns, eating and moods. Another theory is that sufferers may have a lower eye sensitivity to light.

Disorders of the nervous system

Bells palsy

This condition results in the weakness or total physical paralysis of one half of the face. It is caused by a swelling of the facial nerve, which activates the muscles and results in a loss of the covering layers or damage to the nerve fibres themselves. The symptoms appear over a short period of time starting with pain behind the ear and weakness of the face that usually appears after two to five days. It may become difficult to close one eye completely and one corner of the mouth on the same side begins to droop.

Other symptoms include loss of taste, intolerance of loud noise and altered sensation on the affected side. Most people recover within a few weeks, but occasionally the damage may be permanent.

Cerebral palsy

This term refers to a group of motor disorders caused by damage to the brain cells before, during birth or in infancy, to the motor area of the brain. It may be caused when the mother is exposed to rubella in the first three months of pregnancy, if the baby is starved of oxygen during the birth or hydrocephalus in infancy. This is not a progressive disease, but once the damage is done it is irreversible. Most people with cerebral palsy have damage to some degree in the cortex, basal ganglia and cerebellum. The location and severity of damage will determine the symptoms. It may cause deafness, partial blindness, inability to speak, or severe learning difficulties.

Epilepsy

This is a condition marked by seizures, sometimes called fits. A seizure occurs when nerve cells in the brain temporarily go out of control and fire off excessive and random signals. It is a relatively common disorder and it often starts in childhood or teenage years, becoming less frequent after adolescence and sometimes disappearing altogether in adulthood. It often runs in families and most sufferers have no symptoms between seizures, so that they are able to lead relatively normal lives.

Epilepsy may also occur when a person has a progressive condition that affects the brain, such as Alzheimer's disease.

It is thought that a chemical imbalance in the brain causes sufferers to be susceptible to epileptic seizures or there may be a specific cause of disturbance in the brain which sets off a fit. This could include strokes, head injuries, meningitis, damage from alcohol or drug abuse, or other brain infections. In some circumstances, the condition may develop for no obvious reason.

The most common symptom of epilepsy is recurrent seizures, which occur spontaneously and may be preceded by a strange feeling, unusual taste or smell. There may also be a sensory disturbance, known as an 'aura'. Occasionally, a seizure may be triggered by rhythmical flashing lights. A seizure can vary greatly in severity. Major seizures (tonic clonic) occur when brain cells on both sides of the brain are affected at the same time. Tiny seizures (absences) cause only a brief loss of responsiveness.

The seizure often follows a pattern. The person becomes unconscious and may become rigid and arch the back, make rapid twitching or jerking movements, have a rigid jaw or froth at the mouth, breathe noisily and with difficulty.

Minor epileptic seizures are not always noticed as the person may just be staring blankly, appear to be daydreaming, complain of a pins and needles sensation, be twitching his or her mouth, eyelids, head or limb or just be making noises.

Drugs may control the condition, but it is not advisable to use electrical equipment on a client who suffers from epilepsy and medical permission must be sought if other treatments are requested. All members of staff should be aware of the first aid treatment for anyone suffering an epileptic attack:

* Protect them from any danger or hazard.
* Keep others away.
* Speak quietly to the client.
* In the case of tonic clonic:
  - Support or try to ease the fall.
  - Clear a space around the person.
  - Carefully loosen clothing around the neck if possible.
  - Place a soft support under the head.
  - When the attack ceases, place the client in the recovery position (see Figure 5.6 on page 61).

Parkinson's disease

This is a progressive disorder of the nervous system when the nerve cells in the part of the brain that control movement stop functioning properly. The cause is unknown, but a loss of dopamine, a chemical produced by the brain, results in Parkinson's disease. The symptoms – tremors, rigidity and slowness of movement which causes stooped posture, problems with swallowing, drooling and a shuffling gait – do not appear until about 80 per cent of the brain's dopamine has been lost. Other signs include soft, mumbling speech, problems with handwriting, difficulty with everyday activities and depression.

Multiple sclerosis

This is a progressive condition and results from the destruction of the protective tissue around the nerves in any part of the brain or spinal cord. The damage causes interference in the transmission of messages from one neurone to another. The myelin sheaths deteriorate to scleroses (hardened scar tissue with a loss of elasticity) and this happens in multiple areas. It is often classified as an autoimmune disease when the body's own immune system attacks its own tissues.

Some people are genetically susceptible to this condition, but it is thought that a viral infection may also be responsible for triggering it.

Initially, the symptoms are mild, but there is usually an increasing loss of function. There are a considerable number of symptoms, which vary from a tingling sensation and general weakness or numbness to an unsteadiness when walking, slurring of speech and twitching of facial muscles. In more advanced stages, stiffness and spasms may affect the legs and the arms.

Shingles/herpes zoster

This is an infection of the nerves that supply the skin, causing a painful rash of small blisters following the route of a nerve under the skin. It is caused by the same virus which causes chickenpox. After a person has had an attack of chickenpox, the virus can remain dormant in certain nerves, sometimes to be reactivated later to cause shingles. It is not clear what prompts the virus to reactivate or 'awaken' in healthy people. A temporary weakness in immunity may allow the virus to multiply and move along nerve fibres towards the skin. Although children can get shingles, it is more common in people over the age of 50. Illness, trauma and stress may also trigger an attack.

Sciatica

This is a type of neuritis (inflammation of a single nerve) causing severe pain along the path of the sciatic nerve or its branches. It may be caused by pelvic injury, pregnancy, osteoarthritis of the back or slipped disc.

Disorders of the female reproductive system

Amenorrhoea

This is the absence of menstruation. Primary amenorrhoea is when a woman has never menstruated and it can be caused by endocrine disorders in the pituitary or hypothalamus or through genetic abnormalities of the ovaries or uterus. Secondary amenorrhoea occurs to most women at some time and it is when one or more periods are missed. Causes may include changes in body weight; obesity can affect ovarian function, and the extreme loss of weight, which characterises anorexia nervosa, can halt menstrual flow.

Dysmenorrhoea

This is painful menstruation caused by contraction of the uterus during menstruation. In some cases, it may be accompanied by nausea, vomiting, headache, fatigue and nervousness. An underlying gynaecological disorder may cause the pain, conditions such as endometriosis (see below), a backward tilting uterus, fibroids, inflammation of the fallopian tubes or abnormal adhesions (causing structures which should be separate to be bound together). The pain may sometimes extend into the back or thighs and can resemble a constant dull ache or cramps that come and go.

Endometriosis

This occurs when endometrial tissue, normally only found in the lining of the uterus, grows outside the uterus attaching itself to various sites such as the ovaries, cervix, abdominal wall, bowel, ureters, bladder or the vagina. This misplaced tissue still responds to the hormonal changes of the menstrual cycle and therefore may bleed during menstruation causing irritation, pain and sometimes cramps. In time, scar tissue develops and this can cause adhesions which bind structures together that are normally separate and this may interfere with their normal function.

Polycystic ovary disease

This is a hormone disorder due to inadequate secretion of luteinising hormone. The follicles fail to ovulate and remain as multiple cysts distending the ovary. Further hormone imbalance may result in obesity, acne and hirsutism (excessive hair growth).

Uterine fibroids

These are swellings in the muscular walls of the uterus. They are extremely common, benign and mostly cause no problems. Fibroids seem to depend on oestrogen for their growth, growing during pregnancy but shrinking spontaneously after the menopause. They are more common in women over 40 and those of African-Caribbean and Chinese-type origin. The most common symptom is heavy periods, but if the fibroid grows very large, there may be a swelling in the abdomen and if it presses on the bladder will cause frequent urination, or incontinence.

Mastitis

This is an inflammation of the breast caused by bacterial infection through damaged nipples. Chronic cystic mastitis does not become inflamed. It is a lumpiness of the breast due to the presence of cysts and this condition is thought to be caused by hormone imbalance.

Cancer

One in three people will be diagnosed with cancer at some stage in their lives. There are 200 types of cancer. The most common for women are breast, large bowel, lung, ovarian and uterine. The most common for men are lung, prostate, bowel, bladder and stomach. There are several categories of cancer:

* **Carcinomas** account for 85 per cent of cancers and start in the epithelium, the lining covering organs and skin.
* **Sarcomas** account for 6 per cent of cancers and form in the connective tissue such as muscle, bone and fatty tissue.
* **Leukaemias/lymphomas** account for 5 per cent of cancers and occur in tissues where white blood cells, which fight infection in the body, are formed, that is, in the bone marrow and the lymphatic system.
* **Other forms of cancer** such as brain tumours and other rare forms account for 4 per cent of all cancers.

The treatment for cancer can have severe side effects and many treatments are contraindicated. However, depending on the type of cancer, its location in the body and the medical treatment recommended, there are many therapeutic beauty treatments that can be provided with the client's doctor's approval.

Today, because of the diversity of treatments offered in beauty salons and spas, there are increased risks to health and safety. Therapists must be aware of these and maintain a safe working environment for themselves, their colleagues and clients.

Beauty therapists have a duty to ensure that premises, equipment and materials are kept clean and germ free and all sanitary precautions are taken. They must prevent cross-infection within the salon by using appropriate methods of sterilisation. This will also show a high level of commitment to the client who can be assured of a professional and safe place for therapeutic treatments.

Bacteria

Bacteria enter the body in the following ways:
* Airborne through respiration.
* Through contaminated food.
* Through contaminated objects, which have been handled by an infected person.
* Through direct contact by touching an infected person.
* In the salon infection may occur when unsterilised equipment is used or therapists work unhygienically and pass on infection.

Therapists must not work on any person who has visible signs of infection.

Classification of bacteria

Figure 4.1 shows the different types of bacteria and Table 4.1 gives their characteristics.

Useful health and safety terms

Antiseptic – a chemical agent, which inhibits the growth and multiplication of bacteria.

Asepsis – free from bacteria and other micro-organisms that could cause disease.

Bacteria – micro-organisms found nearly everywhere. There are two main types of bacteria: non-pathogenic and pathogenic.

Disinfectant – a chemical agent which destroys bacteria.

Fungus (plural fungi) – simple vegetable life which includes yeasts, moulds and mushrooms.

Non-pathogenic – harmless or actually beneficial to humans.

Pathogenic – disease producing and harmful.

Sanitise – to make clean and sanitary.

Sepsis – infected with bacteria.

Sterilisation – the complete destruction of bacteria.

Virus – a micro-organism smaller than bacteria. Viruses can only live and reproduce within living cells. They cause diseases such as the common cold, measles and poliomyelitis.

Name	Shape	Characteristics
Cocci	Round	Single or in groups
Diplococci	Round, grow in pairs	Causes pneumonia
Streptococci	Round, grow in chains	Pus forming, found in blood poisoning
Staphylococci	Round, grow in bunches or clusters	Pus forming, present in abscesses, pustules and boils
Bacilli	Rod-shaped	Many are spore producers and produce diseases such as influenza, tetanus and typhoid
Spirilla	Curved or corkscrew	Subdivided into other groups including spirochaetal organisms

Table 4.1 *Characteristics of bacteria*

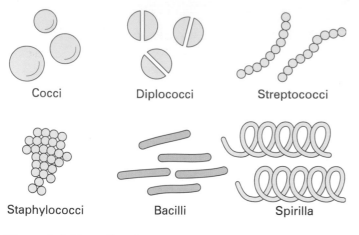

Cocci   Diplococci   Streptococci

Staphylococci   Bacilli   Spirilla

Figure 4.1 *Types of bacteria*

Growth, movement and reproduction of bacteria

Bacteria will grow in a warm, dark, damp environment where there is sufficient food for them to feed on. When the conditions are ideal, bacteria grows and multiplies rapidly, but when conditions are not favourable, bacteria stop multiplying and die.

Bacilli and spirilla move easily as they have flagella or cilia (hair-like projections) which move the bacteria through a liquid.

General infection occurs when the body cannot cope with the bacteria and the build up of toxins, and a localised infection may be transported around the body in the blood.

Viruses

Viruses are living organisms, which are so small they are only visible through an electron microscope. They are many and varied and become active when they are inside the right type of living cell. They are responsible for such things as influenza, chickenpox and measles and, more seriously, AIDS (acquired immune deficiency syndrome) which is caused by the HIV (human immunopathic virus) and Hepatitis B (see Chapter 3 Contraindications).

Fungi

These are microscopic plant organisms consisting of many cells, for example moulds, mildew and yeast. They are unable to manufacture their own food and are

parasitic (obtaining food from other living organisms) or saprophytic (obtaining food from dead plants or animal matter). They can be single-celled yeasts, a network of branching threads, or much larger, formed from interwoven hyphae (long chains of cells) such as mushrooms and toadstools. An example of a parasitic fungus is ringworm.

There are, however, some useful fungi, which are beneficial in different ways:

* Mushrooms are a popular food.
* Penicillin is an effective treatment for illness.
* Some are contained in food such as blue cheese or used as a raising agent for bread.
* Some can be used to produce alcohol.

The body will defend itself from infection in several ways:

* Enzymes present in the mouth, nose, tears, sweat and sebum may kill bacteria.
* The skin is a defence against bacterial invasion as long as it is intact.
* Macrophage cells will engulf bacteria and destroy them.
* White blood cells will destroy bacteria or produce antibodies.
* The lymphatic system will deal with the invading bacteria or virus in the lymph nodes.

Methods of sterilisation and sanitisation

Ultraviolet (UV) radiation

This is one of the most convenient and commonly used methods of sanitisation used in beauty salons today. The UV cabinet has limited sterilisation properties and is efficient in storing previously sterilised equipment.

Small instruments, brushes, ventouses, electrodes, and so on, are sanitised by short-wave UV radiation. All instruments with a fine cutting edge should be wiped first with spirit, for example isopropyl alcohol or surgical spirit.

UV radiation is damaging to the eyes so most modern units have a safety switch built in, to switch off the lamp when the door is opened.

This method of sanitisation is only effective on the surfaces that the rays touch, so the items must be turned during sanitisation, which takes 20 minutes.

Autoclave

The autoclave is a proven method of sterilisation used in health and beauty salons. It boils water under pressure and is suitable for small metal instruments. The vessel itself looks rather like a pressure cooker. It is easy to use and cheap to run. It consists of two chambers: an upper chamber in which the instruments are placed and a lower chamber for the water.

The higher the pressure, the hotter the water has to be to boil, for example at atmospheric pressure water boils at 100°C which is not hot enough to sterilise.

Using the autoclave at 15 lb per square inch, the water boils at 121°C, which is hot enough to sterilise.

For sterilisation to be complete, this procedure should take 15 minutes. The automatic autoclave is recommended as it has an automatic timer and a pressure gauge. The whole sterilisation process is, therefore, automatic once the start button has been pressed.

Figure 4.2 *An autoclave*

Disinfectant

Disinfectants currently available are either prepared and ready for use or need to be diluted. The manufacturer's instructions should be followed for disinfectants which have to be diluted.

A good disinfectant should be:

* easy to use
* non-corrosive
* quick acting
* non-irritating
* odourless.

The quickest method of sanitisation is cleaning with alcohol, either by immersion, or by wiping the surface of the tool with the alcohol before placing it in a dry steriliser such as a UV cabinet. Alcohol-impregnated wipes, which are easy to use, are available commercially and are ideal for use in the salon.

Containers used for disinfecting with alcohol should be washed regularly in hot soapy water. The alcohol should be discarded after one use as it will no longer be sterile.

All equipment should be cleaned before sterilisation to remove surface debris. The best way to do this is as follows:

1 Wash tools in hot soapy water.
2 Rinse with plain water.
3 Dry thoroughly.
4 Use chosen method of sterilisation.

After use, the outer surface of all pieces of electrical equipment should be wiped over with an alcohol such as isopropyl alcohol.

Gamma radiation

This is used to sterilise epilation needles, which come in a sealed pack ready for use.

Salon hygiene

Beauty therapists must ensure that their salons are hygienic at all times.

* All surfaces and curtains must be washed regularly.

* The salon must have up-to-date, effective sterilising units.
* Clean bed linen should be used for each client or the couch should be covered with paper towels.
* Clean towels must be used for each client.
* Towels must be laundered daily.
* Waste must be placed in closed containers.
* Broken glass or contaminated needles must be disposed of in a sharps box.
* Hands must be washed before and after each client.
* Lids should be kept on jars and bottles containing creams and lotions to prevent contamination.
* Spatulas must be used to remove cream from containers.
* Disposable equipment such as spatulas, lip and mascara brushes should be used to prevent cross-infection.
* Salon surfaces must be washed daily with disinfectant and cleaned after each client.
* Therapists must wear a clean uniform.

Personal hygiene

Because therapists work in such close proximity to their clients, it is essential to pay special attention to personal hygiene.

* Take a daily bath or shower.
* Use an effective antiperspirant.
* Teeth should be brushed regularly and mouthwash used if necessary.
* Hair should be kept clean and tied back off the face.
* Uniform and shoes should be spotlessly clean.
* Shoes should be comfortable to prevent poor posture.
* Hands should be clean and nails kept short.
* Nail enamel should not be worn as clients could have an allergy to it. It may also chip during treatment, which would look unprofessional.

The first impression therapists make will be a lasting one. Therefore, it must be a good one, so a clean salon and a professionally turned out therapist will fill the client with confidence.

Figure 4.3 *Therapists should wash their hands immediately before and after treating a client*

Health and safety in the salon

There is a great deal of legislation which protects both clients and employees, and the salon's manager must ensure that all employees are aware of their responsibilities and receive the relevant training in health and safety procedures.

* Statute law is the written law of the land and consists of Acts of Parliament and the rules and regulations which are made in relation to the Acts.
* Byelaws are made at a local level and are enforced by the local council.

It is the manager's task to draw up a health and safety policy for the salon. This is a legal responsibility if the business employs five or more people. The policy must be in written form and available for all members of staff. Employees can be involved in this process and contribute by making suggestions for improvement. This should prevent accidents occurring and provide a safe environment for all members of staff, clients and visitors to enter the premises.

The health and safety policy

The purpose of the policy is to provide information for all employees about the salon's health and safety objectives and how they may be achieved. The policy should include:

* the responsibilities of the manager, supervisors and health and safety representative
* the duties of employees (to include statutory law and company regulations)
* the systems used to monitor health and safety

* the health and safety training provided
* the identification of hazards and risks (see below)
* fire precautions
* accident procedures
* methods of recording accidents and breaches of health and safety regulations.

A **hazard** is something that could cause harm such as a spillage on the floor.

A **risk** is the likelihood of the hazard actually causing harm, for example a client slipping on the spillage.

Beauty Retreat
Policy on health and Safety at work

It is the policy of this establishment to make every reasonable and practicable effort to maintain a safe and healthy working environment for all employees and members of the public.

The establishment recognises that the responsibility for enforcing this policy lies with the management. However, all employees must accept a joint responsibility for the safety of themselves, their colleagues and members of the public.

The coordination and monitoring of the safety at work policy and effective safety communication with the establishment will be the responsibility of Ushma Patel, the elected safety representative. The management will ensure that every effort is made to meet the statutory requirements and codes of practice relating to the activities of the salon and any relevant recommendations from bodies dealing with health and safety.

To achieve this we will:

• provide training in safety procedures
• appoint a safety representative
• implement safe systems of work
• provide information about specific hazards
• issue protective clothing where possible
• monitor safety procedures
• provide training in fire and evacuation procedures
• check all electrical equipment once a year
• provide training in first aid
• record all accidents
• provide adequate rest facilities
• provide a healthy environment.

Since employees are under a legal obligation to cooperate in matters of health, safety and welfare, all must accept personal responsibility for the prevention of accidents.

All employees will be informed of any revision of this policy.

A copy of the health and safety rules of the establishment are displayed in the staff room.

Deborah Baxter
Proprietor

Figure 4.4 *A health and safety policy*

Risk assessment

This involves examining the workplace to identify anything that may cause harm and to decide on the precautions to take to prevent harm coming to anyone who is working in or visiting the premises. The person carrying out the risk assessment will need to consult with all members of staff. Since they are the ones who carry out treatments and follow set procedures daily, they may be more aware of potential risks to health and safety. The category of person who may be at risk, for example therapists, technicians, clients, inexperienced or young staff, or clients and staff with disabilities, will need to be assessed. Then a decision taken as to whether a risk is high, medium or low.

The aim of risk assessment is to reduce risks by taking precautions. If a hazard cannot be eliminated, it is necessary to use control measures such as preventing access to the hazard by unauthorised people, reducing exposure to the hazard or providing personal protective equipment (PPE).

It is important to review risk assessment regularly to ensure that the precautions are working effectively and to alter them when necessary. The hazards in a salon relate to:

* the salon environment
* the equipment used
* the products used for treatment
* the products used for cleaning and sterilisation
* the practical procedures for treatments.

Health and safety procedures

It is the personal responsibility of each therapist to be aware of all hazards in the workplace, reduce the risks by following instructions and using initiative, participate in all health and safety training, use equipment and products according to manufacturers' instructions and use PPE when required. Any breaches of health and safety must be reported to your line manager and you must follow company policies on health and safety.

The manager must ensure that staff receive safety training at induction, when there is any new relevant legislation, to provide safe systems of work and for professional development.

Table 4.2 *Example of risk assessment*

Hazard	Risk	Level of risk	People who may be harmed	Control measures	Responsibility
Hydrogen peroxide	Burning, irritation, bleaching	Medium	Clients, therapists	Train in use; follow Control of Substances Hazardous to Health (COSHH) regulations procedures; use PPE	Therapist, manager/supervisor
Loose wire	Electric shock	High	Clients, therapists	Have equipment checked regularly by an expert; therapist should check before each use	Therapist, manager/ supervisor, electrician, health and safety representative
Steam bath	Heat exhaustion, fainting, scalds	Medium	Clients	Train in use; protect client from direct steam; check that it is set on the correct temperature; do not leave client unattended	Therapist, manager/supervisor
Cuticle nippers	Cutting the skin, cross-infection	Low	Clients	Train in safe use; sterilise before use	Therapist
Wet floor	Slipping, falling, breaking a bone, spraining a joint, pulling a muscle	High	Clients, therapists, visitors, cleaners	Use a sign to inform people; mop up spillages immediately	All staff
Frayed carpet	Falling, tripping, breaking a bone, spraining a joint, pulling a muscle	High	Clients, therapists, visitors, cleaners	Fix the carpet; cover the frayed part; use a sign to inform people	Manager, maintenance, all staff

The health and safety representative

In a small salon the manager will deal with all matters relating to health and safety liaising directly with all members of staff. In larger premises, particularly with different categories of staff, a health and safety representative may be appointed to deal with health and safety matters.

The principal duties of the health and safety representative are to:

* comply with all health and safety legislation and communicate information to all employees
* assess hazards and risks
* provide training and demonstrate safe procedures in matters of health and safety
* implement and monitor safe systems of work and safety procedures
* put right breaches of the health and safety policy
* maintain health and safety records.

Safe systems of work

Accidents involving members of staff and clients will be greatly reduced or even eliminated if safe systems of work are put into practice. A safe system of work is the way a procedure is carried out to ensure maximum safety.

If you are assessing a task the first thing to do is to write down the procedure and list all the equipment and products that are used. Look at where the task is carried out and list any potential hazards or risk to the health and safety of the therapist, client or other person involved. Agree upon the correct procedure to follow and inform all staff orally and in written form. A copy of the procedure should be filed in a secure place for reference purposes. Training must be given to those who need it to ensure that the safe system is implemented correctly by everyone. Regular checks and staff appraisal must be made to maintain standards, and information must be revised and updated when necessary. Regular meetings should be held with employees to check that the systems in place are safe and working effectively.

Acts and regulations

There are several Acts of Parliament and European Union (EU) directives, implemented in the UK, relating to health and safety in the workplace and relevant to spa and beauty therapists. European law has had an impact on legislation in recent years and it is enforced by means of directives, which set out the standards each member state must achieve. The UK implements these directives through regulations. The relevant Acts and regulations are:

* Health and Safety at Work etc Act (HASWA) (1974)
* Management of Health and Safety at Work Regulations (1999)
* Health and Safety (Young Persons) Regulations (1997)
* Workplace (Health Safety and Welfare) Regulations (1992)
* Manual Handling Operations Regulations (1992)
* Personal Protective Equipment (PPE) at Work Regulations (1992)
* Provision and Use of Work Equipment Regulations (1992)
* Control of Substances Hazardous to Health (COSHH) Regulations (2002)
* Electricity at Work Regulations (1990)
* Environmental Protection Act (1990)
* Reporting of Injuries, Disease and Dangerous Occurrences Regulations (RIDDOR) (1995)
* Health and Safety (First Aid) Regulations (1981)
* Fire Precautions (Workplace) Regulations (1997)
* Disability Discrimination Act (1995)
* Health and Safety (Display Screen Equipment) Regulations (1992)

Health and Safety at Work etc Act (HASWA) (1974)

This Act imposes a general obligation on all employers. It forms the basis of health and safety regulations in the UK, even though new regulations have come into effect in response to EU directives stating how these obligations and duties must be fulfilled. The duty of the employer is to ensure, so far as it is reasonably practicable, the health, safety and welfare of all employees. Failure to implement these duties may give rise to criminal liability and to a claim for damages. It also imposes duties on the employee to cooperate with the employer in maintaining health and safety in the workplace.

> **Health** includes mental as well as physical health.
>
> **Safety** is the freedom from foreseeable injury.
>
> **Welfare** – the facilities available for the employees' comfort.

Management of Health and Safety at Work Regulations (1999)

These regulations require the employer to maintain and improve the safe working conditions and environment of the workplace by assessing risks, implementing, monitoring and reviewing preventative measures and completing all health and safety records.

> Health and safety checks must be made:
>
> **regularly** – to comply with current legislation, when they have to be legally documented, or
> to fulfil the requirements of the organisation's own health and safety policy
>
> **randomly** – to ensure all members of staff are fulfilling their obligations in maintaining set standards in health and safety.

Table 4.3 *Duties of the employer and employees under the Health and Safety at Work Act (1974)*

The employer must also appoint one or more competent people to implement evacuation procedures and provide health and safety training as well as keeping all employees up to date with relevant health and safety information.

Health and Safety (Young Persons) Regulations (1997)

These regulations amend the Management of Health and Safety at Work Regulations (1992) by placing new duties on those intending to employ people under the age of 18. No young persons can be employed for work beyond their physical or psychological capacity or be exposed to risks because of lack of experience or training. Employers are required to assess the risk to young people before they start work, taking into account their inexperience, immaturity and lack of awareness of existing or potential risks in the workplace. They must provide information to the parents of school-age children about the risks involved and the control measures taken. The results of risk assessment should be used to determine whether a young person should be prohibited from certain work activities. An exception to this is when the young person is over the minimum school leaving age and the work activity is necessary for his or her training, where risks are reduced as far as is reasonably practicable and where proper supervision is provided by a competent person.

A child may be defined as someone below school leaving age (under 16). A young person may be defined as someone aged 16 or over, who has not reached the age of 18.

Duties of the employer	Duties of employees
To provide and maintain safe systems of work that are safe and without risk to health To ensure safety when handling, using and storing substances and equipment To provide the necessary information, instruction, training and supervision to ensure health and safety To maintain the place of work in a safe condition and without risk to health To provide and maintain access to the place of work and all exits To provide and maintain a working environment with adequate welfare facilities	To take reasonable care of themselves and those for whom they are responsible To comply with statutory duties and requirements Not to intentionally or recklessly misuse anything provided in the interest of health, safety and welfare

It is advisable for a salon to adopt a policy concerning the health and safety of young people employed to ensure that the employer's legal responsibility is carried out.

Workplace (Health Safety and Welfare) Regulations (1992)

These regulations aim to ensure that all places of work meet the health, safety and welfare needs of every employee. Every employer has a duty to ensure that workplaces under their control comply with these regulations and all the facilities that are required by the regulations are provided.

Owners or proprietors of business premises also have duties under these regulations. They must ensure that areas shared by tenants, which are under their control, are well maintained. These may include the reception area, a staircase, landings, office space, stock rooms, rest rooms and toilets. However, owners are not responsible for matters outside their control such as the day-to-day cleaning of toilets, which is the responsibility of the tenant. There should be cooperation between tenants and with the owner to ensure the requirements of the regulations are fully met.

Some of the requirements of the regulations in relation to beauty and spa establishments include the following:

✱ To maintain the workplace so that all the equipment, devices and systems are in good repair and in efficient working order. Repair and maintenance work must be carried out properly and without delay. The maintenance programme should include regular inspection and testing with suitable records being kept on each occasion.

✱ Ventilation must be effective with sufficient quantities of purified air particularly in an enclosed workplace. Windows may provide sufficient ventilation but mechanical methods must be used when appropriate and regularly cleaned, tested and maintained.

✱ The temperature in the workplace should provide reasonable comfort normally at least 16°C. To maintain a comfortable temperature, heating or cooling may be used. In extremely hot weather fans or increased ventilation would be an option. Sanitary and rest facilities and shower and changing rooms must also be maintained at a comfortable temperature. When an employee is required to work in a room which is normally unoccupied (such as a stockroom), then temporary heating should be provided.

✱ Lighting must be suitable and sufficient to enable work to be carried out safely. Lights that are dazzling or cause an annoying glare should be avoided and they must be replaced, repaired or cleaned as necessary. Windows must be kept clean to allow maximum daylight, or shaded if they cause excessive glare or heat.

✱ The workplace floor, walls, ceilings, fixtures and soft furnishings must be kept clean. Waste materials should not be allowed to accumulate except in an appropriate covered bin. Cleaning must be carried out using suitable materials that will not expose anyone to a health and safety risk.

✱ The size of a workplace must provide sufficient room to allow the employee to work in a safe and healthy manner. Workstations should allow ease of movement so that all tasks may be carried out safely and comfortably. Seating provided should give adequate support to the lower back.

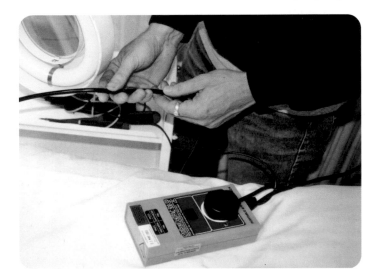

Figure 4.5 *Electrical equipment should be regularly tested by a qualified electrician*

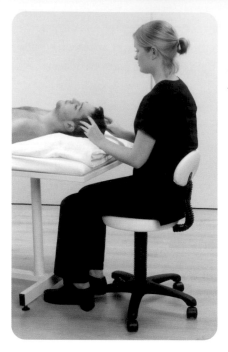

Figure 4.6 *The therapist should be seated correctly to avoid poor posture*

✳ Floors must be suitable for the purpose they are to be used with no uneven or slippery surfaces. They must also be kept free from obstruction that may present a hazard or prevent access. Surfaces of floors that may become wet, for example spa, steam or shower room, must be of a type that does not become unduly slippery.

✳ A secure and substantial handrail should be provided on at least one side of a staircase unless there is a particular risk of falling, in which case two handrails must be provided.

✳ Toilets must be adequately ventilated, lit, clean, easily accessible and sufficient in numbers (see Table 4.4). Suitable means must be provided for the disposal of sanitary items in toilets used by women.

Number of people in workplace	Number of toilets required	Number of wash stations required
1–5	1	1
6–25	2	2
26–50	3	3
51–75	4	4

Table 4.4 *Number of toilets and wash stations required per employee*

✳ Washing facilities must be provided close to each toilet or changing room and there must be a supply of clean cold and hot or warm running water. Soap or other means of cleansing and towels or other means of drying should be provided. Washing areas must be well lit, ventilated and kept clean.

✳ An adequate supply of drinking water should be provided for all people in the workplace. It must be easily accessible and sign posted for reasons of health and safety. A sufficient number of drinking cups must be provided unless a drinking fountain is supplied.

✳ Provision must be made for employees' clothes when they are not worn for work purposes. A changing room must be provided for workers who change into special work clothes and have to remove more than their outer clothing. Clothes must be kept in a secure place such as a locker.

✳ Suitable provision for rest and eating facilities must be supplied that are easily accessible, and for pregnant women and nursing mothers the rest facilities should be conveniently situated near to toilet and washroom facilities, and should include the facility to lie down. Rest areas should be arranged in such a way that non-smokers will not experience discomfort from tobacco smoke.

Manual Handling Operations Regulations (1992)

These regulations were introduced under HASWA (1974). They implement a European directive on the manual handling of loads, to prevent injuries such as strains, sprains, back injuries.

The definition of **manual handling operations** is the transporting or supporting of a load either by hand or bodily force and includes lifting, putting down, pushing, pulling, carrying or moving.

The definition of **load** is any item or object that is being supported or transported.

The limitations of the staff involved

The type of load to be handled

When assessing a task the employer must consider:

The working environment

The task to be completed

The capabilities of the staff involved in the task

Figure 4.7 *Assessment of tasks involving manual handling of loads*

Many injuries which occur are the result of regular mishandling rather than the result of one single incident, so employers are required to assess all tasks which involve manual handling of loads (see Figure 4.7).

Risk of injury may be avoided by eliminating the need to manually handle any load and this can be achieved by delivering goods to the point of use, carrying out any repairs in situ and using trolleys for transportation. Always split large loads to make them smaller and lighter and ask for assistance from a colleague.

When planning the movement of a load, choose the flattest, straightest route and remove any obstacles that you might trip over. Make a note of a place to rest en route and make sure that your storage space is clear for you when you arrive with the load. Check the load has an even weight distribution and there is nothing sharp protruding from it which may cause injury.

Personal Protective Equipment at Work Regulations(PPE) (1992)

Personal protective equipment (PPE) is any equipment which is designed to be worn or held by people at work to protect them from health and safety risks. These regulations are to protect any employees who may be exposed to a health risk or injury in the course of their work. The employer is required to assess the need for PPE and supply it free of charge when it is a necessary requirement of the job. All staff must be trained in the use of PPE, it must be maintained in good working order and fit for the nature of the work.

Provision and Use of Work Equipment Regulations (2002)

These regulations require that all equipment used in a salon, whether new or second-hand, must conform to

Figure 4.8 *The correct procedure for lifting and handling a load*

1 Think about the lift. Where is the load to be placed? Do you need help? Are handling aids available?

2 Get ready to lift. Stand with your feet apart.

3 Bend the knees. Keep the back straight. Tuck in your chin. Lean slightly forward over the load to get a good grip.

4 Get a good grip on the load and lift smoothly.

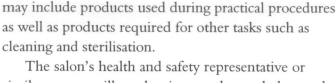

EU safety standards, be suitable for its intended use, properly maintained and in good working order and only used by fully trained staff.

To comply with these regulations:

* all equipment must be regularly serviced
* accurate up-to-date records of when equipment has been checked and repaired should be kept
* a service engineer or electrician should check any equipment bought second-hand
* all members of staff must be trained in the use of the equipment
* training days should be held to update skills and information
* only those trained in the use of specialist equipment should work with that equipment
* written instructions should be provided in addition to training if and when required.

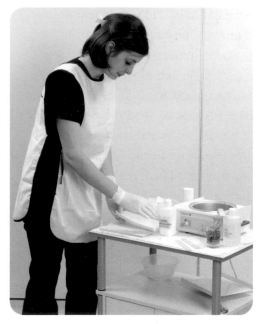

Figure 4.9
Wearing protective gloves and apron when waxing

Control of Substances Hazardous to Health Regulations (COSHH) (2002)

More commonly referred to as the COSHH Regulations, they state that every employer has a legal obligation to assess the risks associated with hazardous substances used in the workplace and to take steps to eliminate or control risks. The regulations apply to all substances which can have an adverse effect on health if they are not handled, stored or used correctly. These may include products used during practical procedures as well as products required for other tasks such as cleaning and sterilisation.

The salon's health and safety representative or similar person will need to inspect the workplace and make a list of all hazardous substances, assess the potential risk to health and evaluate any existing control measures. The law requires suppliers to provide information about the safe use of the products that they are selling on clearly marked labels. To recognise substances that may be hazardous, it is important to read these labels but not to rely solely on this information (see Figure 4.10).

(a) Corrosive

(b) Explosive

(c) Harmful

(d) Highly flammable

(e) Irritant

(f) Oxidizing

(g) Toxic

Figure 4.10 *COSSH labels identify harmful substances*

Exposure to these substances may result in:

* irritation to the skin or eyes
* a burn when they make direct contact with the skin
* irritation to the lungs and eyes if they give off fumes
* breathing difficulties by irritating or restricting the air passages
* allergy, sensitising the skin immediately or after repeated exposure to the substance.

The salon must have measures in place to ensure the safe, storage, handling, transportation, use and disposal of hazardous substances and provide adequate staff training in the use of the hazardous substances. The effectiveness of the control measures needs to be monitored and up-to-date records kept detailing the measures taken and the checks made.

Storage of hazardous substances

Any product which has been identified as hazardous must be stored in a cool dry place, out of direct sunlight, away from naked flames and in a well-ventilated room. It should be stored in a metal cupboard and in the correct container, and if the item is heavy, it should be stored on a low shelf and always out of the reach of children.

Transporting, handling, using and disposing of hazardous substances

When transporting hazardous substances, follow the manufacturers' instructions, wrap them up carefully and label the container. Wear protective clothes when necessary. When mixing and diluting any substance always follow the manufacturer's instructions and never smoke in the vicinity. Always reseal containers after use and wipe up any spillages immediately.

Dispose of unused, excess or old chemicals safely in accordance with the Environmental Protection Act (1990).

Environmental Protection Act (1990)

This Act states that any person disposing of 'waste' has a duty to dispose of it safely in such a way that it does not cause any harm to the environment or the individual. If out-of-date stock needs to be disposed of, it may be necessary to ask the manufacturer for advice. To comply with the Act, you will need to obtain the relevant information from suppliers about the safe use and disposal of products.

Employees should be trained in the safe disposal of products and chemicals. Never dispose of chemical products where they may be found by any unauthorised person, in particular children.

Reporting of Injuries, Disease and Dangerous Occurrences Regulations (RIDDOR) (1995)

Commonly referred to as RIDDOR, these regulations cover all employees, clients or members of the public who suffer injury or a condition resulting from a work activity. The purpose of the regulations is to ensure all information regarding incidents or injury, arising from a work activity, is given to the enforcing authority, by the person responsible within the organisation. The enforcing authority will be either the Health & Safety Executive (HSE) or the local authority. This information is useful to highlight areas which may require improvement or a change in practice, to prevent any future accidents or injury occurring.

Any accident which results in more than three days' absence from work must be reported within ten days of the accident occurring. Fatal accidents or major injury must be reported immediately and dangerous occurrences must also be reported even if they do not result in an injury. Work-related disease must be reported once a written diagnosis has been received in the form of a medical certificate. Records must be kept and can be entered into an accident book along with photocopies of all reports sent to the enforcing authority. These records must be kept for a minimum of three years. All employees must immediately report a suspected infectious disease to their line manager to prevent the risk of cross-infection. An example of an accident report form is shown in Figure 4.11.

Beauty Retreat
24, The Downs, Cheltenham 6AQ 1PY

Date: 20th September 2003

Time: 11.30 am

Name: Jayne Salt

Address: 7 Burton Avenue

Tel. No.: 0789 653421

Status: Client

Description of accident:

Miss Salt had been resting for ten minutes in the relaxation area having a herbal tea after her reflexology treatment. She slipped and fell when the heel of her shoe broke as she was walking to reception to make her next appointment. As she slipped she banged her arm on a shelf, grazing her elbow. The injury was superficial but first aid was applied.

Location of accident: In the reception area next to the product display.

Nature of injuries: Slight graze to the elbow, superficial bleeding.

Action taken: The first aider was called. He provided the necessary treatment by cleaning the graze and covering it with a waterproof dressing.

Witness 1: Kathleen Fitzgerald   **Status:** Therapist   **Signed** _K Fitzgerald_

Witness 2: Faye Ramjaun   **Status:** Manager   **Signed** _Faye Ramjaun_

First aider: Jason Clarke   **Status:** Sports therapist   **Signed** _Jason Clarke_

Signature of casualty: _____ _Jayne Salt_ _____

Figure 4.11 *Accident report form*

In 2001, the Health & Safety Executive launched a new Incident Contact Centre (ICC) for all incidents currently reportable under RIDDOR (1995). It is a joint venture by the Health & Safety Executive (HSE), Convention of Scottish Local Authorities (COSLA) and the Local Government Association (LGA). It provides a central point for employers to report incidents. The primary objectives of the ICC are:

* to improve the current arrangements by offering employers a single address and telephone number for all records, the option to report by telephone, fax, Internet or hard copy, and in the case of telephone calls, a written confirmation on receipt
* to allow injured persons a single point of contact for their rights under the Data Protection Act (1998).

RIDDOR notifications received by the ICC are passed on to the appropriate enforcing authority to alert them to individual incidents. The information collected provides the HSE with valuable information as to where and how risks arise and to highlight trends. Records held at the ICC are constantly updated as new information is received. (Details of the ICC are given in the Glossary of professional associations at the end of this book.)

Health and Safety (First Aid) Regulations (1981)

These regulations set out the minimum requirements for the provision of first aid at a place of work and covers appropriate equipment, facilities and personnel. The requirements vary depending upon the number of staff employed and the type of work involved. First aid at work covers the arrangements an employer must make to ensure that any person who suffers injury or illness in a place of work receives immediate attention and that an ambulance is called in serious cases. The minimum provision is a suitably stocked first aid box and an appointed person to take charge of first aid arrangements.

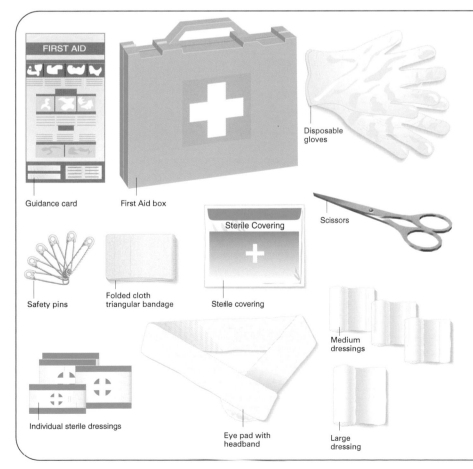

FIRST AID

Guidance card

First Aid box

Disposable gloves

Scissors

Safety pins

Folded cloth triangular bandage

Sterile Covering

Sterile covering

Medium dressings

Individual sterile dressings

Eye pad with headband

Large dressing

Contents of first aid box

For five employees:

* one guidance card
* ten individually wrapped sterile adhesive dressings, assorted sizes
* one sterile eye pad with attachment
* one individually wrapped triangular bandage
* one sterile covering for serious wounds
* six safety pins
* three medium sized sterile unmedicated dressings
* one large sterile unmedicated dressing
* one pair of disposable gloves
* one pair of scissors.

Figure 4.12 *A first aid kit for five people*

Small firms need only provide minimum first aid provision. However, greater provision may be necessary depending on the risks involved, the number of people employed, the distance from emergency services, and if any employee has disabilities or health problems.

Most minor accidents and injuries that occur in the salon may be treated by the appointed person who will hold a current first aid certificate. Qualified first aiders should be able to help with more serious problems while the injured party is waiting to be seen by a doctor. There are many minor accidents which may occur in the workplace and all therapists should be aware of the emergency treatment required (see Table 4.5).

Fire Precautions (Workplace) Regulations (1997), amended (1999)

These regulations provide for minimum safety standards in the workplace. To comply with these regulations the risks of fire in the workplace must be assessed. If five or more people are employed, a formal record of the risk assessments and the proposed measures to deal with them must be kept. All staff must be informed of the results and any written reports should be made available to them on request. Smoke alarms or some other form of automatic fire detection are required, particularly if there is the possibility that a fire could go undetected for some time. All means of escape must be kept clear of obstruction and doors must be unlocked and in good working order. This will help ensure that everyone in the building can get out safely.

Sufficient fire fighting equipment must be provided of the correct type to tackle small fires. It must be easy to find, kept in good working order and all staff trained in its use.

To ensure that everyone knows the procedures to be followed in case of fire, staff training in fire evacuation procedures is essential. Staff must know how to raise the alarm, where the fire extinguishers are located and the quickest way to safety. Regular checks must be made on fire fighting equipment, smoke detection systems, warning systems, means of escape and emergency lighting.

The Fire Precautions (Workplace) Regulations were amended in 1999 to bring larger employers, those that are required to have a fire certificate, into line within the 1997 regulations. It also requires them to carry out fire risk assessment.

Accident	Emergency treatment
Fainting – temporary loss of consciousness	Lie casualty down with legs raised or place in the recovery position if there is any difficulty breathing
Burns from dry heat such as infrared lamp	Cool the area by immersing in or holding under running water, cover with a sterile dressing and seek medical attention
Scalds from hot water or steam	As above
Chemical burn, e.g. undiluted disinfectant	Flush with lots of cold water, remove clothing which may have chemicals on it and cover with a sterile dressing
Shock from fluid loss, fear or pain	Reassure and keep warm, loosen clothing, treat cause and lie in recovery position if there is a possibility of vomiting
Cut – superficial or deep break in the skin which bleeds	Clean with warm water and antiseptic, apply pressure and cover with sterile dressing
Eye injury – from foreign bodies or chemicals in the eye	Wash chemicals out with water, use an eye bath or a twisted moistened corner of a sterile dressing
Asthma attack – muscles of the air passage going into spasm	Reassure, sit comfortably, loosen clothing, allow the sufferer to take medication, provide plenty of fresh air and keep warm

Table 4.5 *Emergency treatment required for minor accidents*

A fire certificate is required:

* if there are more than 20 people employed at any time
* if there are more than ten people working anywhere other than the ground floor
* when the total number of people working in a building exceeds 20.

Once a fire certificate has been granted, it must be kept on the premises as long as it is in force and it will state:

* the greatest number of people who can be safely employed at any one time on the premises
* the means of escape to be used
* the exits to be marked as fire escapes
* any special risks in the structure of the premises
* any breach of the fire regulations could make the employer liable for a fine or imprisonment.

Fire extinguishers

The regulations require all new portable fire extinguishers to be coloured red with an additional coloured panel on the side of the extinguisher to show the contents.

Extinguishers should be marked with:

* the words 'fire extinguisher'
* the type of extinguishing material inside
* the size in kilograms or litres.

The method of discharging the extinguisher should also be described. All fire extinguishers on a premises should have the same operating mechanism.

In the case of a very small fire breaking out which may be easily controlled, fire extinguishers may be used. Two people should always be present to put out the fire as long as it does not endanger their safety. It is essential to use the correct fire extinguisher for the type of fire (see Table 4.6 and Figure 4.13).

Colour	Contents	Use
Red	Water	Paper, fabric, wood, textiles
Blue	Powder	Paper, textiles, wood, burning liquid, electrical
Black	Carbon dioxide	Burning liquid and electrical
Cream	Foam	Burning liquid

Table 4.6 *Contents of portable fire extinguishers*

Water

Foam

Powder

CO₂ gas

Figure 4.13 *Fire extinguishers*

Fire evacuation

In the event of a fire, the safety of staff and clients is the most important consideration. It is important to evacuate the building as quickly as possible. Do not stop to take personal belongings unless they are within reach. Switch off lights and electrical equipment, then guide clients and employees to the nearest fire exit. Close doors behind you. Evacuate the building in an orderly manner and assemble at the designated meeting point. Dial 999 and ask for the fire and rescue service, then check that all members of staff and clients are accounted for.

It is important that all employees are aware of their role and responsibilities in the event of fire. Never use the lift; always use the staircase or fire escape if above ground level and put into action special arrangements for disabled employees, clients or visitors.

There are other incidents that may also require evacuation of the building:

* When a suspicious package is discovered, no one must be allowed to touch it, evacuate the building and phone the police immediately.
* If there is a gas leak, the building must be evacuated. Windows may be left open, but do not turn off light switches or unplug equipment as the tiniest spark may ignite the gas and cause an explosion.

Disability Discrimination Act (1995)

A requirement of this Act is that disabled people are allowed better access to the premises of a service provider (anyone who provides a service to the public) such as a beauty salon and the premises must be modified accordingly. In 1996, it became illegal to treat a disabled person less favourably than others in relation to their disability. In 1999, service providers had to make reasonable adjustments such as providing assistance to disabled people. In October 2004, adjustments will have to be made to premises to improve access to the disabled.

This Act protects the rights of people with sensory and mental disabilities as well as physical disabilities. It includes those with sight and hearing impairment, learning difficulties, long-term illness such as arthritis and those with severe disfigurements.

The premises must be safe and adjustments may have to be made to:

* design features
* the approach to the premises
* fixtures, fittings and furniture
* signs and signage
* other physical elements such as the reception area.

The following will need to be considered when assessing a salon for suitability and ease of access:

* Car parking facilities – are they sufficient, accessible with dropped curbs and even surfaces?
* Ramps may be required for access to a building; doors must also be of a reasonable width and entrance doors, if made of glass may be difficult to distinguish for partially sighted people.

* The reception area may have a high desk, which will provide a barrier to those clients in wheelchairs, and inadequate seating may be difficult to use for those with long-term skeletal and muscular disorders.
* Handles and switches must be located at a level that is easily reached and lighting should be checked for suitability.
* Information and signs should be placed where they can be seen easily and should be recognisable.
* Fire and evacuation procedures must be adequate, e.g. audible and visual.
* Treatment rooms need to be accessed easily, with couches that are adjustable or with steps provided for the client to use.
* Toilets should be easily accessible with a suitable layout.

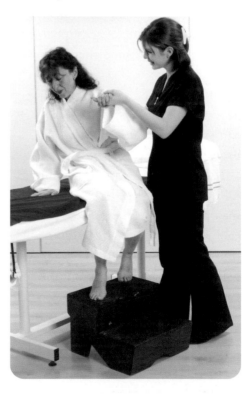

Figure 4.14
Steps should be provided so that all clients can have access to the massage couch

Health and Safety (Display Screen Equipment) Regulations (1992)

These regulations are designed to minimise the risk of occupational ill-health caused by the use of display screen equipment when it forms a large part of a job. With the increasing use of computers in all types of business these regulations must be complied with if any employees are using equipment which may cause the following:

* eye strain
* mental stress
* muscular pain
* other physical problems.

Employers have a duty to:

* assess the equipment and work station for risk of injury or strain to the employee
* plan for breaks or changes of activity
* provide training for employees in the use of the equipment
* provide any special spectacles needed
* provide a properly designed desk and chair.

Enforcing health and safety law

Both the Health & Safety Executive and the local authority are responsible for appointing suitably qualified inspectors whose main role is to ensure that laws relating to health and safety are complied with and also to provide advice and help in matters of health and safety.

Health and safety inspectors may visit a salon at any time to inspect the premises and carry out an investigation. They may take samples, photographs or measurements and have access to all records. They may serve an improvement or prohibition notice if there has been a breach of health and safety and in extreme cases, they may prosecute, which could result in a fine or term of imprisonment.

It is important to ensure that health and safety training is provided on a regular basis for all members of staff. This will maintain high levels of health and safety in the workplace, which will give clients confidence in the salon, and will also contribute to job satisfaction by providing a professional working environment for all employees.

Figure 4.15 *The employer has a duty to assess equipment for risk of injury or strain to the employee*

Electricity and the salon

A beauty salon or spa is dependent on electricity to provide heat and light and to power the equipment used to provide many of the treatments. It is the responsibility of the management to comply with current legislation and provide a safe working environment for staff and clients. It is the responsibility of individual therapists to comply with legislation and follow all rules and regulations in relation to health and safety and the use of electrical equipment, ensuring it is used correctly and following instructions in its storage and maintenance.

It is advisable for the salon to have a contract with a qualified and reliable electrician to regularly service and maintain the electrical systems and equipment.

Electricity at Work Regulations (1990)

These regulations govern electrical safety in the workplace. Employers must ensure that all electrical equipment and electrical systems are suitable for the work involved and safe to use. Care must be taken to buy, install and maintain equipment taking into account manufacturers' instructions and recommendations. A written record of all tests carried out by a qualified electrician must be kept, to include the date and the name of the electrician.

Individual therapists must cooperate with their employer in complying with these regulations. They are responsible for the day-to-day care of electrical equipment to prolong its working life and good condition and keep it safe to use. This may be achieved by following certain rules:

* Store equipment safely in its designated place with all the wires and attachments securely fixed in place.
* Check the wires are not twisted, worn or frayed and that the plug has the correct fuse and is not cracked or loose.

* Do not overload plug sockets by using multiple adaptors and make sure there are no trailing leads which someone could fall over.
* When in use make sure equipment is placed on a stable surface and away from water.
* Always make sure your hands are dry before touching the plug or equipment.
* Always follow manufacturers' instructions and report faulty equipment to your supervisor, then store it safely to be repaired.
* Depending on the type of equipment being used, clean immediately after use or on a regular basis.

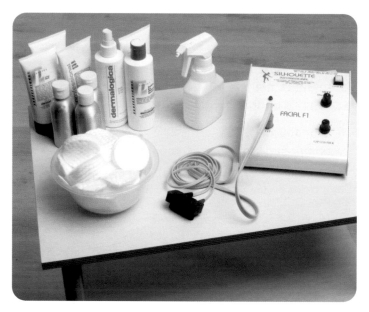

Figure 5.1 *Equipment should be placed on a stable surface within easy reach*

Laser and Intense Pulsed Light (IPL) equipment are regulated under the National Care Standards Commission (NCSC). There are four classes of laser treatment: Class 1 is the safest and Class 4 is potentially the most hazardous. You must apply for registration with the NCSC if your business offers Class 4 laser treatment and IPL for non-invasive cosmetic surgery administered by non-medically qualified staff. (For details, see the Glossary of professional associations and organisations at the end of this book.)

Useful scientific terms

Matter forms all living things and exists as a solid, liquid or gas and is made up of a number of chemical elements.

Chemical elements are substances that cannot be broken down into simpler substances by normal chemical reactions. There are 26 found in the human organism and 96 per cent of the body's mass is made up of the elements, carbon, hydrogen, oxygen and nitrogen, 3.9 per cent is made up of calcium, phosphorous, potassium, sulphur, sodium, chlorine, magnesium, iodine and iron.

Trace elements are chemical elements found in minute concentrations and there are 13 of these in the body.

Compounds are chemical substances composed of two or more elements.

Atoms are the smallest units of matter and consist of:
* a nucleus containing positively charged particles called protons and neutral particles called neutrons
* electrons which are negatively charged particles that move around the nucleus in concentric circles.

Molecules are a chemical combination of two or more atoms of the same or different kinds.

An **ion** is an electrically charged particle or group of particles.

Electrolyte is a solution which can conduct electricity.

How the body conducts electricity

The body is able to transmit electrical current because the tissues of the body are made up of a large proportion of fluid, which contains salt. When salt is dissolved in water the molecules split into ions, electrically charged particles. This turns the fluid in the tissues into an ionised solution. The tissue fluid is therefore an electrolyte which can conduct electricity.

How well the body conducts the current depends on the amount of tissue fluid in that part of the body. The epidermis is very low in body fluid so it will form an initial resistance to the current. This can be overcome by the use of a saline solution or other appropriate product applied to the skin.

Types of electricity

Static electricity

This occurs when two dry insulating surfaces are rubbed together. All substances are made up of molecules and molecules are made up of atoms. Atoms are made up of small particles, which are charged. In the very centre of an atom is a nucleus, which is positively charged, and roaming around this nucleus in concentric circles there are negatively charged electrons (see Figure 5.2).

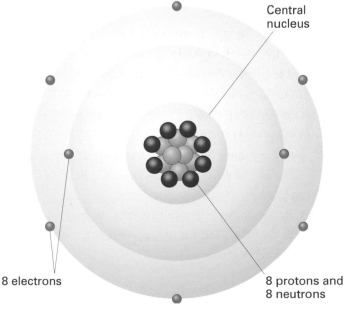

Central nucleus

8 electrons

8 protons and 8 neutrons

Figure 5.2 *An oxygen atom*

Different atoms have different numbers of electrons and protons. The oxygen atom has eight positively (+) charged protons in the nucleus and eight negatively (−) charged electrons in orbits around the nucleus. Under normal circumstances, there are the same number of negative and positive particles making the atom electrically neutral (equal numbers of − and + cancel each other out).

However, under certain conditions such as friction electrons can be rubbed off one surface on to another. There is then a build-up of electrons (negative charge) on one surface and the other surface will have a deficit (lack) of electrons and so be positively charged. Because positive and negative charges attract each other, static electricity is produced.

Example of static electricity

When brushing your hair with a nylon brush the brush gains electrons and becomes negatively charged, the hair loses electrons and becomes positively charged. As positive and negative charges are attracted to each other, the hair will be attracted to the brush. This static charge causes a slight crackling sound.

Current electricity

An **electrical current** is a flow of negatively charged particles called electrons, which requires a complete circuit and a conductor to flow along. If there is a break in the circuit, then current flow will stop. **Voltage** is the driving force (electrical pressure) that pushes the current round.

The flow of current can be changed by the following:

* A resistor reduces the current flow.
* A variable resistor (rheostat) changes the current flow in a circuit.
* A switch completes or breaks an electrical circuit and directs where the current is able to flow (see below).
* A capacitor or condenser is a device which stores electrical charges.
* A potentiometer varies the voltage in an electrical circuit, thus allowing the intensity of a current to be turned up from zero.
* A rectifier converts an alternating current into a direct current (see below).
* A fuse is a safety device which blows when an excessive current flows in a circuit. This can be caused by a fault or because the circuit is dangerously over loaded. Fuses in plugs have different current ratings:
  - **3 amps**, for use with appliances up to 700 watts
  - **5 amps**, for use with appliances between 700 and 1000 watts
  - **13 amps**, for use with appliances between 1000 and 3000 watts.
* A circuit breaker breaks a particular circuit when a problem arises, such as overloading or faulty equipment, so that the electricity supply to only one area will be affected. The circuit breaker can be reset when the fault has been rectified.

Electrical current is measured in **amperes** (**amps**) and these are units of electrical strength. **Resistance** is a term used to describe something which opposes the flow of an electrical current and this resistance is measured in **ohms**. A **volt** is a unit of electrical pressure or force.

To make an electrical current flow along a given path, a supply of energy is needed, for example a battery or the mains supply. The supply of energy will allow the current to flow if there is a conductor along which the current can flow. A conductor is any material which allows electricity to flow through it. An insulator is any material which prevents electricity flowing through it.

How good a conductor is depends on its ability to allow the electricity to flow or its resistance to the flow of electricity. A good conductor has a very low resistance and a poor conductor has a very high resistance (see Table 5.1).

Conductors	Insulators
Copper	Wood
Iron	Glass
Aluminium	Polythene
Carbon	Rubber
Sea water	Paraffin
Sulphuric acid	Earth

Table 5.1 *Conductors and insulators*

Electrical circuit

An electrical circuit is the movement of an electrical current from its source, through the conductors and back to the original source. For example, the current flows from the equipment through the wires to an active electrode, through the body and back to the equipment via an indifferent electrode.

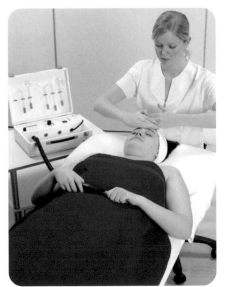

Figure 5.3
A client has an indirect high frequency treatment using an alternating current

Alternating and direct current

An alternating current is a flow of current which constantly changes direction many times per second. It is produced by power stations that provide electricity for the mains supply through power cables. The mains supply feeds electricity into the salon through the mains fuse box, switch and meter (consumer unit). This unit registers the amount of electricity used so that payment can be made to the electricity supplier.

A direct current is produced using either electrically charged cells (batteries) or a rectified, smoothed alternating current. It flows in one direction only, from negative to positive. Chemical energy is converted into electrical energy to power a battery, which is often used in portable equipment.

The effects of an electric current

Heating

When an electric current is passed through different wires, the wire heats up to different degrees depending on:

* the resistance of the conductor
* the thickness of the wire – a thin wire offers more resistance than a thick wire
* the length of the wire – a long wire has more resistance than a short wire.

Lighting

Electrical energy produces light. A light bulb contains a filament, a thin wire with a high resistance, so when an electric current passes through it, it becomes white hot, thus giving out light. The light bulb is filled with an inert gas to stop the filament burning away. Bulbs may be clear providing a bright light or opaque providing a soft light.

Chemical

A current is created by a chemical reaction. The current can also set off a chemical reaction. When a current passes through an electrolyte (solution), the electrolyte splits chemically and this process is called electrolysis. This process is used in epilation for the removal of superfluous hair.

Electrotherapy

This is the application of an electrical current for a therapeutic purpose, to improve face or body conditions. It applies to high frequency treatment, galvanic treatment, faradic treatment (electrical muscle stimulation), inteferential treatment and microcurrent treatment. The types of electricity used in electrotherapy equipment is shown in Table 5.2.

The current intensities are too low to cause any serious injury, but it is essential for the therapist to understand how to use electrical equipment safely, effectively and with assurance.

Equipment	Current
Electrical muscle stimulation (EMS)/faradism or neuromuscular stimulation (NMS)	Interrupted or surged direct
Inteferential	Low frequency alternating
High frequency	High frequency alternating
Desincrustation/galvanism	Direct
Iontophoresis/galvanism	Direct
Microcurrent	Low intensity direct

Table 5.2 *Types of electricity used in electrotherapy equipment*

Wiring a plug

It is essential that all therapists learn how to wire a plug safely as this is one procedure that does not have to be carried out by a qualified electrician and there may be occasions when this procedure has to be carried out to allow the treatment to begin. When wiring a plug you must follow certain safety procedures:

* Never use frayed wires.
* Do not use wires with split or cracked insulation.
* Cut insulation using wire strippers.
* Do not use too long a wire.
* Do not use a fuse of the incorrect value.
* Ensure the cord grip is tightened sufficiently to prevent the wire being pulled out of the plug.
* Power appliances are fitted with a three-pin plug and the three wires are colour coded: Live (L) Brown, Neutral (N) Blue, Earth (E) Green and yellow.

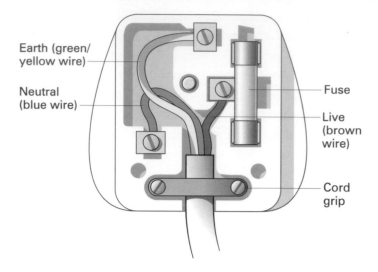

Figure 5.4 *Wiring a mains plug*

Safety precautions before, during and after use of electrical equipment

* Check equipment is in good working order and has had all the required safety checks.
* Make sure all the accessories are available, clean and intact.
* Make sure there are no trailing leads.
* Check that all the controls are at zero at the beginning and end of the treatment.
* Make sure the equipment is not positioned near water.
* Make sure the machine is easily accessible and on a stable surface.
* Always check equipment with a thermostat. Never assume that it is working correctly.
* Test the machine on yourself before use.
* Check the client for contraindications.
* Ensure the client has removed all jewellery including piercings.
* Test the client for skin sensitivity when necessary.
* Never allow the client to touch the equipment.
* Clean and store equipment safely.

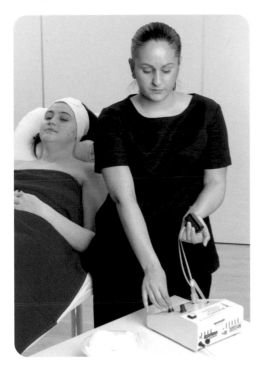

Figure 5.5
A therapist testing equipment on herself

There is very little chance of injury to the therapist or the client when using electrical equipment as long as the therapist follows all the correct procedures and follows the manufacturers' instructions. The risks are then reduced and accidents are prevented. However, electrical injuries may result from faulty equipment, loose wires, cracked plug sockets and switches and frayed cables. Handling appliances with wet hands will also increase the risk of injury.

If anyone suffers an electric shock, switch off the current at the mains or unplug the equipment. If this is not possible, stand on an insulator, for example clothing, paper or a rubber mat, and using a wooden broom handle or chair leg push the equipment or cable away from the injured person or remove their limbs from contact with the source. If breathing is normal, place the injured person in the recovery position (see Figure 5.6, send for medical help and treat for shock by reassuring and comforting the individual. Keep the person warm and loosen his or her clothing.

Hazards and risk

A **hazard** is something that has the potential to cause an accident and a **risk** is the chance that the accident may happen.

Case study

A piece of electrical equipment is sitting on a trolley with a loose screw in one of the legs. A small bowl of saline solution is placed on top of the machine to use during the treatment.

The hazards are:
* the trolley may collapse
* the saline solution will spill over the electrical equipment
* the machine will fall to the floor and break.

The risk of any of these hazards causing an accident is very high but will be greatly reduced if the therapist ensures that all equipment is well maintained and in good working order and no water is placed near to or on a piece of electrical equipment.

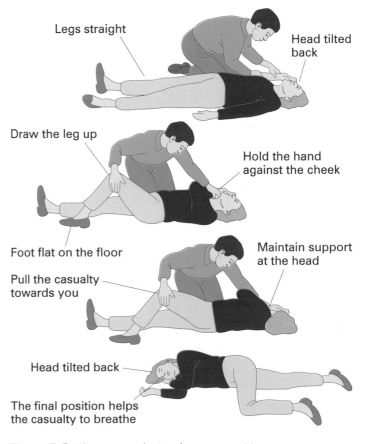

Legs straight | Head tilted back

Draw the leg up | Hold the hand against the cheek

Foot flat on the floor | Maintain support at the head

Pull the casualty towards you

Head tilted back

The final position helps the casualty to breathe

Figure 5.6 *Placing a casualty into the recovery position*

Lifestyle

* Diet and nutrition

* Stress and exercise

Introduction

The type of clients who visit salons and spas has changed in the last 20 years. In the early 1970s, the typical profile of a client who regularly visited a salon for treatment was a married female, with plenty of time on her hands as she did not do a paid job and her children were older and independent. Today, the profile has changed dramatically. The age of a client has fallen as many young girls and boys are now having treatments. Women's lifestyles have changed, with many women now combining a career with bringing up a family. Many now regard beauty treatments as a necessity as well as a luxury and an essential part of their lives. With modern technology, there are many more treatments available, and advertising and the media are constantly reinforcing the message that we deserve to pamper ourselves.

The market for men's beauty treatments is also growing as men are spending more time and money on grooming and to enhance their self-image. They are persuaded by the availability of treatments in specialist spas and health and fitness clubs and celebrity endorsement, as they want to try to be like those people they admire.

Clients' lifestyles will vary widely and this section will help you to assess their lifestyle, to cater for their requirements and be able to offer the most appropriate treatments and advice to suit their individual needs.

The client's lifestyle

There are many treatments available to the client who visits a beauty salon or spa. Although providing these treatments to improve the client's skin or body condition is the main objective, it is only part of the complete treatment programme.

Because of the wide variety of treatments now on offer, you will need to discuss several things with your client during consultation:

* The client's body, facial, hand or foot condition. This will enable you to recommend the correct and most appropriate treatments to achieve the client's objectives.
* The client's medical history. This will tell you if treatment is contraindicated, or needs to be adapted in some way.
* The client's lifestyle. This may require you to adapt treatment, offer advice about complementary treatments and home care products, provide information and motivation and plan when the client may attend for treatment to fit in with his or her schedule.

Most clients comment on the lack of time available to them. They may be working in a high-powered job which requires them to work long hours, sometimes seven days a week. Others are working parents trying to juggle, work, home and their children, often with little help. Some clients will have elderly dependants who need constant care. Their different lifestyles may prevent them from eating regular meals, taking regular exercise or finding time to relax. To compensate for their busy schedule some clients throw themselves wholeheartedly into a hectic social life adding further pressure in their lives by smoking, drinking, eating over rich food and 'burning the candle at both ends'! Some become stressed, tired or run down, often putting others' needs before their own.

Clients may need to alter their lifestyle and follow your home care advice to make sure that any improvement achieved in the salon will be maintained. There is no point having slimming treatments to lose weight or alter body shape and then eating an unhealthy diet and taking no exercise. To be fully effective a course of anti-ageing facials requires correct home care products and the protection of the skin from harmful damage caused by the use of sun beds, smoking, drinking or partying till dawn! The client will need to make an effort to contribute to the improvements expected and the lifestyle the client leads will have an impact on the service you provide.

Male clients

Men now feel that they have as much right as women to look after their bodies and skin as well as relax their minds. The increasing number of gyms with salons and spas has made it far more acceptable for a man to have beauty treatments, as he would be reluctant to enter the rather more feminine type of salons. The treatments and ranges of products should be carefully chosen to appeal to the male client, either unisex or men's ranges. Some product companies are packaging and marketing their products specifically for men even though they are the same as the products already in use for women.

You will need to consider the male lifestyle in the same way as you do for female clients to ensure you provide the right treatments in the right environment.

During consultation, therefore, the client's lifestyle is one of the most important areas for discussion as it will present you with valuable information concerning the client's:

* work and leisure ratio
* job
* family commitments
* current exercise patterns
* methods of relaxation and hobbies
* diet
* social habits
* previous beauty treatments.

Work and leisure ratio

Find out if the client has an occupation. Does the client have to travel far to work or does he or she work from home? The client might have a young family or elderly relatives to look after with very little free time for him/herself. This will indicate the client's possible stress levels and how much free time he or she will have to attend for treatment and what time of the day the client will be available for you to arrange appointments, particularly if the client is embarking on a course of treatments.

Job

The job a client has may contribute to a problem condition that requires your help. It could be that the occupation requires the client to work in an atmosphere that causes skin problems, provides little exercise or increases stress levels.

Examples

A female traffic warden working in all climatic conditions suffers from excessively dry skin and a dense area of broken capillaries on the cheeks.

A hospital nurse, who is involved in sterilisation procedures and does not always wear protective gloves when handling sterilising fluids, is concerned that her nails are very soft and weak.

A student who works four shifts a week in a fish and chip shop suffers from greasy blemished skin.

The customer service manager of a busy superstore providing a telephone sales service often works a 10–12-hour day, supervises a large number of staff and is in the front line for customer complaints. She does not eat at regular intervals and rarely moves from an office environment. She feels permanently run down and suffers with headaches and backache.

Family commitments

Is the client married or single? Does he or she have children, and how old are they? This may indicate how stressed clients might be and also that you may have to fit appointments around their family's daily routine.

Current exercise patterns

These will provide information about levels of physical activity, exercise classes or programmes the client is already following and whether it is regular or if he or she takes no exercise at all. This will provide you with an indication of current fitness level and self-motivation. In order to offer effective advice for clients who are not regular exercisers you will need to consider the barriers and incentives to exercise.

Methods of relaxation and hobbies

If clients manage to make time for themselves and what they enjoy doing, this will also be a good indication of their current stress level, the time they have available for treatments and what treatments may suit them best. For example, they may have several holidays a year, and if they spend this time sunning themselves on a beach with little or no protection, this may have an adverse effect on their skin. Alternatively, they may want an all-year round tan and use sun beds on a regular basis. They may have a sporting hobby which requires certain treatments before and after.

Figure 6.1 *You may need to advise clients on the best method of skin protection*

Current diet

This will be particularly important if the client is hoping to lose weight during the course of treatments. Information on what, when, how much and what cooking methods are used will be required along with any other factors that affect food intake and choice, such as cost, cooking skills and facilities, mood and food preferences. You may need to provide advice about healthy eating to help the client achieve success.

Social habits

Social habits such as consumption of alcohol, how many units the client drinks in a week (one unit is equal to one glass of wine, one measure of spirits or half a pint of beer, lager or cider), and if he or she smokes can have an impact on fitness levels and the condition of the skin. You will also need to consider the number of late nights a client may have in a week, the quality of their sleep patterns or lack of sleep.

Previous beauty treatments

What beauty treatments has the client had in the past? How effective were they?

Once you have established the client's current lifestyle, this will allow you to make professional recommendations for the most beneficial form of treatment to meet his or her individual needs. It also allows you to advise clients about changes they could make to their lifestyle that will help improve their general health and fitness, achieve their objectives and reduce their stress levels.

Figure 6.2 *The client may need to adjust her lifestyle to help achieve her objectives*

Weight problems

When providing body treatments the client's objectives are often weight loss or figure control. There are many reasons for being overweight, one of the most common being poor eating habits that have developed over the years, and which probably began in childhood. Other reasons may include:

* over eating in infancy, which can lead to a large number of fat cells being produced which increase in size as more weight is gained
* eating too many refined and processed foods, which contain hidden fats and sugar
* insufficient exercise to burn off the excess calories.

A disturbance of normal metabolism can be a problem for a small percentage of people and they will need medical advice to deal with the cause.

There are several reasons why people wish to lose weight:

* Because they are obese, that is more than 20 per cent over their ideal weight.
* To reduce the risks of heart disease or high blood pressure.
* To reach an ideal weight.
* After childbirth to regain their figure.
* To lose weight in specific areas, e.g. thighs and hips.
* To ease the pressure on arthritic joints.
* For self-esteem.
* To feel fit and healthy.

Whatever the reason, weight loss must be approached in a sensible manner. It involves eating a healthy, well-balanced diet. This may be achieved by cutting out all the unnecessary foods while eating plenty of the foods that are allowed.

Carbohydrates, proteins and fats are all nutrients, or foods, providing energy.

Metabolism

The food we eat is digested and absorbed by the body and is then converted into the energy the body needs by a chemical process called **metabolism**.

Catabolism and anabolism

Catabolism is the process by which substances (food) are broken down to release energy or are excreted as waste.

The energy which is produced is then consumed by the body for cell reproduction, growth and repair, as well as the manufacture of new products essential to the body. This process is known as **anabolism**.

The body needs food to provide it with calories, which supply the energy required for everyday activities and to maintain the basal metabolic rate, the speed at which energy is released into the body.

Kilocalories

The method of estimating the energy requirements of the body is to measure it in terms of heat. The unit of heat used is the **kilocalorie**.

A kilocalorie is the amount of heat required to raise the temperature of 1000 grams of water 1°C.

The energy value of food is also measured in kilocalories:

1 gram of carbohydrate = 4 kilocalories.

1 gram of protein = 4 kilocalories.

1 gram of fat = 9 kilocalories.

1 gram of alcohol = 7 kilocalories.

Knowing the calorific value of food is important as body weight can then be controlled, by taking in only enough kilocalories to maintain our physical activity.

However, for weight loss the client needs to take in less energy than he or she is using.

Basal metabolism

Basal metabolism is the minimum quantity of energy needed by the body to keep it alive throughout the day and night. **Basal metabolic rate (BMR)** is the rate at which the body burns up energy to keep it alive when resting.

There are some factors which affect the basal metabolic rate and these are as follows:

* Eating will slightly increase the BMR as after a meal energy is required for digestion. Eating food, especially proteins, can increase the metabolic rate by as much as 10–20 per cent.

* With extreme cold the body uses more energy to maintain normal body temperature. An increase in body temperature will also increase the basal metabolic rate.

* Certain drugs such as amphetamines and caffeine will increase the BMR.

* Emotional stress can alter our BMR as can prolonged anxiety.

* Regular exercise will increase the BMR and if the amount of physical exercise taken is increased, then the basal metabolic rate will also be increased to provide the body with the energy required for the physical exertion.

* Thyroid hormones control the rate of metabolism. Too much hormone speeds up metabolism and too little slows it down.

* This function may be affected by age because the basic metabolic rate slows down, as we grow older. Therefore, a smaller proportion of the food absorbed will be converted into energy and there may be weight gain because of the slower metabolic rate.

Figure 6.3 *Older people may need to eat smaller meals*

An adult requires approximately 25 calories per kilo of body weight every 24 hours to maintain the basal metabolic rate. To cope with normal daily activities, additional calories are required and this varies, depending on the occupation and physical activity undertaken.

Women have a lower basal metabolic rate than men and therefore need less calories per day to provide energy.

Individual people's energy requirements vary depending upon:

* their sex
* their age
* their size
* the amount of physical activity they undertake.

Depending on the physical activity undertaken, the calories required by an active man may range between 2700 and 3600 per day, and for an active woman between 2200 and 2500 per day. As many people are sedentary (take no exercise) in their daily activities, it is also helpful to understand sedentary values as well: female 1940 calories and male 2550 calories.

Body mass index

Being overweight must be taken seriously if it becomes excessive because:

* the heart has to work harder
* there will probably be more fat in the blood increasing the risk of heart attack or stroke
* joints will suffer and in the long term may cause arthritis
* there will be a decrease in mobility
* it increases the likelihood of high blood pressure, diabetes, and gallstones
* it may cause backache
* varicose veins may develop.

Being underweight is also undesirable. Therefore, it is important to control your weight.

One way of looking at body weight is by calculating the body mass index (BMI).

This is an index of body fatness. It is the sum of the ratio of body mass expressed in kilograms to the square of height in metres.

$$\text{BMI} = \text{body mass in kg} \div \text{height in m}^2$$

BMI assumes that there is not a single weight for an individual of a specific height, but that there is a healthy weight range for any given height. BMI can be used to classify various grades of weight. A ratio of 20–24.9 is considered to be healthy and desirable for both men and women. Values above this level are associated with increased risk of disease. But care must be taken when applying the calculation to extremely muscular individuals such as sportspeople, particularly those involved in strength sports, as they may show values that are high, but these will not reflect the same degree of risk as those of a sedentary individual with the same BMI.

Body mass index is calculated as:

$$\frac{\text{weight (kg)}}{\text{height (m)} \times \text{height (m)}}$$

For example, if someone weighs 92 kg and has a height of 1.6 metres, the individual's BMI will be:

$$\frac{92}{1.6 \times 1.6} = \frac{92}{2.56} = 36.$$

A BMI of 36 would put the person into the obese category.

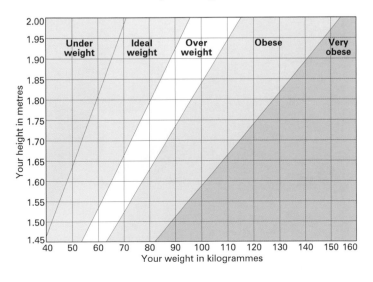

Figure 6.4 *Ideal weight for height chart*

Underweight	Ideal weight	Overweight	Obese	Very obese
BMI of less than 20 You may need to consult your doctor, or start to eat more	**BMI 20–24.9** This is the right weight range for good health	**BMI 25–29.9** Try to lose excess weight	**BMI 30–39.9** It is important to lose weight	**BMI greater than 40** This is serious and it is essential for your health to do something about losing weight

Table 6.1 *Body mass index*

Caution!

There are those people who have a high proportion of muscle to fat and it is a known fact that muscle tissue weighs heavier than fat. This must be taken into consideration when assessing BMI.

How to lose weight

Excess weight is stored under the skin in the form of fat and the fat cells increase in size as more weight is put on.

To lose body fat the energy used by the body must be greater than the energy intake as food. This will cause the body to use some of its stored energy, most of which is fat.

The most sensible thing to do, therefore, is to cut out of the diet those foods that are very high in calories and eat a lot more lower calorie foods while maintaining a balanced diet overall.

There are four rules to follow, which will help:

1 Eat less fat.
2 Eat less sugar.
3 Eat more fibre.
4 Drink less alcohol.

In this way weight loss may be achieved slowly but effectively without feeling starved, deprived, or tired.

A balanced diet

This is a diet which contains a wide variety of foods so that there is an adequate intake of nutrients to maintain health and for the body to function efficiently. This will be made easier by choosing food from each of the four main food groups:

* Starchy foods.
* Dairy products.
* Meat, poultry, fish and alternatives.
* Vegetables and fruit.

Starchy foods

Dairy products

Meat, poultry, fish and alternatives

Vegetables and fruit

Figure 6.5 *The four main food groups*

Starchy foods	Dairy products	Meat, poultry, fish and alternatives	Vegetables and fruit		
			Vegetables, e.g.	*Salad vegetables, e.g.*	*Fresh fruit, e.g.*
Bread	Cheese	Beans and lentils	Broccoli	Cucumber	Apples
Breakfast cereal	Fromage frais	Eggs	Cabbage	Lettuce	Bananas
Chapattis	Milk	Fish	Carrots	Radish	Grapefruit
Noodles	Cream	Meat	Celery	Tomato	Kiwifruit
Pasta	Yoghurt	Meat products	Peppers		Mangoes
Potatoes	Butter	Nuts	Leeks		Oranges
Rice		Offal	Potatoes		Pears
Sweet potatoes		Poultry	Spinach		Grapes
Polenta		Texturised vegetable protein	Turnips		Strawberries
Cous cous					Melon

Table 6.2 *Examples from the four main food groups.*

Meals should be made up mainly from starchy foods with the addition of some foods from the other groups to make a well-balanced meal. Starchy food is filling; it is not high in calories but provides other essential nutrients. Table 6.2 shows some examples from the four main food groups.

The key messages to achieve a healthy balanced diet are to aim to:

* base all your meals around starchy foods
* include at least five servings of fruits and/or vegetables each day
* include milk and dairy foods, if possible three servings per day
* eat smaller portions of meat or fish, and try alternatives such as pulses at least two servings each day
* limit your intake of foods with a high fat or sugar content.

Food labelling

The Food Labelling Regulations (1984) are intended to protect consumers by ensuring that labels on food cans, packets, and so on, accurately reflect their contents and also that they provide additional information, for example whether the product contains nuts or gluten. This is particularly important for anyone with a food allergy or intolerance. The regulations require food for sale or supply to be labelled with specific information such as list of ingredients in weight order and best before and use by dates.

Where the food manufacturer provides information on the nutritional value and content of its products, this must be presented in a standard format specified by food labelling regulations to allow the consumer to compare like-for-like products. Also included on food labels may be any nutritional claims made by the food manufacturer.

The role of the therapist

The therapist may often suggest to clients that they follow a weight reducing diet as part of a course of treatments. It is important, therefore, that therapists have a good understanding of nutrition so that they know their recommendations are healthy, well-balanced and appropriate to the needs of each of their clients.

The relationship between the client and therapist is an important one as it is necessary to find out as much as possible about the client's eating habits, lifestyle and family history. This will enable the therapist to pinpoint the cause of the problem and recommend the appropriate changes to diet and treatment. This will not be a problem if the client has been attending regularly for treatment and a trusting relationship already exists.

The client may, however, be new and feel a little shy and embarrassed, particularly if the therapist is young, slim and looks fit and healthy. The ability of the therapist to put the client at ease, be sympathetic and reassuring is of great importance and ensures that the client will return and persevere in the quest to lose weight.

The importance of food

The body requires food in sufficient quantity and quality for growth, maintenance, repair and energy. Nutrients are substances essential for the well-being of the human body. They provide, energy and material for growth and they include:

* carbohydrates
* protein
* fats
* minerals
* vitamins
* fibre
* fluid.

Carbohydrates and fats provide heat and energy. Fat gives support to certain parts of the body, transports fat-soluble vitamins and is used in the formation of steroid hormones. The body needs sugar for muscle contraction. It is an efficient fuel because it requires less oxygen to work and therefore it is important during physical exercise. Proteins provide materials required for growth of the body and repair of the tissues. Vitamins and minerals are necessary for normal metabolism.

Carbohydrates

Carbohydrates consist of carbon, hydrogen and oxygen. They are found in bread, cereals, potatoes, sugar, fruit and vegetables. If the carbohydrate consumption is in excess of the body's requirements, it will be converted into fat.

There are three major groups:

* sugars
* starches
* cellulose.

Sugars

There are two types of sugar – simple sugars or **monosaccharides** and double sugars or **disaccharides**.

Monosaccharides are:

* **glucose** – found naturally in fruit, plant juices and animal blood
* **fructose** – found naturally in fruit and vegetables and honey
* **galactose** – part of milk sugar (lactose).

Disaccharides are:

* **sucrose** – found naturally in sugar cane and beet sugar; small amounts in fruit and root vegetables
* **maltose** – a product of starch digestion
* **lactose** – part of milk sugar.

Starches

Starches are another major group of carbohydrates called **polysaccharides**. They consist of three or more monosaccharides, but they lack the characteristic sweetness of monosaccharides and disaccharides. One of the chief polysaccharides is **glycogen** which is stored in the liver and skeletal muscles. When the body requires quick energy, liver cells break down the glycogen into glucose and release it for use.

Cellulose (other related materials)

Polysaccharides provide the rigid and fibrous structure of fruit, vegetables and cereals and they are the main component of dietary fibre.

Cellulose consists of many thousands of glucose units and it cannot be digested by humans.

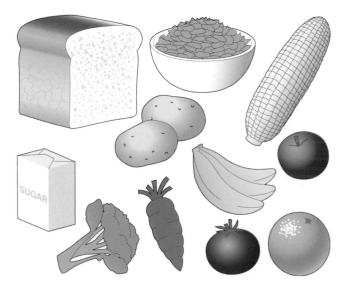

Figure 6.6 *Foods containing carbohydrates*

Proteins

Proteins also consist of carbon, hydrogen, and oxygen, but they also contain nitrogen, and some contain other mineral elements too such as phosphorous and sulphur. Proteins are relatively large molecules of which amino acids form the simplest unit.

There are different proteins, which consist of certain numbers of different amino acids. First-class proteins are those that contain all essential amino acids in the correct proportion and these are meat, fish, milk and dairy products, eggs and soya beans. Second-class proteins are those that do not contain all the essential amino acids in the correct proportions and these are mainly found in foods of plant origin, that is, peas, beans and pulses and nuts.

Fats

Fats consist of carbon, hydrogen and oxygen, but the proportion of the hydrogen and oxygen is different from those in carbohydrates. The fats we eat are animal or saturated fat which is usually solid at room temperature, and vegetable fat which is mainly unsaturated fat and is soft or liquid at room temperature.

The fat from animals comes from meat, milk, cheese, butter and eggs. This type of fat is known to raise the body's cholesterol levels (see below). Vegetable fat is found in vegetable margarine and vegetable oils.

The function of the adipose layer of fat in our bodies is to provide us with energy and warmth. It protects vital organs such as the heart and liver and it provides shape and contour to the body. Essential fatty acids are important as they make up the largest part of the protective membrane surrounding all our body cells and the most common sources of fats are fish and vegetable oils.

There are four different types of fats:
* saturated and trans fats
* monounsaturated fats
* polyunsaturated fats.
* cholesterol, a fat-like material present in the blood and most tissues, especially nervous tissue.

Saturated and trans fats

A diet high in these types of fats increases the level of blood cholesterol, which in time will increase the risk of heart disease. Therefore, we should be reducing the amount of these fats in our diet.

Saturated fats are found in high quantities in animal products like fatty cuts of beef, pork and lamb as well as in hard margarine and lard. They are also in dairy products like full-fat milk, cheese and butter.

Trans fatty acids are artificially created during food processing when liquid vegetable oil is hardened to make a solid fat.

Most cakes, biscuits, pies and pastries contain a lot of hidden saturated and trans fats.

Monounsaturated fats

These are found in high proportions in olives, olive oil, almond oil and avocados. They do not increase blood cholesterol levels and some experts believe it may help to reduce them. In Mediterranean countries where these types of food are eaten, there are much lower rates of heart disease and cancer, and it is thought that this is in part due to the monounsaturated fats that are found in the Mediterranean diet.

Polyunsaturated fats

These are beneficial to health and can help to lower cholesterol levels. Oily fish such as mackerel, sardines and pilchards are an excellent source. They are also found in vegetable seeds and polyunsaturated margarines. Polyunsaturates contain 'essential' fatty acids which are vital to health.

Cholesterol

This is a soft waxy substance found in the food we eat and in our blood and it is known to contribute to heart disease when it reaches a high level. Blood cholesterol is made in the liver and carried in the blood, where it can be deposited on the walls of the blood vessels. It can lead to a narrowing of the arteries, which supply blood to the heart, thus increasing the chance of heart disease. This is known as lipoprotein cholesterol or LDL 'bad' cholesterol. The liver makes another type of cholesterol – high density lipoprotein cholesterol (HDL), a 'good' cholesterol, which helps remove surplus cholesterol from our bloodstream. Egg yolks, offal and shell fish are rich dietary sources of cholesterol.

Minerals

Minerals are only required in small quantities, but they are necessary for the normal functioning of the body. Minerals are found in soil and are absorbed by plants as they grow. We receive minerals from plants, as well as animals which have eaten the plants.

Calcium

This mineral is essential for healthy teeth and bones and clotting of the blood. It is found in milk, eggs, cheese, green leafy vegetables, dried fruits, pulses, tinned fish and white bread.

Phosphorus

This is important in bone and teeth formation, maintenance of body fluids and the transportation of energy inside the cells. Phosphorus can be found in cheese, liver, kidney, eggs, green vegetables and oatmeal.

Sodium

This maintains the fluid balance in the body and is associated with the transmission of nerve impulses in nerve fibres and contraction of muscles. It is found in most foods, especially table salt, processed meat and fish, eggs, milk, yeast extracts, tinned foods and savoury snacks. Any excess sodium is secreted by the body in urine.

Potassium

Like sodium, the functions of potassium are maintaining fluid balance, the transmission of nerve impulses and muscular contraction. In addition, it is necessary for the chemical activities of the cells. It is found in most foods, but cereals and fruit and vegetables are particularly rich in potassium.

Magnesium

This is important to the structure of bones and is found in vegetables and other plant products.

Iron

Iron is essential for the manufacture of haemoglobin in the red blood cells and is necessary to all the body cells in a small amount. Foods rich in iron are liver, kidney, red meat, green vegetables, fortified breakfast cereals, wholegrain bread, nuts and seeds, apricots, cocoa powder and sardines. A diet lacking in iron will cause anaemia. During menstruation some women find it necessary to include iron-rich foods in their diet.

Iodine

Although needed only in minute quantities, iodine is an essential mineral in the formation of thyroid hormones, which in turn are essential for normal metabolism. It is found in seafood, watercress, dairy products and is added to table salt.

Zinc

This is necessary for a healthy skin and is found in meat, fish, dairy products and wholegrain cereals.

Fluoride

This helps maintain healthy teeth by fighting tooth decay and protecting enamel. It is added to drinking water by some water authorities, but is also found in seafood and tea.

Chromium

This is necessary for fat and carbohydrate metabolism and is involved in the production of insulin. It is found in egg yolk, liver, wheatgerm, cheese and wholegrain cereal.

Copper

An essential part of many enzymes, copper helps the formation of red blood cells. It has antioxidant effects combating free radicals (rogue molecules in the body which can have damaging effects) and is found in liver, crab, oysters, carrots, olives, nuts, lentils and wholegrain cereal.

Manganese

This is essential for normal growth and development. It helps regulate blood sugar levels, is required for the body to be able to use vitamin C and is an antioxidant. It is found in beans, beetroot, dark lettuce, oats, pineapples, plums, almonds, hazelnuts and wheatgerm.

Selenium

Selenium is both an essential nutrient as well as a powerful antioxidant. It works in conjunction with vitamin E to protect body cells from damage. It is also necessary to keep the liver functioning healthily and boosts the immune system. It is found in eggs, fish, garlic, liver and yeast.

Silicon

Silicon is vital to the health of bones, cartilage, blood vessels and connective tissue. It helps the body utilise calcium in the bones, and strengthens skin, nails and hair because it helps in the production of collagen and keratin.

Vitamins

Vitamins are chemical compounds which are essential to nerve, muscle and brain function and vital to normal metabolism. They are divided into two groups:

* **Fat soluble** vitamins A, D, E and K.
* **Water soluble** vitamins B complex and C.

Fat soluble vitamins

Vitamin A

Vitamin A is important for healthy eyes and the normal growth of most cells in the body. It stimulates collagen production and strengthens cell walls. A lack of this vitamin can cause very dry scaly skin, mouth ulcers, frequent infections, thrush or cystitis and difficulty in seeing in the dark.

Foods rich in vitamin A include cream, milk, eggs, cheese, butter, fish oils and liver. Carotene can be converted by the liver into vitamin A. The source of this vitamin is carrot, spinach, cabbage and watercress.

Vitamin D

This is essential for the formation of strong bones and teeth as it helps phosphorous and calcium to be deposited in the bones. It is a very important vitamin, particularly for pregnant women and young children.

Foods rich in vitamin D include eggs, cheese, butter, liver, sardines, oily fish and cod liver oil. The action of ultraviolet rays on a substance under the skin forms vitamin D, so sunlight is also a source of vitamin D.

Vitamin E

This is a powerful fat soluble antioxidant with anti-inflammatory properties, helping to protect the skin against ultraviolet radiation. It is said to help prevent scar formation and reduce scars which have already formed. It is now well established that treatment of sunburn with Vitamin E will greatly reduce tissue damage and increase the rate of healing. Vitamin E is found in peanuts, wheatgerm, sunflower seeds, grape seeds, milk, butter and eggs.

Vitamin K

Vitamin K is essential for clotting of the blood. The sources of vitamin K are green vegetables, liver and dairy products.

Water soluble vitamins

Vitamin B complex is a group of water soluble vitamins which include the following:

* **Vitamin B1 (thiamine)** helps to control the water balance in the body, carbohydrate metabolism and maintains a healthy nervous system. It is found in nuts, egg yolk, yeast and wholemeal bread.
* **Vitamin B2 (riboflavin)** helps to keep the skin healthy and helps with the oxidation of foods to provide energy. It is found in liver, milk, cheese, eggs, leaf vegetables, yeast extracts and beef.
* **Nicotinic acid**, also known as **niacin**, affects the normal activities of the skin, the digestive system and the nervous system. It is found in liver, whole wheat, cheese, eggs and yeast extract.
* **Folic acid** affects the formation of red blood cells. A lack of it will cause anaemia. It is found in liver, kidney, yeast and fresh leafy vegetables.
* **Vitamin B6 (pyridoxine)** is necessary for fat and protein metabolism. It is found in egg yolk, meat, liver, peas and beans.
* **Vitamin B12** is essential for the health of red blood cells. It is found in meat, liver, eggs, milk, fortified breakfast cereals and yeast extracts.
* **Pantothenic acid** helps with the metabolism of fats and carbohydrates. It is found in many foods, in particular liver, meat and eggs.
* **Vitamin C** has several functions including helping to form connective tissue, stimulating collagen and contributing to the development and maintenance of healthy bones. It aids the

absorption of iron and helps to strengthen the walls of the blood capillaries. It boosts the skin's immunity by preventing the destruction of langerhan cells, improves healing and aids the metabolism. It is found in green leafy vegetables, soft or citrus fruits and fruit juices, potatoes, white bread and milk.

All of these essential nutrients are present in food in different quantities and for a well-balanced diet suitable to maintain a healthy body there must be adequate proportions from each group.

A well-balanced diet will avoid vitamin deficiency (shortage), but there are other factors which can lead to vitamin deficiency:

* Taking aspirin reduces the amount of vitamin C in the blood. It may be a good idea to recommend vitamin C supplements if you have a client taking aspirin regularly, particularly if the individual does not eat a healthy balanced diet.
* Smoking is associated with low levels of vitamins C and B12.
* The oral contraceptive pill may cause a deficiency of vitamin B6 (pyridoxine) which, in some cases, can result in depression.
* Laxatives taken regularly could lead to a vitamin deficiency as well as a potassium deficiency.

Dietary supplements

Those who may benefit from vitamin and mineral supplements include:

* dieters who consistently consume low calorie intakes
* vegetarians, in particular vegans, who eat a limited variety of foods
* females who are planning to become pregnant, in which case a 400 microgram daily folic acid supplement is advised to reduce the risk of neural tube defects such as spina bifida
* the chronically ill with a poor appetite.

It is important that in these circumstances clients are advised to seek information on vitamin and mineral supplementation from a qualified professional.

Fibre and fluid

The two other essential ingredients for a healthy body are water and fibre.

Water

Water is essential to maintain the body's fluid balance as the body loses approximately two litres per day through perspiration and urine. The human body could survive a lot longer without food than it could without water because water:

* is necessary to maintain the health of most of the body cells
* aids digestion
* makes up a large part of blood and tissue fluid, so aiding the transportation of substances around the body
* dilutes waste products and aids in their elimination
* is essential for maintaining body temperature.

Drinking plenty of water, which contains no calories, is essential when trying to lose weight. Drinking cold water will speed up the body's metabolism, as the body will use calories to heat itself after cooling down. It also helps to dilute and flush toxins (poisons) from the body, so reducing water retention and increasing energy levels.

Fluid balance in the body

Body fluid contains water and dissolved substances and makes up 45–75 per cent of the body weight depending on age and the amount of fat present. The body's need for water is second only to its need for air. Water is essential to maintain a healthy skin and efficient working of body systems. The kidneys regulate the water balance in the body and excessive loss of water causes dehydration.

Body fluid contains sodium and potassium, which together play a major role in fluid balance, and if this balance is upset it can cause problems. Sodium is also essential for muscle and nerve activity.

If water is lost from the body through excessive perspiration, or using diuretics (substances that increase the volume of urine produced which is then excreted via the kidneys), this may result in a lower than normal sodium level, which will be characterised by headaches, hypotension and muscular weakness. Severe sodium loss can result in mental confusion, stupor and coma. The sodium level is regulated by the hormone aldosterone from the adrenal cortex.

Loss of potassium may result from vomiting, diarrhoea, kidney disease or high sodium intake. Symptoms may include cramps, fatigue, increased urine output, shallow respiration and mental confusion. The level of potassium in the blood is under the control of the mineralocorticoids but mainly the hormone aldosterone.

It is important therefore to ensure that sufficient fluid is drunk to maintain a healthy balance and prevent dehydration. Maintaining fluid balance for sedentary individuals requires around 2–2.5 litres of fluid per day, roughly equivalent to six to eight cups.

Fibre

Fibre is sometimes called roughage. It is a carbohydrate found in all vegetable matter. It is indigestible but is important as it helps the process of digestion and keeps the bowels working normally.

Fibre provides bulk, so helping to satisfy the appetite, and is found in pulses such as peas, beans, brown rice, wholemeal bread, flour and pasta, sweet corn, jacket potatoes, green leafy vegetables and dried fruit.

Food high in fibre contains fewer calories but more bulk and it has to be chewed more, therefore creating a feeling of fullness and reducing the appetite, which is helpful when dieting.

Absorption and use of nutrients in the body

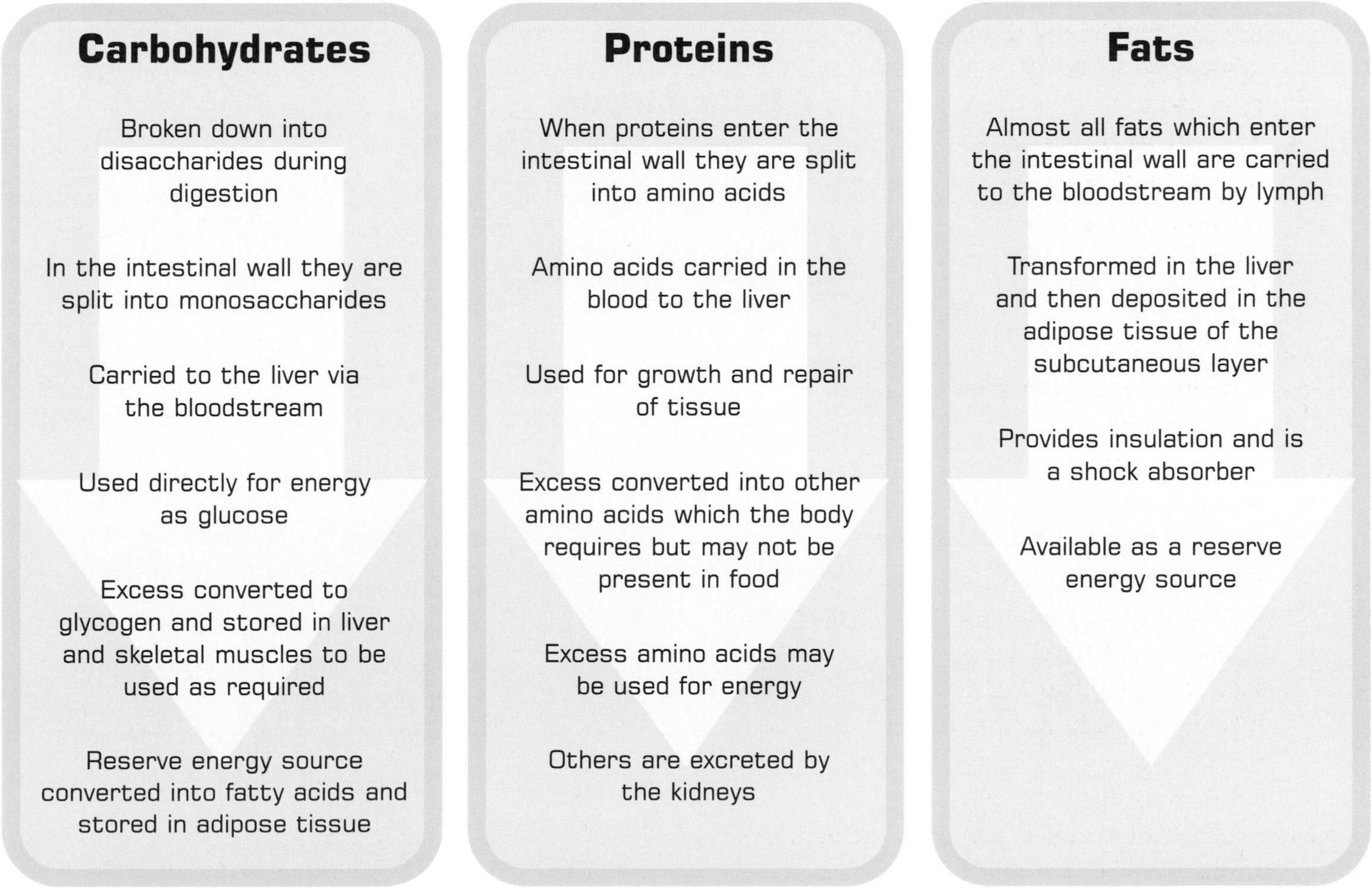

Carbohydrates

Broken down into disaccharides during digestion

In the intestinal wall they are split into monosaccharides

Carried to the liver via the bloodstream

Used directly for energy as glucose

Excess converted to glycogen and stored in liver and skeletal muscles to be used as required

Reserve energy source converted into fatty acids and stored in adipose tissue

Proteins

When proteins enter the intestinal wall they are split into amino acids

Amino acids carried in the blood to the liver

Used for growth and repair of tissue

Excess converted into other amino acids which the body requires but may not be present in food

Excess amino acids may be used for energy

Others are excreted by the kidneys

Fats

Almost all fats which enter the intestinal wall are carried to the bloodstream by lymph

Transformed in the liver and then deposited in the adipose tissue of the subcutaneous layer

Provides insulation and is a shock absorber

Available as a reserve energy source

Figure 6.7 *How nutrients are absorbed in the body*

Providing advice on dietary control

Client consultation

It is important when advising clients about diet that you first complete a detailed record card with as much relevant information as possible to help you devise a healthy and nutritious diet. You will need to ask clients a variety of questions about their lifestyle, height, weight, and so on (see Figure 6.8).

This information will enable you to understand their current diet, ask them to consult their GP if necessary and recommend a healthy well-balanced diet tailored to their requirements and then monitor their progress.

To assist clients in recording how much food they eat in a day, it would be helpful to provide them with a chart or diary, which they should complete for a week. It is useful to include a weekend in the diary, as eating habits are often different from week days.

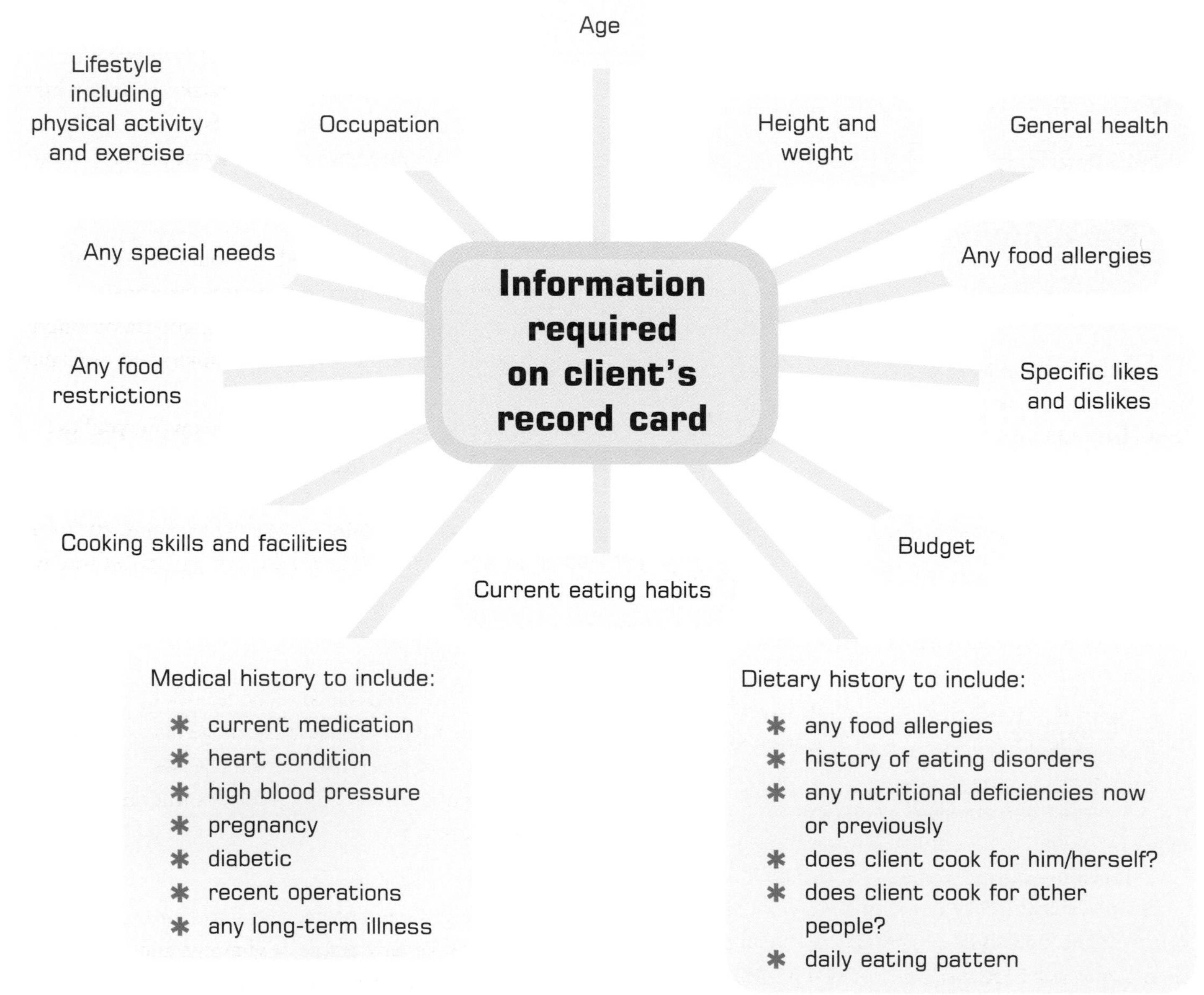

Age

Lifestyle including physical activity and exercise

Occupation

Height and weight

General health

Any special needs

Any food allergies

Information required on client's record card

Any food restrictions

Specific likes and dislikes

Cooking skills and facilities

Budget

Current eating habits

Medical history to include:

* current medication
* heart condition
* high blood pressure
* pregnancy
* diabetic
* recent operations
* any long-term illness

Dietary history to include:

* any food allergies
* history of eating disorders
* any nutritional deficiencies now or previously
* does client cook for him/herself?
* does client cook for other people?
* daily eating pattern

Figure 6.8 *What to include on the client's record card*

You will then be able to assess how much weight the client has to lose. This can be done by working out the ideal weight for the height and build of the client, as well as taking into consideration the client's own wishes.

Figure 6.9 *The therapist weighs a client*

Using all the information provided by the client, you may also recommend some form of exercise. This could be a suitable exercise class or a sporting activity which will fit in with the client's taste and lifestyle.

A combined diet and exercise programme will show results more quickly than either diet or exercise alone. It will serve to increase the metabolic rate and burn up the reduced calorie intake, thus resulting in a loss of weight (see Chapter 7 Stress and exercise for more detailed information).

The goals that are set for clients must be realistic to prevent them from becoming disheartened and giving up.

The four rules to follow – eating less fat, eating less sugar, drinking less alcohol and increasing fibre consumption – can be written into a flexible, eating plan for the client to follow. The eating plan can be used by you to create a personal day-by-day diet plan for those clients who need the discipline of being told exactly when and what to eat.

The flexible eating plan

Eat less fat

Eat only lean meat and chicken or turkey without the skin. Meat in any other form, for example sausages, pâté, pasties or pies should be avoided where possible, or only eaten occasionally due to its higher fat content. The method of cooking should be without the addition of fat, flour or thick sauces which will contain a large number of calories. Mince may be fried using no added fat and the fat from the mince should then be poured away.

Eat fresh fish as it is low in fat and it may be poached, steamed or cooked in a microwave.

Tinned fish is only permitted if it is in brine or water, *not* in oil. Oily fish such as mackerel or herrings should be grilled to remove excess fat.

Remove butter and margarine from the diet but if required, a low-fat spread may be used in minute quantities.

When using a cooking oil, it should be high in polyunsaturates and used only when absolutely necessary, again in minute quantities. Polyunsaturated oils include sesame, sunflower, pumpkin and vegetable oils.

Substitute salad dressings with a low-fat yoghurt flavoured with wine or herb vinegar.

Drink only skimmed milk or semi-skimmed milk when skimmed is totally unacceptable. Try to consume at least half a pint a day. Avoid cream and substitute with low-fat yoghurt or low-fat fromage frais.

Avoid eating biscuits, cakes or pastries, which are very high in fat.

Cheese is high in fat so it should not be eaten at all. An acceptable type of cheese is cottage cheese, which has a low-fat content. Try also low-fat cheeses.

Try to cut out snack foods such as nuts and crisps as they are high in fat.

Drink less alcohol

Nutritionally alcohol provides calories and sugar. A few alcoholic drinks have traces of vitamins and minerals, but other than calories alcoholic drinks do not make a significant contribution to overall nutritional intake, so those attempting to lose weight should limit intake. Drink low-alcohol or no-alcohol drinks, use low-calorie mixers or carbonated water to make a longer drink.

Eat less sugar

Generally reduce and try to remove any sugar that is added to food, for example in tea and coffee or on cereal.

Drink only unsweetened drinks such as mineral water or natural fruit juices.

Eat only fresh fruit as tinned or bottled fruit may contain added sugar.

Avoid processed food, which usually contains added sugar.

Eat more fibre

Foods which are high in fibre are:

* wholemeal bread
* wholemeal cereals
* brown rice
* potatoes cooked in their jackets
* vegetables such as peas, beans, sweetcorn and the green leaf variety, e.g. spinach or spring cabbage
* lentils
* dried fruits.

Fruit and other vegetables contain fibre but not in such high amounts.

Salad foods contain small amounts of fibre and can be eaten in unlimited quantities as they contain few calories. It is the dressing on a salad which contains the calories so this should be used sparingly.

Following these four simple rules, eating moderate quantities of wholesome food and taking some form of exercise five times a week for at least 30 minutes should allow the client to lose weight steadily, while still eating a sensible well-balanced diet.

Eat more vitamins and minerals

By eating a healthy well-balanced diet, you should obtain all the required vitamins and minerals as they are present in food in the form and amounts that the body needs.

Storing and cooking food

To make sure that the fresh foods you eat are as nutritious as possible, they should be stored correctly as prolonged or inadequate storage can lead to a reduction in the nutrient content. 'Convenience' chilled, frozen, dried or pre-packaged foods can be as good a source of vitamins and minerals as fresh food but only if they are stored correctly and cooking instructions followed.

To preserve the vitamin content of fresh fruit and vegetables, you should:

* avoid storing them for too long
* chop vegetables just before cooking them
* avoid overcooking vegetables – use a steamer, microwave or stir fry because water soluble vitamins such as vitamins C and B complex are lost when vegetables are boiled
* eat fruit and vegetables raw whenever possible.

Large amounts of minerals are lost from foods when they are refined, for example during flour milling and rice polishing, so eat whole wheat flour and brown rice whenever possible.

When cooking cut down on the amount of salt used. Try using herbs or other flavourings instead.

Factors affecting diet

Food allergies

There are many people who are intolerant to certain foods, which means they may have an unusual reaction when they eat them. The reaction can be a simple rash, but in some cases it can be severe and life threatening. More often, it will cause headaches, diarrhoea or vomiting. A doctor must be consulted about food intolerance as certain foods may need to be removed from a diet and a qualified dietician should advise on this. Some allergies are hereditary. Children often grow out of allergies, but some people are particularly sensitive to food additives, for example colours, which can produce symptoms of hyperactivity.

Food intolerance can be caused by:

* the lack of a certain enzyme which normally helps to digest food, e.g. people with milk intolerance are lacking in lactose, which helps in the digestion of milk
* certain substances taken in large quantities which act in a similar way to drugs, e.g. caffeine can produce symptoms such as sweating or migraine

* some highly spicy foods which have an irritant effect on the lining of the gut
* some substances that are allergens (a food antigen) (see Sensitisation in Chapter 8 The skin on page 117) and cause an allergic reaction.

Types of food allergy

Coeliac disease

This is a sensitivity to the protein gluten which is found in barley, oats, rye and wheat. It is controlled by eating a gluten-free diet and there are specially prepared gluten-free products available. If this condition is not properly controlled, it may cause poor growth and weight loss.

Egg allergy

This may produce eczema or other forms of rash. Eggs and products containing eggs will need to be avoided.

Fish and shellfish

Allergy to shellfish often produces a rash, but in severe cases it can cause anaphylactic shock (see below) which is a massive allergic reaction in the body.

Milk intolerance

A sensitivity to protein from the milk of cows can cause eczema and because of the lack of an essential enzyme some people cannot digest the lactose present in it. A soya-based milk substitute may be given to babies and children; adults can also drink goats' milk when there is an intolerance to milk from cows.

Peanut allergy

This is known as an anaphylactic food allergy because it produces such severe reactions in the body (anaphylactic shock). These reactions result in a widespread release of histamine which causes swelling (oedema), constriction of the bronchioles, heart failure, circulatory collapse and, in extreme cases, death. It is a serious and potentially fatal condition, which may develop in particularly sensitive individuals within a few seconds or minutes. Sufferers may also be allergic to other types of nut.

Wheat allergy

An allergy to wheat can cause symptoms of asthma, itchy skin and in some cases diarrhoea. Sufferers are sensitive to the whole grain including wheat starch, unlike coeliacs who are only allergic to the wheat protein. It is

important to look closely at the list of ingredients on food labelling to ensure that the food does not contain an ingredient which may cause an allergic reaction.

Pregnancy

It is vitally important to eat a healthy well-balanced diet during pregnancy as the placenta passes nourishment from the mother's bloodstream to the developing baby. There are several dietary recommendations from the Department of Health for pregnant mothers:

* Avoid eating liver and products containing liver, e.g. pâté or sausages, because they are high in vitamin A and, if taken in large amounts, may be harmful to the baby.
* Folic acid intake should be increased before conception and for the first three months of a pregnancy to help prevent conditions such as spina bifida occurring. The Department of Health recommends 400 micrograms per day taken with vitamin B12. Zinc, vitamin B12, folic acid and magnesium help to control nausea during pregnancy. It is found in potatoes, green vegetables, pulses, fortified breakfast cereal, bread, fruit, nuts and yeast extract.
* Avoid eating foods which are associated with the salmonella and listeria bacteria, e.g. soft cheeses, mould-ripened cheeses, raw or lightly cooked eggs, food containing raw egg, pâté, raw or lightly cooked meat.
* Limit the amount of caffeine to no more than 300 milligrams a day. High levels of caffeine can result in babies having a low birth weight. Caffeine is added to some soft drinks as well as occurring naturally in tea, coffee and chocolate.

Figure 6.10 *A healthy, well-balanced diet is important during pregnancy*

Caution!

The Food Standards Agency has recently advised pregnant and breast-feeding women and those intending to become pregnant not to eat more than two medium-sized cans of tuna or one fresh tuna steak a week. This is in addition to earlier advice not to eat swordfish, shark or marlin as the mercury level present in these fish can potentially harm an unborn child's nervous system.

After the birth new mums often want to lose weight and regain their figure. However, if they are breast feeding, energy requirements will be high and they will increase as milk production increases to satisfy the growing baby. It is important to follow a healthy eating plan and eat when hungry to prevent tiredness and to drink plenty of bland fluids such as water, milk or diluted fruit juices. Avoid foods which may upset the baby's tummy and alcohol while breast feeding.

High blood pressure

Having high blood pressure is one factor which increases the risk of heart disease, kidney disease and having a stroke. In people who are at risk it is thought that too much salt in the diet may contribute to high blood pressure.

Salt is required to help maintain the fluid balance in our body. The amount of salt required by the body has been estimated to be just over 1.5 grams per day ($\frac{3}{4}$ teaspoon of salt). This amount is consumed easily from salt which occurs naturally in food, therefore we need no added salt. To help cut down salt intake, you could recommend your client to:

* gradually reduce the amount of salt added to food – taste buds will quickly adjust as the natural flavour of the food starts to come through
* eat reduced salt versions of food products
* use substitutes to provide flavour (clients with a kidney complaint or under medical supervision should seek medical advice)
* avoid high sodium foods such as table salt, smoked fish, dried packet soup, baked beans in tomato sauce, canned soup, bread, breakfast cereal, pickles, salad dressing, dry roasted peanuts, very low-fat spread, cured or canned meats, prawns, stock cubes, sausages, tomato ketchup, hard cheeses, milk, crisps, fish fingers, salted butter and margarine.

Coronary heart disease

A government publication (COMA Report) based on population research has advised that those at risk of coronary heart disease should:

* decrease their fat intake to 30 per cent of calories from food
* decrease their saturated fat intake to 10 per cent of calories from food
* reduce their cholesterol intake to less than 300 milligrams a day
* avoid excess alcohol
* increase starch/fibre rich food
* avoid obesity
* eat a balanced diet
* take regular exercise.

Foods good for the heart

A number of American nutritionists have named the following foods as the ones they believe to be most beneficial to heart health:

* Fish like salmon and trout contain omega-3 fatty acids that may prevent blood clotting.
* Pulses and oats contain soluble fibre, which helps to remove cholesterol from the bloodstream.
* Soya protein helps to reduce 'bad' cholesterol.
* Olive oil lowers cholesterol and may help to prevent blood clotting.

Vegetarian diet

Many people now follow a vegetarian diet or simply eat no red meat. There are those who have adopted a vegan diet which excludes all food of animal origin including dairy products and eggs. It is important that no matter which diet is followed it must be well balanced and include the correct amount of vitamins, minerals, proteins, fats and fibre for good health.

Recent research has shown that a vegetarian diet reduces the risk of heart disease and cancers, but there are other risks involved if the diet is not well planned to include all the requirements for health. Eating no animal foods can lead to health risks, usually a deficiency in iron, vitamin B12, vitamin D, calcium and zinc.

To counteract this, vegetarians should eat plenty of green vegetables such as spinach, broccoli, seeds, nuts, wholemeal cereals and fortified breakfast cereals. They should increase their vitamin C intake, as this will help the absorption of iron into the body, and the foods which contain vitamin B12 such as yeast extract, soya milk and fortified breakfast cereals. Vitamin D intake may be increased by eating egg yolk, dairy products, fortified breakfast cereals and some fish. Calcium intake is dependent on vitamin D and only 30–40 per cent of calcium in the diet is absorbed. Therefore, vegans must eat more peanuts, walnuts, sunflower seeds and green vegetables in their diet and, in addition, vegetarians may eat, milk and cheese. Zinc is required to transport vitamin A around the body and is also involved in red blood cell production. Natural sources include, mushrooms, wheatgerm, brewers' yeast and eggs.

It is also important to look at the amount of fat eaten as some vegetarians base their diet around dairy products which are high in saturated fat and cholesterol. They should limit the amount of saturated fatty foods and replace with vegetable oils such as olive or sunflower.

Diabetes

This is a metabolic disorder and is caused by a lack of the hormone insulin, which reduces the ability of the body to convert food into energy and control the amount of glucose in the blood. There are two types of diabetes:

* Type 1 diabetes, usually referred to as insulin dependent diabetes, is where the body stops producing insulin. The patient requires regular injections of insulin and must follow a healthy diet with regular meals.
* Type 2 diabetes, where the body produces small amounts of insulin but not enough to control glucose levels in the blood, can be controlled by diet and some sufferers may also take tablets. In poorly controlled type 2 diabetes insulin injections may also be required. Many type 2 diabetics suffer with weight problems.

(For more information on diabetes, see Chapter 3 Contraindications.)

Insulin resistance may also occur during pregnancy leading to the condition known as gestational diabetes.

The British Diabetic Association does not recommend a special diet but a healthy well-balanced diet similar to that of any other adult.

Other factors relating to diet

A balanced diet is important at any age. Sometimes poor nutrition is a problem for several reasons:

* Low income may prevent the buying of fresh wholesome foods and poor cooking facilities.
* Illness often means a general lack of appetite or the inability to cook.
* Loss of appetite may occur for many reasons including illness, stress, depression, anxiety or a general disinterest in food.
* Mental lethargy through illness or other medical condition such as Alzheimers, a progressive form of dementia occurring in middle age or later, characterised by loss of short-term memory, deterioration in behaviour and intellectual performance and slowness of thought.
* Disinterest in preparing food could occur with any of the above.
* Over indulging in the wrong type of food such as sweets, cakes, and so on, thus eating an unbalanced diet low in the necessary nutrients and vitamins.

* Eating too many processed and convenience foods, a problem for many people who are too busy to prepare fresh food.

Age

Older people are living longer and enjoying an active life. However, dietary requirements do change in later years so older people should:

* eat a wide variety of food from the four main food groups
* maintain body weight – being underweight can increase the risk of disease; being overweight may restrict mobility and health
* increase the amount of fats they eat such as omega-3 polyunsaturates
* watch salt intake particularly if high blood pressure is a problem
* eat more fibre in the form of fresh fruit, vegetables and cereals
* ensure that the diet has plenty of dairy foods for calcium to keep bones strong and healthy – vitamin D intake should be increased
* eat plenty of vitamin C, which helps with wound healing
* drink plenty of fluid to help the fibre in the diet work.

Calorie-controlled diet

Some clients may prefer to eat their favourite foods and still diet or not have to eliminate any particular food to achieve weight loss. A calorie chart would be helpful to them in choosing their own meals while staying within a calorie limit. Some slimming clubs, dieticians, nutritionists or health centres may provide calorie charts and as all charts vary slightly it is advisable to choose one and use it to compile a calorie-controlled diet to suit personal taste.

Advising the client

Helpful tips

To make sure that a diet or healthy eating programme works, there are several things that can be done:

* Start a diet on a convenient day, which fits in with your routine.
* Plan a week ahead so you have a shopping list of essentials and meals are planned.
* Stock up on healthy low-fat foods.
* Eat regular meals without snacking.
* Take time over meals, enjoy them and do not eat in a hurry.

Wonder diets

There are many different 'fad' diets on the market, which guarantee massive weight loss, but they tend to concentrate on eating a small selection of food instead of eating a well-balanced and healthy diet. They may achieve rapid results, as they are usually 'starvation' diets, cutting the calorie intake so drastically that the dieter is bound to lose weight. In the long term, however, the weight is soon put back on and the body may be deprived of essential nutrients in the process.

There are disadvantages to most of these diets. For example, a diet high in protein such as meat, milk and cheese also contains saturated fat and this is known to increase the cholesterol level in the blood. This is bad for the health and fats contain more calories, weight for weight than other foods. These foods are also low in fibre, which is essential to a healthy diet as fibre provides bulk and satisfies the appetite, as well as being low in calories and aiding elimination of waste from the body.

Low-calorie powders are chemical substitutes for meals and when mixed with water provide a very low calorie intake per day. This is usually in the region of 350–400 calories a day, far below the normal requirements of the body and should only be used on medical advice. Other specialist foods are usually over-refined and over-processed foods which contain artificial chemicals. It is far better for the general health of the body to eat natural wholesome foods in the correct amounts.

Additional help with losing weight

Sweet tablets

These are freely available to buy over the counter and it is recommended that they are taken a short period before eating. They are made from methyl-cellulose or glucose. The former swells up in the stomach and takes the edge off the appetite. This may be achieved in a far more natural way by eating food with a high fibre content. The latter is also said to reduce the appetite, but a piece of fruit eaten before a meal would have a similar effect.

Appetite suppressing drugs

Doctors may prescribe drugs to suppress the appetite, but they often have side effects, which outweigh the benefits. These would normally only be recommended by a doctor if being overweight was a risk to the patient's health.

Slimming clubs

The advantage of a club is the motivation that is received from other members who all have the same problem. In some cases, when enthusiasm is waning it can be motivating to chat to others and the support, advice and encouragement they can give can help achieve targets.

The club may also provide advice about maintaining the weight loss when the target figure has been reached. Having weight loss monitored weekly provides the incentive to keep going as it can be embarrassing to admit defeat in front of others. The disadvantage of a slimming club is that the diet may not always be the best one for the individual.

Eating disorders

Anorexia nervosa

This disorder is characterised by a loss of appetite as well as some unusual eating habits. It is self-imposed starvation, usually subconscious. It is thought to be an emotional response to conflicts of self-identity and a reluctance to accept becoming an adult. The sufferer has a distorted body image. It is a problem which seems to affect mainly young females, but there is increasing evidence that it is also affecting adolescent boys. The condition may be worsened by the media obsession with being slim and the effects are:

* progressive starvation
* huge weight loss
* absence of menstruation

* lowered basal metabolic rate
* depression
* anxiety
* social withdrawal.

The result of this condition is emaciation (wasting) of the body through starvation, which can, in some cases, cause death. Treatment of this condition is usually support from family and friends, but may include psychotherapy and re-education in eating habits. The Eating Disorders Association has a wide range of help available (see Glossary of professional associations and organisations at the end of this book).

Bulimia

Bulimia may also be referred to as binge-purge syndrome. It is characterised by over eating on a grand scale and then forced vomiting, fasting, excessive exercise or over use of strong laxatives. The problem often occurs because of a fear of being overweight, during periods of depression and stress, or because of physiological disorders such as hypothalamic tumours. The effects of this condition can be:

* electrolyte imbalance
* hormone imbalance
* dry skin
* acne
* muscle spasms
* loss of hair
* tooth decay
* ulcers and hernias
* an increased risk of flu and salivary gland infections
* constipation.

Treatment may include support from family and friends, psychotherapy, medical treatment and nutritional advice.

Obesity

This may be defined as a body mass index (BMI) greater than 30 as a result of an excessive build-up of fat (see Figure 6.4). The problems related to obesity are:

* increased mortality
* high blood pressure

* high levels of cholesterol in the blood
* increased risk of heart disease
* increased risk of respiratory disease
* stress on joints
* varicose veins
* difficulties with movement
* difficulties in seating, e.g. on planes
* feelings of unhappiness and inadequacy.

The causes of obesity may be metabolic, resulting from a disorder that reduces the breaking down (catabolism) of fats and carbohydrates, or quite simply eating far more food than the body requires accompanied by inactivity so the body does not burn up the calories. The treatment would be to lose body fat without the breakdown of lean tissue, maintaining some sort of exercise regime and establishing healthy eating habits.

Caution!

Obesity is now a worldwide health problem affecting all socio-economic groups. It is the most important dietary factor in chronic disease such as cancer, cardiovascular disease and type 2 diabetes. People who are overweight are more likely to suffer from, coronary heart disease, gallstones, arthritis, high blood pressure, diabetes and some types of cancer, and women are more likely to have complications during and after pregnancy. The World Health Organisation (WHO) has predicted that one of the consequences of the global epidemic of obesity will be 300 million people with type 2 diabetes by 2005.

People who have excess fat around their middle ('apple shaped') are at more risk of some of these diseases than those who have excess fat around their hips and thighs 'pear shaped'. Men are at increased risk when their waist circumference measures 94 cm; for women risks increase at 80 cm.

The aim of those who want to lose weight is to lose stored fat. Adipose tissue is the body's long-term store of pure, concentrated fat, but fat is also stored in the short term in the muscles. If the body consumes more calories than it uses up in energy, there will be weight gain. If, however, the amount of fat in the diet is reduced, a healthy well-balanced diet is followed, choosing a good selection of food from all four food groups and a regular amount of exercise is taken, then weight loss will result. To lose weight more energy must be spent in physical exercise than is consumed in calories.

Below is a list of contraindications that you could give clients in the form of an advice sheet if they are anxious to lose weight.

Contraindications to diet

A weight reducing diet should not be started without consulting a doctor in the following circumstances:

If you are under 18.

If you are pregnant or breast feeding.

If you have a medical condition for which you are receiving treatment.

If you are suffering from or have previously suffered from an eating disorder such as anorexia nervosa, bulimia nervosa or compulsive eating disorder.

If you are clinically obese.

If you are clinically underweight.

Stress

A client's lifestyle may have quite an impact on his or her life, sometimes more than the individual realises. The client may arrive at the salon in a tense or agitated mood or distracted and worried about the time he or she does not have but is reluctantly fitting in treatments in a busy schedule! It may not always be so obvious to the therapist as stress can have other effects such as lethargy, feeling under the weather or a lack of communication. It is important, therefore, to provide a thorough consultation, particularly if it is the client's first visit to the salon.

I have had many occasions when clients have thanked me profusely after having a full leg wax or an eyebrow shape because they appreciated the short time that they had to themselves and that they were being looked after, even if it was not the most relaxing of treatments. My immediate reaction to this was to recommend an aromatherapy massage, a relaxing facial or Swedish body massage because the therapeutic effects would be increased tenfold. In addition, I would recommend that the client considered exercise in conjunction with relaxation as this helps to alleviate some of the effects of stress and increases energy levels and improves the frame of mind.

During consultation you will need to ask the client specific questions about his or her stress levels. This will help you decide on the correct course and combination of treatments and also what home care advice you can give and recommendations for lifestyle changes.

Stress is a psychological pressure and tension is the body's response to this pressure. It has become an increasingly common problem as the pace of life has increased. In small amounts stress is a normal part of life and it can be stimulating, but when stress changes to 'distress' it becomes a negative and destructive force. Stress is bad when:

* it seems to be continuous with no break
* it makes a person feel out of control
* it disrupts normal everyday living
* it has an effect on personal relationships.

Factors causing pressure will not lead to stress for everyone but will depend on:

* the amount of pressure involved
* how each individual deals with the pressure
* how long the stress lasts for
* the personality of the individual
* the amount of support he or she is receiving.

Figure 7.1 *You will need to be able to recognise stress in your client*

Effects of stress

The damaging effects of stress are not just psychological but also physiological because stress causes the release of the hormone adrenalin into the bloodstream, which prepares the body for 'fight or flight'. When this is happening over a period of time the adrenalin released into the body has an adverse reaction causing physical problems to occur. Emotional trauma, anger and anxiety caused by stress can be transformed into physical ailments with a variety of symptoms, such as headaches and heart palpitations.

Physiological response to stress

Stress affects several systems of the body, as shown in Table 7.1 and Figure 7.2.

Body system	Physiological response
Circulatory	The heart beats faster
	Pulse rate increases
	Blood vessels to muscles and brain dilate
	Blood vessels in the skin are constricted
	Blood clotting ability is increased
	Spleen contracts and discharges stored blood into the circulation
	Body temperature increases
	Perspiration increases
Respiratory	Dilation of bronchioles in the lungs
	Breathing becomes more rapid and shallow
Digestive	Production of saliva slows down
	Decrease in enzyme production in digestive organs
	Rise in glucose levels in the liver
	Butterflies in the stomach
	Bowel stimulation
Muscular	Tension is increased and nodules form
Urinary	Decrease in urine production

Table 7.1 *How stress affects the body*

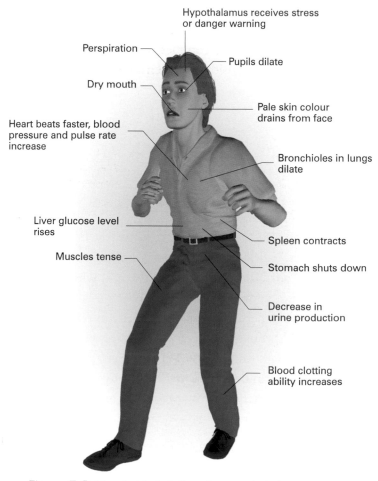

Figure 7.2 *The physiological effects of stress on the body*

Coping with stress

Chronic stress can be linked to heart disease, high blood pressure, disorders of the immune system, allergies, asthma, eczema, irritable bowel syndrome and it can also have an ageing effect on the skin. Often clients are not aware that they are suffering from stress, but it may become clear during the consultation that the client can improve his or her lifestyle and reduce stress, so improving overall health. Stress must be recognised and dealt with effectively to maintain a healthy body and mind.

The realisation that stress is adversely affecting the body is the first step in coping with the problem. Then, in consultation with the client, a plan may be drawn up to minimise the effects or eliminate the causes, as the treatments you can offer in the salon will provide a temporary antidote by relaxing the client. In addition, the client will need to evaluate his or her lifestyle and make changes where necessary. Ask the client to:

* assess his or her current lifestyle and identify the causes of stress
* list the causes that he or she can control
* deal with each one and decide how to overcome the problem
* list the causes that are out of his or her control

* look at the best way to reduce these problems and therefore reduce the stress
* take time to relax, e.g. through therapeutic treatments, sleep, rest, a hobby or favourite sport
* take some form of exercise as this will eliminate pent-up energy, oxygenate the blood and burn up excess adrenalin; it also makes you feel good as endorphins are released into the body
* delegate responsibility to others, at work and at home.

Relaxation

Many clients will suffer from stress to a certain degree, which causes problems such as tension in the muscles. This in turn leads to aches, pains and headaches. Some clients will eat more when under stress, putting on extra weight. This can adversely affect the joints and reduce energy levels. They may also find it difficult to sleep and become lethargic and generally feel unfit.

The adrenaline produced when under stress has adverse effects on the body, increasing the heartbeat and stimulating the nerves. Excess adrenalin causes tiredness and irritability.

It is very important to teach a client how to relax as an antidote to stress. To remove the tension and reduce the anxiety will help in eliminating the harmful side effects of too much stress. Relaxation also helps to store up energy, which is required for important issues. It will also help to concentrate the mind and improve quality of life.

During consultation you will need to evaluate the client's stress level and explain what options he or she will have for relaxation treatment. You may suggest a combination of different forms of relaxation therapy, but these must be agreed with the client.

There are many relaxing therapies available such as heat, floatation and spa therapy, body, Indian head, aromatherapy or facial massage. In addition, you can teach relaxation techniques to the client and he or she will be able to follow your instructions at home when he or she has the time.

To promote relaxation, you will need:
* a warm environment
* a quiet room with no distractions
* low lighting
* comfortable position suited to the client, supported by pillows
* loose warm cover if required
* relaxation tape playing quietly in the background.

The therapist's manner must encourage relaxation and your approach will need to be calm and relaxed. Speak quietly with assurance, smile and do not rush the client.

Relaxation techniques

Clients may attend for relaxing treatments, but if their lifestyle is particularly hectic and stressful they will need to learn how to relax at home or even at work. Advice about how to relax may be provided in the salon, before or after treatment. You will need to make the client aware of the difference in the feeling of tension and relaxation in the muscles and this may be achieved by teaching the client how to contract and relax the muscles, feeling the tension and then slowly releasing it.

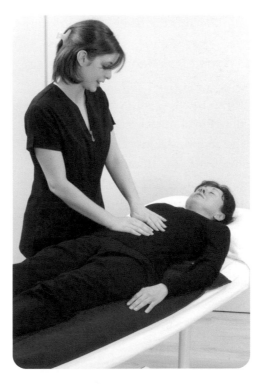

Figure 7.3
A client practises relaxation techniques

The client will be instructed to contract, tighten and relax individual muscles and muscle groups, working in a sequence from the feet up to the head. Clients will soon learn how to do this themselves with practice.

Relaxation procedure

1 Find a suitable location, dim the lights and play relaxing music quietly in the background.
2 Prepare clients with suitable clothing, towels or cover.
3 Ensure clients are comfortable, warm and well-supported.
4 Encourage clients to close their eyes and relax.
5 Begin with some slow, relaxed, even breathing to calm and reduce adrenaline secretion.
6 Ask the client to focus the mind on a special place or single thing to slow thoughts down and empty the mind. It could be a quiet beach in an exotic location, lying in a warm snug bed or anywhere or time which has happy memories.
7 Beginning with the feet ask clients to repeat each movement three times.
   * Breathe in when tightening muscles and out when relaxing them.
   * Pull toes up towards the head (dorsi flexion) and release.
   * Push toes down to the floor (plantar flexion) and release.
   * Push legs into the floor and release.
   * Tighten the gluteal muscles and release.
   * Tighten the abdominal muscles and release.
   * Push the back into the floor and release.
   * Clench the fists and release.
   * Tighten the arm muscles and release.
   * Lift and tighten the shoulders towards the head and release.
   * Press the head into the floor and release.
   * Screw up the eyes and tighten the whole face and release.
   * Tighten all muscles and release.

Allow clients to lie quietly for ten to fifteen minutes. Ask them to practise these techniques at home and suggest further treatment.

Other simple relaxation methods to use in between treatments are stretching and walking.

Stretching exercise

Stretching the muscles exerts a squeezing effect on the blood, compressing veins and capillaries and moving blood back in the direction of the heart. At the same time, waste products are removed more efficiently. Fresh blood enters the muscle bringing with it oxygen and nutrients. Stretching also relieves the tension in the muscles and must be performed slowly and gently while breathing normally. Sessions need only last about 20 minutes and ideally should take place three to five times per week.

Walking

Walking briskly or using an active exercise routine particularly suited to the client can aid relaxation.

Relaxation area

Many salons have a relaxation area that clients can use before, during or after treatment, often lit with candles and essential oil burners. They can sit or lie in a warm comfortable area, have a fruit or herbal tea, read, relax or sleep depending on the time available. It is now popular for clients to have full or half-day packages allowing them to enjoy a combination of treatments designed for their particular needs. This can be offered to individuals or groups and is particularly common in the spa environment.

Figure 7.4 *A client relaxation area in the Elenis Day Spa in London*

Exercising the body

Figure shapes may be improved by diet, which will help in removing fatty deposits stored in the subcutaneous layer of the skin, and by using forms of electrical treatment to tone and firm muscles or improve a cellulite condition. However, exercise also helps to re-shape the body by firming and toning muscles, as well as having other benefits such as an antidote to stress, which will contribute to the overall health and well-being of the client.

Benefits of exercise

The overall effect when exercising regularly is a feeling of well-being and a glow to the skin that is achieved after a very short time. It is enjoyable and will also increase energy levels, stamina and strength. The benefits of exercise include the following:

* Exercise burns off the excess adrenalin caused by stress and increases energy levels.
* Circulation is improved because the increased activity has a pumping action on the blood vessels and pushes the blood towards the heart. The lymphatic circulation is also improved, removing waste products more efficiently.
* Respiration is increased allowing more oxygen in and carbon dioxide to be expelled.
* The heart is a muscle and through regular exercise it becomes stronger as it is made to work harder, faster and more efficiently.
* Muscles increase in tone and strength, as regular exercise causes the muscle fibres to increase in size. The blood supply to the muscles is increased which provides nourishment and oxygen. The elasticity and suppleness of the muscles is also improved.
* Exercise burns calories and helps with weight control. It is important to choose the right type of exercise to suit age, health and lifestyle. If more calories are used than are taken in, this will result in the extra calories coming from the fat stores. Combining aerobic exercise with cardiovascular training is an ideal combination and a good target to aim for is three periods of exercise for up to 30 minutes every week. As fitness levels increase, the amount and type of exercise can be reassessed.
* Bones are nourished and fed through exercise. It increases flexibility and suppleness and mobility in the joints is increased.
* Metabolism is increased which will help those clients who wish to lose weight.
* Tension is relieved, promoting general relaxation and improving the ability to sleep.
* Posture is improved.
* It improves the balance of fats in the blood.
* It lowers the resting blood pressure levels.

Exercise is therefore an excellent way in which to tone all the systems of the body and improve the state of mind. It is most effective when used in conjunction with diet and salon treatments.

Providing advice and making recommendations

A consultation must be carried out to discuss the client's requirements, assess the client's posture, body shape and problem areas, complete a record card and evaluate treatment.

A treatment plan can be devised and an exercise plan suggested to suit the requirements of the client. This may be a general keep-fit programme, an aid to weight reduction or exercises for specific problems. Clients should be advised to seek professional help when embarking on a course of exercise and if your own establishment does not have this facility, then it is important to establish a professional relationship with experts in the field of fitness and exercise.

It is essential to ensure that the exercise recommended is appropriate for the client. Many salons and spas now have experts available to provide one-to-one exercise and training sessions and specialist exercise classes. However, the client often looks to you as his or her personal therapist for advice and guidance.

Maintaining client interest

To encourage the client to participate fully in some form of exercise, the therapist must make sure the exercise chosen is effective, will produce results and maintain the client's interest. This is made much easier for the client if the exercise routine is easy to understand and follow. Also make sure that it is within the client's capabilities as asking clients to do something which is too difficult for them will result in their giving up, or possibly cause them an injury. Encourage the client to change routines or form of exercise as they progress, again to maintain their interest and to accommodate their increasing strength, fitness and endurance.

When objectives have been achieved, re-evaluate the treatment and exercise plan and change to a maintenance programme to prevent problems recurring.

Safety when exercising

Before beginning any exercise programme, it is important to stress the safety aspects to the client. If clients are overweight or have any medical problems such as high blood pressure, diabetes or a heart condition, it is advisable for them to have a medical check first. Advise them to allow at least two hours after eating before starting any exercise and wear the correct clothing, loose-fitting and comfortable, with supportive shoes. They should always warm up before exercising to improve performance as warm muscles respond more quickly, increasing the speed at which they contract and relax, as well as being able to increase the force of the contraction. Failure to do this may lead to a torn muscle. The muscles most likely to tear are the antagonists, the opposing muscles to the agonists, the group that produces the movement.

To be fully effective warming up exercises must include movements for all muscle groups and all parts of the body. Do not perform exercises using the same muscle group repeatedly as this could over work an area. Build up gradually and slowly without pushing the body beyond its limit and trying to achieve too much too soon. Always cool down after exercising and stretch the muscles gently to prevent stiffness. This will keep extra blood flowing through the muscles, helping to disperse waste products such as lactic acid, a by-product of exercise, which can cause stiffness. Stop exercising if there is any pain or giddiness.

Breathing

Whatever type of exercise is undertaken, it is important to breathe properly to provide plenty of oxygen for the active muscles.

Respiration

The function of the respiratory system is to exchange oxygen and carbon dioxide between the atmosphere and the body. Oxygen is inhaled from the atmosphere to the tissues and carbon dioxide is removed from the tissues and expelled into the atmosphere. This interchange of gases takes place through the walls of the capillaries (see Figure 7.5).

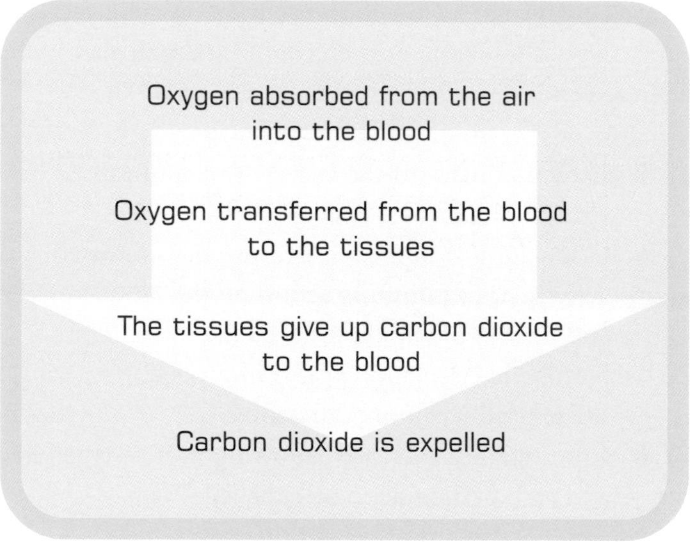

Oxygen absorbed from the air into the blood

Oxygen transferred from the blood to the tissues

The tissues give up carbon dioxide to the blood

Carbon dioxide is expelled

Figure 7.5 *The interchange of gases*

The client should be encouraged to breathe deeply throughout the exercise routine. If a particularly energetic routine is carried out which leaves the client breathless, then a quiet period should be incorporated into the routine to allow the client to regain his or her normal breathing pattern.

Benefits of correct breathing

There are three types of breathing:

* **Apical** or shallow breathing only uses the upper lobe of the lungs and occurs in times of stress, fear or excitement, if the client is asthmatic or has a respiratory disorder.

* **Lateral costal** uses the upper and middle lobes of the lung. It is deeper and slower and is the type of breathing which occurs naturally, interspersed with apical.
* **Diaphragmatic** uses all the lobes of the lung (the upper, middle and lower). It is deep breathing and is used to calm and relax, using the respiratory system effectively. This type of breathing is recommended for the therapist and client prior to Indian head massage, aromatherapy and even reflexology. It is an ideal method of preparing for the treatment to come.

The main benefits of breathing correctly and using breathing exercises include the following:

* Breathing provides oxygen to the tissues.
* It aids metabolism.
* It increases resistance to infection of the lungs.
* It maintains elasticity and strength of the lungs.
* It improves posture.
* It reduces stress level, aiding relaxation.
* It increases circulation.
* It oxidises fat.
* It feeds muscles.

Reasons for exercise routines

Exercise routines can be recommended for different reasons:

* To increase general fitness.
* To increase mobility.
* To strengthen the muscles.
* To correct figure faults.
* For relaxation.
* To increase effectiveness of salon treatments

Fitness

For general fitness a scheme of exercises must be devised to work all muscle groups in the body, without overworking any one area. Exercises must be clearly explained and demonstrated by an expert. The client must assume the correct posture before commencing the exercise routine and start with some simple breathing exercises.

A general routine should follow a set sequence to include a warm-up, breathing exercises and then each area of the body exercised starting with the head and working down to the feet, finishing with more breathing and a cool-down.

Mobility

Mobility exercises are incorporated into most general exercise routines but are often required for an older client to gently stretch and mobilise the muscles before progressing to different types of exercise. The effects of these exercises are to loosen the body and make it more supple enabling the client to progress further. Mobility exercises should be performed fairly quickly in a relaxed manner, without static contractions and the parts being exercised should be moved through as full a range as possible.

Strengthen muscles

Strengthening exercises are used to build up muscle strength, or to correct figure faults and weakness. The muscles are contracted against a resistance, increasing muscle fibres. Isometric exercises can be used with contractions being held for several seconds and the time increased as the muscle strengthens. Using weights while performing the exercises may increase the resistance. It is essential to warm up before strength training and also to breathe correctly. The resistance to the contraction must not be extreme; it is advisable to build up slowly to prevent injury occurring. Sessions should be three times a week and the duration will depend on the physical fitness of the client. Once the required muscle strength has been achieved, exercise sessions are only necessary once a week for maintenance.

Figure 7.6 *Using weights will help to strengthen muscles*

Figure fault	Aim of exercise
Lordosis	Strengthen abdominal muscles and hip extensors. Stretch erector spinae and quadratus lumborum
Kyphosis	Strengthen middle fibres of trapezius, rhomboids and erector spinae. Stretch pectoralis major
Scoliosis	Strengthen the muscles on the outside of the curve. Stretch the muscles on the inside of the curve and balance between the two
Flat back	Strengthen the erector spinae muscles, abdominals and gluteus maximus. Stretch the hamstrings
Flabby upper arms	Strengthen triceps and reduce fat through aerobic exercise
Winged scapula	Strengthen serratus anterior and lower fibres of trapezius
Flabby gluteals	Strengthen gluteus maximus, hamstrings and abductors. Stretch the hip flexors
Flat feet	Increase mobility and strength

Table 7.2 *Correction of figure faults with exercise*

Large muscle groups should be exercised first, as the smaller groups become fatigued far more quickly. The sequence should not include exercising the same muscle group consecutively, as this will cause muscle fatigue.

Correction of figure faults

Some muscles may cause postural and figure problems by either becoming very weak or too strong. Corrective exercises to shorten and strengthen the weak muscles, and mobilising exercises for the stronger over contracted muscles should be given (see Table 7.2). Static muscle contractions can often improve generally poor posture quite quickly.

These conditions may also be helped, by recommending a course of electrical muscle stimulation treatment (see Chapter 18 Electrical treatment).

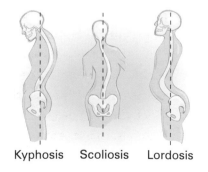

Kyphosis   Scoliosis   Lordosis

Figure 7.7 *Lordosis, kyphosis and scoliosis*

Relaxation

Regular exercise will aid restful sleep and burn off the adrenaline which is left in the body after periods of stress. Muscles become stronger and more flexible, releasing tension and promoting relaxation.

Contraindications to exercise

* Heart conditions or history of heart disease.
* High blood pressure. If the condition is controlled by medication, seek a doctor's approval.
* Arteriosclerosis.
* Respiratory conditions.
* Embolism.
* Obesity.
* Recent injury – sprains, strains, fractures, torn or ruptured ligaments.
* Infections of any kind, e.g. chickenpox, tonsillitis, measles.
* Inflamed joints, e.g. rheumatoid arthritis.
* Acute fevers such as glandular fever, flu or a bad cold.
* Neurological disorders, e.g. multiple sclerosis.
* Painful joints or muscles.
* Pregnancy – exercise should be controlled and gentle.
* After a heavy meal or consumption of alcohol.

If in doubt, the client should seek medical advice. It is advisable to have a medical check before beginning a course of exercise if there is any family medical history, if the client is over 40, diabetic, asthmatic or a heavy smoker.

Medical advice

Some GPs are now embracing alternative methods of dealing with stress and depression, prescribing complementary therapies such as reflexology and aromatherapy. They also encourage exercise to help maintain flexibility in old age, to increase bone density in those at risk from osteoporosis and as an antidote to stress and depression.

Types of exercise

Aerobics

These are exercises that require the efficient use of oxygen by the body throughout the whole exercise routine. Aerobic means literally 'with air'. This form of exercise works the cardiovascular system (heart, blood vessels and lungs) making it stronger and less vulnerable to heart attack and strokes.

Aerobic activities include the following.

Swimming

This is an excellent exercise for most people as it places no strain on any part of the body. It increases the circulation and lung ventilation, muscles are stretched and firmed as most strokes use all the muscle groups. It is a form of exercise which can be undertaken by people suffering from a bad back, arthritis and even high blood pressure, because the water supports the body, and has a relaxing effect when carried out at the client's own pace. The aerobic effect is achieved when swimming at a fast speed for as long as possible giving the body a very efficient cardiovascular workout.

Jogging

This is a very popular form of exercise, particularly when used as a group exercise. As well as toning and strengthening the muscles, this form of aerobic exercise increases energy levels and the client feels invigorated and healthier. It works the heart and lungs, increasing the stamina of the cardiorespiratory system. This is also

an ideal exercise for firming the legs and the gluteal muscles, which can be a problem area.

To prevent injury a good pair of running shoes must be worn and it is not advisable to jog on cement as this may cause injury to the foot and leg. A softer surface such as clay is far easier and kinder on the joints. The warm-up exercise period is essential to loosen the muscles. Allow a five-minute cooling down period for the body to return slowly to normal. This prevents lactic acid remaining in the muscles and causing discomfort.

Figure 7.8 *Aerobic exercise is popular and beneficial to health*

Cycling

This also provides an excellent cardiovascular workout and strengthens the muscles of the back and legs.

Boxercise

This is one of the most effective forms of cross-training available today. It combines use of both aerobic and anaerobic energy systems with the systematic use of both fast and slow twitch muscle fibres in a manner that not only ensures a diverse workout but also enhances sports-specific senses including hand-eye coordination, balance and timing. Boxercise classes are always fun, energetic and are popular with the young and fit!

Skipping

This benefits the heart and lungs and improves the figure as it tones the muscles of the arms, buttocks, thighs, hips and calves as well as firming the pectorals.

Skipping to music makes it more interesting. To prevent wear and tear on the joints, wear a supportive pair of running shoes.

Brisk walking

This is often a preferred form of exercise for older clients as they may do this for fairly long periods even when unfit. It provides a gentle cardiovascular workout. There are many muscles used for walking and these include the foot, leg, back, abdominal and rib, arm, shoulder and neck muscles.

Aerobic exercises all have a sustained rhythm of movement that puts constant demand on the heart, raising the pulse rate to between 120 and 160 beats a minute. This will help to increase the vigour and stamina of the heart, blood vessels and lungs. Aerobics:

* improves the circulation
* tones the muscles
* strengthens bone ligaments and joints
* strengthens the chest wall increasing lung capacity
* increases the efficiency of the heart and blood vessels
* increases overall fitness
* increases energy levels.

Aquarobics

This form of exercise is becoming more popular with many people but in particular older people, pregnant women, those suffering from an arthritic or rheumatic condition or who are unable to participate in other more rigorous forms of exercise. An instructor takes an exercise class with all the participants in the water.

Exercising in the water has several benefits:

* It strengthens and tones the muscles.
* It exercises the whole body.
* It promotes flexibility and balance.
* It increases cardiovascular fitness.
* It provides a safe and invigorating way to work out without putting a strain on the joints.

Yoga

This is a form of exercise which calms the mind as well as improving the suppleness of the body.

Physical or hatha yoga is a series of positions that move all parts of the body improving the general condition. The finished positions should be achieved

without causing discomfort. Therefore, the client must stop when it feels natural and comfortable in each position. The movement into the position should be performed slowly and smoothly and then held for several seconds. Each time the movement is repeated, the stretch will be slightly greater.

The extreme gentleness of yoga makes this form of exercise ideal for someone who cannot take active exercise or older people who want to increase suppleness of the body.

Figure 7.9 *Yoga improves the suppleness of the body*

This type of exercise is, in fact, suited to most people and it can have many uses:

* To improve the general condition.
* To learn how to relax.
* To remove muscular tension.
* To improve figure shape.
* To strengthen the body.
* To improve concentration.
* To improve circulation.
* To improve balance and posture.
* To improve mobility.
* To create a feeling of well-being.

There are other forms of exercise that a client may take without participating in an organised exercise session or energetic exercise routine.

Multigym

This is a set of scientifically designed exercise equipment to exercise different parts of the body.

The client will move from one piece of the equipment to the next, following a personalised exercise programme.

The adjustable weights and resistance factors of each piece of equipment make the multigym ideal for clients with varying degrees of fitness. The multigym also offers several pieces of exercise equipment fitted into a relatively small space, which makes it an ideal addition to a salon that wishes to offer this service.

Figure 7.10 *A multigym*

Toning tables

These have become popular in beauty salons as an addition to the body treatment range already on offer. They are fitness machines in the form of a table that exercises different parts of the body. Tables may be used as a set, with each table performing one particular exercise on one part of the body. Alternatively, one table can combine up to 12 exercises. This is ideal for a small salon lacking in space.

The exercises are isometric, toning the body and increasing flexibility. They are suitable for all age groups and levels of fitness as the body is supported by the table and exercise can be taken without causing fatigue.

The skin

Introduction

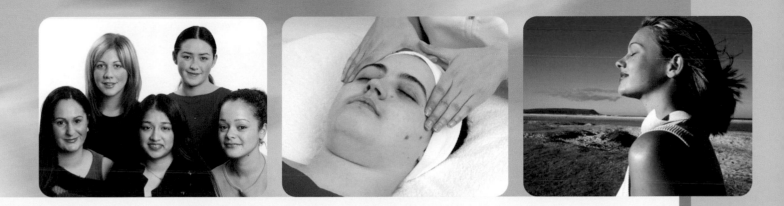

Men and women alike cherish the idea of a perfect skin glowing with health and vitality, free from tension, lines and wrinkles. They hope to give up using concealers and cosmetic camouflage to disguise the shadows and blemishes caused by stress, tiredness, environmental damage and age. They also wish for a body with perfectly proportioned contours, the skin taut and smooth with a texture like silk. The skin is so important to body image that people spend a great deal of time and money restoring it to a more youthful appearance.

Genes and a certain amount of good luck often determine good skin, but the most important factor is the correct care from its owner. Part of this care is to find a good beauty therapist who will contribute in some way to achieving their goal – flawless skin!

The skin is one of the largest, most complex and hard working organs of the body. It has many components including cells, glands, specialised receptors and fibres, all working together making a finely tuned system which maintains optimum health and appearance. Skin reflects emotions, it changes constantly and because of its location it is vulnerable to damage. Many things including nutrition, hygiene, circulation, age, immunity and genes all affect the state of skin.

This section is dedicated to the skin alone as wide knowledge of the structure, function, skin types and conditions is essential to the beauty therapist in providing the most effective forms of treatments and advice for each individual client.

8 The skin

Good skin can make you look healthy. Achieving a clear complexion is a goal for everybody. The appearance, texture and look of the skin is an important factor for most people at any age. It can have quite an effect on girls or boys during puberty if they have spots, blemishes or excessively greasy skin. The onset of acne can destroy their confidence and, in some cases, cause them to become quite introverted. It is quite noticeable among this age group that the more confident and outgoing young people are often those with clear healthy complexions. When I have treated young women with this condition I have noticed a change in personality and confidence in line with the improvement of their skin condition.

At the other end of the scale, many clients will be worried about the state of their skin as they age. They want to hold back the effects of time, improve the moisture-holding capacity of the skin and reduce the obvious signs such as lines, wrinkles and dropped contours.

There are many different considerations in treating all clients, whatever their skin problem and no matter how small, as they will need skin care and lifestyle advice in addition to appropriate treatments and support.

As a therapist, you will gain a great deal of satisfaction from seeing the wonderful results you can achieve for clients after devising a specific treatment plan, carrying out the therapeutic treatments and achieving the objectives agreed between yourself and the client. To be able to do this, you will need to learn as much as you can about the structure and functions of the skin, the different skin types and conditions you may treat, the professional products available to use and the range of treatments you may offer. You should start with a detailed skin analysis.

Skin analysis

Before carrying out any facial treatment, it is important to have analysed the client's skin thoroughly, because it will allow the therapist to:

* recognise the skin type
* recognise any contraindications to treatment
* recognise any disorder, which may need to be treated
* choose the correct products to use for treatment

* recognise which electrical treatments will be most beneficial
* advise the client on home treatment.

Ethnic skin types

Production of the skin pigment **melanin** varies in all ethnic groups. Black skins do not contain any more **melanocytes** (cells that manufacture melanin) than white ones do, but there are differences in the melanin granules (**melanosomes**) in the differently coloured skins. In black skins the granules are larger, whereas in white skins they are less obvious.

* In Asian people, the melanosomes are relatively large in size, and are distributed within the skin cells as a mixture of single and complex forms.
* In African-Caribbean-type skin the melanosomes are even larger. They are heavily pigmented and scattered singly throughout the keratinocytes (epidermal cells).
* In white skin the melanosomes are smaller and have less melanin. They are distributed as clumps in keratinocytes.

White skin

White skin produces less melanin to varying degrees. There are those skins which are pale, often with freckles and accompanied by red, blonde or 'mousy' hair and green or blue eyes. The translucent pale skin is at risk from sunburn, ageing and the formation of skin cancer because of the reduced protection it has from the lack of melanin in the skin. This skin type often complains of the inability to develop a tan and is prone to dehydration and irritation from the environment and other external stimuli. There are white skins that tan more easily and are far less sensitive, and the white Scandinavian skin, while pale in the winter, establishes a deep golden tan easily in the summer without burning and the blonde hair is often bleached almost white by the sun.

White skins age faster than black skins and it is important, therefore, to start protecting the skin from ultraviolet (UV) radiation as early as possible, particularly when living in hot climates such as in Australia and

South Africa. Vascular disorders are more visible on a white skin, sometimes producing a florid complexion in certain people.

Mediterranean-type skin

This skin type has a combination of yellow and red pigment, which provides the beautiful olive colour. It is also oily but not usually prone to spots and acne. This skin type ages much later than white skin and is protected from UV damage by the ability to tan quickly and deeply without burning. A problem for this skin type is sometimes the excess of facial hair, which is strong and coarser than other skin types.

Asian-type skin

This is predominantly yellow in tone with a sallow tinge. It ages very well and does not suffer with the many lines and wrinkles that often afflict white skin. Acne and blemished skins are not so common, but Asian skin types do suffer from hyperpigmentation from operation scars, acne or other skin lesions, therefore must be treated with care.

Chinese-type skin is sallow, often oily but smooth and evenly coloured. It also ages very well.

Black skin

Although all people have the same number of melanocyte cells, black skins have melanocytes that are capable of making large amounts of melanin. This increased melanin is the chief factor in determining skin colour and depth of black skin. There are many different shades of skin as the amount of melanin varies dramatically, so that a person with an abundance of melanin will have deep chocolate-brown skin tone, while a person with less melanin will have a much lighter skin tone. There are numerous shades of black skin, in fact an estimated 35 shades among women of African descent.

The black skin type absorbs 30 per cent more UV light than a white skin. This provides it with increased protection reducing the risk of sunburn, skin cancer and other lesions that form in response to UV exposure. Ageing effects are delayed and collagen and elastin degeneration is very slow allowing the skin to look smooth and remain supple for much longer than other types.

A disadvantage to having more melanin is that it makes the skin more 'reactive'. That means almost any stimulus –

a rash, scratch, pimple, or inflammation – may trigger the production of excess melanin, resulting in dark marks or patches on the skin. These dark areas are the result of **postinflammatory hyperpigmentation**. Less commonly, some black skins will develop a decrease in melanin or **postinflammatory hypopigmentation** in response to skin trauma (burns, etc.). In either case, the dark or light areas may be disfiguring and may take months or years to fade. It is important to handle black skin gently, and wear sunscreen to prevent pigmentation problems.

Sweat and sebaceous glands are larger and more numerous and situated closer to the surface of the skin. This accounts for the oily open-pored appearance of many black skins. If this skin type becomes dry, however, it can have an ashen appearance from dead skin cells that are ready to be removed. Black skin is also more susceptible to developing certain conditions such as keloids, large raised scars that grow beyond the original site of injury. It is also more likely to be affected by several different types of disfiguring bumps. **Dermatosis papulosa nigra** (DPN) is a benign cutaneous condition that is common among black skins. It is characterised by multiple, small, hyperpigmented, asymptomatic papules on the face of adults. DPN resembles seborrhoeic keratoses (superficial yellowish spots).

Mixed skin

People with this skin type will have a combination of characteristics from all of the above skins. The shades and sensitivities will vary greatly depending on the mix.

Recognising the problems that may occur with each of the ethnic groups' skin types and understanding the different types of skin that exist will help the therapist to analyse the skin correctly and prescribe the most appropriate form of treatment.

Figure 8.1
Ethnic skin types

Skin types and their characteristics

There are four basic skin types:

* normal
* dry
* sensitive
* oily.

Normal skin

This is the most rare skin type as once hormones begin changing the body at puberty, the skin will become more oily and with age it becomes drier. This skin type is usually perfectly balanced with cell renewal working in harmony with the exfoliation of dead skin cells. It has excellent moisture-holding capacity and sebum and sweat are secreted at a perfect rate to keep it looking healthy. The way in which the skin is looked after can also be a contributory factor as poor skin care and lack of protection from the environment will soon have a detrimental effect on normal skin.

Normal skin characteristics may include the following:

* The skin looks clear.
* It has an even colour.
* It feels neither tight nor greasy.
* It is soft and supple to the touch.
* The epidermis is of an average thickness.
* It has a high degree of elasticity.

Dry skin

This may be caused by environmental conditions drying it out, lack of sebaceous gland activity, it could be hereditary or the water-holding capacity of the skin has been disrupted.

Dry skin characteristics may include the following:

* The skin is pale in colour.
* It has a thin epidermis.
* It tightens after washing.
* It often looks flaky.
* It has under-active sebaceous glands.
* Fine lines appear prematurely around the eyes.
* Broken capillaries may appear.

Sensitive skin

This skin type is becoming increasingly more common due in part to the environment but also to the sensitivity of many people to external stimulants. Many more clients are complaining of sensitivity or allergy to products that come into contact with their skin. It is a skin type that is easily irritated, therefore the therapist must ensure that specific products and treatments are used that will suit the condition.

Sensitive skin characteristics may include the following. They often accompany dry skin.

* The skin has a thin epidermis.
* It has a translucent appearance.
* It feels very tight after washing.
* It reacts to external stimuli by becoming red and blotchy.
* It is prone to dry flaky patches and broken capillaries.
* It wrinkles prematurely.

Oily skin

This skin type is most common in adolescents and young adults because of the increase in the rate of sebum production influenced by the male hormone testosterone. It is more common in certain ethnic skin types and may be determined by the number of sebaceous glands present that produce large amounts of sebum.

Oily skin characteristics may include:

* a sallow complexion
* a thick epidermis
* over-active sebaceous glands which cause a shiny appearance
* open pores, particularly down the centre panel
* comedones (blackheads) and pustules.

Combination skin

From the age of approximately eleven years onwards, many clients will have characteristics from more than one of the four skin types. This type of skin is referred to as a **combination** and it must be taken into consideration when choosing treatment. There are now many products on the market that cater for a combination skin using ingredients that are suitable for the most sensitive parts while treating the rest effectively.

The characteristics of a sensitive skin may appear with all skin types. In fact, I have treated many clients with acne vulgaris when the skin is particularly sensitive. This is sometimes caused by the overuse of very harsh products to treat the condition. The most common form of combination skin is a greasy centre panel known as the 'T' zone with dry areas on the neck and cheeks.

Determining skin type

To determine skin type you will need to take into account the following.

Skin colour

The paler the skin, the more sensitive it normally is. Sallow complexions may be indicative of a greasy skin or it could be a genetic factor. Redness may indicate extreme sensitivity or very fine skin, which allows the colour from the underlying blood vessels to show through. Freckles are caused when melanin occurs in patches.

> The different colours of skin are determined by its thickness and the **haemoglobin** in the red blood cells showing through a pale skin. They are also the result of the concentration of **carotenoids** (beta-carotene, lutein, lycopene and zeaxanthine) found in the stratum corneum, fatty areas of the dermis and the subcutaneous layer, and **melanin**, a pigment found in the epidermis. The amount of melanin present in the skin will determine its colour from a slightly tanned look through to a black skin. The melanin and carotene together account for the yellow colour of skin. The redness is from the oxygen-rich blood and a blue tinge from oxygen-poor blood which is laden with carbon dioxide.

Skin texture

Very dry skin has a rough surface and is thinner than an oily skin, which feels smoother and has a thicker epidermis. An acne-scarred or blemished skin also feels coarse and bumpy to the touch.

The pore size

Greasy skin has open pores because of the constant production of sebum, and sensitive skin usually has tight, barely evident pores. However, there are many cases in a mature client when open pores are noticeable yet the skin is very dry. This is usually evidence of a previous skin condition which has caused the pores to relax.

Signs of sebaceous gland activity

The sebum present on the skin indicates oily areas and the amount produced will indicate how oily or dry it is. The skin has more sebaceous glands in the centre of the face and hormones may affect the excessive production of sebum.

Evidence of previous skin type or condition

Large open pores, for example, on a mature skin would indicate a previously oily skin or scarring or pitting would indicate an acnefied skin. Very thin skin may be as a result of the use of steroid creams to clear a condition such as severe eczema.

Elasticity

Poor elasticity may be evident in the lines that are appearing on certain parts of the face. They are an indication of how the skin is ageing – naturally or prematurely. Fine lines start around the eyes and sometimes the lips, particularly on a dry skin. Oily skins are more likely to age better than a very dry skin, but this skin type often suffers with spots and blemishes for several years during and after puberty.

Muscle tone

Dropped contours usually indicate a mature skin, as muscles become slack with age.

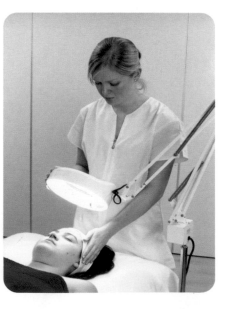

Figure 8.2
A skin analysis

Blemishes

Broken capillaries would indicate sensitivity or a thin epidermis; comedones, papules and pustules would indicate blemished skin; darker pigmented areas may indicate sun damage, age spots or skin disorder. Small raised areas, either pigmented or non-pigmented, may be benign melanomas (moles) or birth marks. Scars may be present due to injury, chickenpox or post acne.

Questioning the client

Asking clients questions about their lifestyle, general health and skin care routine will provide additional information about probable causes of skin problems. The type of information you should be looking for includes the following:

* **Occupation**. They could work in an environment which is dehydrating their skin, e.g. central heating, air conditioning or outdoor work. The atmosphere could be dusty and dirty causing skin blockages and pustules. They may work in different climates thus exposing their skin to extremes of climatic conditions.

* **Lifestyle**. They may be too busy to spend time on their own skin because they are busy people with little time to themselves, or their social life may be hectic and they are going straight out from work and probably have little sleep.

* **Health**. They may suffer poor health and this is often reflected in their skin, or they may be on medication, which can also affect their skin badly.

* **Skin care routine**. What is their regime at the moment? Do they bother using the correct products or do they use incorrect products which may be harming their skin? Do they spend any length of time at all on skin care?

* **Previous problems**. It may be apparent that the skin condition now has something to do with a previous skin problem or condition and there is visual evidence supporting this. However, you may need to question the client to ensure your assumptions are correct.

Skin blemishes and disorders

A skin blemish is a mark on the skin, which may be temporary or permanent, but it will not contraindicate facial treatment.

A skin disorder is a condition of the skin, which may be treated by beauty therapists.

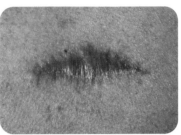

Figure 8.3 *A keloid scar*

Useful dermatological terms

Erythema is a reddening of the skin, due to the dilation of blood vessels, as a reaction to an external stimulus, or an infection.

Macule is a discoloration of the skin, either red or pigmented, which is not raised above the skin's surface.

Lesion is a structural or functional change in skin tissue caused by disease, injury or vascular and pigmentary changes.

Subjective lesions are a burning or itching sensation which can be felt but not seen.

Objective lesions are changes which can be seen clearly on the surface of the skin.

Naevus is a birthmark.

Oedema is the swelling of the tissue.

Scale is an accumulation of epidermal flakes, which may be dry or greasy; they are indicative of an abnormal process of keratinisation.

Vesicle is a tiny elevation in the skin, which contains fluid.

Papule is a small, superficial, raised area of the skin, which may appear red and inflamed. It is usually solid and lacking in fluid.

Useful dermatological terms (cont.)

Pustule is a papule that develops at the mouth of the hair follicle. It becomes infected with bacteria, becoming purulent in the centre (containing pus consisting of dead skin cells, white blood cells and bacteria) with a red, inflamed surrounding area.

Scar is special tissue which forms after the healing of a wound or injury. It is a combination of fibroblasts and blood vessels making collagen to form the scar tissue.

Keloid is a permanent raised scar which is much larger than the original wound and is the result of the fibroblast cells working overtime and longer than is required for the normal healing process.

Disorders of the sebaceous glands

Comedone

This is caused by excess sebum in the follicle and an accumulation of dead skin cells which turn black on exposure to the air.

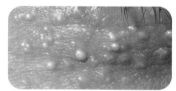

Figure 8.4 *A comedone, or blackhead*

Milium

More commonly called a whitehead, a milium forms when sebum is trapped in the follicle but there is no surface opening, due to an

Figure 8.5 *Milia, or whiteheads*

overgrowth of epidermal skin tissue at the mouth of the follicle. Milia (more than one) are most common on a dry skin and normally appear below the eye and along the cheekbone.

Sebaceous cyst

This is caused by an overgrowth of surface skin tissue which blocks the sebaceous duct, causing a retention of sebum in the

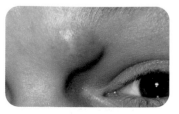

Figure 8.6 *A sebaceous cyst*

follicle and gland. This gradually distends and forms a skin-coloured raised lump, semiglobular in shape, usually with a shiny surface.

Pigmentary disorders of the skin

Lentigo (plural: lentignes)

This is a freckle, a tiny yellow to brown macule which appears on areas exposed to sunlight and is most common on a fair skin.

Chloasma

These are usually irregular areas of increased pigmentation, not raised above the skin's surface, and may be caused by the contraceptive pill, sunburn, pregnancy or disorders of the abdominal organs.

Figure 8.7 *Chloasma*

Vitiligo

These are areas of the skin devoid of pigment, and is caused by the basal layer of the epidermis no longer manufacturing melanin.

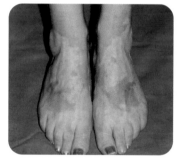

Figure 8.8 *Vitiligo*

Leucoderma

This is an area of the skin with less pigmentation than the surrounding tissue and which therefore appears lighter in colour.

Portwine stain

This can vary in size and is found on the face and neck area. It is a birthmark, pink to purple in colour, and is not raised above the skin's surface.

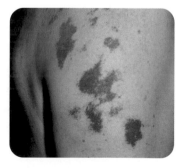

Figure 8.9 *A port wine stain*

Strawberry mark

This develops before or shortly after a baby is born, but normally disappears spontaneously before the child reaches the age of ten. It is raised above the skin and has a cleft surface.

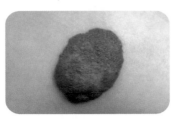

Figure 8.10 *A strawberry mark*

Broken capillaries

These are minute thin-walled blood vessels close to the surface of the skin which dilate and break. They are usually found on the nose and cheek area and are caused by extremes of temperature or over stimulation of the tissues.

Figure 8.11 *Broken capillaries*

Sensitive skin is more at risk from this condition. It often appears blue because of the congestion in the area and transparent skin.

Hypertrophic disorders

Xanthoma

Only slightly raised from the skin surface, xanthoma is a buff-coloured growth, which appears at the inner corner of the eye. It has a texture similar to chamois leather and is caused by

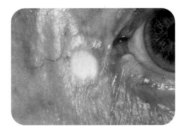

Figure 8.12 *Xanthoma*

inflammation of the deeper layers of skin followed by fat deposits (in some cases, this is due to an excess amount of cholesterol in the blood). They can be surgically removed although they do not contraindicate facial treatment.

Verruca filiformis

Skin tag is the common name given to this condition, a wart which is commonly found on the face and neck. It is a long, thin flexible growth, greyish

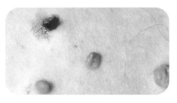

Figure 8.13 *Verruca filiformis*

in colour. It is a benign growth, easily treated with diathermy.

Seborrhoeic warts

These are soft and greasy lesions, that are pigmented with a cleft surface, and affect middle-aged and elderly people.

Figure 8.14 *Seborrhoeic wart*

They are very common and benign.

Benign melanoma

This is commonly called a mole. It is irregular in shape, usually pigmented, light to dark brown, flat or raised, sometimes with

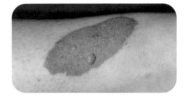

Figure 8.15 *A benign melanoma, or mole*

abnormal hair growth and enlarged sebaceous glands. It can sometimes have a rough warty texture.

Skin conditions

The ageing skin

Ageing of the skin may occur naturally with age or it can be premature, caused by environmental conditions, or ill health or just poor treatment of the skin. The skin shows the signs of age faster because it is exposed to the environment and constant wear and tear.

> **Photoaging** is the effect of chronic and excessive sun exposure on the skin and may be responsible for the majority of age associated changes in the skin's appearance such as rough texture, fine wrinkles, 'age' or 'liver' spots on the hands and dilated blood vessels.

Other factors to be considered are hereditary, health and physical. Taking care of the skin, therefore, should begin at an early age because it is harder to improve a neglected skin or undo the damage already done.

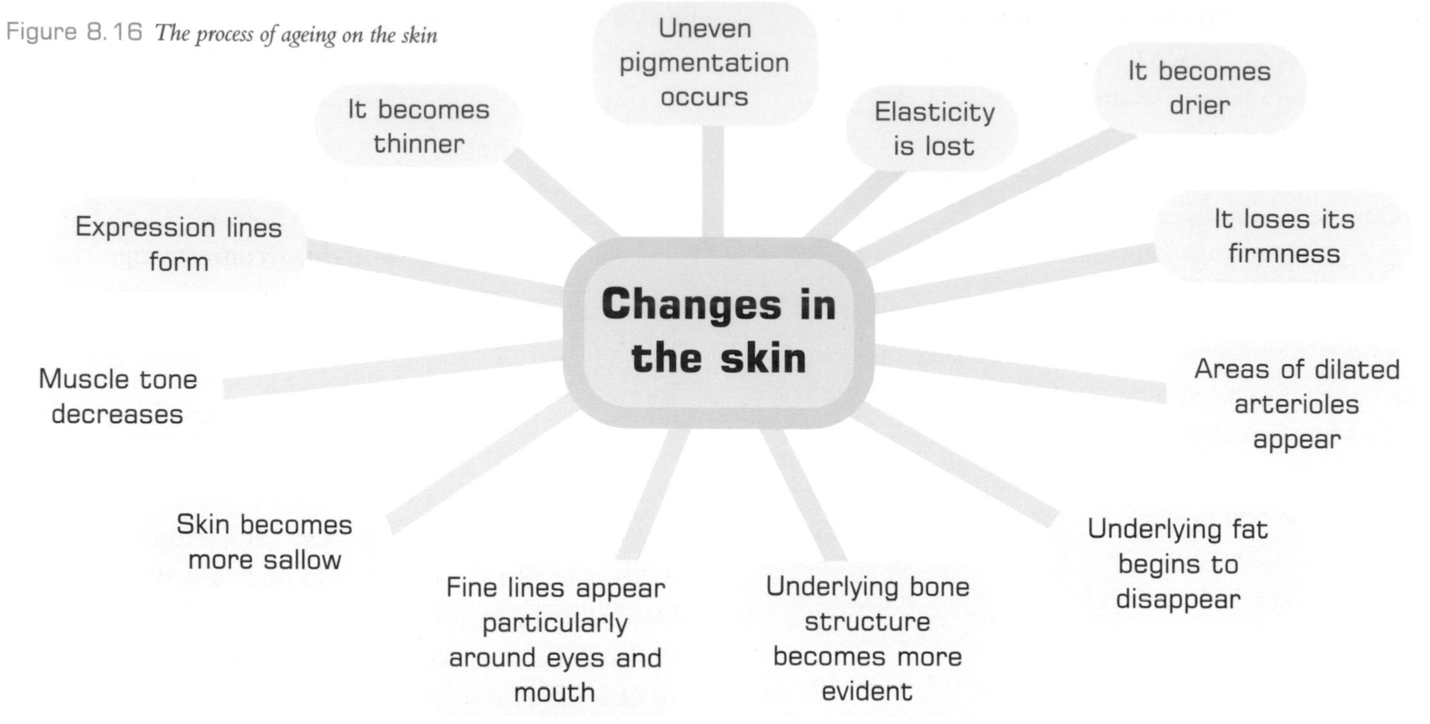

Figure 8.16 *The process of ageing on the skin*

- It becomes thinner
- Uneven pigmentation occurs
- Elasticity is lost
- It becomes drier
- Expression lines form
- **Changes in the skin**
- It loses its firmness
- Muscle tone decreases
- Areas of dilated arterioles appear
- Skin becomes more sallow
- Fine lines appear particularly around eyes and mouth
- Underlying bone structure becomes more evident
- Underlying fat begins to disappear

Figure 8.17 *An ageing skin*

Certain changes take place in the skin as we become older (see Figure 8.16). The reasons for these physical characteristics are described below.

Blood circulation slows down
Essential nutrients the skin requires to remain healthy are not brought to the skin quite as quickly and the removal of toxins (poisons) from the area slows down, affecting the general appearance and health of the skin.

Metabolism slows down
The skin's cell renewal process becomes less efficient and it may appear sluggish and lose its healthy glow.

Chemical changes take place
Tissue repair and cell regeneration slow down and melanin distribution is less even.

Sebaceous glands diminish in number and size
The amount of natural moisture present in the skin is reduced.

Collagen and elastin production breaks down
The skin becomes thinner and fragmented and loses its flexibility and moisture-holding capacity.

Melanin production alters; altered or reduced hormone production
These are particularly a problem during the menopause and may have an adverse effect on the skin.

Environmental factors
Ultraviolet A (UVA) rays penetrate deep into the dermis causing premature ageing, collagen breaks down producing lines and wrinkles. Sun-damaged skin also has a thick epidermis caused by accelerated cell renewal, another defence mechanism of the skin against ultraviolet B (UVB) rays. This occurs to protect the skin from

further damage, and causes the skin to become tough-looking, with an uneven texture and pigmentation.

Air pollution from industry, car fumes, and so on, harms the skin and causes dehydration. Working in a centrally heated or air-conditioned environment dehydrates the skin.

Self-inflicted abuse

Smoking deprives the skin of nutrients and oxygen (essential for keeping it healthy) and vitamin C (which is necessary for the support of healthy collagen). Carbon monoxide, present through smoking, adversely affects the oxygen-carrying capacity of the red blood cells' haemoglobin for many hours.

Alcohol is not harmful to the skin in moderation, but large amounts dilate the blood vessels and over a long period of time weaken the capillary walls. This causes redness and broken capillaries. Alcohol also dehydrates the skin by drawing water from the tissues robbing the body of vitamin B and vitamin C required for a healthy skin.

Crash dieting causes premature sagging and wrinkling of the skin because when weight is lost too rapidly the skin does not have enough time to adjust to the sudden change. This is often noticeable in the face. Essential nutrients may be eliminated from the diet when crash dieting, so the health of the skin is affected.

Lack of exercise can contribute to poor skin conditions. Exercise will stimulate the flow of blood, supplying the skin with oxygen and nutrition, and stimulate the metabolism, encouraging cell renewal and collagen and elastin synthesis.

Lack of sleep causes slackness in the skin, tension in the face, frown lines and makes the skin look lifeless. Cells reproduce most actively between midnight and 4 am. A good night's sleep is a rejuvenating treatment for the skin.

Prolonged and incorrect use of cosmetics can create sensitivity in the skin if the products used are too harsh and can cause excessive dryness, which may lead to premature ageing.

Stress causes tension in facial muscles and restricts blood vessels, so the interchange of blood slows down.

Rosacea

This is a chronic hypersensitivity of the face normally affecting the nose and cheeks. Its characteristics are:

* excessive oiliness
* redness, which sometimes takes on a butterfly shape across the cheeks and nose and often has the appearance of sunburn, accompanying flushing or blushing that occurs easily and lasts longer than normal
* solid papules and pustules
* telangectasia – visible red lines caused by enlarged or damaged blood vessels
* lumpy appearance.

Some people with rosacea also suffer from ocular rosacea causing red sore eyes and eyelids, sometimes with accompanying bumps and eyelashes falling out.

This condition usually appears in middle age and is more common in women than men. The more severe cases when left untreated may develop rhinophyma (a large, bulbous purple-veined nose). The cause is unknown, but the condition is aggravated by:

* eating highly spiced food
* alcohol
* extremes of temperature
* very hot tea and coffee
* sunlight
* emotional stress
* digestive disorders.

All the above cause the already weakened and congested blood vessels to dilate even more and the sensitive skin to become even more inflamed. This condition should be treated by a doctor, particularly in its most severe form, but the therapist may be able to help by giving soothing treatments and lifestyle advice including the following:

* Avoid exposure to sun.
* Always wear a sunscreen and avoid exposure to wind, extreme cold and heat.
* Avoid hot spicy food, alcohol and smoking.
* Do not use harsh products on the skin.
* Avoid stressful situations.

Figure 8.18 *Rosacea*

113

Icthyosis vulgaris

The word *icthyosis* comes from the Greek word for fish because the appearance of the skin in this condition looks like the scales of a fish. It is a condition of abnormal keratinisation and is usually hereditary.

The characteristics are dry, scaly skin which looks as though it has cracked and is darker than normal. It is more common on the extensor surfaces of the body. The condition often improves with age, often disappearing in adulthood and in a warm humid climate.

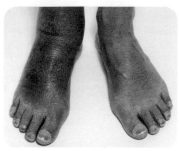

Figure 8.19 *Icthyosis vulgaris*

Psoriasis

This is a fairly common skin disorder which affects about 2 per cent of white people at some time during their lives. Its exact cause is unknown, but it is thought that there is an inherited defect in the skin which causes psoriasis, which is triggered by certain factors:

* Infection. Sometimes psoriasis appears two to three weeks after a streptococcal infection.
* Trauma to the skin can produce lesions.
* Mental stress. This is not a cause, but worry or anxiety can trigger the appearance of psoriasis.

Psoriasis may appear at any time, but it is most likely to develop between the ages of 15 and 30 and to occur in someone who has one or both parents with the disorder. The most common sites affected are the elbows, knees and back, usually areas with less underlying flesh.

The characteristics are:

* dull, red papules round or oval in shape
* well-defined margins covered in silvery scales.

Attacks of psoriasis are quite erratic. There may be long periods of time when the skin is clear of any sign and when it does appear, the length of time it is present varies greatly.

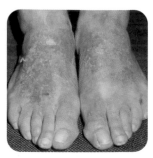

Figure 8.20 *Psoriasis*

A rapid production of skin cells and a tendency of these cells to cling together cause the excessive scaling and flaking. A dermatologist can help to control and improve the condition. The patches can lessen or disappear temporarily when the skin is exposed to natural sunlight. Fortunately, when it does clear it leaves no marks or scars on the skin.

If stress, depression or worry are linked with an outbreak, it would be advisable to find a relaxation technique to counteract these problems.

Eczema

This is a skin condition from which many people suffer and it is a sequence of inflammatory changes triggered by the skin's intolerance to a sensitiser. The characteristics are:

* a red rash
* itchiness
* scaling of the skin which may be loose and thin or thick depending upon how the normal process of keratinisation has been affected
* blisters
* weeping
* cracked skin.

The appearance of eczema may include one, two or several of the above features and one person's eczema may vary greatly from the next. Eczema is not contagious and with treatment inflammation can be reduced, though the skin will always be sensitive to flare up and need special care.

Types of eczema

There are two types of eczema:

* **endogenous** – caused by an internal stimulus via the bloodstream
* **exogenous** – caused by external contact with a primary irritant to which the skin is allergic. This condition is often referred to as **contact dermatitis**.

Some primary irritants are:

* cosmetics
* detergents
* soaps
* rubber
* yeast
* nickel
* dyes.

If the factor that causes the exogenous eczema is identified, then the avoidance of that substance will effect a cure.

There are two common forms of eczema: atopic and seborrhoeic.

Atopic

This usually occurs in childhood and is often associated with a family history of hay fever and asthma. Sufferers are sensitive to allergens in the environment which are harmless to others. One of the most common symptoms is itching (pruritis) which can be almost unbearable.

Seborrhoeic

This type of eczema often affects adults between the ages of 20 and 40 and may appear on the scalp as mild dandruff but can spread to the face, ears and chest. The skin becomes red and inflamed and begins to flake. It is believed to be caused by a yeast growth and if the condition becomes infected, treatment with an anti-fungal cream may be required.

In babies this condition is called 'cradle cap' and usually disappears in a few months, more quickly with the use of moisturising creams and oils.

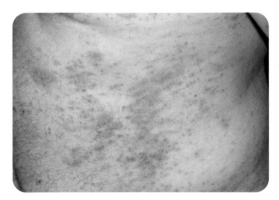

Figure 8.21
Eczema

Seborrhoea

This is a functional disorder of the sebaceous glands, characterised by an over production of sebum, which gives the face a shiny, greasy appearance. Because of this the follicles will appear large and open and the skin looks coarse. The condition often appears during puberty when there is a glandular disturbance and sometimes accompanies acne vulgaris.

Acne vulgaris

This affects adolescents between the ages of 14 and 20 and is an inflammatory condition of the sebaceous glands believed to be an inherited condition. It also affects many adults. It sometimes flares up in women in their thirties or forties (adult onset acne) who have never suffered from skin problems before. Its characteristics are:

*   greasy, shiny skin with enlarged pores
*   inflammation in and around the sebaceous glands
*   comedones
*   papules
*   pustules
*   cysts and nodules (in severe cases).

In most cases, this condition has cleared up by the age of 25. However, it is important to control the condition at a very early age, as the longer it remains, the more stubbornly it resists treatment. It is advisable for the client suffering from acne to seek medical advice before treatment. The incidence of acne in both sexes is similar.

Figure 8.22 *Acne vulgaris*

The stages of acne

1   Acne begins to develop when there is an increase in hormone production during puberty, which stimulates the sebaceous glands.

2   A blackhead forms in the sebaceous duct, caused by an increase rated of sebum production, which blocks the mouth of the follicle preventing the free flow of sebum and this plug of sebum turns black when exposed to the air.

3   Hyperkeratinisation, an accelerated cell production within the basal cells lining the follicle, takes place and these cells are constantly being shed from the walls of the follicle.

4   A papule may be caused by the distension and inflammation of the sebaceous gland, which is caused by the excess sebum leaking through the weakened walls of the sebaceous duct into the surrounding tissue and a blockage of the follicle opening.

5 A pustule is formed when the papule becomes infected with the propioni-bacterium acnes.

6 The bacteria then excrete an inflammatory fatty acid by-product, eventually blocking the follicle completely. This produces acne lesions such as nodules, deep, painful cysts which are characteristic of the more severe cases of acne. They look very much like boils and are usually found on the back of the neck. As the name suggests, they are very painful and slow to heal.

7 Cysts occur when the follicle ruptures near its lowest point. Because this inflammation can take place in the dermis, collagen and elastin may be destroyed resulting in ice-pick type scarring.

> **Propioni-bacterium acnes** is present on the skin even when there is no acne, but it will multiply rapidly under certain conditions.

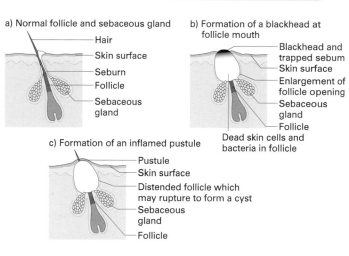

a) Normal follicle and sebaceous gland
- Hair
- Skin surface
- Seburn
- Follicle
- Sebaceous gland

b) Formation of a blackhead at follicle mouth
- Blackhead and trapped sebum
- Skin surface
- Enlargement of follicle opening
- Sebaceous gland
- Follicle
- Dead skin cells and bacteria in follicle

c) Formation of an inflamed pustule
- Pustule
- Skin surface
- Distended follicle which may rupture to form a cyst
- Sebaceous gland
- Follicle

Figure 8.23 *The development of acne*

Causes of acne

Acne can be hereditary. Hormones, which influence the production of sebum and cell activity, trigger most attacks, specifically androgens that are produced by the ovaries and adrenal glands in women. The oral contraceptive changes a woman's hormone level and may cause a breakout in some cases when starting or stopping taking the medication. This is easily remedied by consulting with the GP and finding an alternative.

Some of the newer contraceptives are actually administered by some GPs to help control acne.

Anxiety or stress can worsen the condition and an increase in fatty acids has been found in sebum during periods of stress. Some prescribed medication can cause or aggravate acne, for example testosterone, a male hormone, gonadotrophin used for pituitary disorders, anabolic steroids taken to bulk up muscles and corticosteroids.

Poor hygiene can lead to secondary infection in acne sufferers (see Home care advice below).

Acne and the menstrual cycle

There are many women who experience outbreaks monthly caused by the release of progesterone after ovulation. An increase in skin eruptions and increased sebum production may occur as a result of only minor hormonal fluctuations and it usually occurs five days prior to the beginning of a cycle and lasts for approximately seven to ten days. You will need to take this into account when treating clients and adjust their skin care routine accordingly.

Treatment advice

Sunlight is beneficial to this condition for several reasons:

* The initial erythema and subsequent tanning have a camouflaging effect and this is psychologically beneficial.
* The bactericidal effects penetrate the lower as well as the upper epidermis so may have an effect on the bacteria found deeper in the sebaceous duct.
* The increase in desquamation refines skin texture.

A doctor should treat severe acne, but the beauty therapist can treat milder forms by deep cleansing, skin peeling and offering home care advice on skin care and diet.

Home care advice

* Skin must be kept scrupulously clean, removing excess sebum and the dirt which it attracts and holds on the surface of the skin.
* Spots must not be picked as scarring may occur.
* A gentle pH-balanced soap is ideal as it will cleanse the skin without over stimulating or drying it out excessively. The temptation is to use very harsh products on the skin, but in the long term, the chemicals contained in these products may have an adverse reaction.
* The face must never be dried with a towel as this provides a harbouring ground for bacteria. It is preferable to use tissues and throw them away, or a flannel, which is used only once and then washed.
* The face should be steamed gently, twice a week, to open the pores and eliminate waste matter which has collected in the follicles. A few herbs can be added to the water, e.g. chamomile and sage for their restorative properties.
* Diet should be altered to remove foods high in fat and sugar. Plenty of fresh fruit and vegetables should be eaten since they contain vitamins which are responsible for maintaining a healthy skin. If necessary, a daily vitamin supplement can be taken and plenty of fibre, e.g. wholemeal bread and salads, should be eaten to aid elimination of waste from the body.
* Exercise, particularly in the fresh air, will help to increase circulation, bringing essential nutrients to the skin and removing waste more quickly. It also creates a feeling of well-being and counteracts stress, which often aggravates this condition.

Allergies

Many people suffer from an allergic reaction to products which are used in facial therapy and are more often turning to hypoallergenic or natural products to overcome this problem.

Allergic reaction can happen at any time, even if the substance causing the allergy has been used for many years without causing any adverse reactions.

The skin can be irritated by:

* something being applied directly on to the skin
* something being absorbed systemically into the body.

The skin reacts to the irritant by producing massive amounts of histamine, part of the body's defence mechanism, and usually turns red and blotchy. Other characteristics are eyes watering and stinging, tissues swelling and the nose starts to run. The intensity of the reaction depends upon the amount of irritant applied to the skin.

The best way to deal with an allergy is to locate and remove the cause and this can be done in three ways:

* The client should see a dermatologist, recommended by his or her GP, who will determine by means of patch tests the cause of the allergy.
* Eliminate one product after another, week by week, to determine the cause. This is feasible only if the client already suspects the cause of the problem.
* In the case of a cosmetic product such as make-up it is best to avoid using any cosmetic products for a week and then each week reintroduce one product at a time until the allergic reaction returns, enabling the client to eliminate the cause.

Sensitisation

This is when the body's immune system actually recognises an allergen as alien and the white blood cells react against it causing the unpleasant symptoms of a severe allergic reaction the next time the allergen is used on the skin.

A completely non-allergenic range of products is not possible as there is always someone somewhere allergic to something. A hypoallergenic range of products only guarantees to be less allergy producing than others by omitting as many known allergens as possible.

Skin and the sun

Sunbathing in moderation and with adequate protection is very therapeutic as it promotes relaxation and encourages a feeling of well-being. However, the sun ages the skin and as the face is exposed more than any other part of the body the effects are easily seen.

Most cosmetic companies are now producing skin care ranges as well as make-up which provide protection against UV rays.

UVA rays are absorbed deep into the dermis and are responsible for ageing of the skin because of the damage caused to the collagen and elastin fibres. UVB rays are the burning rays and are absorbed into the epidermis.

Sun protection advice

To protect the face from premature ageing due to exposure to UV rays, the following advice should be followed:

* Use sunscreen products which filter out both UVA and UVB rays even on days that are overcast.
* Use a total sunblock on particularly sensitive skin or parts of the face, that is, lips, eyes, nose, cheekbones.
* Wear a large-brimmed hat.
* Do not sunbathe between 11 am and 3 pm as sunlight is at its strongest.

A suntan is the skin's natural defence mechanism against the harmful effects of UV radiation and the technical term for suntanning is **melanogenesis**.

When the skin is exposed to the UVA and UVB rays an enzyme present in the melanocytes, called **tyrosinase**, is activated causing the amino acid **tyrosin** to produce the pigment melanin. This moves upwards to the surface of the skin giving it a golden suntan.

(Ultraviolet radiation is described in detail in Chapter 19 Ultraviolet, infrared and radiant heat treatments.)

Useful skin terms

Alpha hydroxy acids (AHA) are natural acids found in fruit, milk and sugar which help loosen dead skin cells on the skin's surface, increasing the speed at which they are removed and renewed. These acids are used in treatment creams, cleansers and moisturisers. AHA treatment products do not always have hydrating properties, therefore those used in the morning should be followed by a lightweight moisturiser that also contains a sunscreen to prevent future damage. At night follow the application of the AHA with a good night cream with added ingredients such as antioxidants.

Antioxidants are derived from vitamins such as A, C and E, and form part of the body's natural defence and balance system. Antioxidants protect the skin by attaching themselves to free radicals (see below), thus preventing them from doing as much harm to the skin. Green tea is a powerful antioxidant that protects against UVA and UVB rays, it can soothe sunburn and is 20 times more powerful as an antioxidant than vitamin C.

Ceramides are lipids which are naturally present in the skin and they make up a moisture barrier over the surface. Ceramides added to skin products will help to strengthen this seal allowing the skin to stay moisturised longer.

Collagen is a strong fibrous protein which forms connective tissue in the dermis and provides the support and strength to the skin.

Comedogenic is the ability of a product to block the pores. Certain ingredients are more likely to cause comedones in certain people, e.g. lanolin, glyceral stearate, sesame oil, avocado oil, sandalwood seed oil, tocopherol (vitamin E oil) and jojoba oil.

Useful skin terms (cont.)

Elastin is a highly elastic protein which makes up the elastic fibres in the dermis providing suppleness and smoothness to the skin making it more resilient.

Enzymes are protein molecules naturally present in our bodies and they can be helpful or destructive. They are catalysts, which work by speeding up chemical changes that take place in our cells – some help the skin's natural renewal process and others break it down. When added to skin creams the beneficial enzymes may block the action of skin ageing enzymes and prevent the collapse of collagen.

Free radicals are harmful, highly unstable molecules, created by oxidation (in simple terms, this is what happens when a sliced apple turns brown), which are activated by stress, the release of adrenaline in our bodies, pollution, smoking and UV light. They are molecules which have lost an electron and travel round the body colliding with other molecules trying to replace their lost electron. Unchecked they attach themselves to the skin's surface eventually permeating down to the collagen. These reactive molecules cause skin cells to oxidise and damage the skin by making it less firm and can cause sagging skin, wrinkles, premature ageing and changes in pigmentation.

Hyaluronic acid forms part of the tissue which surrounds the collagen and elastin fibres. It is a natural moisturising ingredient responsible for the skin's plumpness and moisture content, and it has the ability to attract and bind hundreds of times its weight in water. As we age, the amount produced in the skin decreases leaving it less resilient and pliable. Skin care companies often add it to moisturisers.

Liposomes are tiny spheres or lipids made up of water and fat and filled with active ingredients. The liposomes are the transportation system which carries the active ingredients to where the skin needs them. Liposome spheres are smaller than a skin cell, therefore ingredients held inside the liposomes can accurately be delivered into the skin and released precisely as needed.

Nanospheres are smaller versions of liposomes which are supposed to penetrate deeper into the skin because of their smaller size.

Photoageing is the effect on the skin caused by exposure to UV light, the single greatest cause of wrinkles and ageing skin. Most of the damage occurs from casual exposure on a daily basis. Although UVB rays are more intense in the summer, UVA rays are the same intensity all year round and are far more damaging as they penetrate deep into the dermis and destroy collagen, elastin and other connective tissue. The result is fine lines, wrinkling, leathery appearance, hyperpigmentation and loss of elasticity.

Retinoic acid is a derivative of vitamin A, which was once prescribed for the treatment of acne. It does refine the skin reducing wrinkles but the side effects are extreme sensitivity to sunlight, increased reddening of the skin and peeling. Its action is to speed up cell renewal and boost collagen synthesis.

SPF (sun protection factor) is a guide to the effectiveness of sunscreen in screening out UVB rays. For example, a sunscreen with an SPF of 10 will allow the skin to be protected for ten times longer (100 minutes of exposure for a skin which normally burns after ten minutes) from the sun before it starts to burn.

Tocopherol is the technical term for vitamin E. It has healing properties and helps to repair sun-damaged skin. It is an important antioxidant.

Skin care advice

When clients regularly have facial treatments at the salon, it is advisable to recommend that they also use appropriate skin care products at home to reinforce the treatments. It is important to tell clients how to look after their skin at home to prevent premature ageing.

Advice should include the following:

* To drink at least six to eight glasses of water a day to keep moisture levels high, an important factor in cell renewal and hydrating the skin to prevent wrinkle formation. It also helps to detoxify and remove waste.
* To have at least eight hours of sleep a night. While we are sleeping new cells are formed, waste is removed and the skin prepares itself for the day ahead. If sleeping is a problem, advise clients to have a relaxing aromatherapy bath before bed, or listen to a relaxation tape or have a mug of hot milk last thing at night before going to bed as it contains a sleep-inducing amino acid.
* To use a sunscreen every day as damage caused by exposure to UV rays is the single greatest cause of wrinkles and ageing skin. Many skin care products now contain a sunscreen, but if they do not, a sun block could be used under a moisturiser.
* To eat a healthy diet. Skin must be fed from the inside with all the necessary vitamins, minerals and nutrients. Vitamin A keeps skin healthy and prevents it from becoming dry and flaky. Vitamin C is important for the production of collagen and Vitamin E helps to rehydrate the skin and speed up the healing process.
* To use an effective cleanser to remove make-up, dirt and skin blockages caused by a build-up of sebum in the pores.
* To handle the skin gently and use cotton wool or cotton buds to remove make-up. Tissues are too harsh and may scratch or stretch the surface. Use appropriate products, which are gentle on the skin and clean without upsetting the skin's pH balance.
* To take regular exercise, preferably everyday, to increase circulation and lymphatic flow, which helps to improve skin condition and colour, making the skin look younger.
* To keep alcohol intake to a minimum as it dehydrates the skin.
* To avoid smoking. Cigarettes reduce the necessary nutrients and oxygen required for a healthy skin and cause a dull lifeless looking skin. Smoking activates harmful free radicals and weakens collagen and elastin fibres causing premature wrinkling of the skin.

Vitamins and minerals

Effects on the skin through vitamin deficiency

Vitamin A

A lack of vitamin A causes dry flaky skin because one of its functions is to regulate the size and function of the sebaceous glands.

Vitamin B

A lack of one or more of this group results in redness, tenderness and cracks at the corner of the mouth and tiny lines in the skin around the mouth. It also interferes with the transportation of oxygen to the cells and the efficiency of waste removal.

Vitamin C

A lack of vitamin C causes the collagen fibres to break down and show signs of early wrinkling. It also causes the tiny capillaries that supply nutrients to the skin to become fragile, slow wound healing and easy bruising.

Vitamin E

This vitamin is essential to the health of the skin and deficiency causes dry, rough and tired looking skin, easy bruising, slow wound healing and allows free radicals to cause damage.

Effects on the skin through mineral deficiency

Zinc
Skin wrinkles and sags and stretch marks form more easily. In more severe cases, skin healing slows down.

Sulphur
The hair and nails will become weaker and the skin will scale as keratin in the hair, nails and skin is normally rich in sulphur.

Selenium
This mineral is important in maintaining tissue elasticity. A deficiency will contribute to premature ageing of the skin.

Silicon
A lack of silicon causes flabbiness of the skin, weak nails and dull hair.

Sources of vitamins and minerals
Vitamin A: spinach, cabbage, carrots, eggs, fish-liver oils, liver, butter.
Vitamin B: raw fruits and vegetables, whole grains, liver, brewer's yeast, milk, wheatgerm.
Vitamin C: citrus fruits, tomatoes, raw green vegetables, potatoes, spinach, broccoli, strawberries.
Vitamin E: wheatgerm, seeds, green leafy vegetables, whole grains.
Zinc: seafood, meat, liver, nuts, whole grains, oysters, cheese.
Sulphur: fish, eggs, cabbage, sprouts, onions, lean beef, dried beans.
Selenium: wholemeal bread, cheddar cheese, cod, crab, shrimps, garlic.
Silicon: avocado, apples, honey.

Effects on the skin of an efficient blood supply to the skin
When performing any facial or body treatments the blood supply to the area increases. This results in the following:
* Improved skin colour because of the hyperaemia or erythema.
* Increased warmth in the tissues.
* Nutrients, oxygen and vitamins are carried to the area increasing the health of the skin.
* Waste products are removed more efficiently from the area reinforcing the cleansing effect of treatments.
* The dermis contains an extensive network of capillaries, which arise from arteries in the subcutaneous layer. The dermal papillae are supplied with blood via the capillary loops, providing nourishment to the new cells in the basal layer of the epidermis.

Using alpha hydroxy acids

In recent years the use of alpha hydroxy acids (AHAs) has become very popular because of the beneficial effects they have on the skin. Most companies have or are developing ranges of products containing AHAs.

AHAs are mild organic acids that are found in many common fruits and food such as:
* glycolic acid from sugar cane
* citric acid from citrus fruits
* malic acid from apples and white grapes
* tartaric acid from the fermentation process used in making wine
* lactic acid from sour milk.

The action on the skin of these fruit acids is to loosen or break up the thick horny outer layer of skin where an excessive build-up of dead skin cells occurs. This causes a sloughing of the dead skin cells which improves the texture and condition of the skin. They also increase the skin's natural moisture-holding capability and improve the appearance of fine lines and wrinkles.

The use of AHAs dates back thousands of years. Cleopatra used to bathe in sour milk (lactic acid) and other women of her day applied red wine (tartaric acid) to their faces. This made their skin appear fresher and smoother. Today, cosmetic companies provide effective AHA treatments in more stable and elegant cosmetic preparations that will provide excellent results.

Glycolic acid

Glycolic acid has the smallest molecular weight of all the AHAs and, therefore, by virtue of its smaller size, it has greater penetration than other organic acids.

Functions of glycolic acid

* It weakens the intercellular bonds that hold the skin cells together, thereby improving natural exfoliation.
* It helps to rehydrate the skin.
* It stimulates collagen production helping to restructure the dermis and epidermis.
* The stratum corneum is made more permeable to other products and treatments.

The effects of use

The appearance of the skin is greatly improved. It becomes smoother, lines and wrinkles are less noticeable and the skin is softer. The deep cleansing action of glycolic acid helps to eliminate blockages in the sebaceous follicle caused by a build-up of dead skin cells and will help to control an acne condition.

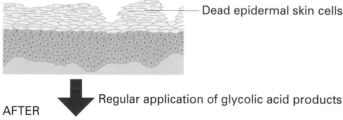

BEFORE
— Dead epidermal skin cells

Regular application of glycolic acid products

AFTER

Softer, clearer, smoother, brighter skin

Figure 8.24 *Effect on the skin of glycolic acid*

Safety in use

The action on the skin can be quite strong and the glycolic acid in retail products is combined with a **buffer**, an ingredient which reduces the irritation to the skin. The best treatment products to use are those that are pH balanced as they are most effective and the least irritating to the skin.

The concentrations of glycolic acid vary between professional products used by the therapist in a salon treatment and the retail products sold for home care. Professional products have a concentration of 40–70 per cent because the application is controlled by an expert and will be applied for the correct amount of time and as often as the therapist feels the client requires treatment. The higher percentages must only be applied under medical supervision.

A client record card must be filled in at the initial consultation to document medical history and the skin care products already in use, and to check for contraindications. Always provide detailed instructions on home care so the client understands how to use the products correctly.

Caution!

After a professional treatment with glycolic acid, sunblock should be applied to the skin and it is advisable for the client to wear a sunblock every day to prevent further sun damage occurring.

Tingling may occur during treatment. This is a normal reaction, which usually lasts for as long as the product is on the skin. If the reaction is severe and the skin becomes very red or stings, then treatment must be discontinued. It is important to monitor the client at all times during treatment.

Contraindications

* Any client on Roaccutane, a medical treatment for acne.
* Any client undergoing radiation treatment or chemotherapy.
* Sunburn.
* Cut or broken skin.
* Irritated skin.
* Recent scar tissue.
* Keloid scars.
* Active eczema, psoriasis or herpes.
* Forty-eight hours before or after:
  – electrolysis
  – waxing
  – using depilatories
  – bleaching.

Botox and injectable solutions for lines and wrinkles

Many salons are now working in conjunction with medical practitioners to provide these treatments which are marketed as anti-ageing treatments, sometimes described as 'extreme cosmetic treatments'. Many clients will at some time ask for these treatments or advice concerning their use. Even if it is not a service provided by your salon, it is your duty as a skin care professional to learn as much as you can and be able to provide information to the client so that he or she can make an informed decision. If you are considering introducing it into your salon, then it may be advisable to ask the doctor concerned to provide detailed information and a demonstration for your clients, allowing them to see these treatments first hand.

Botox

Botox is a wrinkle smoothing agent that has become one of the most popular treatments with clients whose desire is to remain youthful looking for as long as possible. The treatment prevents wrinkles by temporarily blocking nerve impulses and 'paralysing' muscles in the face. Botox is the trade name for Botulinum toxin A, a much diluted form of toxin (poison) from the bacteria that causes botulism.

A series of small injections are administered to a specific area and the toxin works by chemically relaxing the facial muscles and preventing creases and wrinkles formed by common expressions like frowning and smiling. It is used most often to treat the fine lines around the eyes, between the eyebrows and on the forehead.

Collagen replacement therapy

This is a non-surgical treatment used by qualified practitioners to create fuller lips, smooth out facial wrinkles and improve the appearance of deep lines and furrowed brows. Collagen is a natural protein that provides skin with shape and texture and is responsible for the skin's durability and elasticity. Through the process of ageing the collagen in the skin is depleted causing wrinkles and fine lines to appear. Collagen replacement therapy is a method of replenishing collagen beneath the skin with injectable bovine collagen made from sterile purified collagen from cow skin. This cow collagen is so similar to human collagen that the body readily accepts it as part of its own skin.

FDA approval

Botox was only approved by the US Food and Drug Administration Agency (FDA) for cosmetic use in 2002, although it has been approved for the treatment of some medical conditions since 1989 such as blepharospasm – involuntary spasmodic contractions of certain eye muscles, neck spasms and cranial nerve disorders. It is also being used successfully to treat sufferers of hyperhidrosis (excessive sweating) by injecting the Botox into the armpits to reduce sweating.

About 3 per cent of the population is allergic to collagen, so the skin must be tested first for any allergic reaction to bovine collagen, by injecting a small amount into the forearm and observed over a period of a few weeks. Allergy may lead to rashes, joint and muscle pain, headache, blistering and soreness. As long as this test is negative, the client may then be injected with collagen, using a fine needle, beneath the skin's surface to plump out or fill in depressed areas. The results can be seen immediately with little redness or swelling. A local anaesthetic is usually applied to ensure a pain-free treatment.

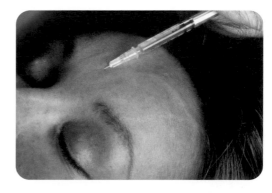

Figure 8.25
Botox treatment

Hyaluronic acid

Hyaluronic acid is a naturally occurring compound created by the body and essential to the texture and quality of the skin. It is a jelly-like compound that fills the space between collagen and elastin fibres. It aids in the transport of nutrients from the blood to the skin and helps to capture and hold water within the cells. This, in turn, acts to cushion and lubricate the cell against damage.

Ageing, environmental toxins and sunlight damage, reduces the amount of hyaluronic acid present in the skin, resulting in loss of vitality, texture and elasticity, leading to wrinkling and sagging of the skin. A synthetic form of hyaluronic acid has been developed and is injected into the skin as an alternative filler to collagen and because it is synthetic, there is little risk of rejection.

Restylane gel

This is a soft tissue filler made of synthetic hyaluronic acid, an inert clear gel, non-toxic and, in general, will not be rejected by the body as foreign tissue. It is applied through injection in the same way as collagen.

Perlane

Similar to other injectable fillers, Perlane, based on a hyaluronic gel, is used to create increases in lip volume. It is a chemically inert and non-toxic compound which may be administered without previous skin tests. Following treatment the lips may be swollen and tender and may show slight bruising, but this should disappear within a couple of days of treatment. Using vitamin C and aloe vera creams will reduce post-treatment discomfort.

Fat injections

These are used to add volume, fill wrinkles and lines and enhance lips. It involves taking fat from another part of the body (abdomen, thighs or buttocks) and injecting it beneath the facial skin. Unlike collagen, allergic reaction is not a factor as the fat is used from the client's own body, but it is a more complicated and time consuming procedure.

Dangers and precautions

Clients should be warned of all the dangers when injecting any foreign substance into the body, that is, allergic reaction and the swelling and discomfort which may occur. Botox has a variety of possible complications:

* bruising
* asymmetry
* droopy eyebrow or eyelid
* unattractive results
* allergic reaction
* dimpling due to thinning of the muscle
* development of immunity to Botox
* interference with a client's ability to eat, speak or blink.

One of the precautions to take after having Botox injections is not to fly immediately, as in rare cases, a drop in pressure during a flight may cause the Botox to move and have an adverse effect on the wrong muscles.

There is a growing trend to have Botox parties and this is causing concern among practitioners. The American Academy of Dermatology has issued a warning against this practice as alcohol and Botox do not mix! Alcohol can intensify bruising and in some cases wash the toxin away from the target muscle.

Facial treatments

* Manual facial treatments

* Eye treatments

* Facial electrical treatments

* Make-up

Introduction

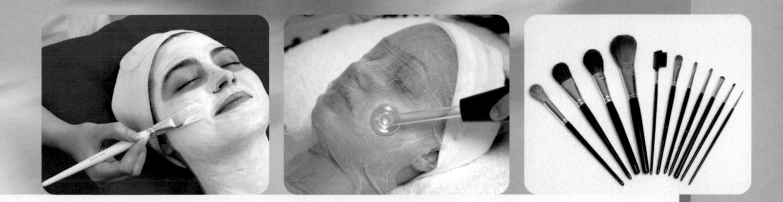

There are several different types of facial treatments offered by salons and spas including manual, electrical, eye and make-up. Many women and an increasing number of men consider a healthy glowing skin an essential. There are many different types of facial treatment available for the client to choose from, providing an option to suit almost everyone. They include manual facials when the therapist provides therapeutic treatments for both the face and mind using her highly developed sense of touch to achieve relaxing, anti-ageing, restorative, healing and stimulating effects suited to the individual needs and requirements of each client.

Technology has advanced in recent years to produce many types of electrical equipment that can be used to reinforce or provide additional effects to manual treatments, achieving results that can be quite dramatic. These may be used in addition to manual facials or as a treatment in their own right.

The type and image of a salon or spa will determine the facial treatments, but they will all provide the eye treatments essential to maintaining the groomed appearance of the face. These include eyebrow shaping, eyelash and brow tinting and eyelash perming. The application of make-up is often an individual treatment for a special occasion or as part of a lesson to teach the client how to apply make-up to her best advantage.

As the face is like a mirror, showing clearly the general health of the body, this section will provide you with the knowledge to help your client achieve the objective of a healthy glowing skin.

There is nothing more soothing than lying wrapped in warm blankets and having a manual facial treatment. The therapist's touch, if just right, can have the same relaxing effects as a few hours' deep sleep. There are some therapists who prefer using their hands for therapeutic effect rather than machines. The manual treatments of cleansing, massaging and applying specialised products require the therapist to develop an acute sense of touch knowing when to adapt pressure and depth and how to adapt movements for different clients.

Cleansing the skin

The cleansing procedure is an essential for all facial treatments. Even if the client has arrived with no trace of make-up, this is the first part of any facial treatment. The aim of cleansing is to improve the efficiency of skin functioning, allow the therapist to analyse the skin accurately and to remove:

* all traces of make-up
* surface dirt and bacteria
* pollution from the environment
* the top layer of dead skin cells
* congestion in the pores.

In the process, skin tissues and circulation are stimulated, thus improving skin colour and cell regeneration. As cleansing is a preliminary to all treatments, it allows the client to become accustomed to the therapist's touch. Cleansing often has to be deeper and exfoliation is used because of the condition of the skin or because it is part of the cleansing routine recommended by the company whose products you are using.

Cleansing should be effective without irritating the skin, and to achieve this the most appropriate products must be chosen. The following will need to be considered:

* the client's skin type
* skin allergies
* age of client
* skin problems present.

Useful cleansing terms

Removing dead skin cells. When the skin has an excess of dead epidermal skin cells, it appears dull and lifeless, the texture may appear rough and uneven and skin congestion or blockages may occur.

Desquamation describes the natural process of the skin shedding its top layer of cells.

Exfoliation describes the manual or mechanical method of removing dead skin cells.

Cleansing preparations

The natural oils on the surface of the skin trap the dirt and bacteria. These have to be removed by emulsifying them with a detergent or dissolving them with more oil.

Most cleansers are mixtures of oil and water, which do not mix, so a third ingredient – an **emulsifier** – is added, which stabilises the oils and forms an emulsion. Depending on the amount of water present, a cleanser can vary from liquid to semi-solid.

A good cleanser will remove make-up effectively without upsetting the skin's pH balance, have a nice smell and feel pleasant on the skin. The different formulations are described below.

Cleansing milk

This is an oil-in-water emulsion and can have up to 90 per cent water. It is a free-flowing milky liquid which is ideal for a younger skin as it feels cool and grease free. It may also contain a detergent element, which helps to control bacteria and grease, but would be drying on an older skin.

Cleansing lotion

Cleansing lotions are recommended only for oily and congested skins as they contain alcohol, an astringent which reduces sebum and leaves the face feeling stripped after use. They are often used with water so are ideal for the client who likes to feel water on her skin.

Cleansing creams

They vary greatly in texture and consistency and are mainly water-in-oil emulsions, so are suitable for dry and mature skins as they are more greasy. The water content, which is small, evaporates and cools the skin and the oil content removes the grease and dirt. The most suitable type for a mature skin is the consistency of a mousse, as it does not drag the skin.

Liquefying cleanser

This cleanser melts quickly on contact with the skin but does not penetrate the epidermis. As it is made mostly of oily material and removes make-up quickly and effectively, it is ideal for a skin which requires the minimum amount of manipulation. It closely resembles petroleum jelly and toning must be thorough as it leaves the skin feeling very greasy.

Soapless cleansers

These are ideal for clients who prefer to use water on their face but do not want the tight stripped feeling from soap. It is a rich but light emulsion applied to the face with dampened hands and rinsed off with water. Gentle in action it deep cleanses without over drying the skin and is suitable for normal, greasy and combination skins.

AHA cleanser

This cleanser contains some form of alpha hydroxy acid, a naturally occurring substance derived from such things as sugar cane, milk or grapes. It acts on the skin by dissolving the intercellular glue binding the dead skin cells together, thus gently exfoliating the skin.

Medicated cleansers

In general, they are used only on an oily congested skin because they have a degreasing effect and contain some anti-bacterial ingredients to reinforce the cleansing process.

Complexion soaps

These are bars of soap which do not leave the skin feeling tight or with an altered pH. Often an oily, blemished skin may also be sensitive, so these soaps are ideal for removing grease without irritating the skin.

Exfoliating cleansers

This is a facial scrub with a soft creamy texture containing very fine exfoliating particles such as oatmeal, crushed nut kernels and cleansing granules that cleanse the skin gently by removing dead cells and impurities, which make the skin look dull and lifeless. They may be used several times a week on greasy skin but less often on dry, sensitive skin. They are applied with the fingertips and mixed with a small amount of water, massaged in and rinsed off with water. They are sometimes used after the deep cleanse in a facial routine if the skin type requires the extra treatment because it is congested, has a rough dry texture, or requires extra stimulation.

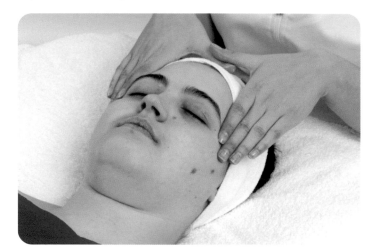

Figure 9.1 *Cleansing the skin*

Skin congestion

Once the skin has been thoroughly cleansed, you will be able to carry out a detailed skin analysis (see Chapter 8 The skin). One of the problems common to many clients is skin congestion. This is when there are blemishes present, often in specific parts of the face. It is a common complaint from many clients that they suffer from spots around the chin, or on the cheeks or around the hairline, a recurring problem that frustrates the client.

These areas of congestion are sometimes caused by internal problems with a particular system so you need to ask clients more probing questions to find out if they have a physiological condition that is affecting their skin in this way.

Table 9.1 identifies the area of congestion and the system that may be contributing to the problem.

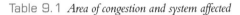

Area of congestion	System affected
The chin	Urinary and digestive systems
The corners of the mouth to the jawline	Endocrine – hormonal
The cheek area	Digestive
Between the eyebrows on the lower forehead	Digestive – the liver
The hairline	Nervous system – stress
The temples and outer jaw area	Lymphatic system

Table 9.1 *Area of congestion and system affected*

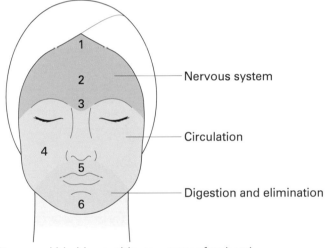

1 Stress and bladder problems – upper forehead
2 Intestines – lower forehead
3 Liver – between the eyebrows
4 Lungs – cheeks
5 Digestive system – above mouth
6 The reproductive system/hormonal – chin and jawline

Figure 9.2 *Common areas of congestion on the face and the three regions relating to different systems*

Toning the skin

This is the second stage in the cleansing routine but may be used for other purposes. Skin toners are necessary:

* after cleansing to ensure complete removal from the skin of all cleansing preparations
* after a face mask to remove all traces of the face mask and refine skin texture
* before make-up to refresh the skin and close the pores.

> ## Caution!
> There are some cleansing products available that do not require the use of a toning lotion or astringent. For example, a cleanser containing glycolic acid that is pH balanced will be removed effectively with warm water and the balance of the skin is not affected by using a toner. Always follow the manufacturer's instructions.

Toners vary in strength and action, but all have a tightening and cooling effect on the skin.

Astringent

This is the strongest acting of the toners and its strength is due to the alcohol content, which irritates the skin causing swelling around the pores, so that they look temporarily less obvious. They are too strong for dry or sensitive skin as they dry out the oils on the skin's surface.

Some astringents contain antiseptic substances, which kill surface bacteria and are useful in treating a blemished skin as they help to dry and heal pustules and prevent the formation of blackheads.

Skin tonics

These may vary in strength achieving a toning and cooling effect without any harsh stinging. The mildest tonics are based on rosewater with added glycerine and may be used on dry, dehydrated or mature skin.

Skin fresheners

The slightly stronger fresheners may contain alkalis which are added to produce stimulating and cooling effects and will act to degrease the surface sebum. They are sometimes applied to the skin from a vaporiser producing a fine mist of distilled water, sometimes containing ingredients such as chamomile or tea tree.

Table 9.2 gives the ingredients of toning lotions.

Toning lotion	Contains
Rosewater Orangewater Chamomile	Flower waters, the mildest ingredients
Witch hazel	A solution of alcohol and water plus extract from the bark of the witch hazel
Glycerine	A humectant and skin softener
Ethyl alcohol Isopropyl alcohol	Alcohols are astringent because of their cooling effect on the skin, which results from their evaporation
Zinc sulphate	Extremely mild astringent
Menthol Camphor Sage	Cooling and refreshing, they are astringent through an irritant effect, triggering the cold sense nerve endings in the skin, which produces a cool sensation
Hexachlorophene	Antiseptic

Table 9.2 *Ingredients of toning lotions*

Face mask treatments

The application of face masks reinforces the beneficial effects of the facial cleanse. A mask is a preparation, which contains various ingredients to which active substances are added to form a paste or gel. They have different actions depending on their formulations.

The choice of mask depends on an accurate skin analysis and a sound knowledge of the effects of the ingredients used. There are several types of mask:

* **Setting masks** use ingredients that set hard after a specified length of time and include clay, astringent and peeling masks.
* **Non-setting masks** never set, therefore do not have such a strong tightening effect on the skin. Gels achieve a tightening effect without setting and include biological masks, which are based on fruit, plant, herbal and vegetable extracts. Natural masks are made from eggs, fruit, honey and oatmeal.
* **Specialised masks** include gel, wax, thermal and oil masks.

Setting masks

Clay masks

These are useful to the therapist because of their range of actions and low cost. They absorb oil, dirt and surface impurities, leaving the skin cleansed, refined and with an improved colour. It is important to analyse the client's skin well before mixing a clay mask and to understand that skin conditions can change. Therefore, each mask must be mixed specifically for the individual client and therapists must have a good understanding of the effects of the ingredients they are using.

Ingredient	Effects
Fuller's earth	Has a fast vascular response causing erythema, deep cleanses, aids desquamation, has a slight bleaching effect
Kaolin	Deep cleanses, draws out impurities, aids desquamation, stimulates circulation and lymph flow
Magnesium carbonate	Gently stimulating, refining, softening, cleansing
Calamine	Soothes, reduces vascularity, cleanses

Table 9.3 *Ingredients and effects of clay masks*

The clays come in dry powder form and have to be mixed with active ingredients to form a paste for easy application. Active ingredients include:

* rosewater and orange flower water – mildly stimulating and toning
* witch hazel – stimulating and drying, refines the pores
* almond oil – slightly stimulating and nourishing
* glycerine – soothing and moisturising.

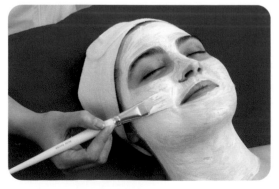

Figure 9.3
Face mask

Suggested clay mask recipes

Normal skin

Two parts magnesium
One part calamine

Mix with rosewater to form a smooth paste.

Effects: To cleanse, refine and soften the skin since there are no skin problems present.

(Kaolin may be added if there are blemishes present or congestion under the skin.)

Dry skin

Equal parts calamine and magnesium.

Mix with almond oil to form a smooth paste.

Effects: Stimulates blood and lymph flow and improves skin colour. Deep cleanses and aids desquamation improving skin texture.

(Kaolin may be added if there are blemishes present or congestion under the skin and the almond oil replaced with rosewater.)

Sensitive skin

Calamine

Mix with glycerine to form a smooth paste.

Effects: Soothes and reduces any vascularity present. Cleanses and softens the skin. The glycerine has humectant properties and therefore prevents the skin from over drying.

Greasy skin

Fuller's earth

Mix with witch hazel to form a smooth paste.

Effects: Has a very fast vascular response causing an erythema, which can improve a sallow complexion. It is deep cleansing and drying and tightens open pores as well as having a slight bleaching effect on the skin.

Clay masks should not be left on any skin for too long. They should be removed when the mask begins to dry or no longer than 8–10 minutes. Even a greasy skin does not require any longer because fuller's earth has a rapid effect on the skin.

When using more than one mask at a time, for a combination skin, the mask should be applied to the area requiring more treatment first, as it has to remain on the skin longer for maximum effect. Both masks can then be removed at the same time.

Astringent masks

These are any masks which include the use of an astringent, for example camphor or menthol, often plant-based, to refresh the skin, boosting circulation, tightening the pores and giving it a healthy glow. They are an excellent pep-up for tired skin but should not be used often as they can have a drying, irritating effect.

Peeling masks

These masks are based on rubber, wax or some type of plastic. When they have hardened on the skin they are peeled off in one piece taking surface dirt and dead skin cells with them. They normally contain a softening ingredient and they form an occlusive layer on the skin preventing moisture loss.

Non-setting masks

Biological masks

These masks are made of:

* fruit
* plants
* herbs
* natural products.

The trace elements in the ingredients create increased cellular activity in the basal layer of the epidermis. This results in refinement of skin texture because of the improvement in respiration and elimination. Plant enzymes trigger a beneficial reaction in the skin's cells even in the deeper layers.

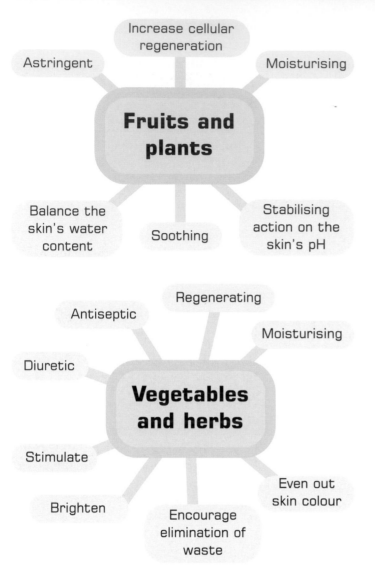

Figure 9.4 *Beneficial effects of plant enzymes on the skin*

Indications for use of biological masks

Biological masks should be used for the following skin types:

Hypersensitive skin conditions. Biological masks may be used when other forms of treatment have been contraindicated, as the action is gentle. Freshens and refines the skin while keeping the acid/alkali balance constant and improving cell renewal.

Dehydrated and dry skin conditions. Those skins lacking in surface moisture and natural oils benefit from the use of biological masks as stimulation is possible without further loss of moisture. The skin is left fresh and soft, free from dead skin cells and with a fine texture.

Mature skins requiring regeneration. The active ingredients aid in regeneration without irritating or reducing moisture.

Oily, blemished skin with sensitivity present. The main benefits are deep cleansing and desquamating. Oil and adhesions are removed from the skin's surface and, because bacteria thrive on this oily film, the skin is left better able to protect itself.

Unstable skin conditions where the pH requires stabilising. Overuse of predominantly alkaline products on the skin progressively destroys the acid mantle and slows down its renewal process, thus allowing the skin to become more susceptible to infection and dehydration. Biological masks help to stabilise the skin's pH.

Skin congestion, due to ill health or incorrect care.

These masks may be applied with a brush, or because of their consistency between two layers of gauze as they will be easier to remove. Removal should be accomplished using tepid water and sterile sponges.

Suggested biological mask recipes

Normal skin

One ripe banana
One tablespoon honey
One beaten egg

Mash the banana and add the honey and egg. Push through a sieve and apply to the face and neck. Leave on for 10–15 minutes.

Effects: Moisturises and softens the skin.

Dry skin 1

One egg yolk
A few drops of almond oil

Mix thoroughly and apply thinly over the face and leave on for 10 minutes.

Effects: Softens and refines skin texture.

Dry skin 2

Two tablespoons oatmeal
Half cup of milk
Two teaspoons of elderflower water

Mix the oatmeal and milk and heat gently until soft, remove from the heat and add the elderflower water and beat together. Apply to the face and leave on for 15–20 minutes.

Effects: Cleanses, refines and softens the skin.

Greasy skin 1

One egg white
A few drops of lemon juice

Whisk together and apply evenly to the face and neck.

Effects: Stimulating and tightening, mildly bleaching with antiseptic properties.

Greasy skin 2

Half a cucumber
Fresh orange or lemon juice

Mash the cucumber and mix with the juice and apply to the face between two pieces of gauze. Leave on for 15–20 minutes.

Effects: Toning and refining.

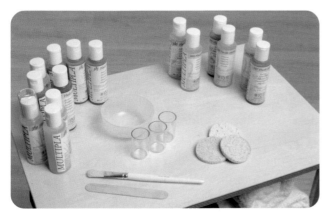

Figure 9.5 *Gel face mask products*

Specialised masks

Wax mask

This is made from a combination of waxes and oils including:

* beeswax
* paraffin wax.
* petroleum jelly
* mineral oil.

It is applied to the skin after it has been warmed to a temperature of 49°C and the face and neck have been covered with nourishing cream.

This mask is most beneficial to dry, dehydrated or ageing skin since it is hydrating and allows the penetration of nourishing creams without over stimulation of the tissues. A congested skin also benefits as the stimulation of the sudoriferous glands causes the skin to perspire, ridding itself of impurities and aiding desquamation.

Actions on the skin include the following:

* The circulation is increased.
* The warmth of the mask opens the pores and softens the skin.
* The nourishing cream is absorbed into the epidermis.
* The skin perspires removing waste.

Gel masks

There are products on the market consisting of active fluids of natural extracts which, when mixed with a gelling agent, create a mask specifically for a particular skin type or condition. This provides a unique skin care programme for the client, as massage and moisturising creams can be made from the same products to complement each other.

Ingredients

Aloe – moisturising
Camphor – stimulating and detoxifying
Ginseng – regenerative
Carrot – stimulates cell reproduction
Azulene – anti-reddening
Horse chestnut – decongestant
Witch hazel – astringent
Rosemary – normalises oil production
Propolis – purifies an oily skin

Oil masks

Oil masks are usually combined with heat treatment to increase the skin's capacity to absorb the oil. They may be used on the following skin types:

* dehydrated
* crepey
* mature
* sun damaged.

The action on the skin is soothing and softening due to the moisturising properties of the oil and the heat produced in the tissues. Respiration and elasticity are also improved.

Hypersensitive and extremely vascular complexions are contraindicated to this type of mask, where heat is used. In this case, the oil mask could be used without the addition of heat.

Thermal masks

This is a thick paste applied to the skin, over a cream, which has been specially formulated to work with the mask for maximum benefit. There are usually a range of creams for different skin types, so once again it is important to analyse the skin type accurately before treatment and, if necessary, use different creams for different areas of the face and neck.

A chemical reaction occurs in the mask causing heat to be produced, which stimulates the skin, improving cellular regeneration and increasing the effectiveness of the skin in absorbing the special cream.

The heat develops as the mask hardens and then gradually subsides after about 20 minutes. The mask becomes rigid and is removed in one piece. The contraindications are:

* highly strung client
* highly vascular complexion.

Ready-made masks

Most companies produce a variety of ready-made masks using different ingredients for a specific purpose and also recommend the use of more than one mask in the same facial treatment to achieve the best results. Ingredients include old favourites such as clays, plants and herbs and also essential oils, marine-based products as well as anti-ageing ingredients.

Suggested specialised mask recipes

Olive oil and ground almonds

Mix together olive oil and ground almonds to form a smooth paste. This mixture should be applied between two pieces of gauze and may be left on the skin for 20 minutes. Once removed, the oil on the skin should be massaged lightly in and the excess removed and the skin toned with rose water.

Hot oil mask

Almond oil should be warmed to a moderate temperature and a piece of gauze to fit the face immersed in it. The eyes should be protected and the gauze applied to the face before positioning the heat lamp in place. The position of the lamp will vary according to the skin sensitivity, intensity of the lamp and previous skin reaction. Timing of the treatment can vary from 5 to 20 minutes for the same reasons as above. After removal of the mask the oil may be used for massage when indicated. The excess oil must then be removed.

Several masks may be involved in a specialised multi-level manual facial and these may include:

* a mask to cleanse and exfoliate dead skin cells
* a mask to rehydrate the skin
* a mask to introduce special products such as collagen into the skin
* a balancing mask to maintain the skin's pH and minimise signs of ageing.

There are also many more scientific masks available such as:

* enzyme masks with active ingredients designed to stimulate skin function at a cellular level and which are antioxidant in effect and also have a tightening effect on the skin

✳ a mask which lowers skin temperature and improves lymphatic drainage

✳ marine masks containing spirulina and alginate with lipo cell complex skin serum, which helps the active ingredients to be transported to the lower layers of the epidermis

✳ anti-ageing masks containing fruit acids, sunflower seeds and juniper oil.

Figure 9.6 indicates the general contraindications to all masks.

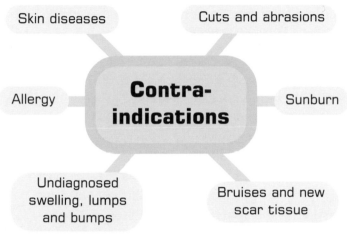

Figure 9.6 *General contraindications to all masks*

Treating discoloured or hyperpigmented skin

Most manual facial treatments that include cleansing the skin and applying a face mask will improve a sallow skin or even out a fading suntan. There are also several facial electrical treatments that have a stimulating, desquamating and hydrating effect, that will improve and brighten the complexion. However, hyperpigmentation may be the problem and can be caused by:

✳ ultraviolet rays stimulating uneven melanin production

✳ hormonal changes occurring during pregnancy and menopause

✳ post-inflammatory hyperpigmentation (dark patches that sometimes show up on Asian and black skin types after acne lesions have healed)

✳ chloasma from the contraceptive pill

✳ hereditary factors, such as dark areas around the eyes.

There are available professional products which will help to reduce hyperpigmentation of the skin effectively. These products include exfoliating and bleaching agents such as tretinoin, hydroquinone, alpha and beta hydroxy acids. They may, however, contain ingredients that will irritate a sensitive skin, so a skin test must be carried out before use. Skin care products that contain alpha hydroxy acids will sometimes help by reducing the areas of pigmentation, but only if used consistently and the client protects his or her skin from ultraviolet rays.

Moisturising the skin

To remain smooth and supple, the skin needs to maintain an adequate moisture level but it is constantly losing natural moisture through evaporation and is particularly affected by:

✳ exposure to the environment – sun, wind, cold

✳ excessive use of degreasing products on the skin

✳ central heating and air conditioning

✳ sebum flow slowing down with age.

It is necessary to prevent further moisture loss and plump out the tissues by using the appropriate moisturiser which conditions the skin making it appear softer and more supple. Moisturisers come in the form of creams from thick to light and fluffy, or very lightweight oil in water emulsions, probably containing a humectant.

Humectants

These are substances which attract particles of moisture from the air and into the skin, for example glycerine urea and rosewater which work well to add to the skin's own moisture level.

Caution!

There are circumstances, however, when the humectant ingredient will do the opposite: In winter when the weather is very cold and dry or in centrally heated homes when the air becomes very dry. If there is no moisture in the air for the humectant to attract, then it will draw water from the skin to its surface causing evaporation and subsequent dehydration of the skin.

To prevent dehydration, a water in oil cream is ideal, made up from a small percentage of water and humectant, blended with oils and made into a liquid or cream. The general rule is the drier the skin and its environment, the richer the moisturiser.

Occlusives

These are moisturisers which trap moisture in the skin preventing evaporation, normally a water in oil emulsion. They form a thin protective layer on the surface helping to preserve the moisture level.

Special creams

These include:

* night creams
* neck creams
* eye creams
* nourishing creams
* skin foods.

These are all rich moisturising creams, using different proportions of oils, waxes, water and other ingredients to create different textures.

A night cream is not necessary before the mid-twenties and even when required, very heavy creams tend to clog the pores and cause puffiness particularly around the eye area.

The neck and eyes do, in fact, show signs of ageing earlier than other areas because the tissues are finer and more delicate and there are no underlying sebaceous glands to provide natural lubrication.

Eye gels are made from gentle plant and herb extracts such as camomile and cornflower. They are suitable for eyes prone to puffiness as they have a decongestant and tightening effect and leave the area grease free.

Neck creams may be much richer – a water in oil emulsion – as the skin is much drier and less sensitive. Used in moderation, they will help counteract a crepey neck.

There are many claims by cosmetic companies that their creams have anti-ageing properties because they contain:

* collagen – protein fibres found in the dermis, which give the skin structural support, provide strength, and allow the skin to stretch and contract
* elastin – a protein which gives the skin its elasticity.

However applied to the skin, these creams do not have much effect on natural ageing but do have humectant properties, plumping out the skin with retained moisture.

Facial massage

Facial massage is the most relaxing and therapeutic part of facial treatment, benefiting all clients, no matter what their skin type. When incorporated into a facial it may also be combined with electrical procedures to increase its effectiveness. Care must be taken in performing the massage manipulations not to overstretch or overstimulate the tissues.

There are many different massage routines and, initially, you will perform the method that has been taught to you in your training establishment. Many experienced therapists combine different types of massage into one routine, for example Swedish and pressure point with lymphatic drainage. Product manufacturers have all developed their own particular massage routines to be used with their products and it is a good idea when learning new techniques to adopt those parts that you feel will most benefit your client .

To ensure total relaxation, it is essential to consider the following:

* The room should be warm and quiet.
* There should be adequate bed covering.
* Ensure the client is comfortably positioned.
* Have all treatment products prepared in advance and close by.
* Avoid talking unnecessarily.
* Warm the massage medium in your hands before applying to the client's skin.
* Do not lose contact with the client's skin before completion of the massage.
* All movements should be rhythmical and flowing.
* Indicate to the client the end of the massage with a gentle but firm pressure on completion of the final movement.

Aims of facial massage

* To relax the client.
* To nourish the skin.
* To improve skin texture
* To improve muscle tone.
* To encourage cellular regeneration.
* To improve lymphatic drainage.

Massage mediums

The medium you choose will depend on the client's skin type, the type of massage and the client's requirements.

Oil

As well as allowing ease of movement and deeper massage, oil nourishes and softens the skin. The oil itself must be light, non-sticky and easily absorbed. Olive and almond oils are most commonly used, but there are many more oils to benefit the skin, used as carrier oils in aromatherapy (see Chapter 16 Aromatherapy).

Essential oils

Essential oils are used quite extensively in body treatment but can also be very effective in treating different skin conditions. They are very concentrated oils extracted from plants and mixed with a suitable carrier oil. Depending upon the effects that are to be achieved, essential oils can be mixed to obtain the required results.

A carrier oil should penetrate the skin easily to allow the essential oils to be absorbed and ideally should have little or no smell. Grapeseed, avocado, almond and wheatgerm are excellent carrier oils.

> ## Caution!
> Always check with the client to see if she has an allergy to nuts before choosing the oil to be used for the massage

Some of the more relaxing essential oils are:

* chamomile
* cypress
* ylang-ylang
* sandalwood
* patchouli
* rose
* neroli
* lavender.

Massage creams

There are creams available for facial massage which contain specific ingredients and are of different textures to suit all skin types. As facial massage should be performed for no less than 20 minutes, one of the most important properties of the cream is that it is not absorbed into the skin too quickly, requiring the therapist to reapply before the end of the massage.

Sensitive skin would benefit from essential oils formulated specifically to treat the accompanying problems or a soothing massage cream.

Dry/mature skin would benefit from a rich cream to nourish the skin but of a light consistency to prevent dragging the tissues, or essential oils.

Normal skin would benefit from all massage mediums provided they were not too heavy.

Greasy skin would benefit from the therapeutic effects of essential oils or a massage cream with a higher water to oil ratio.

Massage manipulations

Effleurage

This is a soothing, stroking, surface movement used at the beginning and end of the facial massage and used during the massage as a linking movement between manipulations.

It can be firm or light without dragging the skin and it is performed either with the palmar surface of the hand or the padded parts of the fingertips. The hand should be completely relaxed and moved over the face and the neck with a gentle but even pressure.

Effects of effleurage

* Increases circulation – the skin is nourished.
* Increases lymph flow – waste products are removed.
* Aids desquamation – improves skin texture.
* Causes an erythema – improves skin colour.
* Soothes nerves.
* Relaxes the client.

Petrissage

These are pressure movements, which are deeper and compress the muscle tissue intermittently against underlying structures. They are classified as kneading, wringing, skin rolling and picking up. These movements are performed with the padded palmar surface of the fingers and thumbs and are all used in body massage but adapted for facial massage. The kneading movements are mainly performed with the padded surfaces of the fingers on the face but using the whole hand around the neck and shoulders. When performing these manipulations the hands should be moulded to the area being treated and movements should be slow and rhythmical.

Knuckling is a method of kneading using the knuckles to knead and lift the tissues in an upward circular movement.

Scissoring is a movement only performed over a flat bony area and the pressure exerted is very gentle. The index and middle fingers of both hands are placed opposite and inside each other and gentle pressure is exerted with both sets of fingers working towards each other lifting and releasing the tissues.

Effects of petrissage

* Increases circulation and lymph flow – the skin is nourished.
* Aids desquamation – improves skin texture.
* Stimulates the skin – improves colour, texture and cellular regeneration.
* Increases muscle tone – improves facial contours.
* Eases away tension nodules – relaxes muscles.

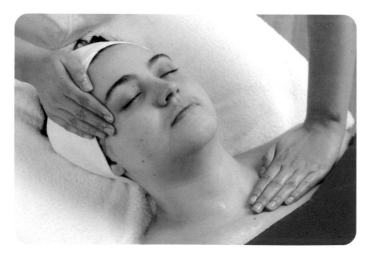

Figure 9.7 *Facial massage*

Tapotement

These are stimulating movements such as tapping and digital hacking performed with the palmar surfaces of the fingertips. Digital hacking to the face is an upward movement with the fingers, rapidly one after the other, lifting the tissues and immediately releasing them. The hands must be relaxed when performing this movement. Tapping is a more rigid movement, usually performed using two fingers together and working along the jaw line.

Effects of tapotement

* Produces an erythema.
* Stimulates the nerve endings revitalising the skin tissues.

Vibrations

Using the palmar surface of the hands and the fingertips on the area to be treated, the muscles of the therapist's arms and hands are contracted and relaxed rapidly creating a fine trembling movement, which promotes relaxation.

Effects of vibrations

* Relaxes the client.
* Gently stimulating.

When to carry out a facial massage

Facial massage is incorporated into a facial after all the cleansing and electrical treatments have been carried out, except for those treatments which, for maximum effect, have to be performed at the end of treatment. A pre-heat treatment such as facial steaming may be included after the deep cleanse (see Chapter 11 Facial electrical treatments).

A basic facial involves:
1 Superficial cleanse.
2 Deep cleanse.
3 Facial massage.
4 Face mask.
5 Moisturise.
6 Protect.

Protection after a facial is important as UV exposure, no matter how limited, contributes to the ageing process of the skin. Many product companies are including sun protection factors in their moisturisers, but if not, apply a factor 15 sun cream to protect the client's skin from further damage.

The effects of facial massage

Table 9.4 shows the effects of facial massage.

* Physical effects are those that can be seen or felt on the surface of the skin.
* Physiological effects are those that occur in the body under the surface of the skin.
* Psychological effects are those that the client feels.

Table 9.4 *Physical, physiological and psychological effects of facial massage*

Physical	Physiological	Psychological
The therapist's hands warm the area The pores relax and open The skin becomes more receptive to absorption of nourishing and hydrating products Puffiness may be removed with massage manipulations Relaxes tense muscles Aids desquamation Softens and lubricates the skin Eases tension lines Removes tension nodules in the muscles Erythema is produced	Increase in blood flow nourishes the tissues and increases cellular regeneration Oxygen is carried to the area, carbon dioxide is carried away Lymph flow is increased, waste products are carried away, reinforcing the external cleansing of the skin Heat and warmth is increased in the tissues because of the stimulation of blood supply Increase in sebum and sweat which helps to remove dirt and grease and maintains the moisture balance in the skin Stimulates and nourishes underlying muscle tissue Stimulates or soothes the nerve endings Essential oils, if used, have a beneficial effect on the body's systems	The client feels relaxed Skin feels rejuvenated Sense of well-being is created Client feels pampered Stress levels are reduced Increases self-confidence Essential oils, if used, have a beneficial effect on the nervous system, calming, uplifting and soothing

Our eyes are working all the time. They provide the face with much of its expression, and are often described as one of the most attractive features of the face. Tired eyes can be relaxed and soothed during facial massage and there are several pressure points around the eyes which can help to ease headaches. There are also several individual eye treatments which may be incorporated into a full facial routine or they may be offered as an individual treatment in addition to any other service. They include eyebrow shaping, eyelash and brow tinting and eyelash perming.

Eyebrow shaping

The eyes are the focal point of the face and the natural shape of the eyebrows normally enhances the features. The eyebrows provide protection for the eyes and the shape should not be altered dramatically, just improved by plucking the stray hairs, which gives a cleaner line, allowing successful application of eye shadow.

The thickness of the eyebrows helps in balancing facial features, so it is important not to over pluck. However, very heavy brows which are close together can make the client appear to frown, so plucking between the brow across the bridge of the nose can greatly improve the appearance. Eyebrows which are very long and taper down the sides of the outer corner of the eye actually make the eyes look as though they have a downward slant and plucking the hair away provides instant lift to the face. Points to consider before shaping begins are shown in Figure 10.1.

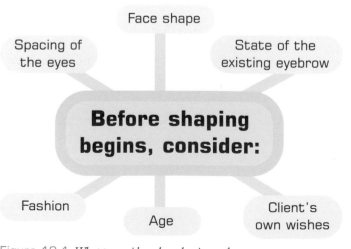

Figure 10.1 *What to consider when shaping eyebrows*

Face shape

Spacing of the eyes

State of the existing eyebrow

Before shaping begins, consider:

Fashion

Age

Client's own wishes

Contraindications

* New scar tissue.
* Highly strung or nervous client.
* Skin disease.
* Bruising.
* Eye disorders and diseases

Eyebrow shaping should be carried out after the cleansing routine and before the soothing massage. If steaming is to be included as part of the facial, it could be applied at this stage, allowing the pores to open, making the treatment less painful.

To cause the least discomfort to the client during treatment, make sure the client's head and neck are well supported, and the area is clean and grease free. Place warm pads of cotton wool over the brows to open the pores and then hold the skin taut when plucking. Always pluck in the direction of growth starting at the bridge of the nose, as this area is less sensitive. On completion of the treatment always apply a cooling, soothing lotion to the area.

Figure 10.2 *Eyebrow shaping*

Determining correct eyebrow width

Rest an orange stick against the widest part of the nose and the inner corner of the eye. The eyebrow should not extend beyond this line.

Move the orange stick so that it makes a diagonal line from the nose across the outer corner of the eye and up to the eyebrow. It should not extend past this point.

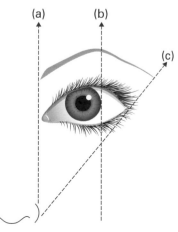

Figure 10.3 *Measuring the eyebrow*

Eyebrow shapes

There are certain shapes, which are more suited to a particular face shape and these should be considered before reshaping.

* **High forehead** – the arch of the eyebrow should be slightly elevated to create the illusion of a lower forehead.
* **Low forehead** – the arch should be as low as possible to give more height to the forehead.
* **Wide set eyes** – the eyes will appear closer by leaving the brows unplucked on the inner corners. You could extend the inner corner using eyebrow pencil.
* **Close set eyes** – to make the eyes appear wider apart, pluck more from the inner corners and extend the outer corner with eyebrow pencil.
* **Round face** – arched eyebrows narrow the face.
* **Oblong face** – the eyebrows should be almost horizontal.
* **Square face** – the eyebrow should have a wide, high arch to create an oval impression.
* **Pear-shaped face** – extra width is needed at the forehead; eyebrows should be arched and extended at the outer corners.

Natural eyebrow   Arched eyebrow

Straight eyebrow   Angular eyebrow

Figure 10.4 *Eyebrow shapes*

Eyebrow and eyelash tinting

This is a very popular salon treatment and can be very effective in accentuating the eyes, which are for most women one of their best features. Even dark lashes are lighter at the ends and will benefit from the tint by making them look longer. The tint usually lasts for up to six weeks but can be repeated more often as long as the client does not have an allergy to the product used. The tinting products available have been formulated for use around the sensitive eye area to reduce the chance of a severe reaction. When mixed with hydrogen peroxide, an essential element in the tinting procedure, a chemical reaction occurs, which changes the character of the tint.

Chemical reaction, or oxidisation

When the tint is mixed with 10 per cent hydrogen peroxide a chemical reaction called oxidisation occurs (see Figure 10.5).

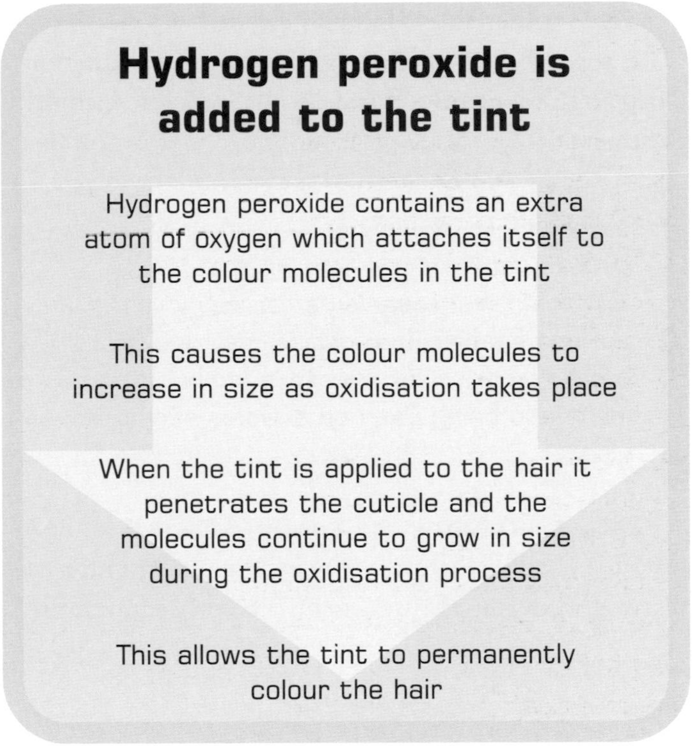

Hydrogen peroxide is added to the tint

Hydrogen peroxide contains an extra atom of oxygen which attaches itself to the colour molecules in the tint

This causes the colour molecules to increase in size as oxidisation takes place

When the tint is applied to the hair it penetrates the cuticle and the molecules continue to grow in size during the oxidisation process

This allows the tint to permanently colour the hair

Figure 10.5 *Effects of adding hydrogen peroxide to a tint*

The mixing process must be carried out immediately before applying the tint as once the oxidisation process starts, it may not be stopped. If you delay applying the tint to the lashes or brows, the oxidisation process may have finished and the colour molecules will be too large to penetrate the cuticle of the hair making the tinting procedure ineffective.

Skin sensitivity test

It is essential before tinting the client's brows or lashes to carry out a skin sensitivity, or predisposition test. This should take place 48 hours before treatment to determine if the client is allergic to the products.

A small amount of the tint should be mixed according to the manufacturer's instructions and applied to the skin, in an inconspicuous position, such as behind the ear or on the inside of the elbow.

If there is a **positive reaction**, the skin will become red in the area of the patch test and there will be severe itchiness and in some cases swelling of the tissue. The treatment is therefore contraindicated.

If the client experiences no discomfort or irritation – a **negative reaction** – then you may proceed with the treatment.

Caution!

The skin may become sensitive to a particular product even after many years of use and an allergic reaction may occur. Regular testing for allergy is important as the dye is being used on a highly sensitive area.

Even if clients have had a negative reaction to the test, it is possible that they may experience irritation or discomfort during the treatment. The procedure must be immediately halted and the tint removed by wiping it away with damp cotton wool and then flushing the eye by squeezing distilled water from a special sterile bottle with a flexible tube.

If the tint stains the skin for any reason, a stain remover, which may be obtained from the manufacturer, should be used. However, this should not occur if the skin surrounding the area to be treated has been protected by applying petroleum jelly, creating a barrier on the skin.

Reasons for eyelash and eyebrow tinting

This treatment will enhance the general appearance of the eyes and provide an alternative to mascara for those clients who are very sensitive to eye make-up or contact lens wearers whose eyes may be irritated by the fibres in mascara. Because it does not smudge, tinting is ideal for any sporting activity, in particular swimming, when mascara cannot be worn. It will increase the colour intensity of those with blond, red or grey hair and provide definition for the client who does not have the time to apply make-up or who has fine or thin eyebrows. Both red and white hairs are more resistant to the tint and may take longer to develop than other colours.

Contraindications to eyelash and eyebrow tinting

* Skin disorders.
* Skin diseases.
* Eye disorders and diseases (see Chapter 3 Contraindications).
* Excessively dry or flaky skin.
* Cuts or abrasions in the skin.
* Immediately after eyebrow shaping.
* Clients who are unable to keep their eyes still for any reason.
* History of sensitivity to eye make-up.
* Positive reaction to tint test

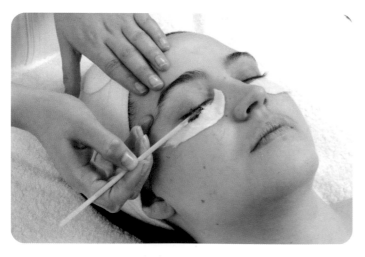

Figure 10.6 *Eyelash tinting*

Eyelash perming

Eyelash perming is offered to clients who want their eyes to look wider and their lashes longer, so providing definition. It is ideal for the client on a special occasion, the client who has very straight lashes and for those who use lash curlers regularly as this may be damaging in the long term. It also enhances the eyes of those clients who are unable to wear make-up for work or because they participate in a sporting activity.

Manufacturers will provide training in their particular system, but the method of use is similar whichever product you use.

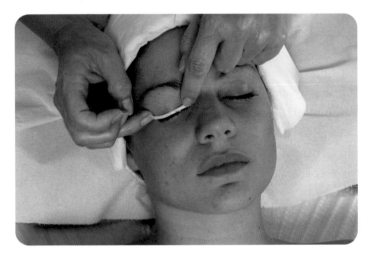

Figure 10.7 *Eyelash permimg*

The eyelash perming procedure

A slim, flexible mini-roller, which comes in different sizes, is placed along the upper lashes and the lashes are curled round the roller, which is covered in a mild water soluble adhesive, to fix the lashes in place. The roller size depends on how straight the lashes are, their thickness and texture. It is important to make sure that the lower lashes are not caught up in the curling process, as they will be permanently fixed in the wrong position! A mild perming solution in the form of a gel or cream is then applied to the lashes to create the curl. Dry, lint-free pads are then placed over the eyes and the solution is left to develop for about 10 minutes on fine hair and 15 minutes on coarse hair. The lashes will then be treated with a fixing solution or neutraliser to ensure the curl is permanent. After the required time, the glue and perming solution are then gently removed. The final part of the treatment is the application of conditioner brushed on to the lashes to hydrate them.

Safety precautions

Check the client for contraindications, which are the same as for eyelash tinting (see above). It is advisable to carry out a skin sensitivity test first in the same way that the test is carried out for eyelash tinting, as this will check whether the client is allergic to the products.

Make sure that the correct sized roller is used. If it is too large, there will be very little curl and if it is too small, the curl may be excessive.

If irritation occurs at any time during the treatment, the products must be removed immediately and the eye flushed with water from a sterile bottle of distilled water with a long flexible tube.

Maintaining healthy eyes

Good health is reflected in the eyes, as it is in the skin, and it is important to look after the eyes and the skin surrounding them.

For sparkling eyes as well as healthy teeth, fluoride is an essential part of your diet. Foods rich in fluoride are seafood, watercress, spinach, cabbage, egg yolk and porridge oats.

The skin under the eyes is thinner than on the rest of the face and there are very few sebaceous glands. As a result, this area is prone to dryness and crows' feet, or expression lines appearing.

Fine lines (crows' feet)

Caused by constant facial expressions, fine lines are more commonly called laughter lines and are found particularly on a fairly dry skin. They appear with age and exposure to ultraviolet rays and may be aggravated by poor eyesight or rough handling when applying or removing cosmetics.

Treatment

Use a good eye cream which plumps out the tissue temporarily, but care must be taken not to apply too much, as this may cause swelling and irritate the eyes. Always apply with the ring finger, using a gentle tapping movement, to prevent stretching of the skin. A gel is very soothing and cools the eye area if there is any sensitivity present. There are now eye creams available which contain alpha hydroxy acids (natural acids found in fruit, milk and sugar), and these may be used to reduce lines around the eye, but care must be taken not to overuse these products and to apply a sun protection cream after use.

When cleansing eye make-up, use a non-oily, special eye make-up remover and protect the skin under the eye with a small piece of damp cotton wool. Then gently remove the eye make-up on to the cotton wool and not the skin.

When performing facial massage be particularly careful that movements are gentle and always from the outer corner to the inner corner of the eye. Slight pressure on the inside corner of the eye relieves tired eyes and removes tension. A small circular pressure movement on the temples, at the sides of the eyes, helps to relieve headaches.

Dark circles

Dark circles may be caused by:

* anaemia
* liver disease
* tiredness due to lack of sleep
* poor elimination of waste from the body, creating a build-up of toxins (poisons) in the system
* too much sugar and starch in the diet
* lack of fresh air and exercise
* genetic.

Treatment

If the client smokes, recommend stopping, as it encourages carbon dioxide and lowers the oxygen content of the blood. Deoxygenated blood shows up with a blue tinge under the skin particularly on the under eye area, which is very fine. Also recommend a diet to help detoxify the system and reduce starch (cakes, bread, cereals and sweets), which also increases carbon dioxide content in the blood. Camouflage make-up or light reflecting foundation can be used to disguise this problem.

Swollen eyes

This could indicate a medical condition which causes fluid retention and is often related to kidney problems or a sluggish lymphatic system. The skin around the eyes may have been overstretched and the contours dropped or fatty deposits around the eyes may have caused them. A night cream may have been used which is too heavy or the client may be suffering from an allergic reaction and, in some cases, the problem could be hereditary.

Treatment

If you suspect a medical condition, then refer the client to a doctor. Use cold compresses on the eyes to cool and soothe.

Electrical equipment used in facial therapy is becoming increasingly more sophisticated and is designed to improve skin conditions, hydrate and protect and delay the effects of ageing. There are many different types of equipment on the market, but whatever the design, they all work in a similar way. It is important, however, to follow the instructions for use provided by the manufacturer of the equipment.

There are several pieces of equipment which may be incorporated into a facial treatment to reinforce the effects of manual treatment or to achieve effects not possible with manual treatment alone. Not all the treatments pass an electrical current through the body but instead use the current to work the machine, producing the required effect.

Choice of equipment

It is important for therapists to recognise when it is appropriate to incorporate a piece of electrical equipment into a facial routine. Most pieces of equipment achieve one or more of the following effects:

* cleansing
* tightening and firming
* stimulating
* relaxing
* anti-ageing
* nourishing.

Some skin conditions may be improved or corrected more quickly by use of the most appropriate equipment. It is important, therefore, to analyse the skin correctly and have a complete understanding of the effects of all equipment.

It is also essential to understand how each piece of equipment works and how to use it safely and effectively.

General contraindications to electrical treatment

* Any skin diseases to prevent cross-infection.
* Recent scar tissue.
* Heart disease. A weak heart may not be able to maintain an increase in blood pressure caused by a dilation of the blood vessels, an effect of an electrical current flowing through the body.

* Arteriosclerosis – often referred to as hardening of the arteries. The arteries are unable to open up to allow the increased flow of blood, which is a natural response to stimulation of the circulation, and fainting may occur.
* Hypersensitive skin. Irritation or itching may occur as the skin is very easily stimulated. Broken capillaries may worsen due to the increased dilation of the capillaries in response to the increase in circulation.
* During pregnancy. It is not advisable to use electrical equipment that allows an electrical current to flow through the body.
* Epilepsy – electrical treatment may cause an epileptic episode.
* Cuts, abrasions or bruising.
* Metal pins and plates.

In addition to the general contraindications, there are also specific contraindications to each piece of equipment that must be considered. These are listed in the relevant section below.

Facial steaming

The facial steamer is one of the most versatile treatments. It is beneficial to all skin types and can be incorporated into most skin care routines.

There are free-standing models with a height adjusting facility and an adjustable head, allowing accurate placement of the steam vapour, as well as control of steam pressure. Most new models are easy to empty and have an indicator that makes a beeping noise when the water reservoir is almost empty.

Figure 11.1
A free-standing steamer with adjustable head

To prevent calcium and mineral deposits building up in the machine, it is advisable to use distilled water in the steamer instead of tap water. Some models produce ozone, which has an anti-bacterial effect on the skin and promotes healing. These models contain a high-pressure mercury vapour lamp, over which the vapour passes and ozone is produced.

The small hand-held model is a specialised steamer, which emits a very fine spray to the face, carrying plant extracts, herbal solutions or skin fresheners. On the side of the steamer are two glass beakers, one to hold the special solution, which is drawn up and mixed with the distilled water in the main reservoir of the steamer. The other beaker catches the drips of water produced by the vapour.

Effects and benefits of steaming

* Opens the pores and softens the skin.
* Stimulates the sudoriferous glands to produce sweat helping to eliminate waste.
* Oily deposits in the follicles are softened and comedones are removed more easily.
* Sebaceous glands are stimulated, helping to lubricate the skin.
* Softens dead skin cells, aiding desquamation.
* Increased circulation causes an erythema, improving skin colour.
* Prepares the skin for further treatment.
* Relaxing.
* Increase in circulation brings nutrients to the skin and carries away waste products.

Although most steamers on the market have a facility for the use of ozone, there has been recent legislation proposed to reduce or remove the use of ozone in facial therapy. The principle of this is that the concentration of ozone being emitted by these units could exceed the specified safety levels of 100–120 micrograms per cubic metre and the ozone produced is inhaled directly into the lungs. Some examining bodies have pre-empted any official legislation by removing the use of ozone in steam therapy, although it is still commonly used within the industry.

Uses of steaming

Steaming is effectively a gentle cleansing or skin preparation treatment suitable for all skin types and would be performed after the superficial and deep cleanse. It may be used on different skin types for different reasons and for a varying length of time (see Table 11.1).

The general rule for placement of the steamer is the oilier the skin, the closer the vapour and the more sensitive skin, the further away the steamer should be placed. The length of time the steamer is used for would depend upon the skin type and condition. The average time within a facial routine would be five minutes, less if the skin were very sensitive or mature and longer if it was very congested. Any area of high colour should be protected with cotton wool pads to prevent over stimulation.

Dry skin (5 mins)	Sensitive skin (3–5 mins)	Mature skin (5 mins)	Normal skin (5–10 mins)	Oily skin (10 mins)
Deep cleanses Desquamates Hydrates Improves colour	Gently cleanses Hydrates	Increases cellular regeneration Desquamates Hydrates Improves skin colour	Maintains function and texture Cleanses Hydrates	Unblocks congestion Deep cleanses Improves skin colour

Table 11.1 *Effects of steaming on different skin types*

Specific contraindications to steaming

* Sunburn.
* Acne rosacea.
* Extreme vascularity.

Exfoliation

Exfoliation is the method by which skin cells are removed from the outermost layer of the epidermis. It may be achieved in varying degrees by manual cleansing, brush cleansing, pore grains, oatmeal scrubs, abrasive sponges and masks, biological and chemical peels and alpha hydroxy acids (AHAs).

The effects of exfoliation are to improve skin texture and colour by removing dead skin cells, remove skin blockages, increase cellular regeneration and increase the absorption of creams into the epidermis.

With modern technology a new system has been developed which exfoliates the dead skin cells and also refines fine lines and wrinkles to achieve a smooth and rejuvenated skin and this is known as microdermabrasion.

Microdermabrasion

This is a 'state of the art' therapeutic method of skin abrasion providing more than the standard skin peeling treatment. It will provide exfoliation of the surface skin cells in a gradual and controlled manner. Initially, this form of treatment was used by dermatologists, but it is becoming increasingly popular as a treatment used by beauty therapists in salons and spas.

There are now many different forms of this treatment available, but in general, each unit will consist of a compressor and a low-pressure suction pump which delivers a controlled stream of micronised aluminium oxide crystals to the skin through a disposable sterilised nozzle. The used crystals and exfoliated skin cells are then removed by the controlled vacuum action of the unit leaving the skin instantly smooth and fresh, promoting new skin and collagen growth.

The pressure used to deliver the stream of crystals is fully adjustable which allows the therapist to treat many different skin types and conditions on the face and body. It is a completely painless treatment and is simple to operate.

To allow the therapist to work on all the different skin types – from thick coarsened skin to thinner ageing skin – there are usually different levels at which the microdermabrasion unit will work. For example:

* Level 1, the most superficial of the treatments, is often used as an introduction to the client in preparation for the higher levels. This will exfoliate the skin and help in the removal of milia and comedones.
* Level 2 provides a more concentrated procedure and is particularly good for the treatment of fine lines and wrinkles, pigmentation and acne scarring. This level complements the use of microcurrent, electrical neuromuscular stimulation treatment (MENS).
* Level 3 is the level, which focuses on the treatment of scars, stretch marks and lip and frown lines.

After treatment, it is important to instruct clients in the care of their skin as they will have exposed new skin to the elements and it takes up to three days to restore the protective barrier.

* Do not swim or use heat therapy such as sauna and steam.
* Do not sunbathe or use a sun bed.
* Do not use make-up for two days if possible.
* Use a high factor sun protection even in winter.
* Always make sure that hands are clean before applying anything to the skin.
* Do not apply products to the skin which have an exfoliating or peeling effect such as AHAs.

This treatment may also be used for body exfoliation, by using a body nozzle to remove dead skin cells and stimulate circulation. It helps in the treatment of cellulite by helping to reduce the orange peel effect on the thighs and other parts of the body. It is also an excellent preparatory treatment for false tan application.

Specific contraindications to microdermabrasion

* Hypersensitive skin.
* Eczema.
* Psoriasis
* Broken capillaries.
* Bruising.
* New scar tissue.
* Skin disease.
* Asthma.
* Hepatitis.

Benefits of microdermabrasion

* Reduces fine lines and wrinkles.
* Refines acne-scarred skin.
* Removes skin congestion.
* Improves skin colour.
* Treats pigmentation disorders and age spots.
* Increases cellular regeneration.
* Improves a sun-damaged skin.
* Improves the rate at which the skin absorbs other moisturising and active ingredients.

Although some manufacturers recommend this treatment to even out hyperpigmentation, occasionally, it may actually cause hyperpigmentation in some skin types. It is important always to carry out a thorough and detailed consultation with the client and follow the manufacturer's instructions for treatment to prevent problems occurring. For the treatment of lines, wrinkles and scars, a course of ten treatments is recommended once a week and this should be followed by monthly maintenance treatments.

Some manufacturers have now produced equipment that provides other treatments in addition to the exfoliation such as ultrasound, oxygen and light therapy.

Cosmetic brush treatment

This has been used for many years as an effective exfoliating system and although the newer, microdermabrasion units have superseded them, they are still useful for mobile therapists and those who have a small budget and cannot afford the more expensive equipment.

The machines vary in size from small hand-held units to a large individual machine or in a combined unit with other equipment. The brushes come in various sizes and textures made from natural hair or bristle. The machines have a controllable brush speed and can be rotated clockwise and anticlockwise.

Brush cleansing reinforces the manual cleanse. This method desquamates by gently removing the dead surface skin cells and helps to remove skin blockages. It stimulates circulation and improves skin colour and cellular regeneration. The skin should be thoroughly cleansed and steamed if required and depending on the skin type, a cleansing medium should be applied with a mask brush:

* soap – oily/blemished skin
* cleansing lotion – oily/combination skin
* facial scrub – congested skin/thick epidermis
* cleansing cream – dry/mature/sensitive skin.

The correct brush size must be used for the area treated. For example, the neck would need a larger size than the sides of the nose. The brush should always be moistened with water before use to soften the bristles.

Slower speeds should be used on dry/sensitive skin for a more gentle effect and faster speeds on coarser skins with a thicker epidermis. Pressure and speed should be reduced over bony areas. The brushes must be guided over the skin gently. It is not necessary to rotate the brush at all since the machine does that for you. It is advisable to apply damp cotton wool pads to the client's eyes during treatment to prevent any of the cleansing medium going into the eyes.

The cleansing medium should be removed with damp cotton wool pads and the facial routine continued, or the appropriate moisturiser applied. After use, the brushes must be thoroughly cleansed in hot soapy water and then disinfected. They should be stored in a dry steriliser.

Figure 11.2
Brush cleansing equipment

Specific contraindications to brush treatment

* Acne – to avoid irritation and spread of infection.
* Sensitive skin with broken capillaries.
* Bruising, cuts and abrasions.
* New scar tissue.

Vacuum suction

This is a mechanical method of lymphatic drainage, the removal of waste products from the skin via the lymphatic system. The machine contains an electrically driven vacuum pump connected to a perspex or glass ventouse by a flexible plastic tube. The pump draws air from the ventouse, causing the air pressure beneath to be reduced and forms a partial vacuum, which lifts the underlying skin tissue into the ventouse. A control valve sets the degree of suction and a gauge indicates the vacuum within the ventouse.

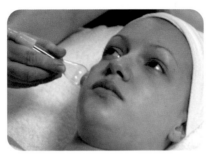

Figure 11.3 *Facial vacuum suction*

The ventouses come in different shapes and sizes, the larger apertures for lymphatic drainage and the smallest for comedone extraction. Some have a small hole on the side, which is covered by a finger to create the vacuum, and at the end of each stroke, the finger is lifted away from the hole to release the vacuum. For those ventouses without a hole the little finger should be used to break the suction at the end of each stroke.

Vacuum suction machines with a pulsating action are beneficial to mature and wrinkled skin, as the vacuum is intermittent and less stimulating. In this case, two ventouses are used, one on either side of the face working in unison. The frequency and the pulse width can be adjusted to suit all skin types and different areas of the face.

Precautions when using vacuum suction

* Before use, make all electrical checks.
* Select the correct ventouse size.
* Ensure there are no cracks or chips in the ventouse.
* Test the vacuum on yourself first.
* Use the necessary lubrication for the skin type. For oily skin, use a cleansing lotion; for dry/mature/sensitive skin, use oil or massage cream.
* Ensure the vacuum is not excessive, that is, tissue should not be lifted into the ventouse more than 20 per cent.
* Always break the suction before removing the ventouse from the face.
* All strokes should be towards the lymph nodes.
* After use, ventouses should be cleaned in a sterilising fluid and tubes should be washed in warm soapy water, dried thoroughly and then placed in a sanitised container.

Effects and benefits of vacuum suction

* Waste products are removed via the lymphatic system improving elimination, absorption and general skin health.
* Deep cleansing to the skin helps in the removal of skin blockages and congestion. The cleansing action may be increased with the application of a special cleansing medium.
* The desquamation of dead skin cells improves skin texture.
* The skin is nourished because the increase in circulation brings nutrients and oxygen to the area.
* Skin colour is improved due to the increase in circulation.
* The skin is hydrated and moisturised when a rich lubricant is used.

Aim of treatment

The aim of treatment is to increase the lymphatic circulation and remove waste products from the skin of the face and neck to the superficial lymph nodes. Manual massage will be performed after vacuum suction to remove the waste from the lymph nodes to be absorbed back into the main system for elimination.

Drainage is performed:

* from the neck to the superficial and deep cervical nodes or sub mandibular nodes
* from the chin and jaw line to the sub mental and sub mandibular nodes
* across the lower cheek area to the buccal and parotid nodes
* from the nose to the buccal nodes
* across the upper cheek area to the pre auricular nodes
* from the forehead to the pre-auricular nodes (see Figure 11.4).

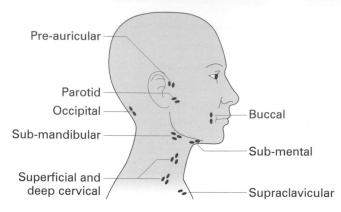

Figure 11.4 *The lymph nodes of the face and neck*

Specific contraindications to vacuum suction

* Sensitive skin with dilated capillaries, as the suction could worsen the condition.
* Thin overstretched skin, as the loose tissue would be sucked into the ventouse causing discomfort.
* Recent scar tissue.
* Bruised or broken skin.
* Bony areas.
* Acne rosacea.

High frequency

This is a rapidly oscillating current with a frequency of 200 000 cycles per second. It is so rapid that it does not stimulate motor or sensory nerves. The current produces heat in the tissues and depending upon the method of application used, the physiological effects are stimulating or soothing. The two methods of high frequency are:

* direct
* indirect.

The machine has an on/off switch, an intensity control and an ebonite handle, connected to the machine by an extendable cord. Each machine has a selection of glass electrodes, which fit into the handle and come in different shapes and sizes:

* The saturator electrode is used for indirect high frequency and is held by the client to complete the circuit.
* The mushroom-shaped electrode is the most frequently used and normally comes in two sizes to suit all areas of the face and neck.

* The horse-shoe shaped electrode is shaped to fit the back of the neck and across the shoulders.
* The fulgurator electrode is long and thin with a tiny pointed end used to spark pustules.
* The roller electrode is used to cover all areas but particularly larger areas such as the back and décolleté (see Figure 11.5).

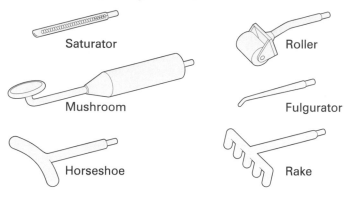

Figure 11.5
The facial electrodes used in high frequency treatment

Direct high frequency

Using the appropriate glass electrode in the ebonite handle, the high frequency current is passed directly into the client's skin, using small circular movements and starting on the neck area. The lighter the contact, the more stimulating the treatment. Talc should be used as a lubricant to allow the electrodes to move smoothly over the skin if it is oily. A special oxygenating cream and gauze may be used for all skin types. This will provide the skin with oxygen when the high frequency current passes over the cream and because the gauze creates a tiny gap between the skin and the electrode, this helps to produce more ozone.

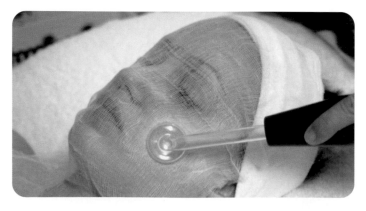

Figure 11.6 *Direct high frequency treatment*

How ozone is produced

The glass electrodes are partial vacuums, that is, hollow tubes with a low density of air and inert gas, which in most machines produces a blue, orange or pink light. This provides a passage along which the current flows and the high frequency energy is discharged into the skin where the electrode makes contact.

When the high frequency (HF) current is passed through oxygen, it produces ozone. This occurs between the electrode and the skin and more intensely when the electrode is lifted very slightly off the face to 'spark' the pustules.

HF + oxygen = ozone

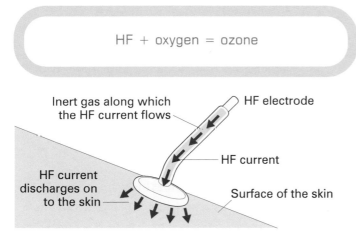

Figure 11.7 *How ozone is produced in direct high frequency treatment*

Effects of high frequency

* Increases circulation, which produces heat in the tissues, brings nutrients to area, removes waste.
* Produces an erythema improving skin colour.
* Aids desquamation, refining the skin.
* Dries the skin helping to heal pustules.
* Cleansing effect due to increase in sebum flow and perspiration.
* Germicidal effect due to the formation of ozone which helps to kill bacteria.

Benefits

Direct high frequency will be beneficial to:
* oily, blemished and pustular skin – heals and dries
* sallow skin – improves skin colour
* sluggish skin – stimulates and encourages cell renewal.

For oily skin to gain maximum benefit from this treatment, it should be performed at the end of a facial to allow the ozone produced to be left on the skin. It is advisable not to wear make-up after treatment.

Indirect high frequency

This treatment is combined with facial massage and is performed after all cleansing treatments have been carried out. With this method of high frequency, the saturator electrode is placed in the ebonite handle and given to the client to hold. The therapist then performs the facial massage and the high frequency current discharges from the client to the therapist's hands at the point of contact. Depending on the client's skin type, oil, cream or special creams may be applied to the skin. Whichever medium is chosen, it must not penetrate into the skin too quickly, as the treatment must not be interrupted to apply further applications. All massage manipulations may be used, apart from tapotement, as at least one hand must remain in contact with the client's skin at all times.

Effects of indirect high frequency

* Relaxation – warmth is created by the energy produced and a sedative effect is achieved.
* Removes tension – a combination of massage and warmth in the area relieves muscular tension.
* Produces a mild erythema and aids desquamation improving skin texture and colour.
* Improves circulation, bringing nourishment to the area, removing waste products and increasing warmth in the tissues.
* Nourishing – the creams applied to the skin are absorbed more readily when high frequency is applied indirectly.

Benefits

Indirect high frequency will be beneficial to:
* muscular tension – eases aches and pains
* sensitive skin – gently decongests areas with thread veins

* dry/mature/dehydrated skin – gently stimulates and nourishes
* tense clients – promotes relaxation.

Specific contraindications to indirect high frequency

* Headaches/migraines.
* Highly nervous clients.
* Epilepsy.
* Excessive number of dental fillings/braces.
* Metal pins and plates.

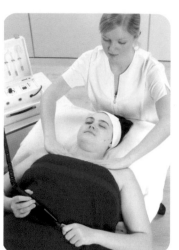

Figure 11.8 *Indirect high frequency treatment*

Precautions when using high frequency

* Always inform the client about the loud buzzing noise the electrode makes when it is in use, as it can sound quite alarming.
* Remove all the client's jewellery and your own particularly when performing indirect high frequency.
* Before use, make all electrical checks.
* Do not allow the client to come into contact with metal and avoid touching any metal parts of the facial couch.
* The electrode or one hand, depending upon which method is used, should be placed on the neck or shoulder before switching on the current. Alternatively, place your finger on the electrode, switch on the machine and when the electrode is in contact with the client's skin you may remove your finger and the current will be discharged into the client's skin.
* Do not remove the electrode from the client during treatment with direct high frequency and always keep one hand in contact with the client's skin during indirect high frequency.
* Do not touch your client with your other hand when performing direct high frequency.

* Timing of treatment would depend upon the skin type being treated, the reaction of the skin and the client's tolerance to treatment. The following may be used as a guide:
  Direct:
    – Oily and blemished skin – 10 minutes
    – Dry or mature skin – 5–10 minutes
    – Sensitive skin – no more than 5 minutes.
  Indirect:
    – A normal 20-minute massage unless the skin has an adverse reaction.
* After use, the electrode should be cleaned and sanitised and put away safely. It is also essential to clean the machine itself and the ebonite holder with surgical spirit. When residues of grease or talc remain, this acts as a conductor to the high frequency current and the therapist may feel an electric shock in her hand.

Electrical muscle stimulation or faradic treatment

This treatment is commonly known as faradic treatment. It is used to stimulate muscles and is classed as a passive exercise treatment. There are special facial units available or body machines with a facial outlet.

The facial unit has an on/off switch, a pulse indicator switch, an intensity control and a single output with a facial electrode attachment. The positive and negative electrodes are both built into the facial attachment to complete the circuit.

The faradic current is an **interrupted** or **surged direct current**, that is, a direct current that is rapidly switched on and off. There is a 'stimulating' period

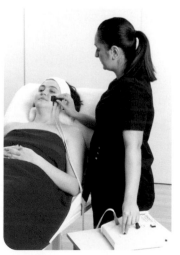

Figure 11.9 *Facial faradic treatment*

154

while the current flows and the muscle contracts and a 'rest' period when the current does not flow and the muscle relaxes. The contraction produced should resemble normal facial exercises.

Benefits of faradic treatment

* Tightens and firms muscles and improves facial contours.
* Stimulates an exhausted skin and improves colour.
* Delays the effects of ageing by increasing cellular regeneration.

Physiological effects of the current

* The sensory nerve endings in the skin are stimulated and the client will feel a pins and needles sensation.
* The muscle contracts when the motor point is stimulated.
* The circulation to the area is increased bringing nourishment.
* The contraction causes a pumping action on blood and lymph flow, which speeds up the elimination of waste.
* An erythema occurs in the area of the working electrode.

> To obtain a good contraction the electrode should be moistened with saline solution, applied to a grease-free skin, and positioned correctly over the motor point of the muscle (where the nerve enters the muscle).

Treatment time is usually about 15 minutes to exercise the facial muscles in a general toning routine. The number of contractions applied to each muscle will depend on the client's tolerance and the reaction of the muscles to treatment and as treatment progresses, the number of contractions may be increased.

For greatest effect the treatment should be given several times a week over a period of weeks and then reduced to a maintenance programme to suit the client's needs.

Faradic treatment can be incorporated into a facial after the cleanse to ensure the skin is grease free and before the massage which may be used to relax the client. A skin sensitivity test should be carried out before treatment.

> ## How to determine skin sensitivity
>
> To prevent any injury to facial muscles and ensure the sensory nerves are responding, you must carry out a skin sensitivity test before treatment. For this test clients are required to close their eyes while a sharp object (the end of an orange stick) and a soft object (piece of cotton wool) are placed randomly on the face and neck. If the client can differentiate between the two, then the individual has good sensitivity and treatment may proceed. If the client cannot, then treatment is contraindicated.

The most common method of treatment is to work on individual muscles, starting on the neck as this is the least sensitive area and the muscles are larger and respond well to stimulation. Clients should be in a fairly upright position for comfort and to allow the therapist to work with ease. The muscles worked should be those that have a lifting and firming action on the face. All the superficial muscles of facial expression may be exercised together by stimulating the seventh facial nerve. This can be activated in front of the ear where it enters the cheek. The branches of this nerve innervate different areas of the face and neck.

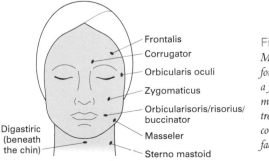

Frontalis
Corrugator
Orbicularis oculi
Zygomaticus
Orbicularisoris/risorius/buccinator
Masseler
Sterno mastoid
Digastiric (beneath the chin)

Figure 11.10
Motor point positions for pad placement in a facial electrical muscle stimulation treatment to produce contraction of the facial muscles

Safety precautions

* Before use, make all electrical checks.
* Make sure the client is comfortable.
* Carry out a skin sensitivity test.
* Use saline solution on the electrode to help current flow.
* Position electrode before turning on the current.
* Turn up intensity during the contraction.
* If it is necessary to reposition the electrode, turn down the intensity before moving the electrode.
* Avoid working the mouth area if there are a large number of metal fillings or braces as this may cause discomfort.
* Never turn the intensity beyond the client's tolerance, all contractions should resemble normal facial exercises.

Specific contraindications to faradic treatment

* Muscular disorders.
* Disorders of the nervous system.
* Highly strung, nervous client.
* Fatigue or tremor in the muscle.
* Lack of skin sensitivity.
* Epilepsy.
* Hypersensitive skin.

Galvanism

A galvanic current is a constant direct current, which may be used in facial treatment in two ways:

* **desincrustation** – to deep cleanse and remove oil and skin blockages
* **iontophoresis** – to introduce active water soluble substances into the skin for specific effects.

How galvanism works

The current, which flows through the skin, forms a circuit between the active and indifferent electrodes and the active substances pass into the epidermis on a galvanic charge. The active electrode can be either negative or positive. The active substances to be introduced into the skin are either negatively or positively charged.

Useful terms

An **active electrode** is a working electrode, which is applied to the face during treatment.

An **indifferent electrode** is a non-working electrode, which the client holds to complete the circuit.

A **milliamp meter** measures the amount of galvanic current being used and indicates the level of the skin's resistance.

An **anode** is the positive pole.

A **cathode** is the negative pole.

An **ion** is an atom carrying an electrical charge.

Ionisation is the use of active ions or electrically charged elements in treatments.

Anions are ions with a negative charge.

Cations are ions with a positive charge.

Anaphoresis is the movement of negative ions to the positive pole.

Cataphoresis is the movement of positive ions to the negative pole.

Saponification is 'soaping' or cleansing of the skin using a negative charge with saline solution or desincrustation fluid.

The polarity selected for the active electrode must be the same as the polarity indicated on the active substances to be used if they are to penetrate the epidermis, as 'like poles repel, opposite poles attract'.

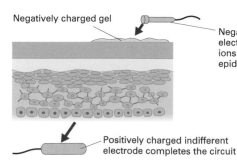

Negatively charged gel

Negatively charged active electrode repels negative ions in the gel into the epidermis

Positively charged indifferent electrode completes the circuit

Figure 11.11
Penetration of ions into the epidermis

Table 11.2 shows the effects on the skin of the chosen polarity.

Effects of positive pole	Effects of negative pole
Hardens the skin	Softens the skin
Closes the pores	Opens the pores
Decreases the circulation	Increases the circulation
Soothes the nerve endings	Stimulates the nerve endings
Produces an acid reaction	Produces an alkaline reaction
Fluid moves away	Fluid drawn towards

Table 11.2 *The effects on the skin of the chosen polarity*

The galvanic machine

The machine may be an independent piece of equipment or part of a combined unit. Its main features include:

* a pilot light
* an intensity control
* a polarity changer
* a milliamp meter
* a socket for the electrode.

As galvanic units operate from the mains, the alternating current is converted into the smooth direct current used for galvanism by the following devices contained within the machine:

* The transformer which reduces the voltage of the alternating mains current.

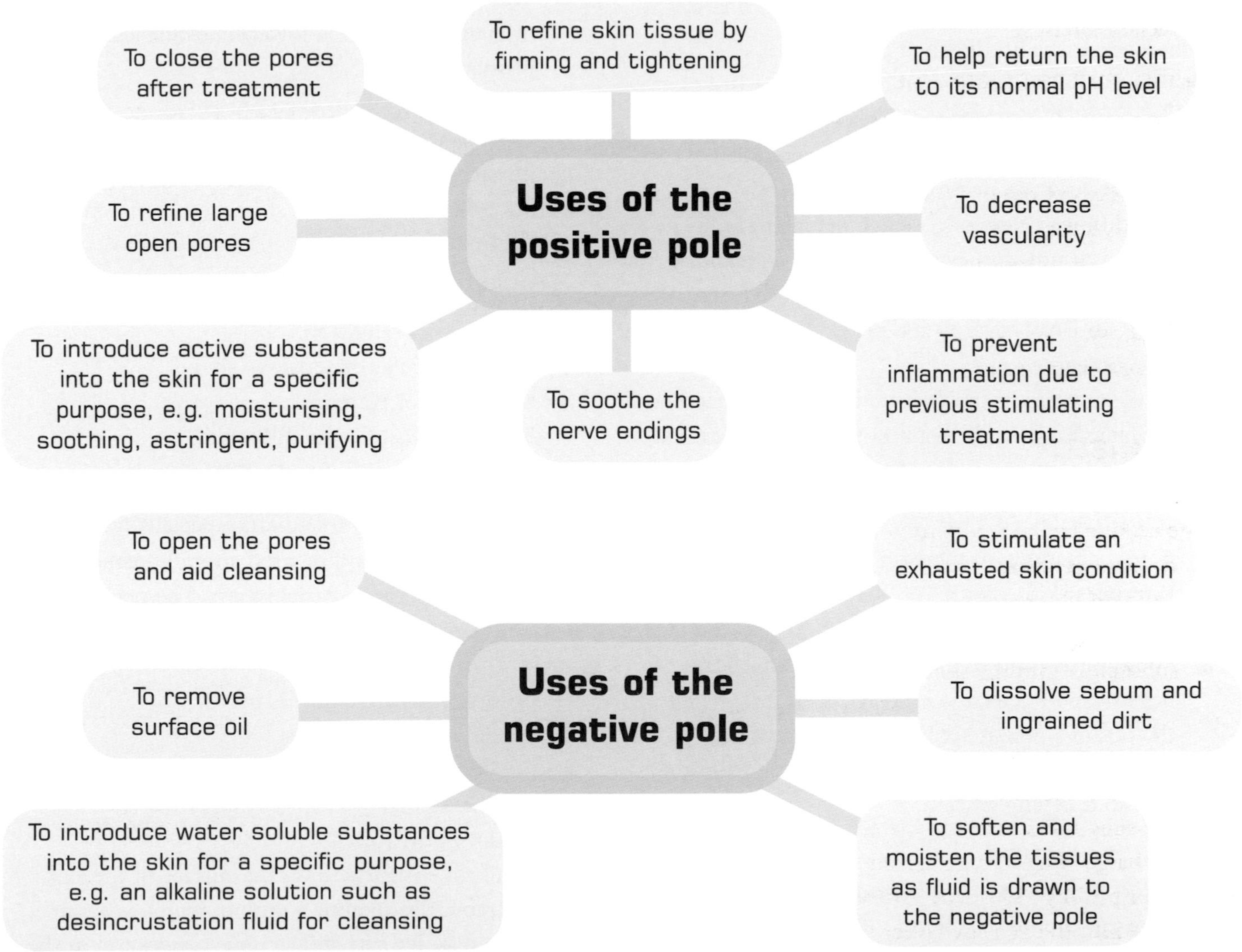

Uses of the positive pole

- To close the pores after treatment
- To refine skin tissue by firming and tightening
- To help return the skin to its normal pH level
- To refine large open pores
- To decrease vascularity
- To introduce active substances into the skin for a specific purpose, e.g. moisturising, soothing, astringent, purifying
- To soothe the nerve endings
- To prevent inflammation due to previous stimulating treatment

Uses of the negative pole

- To open the pores and aid cleansing
- To stimulate an exhausted skin condition
- To remove surface oil
- To dissolve sebum and ingrained dirt
- To introduce water soluble substances into the skin for a specific purpose, e.g. an alkaline solution such as desincrustation fluid for cleansing
- To soften and moisten the tissues as fluid is drawn to the negative pole

Figure 11.12 *Uses of the positive and negative poles*

* The rectifier which changes the alternating current to a direct current.
* The capacitor which smoothes out any irregularities in the direct current.

Modern machines are safe to use, but manufacturers' instructions must be followed and treatment time must not exceed ten minutes. In fact, six minutes is adequate time to carry out effective treatment.

The electrodes

The active or working electrode which introduces water soluble substances into the skin takes different forms:

* metal rollers
* metal ball electrodes
* tweezers
* rod with a round flat applicator head.

The tweezer electrode when used for desincrustation must be covered by 16 thicknesses of lint. The flat applicator must also be covered with lint, but it is not necessary to use more than one thickness as the surface area of the electrode is much larger.

The indifferent electrode, which the client holds to complete the circuit, comes in the form of a metal rod which must be covered with viscose sponge, or a small metal plate similarly covered and placed behind the client's shoulder.

Both electrodes are attached to the galvanic machine by leads. The skin must be kept moist during treatment to aid the flow of current.

General effects of the galvanic current

* Tonic as there is an increase in circulation.
* Improves skin colour.
* Relaxing as warmth is produced in the tissues.
* Soothing as fluid in the tissues is drawn to the negative pole (electro osmosis); therefore, when the positive pole is applied fluid is drawn away and waste products will be moved away from the area so relieving tension.

Safety precautions

* Check the client for contraindications.
* Remove client's jewellery.
* Make all electrical checks.

* Ensure that all wires are securely attached to the electrodes.
* Ensure all dials are at zero.
* Test the client for skin sensitivity.
* When lint is used make sure it is folded without any creases to prevent concentration of the current.
* Lint must be evenly damp and not dripping wet.
* Always warn clients that they may feel a slight tingling sensation and experience a metallic taste in their mouth, particularly if they have a lot of metal fillings.
* The area to be treated must be clean and grease free.
* Turn up the current slowly and watch the milliamp meter for a lowering of the skin's resistance.
* Always apply a firm even pressure.
* Do not overtreat for too long or at too high an intensity.
* Turn down the current slowly on completion of treatment.

Specific contraindications to galvanism

* Lack of skin sensation.
* Highly vascular or sensitive skin.
* Metal pins or plates.
* Braces or lots of metal fillings.

Desincrustation

This is a deep cleansing treatment especially for oily congested skins. It would be used after cleansing and if appropriate after a gentle facial steam. The negative pole is used and a negatively charged alkaline gel is applied to the skin.

Because the negative pole is used:

* the circulation increases
* the skin is softened
* the pores open
* sebum in the follicles liquefy
* an alkaline is formed on the surface of the skin.

In addition, the alkaline solution, which is applied, will help to dissolve dirt and remove congestion in the skin.

The electrode must be moved over the face in small circular movements and the skin should remain evenly moist throughout the treatment. Depending on the area to be treated, timing should be between three and five minutes, which is normally sufficient for the effects of the pole to work and the active substances to penetrate the epidermis. For a small area such as the centre panel, the treatment should take about three minutes and the whole face should take approximately five minutes.

The desincrustation fluid must then be thoroughly removed after lowering the current and switching off the machine. Some manufacturers recommend the use of a cleanser to ensure complete removal of the fluid and then wiping over the skin with the appropriate toning lotion.

The polarity of the machine should then be reversed to positive to neutralise the effects of the negative pole, which are stimulating, and the new lint should be evenly soaked in an astringent before applying to the face for half the length of time that the desincrustation was performed.

This treatment would actually stimulate the sebaceous glands and produce more sebum if performed too often, so the treatment should not be repeated within two weeks.

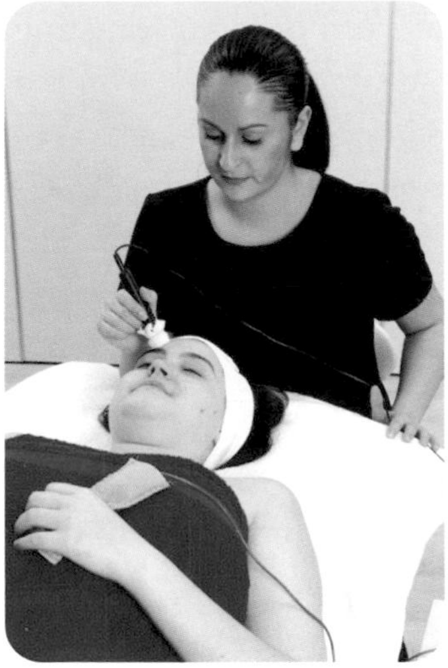

Figure 11.13 *Desincrustation*

Iontophoresis

This treatment is used to pass active substances through the skin on a galvanic charge. It is normally carried out at the end of a facial and the active elements stay in the skin and continue working after treatment. The introduction of active substances into the skin by iontophoresis is quicker and more intensive in effect and results in deeper penetration than by manual applications. The skin also benefits from the effects of the pole used, which in most cases, unless indicated by the manufacturer, is the positive pole.

The active substances are gradually absorbed into the bloodstream through interchange of blood and tissue fluids. It is not necessary for a galvanic current of high intensity to be used to pass active substances into the skin. All that is necessary are:

* an uninterrupted flow of current
* the electrodes should be in good contact
* the skin should be evenly moist.

The skin should be thoroughly cleansed and a massage performed, possibly with a cream which complements the active substances used for iontophoresis.

For this treatment to work efficiently the creams applied to the face must be water soluble (oil in water) as a water in oil cream will leave an oily film on the skin preventing effective penetration of the active substances.

Treatment time should take approximately three to four minutes for one part of the face or six minutes for the whole of the face and neck. Little time is needed to allow full penetration of the products into the skin. Sensitive skin may require even less time, or to set the machine at the lowest possible intensity, to avoid irritation of the skin.

The polarity used to introduce these substances into the skin should be the same as that indicated by the manufacturer. Normally, the positive pole is used as the products used for iontophoresis are positively charged.

Polarity is normally indicated clearly on the product itself or on the container pack. In the case of a product labelled positive and negative, always begin on negative and reverse the polarity to positive.

The skin should be left free from make-up after iontophoresis in order to gain maximum benefit from treatment.

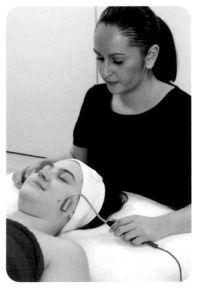

Figure 11.14 *Iontophoresis*

Microcurrent or MENS

Microcurrent Electrical Neuromuscular Stimulation (MENS) is often described as 'anti-ageing' as it helps to rejuvenate and recontour the client's facial muscles. There are many different makes of microcurrent machines all using similar currents and wave forms, but they are different in design with their own distinguishing features and different methods and procedures.

The origins of this treatment are medical with physiotherapists using the current to stimulate soft tissue and muscle damage from injury or illness, for example torn ligaments and Bells palsy. The effects of the MENS used in healing have been well documented, with the recovery of the facial profile improving dramatically in six to twelve weeks in Bells palsy sufferers. Athletes who were treated with the MENS current have recovered from ruptured ligaments and tendons in six months instead of the usual eighteen.

This success led a pioneering doctor to apply the current cosmetically to:

✱ correct sagging muscles
✱ rejuvenate skin tissue
✱ refine fine lines and wrinkles.

The treatment works by using a low frequency microcurrent, which is a thousand times smaller than the current used in other electrotherapy equipment. This current stimulates the golgi tendon organ which is present in every muscle in the body.

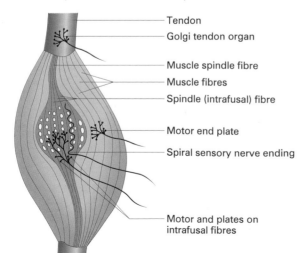

Tendon
Golgi tendon organ

Muscle spindle fibre
Muscle fibres
Spindle (intrafusal) fibre

Motor end plate

Spiral sensory nerve ending

Motor and plates on intrafusal fibres

Figure 11.15 *A golgi tendon organ*

The golgi tendon organ

The golgi tendon organ is a sense organ located near the end of a muscle and adjoining tendon. It is responsible for keeping a muscle toned and healthy, acting as a safety mechanism to prevent excessive contraction of the muscle. If tension on a muscle and its tendon is excessive, this sense organ responds by initiating an inhibitory response which relaxes the muscle. This protects muscles and tendons against breakage and rupture. Together with the muscle spindle fibres the golgi tendon organ is responsible for muscle tone and the control of body posture.

Microcurrent is completely safe, pleasant, relaxing and gently stimulating to the area being treated. It will imitate the body's own bio-electrical impulses to stimulate the regenerative processes of the skin and muscle and there is little, if any, sensation experienced by the client. It is suitable for all ages, as the treatment is as much preventative as it is corrective. It enhances existing features and defines facial and body contours.

Effects of microcurrent treatment

✱ Speeds up the circulation, increasing oxygen and nourishment to the area.
✱ Speeds up lymphatic flow, draining away toxins leaving the skin fresher, clearer and smoother in texture.
✱ Speeds up mitotic activity improving cellular regeneration.
✱ Speeds up collagen production by increasing the activity of the fibroblasts that produce collagen.
✱ Increases ATP, a chemical found in the body which provides energy. This helps to activate and rejuvenate the skin and muscles, increasing a sense of well-being.
✱ Refines deep lines and wrinkles making them less evident.

* Reduces a double chin.
* Re-educates muscle tone, shortening muscle fibres when slack.
* Lifts the eyebrows and overhanging lids.
* Lifts the corners of the mouth.
* Revives the skin's ability to hold water.

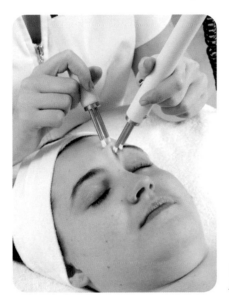

Figure 11.16
Microcurrent treatment

Specific contraindications to microcurrent treatment

* Clients with a pacemaker.
* Epilepsy.
* Pregnancy
* Sunburn.
* Pustular acne.
* New scar tissue or recent operation.
* Recent Botox injections.
* Recent collagen treatment.
* Facial implants, metal screws or prosthesis.
* Cancer.
* When muscle relaxants have been prescribed.

When to use electrical equipment

Once you have learned to analyse the skin correctly and understand the uses of all available electrical equipment, you should instinctively know when to use the equipment at the most appropriate time during the facial routine. The following is a guide:

* Steaming, brush cleansing, desincrustation, vacuum suction are all treatments that reinforce the general cleansing of the skin and prepare it for further treatment. They will be used, therefore, after the deep cleanse. The skin must be totally clean and grease free before application.
* Electrical muscle stimulation may be uncomfortable for the client so it should be incorporated just before the facial massage. The treatment responds more readily to warm relaxed muscles, so it can be beneficial to steam the face first.
* Indirect high frequency is always performed with the facial massage. The use of the current combined with manual massage increases the warmth of the skin tissues by stimulating circulation. The effect also helps the skin to absorb the nourishing products being used.
* Direct high frequency has a bactericidal effect on the skin, so it is advisable to use it after all the other treatments have been carried out. The skin will gain maximum benefit if nothing is applied after the high frequency.
* Iontophoresis is a nourishing treatment and the effects of the pole are all soothing, so this treatment should complete the facial routine. The client should also be advised not to wear make-up for at least eight hours after treatment.
* High frequency and galvanism are often combined in one facial as they complement each other very well to provide a specialised facial, often referred to as the 'queen' of facials.
* Microcurrent treatment often incorporates a complete facial treatment, so it is important to follow the manufacturer's instructions.

The electrical treatments you provide will help to improve the client's skin condition. However, it is important that the client also follows your home care advice to reinforce the beneficial effects of salon treatments. Table 11.3 shows some real examples of skin conditions that have improved greatly with the treatments and advice suggested.

Condition/problem	Suggested treatment and home care advice
Janet is 15 years old. Her skin is oily and she has congestion in the chin area and pustules on the forehead. She has a fringe and her hair is very greasy.	Desincrustation to unblock and decongest the skin and control oil production Direct high frequency to cleanse and dry the skin Use of glycolic acid skin care to improve skin texture and use SPF15 to protect the skin Eat a healthy balanced diet
Mrs McMorrow is 52 years old. She has a pale complexion with a few broken capillaries on her cheeks, her skin is dehydrated and dull, she smokes heavily and has vertical lines around the mouth.	Indirect high frequency to provide hydration and gently decongest the areas of broken capillaries Massage cream specially made from a mixture of aloe vera to soothe, horse chestnut to decongest and carrot to add oil Facial faradic to improve muscle tone particularly around the mouth area Use of glycolic acid skin care and glycolic acid peel every month. SPF30 to protect the skin
Mrs Macaulay has recently had her third baby. She is very tired and has tension in her shoulders, her skin has become very dry and she has an outbreak of pustules around her mouth.	Facial massage with essential oils to relax and hydrate the skin Iontophoresis using products to purify the skin and rehydrate Eat plenty of energy giving foods and foods rich in essential fatty acids, and drink two litres of water a day to rehydrate the body and increase energy
Mrs Bennett is worried about the signs of ageing on her face. She has lines under her eyes, overhanging eyelids and a sagging jaw line. Her skin is dull looking and she complains of fluid retention under the eyes.	A course of microcurrent treatment to counteract the signs of ageing Facial vacuum suction to improve lymphatic flow and reduce fluid under the eyes Iontophoresis to rehydrate the skin
Isabelle is six months pregnant. She is tired and is suffering regular outbreaks of spots down her centre panel but has very dry patches over the cheeks	Manual facial massage for relaxation and hydration Vacuum suction to stimulate lymph flow and deep cleanse and decongest the centre panel

Table 11.3 *Suggested treatment and home care advice for various skin conditions*

The key to effective treatment is to provide a thorough consultation, a detailed skin analysis, devise an appropriate treatment plan and offer the home care and lifestyle advice that will reinforce the beneficial effects of the salon treatment.

New developments

A treatment called BioSkinJetting has recently been introduced into the UK market. It is a 'biological method' of correcting wrinkles and scars, based on the skin's own regenerative capacity. The treatment stimulates the skin to produce new collagen and fill up the wrinkle or scar. The manufacturer claims that fine wrinkles disappear and deep wrinkles become less visible.

The treatment begins with the application of an anaesthetic cream to make the skin less sensitive, then a special technique is used to separate the wrinkle from the underlying skin using a fine needle. This stimulates the skin immediately below the wrinkle speeding up cell division and new tissue formation. It also increases collagen fibres, which has a cushioning effect, lifting the wrinkle. Blood circulation is increased bringing extra oxygen to the skin cells improving cellular regeneration. A reaction to treatment is the formation of fine red lines, which will disappear within a few days but it is possible to cover these red lines up with a camouflage cover cream immediately after the treatment. For lasting results the company advises the client to have five treatments. How long the results last will depend on lifestyle, skin care and hereditary factors.

Lasers and pulsed light equipment

These treatments are becoming increasingly popular, particularly for their skin rejuvenation effects.

There are many types of laser but all have the ability to produce a very particular type of light energy. The light is highly concentrated with a beam that is capable of travelling in a narrow and precise straight line over enormous distances. The laser, however, is very versatile because of its ability to produce these beams in different concentrations of frequency and intensity.

Depending upon the effects and intensity of energy required, any part of the light spectrum can be used, from the blue-green high intensity beam of the argon laser, to the invisible white and red cool beams of the gallium arsenide and helium neon lasers. The former is used in medicine to cauterise blood vessels responsible for producing a bleeding stomach ulcer, for example. The latter is used in many beauty salons to rejuvenate the skin, smooth wrinkles, firm sagging facial muscles and reduce stretch marks.

Those used for medical and dermatological reasons can be hot or cold, some with deep penetration and others which bathe the surface of the skin with a gentle light. The four main types used in clinics and hospitals are described below.

The argon laser

This produces a blue-green light and causes a reaction in red objects only. It is used in the treatment of port wine stains and dilated blood vessels under the skin leaving the area lighter in colour. The blue-green beam can be passed through the clear cornea, lens and vitreous humor of the eye without causing any damage, but it is absorbed by the pigmented retina allowing eye surgeons to treat detached retinas in less than two milliseconds.

The ruby laser

This has a pure red light and is absorbed by tissues which contain pigment, leading to its use in destroying melanomas and also to remove port wine stains.

The carbon dioxide (CO_2) laser

This can be finely tuned to produce either a powerful beam capable of penetrating almost anything in its path or a low-powered beam that merely pricks the surface of the skin. The low-powered version is used to remove tattoos, warts and skin tags. This beam is invisible so helium is incorporated into the laser tube to produce a red beam that will guide the operator.

The helium neon (cold beam) laser

This is the laser used by beauty therapists because it has a very gentle beam of low wattage which will not burn or vaporise tissue. The light excites the cells on which it is directed, thus stimulating them electrically and bio-chemically, minimising fine lines, stimulating muscles and improving the skin tone.

How the laser works in facial treatment

A mixture of gases, usually helium and neon, are placed in a tube through which a light source, which has been energised by an alternating current, is passed. The light rays then bombard the molecules of gas, further radiation is produced and added to the existing light producing an intense beam of light. This laser beam is passed through a fibre-optic cable to an applicator head which is then placed over the facial acupuncture points one at a time. Circulation to the whole face is increased.

Effects of laser treatment

Heat is transferred to the skin tissues and has a soothing effect. The blood supply is stimulated which encourages the acceleration of tissue repair, so improving skin texture. An increase in cell activity helps the synthesis of collagen and elastin improving elasticity. The combined effects reduce lines, improve muscle tone and enhance the appearance of sun-damaged or photo-aged skin (hyperpigmentation caused by the sun) and revitalise and brighten a sallow or dull complexion.

For maximum effect a course of 10–15 treatments is recommended. Each treatment should last for no more than 25 minutes.

Caution!

Your salon must register with the National Care Standards Commission (NCSC) if it uses laser or pulsed light equipment. (See Glossary of professional associations and organisations at the end of this book for further information.)

Precautions

* Laser therapy should always be applied in an enclosed area.
* Any equipment in the immediate vicinity with a reflective surface should be removed or covered.
* A permanent sign should be placed on the door of the treatment room to advise that a laser is in operation.
* Clients should not be left alone with the equipment.
* Special matte-black goggles supplied with the laser must be worn by the client at all times during treatment. No other goggles will do because those provided have been specially treated to prevent exposure to the beam.
* Glasses are also supplied for the operator and must be worn during treatment.
* Eye contact with the beam must be avoided at all times.
* Use of the laser machine must be restricted to those specially trained in its use.
* All staff must be aware of the dangers of laser equipment and to avoid any interruption during laser treatment.
* Equipment must be locked away when not in use to prevent unauthorised use.
* A record of treatment must be kept for each client.

Contraindications to laser treatment

* Infectious skin disorders.
* Infectious eye disorders.
* Heart or blood pressure problems.
* During pregnancy.
* On the thyroid area.

12 Make-up

Most facial treatments carried out in a salon require that make-up should not be worn for several hours or more afterwards to allow the skin to benefit from the effects of the treatment. The separate application of make-up, therefore, is a service offered in all salons and make-up lessons have proved to be a very popular addition to the list of salon treatments.

A make-up service may be required:

* for a bride on her wedding day
* to camouflage a birthmark, scar or other imperfection
* to provide a make-up lesson
* for photographic make-up
* for evening make-up
* for demonstrations.

Make-up equipment

To offer a make-up service therapists will need:

* a large mirror
* lighting above and on the sides of the mirror
* a comfortable and adjustable chair
* an attractive and well-stocked make-up display
* a set of make-up brushes
* six cosmetic sponges
* tissues
* cotton wool
* tweezers
* headband
* make-up palette.

Make-up brushes

Brushes made from natural hair are the most attractive and they last much longer, maintain their shape better and provide easier application than synthetic varieties. The most commonly used brushes are sable, pony, squirrel and goat. They come individually or as sets and are usually presented in a wallet or pouch with compartments for each brush. This will protect the brushes and keep them clean if they are being carried around, but when in constant use an upright container is more convenient to use.

Types of brushes

The **powder brush** is the largest brush in the set. Very full and round in shape, it is used for the application and removal of loose powder.

The **blusher brush** is half the size or less of the powder brush and slightly flatter in shape. It is more flexible, allowing the therapist to apply the blusher evenly and in the correct position.

The **contour brush** is similar in shape to the blusher brush, but the end is straight. It is used for shaping the face and blending the blushers and shaders.

The **eyeliner brush** is the smallest brush with a fine tapered end. It is made from natural hair such as sable so that it holds the point well, allowing the finest of lines to be drawn around the eye.

The **concealer brush** is shaped like a very small flat paintbrush. It is useful when concealing blemishes or areas of pigmentation and blending eyeliners to soften the line.

The **angled eyeshadow brush** is similar in shape to the concealer brush but with the tip cut off at an angle. This is to allow the greatest control over the placement of eyeshadow on the lids and in the socket area.

The **eyeshadow brush** is a tiny version of the blusher brush and is most useful for blending eyeshadows or allowing a very light application of colour.

The **eyeshadow sponge** gives more coverage and depth of colour and is ideal for blending and applying the eyeshadow more cleanly than a brush, which if very soft sometimes flicks the eyeshadow on the surrounding area.

The **eyebrow brush** looks like a very thin toothbrush and is used to remove any trace of powder in the eyebrows, as well as brushing them into shape.

The **lipstick brush** is a small, flat, fairly stiff brush with a straight edge. It is used to outline the lips or correct their shape, as well as applying the colour for a lasting effect.

Figure 12.1
Make-up brush set

Care of make-up brushes

They must be washed regularly in a mild detergent or in alcohol if they are made from natural hair. To dry they should be laid flat and if possible left with the air circulating around them.

Other make-up items required

In addition to brushes, therapists need the following essential items:

* cosmetic sponges for applying foundation and other cream products
* tissues for protecting the face when applying eye make-up and lipstick
* a make-up palette to mix and blend colours, e.g. foundations and lipsticks
* tweezers to remove any stray eyebrow hairs which would spoil the eyeshadow application
* a pencil sharpener, preferably a special one used for make-up, and pencils that are very soft and quite often larger or smaller in size then a normal pencil.

Reasons for use of make-up

* It provides protection from the environment. Worn in cold weather, it is a barrier which will help prevent loss of moisture. In the summer there are products which provide protection against the harmful effects of ultraviolet (UV) light as many foundations now contain a sun protection factor (SPF) of 15.

* Make-up highlights good features and masks imperfections.
* Birthmarks, tattoos or other pigmentary disorders can be camouflaged with skilfully applied make-up.
* In certain cases, it can be used to improve looks.
* Different colours and styles may be used to change an image.
* Make-up changes with each season so it may be used to make a fashion statement.
* For special occasions, when something a little out of the ordinary is required.

Selection of make-up

No two make-ups are ever the same – each one is personal to the individual, so before selecting make-up you will need to consider a number of points, as shown in Figure 12.2.

Decisions may then be made about the type of make-up to be used, the amount of corrective work to be undertaken and the colours to be applied.

Everything should be placed close to hand and stored neatly with each item easily accessible, preferably in a special make-up box, which has adequate sized compartments.

Application of make-up

The skin must be thoroughly cleansed and toned before applying moisturiser. It should then be rested for about

Figure 12.2 *Points to consider when selecting make-up*

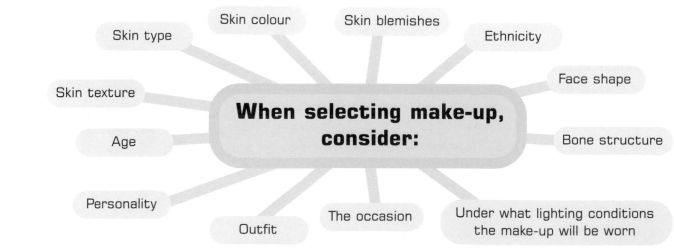

Skin type · Skin colour · Skin blemishes · Ethnicity · Face shape · Skin texture · Bone structure · Age · **When selecting make-up, consider:** · Personality · Outfit · The occasion · Under what lighting conditions the make-up will be worn

five minutes to allow the skin to absorb the moisturiser and then the excess blotted with a tissue. When foundation is applied immediately over moisturiser some of it will be absorbed into the skin and may cause a blotchy effect.

Order of work

1 **Colour correction.** The products for this are similar in texture to a moisturiser and come in two shades:
   * green – to tone down a highly coloured area caused by sensitivity or dilated capillaries
   * purple – to brighten a sallow skin.

2 **Concealer.** To cover blemishes or areas of uneven pigmentation often found around the eyes and lips and any other shadows on the face.

3 **Foundation**. To even out skin texture and colour and to provide a base for the rest of the make-up.

4 **Cream or gel blushers and shaders.** Cream products must always be applied before any powder product is used.

5 **Cream eye make-up.**

7 **Loose powder.** To set the make-up already applied and to provide an ideal base for the powder products still to be used.

8 **Powder blushers and shaders, powder eyeshadows.**

9 **Mascara.**

10 **Eyebrow pencil.**

11 **Lip pencil, lipstick and or lip gloss.**

Make-up products

Concealer

This is often an essential item required for covering imperfections. It is important to choose the right shade, texture and formulation for a natural look. When concealing a spot the aim is to find a concealer that will

hide it, dry it out and stay in place. A good product combined with a good application technique will ensure the flaw does not look worse after application than before.

Some concealers are more than just camouflage. They contain ingredients that help to heal blemishes such as salicyclic acid, make the concealer waterproof or provide a sun filter. They are now available in different shades to match skin tone. Choose an orange shade for ethnic and black skin tones to lift and disguise darker areas, yellow shades to counteract purple or blue circles. They are also made in a variety of formulations:

* Stick or pot concealers offer the greatest coverage because they are thicker and contain more pigment. Always use sparingly.
* Tubes, wands and pens are less opaque, lighter in texture and easier to blend, which makes them more suitable for clients who do not wear very much make-up or just a tinted moisturiser.

When choosing a concealer, apply it along the jaw line and look at it in natural light to make sure that it is a good match for the skin tone. Concealer may be applied in several ways:

* Wedge-shaped sponges may be used to evenly conceal dark under-eye circles. Too much concealer can make the skin look crepey and it is best to use a creamy formula that is not too matt to cake on dry skin and not too greasy to slide off the skin. Using a moisturiser first will make application easier and prevents the concealer settling in the fine lines around the eyes.
* A cotton bud or washable applicator is more hygienic than using fingers and both are ideal for applying over a tiny blemish or spot.
* A small firm bristled brush is ideal for camouflaging small scars and thread veins.
* Set the concealer with a yellow-based pressed powder as pink tones emphasise redness and this will also guarantee a longer lasting cover.

Foundation

The main purpose of foundation is to even out the skin's texture and colour and to cover minor imperfections. Foundations have different characteristics such as pore reducing, light reflecting, moisturising or providing a matte finish. In addition to concealing, foundations may add radiance to the skin, brighten the complexion, moisturise, medicate, balance or even protect from UV if they contain a SPF. Today, the colour range is extensive, from flat white to the deepest mahogany, but colour should always match the skin tone. Foundations come in several forms as described below.

Liquids

These provide only a light protective film as they have a high percentage of water and a low percentage of oil. Because of the low percentage of oil, they are suitable for a greasy skin but not a blemished skin, as they do not provide adequate cover.

Gels

These are essentially liquids with special gelling agents added. The purpose of a gel foundation is to give a natural tanned look to the skin and they are most effective on a clear skin.

Creams

These are thicker and heavier with a higher oil content, which makes them more suitable for a drier skin type. They are usually waterproof and give extra protection to dry skins, particularly in the winter. For mature skins choose a light reflecting formula containing tiny light reflecting particles which give the illusion of smoothness and even out the appearance of lines and wrinkles.

Cream mousse

These are suitable for most skin types and are very popular because they are light in texture and give a good cover without feeling heavy on the face. They normally come in an aerosol or pump dispenser.

All-in-one foundation

These are made from a mixture of cream and powder and require a damp sponge for application because they can be difficult to apply. They are not suitable, therefore, on a dry or sensitive skin.

Block foundation

These consist of an emulsion of fats and waxes in water with plasticising agents and pigments compressed into a solid cake form. They provide excellent cover for a discoloured or blemished skin, but they can dry it out and are not suitable to use on a dry skin.

Figure 12.3
Applying foundation

To apply any foundation successfully, a damp sponge should be used to give a natural look and to help blend it in around the hairline. A dry sponge will give a heavier coverage when this is required. Foundation should also be applied to the eyes and lips to provide a base for longer lasting eyeshadow and lipstick. If, however, the foundation feels too heavy on the eyelids, a special eyeshadow base may be used to prevent creasing of the eyeshadow during the day.

The make-up expert Bobbi Brown says: 'The right foundation should not be heavy or artificial. It should in fact be so perfectly matched to your skin tone and texture that it disappears. You see not make-up but smooth flawless skin.'

Contour cosmetics

These cosmetics are used to accentuate and enhance good features or to minimise not-so-good features! They include:

* **shaders** that are darker than the foundation and are used to shape the face or diminish prominent features
* **highlighters** that are lighter than the foundation and are used to accentuate good features
* **blushers** which add warmth and shape to the cheeks and balance out the eyes and lips never overpowering the other features.

As with foundation, contour cosmetics are available in several forms:

* **creams** that will add moisture as well as colour and are used over the foundation but before the face powder
* **powders** that are always applied after the face powder
* **gels** that are transparent for a natural look, applied over foundation but never covered with face powder
* **sticks** which are solid creams and are applied over foundation but need to be well blended.

Remember!

* Light colours will highlight a feature.
* Dark colours recede or fade out.
* Bright colours attract attention.
* Always blend blushers upwards and outwards and never apply too near the eyes or nose.
* Never overdo the use of contour products as the effect should be natural for normal use.

Shaders

Common areas for correction with shaders are:

* all face shapes
* a square jaw line
* a double chin
* a wide, crooked or long nose
* below the cheekbone to create a hollow.

Highlighters

Highlighters can erase deep lines such as the naso labial folds. Used above the cheekbones, a highlighter will emphasise good bone structure and used on the eyes, it will highlight and draw attention to them.

Blushers

Blusher gives the face a healthy glow if applied correctly. It draws attention to the eyes and emphasises good bone structure. For those with colour already in the cheeks, blusher evens out the natural skin tones.

A good selection of colours should be available. Blusher can be matched up to clothes and make-up and not just the skin tone. The finish on a blusher can be matt (suitable for day wear) or iridescent (suitable for evening make-up).

Blushers come in the same forms as foundation: powder, cream, gel, liquid and mousse.

The same principle applies when applying the blusher. Creams, liquids and gels are applied before the face powder and the powder blusher is applied afterwards.

Figure 12.4
Applying blusher

Face powder

Face powder is essential to help set the make-up, keeping it fresh looking all day and providing a surface suitable for powder blushers and shaders, which if placed directly on to foundation would go streaky. It also removes the shiny appearance leaving a matt finish and a smooth complexion.

Probably the best powder to use is a translucent one. Translucent powder is always used by make-up artists because it is semi-transparent and allows the light to shine through. Sometimes even translucent causes a chalky look on the skin. To counteract this, apply a small amount of yellow powder. Coloured powder tends to give the face an unnatural or heavily made-up look and often it changes colour when oils are absorbed from the skin.

Face powder comes in two forms:

* loose
* pressed.

Loose powder

Loose powder usually comes in a large container with a removable lid. There are also smaller containers, rather like talcum powder shakers, that enable the therapist to

dispense the face powder more economically. For professional use, the larger container if used economically and hygienically is more appropriate and the smaller shaker is suitable to be carried around without fear of spillage.

Figure 12.5
Applying face powder

Pressed powder

This is the traditional face powder, which comes in a compact with a powder puff and is carried in a handbag or pocket. It may be used to touch up make-up or remove shine during the day. This type of powder has its drawbacks. The powder puff needs to be washed frequently because the oils from the face will be transferred on to the pressed powder after each use causing the surface of the powder to harden. Bacteria may also be transferred to the powder, so it is advisable to use small disposable cotton wool pads to apply the powder and then discard them for a fresh one.

Matt powder is ideal for everyday use. For a special effect, iridescent powder with touches of silver or gold in it may be used for an evening make-up.

Bronzing powder is popular in the summer to provide a golden glow to the skin, but it should be used sparingly to prevent a blotchy finish.

Properties of face powder

The main constituent of powder is talc. Adding fine aluminium powder, guanine or mica coated with titanium dioxide produces the iridescent or glittery effect. Zinc oxide is incorporated to mask blemishes. Magnesium stearate determines the cling of the powder and the degree to which it is waterproof. Magnesium carbonate contributes to the smoothness of the powder and absorbs any perfume added.

Eyeshadow

The skilful use of eye make-up draws attention to one of the best facial features. It can enhance already beautiful eyes and it can make quite ordinary eyes look glamorous. Eyeshadow adds colour and dimension and comes in several forms:

* **Cream** – oil-based, it spreads easily and blends well, but it needs to be set with powder as it tends to crease.
* **Powders** – compressed powder with added moisture to provide cling. Its staying power is good, but it may feel taut on very dry skins.
* **Gels** – easy to apply but add gloss rather than depth of colour so may require several coats to obtain a good colour.
* **Water colours** – a cake eyeshadow applied with a wet brush to give a long lasting finish, with a depth of colour stronger than powder.
* **Crayons and pencils** – soft wax pencils, which are easy to apply without dragging but need to be blended well.

Figure 12.6
Applying eyeshadow

Eyeliner

Eyeliner is used for defining the eye shape and making the eyelashes look longer. There are many colours available in the form of a pencil to complement the colour of the eyeshadow, but a colour to match the natural hair colour may be preferred. Eyeliner may be applied in different ways:

* **Liquid** – oil-based in water and applied with a fine sable brush.
* **Cakes or blocks of water colour powder** – applied with a fine dampened brush; easier to control than the liquid.
* **Crayon or pencil** – a wax stick which is easier to use when kept sharp.

The thickness of the line can vary, but it should be placed close to the lashes and it can be softened with a brush, cotton tip or sponge to achieve the effect required. Special effects may be achieved by applying kohl to the rims of the upper and lower lids. Using white pencil on the inner rim will extend the whites of the eyes making them look larger.

Figure 12.7
Applying eyeliner

Eyebrow pencil

This is a wax crayon but of a harder consistency to define eyebrow shape and colour. Colours should always blend with the natural colour of the eyebrow and the hair colour. An eyebrow powder may be used instead if the effect of the pencil is too harsh.

Figure 12.8
Applying eyebrow pencil

False eyelashes

The application of false eyelashes is dictated by fashion, but the application of make-up will sometimes include using false eyelashes to enhance the finished result. False eyelashes may be used for a variety of reasons as shown in Figure 12.9.

There are two types of false eyelashes:

* semi-permanent individual lashes
* temporary strip lashes.

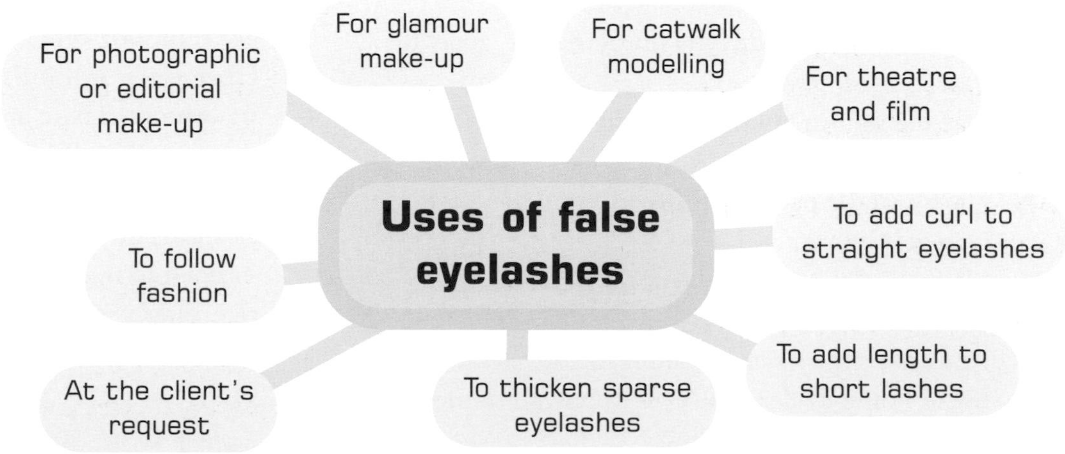

They are made from synthetic fibres that hold a permanent curl and they vary from very realistic lightweight lashes to very thick, dark, heavier lashes.

Semi-permanent individual lashes

For a more natural effect, it is best to choose individual lashes. They may be single or in groups of varying lengths and may be trimmed to suit the client. They are applied directly to the lashes using a semi-permanent glue to maintain their appearance, but they do have to be replaced as they fall off. They will become detached through rough handling, by using an oily eye make-up remover or they will fall out when the natural lash to which they are attached falls out. Because the glue is stronger than that used for strip lashes, great care must be taken with its application so that glue does not enter the eye.

Figure 12.10
Applying individual lashes

Uses of false eyelashes

- For photographic or editorial make-up
- For glamour make-up
- For catwalk modelling
- For theatre and film
- To add curl to straight eyelashes
- To add length to short lashes
- To thicken sparse eyelashes
- At the client's request
- To follow fashion

Figure 12.9 *Uses of false eyelashes*

Temporary strip lashes

Strip lashes will appear heavier than individual lashes and quite long, but some strips are fairly sparse or may be trimmed very effectively to make them look as natural as possible. To achieve a more natural effect, the length of strip can be trimmed, the lashes can be thinned out or reduced in length. Always trim the outside longer edge of the strip to fit the client's eye, never the inner corner or you will distort the natural shape. Strip lashes can add drama to the eyes for photographic, evening or editorial make-up by using colour, extra length or sparkle.

Figure 12.11
Applying strip lashes

Contraindications to false eyelashes

These include any eye disorder or allergic reaction to the adhesive used. A skin test must be performed 24 hours before application of the lashes. A small amount of adhesive should be applied in an unobtrusive spot and covered. Watch for a reaction. If there is an allergy to the glue, the skin may become red, itchy or inflamed.

Safety precautions

* Check client for contraindications.
* Carry out a patch test particularly if client has sensitive eyes.
* Sit client in a comfortable semi-reclining position.
* Remove all traces of eye make-up and grease.
* Use tweezers to hold the false lashes.
* Do not apply glue directly on to the eye, apply to the false lash first.
* Use the minimum amount of glue to apply the lashes.
* Have a sterile eye bath ready to bathe the eye if glue gets into it.
* Use a special eyelash solvent for removing the semi-permanent lashes.
* Recommend a special cleanser for the client to use at home to clean the eyes to prevent removing the semi-permanent lashes.

Mascara

The purpose of mascara is to colour, lengthen and thicken eyelashes. The qualities of an ideal mascara are shown in Figure 12.12.

Figure 12.12 *Qualities of an ideal mascara*

There are several different types of mascara on the market:

* The **block** or **cake mascara** is the oldest and most economical variety and is made from waxes and pigments. Although not as popular as the more convenient wand with a brush, it is still in use and has to be applied with a wet brush.
* The **cream mascara** is applied and removed easily but is not run proof or waterproof.
* The **automatic liquid mascara** is probably the most popular having most of the ideal qualities required from a mascara. It consists of pigments, water, or alcohol and water with an oil to soften for ease of use. It may also contain filaments to thicken and lengthen lashes. It is long lasting and, given the correct cleanser, is easy to remove. However, it is not always run proof and waterproof. There are some on the market with these qualities, but they are often resistant to cleansing and can be difficult to remove requiring a special eye make-up remover.

Figure 12.13
Applying mascara

Lipsticks

The skin on the lips is very thin and it lacks the oil and sweat glands that protect our skin causing a common problem – dry lips. The lips are made from the same mucous membrane as the mouth's lining. They are red-pink in colour because the membrane is quite transparent and allows the colour of the underlying blood capillaries to show through. The purpose of a lipstick is to add balance and colour to the face, but it also acts as a barrier between the lips and the sun, wind and cold providing protection.

Applying lip colour is the most effective way to alter a make-up 'look', as colour expresses personality and sense of style. Lipsticks come in several forms:

* A conventional stick which provides excellent coverage.
* A tube with a sponge applicator which provides a creamy and glossy finish.
* Crayons and pencils which are excellent for outlining the lips and providing a longer lasting matt colour. They also help to prevent lipstick from 'bleeding' on to the skin. They are made with harder wax and less oil than a lipstick. They are usually chosen to match the shade of lipstick or natural lip colour.
* Colour or gloss in a pot, which adds sheer colour to the lips or gloss over a lipstick. There are also many shades of lip gloss available to provide a sheer glossy covering in a favourite shade.

Lipsticks may be:

* **matte** – longer lasting but more drying than other formulations; gloss may be added to provide lustre

Figure 12.15 *Applying lipstick*

Figure 12.14 *Applying lip liner*

* **sheer** – provides a transparent stain on the lips for a natural look
* **glossy** – creates the illusion of fuller lips, provides glamour but comes off very easily
* **iridescent or frosted** – provides more drama and is useful for evening make-up.

There are many requirements for an ideal lipstick, which makes a good one hard to produce:

* It should be easy to apply providing an even coverage.
* It must adhere well to the lips.
* The colour should not change once applied.
* Its appearance should be attractive.
* It should feel and taste pleasant.
* The physical properties of the lipstick should not change.
* The texture should be firm but not brittle and it must not bend during use.

Problems with lipsticks

'Bleeding' of the lips

This occurs when the lipstick is applied and it spreads outwards causing an unsightly messy outline. This happens when:

* the formula is very creamy and glossy and even normal body temperature causes it to melt slightly
* fine vertical lines are present around the lips and they allow the lipstick to seep into them.

Applying foundation and powder to the lips and outlining them with a pencil before applying the lipstick or using a special fixative prior to lipstick application can rectify this problem.

The lipstick changes colour

This happens particularly with the darker shades and the blue tones in the lipstick are emphasised. To prevent this happening the lips can be prepared as detailed above with the foundation creating a barrier between the lips and the lipstick. Alternatively, a white cream fixative can be applied.

Lipstick dries the lips

The use of frosted shades or an overuse of fillers and binders in the ingredients usually causes this. Avoid using frosted shades and moisturise the lips well, particularly in the winter.

Making a lipstick

This is a two-stage process where all the ingredients are blended into a base and the mixture is then moulded into sticks. The ingredients consist of a mixture of fats, waxes and oils. The waxes encourage the lipstick to set and allow it to be formed into a stick. The more wax that is used, the harder the lipstick will be, but too much wax will make it difficult to apply. The oils moisturise, lubricate and soften the lips, but the balance must be right to prevent the lipstick from becoming too greasy.

The waxes most commonly used are **carnauba** from Brazilian palm trees, **gandelilla** from plants grown in Mexico and **beeswax**.

The oils most commonly used are **castor oil**, used in more expensive lipsticks, and **mineral oil**.

Other ingredients are then added to this base:

* **Emollients** for soothing and softening are added so that lipsticks can then be sold as 'lipcare' rather than just as a cosmetic product. These include almond oil, wheatgerm oil and more recently, a sun filter for protection against UV rays.
* **Colour** in the form of dyes and pigments which must be safe to use as they are being applied to the lips.

* **Pigments** are much more difficult to add to the base as they are insoluble and they have to be ground into a paste first. Because they add colour without actually dyeing the skin, they come off with the lipstick. Natural organic pigments are used to produce the bright shades of pink, red and orange. For a frosted finish, tiny particles coated with the light reflecting titanium dioxide are added.
* **Dyes** are used less frequently than pigments. They are soluble and therefore mix more easily with the base. They also give a longer lasting effect but are more likely to cause an allergic reaction.
* **Perfumes** are added to some lipsticks in the form of essential oils with light floral scents.

When the extra ingredients have been added to the base the mixture is heated and any air trapped in the mixture rises to the surface preventing the formation of unsightly bubbles. The finished product is then poured into stainless steel moulds to harden and then tested for consistency and texture before being packaged.

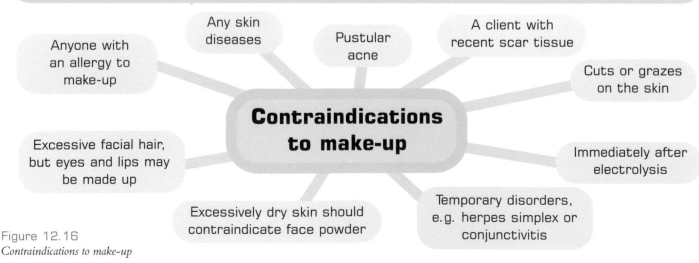

Figure 12.16
Contraindications to make-up

Corrective make-up

This is sometimes necessary to disguise prominent features or to cover blemishes on the skin.

Facial contouring is used for correcting face shapes and the principle of most corrective work is that dark colours recede and light colours accentuate.

Common faults

Florid complexion

This can be a general redness of the skin or an abundance of dilated arterioles. To counteract this problem, a green moisturiser may be applied to the area before applying a beige foundation.

Sallow complexion

This often accompanies a greasy skin or is a characteristic of certain ethnic skins. It can be improved and brightened by applying a purple-tinted moisturiser underneath the foundation.

Dark circles under the eyes

These may be successfully disguised by using a white masking cream sparingly over the darker areas or a lighter shade of foundation.

Puffy eyes

These cause a crease underneath the 'bags' (puffy tissue), which may be disguised by using a lighter shade of foundation in the crease. A darker shade of foundation should be applied to the puffy areas to diminish their size.

Protruding eyes

Dark shadow should be applied all over the lid and highlighter on the browbones.

Figure 12.17
Make-up correction for protruding eyes

Deep-set eyes

Use light coloured shadows all over the lid to accentuate the eyes and a slightly darker shade may be applied to the extreme outer corner blending upwards and outwards.

Figure 12.18
Make-up correction for deep-set eyes

Wide-apart eyes

To draw them together a darker shade of eyeshadow must be applied to the inner part of the eye and lighter shades used on the outer part.

Figure 12.19
Make-up correction for wide-set eyes

Close-set eyes

The eyes can look smaller because they are close together, so apply lots of highlighter to the inner corners next to the nose and then other colours applied upwards and outwards.

Figure 12.20
Make-up correction for close-set eyes

Nose shapes

* A **wide nose** will appear narrower if shader is applied to the sides.
* A **long nose** will appear shorter if shader is applied to the tip and highlighter to the sides.
* A **short nose** will appear longer if highlighter is applied down the centre to the tip.
* **Nasolabial folds** – deep creases which run from the nose down to the corners of the mouth. A lighter shade of foundation may be applied using a fine brush and then blended into the foundation to remove harsh lines.

Face shapes

Round face

The cheeks are full and rounded, so a darker shade of foundation could be applied to the outer edges of the lower half of the face to achieve a slimming effect, and highlight applied to the chin to increase the overall length.

Square face

This shape has a broad forehead with a square jaw line. Therefore, the sides of the forehead and the angles of the jaw should be shaded to soften the angular shape and the outer part of the cheekbone highlighted to emphasise the centre of the face.

Long face

The top half of the forehead and the chin should be shaded to reduce the length of the face and the cheeks should be highlighted to create width.

Heart-shaped face

This shape is wide at the forehead and narrows to a point at the chin. Width is needed at the cheeks and the jaw line and this may be achieved by applying blusher on the cheek area and highlighting underneath at the angle of the jaw. A small amount of shader may be applied to the point of the chin.

Diamond-shaped face

This face shape has a narrow forehead and chin with wide cheekbones. The width is increased at either side of the forehead and at the angles of the jaw by applying highlighter. The point of the chin can be shaded to reduce the length.

Pear-shaped face

This face shape has a narrow forehead and a wide jaw line. The forehead should be highlighted at either side to create width and the angle of the jaw can be diminished by using a small amount of shader.

Lip shapes

The problems which occur are as follows:

* Both lips are too thin.
* Either the upper or lower lip is too thin.
* Large full lips.
* Very small mouth.
* Drooping mouth.
* Asymmetrical mouth or one side smaller than the other.

■ Shader   ■ Highlighter   ■ Blusher

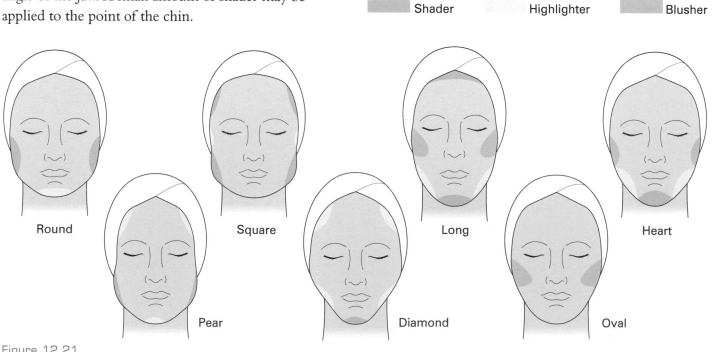

Round   Square   Long   Heart

Pear   Diamond   Oval

Figure 12.21
Correcting face shapes

Whatever the problem, it is advisable to block out the shape as much as possible with foundation and powder before applying the lipstick. Lip liners can then be used to draw in the correct shape, either just inside the natural lip line to reduce the size, or just outside the natural lip line to increase the size.

Highlighter may be applied in the cupid's bow to accentuate the lips, and gloss applied over the lipstick will also highlight the mouth.

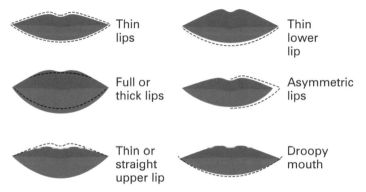

Thin lips

Thin lower lip

Full or thick lips

Asymmetric lips

Thin or straight upper lip

Droopy mouth

Figure 12.22 *Correcting lip shapes*

Clients who wear glasses

There are several problems which occur when clients wear glasses and they are caused by the type of lens used.

* For long sight, the lens will make the eye more prominent. To rectify this, use neutral shades and avoid bright or pearly type eyeshadows.
* For short sight, the lens will make the eye seem smaller. To rectify this, use light colours to accentuate the eyes.
* Tinted lenses will alter the colour and effect of the eye make-up, so this should be taken into consideration.

Frosted shadow and heavy foundation should be avoided as it creates a crepey appearance.

Make-up should be applied to suit the frames: smaller light-coloured frames will require less colour than larger brightly coloured frames.

For those clients who wear contact lenses, it is essential to avoid very greasy products that may cause blurring if they attach to the lens. Avoid mascara containing filaments that may irritate the eye if trapped under a lens. Take great care when applying powder products as these will feel gritty under a lens.

Mature make-up

As we age, we lose colour in our skin and hair, lines appear, the skin becomes drier and pigmentation may become uneven.

Always moisturise the skin well and allow the moisturiser to settle into the skin for about ten minutes and then reapply if necessary. Many companies recommend a product applied under the foundation to tighten and firm the skin and brighten a dull complexion.

Light reflecting foundation is ideal to deflect light away from the lined areas. Use lightweight hydrating foundations that are easily applied to reduce skin handling or stretching, but do not apply too much or the foundation may settle in the lines. Use powder sparingly as this may be drying to the skin and make it appear dull.

Cream blushers in soft shades of peach or coral will lighten the skin while providing definition to face shape.

Avoid shimmery eyeshadows and blushers as they make the skin look crepey and accentuate imperfections. If an eyeliner is used, blend it well as the line may appear harsh.

There may be fine vertical lines around the lips, so apply foundation and powder before outlining with a pencil to prevent lipstick bleeding. Bright lip colours such as red may be used with certain colouring such as white hair, but in general, softer shades are more flattering.

Figure 12.23 *Mature make-up*

Evening make-up

When applying make-up for the evening therapists have the opportunity to apply all their artistic talents to the full. The normal everyday make-up can be adapted as follows:

* Foundation can be lighter or darker than the normal skin colour and can be applied a little more heavily if required to create a flawless finish.
* Face powder can have added sparkle but must not be used all over the face, just along the cheekbones to highlight them.
* Contour cosmetics can be used with more definition, particularly under the cheekbones to create a hollow and emphasise bone structure.
* Eyeshadows can be very bright or very dark with lots of shine and glitter, using several shades blended together for maximum effect.
* Eyeliners can be used more boldly and kohl pencil applied to the inside of the eye in a colour to complement the eyeshadow. Mascara may be applied in the bright shades of green, blue or violet to match eyeshadows.
* False eyelashes can be applied either in strips or individually to make the natural lashes appear longer and thicker.
* Vivid shades of lipstick, with silver or gold frosting, applied to the lips in the centre will create a pouting effect, or a highlighter painted in a thin line above the cupid's bow emphasises the shape. Gloss may be used for a gleaming finish but too much may cause it to smear.

Figure 12.24
Evening make-up

Lighting

When applying an evening make-up a clear white light should be used. It is important to bear in mind the effects that different lighting will have on the make-up. Lighting varies from very dark with disco lighting to very dark and candlelit, or just different coloured lights.

* Pink light causes make-up colours to look warmer, so the deeper pink shades of blusher may look red. Therefore, use a slightly lighter pink or tawny shade which contains no red. Pink light will also dull green and blue eyeshadows, so if these colours are to be used, try the type with added sparkle or highlight the centre of the lid over the eyeshadow.
* Red light alters make-up colour drastically, particularly the yellow, gold and tawny hues which will look very much deeper. It also causes the blusher to fade away.
* Rose light is flattering to all skins and will enhance any make-up.
* Blue light turns make-up grey. It is a very hard colour and makes blusher or shaders look much deeper than they really are, so a lighter touch is advisable.

Ethnic skin types and make-up

There are several points to consider when making up an ethnic skin. The most important one is the number of different shades that there are. For example, black skin may include African, African-Caribbean and African-American skin types; East Asian skin may include Chinese and Japanese skin types; Indian Asian may include Indian, Sri Lankan and Pakistani skin types; the Middle East may include Egyptian and Saudi Arabian skin types, and so on. The shades and tone of skin varies from a pale brown to a deep ebony colour. The pigmentation on the face may also be different, often darker around the eyes and lighter on the forehead. The darker the skin is, the more melanin it contains and therefore the more protection it receives from UV radiation. This will delay the ageing effect that exposure to UV radiation has on the skin.

Black skin types are also much oilier as there are many more sebaceous glands present. However, they may still dry out when exposed to the environment and if not properly looked after, so it may also be a combination skin.

Ethnic features vary considerably. Chinese-type features may include a flatter rounder face, sometimes with a square jaw line, round cheek bones, small generous lips and brown eyes. The eyelid may be flatter with a large area and no deep socket and the skin has yellow undertones. Black skin-type features may include a defined bone structure, full lips, deep-set eyes, broad nose and the skin tone varies from pale brown to deep black brown.

Application of make-up

Black skin types

To begin with, a water-based moisturiser must be used to combat any oiliness and prepare the skin for further application.

There are now several ranges of make-up which have been developed for black skins and the colour range of foundations will suit most shades of skin. The consistency of the foundation is also important. Gels are ideal to enhance a good colour without too much cover. The foundations which provide cover contain products such as titanium dioxide which when applied to a very dark skin will have an ashy effect.

Face powder should be transparent and used very sparingly as it can dull the skin.

Blushers and shaders may be used in cream, gel or powder form and in shades strong enough to be seen such as deep bronze, cocoa and red browns that also tone well with the foundation, eyeshadows and lipstick.

Eyeshadows that are more intense in colour such as

bronze, mahogany and copper are better as paler colours can look washed out.

Lips are enhanced using deep shades such as burgundy, plum or deep berry colours.

Choice of colours should be selected in consultation

Figure 12.25
Black skin make-up

with clients to suit their age, the occasion, the clothing they will be wearing, and the therapist's advice.

Chinese-type skin

This skin type is often more sensitive than others, so use products that will not irritate. Whatever the depth of colour, there is always a yellow undertone, so use a foundation and powder with a yellow base.

Apply blushers that will lift the yellow undertone, such as soft plum, pink and berry shades.

The Chinese-type eye shape may be enhanced with the use of eyeliner and iridescent pale shades to lighten

or disguise if the client wishes by using darker shadows on the lid and slightly below the outside corner. Eyelashes are sometimes sparse and straight, so could be permed or curled using black mascara to define and lengthen.

Figure 12.26
Chinese-type make-up

Asian skin types

Asian skins tend to be smooth and poreless with yellow undertones. Mix a yellow base with the foundation closest to the client's skin tone. However, one of the problems with this skin type is uneven pigmentation, so you must take great care to use a concealer close to the skin tone.

Asian eyes suit definition. Line the top and bottom and smudge the colour to open up and draw attention to the eyes. Bold lip colours such as plums with brown, red or mauve undertones suit an Asian skin. Dusty pink or plum blusher will brighten the complexion.

Figure 12.27
Asian make-up

Bridal make-up

Bridal packages are very popular with young and old alike. It is an occasion when even those who do not normally have beauty treatments will consider such treatments as manicure, pedicure, eyelash tinting, waxing and make-up.

It is important to ensure the finished result is suitable for clients and they are happy with the make-up as there will be photographic and video evidence to mark the occasion. There are a number of things to consider when booking a bridal make-up:

* Discuss the requirements with the bride well in advance.
* The time and location of the appointment must be arranged to fit in with your other clients and the bride's wishes. It also allows the bride to have her appointment at home if she prefers.
* Consider the dress – colour, fabric and neckline – and if a headdress or veil will be worn. It may be necessary to use a self-tanning cream one or two days before the wedding if the neckline is low or cut out. Make-up colours should complement the dress and the bridal flowers, as well as enhancing the bride's best features.
* It is advisable to have a trial run before the wedding. Discuss how long the make-up is to last for, if it requires to be changed from day to evening. Any problems can be ironed out and changes made if necessary. This is most important if the client does not normally wear make-up or if she has requested something rather unusual which needs to be tried out first.
* Discuss the cost and include the trial run and additional charge for a home visit.
* Discuss any other make-up that may be required such as the bride's mother, bridesmaids or other relatives. Extra time or additional therapists may be required.

Ensure that the client has purchased any make-up required for freshening up during the day.

In general, choose colours, which suit the client's colouring and coordinate well with the overall colour scheme.

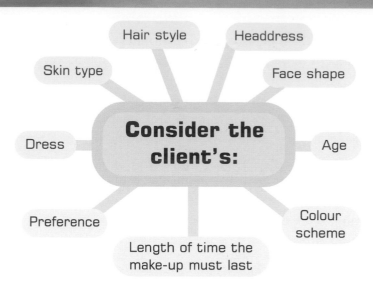

Figure 12.28 *Considerations for bridal make-up*

Use subtle shading techniques to highlight good features and detract from bad ones.

Use matt shades on the eyes and for the blusher. Pearly colours look hard and will reflect in photographs.

Apply lipstick, blot, then powder and re-apply for a longer lasting effect or apply a lip pencil in the same shade as the lipstick as the first coat and then cover with a coat of lipstick or gloss.

Powder should be applied lightly and then set with a fine mist of mineral water to set and prolong the make-up.

Use a waterproof mascara as the occasion can be very emotional for some brides.

For a very subtle effect, one shade of blusher can be used on the cheeks, on the eyes and on the lips, with a hint of gloss. This is a very natural effect ideal for the younger bride with a flawless complexion.

Figure 12.29
Bridal make-up

Semi-permanent make-up

This is a new treatment which is being offered by many salons to correct problems and enhance looks. The procedure is known as micro pigmentation and small amounts of natural pigment are placed into the skin using techniques that are more refined than tattooing and do not penetrate the skin as deeply.

The cosmetic procedures that are available are:

* lip liner
* full lip colour
* eyebrows
* eyelash enhancement
* eyeliner
* beauty spots.

The corrective procedures available are:

* areola restoration
* camouflage of scars, burns, cleft lip, alopecia and restoration of hairline after cosmetic surgery.

Semi-permanent make-up offers effective results for those people who do not want to or cannot apply make-up on a daily basis and it may be applied to the young or old. Micro pigmentation is a treatment which will benefit many people and for many reasons:

* Those people with a very busy lifestyle who would prefer not to spend time applying make-up.
* People who are allergic to conventional make-up.
* Some physical disabilities may prevent the application of make-up unless assistance is available.
* For the correction of asymmetrical features such as uneven lips.
* Partially sighted people who find it difficult to apply make-up.
* Those who wear glasses.
* Those who have an unsteady hand and wish to create a soft line around the eyes.
* Skin disorders such as uneven pigmentation or other flaws in the skin.
* To camouflage minor disfigurements.
* People who live in a hot climate.
* Sportspeople.

The treatment lasts between one and three years, depending on the client's skin type and age. The colour will fade gradually over that period of time.

A topical anaesthetic cream is usually applied before treatment to minimise discomfort, and the sensation the client feels should be no worse than that felt with electrolysis.

Precautions

* Specialist training is required in these procedures.
* Work must be carried out under sterile conditions.
* Disposable needles must be used.
* Machine tips that come into direct contact with the skin must be discarded after one use.
* The local council must be contacted when this service is to be introduced to ensure that the beauty therapist is licensed to carry out the treatment.
* Client consultation is important and a skin test will be required on the client before treatment.
* High quality colours must be used. The ingredients are titanium oxides, alcohol, glycerine and distilled water. They are put through a process which makes them safe and allows them to remain true in colour.

The treatment is not regulated by any official body but is being investigated at the time of writing. Some suppliers have indicated that one outcome could be that certain areas such as the eyes may only be treated under medial supervision. Legislation is considered necessary, as the procedure is similar to tattooing and is thought to carry the same health risks. Standards in hygiene should be similar to the recommendations applied to tattooing:

* The area being treated should be thoroughly cleansed first and dressed afterwards.
* Every client should have a separate container of each pigment used.
* Any item which comes into contact with blood must be disposed of safely and immediately.
* Aftercare instructions must be given.
* Sterilisation of equipment should be thorough using the appropriate methods.

Popular areas for treatment

Three of the most popular areas for treatment are: the lips, eyebrows, eyeliner.

The lips

A new lip line or full colour can appear to change the size and shape of the lips as well as adding colour. The procedure can help to balance uneven lips, prevent lipstick from bleeding and camouflage facial lines around the lips as a result of ageing. The finished look can be natural or dramatic as the client wishes.

The eyebrows

This procedure aims to give the appearance of hair in the browline and fullness can be achieved for sparse or no eyebrows. It is especially helpful to alopecia sufferers eliminating the need for eyebrow pencil.

Eyeliner

Pigment can be applied between the lashes for a soft natural look, giving the appearance of thicker lashes. A more definite look may be achieved with a bold eyeline or a soft smudgy effect at the corners of the lid. (Some companies will not treat this area but will recommend that a doctor rather than a therapist carry out the procedure.)

Expected results after treatment

In some cases, there may be some swelling after the procedure, accompanied by redness to the area, but this will subside fairly quickly. Aftercare advice will be given to the client according to the treatment procedure and the area treated. Contraindications are shown in Figure 12.30.

If there is any doubt, it is advisable to obtain a doctor's note before treatment.

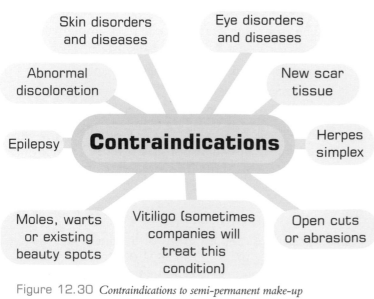

Skin disorders and diseases

Eye disorders and diseases

Abnormal discoloration

New scar tissue

Epilepsy

Contraindications

Herpes simplex

Moles, warts or existing beauty spots

Vitiligo (sometimes companies will treat this condition)

Open cuts or abrasions

Figure 12.30 *Contraindications to semi-permanent make-up*

Photographic make-up

A much greater effort is required when applying make-up for photographic work because there are more problems created with the use of lighting techniques than in natural daylight.

The lighting can drain colour from the face or throw it into relief. This causes unnatural effects and contours emphasising prominent features and where overhead lighting is used, the eyes are thrown into shadow.

These problems can be overcome by adapting the application of the make-up:

* Uneven skin colour or dark circles around the eyes should be blanked out using a white masking cream which is longer lasting and more effective than a concealer.

* Foundation must be even and matte, providing a good coverage without heaviness, and a shade darker than usual may be used to counter the draining effect of the lighting.

* Powder is essential in photographic make-up as an oily finish will cause a reflection.

* For a very soft effect for bridal make-up, shading and highlighting should be carried out with cream products and then set with a fine translucent powder.

* Colour blending is very important to avoid harsh lines, particularly as a more obvious colour contrast can be used under artificial light.

* When applying blusher it should be placed slightly lower than usual in a more angular line because the camera has a bleaching effect on the rounded parts of the face. Therefore, to accentuate the blusher, highlighter and shader must be used.

* The socket line must not be over emphasised when applying eyeshadow because the shadow will appear deeper if there is overhead lighting.

Figure 12.31
Photographic make-up

Remedial camouflage make-up

There are many conditions of the skin that can be treated with camouflage make-up by beauty therapists, but to treat the more severe cases a specialised course in remedial make-up must be undertaken.

There are several different types of camouflage make-up to conceal and disguise skin imperfections such as scars, tattoos, burns, birth marks and pigmentary disorders. You will need to ensure the products you use have certain qualities, in order to:

* provide a good cover – enough to last a whole day and, in some cases, when used on other parts of the body for several days, providing the area is not washed with soap
* be waterproof – to enable the client to take part in all activities including watersports and swimming; however, care must be taken when drying with a towel and a blotting action must be used to keep the make-up in place
* be sun proof – the skin that is being camouflaged may be quite delicate and sensitive and most products contain titanium dioxide to protect against ultraviolet rays
* have a good range of colours – this is essential so that all skin colours can be matched exactly and if an exact match is not available, then different shades can be mixed to the required colour
* be hypo-allergenic and suitable for everybody who requires camouflage make-up.

Therapists may be asked to treat the following conditions:

* Port wine stain – a deep red birthmark on the face and neck, which is not raised above the skin's surface and may be successfully camouflaged.
* Rosacea – red area of dilated capillaries caused by the skin condition. It often looks like a red butterfly shape across the cheeks and nose.
* Vitiligo – an area of skin with no natural pigment giving the appearance of white patches.
* Dark circles around the eyes – often a genetic condition but can be caused through illness, stress and exhaustion.
* Tattoos – these are permanent and may often be in

a conspicuous position.
* Chloasma – areas of darker pigmentation than the surrounding skin.
* Dilated arterioles – still show through a normal make-up.
* Burns and scar tissue – difficult to cover because they are non-absorbent and the creams may slip.

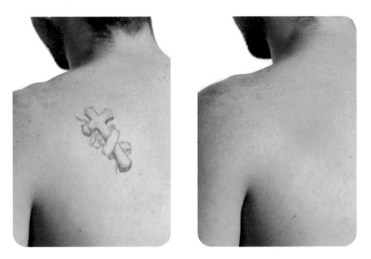

Figure 12.32 *A tattoo – before and after camouflage make-up*

* Varicose veins.

Referral from a doctor

It is very important when dealing with clients (men, women or children) who have been referred to you by their doctor to be sympathetic, reassuring and positive in your approach. Details of the problem will be included in a note from the doctor, but it is also necessary to listen to the client's own requirements.

The main objective is to teach clients how to apply their own camouflage make-up as quickly and effectively as possible so that they can use it everyday with total confidence. The number of visits required will need to be decided with each individual client, as the time it takes to become proficient will vary from client to client. Children may need extra help and it might not come very easily to a male client who has had no previous experience of make-up application.

Advice to the client

You will need to explain to clients that they will need to allow ample time in the morning to apply the make-up, but as they become more proficient, application will not take as long.

It is important to make up in a good light, preferably daylight.

When applying the creams apply them sparingly, building up the layers gradually rather than using one heavy application.

Advise clients to return at any time if they feel that the results they are achieving are not satisfactory.

Application of remedial camouflage make-up

Colours should be chosen to match as closely as possible the shade of skin surrounding the blemish and if necessary, use a second shade over the first for a perfect match.

The skin should be totally clean and grease free. Moisturiser must not be applied to the area of skin to be treated because any moisture on the skin will repel the cream and the application will be difficult.

When deep colours in a tattoo are to be camouflaged a white colour should be used first and then a colour mixed to match the client's skin tone. If the mark is predominantly red, then a green base may be used first before the colour is added.

The cream should be pressed on to the blemish – never rubbed – until the blemish or discoloration has disappeared. The colour should be blended beyond the edges of the blemish into the surrounding skin. If the client's skin is freckled and you have covered a large area, then it is a good idea to add some freckles using the make-up so the finished result is more natural.

A special fixing powder should then be applied generously over the treated area. The powder should be left for ten minutes for the cream to set, then lightly brushed with a soft powder brush to remove the excess.

Normal foundation may now be applied to the face but gently, without rubbing, to avoid disturbing the camouflage cream. The application of make-up may now continue in the usual way.

To remove the camouflage make-up, a special removing cream is normally available from the manufacturer of the make-up. This should be gently massaged in until the cream begins to dissolve, gently wiped away and then the face or area treated may be cleansed in the usual way.

Spa and heat therapies

Introduction

There has been a huge increase in the number of spas opening in the UK and worldwide in the last few years. Many beauty salons are now converting to spa therapies or using them alongside popular beauty therapies.

There are several categories of spa, including:

* the destination or resort spa located in beautiful surroundings, in the mountains on the edge of an ocean, or in an exotic landscape

* the urban spa situated in the hub of a bustling city centre providing a sanctuary for the client with a busy lifestyle who would like the spa therapies offered in the resort spa but within easy reach

* the themed spa that has a particular vision such as eastern philosophies, health and fitness, spiritual, wellness and many others

✱ the hotel spa providing the ultimate in luxury treatments for guests and the large sports clubs supplying the therapeutic treatments required to counteract the stresses and strain of a sporting lifestyle.

Whatever the location or vision, the treatments will include relaxing, holistic therapies, hydrotherapy and heat treatments, massage therapies and many other complementary treatments using ingredients based on natural elements.

This section discusses many of the options available to the beauty therapist working in or hoping to open her own spa.

The spa

The word spa conjures up many different things to different people, but the traditional definition is: 'A place of naturally occurring thermal or mineral waters'.

The Latin words:

Sanus

Per

Aqua

mean 'health through water'.

There are also those who associate Spa with the name of a town in Belgium that drew people from many areas to its healing waters during the sixteenth century. Water therapy has, in fact, been in existence for thousands of years and there is evidence that the Indians, Egyptians and Assyrians used mineral waters for curative purposes. Many peoples including the Japanese, Chinese, Greeks and in particular the Romans used warm baths for therapeutic purposes, relaxation, reducing fatigue, promoting wound healing and increasing a sense of well-being.

Figure 13.1 *Turkish baths*

Today, however, many people look upon a spa as a concept combining leisure, health, beauty and relaxation. Because of this, the word spa is often used inappropriately to describe many establishments in the health, leisure and relaxation industry. These may include the hotel with a swimming pool or a small salon with a jacuzzi. While they may provide excellent treatment and service, they are not a true spa which uses natural resources and provides longer lasting health benefits.

People have become far more health conscious and are aware of the many therapeutic treatments available to counteract the stress of modern-day living. The beauty therapy industry is responding to their needs by introducing more spa destinations and treatments. Water is the basis of spa treatment and in addition to the water therapies available, salons and spas are introducing beneficial treatment using derivatives from the sea and other sources of thermal or mineral waters as well as the popular heat treatments using sauna and steam baths.

Heat therapy

There are several different forms of heat treatment, which may be used either for their own beneficial effects or to increase the benefits of other forms of body therapy. Most treatments are available in beauty salons, spas, health clubs, health farms and fitness centres and may include:

* steam baths
* sauna baths
* foam and aerated baths
* whirlpool or spa baths.

These forms of heat therapy all have similar effects, although they differ in application. In general, because they are heating the body they:

* relax tense muscles
* have an overall soothing effect.

The physiological effects of heat on the body

Heat therapy can have the following effects:

* The circulation is increased warming the body.
* An erythema is produced which improves the overall skin colour.
* The surface capillaries dilate helping to control body temperature.
* The sudoriferous glands are stimulated to produce sweat, which also helps in controlling body temperature, and waste products are removed.
* The lactic acid accumulated in the muscles through exercise is dispersed with the increase of circulation.

* The body temperature rises slowly causing the heartbeat to quicken in the same way as taking exercise.
* Tense muscles are relaxed.
* It promotes a sense of well-being.
* The tissues are softened preparing them for subsequent treatments such as G5, body massage, vacuum suction and electrical muscle stimulation (faradism).

The uses of heat

The application of heat prior to body massage or electrical body treatment will improve the effectiveness of the treatment. If no heat treatment is available, even a warm shower can be effective as clients will feel refreshed and warm. The skin is also cleansed and any barrier from body lotion or cream previously applied to the skin will be removed. Tension in the muscles is reduced allowing treatment such as electrical muscle stimulation to be carried out more comfortably. Heat is also very soothing and relaxes the client, so providing an ideal preparatory treatment prior to other therapies.

Contraindications to heat

If clients are taking any medication or are having treatment for a medical condition, it would be advisable for them to obtain their doctor's permission before having heat treatment. Reasons to avoid heat treatment include:

* very high or very low blood pressure
* history of thrombosis
* angina pectoris
* acute respiratory conditions such as pneumonia or bronchitis
* skin diseases
* diabetes (unless clients have the doctor's approval)
* epilepsy
* immediately after a heavy meal
* after alcohol consumption
* those on a strict diet as the heat will cause them to become light-headed and possibly faint
* during the heavy days of a period
* during the later stages of pregnancy.

Blood shunting

There are occasions when the body has to make adjustments to blood flow, re-routing blood to various parts of the body and sending it to where it is most needed. At rest, approximately 40 per cent of the entire output from the heart goes to the liver and kidneys, but with the onset of a vascular shunt, this may be reduced to as little as 5 per cent.

Shortly after exercise begins, blood shunting occurs when blood is re-routed to the muscles to cope with the increased demand. It is also shunted away from the abdominal organs and the skin as well as the liver and kidneys. For those people who are not very fit, the blood shunt away from the liver may cause a 'stitch'.

During heat treatment such as sauna or steam, blood is shunted to the skin and away from the vital organs to help the body maintain a normal temperature.

After eating a large meal, blood is shunted to the intestines to help with digestion. It is important, therefore, that heat treatment and exercise are not taken after eating a heavy meal or consuming alcohol.

Steam baths

The original steam baths were Turkish or Roman baths and they were very large buildings with many different rooms, all of varying temperatures. The principle of this type of treatment was to progress through the different rooms from the lowest temperatures to the highest and according to personal taste, a plunge into a pool of cold water at the end. Then there would be a room for relaxation where the participant would also be able to benefit from a relaxing body massage. It was a very sociable and leisurely form of treatment enjoyed by many.

A typical Roman bath would consist of the following:

* The *apodyterium*, or changing room.
* The *tepidarium*, a warm room, for relaxation where slaves would massage scented oils into the skin.
* The *caldarium*, or hot room, for sweating, so the oil and sweat would release dirt from the skin and then it would be scraped away using a 'stigril'. The remaining oils would then be rinsed off in a plunge pool of warm water before moving on to the final room.
* The *frigidarium*, a cold room, to have a refreshing plunge into a cold pool.

The Romans would then finish their treatment in the great bath, a communal pool, to relax.

Figure 13.3 *A modern steam bath*

Figure 13.2 *The Great Bath in the spa city of Bath*

There are very few Roman baths in existence today, although they are more common in spa towns and particularly in some European countries. There are, however, smaller scale versions of steam rooms at health farms, modern spas, salons and leisure centres.

The modern, more private, equivalent is the small steam bath made from metal or fibreglass and this type of bath may be fitted into even the smallest of beauty salons. It uses moist heat caused by hot water vapour. Steam is produced when the water is heated in the base of the bath.

Metal steam baths are extremely durable and are good value for money but are harder to keep clean.

They also require a lot of towels to be used to protect the client, as well as being more cumbersome than the fibreglass model. Fibreglass looks more attractive but costs more to buy, less towels are required for client protection and the bath is far easier to keep clean.

The steam bath is constructed like a cabinet with a solid hinged door or a zippered plastic covering, each with an opening for the head. It has an adjustable seat to accommodate all different sizes, with a small tank underneath to hold the water, which is heated by an electrical element. The size of this water reservoir must be adequate for the number of times it is to be used, for example a large capacity tank would provide eight treatments without being refilled and a smaller tank would provide approximately five treatments. If the steam cabinet was in constant use, therefore, the larger tank would be essential, but in a small salon, which would only use the bath occasionally, a smaller model would suffice.

Clients must be supervised while in the steam bath just in case the heat overcomes them. Discussing their personal treatment plan and their progress so far may use this time most effectively.

The effects of steam bath treatment are shown in Figure 13.4.

Case study: Bath spa

Modern spas are now recreating the old Roman baths in a more up-to-date style. The most recent example is the new spa in Bath.

Bath's natural thermal waters will once again be used for bathing and healing in a complex combining restored historic buildings and a new spa. This will be a spa with a difference – it already has more than 2000 years of history, and the water in which people will bathe, relax and recuperate fell as rain thousands of years ago.

The Bath Spa Project and the revival of the new spa has been made possible by a £7.78 million grant from the Millennium Commission, and a collaboration between: Bath & North East Somerset Council, Thermae Development Company, the ERDF KONVER Fund and the Bath Spa Trust.

The open-air rooftop thermal pool will be one of the greatest attractions of the new spa. Visitors will be able to enjoy the natural warmth of the water all year round, while enjoying the views across the city out to the hills. The rooftop pool contains two whirlpools.

On the third floor is a Turkish bath, with four circular glass steam rooms and a central shower-mist feature. With the outside walls permeated by glass lenses, this will be a unique space, with steam and shafts of natural light creating an amazing atmosphere in which to enjoy Bath's mineral-rich water to its full. On the second floor of the building are four massage rooms as well as an exercise area, offering free meditation, yoga classes throughout the day.

Source: Adapted from www.bathspa.co.uk

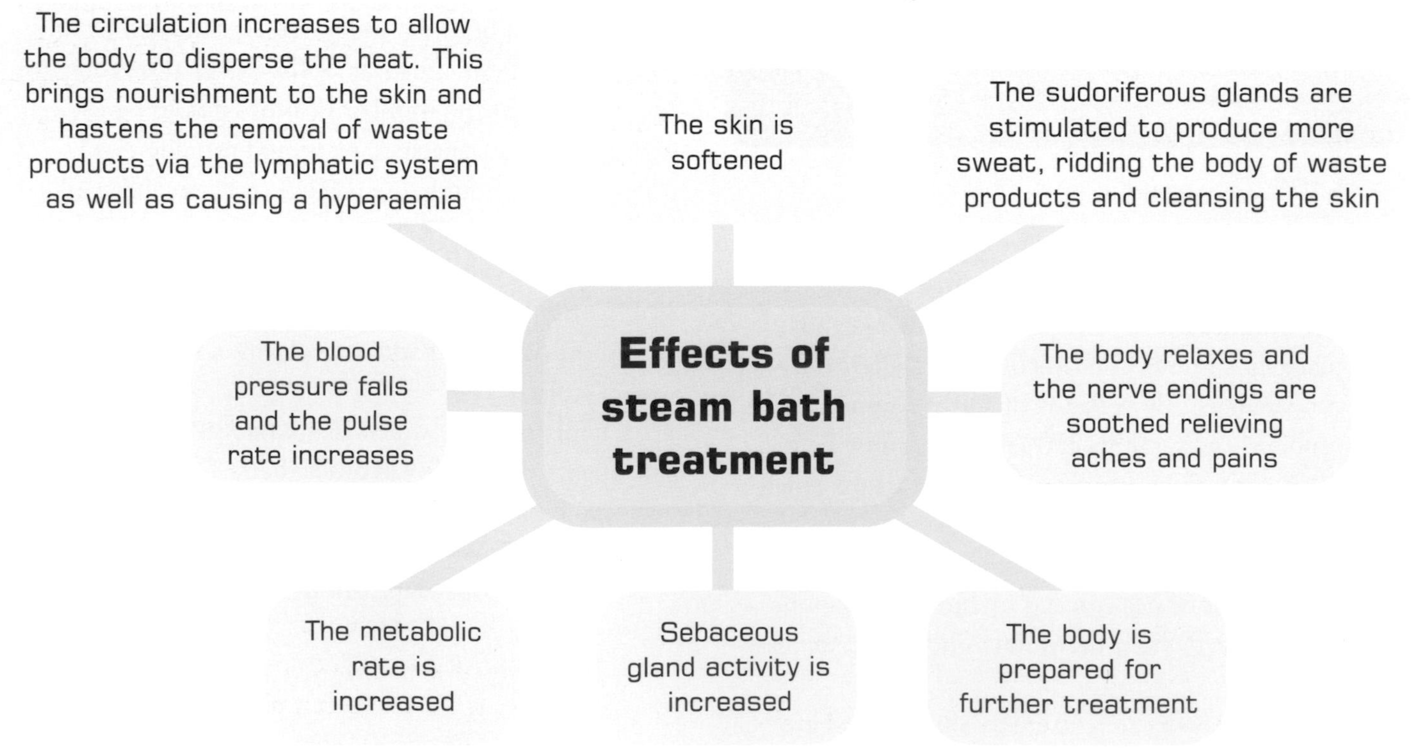

The circulation increases to allow the body to disperse the heat. This brings nourishment to the skin and hastens the removal of waste products via the lymphatic system as well as causing a hyperaemia

The skin is softened

The sudoriferous glands are stimulated to produce more sweat, ridding the body of waste products and cleansing the skin

The blood pressure falls and the pulse rate increases

Effects of steam bath treatment

The body relaxes and the nerve endings are soothed relieving aches and pains

The metabolic rate is increased

Sebaceous gland activity is increased

The body is prepared for further treatment

Figure 13.4 *Effects of steam bath treatment*

Precautions

The steam bath must be checked prior to the client's arrival, to ensure that it is filled with the necessary amount of water. The seat must be prepared by covering it with towels. The temperature of a steam bath should be 50–55°C and the client should shower before taking a steam bath. Demonstrate to clients how they may leave the steam bath if they feel unable to continue with the treatment. It will also dispel any worries they may have about being confined in a small space. Once the steam bath has reached the required temperature, the client should be seated to the correct level. A towel must then be tucked around the client's neck to prevent steam escaping.

Treatment time will depend on the individual client, but it can vary from 10 to 25 minutes. It is important not to allow the client to remain in the steam bath longer than is necessary. A warm shower should be taken after the steam bath and if clients are not having further treatment, they must rest for at least 15 minutes. Offer them a glass of water and continue with further treatment – a relaxing massage is an ideal accompaniment to any form of heat therapy.

The steam bath must be cleaned with an anti-fungal disinfectant solution and dried thoroughly after use because the warm moist conditions are an ideal breeding ground for germs. When all treatments for the day have finished the steam bath must be left open to allow it to dry thoroughly.

Sauna baths

The sauna is another form of heat treatment, but whereas the steam bath uses hot water vapour (moist heat), the sauna uses dry hot air (dry heat) to achieve similar effects. The traditional Finnish sauna would have been made from pine logs and situated on the side of a lake so that after sitting in the sauna for the required length of time, participants could then take a plunge into the cold lake.

The saunas mainly used today are made from log pines or panels of pine with a space in between filled with an insulating material to keep all of the heat within the sauna. All the internal fittings, the resting benches,

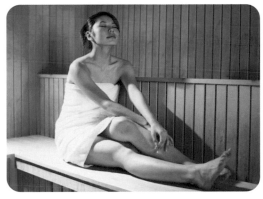

Figure 13.5
A sauna bath

the guard rail for the stove, the duck boards, bucket and ladle as well as the flooring are also made of pine as any metal used within the sauna would become too hot and burn the occupants.

Pine material is ideal because it absorbs any condensation produced, so remaining dry. The sauna can be built into a space or be free standing as long as there is enough room around the sauna to allow the air to circulate freely. The wood also absorbs the heat produced and then radiates it back into the sauna increasing the temperature within the cabin.

The heat is produced by an electric stove, which has a small tray on top containing special stones. The heater is controlled by a thermostat, which should be situated out of reach of the clients who may be tempted to alter the temperature. There should be a thermostat placed as near to the ceiling of the sauna as possible to give the most accurate reading.

Effects of sauna baths

* The effects are the same as the steam bath, but although the sweat produced is profuse, it quickly evaporates leaving the skin fairly dry.
* The body feels refreshed.
* The body is relaxed by alternating the sauna with warm showers and rest periods, allowing the body time to return slowly to its normal temperature.
* Depending on the fitness of the client, a plunge pool may be used alternately with the sauna, which will have the effect of raising and lowering the temperature rapidly, providing a more stimulating treatment but placing greater strain on the heart. This method tends to be more popular among male clients.

Precautions

To reach the required temperature, the sauna bath must be switched on approximately 45 minutes before use for a larger model and 30 minutes for an average-sized sauna. The pine bucket must be filled with water ready for use and towels placed on the resting benches. A pine fragrance or eucalyptus oil may be added to the water used in the sauna to provide a fresh smell when poured over the coals.

The time taken for a complete sauna treatment is usually between 10 and 25 minutes. The temperature of the sauna bath is normally set between 70°C and 85°C. In a larger model, which has more air circulating, it may be set to a higher temperature. Male clients often have the sauna at a much higher temperature, as do female clients who are used to sauna treatment. The larger establishments have two or more saunas set at different temperatures to suit all clients, whatever their preference.

The air vents in the walls of the sauna should be opened to allow movement of air through the sauna.

It is important to ensure that the client is fit to participate before taking a sauna. The sauna routine must be explained to each new client and there should be ample supervision available during treatment. Clients are advised to start on the lower benches to acclimatise themselves to the heat and then move up where it is hotter when they are ready. Tepid showers or rest periods outside the sauna may be taken to maximise the relaxation effects of treatment.

Water should occasionally be poured on to the coals which will produce steam and increase the humidity, which in turn will reduce the evaporation of sweat from the body so that less water is lost reducing the risk of dehydration.

The sauna should be regularly scrubbed with disinfectant and clients could be provided with disposable sauna slippers to prevent the spread of infection such as verrucae or athlete's foot.

At the end of the day, the doors should be left open to allow the fresh air to enter the sauna, ensuring that there is no stale odour and it is always pleasant smelling.

The vibratory sauna machine

The sauna has been incorporated in a body conditioning machine as part of a special combination treatment to alleviate stress and to condition the body. The machine provides:

* **dry heat** which helps to deep cleanse the skin, improve the circulation, ease aches and pains and detoxify the body
* **detoxification** – toxins are eliminated from the body through perspiration improving skin tone and helping to combat the problems associated with water retention
* **massage** as it simulates the effect of exercise and massage (provided by the gentle vibration, set to a frequency to reduce stress), so promoting mental and physical relaxation
* **sound** – it has a built-in stereo system allowing the client to listen to a selection of music or therapeutic tapes, again to promote mental relaxation
* **aroma** – aromatic oils are used for their beneficial effects and the benefits are obtained through inhalation and absorption.

Figure 13.6
A vibratory sauna

How the vibratory sauna works

The vibration relaxes the muscles while the introduction of heat dilates the blood vessels, thereby increasing the heart and pulse rate. This, in turn, increases the blood flow and intake of oxygen. The body cells use oxygen to burn up carbohydrates and then they burn up the fat cells. It also accelerates the kidney function in the removal of lactic acids and body waste.

Benefits

* Relieves muscular aches and pains.
* Relieves backache.
* Increases the circulation.
* Therapeutic for sufferers of arthritis and rheumatism.
* Helps with weight control.
* Helps eliminate body waste and stimulates kidney function.
* Helps in the treatment of cellulite.
* Provides a soothing and relaxing environment, which helps relieve tension and stress.

The machine

The machine consists of a comfortable couch with a built-in headrest and its own fan to supply cool fresh air. It has a hinged lid which, when closed over the couch, reaches the client's neck to form a heating chamber. There is an aperture similar to that in a steam bath so that the client's head is not enclosed during the treatment. There is a control panel on the outside for the therapist to pre-set the heat, vibration, time, fan and stereo cassette. There is also a panel inside the unit so that the client may adjust the heat, fan and volume of the stereo cassette. The display panel to show the settings is positioned for the client to monitor easily.

Advantages over an ordinary sauna

* It is a complete model, compact and transportable.
* It can be fitted into relatively small areas.
* No pre-heating is required.
* It is private.
* It is a personal treatment because the temperature can be adjusted to individual needs, whereas with a sauna the temperature is the same for everyone.
* It is more comfortable for those who have difficulty breathing in hot air because it protects the nasal and bronchial passages.
* The pleasantly vibrating couch is more comfortable than wooden benches.

Floatation spa therapy

This treatment provides not only the essential qualities and benefits of traditional spa and hydrotherapy but also the additional advantages of weightlessness and is used for total relaxation of the body and the mind. It is quite different in application and effect from the more popular forms of heat or hydrotherapy and is in a category of its own, as the chief aim is to relax the client and provide an antidote to the stresses and strains of a busy life.

The floatation tank was pioneered in the United States in the 1950s by Dr John Lilly, an American neuroscientist based at the National Institute of Mental Health in Maryland. During his research, Dr Lilly created a device that eliminated as many external stimuli as possible to enable him to study the origin of consciousness and its relation to the brain. It was originally called a sensory deprivation chamber and floatation tank therapy is now known as 'Restricted Environmental Stimuli Therapy' or REST. It is a very popular form of relaxation in the USA and there are also hundreds of floatation tank centres in France and Japan.

They are becoming increasingly popular in the UK and around the world with spas, health farms and natural health centres offering floatation tank therapy. Many beauty therapists are now seriously considering the value of this form of relaxation.

The floatation tank

The tank is made of fibreglass and is rectangular or oval in structure, either with sides, a roof and a door, or similar to a large bath. It is sometimes the size of a bed or larger. The tank contains approximately 30 cm of concentrated salt water that is heated to a temperature of 35.5°C, which allows the body to float effortlessly. Epsom salts may be used, but the more sophisticated treatments utilise Dead Sea salts which provide the water with a high density, leaving the floater with a sense of weightlessness.

To ensure privacy, each floatation tank should be in its own room with a shower and filtration plant close by. A quiet room or area should be available for the use of the client after using the tank.

All first-time floaters should be given clear and thorough instructions in the use of the tank, with particular reference to any fears the client might have which would prevent the treatment being totally relaxing. The side of the pool should be low to facilitate easy entry and exit with safety handles to assist.

Figure 13.7
A floatation tank

Before treatment

The client should take a shower before treatment for hygiene reasons. Earplugs need to be used to protect the ear canals from filling with water. These are the only preparations required before entering the tank.

Sometimes soothing music is played for several minutes at the beginning of the treatment, providing time to acclimatise to the total darkness and losing all sense of space and time.

Treatment time

This is normally 50 minutes to one hour, time enough for the body to relax completely. Most people emerge feeling as though they have had a good night's sleep and others do fall asleep. The end of the treatment may be indicated gently to the client, who has probably lost all track of time, by music being played again for several minutes.

After treatment

A shower should be taken to remove all the salt from the body and the client may then sit or lie in the quiet area before leaving or having further treatment.

Benefits of floating

Easing pain

The dense salt solution provides the body with buoyancy and eliminates the body's specific gravity. This allows the floater to experience almost total weightlessness and provides relief from a bad back, aching feet, painful joints and muscular tension. There is a decrease in the production of lactic acid and an increase in its elimination from the system and as lactic acid is associated with muscular pain, this is reduced.

Relaxation

The brain produces slower brain waves during a float and these are known as theta waves, normally only experienced during deep meditation or while under hypnosis. This is total relaxation and is almost immediate. As floating frees the brain, muscular system and the skeletal system from gravity, vast amounts of energy are available to deal with matters of the mind. The absence of external stimuli – light, vision, noise, gravity and touch – enables relaxation to occur more powerfully than with other methods of relaxation.

An increased sense of well-being

Research has shown that floating can reduce blood pressure and heart rate. It can also reduce the levels of stress-related chemicals in the body such as adrenalin and cortisol which cause tension, irritability and anxiety and relieve depression. Equally, the body produces more beta-endorphins, the body's natural opiates, which have a soothing effect, decreasing the perception of pain and creating a sense of well-being which can last for some time after floating. Therefore, the more regularly the client floats, the more cumulative the effect.

Restores body to a state of homeostasis

External stimuli can disrupt homeostasis. Removing external stimuli allows the body to focus all its energies on restoring balance and harmony.

Contraindications to floatation

* People who are claustrophobic should be advised against entering a floatation tank because of the confined space. However, if it has a door, it does

not have to be shut but may be left open during treatment, which may help some sufferers.

* Epileptics may not use the tank unless they are under medication and have permission from their doctor.

* Anyone who has consumed alcohol.

Sanitation

* The tank rooms and shower facilities must be cleaned between uses.

* The complete volume of water must be filtered between uses and the level of the water must be checked daily.

* The condition of the water and the tank must be monitored between uses. The water must at all times be free from scum, oils and hair, and so on.

* The temperature of the water must be checked between uses.

* The pH of the water must be checked daily – the correct pH is 7.6.

* The inside of the tank above the solution line must be cleaned weekly or more often if necessary.

* The specific gravity of the water must be checked at least once a week – the acceptable range is 1.22 to 1.28.

* The bromine level of the water must be checked daily – the reading should be no higher than 2ppm.

* The tank will be tested regularly for purity either by the local Environmental Health Department or by an outside laboratory.

Foam baths

The foam bath is a very efficient way to heat the body and is commonly used in health farms and spas. However, it can be made fairly cheaply for a small salon, from an ordinary bath, with the correct accessories to adapt its use. A plastic duck board perforated with hundreds of holes may be placed in the bath and air compressors force air through the holes in the duck board. Only a small amount of water is required (about 10 cm), enough to cover the duck board, and it is heated to a temperature of 38–43°C. Some concentrated foam essence such as seaweed or pine may be added to the water.

The air compressor is switched on to aerate the water and left until the foam reaches the top of the bath. Clients are then helped into the bath where they will rest, with only their head above the foam, in a semi-reclining position.

The foam provides excellent insulation, generating heat in the client's body, which cannot escape so that it builds up and induces more perspiration.

The aerated bath is similar. It is filled with the normal amount of water used when taking a bath but with an essence added. The built-in compressor then aerates the water. The client sits or reclines in a comfortable position allowing the water, which is full of bubbles from the increased oxygen, to gently massage the body. These baths may also be installed for home use.

Treatment time is normally 15–20 minutes for both types of bath. The effects on the body are the same as for steam bath treatment.

Safety precautions

* Baths should be well maintained and regularly serviced.

* All electrical precautions should be taken before treatment and the manufacturer's instructions followed.

* The client must be checked for contraindications, given a thermal skin test (see below) and a record card should be filled in.

* The shower must be cleaned regularly and a shower mat provided to prevent slipping

* Towels should be placed in easy reach of the client. Clean towels should be provided for each client.

* Soap must be provided in a liquid soap dispenser for ease of use and hygiene purposes.

* Water on the floor in wet areas must be regularly mopped up to prevent accidents.

* The client's pulse must be taken before treatment to ensure that it is normal and after treatment to ensure that it returns to normal (see below).

Pulse

Pulse is a wave of pressure, which passes along the arteries indicating the pumping action of the heart. The pulse is normally taken at the wrist just under the thumb on the palmar surface of the hand and it is called the radial pulse. The fingertips should be placed into the hollow at the base of the metacarpal of the thumb and pressed lightly over the artery (see Figure 13.8). The number of beats in a minute should be counted, using a watch with a second hand count.

The average pulse rate in an adult is 72 beats per minute, but varies between 60 and 80 beats. The pulse rate may increase due to stress, exercise, illness, as a result of injury and while drinking alcohol. A normal pulse will feel regular and strong.

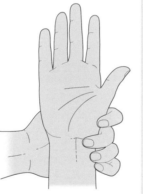

Figure 13.8
Where to take a pulse

Thermal skin test

A thermal skin test may be used to check the client's tolerance to heat. To do this the therapist should fill two test tubes, one with cold water and one with hot. Place the test tubes alternately on the client's skin asking the client to identify which is hot and which is cold. If the client lacks sensitivity to the cold and hot, then the treatment is contraindicated.

Whirlpool or spa baths

The whirlpool spa was invented 35 years ago in the United States and is becoming increasingly popular. It is an essential part of all new health spas and clubs, the larger baths accommodating up to eight people at a time.

The weight of the spa is quite considerable, so the floor must be tanked, drained and reinforced sufficiently to take the full weight of the spa when filled with water.

The plant room should not be sited more than five metres from the spa itself in a well-ventilated area with sufficient power to supply it. The wet area around the spa must have a non-slip surface to prevent accidents and good drainage facilities are required.

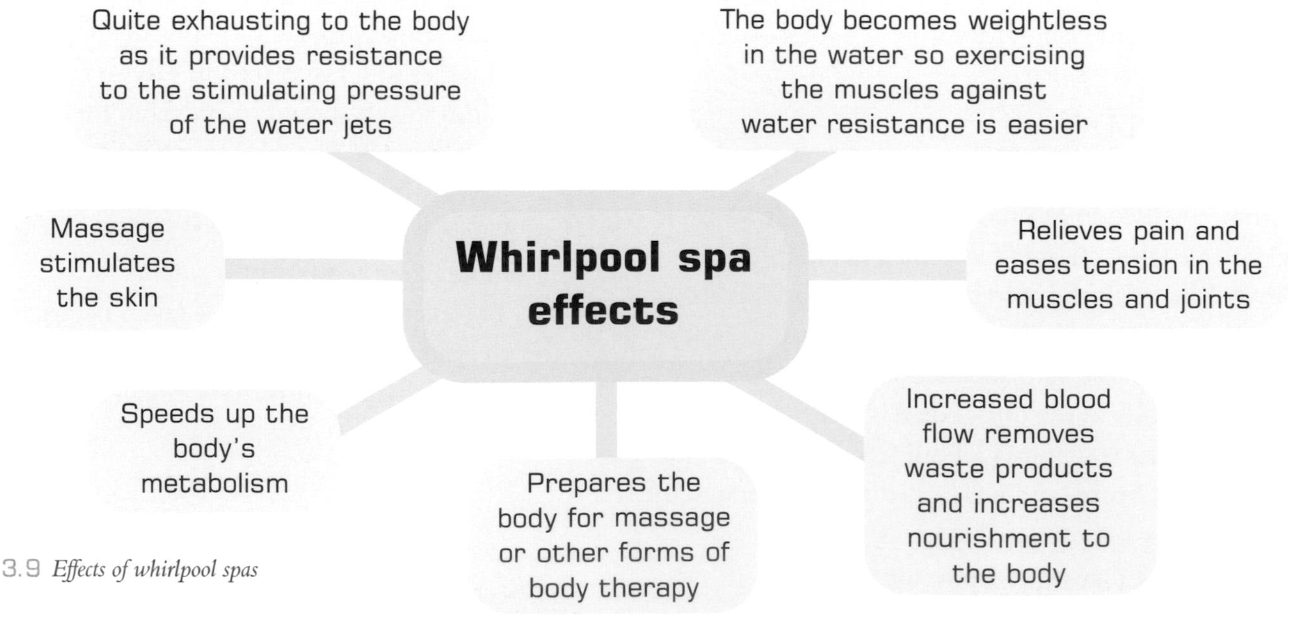

Quite exhausting to the body as it provides resistance to the stimulating pressure of the water jets

The body becomes weightless in the water so exercising the muscles against water resistance is easier

Massage stimulates the skin

Whirlpool spa effects

Relieves pain and eases tension in the muscles and joints

Speeds up the body's metabolism

Prepares the body for massage or other forms of body therapy

Increased blood flow removes waste products and increases nourishment to the body

Figure 13.9 *Effects of whirlpool spas*

A good whirlpool spa should have the following features:

* an efficient filtration system
* an automated level deck system with overflow channel so that as clients enter or leave the pool, there are no unsightly marks around the sides
* a heavy duty control panel
* two types of massage system, which can be used separately or together.

For a soothing spa effect, air channels underneath the pool are pressurised by an air compressor and forced up through tiny apertures to produce a gentle massage.

The more stimulating whirlpool massage is produced by jets of water that are positioned around the sides of the bath to work on specific parts of the body and the jet nozzles can be angled to suit the requirements of individual needs.

When the two systems are combined they produce a turbulent stream of bubbling aerated water which provides an all-over massage.

Health and safety in the spa

In any environment that has a mixture of water and heat there is a strong possibility that bacteria will reproduce rapidly, particularly if there are a large number of people using the spa. It is essential, therefore, that the spa water is constantly monitored and kept within a safe limit for all users.

This can be done manually using a comparitor (a colour wheel against which the tested water is compared), or by a chemical controller

Figure 13.10 *A spa*

that is situated in a plant room. This is a computerised system that is constantly monitoring the **chlorine** content and the alkalinity of the water and adjusting the levels to maintain a safe environment for the clients.

Chlorine is the chemical used for cleaning the water, however because it is alkaline and has a high pH factor, when it is added the pH level is increased to a level which will irritate the skin and eyes. Therefore, an acid must be added to the water in the form of **sodium bisulphate** (dry acid) to reduce the alkalinity.

pH levels

The pH of the skin is 4.0–5.5.
The eyes have a pH of 7.4–7.6.
Chlorine has a pH of 11.

The plant room

The water from the spa goes into a balance tank before returning to the plant room where it passes through a strainer basket to catch any large objects (such as hair, plasters, ear rings) (see Figure 13.11). The water is then pumped into a filtration tank at high pressure and smaller contaminates such as sweat, deodorants, body fat, skin products and waste matter are filtered out.

The water is then heated in a heat exchanger to a temperature of 37°C. At this stage, the water still contains contaminates (such as bacteria and viruses) which are too small to be trapped by the strainer and filter, so they have to be removed by using chlorine. As well as killing pollutants, chlorine also makes the water crystal clear. The chlorine and the dry acid are both kept in large containers in the plant room. They

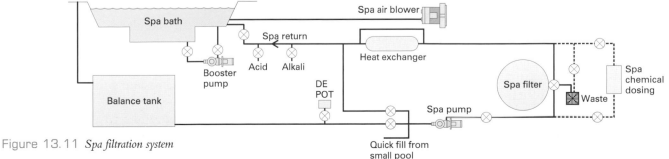

Figure 13.11 *Spa filtration system*

are stored separately from each other as if they were mixed, they would give off a chlorine gas which is toxic and may be lethal.

Personal protective equipment

A qualified or fully trained operative should only handle the chlorine and dry acid as they are hazardous chemicals. Personal protective equipment (PPE) must be worn to prevent irritation of the skin or inhalation. In a large plant room in a hotel, health club or large spa it would be the responsibility of the maintenance staff and they would wear a face mask and/or a respirator, a full set of overalls, special gloves and wellington-type boots.

Body wraps

There are several methods of body wrapping or inch-loss treatments using bandages, linen, plastic, rubber or foil combined with the application of active natural products on the skin and heat to increase the elimination of toxins from the body. Body wraps may also be used as a pampering treatment and alternative to massage.

Choosing the right combination of active products and wrap system provides an effective treatment for clients wishing to relax, improve their body shape and the texture of the skin or motivate them to diet.

Natural products

Therapists are responding to the increasing trend towards all things natural and holistic by using body care products which are based on natural ingredients using marine products such as plankton and seaweed, essential oils, mud and flower and herbal infusions. The active ingredients come in different forms – paste, powders, oils and solutions – and they all have specific effects on the tissues.

Marine products

Active ingredients, for example trace elements and salts, are extracted from marine algae plants (more commonly known as seaweed) and used for their therapeutic value in body and skin care products. It is the intensity and access to light that determines the colour of seaweed and they tend not to grow below eight metres as they need the light to synthesise. The three types most commonly used are fucus, ascophyllum and laminaria.

Thalassotherapy

Thalassotherapy is derived from the Greek word thalassos meaning sea and it involves treatments that incorporate the use of sea water and seaweed. The benefits of these treatments have been well documented over the centuries. It includes sea water baths, algae masks and sea mud wraps.

Seaweed or marine algae is believed by some to be nature's source of complete and balanced nutrients, containing many elements that are essential to the human body because the algae soaks up all the minerals that exist in their immediate environment. The chemical composition of sea water is similar to human plasma, although the protective nature of the skin does not allow most of these ingredients to penetrate to the lower living layers of skin cells. Some therapists have reported the benefits of sea water experienced by people with atopic dermatitis and psoriasis. At spas, the sea water bath is usually heated to approximately 40.6°C. It provides relaxation and often soothes sore muscles.

Fucus

Deep-water brown seaweed works by activating the sweat glands, eliminating water containing toxins and increasing the body's temperature. Its main actions are diuretic and internal cleansing. Therefore, it will complement a slimming programme by helping to detoxify the system. Fucus comprises:

* iodine – this has a general cleansing effect on the bloodstream, regulates metabolism, boosts energy and stimulates the thyroid gland
* vitamins – these have an antioxidant effect, counteracting free radical damage
* amino acids – these are essential for maintaining health in all body systems
* potassium – this reduces fluid retention and replaces trace minerals that are lost when detoxifying

* magnesium – this helps to keep the circulatory system healthy and counteracts stress.
* phytin – a natural antioxidant which promotes metabolism regulation and increases oxygen transportation.

Ascophyllum

This is also brown and often associated with fucus. It is rich in amino acids and minerals, and it is balancing, helping to induce a sense of relaxation.

Laminaria

This is a deep-water, brown seaweed which contains a high percentage of organic iodine, vitamins, amino acids and trace elements. It helps to regulate the thyroid gland and the metabolism and stimulates the lymphatic system.

Detoxifying wraps often consist of full body skin brushing to stimulate the lymphatic system, then full body exfoliation to cleanse and refine the skin's surface. The detox product is applied to the skin and the body is wrapped up to allow the algae to penetrate the skin, the therapist will then provide a relaxing scalp massage.

Blue seaweed is microscopic and unicellular. It helps to regenerate tissues while firming and rehydrating. Spirulina is rich in proteins, vitamins, beta carotene and iron and helps to stimulate cellular metabolism.

Red seaweed grows at the deepest level and is good for re-mineralising, exfoliating and softening the skin.

Figure 13.12
A body wrap treatment

Essential oils

These oils are incorporated into products for their specific effects, to:

* improve the elimination of toxins
* tone tissue
* stimulate the circulation
* relax
* revitalise.

Mud

Marine and volcanic mud, healing clays and earth are rich in minerals and may be used for hydrating, re-

Figure 13.13
A mud wrap treatment

mineralising, detoxifying and refining skin texture and body shape. Mud may also be used as an antidote to stress, fatigue and feeling run down. It is available in many countries as a special spa treatment and mud such as that from Arizona contains copper, magnesium and zinc. Copper has been used for hundreds of years to ease painful joints and muscles, repair damaged skin and heal wounds. It is also used by the body for the healthy formation of nerves and bones, to maintain healthy thyroid function and to protect the body against infection and disease. Magnesium is recommended for strong bones, teeth and healthy muscle function. Zinc is required for repairing damaged tissue and bolstering the immune system.

Before applying the mud, it is advisable to exfoliate the skin as this will increase the circulation and aid mineral absorption. The mud comes in powder form and is self heating. When mixed with cool water it will begin to bubble and this paste is then applied to the client's body before wrapping the client in loose layers of plastic sheeting, foil and blankets to keep warm and maximise absorption of the minerals. This is left for 20–30 minutes, then showered off before massaging the skin with a hydrating cream.

Rassoul is a popular spa treatment using micronised brown mud, which comes from the warm fertile valleys of Morocco. Since the twelfth century, Moroccans have used Rassoul as a daily therapeutic source for skin cleansing and purification, dermatitis, skin sensitivities, smoothing rough or scaly skin, seborrheoic skin and scalp and hair treatments. Rassoul contains the earth's most natural and necessary health and beauty elements – silicium, magnesium, iron, calcium, potassium and sodium.

A popular spa therapy involves combining heat and steam with mud, which works on the skin to exfoliate and smooth as well as drawing out the impurities.

Mud wrap and floatation therapy

Using a combination of floatation therapy and mud wrap provides a highly therapeutic treatment for mind and body. Being in a floatation bed for 45 minutes gives the equivalent benefit of several hours of deep sleep. Add the mud body mask full of skin nourishing natural minerals and the effect is amazing!

While sitting on the floatation bed, the client will be smothered in warm beach mud collected from a specific location, then wrapped in cling-film and finally the water-filled blanket will be enveloped around the client. The next stage is sinking into the massage bed (the base of the bed is mechanically lowered). The client should be left for around 45 minutes in a candlelit room while floating, though the therapist should check regularly throughout the treatment. Total treatment time is about 55 minutes.

The water-filled blanket creates a weightless womb-like place to float within the floatation bed. Meanwhile the heat opens up the pores so the mud's properties can soak into the skin and eliminate toxins. Most people fall asleep during the treatment. At the end, the client is raised up again. Lying on a completely flat surface may initially feel strange after floating, but the therapist should ensure the client sits up slowly.

Immediately after the client has been unwrapped, has climbed from the floatation bed and showered, the skin should feel incredibly smooth and soft and the body deeply relaxed.

Popular mud treatments

Three of the most popular healing mud or earth treatments are described below.

Dead Sea mud

This contains magnesium which provides energy, bromine for relaxation and the alleviation of stress, iodine to improve gland functioning and help fat burning, and potassium, a natural detoxifier.

Fango

This is a volcanic thermal mud rich in vitamins, trace elements and minerals. In addition to magnesium, iodine and bromine, it contains sulphur which stimulates healing and sodium chloride to help rid the body of toxins.

Peat mud

Peat mud is packed with amino acids, often having a low pH. These have the ability to stimulate the autonomic nervous system and help to regenerate the skin's protective layer.

Flower and herbal infusions

Pure and natural linens are soaked in hot flower and herbal infusions, the body is then cocooned in blankets and a marma pressure point massage is applied to the face and head to calm and revitalise the mind. The wrap helps to reduce the build-up of fluid, and increase metabolism. It reduces aches and pains and the skin is purified by the heat and the texture of the linens and revitalised by the flower and herbal extracts.

Inch-loss wraps

The most effective wraps are those that do not rely on water loss alone to achieve results as this would only be temporary. Sea clay wrap is an excellent treatment, which provides inch loss for clients who are trying to lose weight and improve their figure as well as removing toxins from the body. It is a treatment which does not require a large working area – just a private room or cubicle with enough space for measuring and wrapping clients comfortably. It will benefit the following:

* Clients on a diet – to provide motivation.
* After pregnancy or weight loss – to improve and firm the skin.
* Clients with stretch marks – to tighten the skin and make them less noticeable.
* Areas of cellulite.
* Anyone who may wish to lose inches for a special occasion.
* Those who just wish to improve their shape even if they are not overweight.
* The client who wants to detoxify the body.
* A dry or rough skin condition.
* To help reduce weight as part of a course of treatments.

Consultation

With any wrap system it is important at the initial consultation to explain the treatment to clients, the sensation they will feel, the initial tightness of the wrap, the exercises they will do once wrapped, the time it will take (approximately 2–2$\frac{1}{2}$ hours) and the frequency of treatments. It is also important to discuss the results that are likely to be achieved, making no false promises as these may lead to disappointment.

The benefits to the client are:

* by tightening and toning soft tissue, a few inches will be lost
* the skin will be deep cleansed and detoxified
* the cellulite condition will be improved
* stretch marks will be tightened
* scars and blemishes will become less noticeable.

The client's medical history must be checked as there are certain medical conditions that must be avoided and some that may require the treatment to be adapted.

Contraindications to inch-loss wraps

* Never wrap a client who is allergic to natural elements. If in doubt, carry out a patch test before treatment.
* Pregnancy.
* Emphysema.
* Phlebitis.
* Unhealed wounds in the skin.
* Recent operations.
* New scar tissue.

Care must be taken with the following:

* Circulatory or respiratory problems. Do not wrap too tightly.
* High blood pressure. Ask clients if they are on medication to control the condition and if they are, wrap as normal.
* Skin disorders such as eczema or psoriasis usually benefit from treatment. However, if the condition is severe and there are open sores, treatment is contraindicated.
* Breast-feeding mums. Wrap to underneath the bust. There is no medical reason for not wrapping the whole body but it might cause discomfort.
* Epilepsy, as it would be difficult to move the client into the recovery position when wrapped.

There is nothing in the wrapping procedure or solution used that would precipitate an attack, however.

* Heart conditions. A doctor's permission must be obtained.

Figure 13.14
A body wrap treatment

Treatment application

The equipment required for treatment includes:

* elastic contour wrap bandages about 15 cm wide
* the natural sea clay solution
* a heating tank to warm the solution and bandages prior to use
* a pair of tongs to handle the hot bandages after heating; they may be placed in a bowl to cool before use
* a large mirror and measuring tape
* a vinyl suit, to keep the client warm while wrapped
* towels for clients to dry themselves after treatment
* a large bowl or bucket to place the dirty bandages after wrapping
* a laundry basket to place the clean bandages ready for rolling.

Precautions

Clients must use the bathroom just before they are wrapped, as they will be unable to go to the toilet for some time afterwards. Clients must then be measured and their statistics recorded. Weigh clients first to ensure they are at least maintaining their weight during the course of treatments and it will also prove to them that this is not a water-loss treatment, which provides only temporary weight loss.

Measure clients ensuring that they are standing correctly. They must stand straight, legs together, hands interlocked behind their head, and elbows to the side. This will provide more accurate measurements.

Wrapping always begins at the lowest extremity working upwards and always wrapping towards the heart to ensure adequate blood supply to all parts of the body.

There are certain areas of the body, which must be wrapped with extreme caution as they have relatively little muscle protection for underlying arteries and nerves. Wraps therefore must not be too tight in these areas as this could result in loss of blood circulation or loss of feeling in the extremities. These areas are:

* back of the knee joints
* inside groin area
* lower lumbar area of the back
* inside of the elbow.

Pressure must be reduced across the back of the knee, in the groin and inside of the elbow and the edge of a bandage must not go across the joint of the knee or elbow. The middle of the wrap should always cross the joints. Clients must always be in an erect position when wrapping the lower back so there is no additional pressure to the back if they stand upright after being wrapped in a forward position.

It is important that if clients experience any tingling sensations or loss of feeling in any part of the body, they are immediately unwrapped.

Once clients have been wrapped, they are helped into the vinyl suit and they may be taken to an exercise area to stand and walk around or to do some light isometric movements. The benefits of exercise while wrapped are:

* the pores of the skin open
* the solution works on the toxins
* there is a resistance to the bandages during movement-providing isometric exercises.

The last 15 minutes of the full 60–70 minutes should be used to cool down and then the vinyl suit is removed and the wraps are removed in the reverse order to application. Clients are then re-measured and the results recorded.

Home care advice

* Shower with tepid water only so as to retain the solution in the pores to carry on working.
* Limit soap to feet, underarms and groin area to prevent soap removing solution from the pores.
* Avoid creams and lotions.
* After three or four days, have hot showers with plenty of soap to open the pores and eliminate toxins and solution.
* Drink plenty of water (mineral and tap water only) – about 1.7 litres a day to flush out toxins.
* Avoid tea, coffee, sugar, salt, alcohol, fried or fatty foods and carbonated drinks.

Hot stone therapy

This is an ancient healing art recently rediscovered. It is a manual form of massage, which uses smooth heated and cooled stones to relieve muscle stiffness and soreness and induce relaxation. Stone massage involves the application of water-heated stones of varying sizes to key points on the body which are then incorporated into a massage. The combination of the warm stones and the deep and flowing massage is extremely soothing and the heat allows manipulations of a greater intensity than with other forms of massage.

The stones come from places such as Mexico and Arizona and they are made from basalt, an igneous rock shaped by the elements, which holds and transfers heat to aching muscles. In addition, cool marble stones, a sedimentary rock, are used. These are hand carved from high quality marble into shapes and sizes that are adaptable for treating different parts of the body.

Hot stones are also used in pedicures and for facials. The warmer stones expand the blood vessels, pushing blood and unwanted waste materials through the body. This has a sedative effect on the nervous system. The cold stones cause the blood vessels to constrict, stimulating the nervous system and drawing blood and waste products along the body. This ensures that every cell in the body receives more oxygen and nutrients while, at the same time, waste material is removed more effectively through the corresponding increase in lymph flow.

Those experiencing a hot stone massage should notice an improvement of the following symptoms:

* muscular aches, pains, sprains and strains
* poor circulation
* rheumatic and arthritic conditions
* fibromyalgia
* multiple sclerosis
* back pain
* stress, anxiety and tension
* insomnia
* depression.

Adding aromatherapy to hot stone treatment has additional effects on the client depending on the oils chosen.

There are also chakra stones, which can be placed on the chakra points to remove blocked energy. This treatment was introduced in 1995 from the United States and has fast become one of the most popular spa treatments.

Body treatments

* Body assessment

* Body massage

* Aromatherapy

* Indian head massage

* Electrical treatment

* Ultraviolet, infrared and radiant heat treatments

* False tan

Introduction

For many people being slim is synonymous with being beautiful and there are some clients who are on an eternal quest to achieve the perfect shape. We as beauty therapists owe it to clients to help them achieve realistic goals as far as weight and body shape are concerned. We must teach them to accentuate their good points and improve on the rest. Every individual has his or her own unique shape and some people find it very easy to maintain while others have a constant battle to prevent the pounds piling on, the waistline spreading and the muscles losing tone.

This section deals with all aspects of body treatments that will provide the 'feel good' factor and motivation for those who are overweight and need practical help and advice. Body massage, aromatherapy and Indian head massage are all therapeutic treatments that relax the body as well as the mind, providing a wonderful antidote to a hectic lifestyle. Mechanical and electrical treatments are used to lift, tone, tighten and firm the contours, improve skin condition, fight cellulite and lose inches.

There is also useful information about the effects of ultraviolet and infrared radiation, the safe use of sun beds and alternative false tan treatments.

Client consultation for body treatments

A good body requires a combination of good genes, plenty of exercise, sensible eating and lots of self-discipline. Having a good figure provides confidence in both men and women, so the eternal quest to develop the body beautiful has led to a huge increase in the number of:

* salons offering slimming treatments
* spas
* health clubs
* fitness studios
* exercise and diet classes
* toning table centres.

Many people are now also aware of the need for a fit and healthy body to combat the stresses and strains of everyday life, and the benefits of relaxation in the forms of heat therapy, body massage and aromatherapy, and physical forms of exercise.

When the body is not fit and healthy it will become more susceptible to illness, premature ageing, fatigue and poor skin and hair condition. As well as exercise, therefore, a good diet is essential to rejuvenate the body and the mind.

In addition to self-discipline, the beauty therapist can offer all that a client needs to become fit and healthy (see Figure 14.1). The main reasons that clients attend for body treatments are:

* relaxation and as an antidote to stress
* spot reduction – treating specific areas to lose inches or tone the muscles
* figure correction after rapid weight loss or after giving birth
* to lose weight.

Although there are many varied treatments on offer, it is important to remember that one form of treatment alone will not usually succeed. The combination of diet, exercise and the application of treatments in the salon is essential in achieving the required results. A trusting relationship between client and therapist is therefore very important so that the correct combination of treatments is used to maximum effect and the client will follow the diet given and carry out any home care advice such as follow-up exercises.

Consultation is a very important first step in planning the course of treatment for the client to enable you to choose the most appropriate treatments to achieve the client's personal objectives. The client may already be a regular for facial therapy, electrolysis or other treatments, in which case you will probably have built up a good relationship with him or her. If clients are new to the salon, then it is important to put them

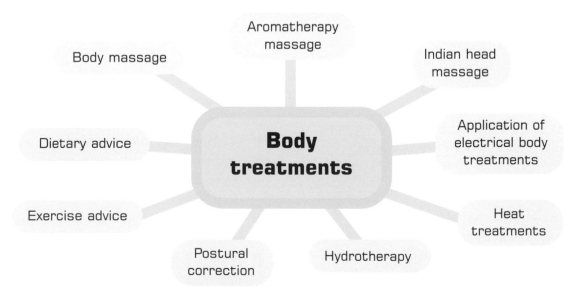

Figure 14.1 *Body treatments offered by the therapist*

completely at ease as they may feel embarrassed about their weight problem or their figure shape.

It is probably a good idea to combine a relaxing body massage with the initial consultation and in this way clients will talk more freely to you without feeling as if they are under close scrutiny.

Figure analysis is important when planning treatment and this will require the recording of clients' statistics. They probably will not feel as embarrassed being measured after the massage than if they had come straight in to be measured and weighed.

Record cards

A detailed record card must be filled in for the usual reasons of efficiency, client confidence and professionalism and also to provide other necessary information including:

* medical history
* lifestyle
* figure faults.

The record card will provide you with the information on which you base your treatment plan.

Medical history

This should include:

* the number and the age of any children and gynaecological operations in particular, as these are often the cause of figure faults
* the type and date of any recent operations or medical conditions, which may require you to adapt or modify treatment
* any form of medication that is being taken which may cause weight gain, e.g. steroids, contraceptive pill or hormone replacement therapy.

If the client has recently had a baby, then medical approval must be given before treatment begins.

Lifestyle

It is important to:

* assess the client's eating habits as this will allow you to suggest a healthy eating plan if necessary
* recognise any factors which may contribute to figure faults such as lack of exercise, or a job which entails sitting for long periods

* recognise any underlying causes of stress
* plan times when the client will be available for treatment and how much work must be done at home to enhance results from treatment.

Recording a client's age will indicate whether the client may be suffering from problems caused by the menopause and, if so, it may be necessary to seek doctor's approval before treatment. This can be a tricky question as many women do not want to divulge their true age, but with some thorough questioning and a good relationship this should not be a problem.

Other information you should obtain:

* **Weight**. Always weigh the client with the same clothing on each week, e.g. bra and pants so that the weight loss or gain is accurate. You can make a visual assessment as the client is being weighed, noting any changes as they occur. Remember that weight may fluctuate considerably during menstruation because of fluid retention.
* **Initial measurements**, if clients will allow their measurements to be taken. (Some clients may be too embarrassed while others will find the recording of measurements an incentive to lose the excess weight.) When measuring the client make sure the tape fits the area, as if it is too loose, the measurement may be inaccurate. Measurements should be taken at regular intervals to chart the progress of clients and to motivate them. If clients are obese, then medical approval must be given before treatment begins.

Figure faults

A figure diagnosis should be carried out to provide information regarding:

* the figure type and condition
* fat distribution in the body which will vary depending on the sex, size and medical condition of the client
* specific figure faults which may require special attention
* postural faults which may be corrected or improved.

Fat distribution with age

In general, an older body is fatter than a younger body, older women tend to be fatter than older men and the body shape changes as we age. The main reason for this is oestrogen. In our teens and twenties any excess fat is evenly distributed, in our thirties and forties extra weight goes on the hips and thighs, in our fifties to our waist and in our seventies a pear shape is common.

Treatment plan

A treatment plan should be devised and a record should be made of all treatments as they are completed to enable progress to be assessed and indicate to the therapist when a change in the treatment plan is required. This ongoing record also provides up-to-date information for other therapists who may treat the client, so providing consistency in the treatment programme.

As each client will have individual requirements depending on their particular problem, it is important to assess how many treatments are required, how long the course will take and the regularity of attendance so that clients will be aware of the cost and the time involved. It is important to set realistic goals so that motivation is maintained.

Special offers on courses of treatments should be available to make it a more attractive proposition to clients and ensure that they attend for the minimum number of treatments necessary to produce the required results.

Figure analysis

It is important to analyse the figure and posture of clients before beginning any course of body treatments for weight reduction or body shaping for the following reasons:

* This will ensure that the treatments recommended will be the most effective for clients and their particular requirements.

* It will ensure that the treatment chosen will not cause any harm or discomfort.
* It will help therapists to recognise any faults which are not to be treated by them and may need to be referred to a doctor.
* When using more than one form of treatment it will influence the therapist's decision about which treatments to use.
* It will ensure that treatment is not given unnecessarily if figure faults are caused by some simple postural problem.

The initial figure assessment of clients is a visual one. This will show any problems they may have with their range of movement and even when clients are fully dressed, it is easy to assess figure shape.

The next part of the assessment will require clients to remove their clothing as far as their underwear. Check for postural and figure faults in front of a full-length mirror. The clients can then see how their posture may be corrected, while the therapist explains the treatments which may help any problems of excess weight, cellulite or poor muscle tone.

Correct posture

Good posture depends a great deal on muscle tone. By observing the client from the front, back and side, the therapist should note any deviation from the norm as far as posture is concerned, as this will be a good indicator of the problems the client has to overcome.

A client who has good posture will stand tall and straight without strain and without having to hold in any part of the body with any effort.

Weight must be evenly distributed on both legs and carried on the arches of the feet.

For good posture:
* The head and shoulders should be level.
* The scapulae should be an even distance from the spine.
* The vertebral column should be straight down the back and not curved in either direction.
* The abdomen should be flat and the buttocks not protruding.
* The waist should be evenly curved with the hips level.

* The arms should be in a relaxed position at the side and hang evenly.
* The legs and knees should be straight with the feet together or just slightly apart and facing forward.

The benefits of good posture

* Breathing may be full and deep, as the chest is not contracted.
* The digestive organs function more efficiently if they are not compressed.
* An even distribution of body weight ensures that the body does not become too tired with certain muscles working overtime.
* Postural defects will not occur if the bones are held in their correct positions.
* The figure looks its best when the posture is correct.

The maintenance of good posture

To maintain the correct posture and allow the body to remain standing correctly, the body relies on the **antigravity muscles**. These muscles are in a state of partial contraction all the time, except when we sleep or lose consciousness.

The antigravity muscles include:
* the **pectorals** on the chest
* the **biceps** on the upper arms
* the **trapezius** on the back
* the **gluteals**, or buttocks
* the **quadriceps** on the thigh
* the **gastrocnemius** on the calf.

Body types

Posture, exercise and diet can change the overall shape of the body. However, the one consistent factor is the body type. This is hereditary and is determined by the genes. The therapist can recognise the body type by its characteristics and can help clients with figure faults or help them to come to terms with their problems.

There are three body types:
* endomorph
* ectomorph
* mesomorph.

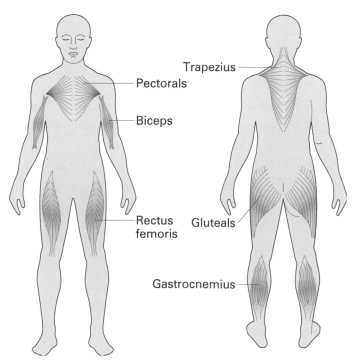

Figure 14.2 *The antigravity muscles*

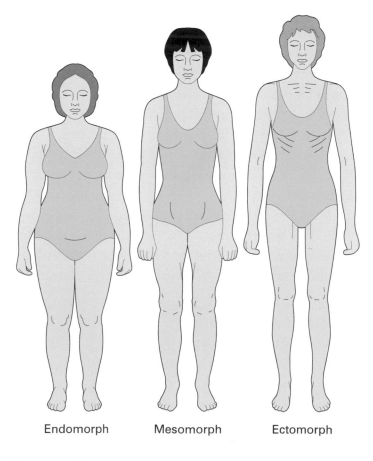

Figure 14.3 *Endomorph, ectomorph and mesomorph*

Endomorph

Round in shape, with a higher proportion of fat to muscle, this body type tends to put on weight easily and fat is deposited around the hips, abdomen, thighs and shoulders. The limbs and neck are short and hands and feet are small.

Ectomorph

This body type is lean and angular with long limbs and small joints. There is very little body fat with none of the usual female curves and a lack of muscle bulk.

Mesomorph

Usually strong with an even distribution of weight, this body type normally has broad shoulders and well-toned muscles. This body type is characteristic of an athletic person who normally has no weight problems while active.

Figure faults

The most common figure faults (particularly in female clients) are the pear shape with heavy hips, thighs and buttocks, round shoulders, protruding abdomen and a large bust which can lead to round shoulders. The male client often has a protruding abdomen, round shoulders and a forward pelvic tilt. Many of these faults are due to slack muscles or excess fat. Slack muscles may be caused by:

* the client's sedentary life style
* lack of exercise
* the normal ageing process
* pregnancy
* illness
* stress.

Excess fat is usually caused by a higher intake of calories than are burned off through normal exercise.

Body fat

Women have a higher ratio of fat to muscle than men, a large proportion of which lies just beneath the skin.

> The body will burn carbohydrate for fuel for the first 20 minutes of exercise and then it begins to burn fat.

This provides support and insulation, contouring the body and keeping the skin firm and supple. Encourage the client to exercise after weight loss because it helps to burn fat as a primary fuel.

If there is excess fat, the skin loses its shape by becoming dimpled and more solid. If a large amount of fat is lost, the body will lose its shape as the skin sags when the underlying support shrinks away.

Spinal curvature

There are figure faults which require medical attention but are easily recognised by the therapist when carrying out her visual assessment. In these cases, medical approval must be sought before planning any exercises or treatments.

Kyphosis

This condition causes the thoracic part of the spine to curve outwards. Round shoulders and tightness of the pectoral muscles often accompanies this figure fault.

Lordosis

This condition is an inward curve of the spine in the lumbar region and is commonly referred to as a **hollow back**. It is sometimes associated with the forward tilting of the pelvis.

Scoliosis

This is a fault which shows itself as a lateral curve and rotation of the spine, either to the right or the left. This fault causes changes in the muscles, ligaments, bones and joints which may lead to further faults such as:

* one leg longer than the other
* one shoulder slightly higher than the other
* uneven scapulae
* pelvic tilt.

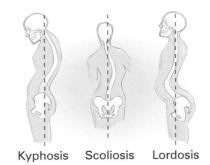

Kyphosis Scoliosis Lordosis

Figure 14.4 *Kyphosos, lordosis and scoliosis*

Dowager's hump

This figure fault often affects women as they grow older. The head is tilted forward slightly and with age fatty deposits accumulate at the back of the neck over the spine and when established it is very difficult to correct.

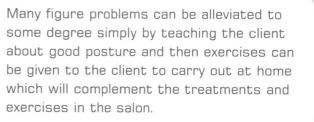

Figure 14.5
Dowager's hump

> Many figure problems can be alleviated to some degree simply by teaching the client about good posture and then exercises can be given to the client to carry out at home which will complement the treatments and exercises in the salon.

Manual assessment

This is something the therapist can do quite easily when performing a massage. The condition of the muscles as well as the skin can be noted and contraindications to some forms of electrical treatment may be apparent.

Manipulation of the muscles allows the therapist to determine their tone and strength, indicating the client's physical condition. Tension – tightening of the muscles or nodules in the muscles – also shows how much stress clients are feeling, or whether they are suffering discomfort from an injury or a figure fault.

The skin condition may affect the form body treatment will take and manual assessment will show the elasticity of the skin and how different skin conditions may affect treatment, for example severe stretch marks from pregnancy or rapid weight loss. With age, whether it is natural or premature, the skin becomes loose and crepey and this will cause treatment to be modified or contraindicated.

Testing for mobility and muscle strength

There are several simple tests, which may be carried out by the therapist on the client, particularly before recommending any form of exercise or applying electrical muscle stimulation treatment.

Determining the strength of the client's muscles will allow the therapist to judge the intensity of current to be used with electrical muscle stimulation for the first few treatments until the muscle reaction can be seen after several applications.

It is important to determine how flexible or mobile a client is before recommending any type of exercise. The general fitness and strength of clients varies considerably and the tests given must not be too difficult or rigorous.

There are three different types of movement:

* **Passive** movements that are performed by the therapist on the client who takes no active part in the exercise.
* **Active** movements are those which the client performs with or without assistance from the therapist.
* **Resisted** movements are those performed against a resistance.

Mobility

Mobility can be inherited or acquired and it can be determined by the ease with which the joints can move through their full range of movement. Most people, with age, begin to lose mobility. Therefore, some form of exercise plays an important role as we get older. There are some simple exercises to test for mobility and these are outlined below.

Shoulder

The client should place the left arm along the back and bring the right arm over the shoulder to meet it. If the

Figure 14.6 *Exercise to show shoulder mobility*

client is able to clasp fingers, then mobility is good at the shoulder, but if they fail to touch, it is poor. There could be a difference when both sides are tested as quite often there is more mobility in one side than the other.

Spine

The client should kneel down on hands and knees, drop the forehead down and bring the knee up to meet it. If this is achieved without discomfort, then mobility of the spine is good.

Finally, the client could be asked to perform a few simple exercises such as side bends, touching the toes and arm rotations to indicate how supple and mobile they are.

Strength

Physical strength is determined by the strength of the muscles. Strong muscles are firm and allow the body to perform all movement easily. Muscle strength is tested by asking the client to perform certain movements for different areas of the body.

Sitting up from a lying position with the knees slightly bent will test the strength of the abdominal muscles.

From a lying position, ask the client to lift one leg at a time and hold for several seconds. The ease with which this position can be held indicates the strength in the muscles of the leg.

Supported in a sitting position with the arm extended out to the side, palm facing up and then against the resistance of the therapist's hand, the client should try to bring the arm back towards the shoulder. This exercise will test the strength of the muscles in the arm.

Cellulite

This is a condition that affects a great many women (probably 80–90 per cent), although its existence is questioned by experts in the medical field. For those women who have slim figures yet suffer with specific areas of cellulite, normally on the bottom and thighs, its existence is very real and problematic to them. It appears in the subcutaneous layer and varies in thickness. It is made up of fat cells interlaced with collagen and other fibres.

These fatty areas differ from normal fat in several ways:

* Cellulite is very stubborn and resistant to normal forms of dieting and exercise.
* The areas of cellulite have more water content than other areas of fatty tissue.
* This condition does not affect men to the same extent as women and is not as noticeable because of the difference in skin structure.
* There is a pitting of the skin in the area, which resembles orange peel, and the fat feels harder than normal.
* In more extreme cases, cellulite can be painful.

The appearance of cellulite varies in different people, but the areas most affected are:

* the thighs and inside of the knee
* the hips
* the buttocks
* the abdomen
* the upper arms and back (less commonly affected).

Cellulite is more likely to occur in areas of poor circulation due to inactivity. The hips and upper thighs of women who have a job requiring them to sit down for long periods of time are more likely to suffer from this condition than women who have an occupation which allows them to move about and exercise.

Poor circulation also interferes with the normal process of waste removal via the lymphatic system and prevents the tissues from receiving proper nourishment.

Tension in the muscles also restricts the circulation. Poor circulation will eventually lead to congested areas forming, the interchange of tissue fluids and removal of waste products slow down, so there is an accumulation of fluid and waste in an area of fatty tissue which leads to the cellulite condition.

Causes of cellulite

Toxins enter the body via the air we breathe, the food we eat and the water we drink, and the body normally deals with them quickly and efficiently. Sometimes, however, the body cannot deal with these toxins if there is an excess of them, so they remain in the tissues.

Elimination problems or poor liver and kidney function causes a build-up in the body of the by-products of normal metabolism and waste products.

Eating the wrong kinds of food and lots of processed meals contribute to this condition. An excess of sodium (salt) in the body, which encourages water retention, and not exercising sufficiently, or doing the wrong type of exercise may cause cellulite.

Stress can prevent the normal physiological functions of the body from working effectively:

* It can upset the digestive system and therefore the process of elimination.
* It affects the circulatory system, which provides the body with nourishment and removes waste products.
* It disturbs our normal breathing process, which helps in the stimulation of lymph flow and increases the amount of oxygen that the body receives.

For many people, when under stress one of the first reactions is to eat. Unfortunately, it is usually too much of the wrong types of food. With age, the skin becomes thinner and looser as the connective tissue loses its elasticity, allowing fat cells to migrate to the area and to enlarge. Hormones are a contributory factor as the female body has large amounts of oestrogen, which actually encourage the laying down of fat cells in the body. Therefore, it is uncommon for a girl to suffer from cellulite before puberty, even if she is overweight. Most women are predisposed to the formation of cellulite at times of hormonal change and these include:

* puberty
* when taking an oral contraceptive
* pregnancy
* menopause.

Treatment of cellulite

It is important when dealing with a cellulite condition that you explain to the client that there is no one treatment alone which will rid the body of the problem. It must be approached in several ways:

* Detoxify the body by eliminating stored waste.
* Prevent fluid retention.
* Exercise the body more and increase the metabolism.
* External application of treatments by the beauty therapist.
* Eat a well-balanced diet.
* Control stress.
* Improve posture.

Cellulite and diet

For any treatment provided by the beauty therapist to be effective, there must be cooperation from the client as far as diet is concerned. However, it should be stressed that clients do not have to go on a deprivation diet, but just need to look at the way they eat and the types of food they are eating. A few adjustments will need to be made with guidance from the therapist. The client may not necessarily be over eating but may just be eating the wrong types of food.

Common faults in diet

* Too much fat.
* Too much salt.
* Too much sugar.
* Eating too much processed food.
* Eating too many sweet and salty snacks.

As a result, the body has less energy, puts on weight and develops problems such as cellulite.

Dietary advice to combat cellulite

* Reduce the amount of meat, especially red meat, as it contains chemicals, synthetic hormones and antibiotics given to the animals for growth. Choose very lean meat, only eat it a couple of times a week and prepare it without using fat.
* Reduce the intake of fat as this is a major cause of weight gain and high cholesterol levels. The body only requires 15–20 per cent of fat in a balanced diet.
* Reduce the amount of sugar consumed because it depletes the body of potassium which is essential to keep the sodium balance in the body as well as causing excess weight gain.
* Reduce consumption of chocolate, caffeine, fizzy drinks and alcohol.

* Reduce the amount of salt in the diet. It is unnecessary to add salt to food as the amount of salt the body requires to remain healthy is contained in food naturally. When sodium and potassium levels are well-balanced they help the cells of the body to receive nutrients and remove waste products. Too much salt causes water retention and cellulite.

* Advise clients to cut out as many processed foods from their diet as possible. These contain large amounts of fat, sugar and salt, as well as chemicals which are of no benefit at all and will be stored in the body. In excess, processed foods are hard to eliminate.

* Increase the intake of foods rich in potassium as a low potassium level can cause fluid retention and flabbiness, characteristics of cellulite. The foods which are rich in potassium are fresh fruit, fresh vegetables, pulses and whole grains.

* Eat raw fruit and vegetables to receive the maximum nourishment.

* Drink plenty of water (2–3 litres a day) as this will help to flush out all the toxins and prevent the formation of cellulite. It also aids digestion and the absorption of food. Drink a large glass of water first thing in the morning and also before and after exercise to replenish the body's supply which is lost from the body through perspiration. To ensure its purity, filter the water before drinking to remove chemicals which otherwise would deposit themselves in the tissues.

Suggested treatments

* Swedish massage, G5 massage and aromatherapy using diuretic and stimulating essential oils.
* Manual lymphatic drainage.
* Body brushing.
* Body wrap.
* Electrical treatments – vacuum suction, galvanism and microcurrent.

Body massage is a treatment which may be provided on its own or after some other form of treatment. It is used as a treatment to maintain physical health and well-being as well as inducing relaxation. It has become increasingly popular in recent years as more and more people are becoming aware of the need to counteract stress in their lives and help eliminate the resulting problems. Some of the more common problems caused by stress are shown in Figure 15.1.

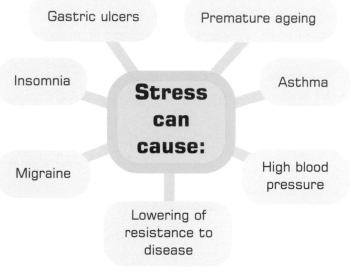

Figure 15.1 *Common problems caused by stress*

Prolonged bouts of stress cause tension in all parts of the body but particularly in the muscles. The ability to perform a relaxing massage, therefore, is an essential key to success for therapists who provide body treatments.

Client care and consideration

Performing a relaxing and enjoyable massage is very important in ensuring a successful treatment. However, the salon atmosphere and the attitude of the therapist are both factors to be considered in providing a truly effective treatment. If clients are not in a relaxed frame of mind before the massage, it will take the therapist longer to achieve this effect, so client care and consideration is vital.

The salon

The treatment room should be warm and well-ventilated as clients will have to remove most of their clothing for a general body massage or they may have had some form of pre-heat treatment. The room or treatment area should be private, so curtains are essential if a separate room is not used.

Ideally, the light should be natural, but if not, it should be indirect or dimmed so that it does not shine brightly into the client's eyes.

The treatment couch should be covered with a sheet and blanket or other form of covering so that either or both may be used. In the summer months clients may only need to be covered with a large bath towel to maintain their modesty as a heavier covering may be too warm.

There should be a calm atmosphere and soothing music may be played quietly in the background to promote relaxation.

The equipment

A comfortable massage couch at the correct height is essential. It must be positioned to allow therapists to work without getting backache. There are also couches available that have extra width for different forms of massage such as 'Balinese'. Electrically adjustable couches will allow the therapist to control the height of the massage couch either to suit herself, or for each client. This allows clients who would normally find it difficult to get on to the couch, because of their age, medical condition or disability, to position themselves comfortably before the therapist adjusts the height.

There are different cushioned accessories available to allow the client to lie face down and still breathe easily. Some couches have a small hole to allow the mouth and nose to be free to breathe.

The bedding should be warm and clean. Protective paper towelling may be used to protect the bedding, maintaining hygienic conditions and reducing laundry bills. Pillows for client comfort should be provided and spare pillows or cushions to support the client's limbs during the massage should be kept nearby.

Spare towels should be readily available to be used when uncovering different parts of the body for treatment.

A trolley should be set up with all the necessary equipment for the treatment so that the therapist does not have to leave the client during the massage. A massage medium should be chosen according to the client's skin type and treatment. These should include the following:

* **Talcum powder** – used mainly on the therapist's own hands rather than on the client, to provide ease of movement.
* **Oils** – there are many different types of oils which may be chosen to suit a particularly dry skin type or the client's own preference.
* **Creams** – these are more readily absorbed into the skin than the oils but some clients may have a preference for a particular cream.
* **Essential oils** – these are now in common use in aromatherapy treatment and are mixed especially for each client to suit particular needs.

Whichever lubricant is chosen, it should be applied on to the therapist's hands and not placed directly on to the client's skin.

The therapist

Because of the therapist's close proximity to the client during a body massage, which can last up to one hour or more, personal hygiene is very important. An immaculate appearance is essential too, and a clean uniform should be worn. It is often quite difficult to keep a white uniform clean as the oil used for massage easily marks the fabric, making it look grubby. Talcum powder clings to black and navy and some therapists choose to wear aprons made in the same fabric when performing body massage and then removed for other treatments.

Hair must be tied up if it is below chin level to prevent it falling over the therapist's face during treatment. Therapists' hands must be clean and nails must be kept short so that they do not dig into clients, particularly when performing finger kneading or frictions. Low-heeled comfortable shoes must be worn to prevent poor posture and backache.

To be able to relax clients completely, therapists themselves must be quiet, calm and reassuring. They must know when to listen attentively and when to discourage clients from talking, allowing them to gain maximum benefit from the massage.

Therapists should stand in an upright position and use their body weight to increase pressure in a movement when necessary. The correct working position must be assumed to allow freedom of movement and good massage technique while preventing backache.

Walk standing

This is the position assumed when the therapist is working longitudinally down the length of the muscle, with one foot in front of the other and the therapist facing the client's head. The front knee can then be bent slightly when moving forward rather than bending the back.

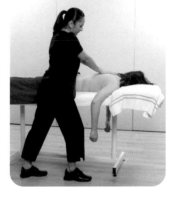

Figure 15.2 *Walk standing*

Stride standing

This is the position assumed when working transversely across the muscles. The therapist's feet should be slightly apart and the therapist facing the side of the massage plinth.

Figure 15.3 *Stride standing*

The client

The working area must be prepared in advance of the client arriving so that the therapist may concentrate solely on the client's needs.

Allow clients to remove their clothing in private, providing them with a suitable gown to retain their modesty, and then help them on to the couch making sure they are comfortable and warm.

When a client is visiting the salon for the first time, a record card must be filled in. This is an ideal opportunity to get to know clients and put them at their ease. It is at this point that the therapist will note if there is any condition that will prevent her carrying on with the massage or having to adapt it in some way. If there is any doubt about a possible medical condition, then the therapist should ensure that clients speak to their doctor before treatment commences. Alternatively, therapists can contact the client's doctor and seek professional advice themselves.

It is common practice to have some form of heat treatment prior to massage, such as a sauna or steam, and the therapist should accompany clients and instruct them about the procedure as well as ensuring their safety.

When clients are wrapped in blankets for their massage, towels may be placed strategically underneath them so that different areas can be massaged without disturbing the client unduly to rearrange the bedding.

At the conclusion of the massage clients should be allowed to sit up slowly and placed in a semi-reclining position to regain their balance. If there is an excess of oil or cream remaining on the client's skin, then it may be removed with hot towels or a fragrance or toning lotion if the client wishes. However, this can feel very cold and the client may prefer the oils or cream to be left on to nourish their skin.

The general massage routine

Body massage must always be tailored to suit the needs of the clients but, in general, a full body massage, excluding the face and head, should last for approximately one hour and should include:

* both arms
* neck and chest
* both legs
* abdomen
* buttocks
* back, neck and shoulders.

There are many different schools of thought concerning the specific order of work to follow, but it is entirely up to individual therapists to decide since they alone will know the requirements of their clients. Whichever order is adopted, the back should always be the last area to be treated as it is the most relaxing part of the general body massage.

222

It is also important to maintain continuity, keeping one hand in contact with the client at all times, and the rate of movement should be moderate unless the condition requires movements to be speeded up. The flow of movement should be even and consistent with the hands moulded gently to the part being worked on.

The amount of pressure exerted will vary on different parts of the body and on different clients. With practice, therapists will develop a sense of touch enabling them to treat each client more effectively.

When working on a specific area only, for example the back, 20–30 minutes should be allowed.

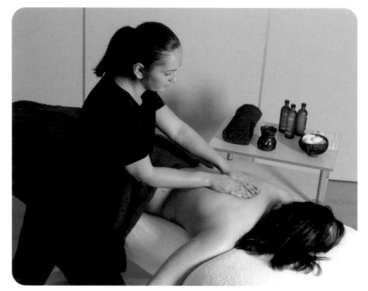

Figure 15.4 *Body massage treatment*

General effects of body massage

* Increases the circulation:
  – thereby, increasing the interchange of tissue fluids, which relieves fatigue in the muscles
  – which causes a hyperaemia, so improving skin colour
  – which brings nourishment to the skin, so improving its functions.
* Removes physical tension in the muscles.
* Stimulates the lymphatic system to remove waste products more efficiently.
* Softens and breaks down fatty tissue.
* Stimulates or soothes nerve endings in the skin.
* Improves texture of the skin through desquamation.

* Improves skin elasticity.
* Induces relaxation.
* Rejuvenating.
* Promotes a sense of well-being.
* Encourages some clients to stick to their diet.
* Softens and moisturises the skin.

Massage can be beneficial to most people even if it has to be adapted in some way. If clients are attending regularly for other treatments, then there will be a record of their medical history. If not, this information must be recorded and, if necessary, clients should be advised to seek medical approval before starting any form of treatment.

Contraindications to massage

It is important that the therapist assesses each client's suitability for treatment and understands that some contraindications are temporary and others just local so that only a small area needs to be omitted from the procedure, for example varicose veins or hairy skin.

* Any condition that would require medical supervision.
* Any recent operations or injuries such as a fracture.
* Skin diseases.
* Recent scar tissue.
* Undiagnosed lumps.
* Circulatory disorders.
* Heart disease.
* High blood pressure.
* Neuritis – inflammation of the nerves.
* Lung disease.
* Haemophilia – danger of bleeding if bruised.
* Around painful joints.
* Very thin bony clients.
* Very thin overstretched skin.
* High fever.
* Sunburn.
* Later stages of pregnancy.

When the client appears to be in extreme muscular pain a doctor must be consulted as this may mask a more serious problem such as a slipped disc.

Massage manipulations

Massage is the manipulation of body tissues, either manually or mechanically, to produce beneficial effects on the muscular, vascular and nervous systems of the body. The manipulations used are:

* effleurage and stroking
* petrissage
* tapotement
* vibrations.

Effleurage and stroking

These are soothing, smooth stroking movements which are divided into:

* deep and superficial effleurage.
* deep and superficial stroking.

The technique is exactly the same for the deep movement as the superficial, the only difference being the pressure applied.

Effleurage

Effleurage starts and concludes any massage sequence and is interspersed with other movements during the massage to provide continuity and ensure that the massage is as relaxing as possible, keeping the hands constantly in touch with the client.

Effleurage is performed with the whole palmar surface of the hand following the direction of the blood flow back to the heart (commonly termed venous return) and the lymphatic flow, ending in a group of lymph glands.

The movement should be slow, smooth and rhythmical, with the hand moulded to the area being treated, ending in slight pressure and returning to the point of origin without breaking contact but exerting no pressure. The hands may perform the movement alternately or together.

Figure 15.5 *Effleurage*

Effects of effleurage

* Improves general circulation.
* Increases the flow of lymph, removing waste products more efficiently.
* Soothes the sensory nerve endings, so inducing relaxation.
* Provides continuity of movement which promotes relaxation and allows the client to become accustomed to the massage.
* Aids desquamation.

Stroking

Soothing stroking is a slow rhythmical movement performed in any direction very gently with the hand moulded lightly to the part. One hand may follow alternately from the other or both hands may be used together. It stimulates the superficial nerve endings in the skin and revitalises lethargic clients.

Stimulating stroking is performed much more vigorously and again in any direction.

Effects of stroking

* Soothes the superficial nerve endings in the skin.
* Relieves tension.
* Cools down a hot area of skin.
* Promotes relaxation.

Petrissage

These are pressure manipulations and include the following movements:

* kneading
* picking up
* wringing
* rolling
* friction.

Pressure is applied to the muscle and then it is released systematically working over a muscle or group of muscles. The amount of pressure exerted on the muscle will depend upon the area being worked and the purpose of the massage. A greater degree of pressure may be used on a large muscle area, for example the gluteal muscles and reduced on a smaller area, for example biceps and triceps.

Whichever movement is employed, it will follow the shape of the muscle and normally towards the heart. The pressure may be applied by pressing the muscles down on to the underlying structures or lifting tissue away from the underlying structures.

Kneading

Kneading can be adapted for different parts of the body to cope with the difference in size and shape of the muscles. The tissues are pressed down on to the underlying structures and there are several types of kneading performed either with one or both hands:

* **Flat-handed kneading**. This can be single-, double-handed or alternate. It is usually performed on the back as the muscles are large thin sheets.
* **Squeezing kneading**.
* **Circular kneading**. This is a deep movement when the muscles are pressed against the bone in a circular motion.
* **Finger kneading**. This is a circular movement, but this time performed with the padded palmar surfaces of the thumb or first and second fingers. It is normally performed on small areas such as the feet and around the shoulders or down either side of the spine.
* **Ironing**. Also known as reinforced kneading, the hands are placed one on top of each other to obtain greater depth.

Figure 15.6 *Ironing*

Effects of kneading

* Increases blood supply to nourish and remove waste products.
* Promotes relaxation and removes tension from the muscles.
* Prevents fatigue by removing lactic acid from the muscles.
* Relieves aches and pains.
* Aids joint mobility.

Picking up

Double-handed picking up is when the muscle is lifted, squeezed and relaxed with both hands working alternately along the length of the muscle. **Single-handed** picking up is performed with one hand on a small muscle area, for example the deltoid and, in this case, the muscle is lifted and squeezed with the thumb on one side and the fingers on the other.

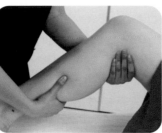

Figure 15.7
Single-handed picking up to gastrocnemius

Effects of picking up

* A deep movement effective on stubborn areas of fatty tissue.
* Increases the circulation and lymphatic flow.

Wringing

This is a picking up of the muscle and then wringing it from side to side using both hands and pressing the tissue between the thumb of one hand and the fingers of the other, again working along the length of the muscle.

Figure 15.8 *Wringing*

Effects of wringing

* Increases the circulation.
* Warmth is produced quickly in the tissues.
* Effective on fatty areas.

Rolling

The fingers of both hands grasp the superficial tissues over underlying bone and the thumbs roll them gently against the fingers.

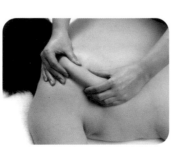

Figure 15.9 *Skin rolling*

Effects of rolling

Apart from the normal increase in circulation with its accompanying benefits, this manipulation can be used to loosen skin over tight areas.

Frictions

These movements are performed with the thumb or finger tips. They are deep pressure movements and can be performed in a small circular movement or transversely, across the muscle, pressing down on the underlying structures.

Effects of frictions

* Breaks down adhesions in muscle.
* Loosens scar tissue.
* Increases joint mobility.

Tapotement

These are also known as percussion movements. They are all stimulating and come in several different forms:

* hacking
* clapping or cupping
* beating
* pounding.

When performing this movement the hands should be totally relaxed and at right angles to the wrists with the elbows bent and the arms away from the body.

Hacking

The hacking is performed across the muscle fibres with both hands working alternately and the fingers should strike the area rapidly leaving the area as soon as they make contact, to produce light flicking movements.

Figure 15.10 *Hacking*

Effects of hacking

* Has a stimulating effect on the nerve endings.
* Has a revitalising effect on tired muscles.
* The increase in circulation warms the area.

Clapping or cupping

This movement is performed with the hands in a cupped position and the wrists relaxed. By flexing and extending the wrist, the hands are lifted and dropped in quick succession rapidly but with a light touch. When performed correctly there will be a hollow cupping sound.

Effects of cupping

* Increases circulation bringing nourishment and removing waste.
* Increases warmth in the area.
* Helps in breaking up fatty tissue.

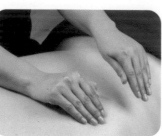

Figure 15.11 *Cupping*

Beating

Loosely clenched fists are used to perform this movement and it is slightly heavier than clapping but performed in a similar manner, dropping the fists from just below shoulder level, alternately and rhythmically.

Pounding

With loosely clenched fists and the elbows abducted, the ulnar side of the fist strikes the area, moving towards the body rapidly alternating with both hands and moving away from the area as soon as it is struck.

Effects of beating and pounding

* Stimulates.
* Helps to soften adipose tissue.
* Increases circulation.
* Warms the area.
* Tones.

Vibrations

These are fine trembling movements using the whole palmar surface of the hand or with the fingertips only. By contracting and relaxing the muscles in the forearm, the fine trembling movement or vibration occurs. The movements can be:

* fine
* coarse
* static (in one place)
* running (moving over an area while vibrating the hands).

Effects of vibrations

* Stimulating to the nerve endings when the vibrations are coarse.
* Can induce relaxation when the vibrations are fine.

The effects of massage on the body

The circulation

The circulation of blood carries food and oxygen to all parts of the body and provides a defence against infection. It also carries away waste products via the lymphatic circulation. Therefore, an increase in circulation as a result of massage will:

* improve nutrition in the tissues and remove waste products more effectively
* increase cellular regeneration.

The tissues are warmed because of the increased circulation. However, some massage movements will cause the surface capillaries to contract and this will have a cooling effect on the body.

The skin

A massage will have the following effects on the skin:

* The colour of the skin is improved because of the increase in circulation which causes the capillaries to dilate.
* Removal of waste products is speeded up through the lymphatic system and the sweat glands, so cleansing the skin.
* Skin texture is improved as the dead skin cells are desquamated from the surface.
* The activity of the sebaceous glands is increased, producing more sebum so making the skin soft and supple. This helps to keep it intact preventing bacteria from entering.
* The skin is also nourished externally by the application of the special oils or creams applied as a massage medium. Different skin conditions may be treated with the appropriate product.
* The skin functions more efficiently helping to maintain its elasticity.

The muscles

When muscles have been working hard or exercising they require more oxygen, which in turn produces more waste or lactic acid, causing the muscles to stiffen.

Massage increases the circulation, bringing more oxygen and removing the build-up of lactic acid so leaving the muscles feeling refreshed. The increased circulation also provides the muscles with nourishment. The muscles are relaxed and elasticity is improved.

Massage also helps weak muscles to improve in tone, and aids joint mobility, which helps in movement of muscles attached to the joints. Tension nodules in the muscles can be eased away gently.

The nerves

The nervous system is soothed when the massage is slow and rhythmical. Some massage movements, particularly tapotement, can be stimulating to the nerves.

Adipose tissue

This is the fatty tissue of the body and is very difficult to remove with massage alone. Therefore, for maximum effect massage should be accompanied by a good diet and regular exercise.

Poor circulation and fat deposits together may be treated effectively with massage by moving the tissue fluids and allowing absorption of the adipose tissue through increased metabolism.

Metabolism

Metabolism is the process by which the body converts food and other substances into energy for its own use, growth, repair and maintenance of a fit and healthy body. Part of this process is the digestion of food which when broken down is absorbed and used in the metabolic process, providing energy.

Incorrect metabolism can cause minor health problems, that is, sluggish skin, overweight, greasy or spotty skin. Massage can help to stimulate the metabolism improving the general health of the body.

There are several reasons why a client will want a body massage and the most common ones are:

* relaxation
* to lose weight
* to loosen stiffness in the joints
* to remove aches and pains
* to tone up slack flabby muscles
* to relax contracted or tight muscles.

Relaxation

The client must be discouraged from talking and a relaxation tape may be played in the background. All stimulating movements such as hacking, clapping, etc. must be omitted and the number of effleurage strokes can be increased accordingly. The rate of movement should be slow and the depth of pressure increased slightly, particularly when performing petrissage movements.

More time should be spent working on the back, especially on the areas of tension normally found in the trapezius muscle and down the sides of the spine.

Soothing stroking could be incorporated into the massage interspersed with effleurage.

Weight problems

Many clients believe in the popular misconception that massage will help them to lose weight. In fact, massage alone will not cause weight loss, but as part of a carefully controlled treatment plan which includes diet, exercise and use of electrical equipment, it can be effective.

The fact that clients have approached therapists for body massage shows that they are keen to work on their weight problem and if therapists can find out the cause, they can then offer a treatment plan which will include massage. The most common cause is over eating the wrong types of food and taking insufficient exercise. Therapists who can teach clients to eat more sensibly, take more exercise and have regular body massage, when progress will be monitored, can easily rectify this. The problem may be hereditary and therefore results may take longer to achieve, but regular body massage will maintain contact with clients allowing therapists to provide encouragement and support as well as working out a long-term treatment plan.

Hormonal imbalance

This can be responsible for a client who is obese, for example under-active thyroid gland or possibly medication such as steroids which the client is taking for a medical condition. The menopause may also cause water retention and fat storage, which often settles in the area of the abdomen and hips creating the typical pear-shaped figure. In these cases, the benefits of relaxation through massage will be most effective. Whatever the cause, before treatment it is important that the general health of the client is good and a doctor confirms that treatment may go ahead.

Ideally, massage should be combined with diet and gentle exercise, possibly increasing as the weight problem improves. The areas which have the most excess fat should be worked on, using the more stimulating movements, wringing, picking up, skin rolling, hacking, clapping, beating and pounding. Depth of pressure must be increased considerably. If appropriate to the client, a heavy-duty gyratory vibrator may be used instead of or in addition to manual massage.

Joint stiffness

It is always advisable to obtain the permission of the client's doctor before treating joint stiffness. Massage should be applied to all muscles which act on the particular joint in question. Frictions and finger kneading may be applied to the joint itself. Plenty of effleurage movements should be interspersed during the massage. Mobility exercises and passive movements could be done during treatment and then strengthening exercises which can also be carried out at the client's home.

It could prove effective if some form of heat treatment was applied before treating the joints, to help with mobility. Paraffin wax is a gentle form of heat and has a soothing effect.

Muscular aches and pains

First of all, it is important to eliminate a medical condition as the cause of the aches and pains. Therefore, clients should consult their doctor. The pain may be caused by knots of tension in the muscles, and deep kneading, particularly with the thumbs and fingers, will help to relax the tension in the muscle. These movements should then be interspersed with lots of soothing relaxing effleurage. More time should be spent on the areas which are particularly affected, and these areas must be pointed out by the client.

Before performing massage, the muscles may be warmed by applying heat in the form of a sauna or steam.

Slack muscles

This can occur for several reasons:

* after pregnancy
* as a result of rapid weight loss
* through the natural ageing process.

The elasticity of the muscles has been lost and massage must be combined with gentle exercise which can be increased as the muscles regain some strength. Nourishment will be increased to the muscles because of the increase in circulation. The massage should be more stimulating using deep kneading and tapotement. As the muscles' tone improves, some of the petrissage movements may be incorporated.

Tight or contracted muscles

Muscles may be tight due to excessive exercise or to a postural problem. Many sports men and women suffer from this problem.

The movements performed must be slow and rhythmical, in particular kneading and effleurage, to help in stretching the muscles. Tapotement must be eliminated as this could prove painful.

Massage for men

The muscle bulk in men is larger and stronger than in women. Their muscles are firmer, there is less fatty tissue and their skin is far thicker and tougher and normally quite hairy. The depth of pressure will have to be increased and more body weight used. A good massage cream or oil must be used to allow ease of movement. The movements should consist mainly of kneading, picking up, wringing and tapotement interspersed with deep effleurage. Excess cream must be removed with cologne or astringent.

16 Aromatherapy

Aromatherapy has become one of the most requested treatments in beauty salons. It is increasing in popularity to such a degree that manufacturers of skin care and other cosmetic products are incorporating essential oils for their therapeutic effect. Aromatherapy massage is not only relaxing in its application but with the careful use of essential oils has other beneficial effects on the body and mind. It is the most effective way of introducing essential oils into the body and it is known to benefit both physical and psychological problems. As the word suggests, aromatherapy means:

aroma – a pleasant sweet smell or fragrance

therapy – healing treatment serving to improve or maintain health.

The sense of smell

We respond to odours emotionally rather than intellectually. The smell receptors in the nose are directly linked with the limbic system, which is responsible for a great range of emotions as well as regulating reproductive cycles and sex drive. Certain smells stimulate intense experiences and may evoke past experiences. Smells can warn, frighten, arouse or console us.

Aromatherapy is a holistic treatment using essential oils to promote balance and harmony within mind and body. Essential oils are found in:

* **herbs** such as rosemary and thyme
* **flowers** such as rose, geranium and lavender
* **leaves** such as basil, sage and clary sage
* **fruits** such as tangerine, lemon and grapefruit
* **berries** such as juniper and cypress
* **bark** such as cinnamon
* **resin** which may be made into incense, e.g. myrrh and benzoin

* **wood** such as sandalwood or rosewood
* **seeds** such as anise and caraway
* **roots** such as angelica and vetiver
* **nuts** such as nutmeg
* **grasses** such as lemon grass.

These essential oils provide not only the aroma of a plant but also many complex chemicals that treat the body in many ways. The beneficial properties of essential oils, which are sometimes referred to as the life force of a plant, are far more effective than the aroma produced from the flower or plant as they are more concentrated.

Together the use of essential oils and massage helps to maintain optimum health. They will work on the autonomic nervous system and the central nervous system, affecting the energy fields of the body. Stress causes suppression of the immune system and this treatment is an excellent antidote helping to establish and maintain balance between the nervous systems and organs of the body.

Pressure point massage, particularly on the face, working on specific energy lines or meridians, is used to prevent energy blockage that causes imbalance in the body and is often combined with essential oils.

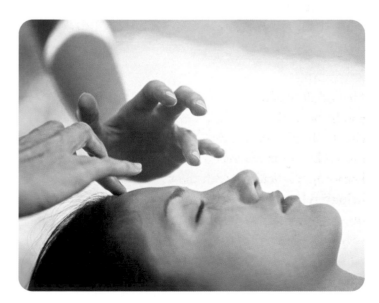

Figure 16.1 *Pressure point massage to the face*

How essential oils are extracted

Steam distillation

The raw materials are collected and placed in large vats with water and then heated. The steam extracts the oil from the plant and the vapour produced passes into a condenser and is then cooled with the essential oil separating from the flower water. This is the most commonly used method.

Figure 16.3 *Enfleurage*

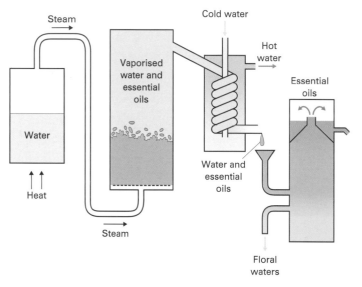

Figure 16.2 *Steam distillation*

Expression

This method, also known as the cold press method, is used for citrus oils. The essential oil is expressed by squeezing it from the rind or peel of the fruit. The best source of raw material would be organically grown fruit which has not been sprayed with pesticides.

Solvent extraction

The raw materials are covered by a solvent such as ether, benzene, petroleum, hexane or acetone and then heated to extract the essential oil. This is then filtered, which leaves a paste made up of wax and fragrance called concrete that is then mixed with alcohol and distilled at low temperatures. The alcohol absorbs the fragrance and when the alcohol is evaporated off an aromatic absolute remains.

Enfleurage

This is one of the earliest methods used to extract essential oils from flowers. A pure, odourless, cold fat is placed in a thin layer on a glass frame and the flower petals are placed in layers on top. After 30 hours, the fat will have absorbed the essential oils. The glass frame is turned and new flowers take their place. Once the fat is saturated with the essential oils, it is washed with alcohol, which absorbs the essential oils, and finally the alcohol is evaporated off leaving pure essential oil. This is an expensive method of extraction, which is not in common use.

Maceration

The flowers or petals are slightly ruptured and placed in warm fat. This is repeated many times until the fat becomes saturated with essential oil and is then bathed in alcohol, which evaporates leaving essential oil.

Quality of essential oils

For the best results, the highest quality oils should be used and you will need to consider the following when choosing oils:

* Choose a supplier who buys raw materials from areas with the best growing conditions – such things as altitude, soil, climate and time of harvesting affects the quality.

* Organically grown plants yield the highest quality essential oils.
* The more expensive oils are usually of the highest quality.
* Watch for blended oils that mix high quality oils with less expensive ones as the result will be an inferior product which reduces the healing properties of the oil.
* Always buy oils which have the Latin name on the bottle as well as the common name.

Absorption of essential oils

Oils may be absorbed into the body:

* manually
* by inhalation.

When applied to the skin manually the oils will be absorbed into the skin, muscular tissue, the joints and the bloodstream where it will reach all the body tissues and organs.

As vapour, oils will be inhaled through the nose and into the lungs. From the lungs it will enter the bloodstream and from the nose it will reach the brain causing hormonal and neurochemical release which has emotional and psychological effects.

The olfactory sensations

Special senses allow us to detect changes in the environment and the sense of smell has a connection with the part of the brain that is the sorting house for emotional responses. Our sense of smell provides us with a warning system giving us valuable information about the environment and it is closely linked with our sense of taste.

The olfactory system

For information on the structure and function of the olfactory system, see Chapter 36 The special senses, page 411.

To be smelled a substance must be:

* volatile – capable of giving off a gas so that it may enter the nostrils
* water soluble so that it can dissolve in the mucus of the cilia (fine hairs) in the nose and make contact with the olfactory cells
* lipid (fat) soluble – as the plasma membranes of the cilia are largely lipid so the substance must be able to dissolve in this lipid covering to make contact with the hair in order to initiate a response.

The limbic system

The limbic system is closely connected with the part of the brain that receives the messages from the olfactory cells in the nose. For more information on the limbic system, see Chapter 36 The special senses, page 412.

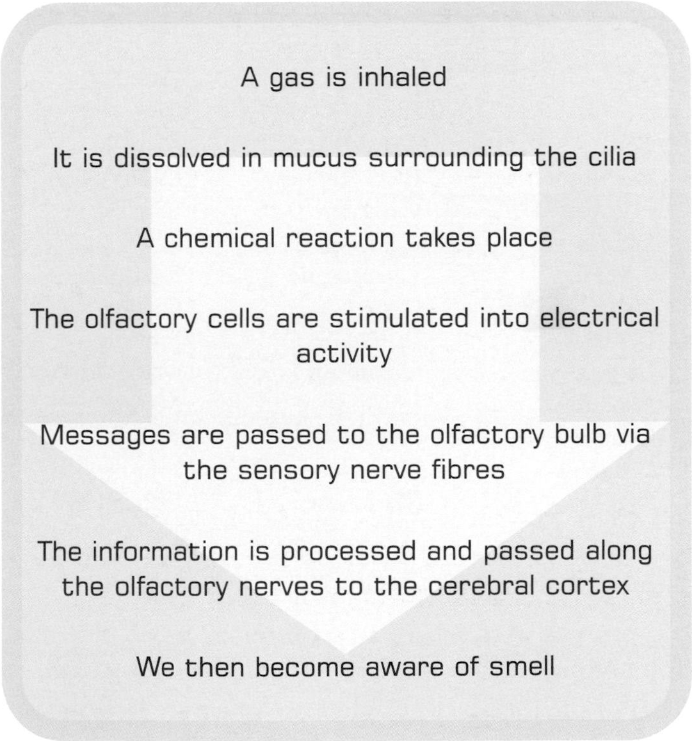

A gas is inhaled

It is dissolved in mucus surrounding the cilia

A chemical reaction takes place

The olfactory cells are stimulated into electrical activity

Messages are passed to the olfactory bulb via the sensory nerve fibres

The information is processed and passed along the olfactory nerves to the cerebral cortex

We then become aware of smell

Figure 16.4 *How we smell*

Essential oils

Classification and properties of essential oils

Essential oils are divided into top, middle and base notes.

Top notes	Middle notes	Base notes
Sharp and immediate aroma	Flowery aroma, slower to register	Heavier, spicy, woody and floral aroma
Evaporate very quickly	Evaporate moderately quickly	Evaporate slowly
Absorbed into the skin quickly	Absorbed into the skin moderately quickly	Absorbed into the skin very slowly
Last for about 10 hours in the body	Last for 24 hours in the body	Lasts up to five days in the body
Originate from citrus plants and herbs	Originate from herbs and flowers	Originate from woods, resins and flowers
Generally stimulating	Generally balancing oils	Generally relaxing to mind and body
Thinnest of the oils	Affect the body organs	Some are sedative and aphrodisiac
	Slightly sedative	Fix the top and middle notes

Table 16.1 *Top, middle and base notes*

Top	Middle	Base
Basil	Aniseed	Benzoin
Bergamot	Black pepper	Cedar wood
Eucalyptus	Camphor	Cinnamon
Lemon	Caraway	Clove
Cajeput	Chamomile	Frankincense
Clary sage	Cypress	Ginger
Coriander	Fennel	Jasmine
Lemon grass	Geranium	Marigold
Niaouli	Hyssop	Myrrh
Orange	Juniper	Neroli
Petitgrain	Lavender	Nutmeg
Sage	Marjoram	Origanum

Table 16.2 *Essential oils classified as top, middle and base notes*

Properties of oils

Sensitive to heat and light

Not greasy or oily, as the name suggests

Not lubricating

Have a fragrance

Do not mix with water

Volatile as they evaporate when exposed to air

Mix well with alcohol, vegetable and mineral oils

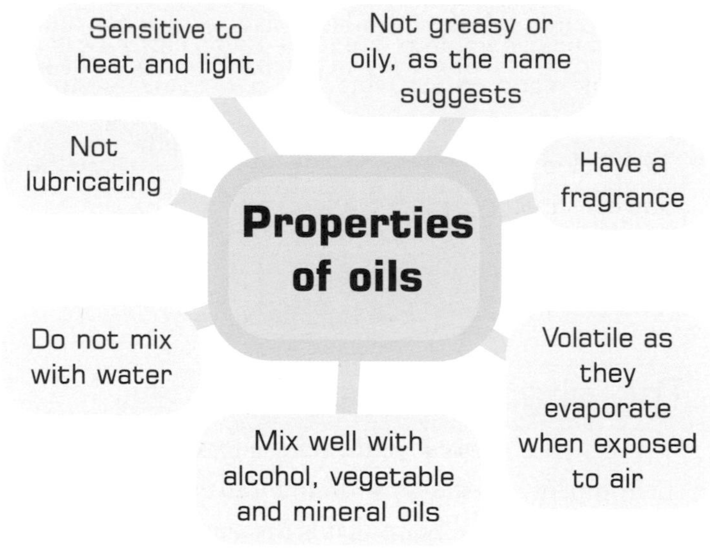

Figure 16.5 *Properties of essential oils*

Top notes are fresh and light, the middle notes are the heart of the fragrance and the base notes are rich and heavy in their aroma.

Characteristics of essential oils

* Essential oils come in many shades, from pale yellow to straw-coloured, and some more vibrant colours such as chamomile which is blue, sage which is pale lime and patchouli which is orange.
* The viscosity is thin like water rather than thick like an oil.
* They are volatile and evaporate quickly when exposed to the air, top notes evaporate quicker than base notes. Therefore they must be stored in a dark glass bottle which is tightly stoppered. Plastic containers cannot be used as essential oils will corrode plastic.

* They are inflammable so will catch fire easily. Care must be taken when using oils in a burner.
* They are soluble in vegetable oils and alcohol.
* They mix well with soap and honey.

Synergy

All essential oils work more effectively in a synergistic blend, the oils interacting with each other for greater effect than if they were used alone. Some essential oils when used together have a mutually enhancing effect, for example the anti-inflammatory effect of chamomile is more effective when mixed with lavender. When creating a synergistic blend you will need to consider:

* the symptom to be treated
* the underlying cause
* psychological or emotional factors.

Creating a synergistic blend

Oils can be divided into families – floral, citrus, herbs, trees, spices and resins. Table 16.3 gives some examples of oils and the families to which they belong. Oils which belong to the same botanical family or share the same constituents generally blend well.

Oils also blend well with adjacent groups. For example:

Floral → Citrus → Herbs
Citrus → Herbs → Trees
Herbs → Trees → Spices
Trees → Spices → Resins
Spices → Resins → Floral
Resins → Floral → Citrus

Methods of use

* Aromatherapy burners
* Candles
* Ceramic ring
* Compress
* Directly on to the skin
* Dry inhalation on a handkerchief
* Facial steamer
* Foot spa
* Fragrance bowl
* Hair care products
* Humidifier
* In the bath
* In the car
* Inhalation
* Massage
* Ointment
* Pot pourri
* Sauna
* Skin care products
* Tea infusions

Aromatherapy massage combines the use of the relaxing effects of the massage itself with the therapeutic effect of the oils and the sense of smell. The mind and body is soothed and the body's natural energy flow is stimulated.

As a therapist, using massage to apply essential oils to the body will be the principal form of treatment. You may also wish to use a burner, humidifier or fragrance bowl in the treatment room and you can give your client

Table 16.3 *Examples of botanical families*

Floral	Citrus	Herbs	Trees	Spices	Resins
Chamomile	Bergamot	Basil	Bay	Aniseed	Amyris
Geranium	Citronella	Bay laurel	Birch	Black pepper	Benzoin
Jasmine	Grapefruit	Coriander	Cajeput	Cinnamon	Camphor
Lavender	Lemon	Fennel	Cedar wood	Cloves	Frankincense
Mimosa	Lemon grass	Loveage	Eucalyptus	Nutmeg	Myrrh
Neroli	Lime	Marjoram	Juniper	Tea tree	
Rose	Mandarin	Patchouli	Niaouli		
Violet	Melissa	Rosemary	Petitgrain		
Ylang ylang	Neroli	Tarragon	Pine		
	Orange	Thyme	Rosewood		
	Petitgrain		Sandalwood		

advice in using oils for home care. The methods listed above are all useful to clients, particularly when you choose and blend the essential oils for their own specific needs.

When recommending oils to be used at home in the bath do not forget that they can be mixed with an appropriate carrier oil, full fat milk or specially formulated bath products. Resins or absolutes must not be used in the bath as they will stain the surface.

Precautions

* Always check for contraindications.
* Do not use undiluted oils.
* Do not administer essential oils internally.
* Ensure the client likes the fragrance of the oils.

Carrier oils

Essential oils may not be applied directly on to the skin but should be diluted in a base oil. When choosing a carrier oil to mix with essential oils for aromatherapy massage, the best quality vegetable oils should be used. They are obtained from the seeds of plants from around the world and extracted by 'cold pressing' to ensure they are in their purest form.

Benefits of a carrier oil

* Dilutes the essential oil to make it safe.
* Helps to spread the essential oil evenly.
* Slows down the evaporation rate of the essential oil.
* Increases the absorption of the essential oil into the skin.

The following are a selection of carrier oils, some of which may be used for a particular purpose, as shown in Table 16.4:

* aloe vera
* apricot kernel★
* avocado
* calendula
* coconut★
* evening primrose
* grapeseed
* hazelnut★

* jojoba★
* olive
* peach kernel★
* peanut★
* soya bean
* St John's wort
* sweet almond★
* vitamin E
* wheatgerm.★★

★ Avoid the use of these oils for those with an allergy to nuts.
★★ Avoid the use of this oil for those with an allergy to gluten. Use vitamin E or soya bean instead.

For the body	For the face	For healing
Grapeseed	Aloe vera	Almond
Peanut	Apricot kernel	Calendula
Sesame	Avocado	Jojoba
Soya	Evening	Olive
Sunflower	primrose	St John's wort
Sweet almond	Jojoba	
	Peach kernel	
	Sweet almond	

Table 16.4 *Specific uses of carrier oils*

Effects of individual oils

* **Aloe vera oil** contains enzymes, vitamins, proteins and minerals that support all skin functions and it activates the skin's own healing powers. It will help in skin rejuvenation and is soothing to a sunburned skin. It will be useful when mixed with essential oils for the treatment of psoriasis, eczema and skin allergies.
* **Apricot kernel oil** is especially good for prematurely aged, dry and sensitive skin.
* **Avocado pear oil** contains vitamins, protein and fatty acids and is useful for all skin types but especially dry, dehydrated skin and eczema.
* **Calendula oil** is excellent for healing and may be used on irritated skin, for muscle pain and on children.
* **Evening primrose oil** is used for PMT, menopausal problems, eczema, psoriasis and helps

in preventing premature ageing. It contains a high level of gamma-lanolin acid, a substance much like the body's own chemical metabolism regulator.

* **Grapeseed oil** is a commonly used oil and may be used on all skin types.
* **Hazelnut oil** is good for dry or damaged skin, and blends well with sandalwood, rosewood, ylang ylang.
* **Jojoba oil** contains vitamin E. It is highly penetrative, having healing and anti-inflammatory properties, and is good for eczema and psoriasis, and is nourishing to the skin.
* **Olive oil** has disinfecting and wound healing properties and is soothing to rheumatic joints, but it has a strong odour which some people do not like.
* **Peanut, safflower, soya bean and sunflower oil** can be used for all skin types.
* **Sesame oil** is useful for all skin types, in particular psoriasis, eczema, rheumatism and arthritis; also good for stretch marks.
* **Sweet almond oil** is nourishing and penetrating, and is excellent for a dry sensitive skin.
* **Wheatgerm oil** aids regeneration of the skin, is soothing and healing and is particularly good for dry and ageing skin.

Effects on the body

Depending on the blend of oils chosen, they can have different effects on the body. For example, they can:

* penetrate into the dermis in approximately 6–10 seconds
* stimulate or soothe the nervous system
* promote healthy cell growth
* relieve aches and pains
* soothe aching muscles
* refresh the mind and increase concentration
* relieve headaches
* be antiseptic in effect
* be anti-inflammatory in effect
* be uplifting
* be balancing

* have anti-viral properties
* help to stimulate the body's immune system
* can be sedative in effect.

Useful terms: effects of essential oils

Term	Effect
Analgesic	Relieves pain
Antidepressant	Alleviates depression
Antiphlogistic	Reduces inflammation
Antiseptic	Helps to stop bacterial growth
Antisudorific	Reduces perspiration
Antitoxic	Counteracts poisons
Astringent	Local constriction of tissue
Bechic	Relieves coughing
Carminative	Helps flatulence and colic
Cephalic	Stimulates the brain
Cicatrisant	Helps formation of scar tissue
Cytophylactic	Helps cell growth
Decongestant	Relieves catarrh
Diuretic	Stimulates urine excretion
Emmanagogic	Induces menstruation*
Haemostatic	Stops bleeding
Hepatic	Liver tonic
Hypertensive	Raises blood pressure
Hypotensive	Lowers blood pressure
Nervine	Nerve tonic
Rubefacient	Stimulates local circulation
Sedative	Induces sleep
Stimulant	Increases general activity
Sudorific	Promotes perspiration
Tonic	Generally or locally stimulating
Vasoconstrictor	Constricts blood vessels
Vulnerary	Can help heal external cuts, and so on

* May also be abortifacient (causes miscarriage)

Composition of essential oils

The basic chemical constituents of essential oils are:

* carbon (C)
* hydrogen (H)
* oxygen (O).

Essential oils are made up of many different organic molecules and the aroma and properties of each oil is dependent on the combination and concentration of these molecules, which may vary from harvest to harvest and plant to plant. The constituents belong to different chemical families, as described below.

Acids. They are quite rare, occurring in minute quantities and usually found in a combination with esters.

Alcohols. They are the largest group found in essential oils. Germicidal in effect, they may be subdivided into:

* monoterpenol, which are anti-bacterial and anti-viral – they are stimulating with a tonic effect and can be used on all ages as they are non-irritating
* sesquiterpenol, which have a decongestant effect on the circulatory system, have a tonic effect and are also non-irritating
* diterpenol, which have a similar structure to human hormones so have a balancing effect on the hormonal system.

Aldehydes. They are anti-inflammatory, calming to the nervous system and they often have a powerful aroma. Some aldehydes are skin sensitisers.

Esters. They are balancing and anti-inflammatory and therefore effective for skin problems. They are also calming and uplifting, so beneficial to the nervous system.

Ethers. They occur rarely in essential oils and the properties are antidepressant, antispasmodic and sedative.

Ketones. They have a calming and sedative effect and help to break down mucus and fat, and they promote healing in scar tissue. Some may be toxic, so oils containing ketones should be well diluted and not used too often or for too long.

Lactones. They occur mostly in expressed oils such as lemon, orange, grapefruit and are generally regarded as non-toxic but are responsible for skin photosensitisation.

Oxides. They are rare in essential oils apart from cineole (eucalyptol) which has mucolyptic properties and is found in oils such as eucalyptus, peppermint, camphor, marjoram. They are used to help with colds and infections of the respiratory tract but may be irritating if used in large quantities and should be used with care.

Phenols. They are very strong in action so should be used in low concentrations for short periods of time. They make powerful antiseptics and are stimulating to the nervous system and the immune system.

Terpenes. They are hydrocarbons made up solely of hydrogen and carbon atoms and may be classified as:

* monoterpenes – occur in most essential oils; although weak in effect, they are antiseptic, anti-inflammatory, stimulating, expectorant and slightly analgesic
* sesquiterpenes – have similar properties to monoterpenes; they are calming
* diterpenes – not found in many essential oils as the molecule is heavy and may not always be extracted in the distillation process.

The more that essential oils are interfered with chemically, the less effective they are. It is also important to use the correct strength of oil as excessive use may have the reverse effect of that which is wanted.

Physiological effects of essential oils

Essential oils are non-invasive and when used correctly are non-toxic. They stimulate the body's own natural healing processes. The body absorbs the oils very quickly and they remain in the body for between ten hours and several days when they are secreted or excreted in the normal way via the excretory system, respiratory system and the skin. It may take less time in a fit and healthy person than in someone who is obese or unhealthy for the oils to be excreted, depending on the note of the oil (see above).

Figure 16.6 *Common problems of the cardiovascular system*

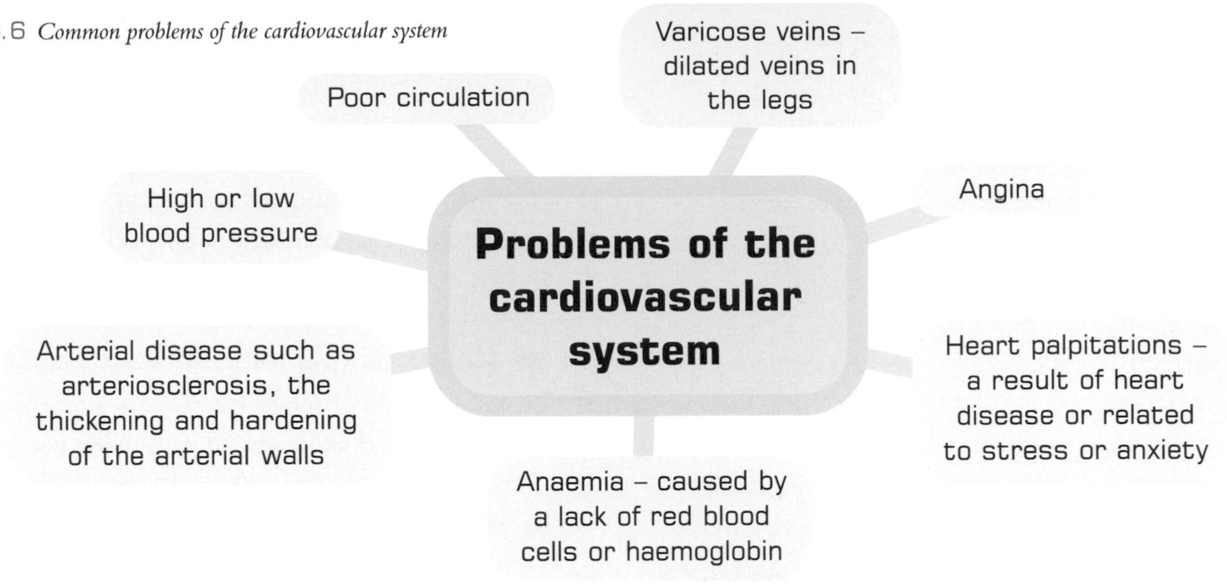

Poor circulation

Varicose veins –
dilated veins in
the legs

High or low
blood pressure

Angina

**Problems of the
cardiovascular
system**

Arterial disease such as
arteriosclerosis, the
thickening and hardening
of the arterial walls

Heart palpitations –
a result of heart
disease or related
to stress or anxiety

Anaemia – caused by
a lack of red blood
cells or haemoglobin

The cardiovascular system

The cardiovascular system consists of the heart and the circulatory system. A healthy heart and circulatory system is essential to the normal functioning of all the body organs and tissues. Some common problems of the cardiovascular system are shown in Figure 16.6.

Some of the recommended oils for the circulatory system include the following:

* Lavender, geranium, marjoram, chamomile, ylang ylang, clary sage to **reduce blood pressure**.
* Rosemary, thyme, camphor to **raise blood pressure**.
* Black pepper, rosemary, peppermint, marjoram, ginger, rose to **improve blood circulation**.
* Rose, melissa, orange, neroli for **antispasmodic action on the heart**.
* Cypress, lemon, geranium for **varicose veins**.

The digestive system

Problems of the digestive system include those shown in Figure 16.7.

Recommended oils include the following:

* Marjoram, rosemary, ginger, fennel, camphor, black pepper, peppermint for **laxative effects**.
* Sandalwood, rosemary, chamomile for **antispasmodic action**.
* Basil, bergamot, sage, coriander, cardamon, peppermint, fennel, lavender, aniseed, melissa for **indigestion** and **flatulence**.

* Eucalyptus, sage, chamomile, peppermint, cypress, sandalwood for **diarrhoea**.
* Lemon, sage, peppermint, rose for the **liver**.
* Coriander, ginger, tarragon, nutmeg, myrrh to **stimulate digestion**.
* Eucalyptus, lemon, chamomile, camphor, ylang ylang for **gall stones**.

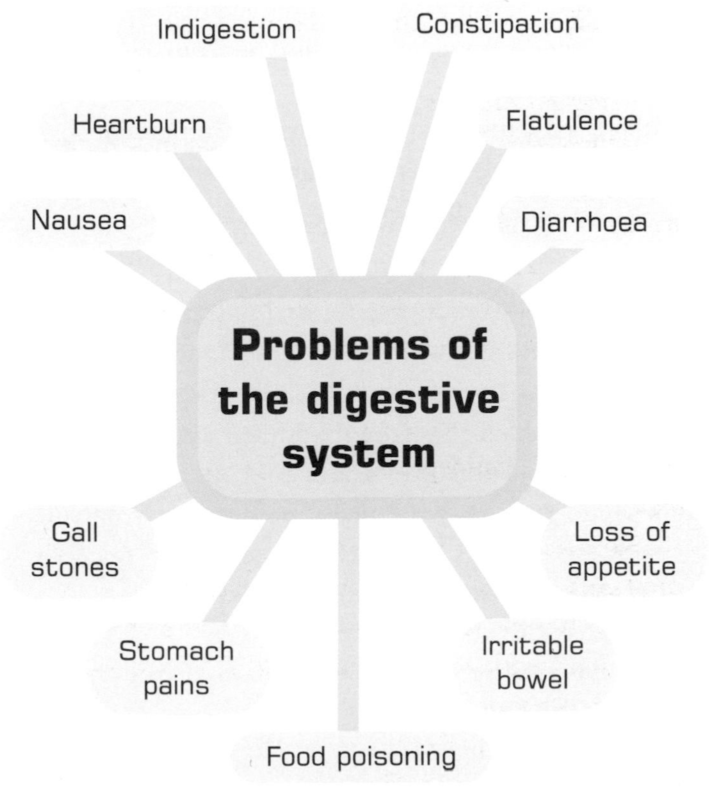

Indigestion

Constipation

Heartburn

Flatulence

Nausea

Diarrhoea

**Problems of
the digestive
system**

Gall
stones

Loss of
appetite

Stomach
pains

Irritable
bowel

Food poisoning

Figure 16.7 *Problems of the digestive system*

Body treatments

The respiratory system

The respiratory system, which includes the nose, throat and lungs, is prone to infection and essential oils can be inhaled for effective results as well as massaged into the back and chest. The effects are antiseptic, helping to control bacterial growth; expectorant, to increase the output of respiratory fluids; and antispasmodic, to lessen the spasm in smooth muscle fibres.

* **Antiseptic oils** include angelica, cinnamon, thyme, tea tree, eucalyptus, pine, camphor, clove, lemon, peppermint and cajeput.
* **Expectorant oils** include eucalyptus, camphor, pine, thyme, rosemary, hyssop, lemon, myrrh, cajeput and benzoin, which all help to clear the respiratory tract of mucus.
* **Antispasmodic oils** include clary sage, aniseed, hyssop, cypress, frankincense, rosemary and basil, which will help to alleviate and soothe coughs.

The following conditions will benefit from specific oils:

* Basil, lemon, thyme, cypress, pine, clove for **asthma**.
* Basil, bergamot, cajeput, eucalyptus, tea tree, lavender, pine, peppermint, benzoin, clove for **bronchitis**.
* Eucalyptus, lemon, sage, thyme, chamomile, camphor, lavender, pine, benzoin, sandalwood for **flu**.
* Hyssop for **hayfever**.

The lymphatic system

This system is responsible for draining and removing waste from the body as well as removing excess fluid. A poor lymphatic system will result in a build-up of toxins and fluids which results in fluid retention or oedema and cellulite. Therefore, stimulating oils and those with antiseptic properties are used for a sluggish lymphatic system.

* **Stimulating** – fennel, geranium, juniper, lavender, rosemary and sage.
* **Antiseptic** – eucalyptus, lemon, thyme and tea tree.

The urinary system

The urinary system consists of two kidneys, ureters and the bladder. An efficient urinary system is essential to help with excreting waste fluid and detoxifying the body and regulating the fluid balance. Essential oils are used to maintain an efficient system and have an antiseptic effect on the urinary tract to help deal with infections such as cystitis.

* **Fluid retention** is improved by using diuretic essential oils such as eucalyptus, sage, juniper, cypress, fennel, lavender, rosemary, patchouli and sandalwood.
* **Urinary tract infections** would benefit from essential oils such as bergamot, cajeput, eucalyptus, niaouli, fennel, juniper, pine, sandalwood, benzoin, frankincense and tea tree.
* **Kidneys** benefit from eucalyptus, lemon, sage, thyme, juniper, fennel and sandalwood.

The immune system

The immune system is responsible for fighting infection and produces white blood cells and antibodies. Essential oils are effective in stimulating the immune system to help the body destroy invading bacteria and viruses and to strengthen the immune system so that it works more efficiently.

* **Strengthening** the immune system – bergamot, eucalyptus, ginger, lavender, lemon grass, rosemary and tea tree.
* **Stimulating** the immune system – eucalyptus, lavender, tea tree, pine, chamomile and sandalwood.
* **Antibacterial** and **anti-viral** – camphor, clove, cajeput, eucalyptus, niaouli and tea tree.

The nervous system

This system is the link between the mind and the body and the pace of life today is such that we overwork our nervous system causing many physical and psychological problems. The use of essential oils will help as they have many different properties. They will soothe or stimulate, regulate or balance the nervous system. Oils will be chosen for their specific effects, stimulating oils will be chosen for depression or nervous fatigue whereas soothing oils will be chosen for insomnia, hysteria, nervousness or anxiety.

* Basil, bergamot, thyme, clary sage, chamomile, juniper, lavender, geranium, marjoram, patchouli, melissa for **anxiety** and **tension**.
* Chamomile, clary sage, lavender, neroli and sandalwood are sedating **antidepressant** oils. Jasmine, geranium, rose, melissa, basil, bergamot are **uplifting antidepressant** oils. Both can be used for **depression**.
* Chamomile, camphor, juniper, marjoram, neroli, thyme, rose, ylang ylang for **insomnia**.
* Basil, bergamot, chamomile, cedar wood, geranium, jasmine, juniper, lavender, neroli, rose for **stress**.
* Basil, bergamot, clary sage, chamomile, lavender, geranium, jasmine, neroli, rose, sandalwood, ylang ylang for **nervous tension**.

The reproductive system

Treatment with essential oils will help with problems caused by hormonal changes or infection. Essential oils can be used for heavy, irregular and painful menstruation or absence of menstruation altogether. Some oils will have a regulating or strengthening effect while others have aphrodisiac qualities.

* Basil, clary sage, thyme, chamomile, lavender, melissa, peppermint and rose for **irregular menstruation**.
* Cajeput, sage, chamomile, aniseed, juniper, marjoram, melissa, rosemary, jasmine, tarragon for **painful menstruation**.
* Clary sage, sage and thyme, chamomile, fennel, melissa, rose for **absence of menstruation**.
* Juniper, fennel, parsley, angelica, cypress, myrrh, marjoram to **induce menstruation**.
* Clary sage, chamomile, lavender, geranium, neroli, rose otto for **PMT**.
* Clary sage, sage, chamomile, cypress, fennel, geranium for **menopause**.
* Jasmine, ylang ylang, neroli, rose, sandalwood, patchouli, vetivert, clary sage for **aphrodisiac**.

The muscular and skeletal system

This system receives a great deal of wear and tear and to maintain a good balance between the structure and flexibility of the two requires a healthy diet, moderate exercise, relaxation, good posture and the minimum of stress. Apart from minor aches and pains, problems such as rheumatism, arthritis, backache and osteoporosis can affect these systems.

* **Muscular aches and pains** will benefit from cajeput, caraway, eucalyptus, sage, thyme, black pepper, camphor, marjoram, chamomile, lavender, clove and nutmeg.
* **Arthritis** will benefit from caraway, lemon, sage, thyme, camphor, chamomile, juniper, cypress and benzoin.
* **Rheumatism** benefits from cajeput, coriander, eucalyptus, lemon, sage, thyme, chamomile, juniper, lavender, marjoram and rosemary.
* **Sprains** benefit from eucalyptus, camphor, lavender, marjoram and rosemary.
* **Cramp** will benefit from basil, cypress and marjoram.
* **Lack of muscle tone** will benefit from lemon grass, black pepper, lavender and rosemary.
* **Stiffness** will benefit from thyme and rosemary.

The skin

Skin is protective and semi-permeable. It absorbs, secretes and excretes substances from the body as well as maintaining normal body temperature. The skin may become imbalanced, due to internal and external factors, or inflamed or infected. It can be helped with the use of essential oils. Essential oils will nourish, cleanse, detoxify, tighten and calm the skin and there are many conditions which may be improved such as:

* acne
* psoriasis
* eczema
* dermatitis
* mature skin
* sensitive skin
* oily skin
* dry skin

Body treatments

* broken capillaries
* sunburn
* inflammation
* bruises
* burns.

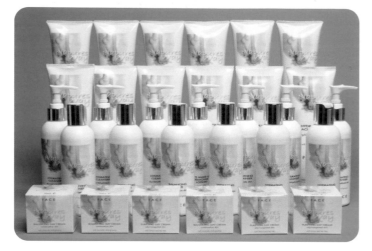

Figure 16.8 *Skin care products*

Essential oils may be blended with a carrier oil to improve certain skin conditions.

Skin conditions

* **Acne**. Lavender, bergamot, geranium, sandalwood, tea tree – antiseptic, healing and oil regulating; chamomile – anti-inflammatory.
* **Broken capillaries**. Lemon, cypress, neroli – calming vascular constrictors; rose, chamomile, geranium – soothing and anti-inflammatory.
* **Bruises**. Sage, fennel, camphor, marjoram.
* **Burns**. Lavender and tea tree – soothing, healing and antiseptic; chamomile, geranium, rose – soothing.
* **Dry skin**. Chamomile, geranium, lavender, marigold, neroli, rose – moisturising and soothing.
* **Eczema**. Chamomile, lavender, geranium, rose, melissa – moisturising, soothing and healing.
* **Fungal infection**. Lavender – antiseptic; tea tree – antifungal; geranium – anti-inflammatory; lemon grass – drying and deodorising.
* **Mature skin**. Rose, neroli, frankincense, geranium, lavender – rejuvenating; chamomile – soothing.

* **Oily skin**. Bergamot, lemon, cedar wood, geranium – rebalancing and antiseptic; lemon grass – open pores; lavender – healing.
* **Psoriasis**. Bergamot and chamomile – soothing and anti-inflammatory; lavender – healing.
* **Sensitive skin**. Jasmine, lavender and chamomile, neroli and rose – moisturising and soothing.
* **Sunburn**. Lavender, chamomile, geranium or rose – soothing and anti-inflammatory

Effects

* **Antiseptic** – chamomile, lavender, tea tree, lemon, pine, thyme, eucalyptus, clove, cinnamon, bergamot, lemon.
* **Anti-viral** – lemon, patchouli, tea tree.
* **Anti-inflammatory** – chamomile, jasmine, lavender, myrrh, neroli, frankincense, rose.
* **Healing** – lavender, chamomile, geranium, frankincense, myrrh, benzoin.

Contraindications to essential oils

Essential oils used in the correct way produce no side effects. They actually stimulate the body's own self-healing powers and work holistically treating mind and body. There are very few contraindications, but care must be taken in the following circumstances:

* Pregnancy. It is advisable not to use essential oils in the first five months of pregnancy. Care must be taken to use only the safest oils in the latter stages. (See also below.)
* Cancer – unless with doctor's permission.
* Heart disease – unless with doctor's permission.
* Skin conditions. Do not massage directly over skin infections, inflamed bites and stings, varicose veins, scar tissue, bruises or acute inflammations.
* Fever or high temperature.
* Recent inoculations. Treatment must not be within 24 hours or 36 hours after typhoid.
* Client receiving homeopathic treatment as essential oils can cancel out the effects of the homeopathic remedies.

* After major surgery. The doctor's advice should be sought but treatment should be delayed for six weeks to three months depending on the surgery.
* Conditions requiring medical attention. The doctor's permission must be sought for asthma, diabetes, multiple sclerosis, thyroid conditions and any other condition receiving medical attention.
* Strong drugs or medication. Effects of drugs may be magnified by treatment. Where a client is taking medication, the doctor's permission must be sought.
* Sensitisation – when the skin becomes intolerant to essential oils. This may happen suddenly or over a long period of time and it may be characterised by some of the following – itching, rash appearing, runny eyes, blotches on the skin, coughing, wheezing, sneezing or shortage of breath. To ensure the client will not have an allergic reaction to an oil, it is advisable to carry out a patch test and apply the oil, leaving it for 24 hours.

The following oils are contraindicated for certain conditions:

* High blood pressure. Do not use hyssop, rosemary, sage and thyme.
* Epilepsy. Do not use fennel, hyssop, rosemary and sage.
* Babies. Do not use aniseed, camphor, cinnamon leaf, clove, eucalyptus, fennel, hyssop, lemon grass, marjoram, nutmeg, origanum, parsley seed, peppermint, sage and thyme (red).

Uses during pregnancy

Some therapists advocate certain oils for particular problems suffered during pregnancy. Mandarin essential oil used in a vaporiser can help towards eliminating nausea and melissa has been a traditional French remedy for morning sickness for many years.

* Pregnancy (first five months). Do not use aniseed, basil, camphor, cedar wood, cinnamon leaf, clove, cypress, fennel, hyssop, juniper berry, marjoram, myrrh, nutmeg, origanum, parsley seed, peppermint, rosemary, savory, sage. For six to nine months the following oils may be used in weak dilutions – cedar wood, cinnamon leaf, cypress, marjoram, nutmeg, origanum, parsley seed, rosemary, savory.
* Exposure to ultraviolet light. Do not use angelica, bergamot, cumin, ginger, lemon, lime, mandarin orange and verbena as they may cause skin pigmentation when exposed to sunlight.

Essential oils must NEVER be given:
* in too high a proportion to carrier oil
* for too long
* too frequently.

Problems with use

Irritation

If certain oils are applied in too high a percentage, too frequently or for too long, irritation of the skin or mucous membrane may occur causing inflammation in the area treated. Therefore, dosage must be very carefully measured. When decanting essential oils it is important to wear protective gloves and glasses and work in a well-ventilated room. If the oil comes into contact with the skin, wash off immediately. If the oil enters the eye, flush with water.

Sensitisation

Sensitisation occurs when there is an allergic reaction to an essential oil. When this occurs test other oils on the client that have similar therapeutic effects. It would be exceptional if a client had an allergic response to all essential oils.

Toxicity

This is a term used to describe a level of poisoning. There may be an occasion when an oil causes toxicity, so great care must be taken in the use of essential oils. Avoid those that are known to be toxic and use the correct dilutions so there is not a build-up in the body and do not treat too often. The effect of an oil's toxicity will vary from individual to individual depending on the person's size and age. However, toxicity is dose dependent and essential oils should be administered in much smaller doses in children than in adults and the duration of treatment should be shorter and less frequent. Aniseed and hyssop are thought to damage the nervous system if used for long periods of time.

Storage of essential oils

Pure essential oils should be stored:

* in a cool, dry place
* in dark glass bottles
* in an airtight container
* out of direct sunshine
* out of reach of children.

The average shelf life of essential oils is six months to two years. The therapeutic effect of the oils diminishes with age. When exposed to the air the oxygen combining with some of the constituents of the oil will cause it to oxidise and deteriorate.

Do not store ready-mixed essential oils in a carrier oil as the essential oils have a much longer shelf life when they are stored in their pure state. When using oil for aromatherapy massage, mix only the amount you require for the treatment.

Figure 16.9 *Essential oils which should never be used*

Blending essential oils

Massage is the most common way of using essential oils, blending them with a suitable carrier oil, combining to great effect the senses of smell and touch. It is a therapeutic treatment providing benefits to both mind and body:

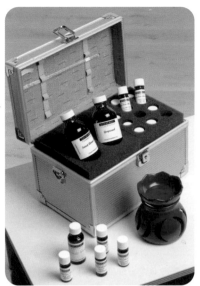

Figure 16.10 *Essential oils*

* Circulation is stimulated allowing the oils to be dispersed more rapidly around the body.
* The warmth of the skin makes the oils smell stronger.
* The carrier oil prevents the essential oil from evaporating too quickly.
* The carrier oil allows the essential oils to be dispersed evenly.
* Essential oils can be chosen to meet the individual needs of each client.

Because of their potency essential oils should not be used undiluted but should be mixed with a carrier oil in specific proportions. Using double the dose of essential oils does not mean that the client will receive twice the benefit. On the contrary, some oils will have the opposite effect than that stated. They may make the client feel nauseous and some are highly toxic.

Essential oils are always measured in drops because of their potency and concentration, and the general rule is to add half the number of drops of essential oils to the number of millilitres of carrier oil. For example:

25 drops of essential oil will be added to 50 ml of carrier oil

5 drops of essential oil will be added to 10 ml of carrier oil.

For a full body massage, you will need about 20 ml of carrier oil and 10 drops of essential oil. For massaging a smaller area, reduce the amount of oils accordingly, for example 6 ml of carrier oil with 3 drops of essential oil.

Essential oils are normally sold in dark glass bottles fitted with a dropper for accurate measurement. Because they are volatile and evaporate fairly rapidly the drops should be measured quickly and accurately in small quantities enough for the particular treatment being carried out.

You will need to consider the following when blending essential oils:

* Use the most appropriate essential oils for the client.
* Use essential oils that complement each other. Some oils may inhibit each other's effects.
* Blend together a top, a middle and a base note oil as they work together synergistically.
* Base notes last longer so may be used in smaller quantities.
* Top notes evaporate quicker so may be used in slightly higher quantities.
* Ensure the client likes the aroma of the blend.
* Look at plant families.
* Look at chemical constituents.
* Choose the carrier oil for its effectiveness, lack of smell, penetrative qualities or price.
* Mix the carrier oils when required, e.g. wheatgerm oil is rarely used alone as it is so rich but adding it to another oil will help to preserve it because of its antioxidant quality.

Figure 16.11
A therapist blends oils

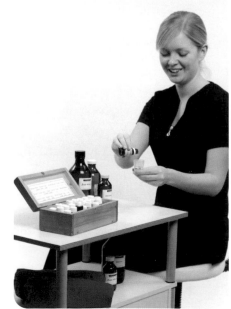

Essential equipment

10 ml ($\frac{1}{2}$ fl oz) dark glass bottles with a dropper for storing pure essential oils

Pipettes or eye droppers for testing or measuring

Strips of blotting paper to test oils

Small funnel for pouring carrier oils into small bottles

Small bowl or measuring beaker to hold blend for massage

Glass rod for mixing

Client consultation

The initial consultation with the client will take quite a long time as it is important to obtain as much information as possible about the client's:

* medical history
* lifestyle
* requirements
* physical condition
* mental condition
* personality.

A detailed record card must be filled in with the client's personal details and medical history to include the following:

* Illnesses the client may have had.
* Operations, with details.
* Accidents and injuries sustained.
* Reoccurring problems.
* Muscular or skeletal problems.
* Digestive problems.
* Circulation (heart, blood, fluid, cellulite, kidneys, bruises, etc.).
* Gynaecological problems.
* Nervous problems.
* Immune problems.
* Other (allergy, asthma, hayfever, epilepsy, diabetes, etc.).
* Is the client currently undergoing any form of medical treatment?
* Is the client taking any medication?
* Does the client smoke?

Lifestyle will include:

* marital status
* professional capacity
* description of work
* time management
* personal time
* hobbies or interests
* exercise taken
* energy level
* ability to relax
* sleeping pattern
* degree of stress (1–10)
* diet: what is eaten; how it is eaten; drinks daily
* food allergies or problems
* condition of the skin
* general comments
* yin or yang qualities.

Postural analysis will include:

* Standing – posterior, anterior and lateral views.
* Look at specific points – from the back, the shoulders should be level, the scapulae should not protrude on either or both sides, the spine should be straight with no sign of scoliosis and the hips should be level. Check the knees and ankles that they are level and there is no swelling present.
* From the side, check that the chin does not lean forward, there is no stooping or dowager's hump present at the top of the back, the abdominal muscles are not protruding and weak, there is no pelvic tilt and the feet are not flat.
* From the front, check that the shoulders are not curving inwards indicating poor posture and that waist, hips and knees are level.
* Sitting down again, check the shoulder level and the spine.

Connective tissue test

With the client in a prone position on the couch, using your index finger and starting at the base of the spine, move gently upwards rolling the skin and it should ripple naturally if there is no tension present. If there is tension, it will show up as a tight area with little or no rippling.

AROMATHERAPY CONSULTATION RECORD CARD

Personal details	
Name	Janine Kay
Address	12 Portland Place The Glen Manchester M20 3DJ
Tel. no./email	0161 347 2968 janine@ntl.com
Date of birth	20/05/72
GP's name, address and tel. no.	Dr Brown 0161 347 6994 The Clinic Manchester M20 5BJ
Reasons for trying aromatherapy	Stress and lack of energy, backache
Medical details	
General state of health and well-being	Good normally. Has had a bad cold recently, can't shake it off
Illnesses	Glandular fever, measles and chicken pox
Accidents	None
Operations	Appendix removed
Muscular problems	Has occasional muscle spasm in the upper back area
Skeletal problems	None
Digestive/excretory problems	Irritable bowel
Circulatory disorders	None
Gynaecological problems	None
Nervous problems	Stress from working long hours, feels run down
Emotional trauma	None
Immune problems	Recurrence of cold and flu-like symptoms
Allergies	Eczema, from allergy to some metals
Medical treatment	None
Current medication	Contraceptive pill
Family medical history	Asthma, hay fever and eczema
Skin type	Dry
Skin colour	Pale
Skin problems	Occasional spots around the chin

Lifestyle	
Marital status	Married with three children
Professional status	Working part time in a school and is training to be a JP
Exercise	Tennis in the summer, salsa classes in the winter. Member of leisure centre, tries to go twice a week
Energy level 1–10	5
Sleep pattern/ability to relax	Not sleeping very well at the moment
Stress levels (1 = low, 10 = high)	7
Yin/Yang quality	Yang
Diet	Good, balanced
Do you eat in a hurry?	Yes
Type and no. of drinks daily	Tea – 5, water – 3, glasses of wine – 6 a week.
Vitamin suppliments	No
Food allergies/ intolerances	None
Smoke/drugs	No
General comments	

Client's signature Janine Kay	Therapist's signature Lynne Daley		Date 23/01/04
Date	**Treatment**	**Oil Chioce**	**Homecare**	**Therapist**
23/01/04	Full body	Black pepper Grapefruit Frankincense	Lavender in a burner or the bath	Lynne Daley

Figure 16.12 *An aromatherapy record card*

Flare reaction test

Run the sides of your thumb nail slowly down either side of the spine and note the pink areas, which will indicate a good circulation, and those areas where it looks white or the redness fades away quickly. This will indicate poor circulation and tension.

Aftercare advice

Once the client has had an aromatherapy massage offer him or her a glass of water. Allow the client to sit quietly as he or she may feel quite sleepy and discuss home care advice. This will reinforce the treatment and encourage clients to continue receiving benefit from the effects of the treatment.

* The client should relax after treatment and, if possible, not drive.
* Do not take a bath or shower for eight hours.
* Drink plenty of water or herbal teas.
* Do not drink alcohol for 24 hours.
* Do not eat straight away.
* Do not use a sun bed or sunbathe for 24 hours.
* Recommend essential oils to use at home.
* Advise clients about the different methods of application available to them.
* Instruct clients in their use – measure in drops, do not use undiluted on the skin and do not take internally.

Effects of essential oils

Aniseed

Antiseptic, antispasmodic, carminative, diuretic, expectorant, galactagogic, stimulant, stomachic.

Used to treat bronchitis, whooping cough, catarrh, flatulence, colic, painful periods and to stimulate breast milk.

Basil

Antidepressant, antiseptic, antispasmodic, carminative, cephalic, digestive, emanagogic, expectorant, galactagogic, nervine.

Used to treat anxiety, depression, melancholy, fatigue, insomnia, migraine, to clear the mind, muscular aches, pains, rheumatism, bronchitis, coughs, sinusitis, flatulence, stimulates menstruation.

Benzoin

Anti-inflammatory, antioxidant, antiseptic, astringent, carminative, diuretic, expectorant, sedative, vulnerary.

Used to treat asthma, bronchitis, coughs, laryngitis, flu, arthritis, poor circulation, rheumatism, cuts, inflamed skin, stress and nervous tension.

Bergamot

Uplifting, antidepressant, refreshing, appetite and digestive stimulant and antiseptic.

Used to treat depression, stress, tiredness, irritability, cystitis, urinary tract infections, fever, anorexia, colic, flatulence, indigestion, sore throat and bad breath (photosensitive).

Black pepper

Stimulating, anti-toxic and gently analgesic.

Used to treat nausea, cold, cough, fever, cystitis, constipation, loss of appetite and digestion and aches and pains, and to warm up before sport.

Cajeput

Analgesic, antispasmodic, antiseptic, diaphoretic, carminative, expectorant, tonic.

Used to treat colds, flu, bronchitis, throat infections, urinary tract infections, diarrhoea, stomach cramps, rheumatism, neuralgia, oily skin, insect bites, arthritis, rheumatism.

Chamomile

Anti-inflammatory, healing, calming, sedative, relaxing, antiseptic, digestive stimulant.

Used to treat stress, anxiety, hysteria, irritability, insomnia, headaches, rashes, inflammation, bites, burns, cuts, toothache, earache, indigestion, liver disorders, loss of appetite, aches and pains, menstrual and menopausal problems.

Clary sage

Antidepressant, antiseptic, astringent, carminative, digestive, emmenagogic, nervine, euphoric, antispasmodic, aphrodisiac, relaxing, revitalising.

Used to treat high blood pressure, sore throat, painful or irregular periods, depression, nervous anxiety, stress, dyspepsia, flatulence, PMS, amenorrhea, frigidity, impotence, asthma and night sweats.

Cypress

Antispasmodic, antiseptic, astringent, deodorising, diuretic, expectorant hepatic, sudorific, tonic.

Used to treat asthma, bronchitis, dysmenorrhea, menopausal problems, nervous tension, stress, greasy skin, hyperhidrosis, varicose veins and wounds.

Eucalyptus

Stimulating, antiseptic, antispasmodic, diuretic, expectorant, anti-viral, aids concentration.

Used to treat bronchitis, asthma, catarrh, fever, flu, sinusitis, throat infections, kidney infection, measles, muscular aches and pains, neuralgia, rheumatism, herpes, cuts, burns, insect bites, wounds and ulcers.

Fennel

Anti-inflammatory, antiseptic, antispasmodic, carminative, diuretic, emmenagogic, expectorant, galactagogic, laxative, stimulant, stomachic, tonic.

Used to treat cellulite, oedema, obesity, rheumatism, asthma, bronchitis, anorexia, colic, constipation, dyspepsia, flatulence, nausea, amenorrhea, menopausal problems and insufficient milk in nursing mothers.

Frankincense

Relaxing, sedative, calming, uplifting, mildly antiseptic.

Used to treat chest infections, catarrh, bronchitis, hayfever, insomnia, depression, bereavement, immune deficiency, wounds, scars ulcers, dry, damaged and wrinkled skin.

Geranium

Sedative, relaxing, balancing, anti-inflammatory, tonic, antiseptic, mildly diuretic.

Used to treat cellulite, fluid retention, poor circulation, hormone imbalance, mood swings, wounds, bruises, burns, broken capillaries, endometriosis, haemorrhage, throat and mouth infections, eczema, acne and mature skin.

Hyssop

Astringent, antiseptic, antispasmodic, anti-viral, carminative, cephalic, cicatrisant, digestive, diuretic, emenagogic, expectorant, febrifuge, nervine, sedative, tonic, vulnerary.

Used to treat anxiety, fatigue, lack of concentration, stress, amenorrhea, leucorrhea, indigestion, asthma, bronchitis, coughs, sore throat, tonsillitis, rheumatism, low or high blood pressure, bruises, cuts, inflamed skin and eczema.

Jasmine

Analgesic, antidepressant, anti-inflammatory, antiseptic, antispasmodic, aphrodisiac, carminative, cicatrisant, expectorant, galactagogic, balancing, sedative, tonic.

Used to treat dry, irritated or sensitive skin, eczema, catarrh, coughs, laryngitis, insomnia, low esteem, depression, nervous exhaustion, stress, frigidity, impotence, joint and muscular pains and sprains.

Juniper

Diuretic, antiseptic, uplifting, relaxing.

Used to treat cystitis, fluid retention, cellulite, colic, indigestion, cramps, gout, circulatory problems, menstrual problems, anxiety, stress, eczema, acne and oily skin.

Figure 16.13 *Juniper*

Lavender

Relaxing, antiseptic, antispasmodic, diuretic, healing, calming, uplifting, stimulating.

Used to treat high blood pressure, lymphatic congestion, cellulite, fluid retention, colic, flatulence, indigestion, nausea, cystitis, conjunctivitis, headache, migraine, nose and throat infections, flu, catarrh, bronchitis, asthma, irregular or scanty periods, anxiety, depression, irritability, insomnia, acne rosacea, eczema, insect bites, burns, inflammation and sunburn.

Lime

Antiseptic, anti-viral, antibacterial, stimulating, carminative, diuretic, tonic.

Used to treat warts, verrucae, varicose veins, poor circulation, arthritis, rheumatism, flatulence, colds, flu, fever, infection asthma, greasy skin (photosensitive).

Lemon

Stimulating, invigorating, astringent, deodorising, diuretic and antiseptic.

Used to treat acne, anaemia, greasy skin, poor circulation, rheumatism, hypertension, migraines, sore throat, loss of appetite, regulate stomach acidity, liver complaints, asthma, colds, flu, warts and verrucae, scabies, bites and stings.

Melissa

Antidepressant, antihistaminic, antispasmodic, carminative, emmenagogic, nervine, sedative, tonic.

Used to treat allergies, insect bites, eczema, asthma, bronchitis and dry coughs, colic, indigestion, nausea, menstrual problems, anxiety, depression, insomnia, migraine, shock.

Marigold

Anti-inflammatory, antiseptic, antispasmodic, astringent, emmenagogic, tonic, vulnerary.

Used to treat burns, cuts, insect bites, wounds, eczema, menstrual irregularities, varicose veins, haemorrhoids, conjunctivitis.

Myrrh

Anti-inflammatory, antiseptic, astringent, carminative, emmenagogic, expectorant, fungicidal, revitalising, sedative, stimulant, tonic, vulnerary.

Used to treat colds, asthma, bronchitis, catarrh, coughs, gingivitis, mouth ulcers, sore throats, laryngitis, arthritis, amenorrhea, thrush, athlete's foot, ringworm, chapped skin, mature skin, eczema, wounds and wrinkles.

Neroli

Antidepressant, antiseptic, antispasmodic, carminative cicatrisant, deodorant, digestive, fungicidal, stimulant, tonic.

Used to treat anxiety, depression, PMT, shock, stress, palpitations, poor circulation, diarrhoea, colic, flatulence, dyspepsia, scars, stretch marks, mature, sensitive skins, wrinkles.

Niaouli

Antiseptic, analgesic, relaxing, uplifting, healing.

Used to treat insect bites, wounds, burns, poor circulation, flu, fever, sore throat, sinusitis, bronchitis, cystitis, oily skin, indigestion, gastroenteritis and rheumatism.

Peppermint

Analgesic, anti-inflammatory, antiseptic, antispasmodic, anti-viral, astringent, carminative, emmenagogic, expectorant, hepatic, nervine, vasoconstrictor.

Used to treat fainting, headache, fatigue, migraine, stress, colds, flu, fever, cramp, colic, flatulence, nausea, indigestion, asthma, bronchitis, sinusitis, halitosis, neuralgia, muscular pain, acne, ringworm and scabies.

Petitgrain

Relaxing and stimulating, antiseptic, tonic.

Used to treat stress, nervousness, tiredness, tension, insomnia, fatigue, dyspepsia, flatulence, backache and muscular tension.

Rose

Uplifting, balancing, relaxing, soothing, antiseptic, tonic, cooling, healing, aphrodisiac.

Used to treat stress, depression, headaches, hangover, migraine, insomnia, irregular menstruation, frigidity, sterility, vaginitis, constipation, nausea, conjunctivitis, fever, wounds, shingles, gingivitis, eczema, herpes simplex, sorrow, disappointment, sadness and post partum depression, all skin types (especially dry, mature, inflamed, allergy prone) and baby skin care.

Rosemary

Antiseptic, diuretic, stimulating, cleansing, astringent, tonic.

Used to treat headaches, migraine, mental fatigue, breathing problems, fluid retention, lymphatic congestion, poor circulation, lack of periods, colitis, constipation, diarrhoea, flatulence, gall stones, gastroenteritis, stomach pains, aches and pains, arthritis, asthma, coughs and flu, alopecia and dandruff.

Figure 16.14 *Rosemary*

Sandalwood

Antiseptic, astringent, relaxing, sedative, aphrodisiac, antidepressant, expectorant.

Used to treat cystitis, colic, diarrhoea, gastritis, hiccups, vomiting, depression, tension, insomnia, frigidity, impotence, aggression, bronchitis, catarrh, coughs, sore throat, dry, inflamed or cracked skin.

Tea tree

Anti-inflammatory, antiseptic, anti-viral, antibacterial, expectorant, fungicidal, immuno-stimulant, vulnerary.

Used to treat asthma, bronchitis, catarrh, colds, coughs, fever, flu, sinusitis, tuberculosis, whooping cough, cystitis, thrush, abscess, acne, oily skin, athlete's foot, verrucae, warts, cold sores, burns, insect bites and wounds.

Thyme

Antioxidant, antiseptic, antispasmodic, anti-toxic, astringent, aphrodisiac, carminative, cicatrisant, diuretic, emmenagogic, nervine, rubefacient, immuno-stimulant, sudorific, tonic.

Used to treat headaches, insomnia, stress, colds, flu, cystitis, dyspepsia, flatulence, diarrhoea, asthma, bronchitis, catarrh, sinusitis, sore throat, cellulite, arthritis, muscular aches and pains, poor circulation, sprains, burns, bruises, cuts, oily skin, acne, eczema and dermatitis.

Ylang ylang

Aphrodisiac, antidepressant, antiseborrheic, antiseptic, euphoric, hypotensive, nervine, sedative, stimulant, tonic.

Used to treat depression, frigidity, impotence, insomnia, nervous tension, stress, high blood pressure, palpitations, acne, insect bites, irritated and oily skin, skin care in general.

Figure 16.15 *Ylang ylang*

There are several different forms of massage available to the beauty therapist and Indian head massage is a method, which may be used in addition to those already discussed. It has additional benefits in that it may be performed in environments other than the salon, for example the client's home, workplace, hospital or care home, and the client does not have to remove any clothing to enjoy a treatment. It is a useful treatment for the mobile therapist to offer clients as little in the way of equipment is required and oils may be used only if needed. In fact, it is a service that is available in many hairdressing salons as an addition to other services and to benefit the clients' hair condition.

The history and origins of Indian head massage

Massage has been practised in India for thousands of years dating back to the beginning of the Hindu religion, and Indian families have made it an essential everyday part of family life for generations, with tiny babies receiving a daily massage to promote good health. As children grow older, they are taught the massage techniques themselves, giving and receiving massage for its soothing and calming effects, the therapeutic effects on the muscles and skin and to encourage the body's own natural healing abilities.

Traditionally, the women of India practised the art of Indian head massage as part of their cosmetic and grooming process, to keep their hair strong, in good condition and sweet smelling, as they used oils such as coconut, jasmine, olive, sesame, almond and mustard for their beneficial effects.

Figure 17.1 *Selection of oils used for Indian head massage*

The different generations of women in the family would provide the treatment for each other, thus ensuring that the practice continued and the skills were passed down through the generations. It is also traditional that brides and grooms are massaged by other family members as part of the wedding preparations. This aids relaxation, improves the beauty of the skin and hair and increases physical stamina. Wealthier women would use more expensive oils containing essential oils such as sandalwood, which calms the mind and cools the head, or henna to enhance colour.

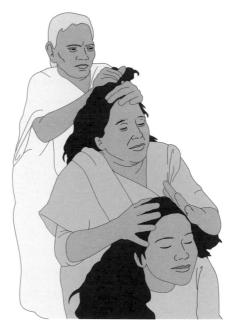

Figure 17.2 *Indian head massage performed by three female generations*

Men also received head massage when they visited the barbers, although it differed from the relaxing techniques employed by the women. The barber would provide a very stimulating scalp massage to invigorate and revive the client. As with the women, the barbers would pass on their knowledge and skills to their sons to provide the treatment for the next generation. The Hindi term for head massage is *Champissage*.

Head massage is also offered in many public areas such as the market place, on the beach and any other general meeting place. At different times of the year, particular oils are used, cooling in the spring and summer and warming in the winter.

Coconut oil

Coconut is nature's wonder emollient, high in Vitamin F, which contains linoleic, linotenic and arachidonic fatty acids. It is a medium to light oil, has a wonderful aroma, is an excellent moisturiser for the skin and is used traditionally in the spring. As it comes in a solid form, it requires gentle heating in a small bowl placed in a larger bowl of warm water. This oil is also used for Balinese massage techniques.

Jasmine oil

Fragrant, white jasmine flowers are cooling and calming, their oil helps relieve fever and sunstroke. Aromatherapists say that jasmine carries important psychic influences, making the mind more receptive, increasing feelings of love and compassion. Widely used in perfumery and aromatherapy, jasmine is one of the most expensive fragrances in the world. Flowers must be hand-picked before dawn when essence is at its peak. It is a highly perfumed oil which provides a beautiful aroma to the hair and leaves it shiny and lustrous.

Olive oil

Olive oil is a heavier oil, good to use in the summer and has a distinctive smell. It is excellent for very dry hair and scalp and because of its purity is suitable for children. It also relieves pain and stiffness, increases body heat and reduces swelling.

Sesame oil

This is the most popular oil used for Indian head massage. The oil, expressed from tiny seeds, is a key health and beauty aid valued for its rejuvenative properties. Sesame is the base for most authentic Ayurvedic oils and emollients and recommended by Ayurvedic practitioners as it contains iron and phosphorous. It relieves muscular pains and reduces swelling and stiffness. Some users claim that it will delay the onset of grey hair. In India, this oil is commonly used in the summer and it has balancing effects.

Almond

Almond is a light oil that is suitable for all clients. It is warming and helps to ease pain and stiffness. It is used for hair that has become dry following chemical treatment.

Mustard oil

This is a pungent, stimulating oil, recommended for use in the winter as it is warming, and useful for increasing body temperature. It also relieves aches and pains and relaxes muscles. It is popular with male clients because of its invigorating effect and should be used with care to prevent irritation.

Ayurveda

This is a closely followed practice in India based on holistic healing. It is a form of preventative medicine dating back 5000 years. The literal translation from the Sanskrit words *ayus* and *veda* is science of life. It is said to promote positive health, beauty and long life and is becoming ever more popular in the west with the increased interest in holistic therapies.

Ayurveda is based on the principle that health is maintained by the balance of three *doshas* (energies or forces), known as Vata, Pitta and Kapha. Every client will have his or her own personal combination of these forces, known as their *Prakruti* (literally meaning the first creation), a unique blend of qualities that makes the individual who he or she is at the moment of conception.

Doshas

Kapha – all forms of matter.

Vata – the force and direction they move.

Pitta – the transformations they go through.

These doshas are combinations of different elements:

* Kapha – earth and water, responsible for physical stability, body structure and fluid.
* Vata – air and ether, responsible for movement of the body, mind, senses and the process of elimination.
* Pitta – fire and water, responsible for heat, metabolism, energy production and digestive functions.

The Ayurvedic practitioner offers advice and provides different treatments to balance these energies to promote physical, emotional and spiritual harmony. One of the treatments they use is Indian head massage, which has been adapted for the beauty therapist in the west to include massage of the neck, shoulders, upper back and arms, not just the head and scalp. It is necessary to assess the client first and recognise his or her dosha characteristics, then provide the most suitable treatment and choose oils to benefit the individual.

Each person contains elements of all three energies and this mix is constantly changing based on age, lifestyle choices and external influences. Finding and maintaining the right balance of energies is the Ayurveda's secret to both health and beauty.

To establish your own doshic tendencies, look at Table 17.1 and consider the attributes that apply to you. The column in which you have the most attributes is your primary doshic tendency. Most people, however, are a mix of two primary tendencies and, in rare cases, they may be tridoshic, having equal tendencies of all doshas.

Indian head massage is an excellent treatment, which may be used without or combined with specific oils, to contribute to maintaining balance in the body and counteracting stress.

Stress may be defined as 'a response by the body to a situation, which is perceived as threatening' and this may then have an adverse effect on any of the systems of the body. We all experience stress to some degree and a healthy amount of stress can be a powerful motivating force on which some individuals positively thrive. However, having more stress than the individual can handle is one of the greatest threats to our health, as the positive effects are replaced by exhaustion and the individual may find it difficult to cope. A great deal of stress over a long period can lead to illness, burnout or eventual breakdown.

Stress is an individual response internally to external factors that threaten our security. It is not always caused by traumatic events, even good experiences such as planning a holiday, party or wedding can prove stressful. In small amounts, stress is a normal part of life, but when stress builds up to such a degree that it changes to

Table 17.1 *The characteristics or qualities of the doshas*

Vata – air and ether	Pitta – fire and water	Kapha – earth and water
Dry skin	Blemish prone skin	Oily skin
Rough wiry hair	Fine hair prone to grey early	Thick, wavy slightly oily hair
Tans easily	Sunburns easily	Tans slowly and evenly
Brittle nails	Strong flexible nails	Strong, thick nails
Cold hands and feet	Tends to perspire easily	Moderate perspiration
Thin build	Medium build	Generous build
Difficult to gain weight	Can gain or lose weight easily	Difficult to lose weight
Nervous, anxious	Moody, irritable	Calm, placid
Prefers warm, sunny climate	Prefers shade, cool climate	Dislikes humidity
Fast metabolism	Strong metabolism	Sluggish metabolism
Prone to poor digestion, pains	Prone to fever and rashes	Prone to excess fluid retention
Artistic, creative	Ambitious, passionate	Steady, reliable, easy going

distress, it becomes a negative and destructive force. Every person is different, however, because a source of stress to one person could be a motivating factor for another. Some people need to create a small amount of stress in their lives to help them achieve a goal or rise to a challenge. Each individual will react differently to a given situation or experience, so the stress level and the reaction to it will vary in every case. Indian head massage is an excellent antidote to stress as it is a quick treatment that may be performed in the workplace and does not necessitate the removal of any clothing.

Effects of Indian head massage

Physiological effects

* Increases circulation to the head, scalp and neck, providing extra oxygen, nourishment to the area being treated and improving cellular regeneration.
* Increases lymphatic circulation, speeding up the elimination of waste products (lactic acid), it aids fluid removal and improves the immune system.
* Stimulates the sudoriferous glands to produce sweat, improving waste removal.
* Stimulates the sebaceous glands to produce sebum which will help to lubricate the hair and scalp.
* Relaxes muscles and eases tension.
* Breaks down adhesions in the muscles.
* Increases flexibility in the neck and shoulders and improves posture.
* Improves the range of movement in the joints.
* Soothes the nerves.
* Reduces sinus congestion.
* Eases headaches.

Figure 17.3 *Indian head massage movement*

Physical effects

* Stimulates hair growth and cellular regeneration.
* Improves hair condition with the increase in circulation and sebum flow.
* Improves skin condition by aiding desquamation and increasing sebum production.

Psychological effects

* Increases a sense of well-being.
* Improves sleep-related problems.
* Increases energy levels.
* Counteracts stress.
* Induces a sense of calm.
* Improves the ability to concentrate.

Contraindications

* The client has consumed alcohol.
* The client has an infectious skin disease of the areas to be treated. If the infection is localised, i.e. herpes simplex on the upper lip, the scalp neck, back, shoulder and arms may be treated.
* Avoid areas with cuts, abrasions and bruising.
* New scar tissue must be avoided, but once healed gentle massage will help to prevent adhesions forming.
* Any eye infection will contraindicate treatment of the face but other areas may be treated.
* A high temperature or fever indicates infection present generally in the body and Indian head massage may worsen the condition by increasing the circulation.
* Infections of the scalp such as pediculosis, which is an infestation of lice found in the hair characterised by itching and the appearance of tiny eggs firmly attached to the hair shaft. The client may have irritated the scalp by scratching and it may look red and inflamed. Tinea capitis is ringworm of the scalp, a fungal infection characterised by itchiness and small round lesions.
* Head or neck injury such as whiplash, concussion or a blow to the head or after a recent operation.
* Spondylitis (inflammation of the vertebrae) or spondylosis (a degeneration of the vertebrae).
* History of thrombosis or embolism.

Doctor's approval may be required for clients with high or low blood pressure, heart conditions, epilepsy, diabetes or cancer. Extreme care must be taken with frail clients or those suffering with osteoporosis.

Common hair and scalp disorders

Alopecia

Alopecia is a loss of hair either partially or completely. The disorder may be temporary or can become progressively worse. The most common form is male pattern baldness (androgenetica alopecia), a genetic disorder which causes the hair to shrink so that it becomes thinner and shorter. This may occur any time after puberty. Alopecia is a condition, which sometimes affects women, particularly after the menopause.

Stress, shock, illness, surgery or chemotherapy may also cause different types of baldness:

* alopecia areata – hair lost in patches
* alopecia totalis – hair lost completely from the head
* alopecia universalis – total loss of all body hair.

Dandruff (pityriasis capitis)

This condition is an excessive shedding of the skin from the scalp. It is characterised by dry white flakes of skin when there is little sebum present and yellowish, oily flakes with an overproduction of sebum on the scalp. Overuse of shampoo, chemical treatment or a lack of B vitamins and essential fatty acids in the diet may also cause this condition.

Greasy hair and scalp

Caused by an overproduction of sebum from the sebaceous glands, this condition can be worsened by an imbalance of hormones.

Dry hair and scalp

This may be caused by an underproduction of sebum from the sebaceous glands, bleaching, colouring and perming the hair, using heated rollers, hair straighteners and using excessive heat to dry the hair.

Equipment and materials

A comfortable chair is the only essential item required to perform this treatment and an easily transportable model would be ideal for the mobile therapist. If you are providing treatment in the workplace for a particular company or in a building shared by several companies, a chair may be left in a room designated for treatment.

There are now quite substantial, specially designed, folding chairs available which provide extra support for the client, but the traditional method of Indian head massage only requires a small comfortable chair, preferably with lower back support. The most important consideration for the therapist is to make sure the height of the chair is such that there is no awkward bending to reach the client as this may prevent an efficient massage

or cause injury, so a height adjustment facility on the chair will help.

Figure 17.4 *A therapist performing Indian head massage on a client sitting on a portable chair*

A choice of massage oils should be available for those clients who require oil and also a selection of essential oils, which may be blended by therapists qualified to use them (see Chapter 16 Aromatherapy, page 243).

Selection of oils for each dosha

The essential oils chosen should be to balance the doshas and you will need to consider the aroma, the heating or cooling effect and the benefits they provide (see Table 17.2).

Pre-blended oils may be used, but it is important that the therapist understands the effects of the oils and the possible contraindications. Special oils which contain traditional eastern herbs and spices may also be obtained from a specialist supplier, if required.

Because it is a mobile treatment, the therapist may not have easy access to washing facilities, so antibacterial

Dosha	Suggested carrier oils	Suggested essential oils
Vata – unique characteristic is dryness	Sesame oil, as it is warming and grounding, nourishing and calming and highly penetrative. Avocado and vitamin E for their nourishing effect on dry skin	Clary sage, clove, cypress, cinnamon, geranium, rose, jasmine, musk, orange and sandalwood
Pitta – unique characteristic is heat	Coconut is the best carrier oil, but sunflower, jojoba, safflower and sesame are also beneficial when mixed with cooling essential oils	Chamomile, jasmine, lemongrass, melissa, mint, rose, rosewood, sandalwood and vetivert
Kapha – unique characteristic is heaviness	Mustard, jojoba, olive and almond oils	Cedar, cinnamon, musk, eucalyptus, myrrh, patchouli, pine and sage

Table 17.2 *Suggested carrier and essential oils for each dosha*

cleansing wipes could be used for cleansing the hands between treatments. Several small towels should be available to cover the client's shoulders and upper back when working on the scalp if oils are used.

A mirror, brush and comb for the client to use at the end of treatment and a sterilising solution for all items used during the treatment are also required.

The room itself should be warm, well ventilated and, if required, have relaxing music playing quietly in the background to promote relaxation. Lighting should be subdued as strong lights may cause eye strain or headaches. Oil burners or candles may be used to introduce a relaxing aroma into the room or oils specifically chosen to complement the client's treatment.

Massage movements

The movements used in Indian head massage are basically the same as those used in body massage – effleurage or stroking, petrissage or compression movements, tapotement or percussion, frictions and vibrations. These movements are discussed in detail in Chapter 15 Body massage. In addition, there is a movement called champi which is similar in effect to hacking. It is performed by placing the hands together in a prayer position with the wrists and hands completely relaxed and, using the little fingers, strike the muscles of the area being worked very lightly and quickly.

Figure 17.5 *Champi massage movement*

Chakras

An important element of Ayurvedic medicine is Chakra energy balancing. The body is said to have seven energy centres, each one of them being associated with one of the endocrine glands. Energy flows through these points in the body and this energy flow is thought to have a great effect on the individual's well-being. When energy flow is impeded it is thought to create an imbalance in the body that may have a detrimental effect on different systems of the body. The chakras are situated in line with the spine and they are the crown, the brow, the throat, the heart, the solar plexus, the sacral and the base, and each one is associated with a particular colour (see Table 17.3). When combining Indian head massage with Ayurvedic energy balancing, the overall effects of treatment are greatly increased.

Chakra	Position	Gland	Colour
Crown	Top of the head	Pineal	Violet
Brow (third eye)	Centre of the brow between the two eyebrows	Pituitary	Indigo
Throat	Between the two clavicle bones at the base of the neck	Thyroid	Blue
Heart	Between the fourth and fifth thoracic vertebrae	Thymus	Green
Solar plexus	Between the twelfth thoracic vertebrae and the first lumbar vertebrae	Pancreas	Yellow
Sacral	Halfway between the pubis and the navel	Adrenal	Orange
Base	Base of the spine	Reproductive	Red

Table 17.3 *The chakras*

Figure 17.6 *The seven chakras*

When providing an Indian head massage the therapist will be working on the three higher chakras of the upper body – the crown, the brow and the throat. Working on these chakra points at the beginning of treatment will help to open up the energy channels and at the conclusion of treatment will help to re-energise the client.

The higher chakras

The crown chakra *sahasrara* represents infinity and it governs spirituality, enlightenment, wisdom, creativity and understanding. Imbalance may lead to exhaustion, inability to make decisions, frustration and depression.

The brow chakra *ajna* is often referred to as the third eye and it governs intuition, vision, intellect and ingenuity. Imbalance may lead to problems with the sinuses, neuritis, migraine, tiredness, over sensitivity, irritability and stress.

The throat chakra *vissuddha* is the creative centre and governs communication, vocation and talent. Imbalance may lead to fatigue, laryngitis, sore throat, asthma, anaemia and upper respiratory problems.

Marma pressure point application

Part of the Indian Ayurvedic system of medicine, Marma therapy is a treatment manipulating marman or vital points in the body using a mixture of slow, gentle strokes, brisk invigorating movements and warming techniques, such as rubbing and squeezing.

The Marma points on the body are the junction points of blood vessels, ligaments and nerve centres. Marma means secret, hidden and vital. There are

107 points in the body, 37 of which are in the treatment area of Indian head massage and when they are massaged help to release blocked energy, restore normal function, energise or relax. These points correspond to internal organs and systems of the body which react to manual stimulation.

The ancient form of Marma massage therapy dates back to 1500–1200 BC and the word *Marma* was used for the first time in Atharva Veda (ancient Indian scripture). *Marma shastra* is an ancient Indian martial art form that manipulates vital points in the body. It can be used both for self-defence and also for healing. Healing was an important part of martial arts, as the fighter had to know how to heal his wounds. It is said to take between eight and ten years to become a Marma healer in India for the purpose of healing, massage and increasing flexibility. A student may only heal independently after he has completed his course and works as an apprentice with his guru for two to three years. The basic principles of Marma pressure point massage have been adapted for use with many holistic and beauty therapies, including Indian head massage, and the points are massaged with the thumb or index finger in small circles slowly clockwise and then small circles anticlockwise, gradually increasing and decreasing pressure.

Preparation before treatment

After completing a detailed consultation with the client, including the completion of a record card, he or she must remove spectacles, earrings, piercings, necklaces and make-up and, if necessary, brush the hair to remove all traces of hair spray or gel. Although this treatment is carried out over clothing, it may be necessary to ask the client to remove some items such as a bulky jacket or a male client to loosen his collar to allow comfortable access to the neck area.

The client must be seated comfortably with shoes removed and feet positioned flat on the floor with the hands in a relaxed position on the lap. Legs must not be crossed at the knees or ankles.

Standing in a relaxed position behind the client, lay both hands lightly on the top of the client's head and ask the client to begin with breathing exercises. Breathe in and out through the nostrils, slowly and deeply three times; this allows you and the client to become relaxed and grounded, it stills the mind and allows you both to concentrate on the massage therapy to come and helps maintain the stamina of the therapist throughout treatment.

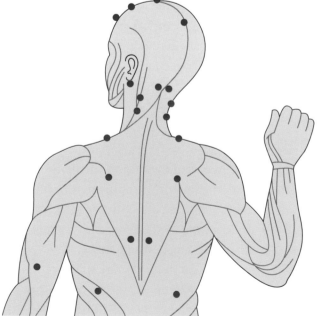
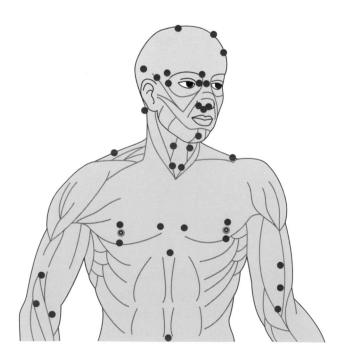

Figure 17.7 *The Marma pressure points*

Aftercare advice

At the conclusion of treatment, the client may be accompanied to a rest area or allowed to sit quietly in the treatment area while you provide the correct aftercare advice. Offer the client a glass of water or herbal infusion and explain that to benefit from the treatment he or she should avoid smoking, caffeine and alcohol, drink plenty of water and eat only light meals for the remainder of the day. The client should also avoid, strenuous activity, swimming, shampooing the hair and driving a long distance.

Contra-actions

The results of treatment are usually beneficial, with the client providing you with positive feedback about his or her sense of calm and relaxation, increased vitality, relief from pain or even a reduction in muscular tension. However, when the body is eliminating toxins as a result of the treatment, a 'healing crisis' may sometimes occur. These are symptoms, which may appear to be negative but are, in fact, part of the cleansing and balancing process. They may include some of the following:

* increased or lowered energy levels
* increase in bowel movements or urination
* headaches and/or flu-like symptoms
* becoming emotional and tearful
* feeling nauseous, dizzy or, in extreme cases, fainting
* slight increase or lowering of body temperature.

None of these symptoms is anything to worry about as it may only last for 24 hours, but if any symptons continue, it could be an indication that the client has a medical condition which may require medical advice. Always discuss the client's previous treatment and reactions to it and record any details that may be relevant.

Most body electrical treatments are used as part of a programme designed specifically for clients to allow them to lose weight or re-contour their body. Electrical equipment may be introduced:

* when the client is on a weight reducing diet – the use of electrical equipment can increase the effectiveness of the diet
* to provide a variety of treatment, motivating and maintaining the client's interest
* when specific areas only need to be treated to effect a localised reduction.

It must be stressed to the client that use of electrical equipment alone is not enough to lose weight or re-contour the body. The essential ingredients in an effective body treatment programme are:

* to follow a well-balanced, weight reducing diet
* to increase the amount of physical exercise taken
* the application of appropriate body treatments by a beauty therapist.

The electrical treatments offered by the beauty therapist include:

* vibratory treatment
* vacuum massage treatment
* electrotherapy, which includes high frequency treatment, galvanic treatment, electrical muscle stimulation and microcurrent treatment.

Vibratory treatment

Vibratory treatment is a form of mechanical massage and there are three types:

* **Percussion**. Machines work only on a vertical plane, which means that the movements they make are only up and down and physiologically are equivalent to tapotement or hacking. The percussion vibrator is used mainly in facial therapy.
* **Gyrators**. Machines work on a vertical and horizontal plane. The movements are up and down as well as circular, simulating the actions of effleurage, petrissage and kneading, and are used in body therapy.

* **Audio sonic**. Machines use sound wave vibrations to achieve their effects and may be used when other types of vibratory treatment are contraindicated.

Gyratory vibrator (G5)

This machine was designed by M. Henri Cuinier and is usually known as the G5. G5 was the original model number and this model is still used today.

The gyratory vibrator is the most commonly used type of mechanical massage machine and the models used for body work are normally free-standing, on a pedestal, with castors for ease of movement. The motor is heavy-duty with an air-cooling system so that it does not overheat with prolonged use. From the motor comes a flexible insulated arm, to which the applicator heads are attached to perform the treatment. All the applicators are kept in an accessory tray on the pedestal base.

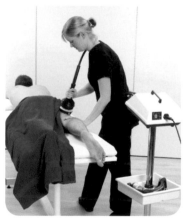

Figure 18.1 *The G5*

The machine has several different applicator heads, made from polyurethane or rubber, and they come in various shapes and sizes. They are all used during treatment to achieve similar effects to those of manual massage:

* The sponge heads are used for effleurage.
* The hard rubber heads are used for petrissage.
* The spiky and brush heads are used to simulate similar effects to those produced by tapotement.

The selection of the applicator head used depends upon the area being treated and the depth may be controlled, by varying:

* the pressure applied
* the type of applicator used.

Applicator heads

* The **round sponge applicator** is used with light pressure at the beginning and the end of treatment. It produces a hyperaemia and relaxes the client.
* The **curved sponge applicator** is used on those parts of the body that it moulds to, such as the limbs and shoulders. It is similar in action to effleurage in manual massage.
* The **pin cushion applicator** is made from rubber with many round-ended protrusions and is effective in the treatment of rough skin. It produces a hyperaemia and desquamates the skin.
* The **heavy pronged applicator** is a rubber applicator with larger protrusions than the pin cushion. It provides depth to the massage movements and is used in areas of solid subcutaneous fat or thick tissue.
* The **football applicator** is made of rubber and is used on dense areas such as the gluteals. It is also used for kneading of the colon.
* The **egg box applicator** is a rubber applicator and is used with deep pressure in dense fleshy areas such as gluteals and thighs.
* The **lighthouse applicator** is rubber-tipped and may be used on either side of the spine, but great care must be taken to avoid irritation or damage to the vertebrae. It is also used on the colon.
* The **sucker applicator** is a round rubber head, the surface of which is covered by small suckers. It is suitable when treating a client who has a cellulite problem.

The treatment should combine some manual massage movements with the mechanical application, thereby combining the depth of the vibratory treatment with the personal touch of the manual massage.

Effects of G5

* It stimulates the circulatory system, increasing blood supply to the area being treated, so providing nourishment to the skin and muscles and improving skin colour.
* It improves lymphatic flow and aids the removal of waste products. This is particularly important for a cellulite condition.
* It has a desquamating effect on the surface of the skin.
* It relaxes tense muscles.
* It eases muscular pain.
* It penetrates deep into the subcutaneous layer helping the dispersal of fatty tissue.
* It motivates clients by helping them to achieve the desired results in weight reduction and body shaping.

Advantages of G5

This treatment has certain advantages over manual massage:

* It is a far less personal treatment than manual massage and is therefore ideal for treating male clients.
* It can produce a depth of massage far greater than that of manual massage.
* It is far less tiring than manual massage, particularly for weight reducing purposes.

Round sponge – general purpose head, starts and finishes treatment, similar to effleurage

Football – used on heavy areas of adipose tissue, may also be used for colonic kneading on the abdomen as it improves digestion and peristalsis

Pin cushion – a surface stimulating head causes a hyperaemia. Not used on fine or sensitive skin. Aids desquamation, improves skin texture, used on heavy areas of adipose tissue

Curved sponge – effleurage head contours to certain parts of the body

Heavy prong – simulates petrissage, used for deep application on heavy areas of adipose tissue

Egg box – simulates petrissage, used on heavy areas of adipose tissue

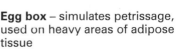

Lighthouse – emulates frictions, may be used down the sides of the spine and around the joints on soft tissue. May also be used for colonic kneading

Figure 18.2 *G5 applicator heads*

The client

Ideally, the client should have some form of pre-heating treatment which will relax the muscles in preparation for treatment.

The movements used should be towards the heart and following the natural contours of the body. For maximum comfort effleurage strokes should be interlinked with manual effleurage and kneading should be performed with the therapist's hand providing support and resistance. To provide continuity, manual effleurage must be used throughout the treatment and any unnecessary changing of applicator heads should be avoided.

The machine

When this machine is in constant use it will be necessary to have several sets of applicator heads to allow enough time between treatments to clean and dry them.

Talcum powder is the only medium which should be applied to the client's skin for use with this machine because oils or cream have an adverse effect on the applicator heads and over a period of time will cause them to disintegrate.

Contraindications to vibratory treatment

* Skin disorders and diseases.
* History of thrombosis or phlebitis.
* Systemic conditions.
* Bruising or scar tissue.
* Swelling.
* Raised abnormalities on the skin.
* Thin or elderly clients.
* Varicose veins if in the area of treatment.

Audio sonic vibrator

This is a sound wave vibrator which is placed on the skin, vibrating smoothly up and down and gently massaging the tissues. Contact is maintained over the area being treated and the vibrations penetrate quite deep into the underlying tissues.

Sound waves are transmitted to the area requiring treatment through a sound head which is applied without pressure to the surface of the skin. There are two applicators – a round ball-shaped head, which provides sound waves to a small area, and a disc-shaped

Varicose veins

These occur on the legs when the valves in the veins become weakened and because of this, large amounts of blood are forced by gravity backwards into the vein. This has the effect of overloading the vein, which then pushes the walls of the vein outwards where there is a build-up of blood. The veins closest to the surface of the legs are most susceptible to this condition.

When this happens repeatedly the walls of the veins lose some of their elasticity and become overstretched and loose. A vein in this condition is called a varicose vein and it is often caused through pregnancy and standing for long periods of time. These swollen areas caused by the accumulation of blood force fluid into the surrounding tissue.

This condition can be very painful and causes tiredness and aching. It will contraindicate any treatment which is stimulating to the area.

head with a larger surface area for normal use. The sound waves can penetrate up to 6 cm within the body, allowing the therapist to treat areas which are inaccessible to conventional manipulative techniques. When the sound wave energy produced has been absorbed by the body tissues the sound waves cease to travel further.

The vibrator is used normally for the specific effect of relieving tension in tense contracted muscles but may also be used when the use of gyratory vibrators is contraindicated because of hypersensitivity.

The unit is quite small and is handheld. Therefore, only small areas can be treated effectively

The tissues are very gently stimulated and this treatment is most effective on areas of soft tissue which offer little resistance. The effects achieved are deep in the tissue, causing little stimulation to the surface of the skin, making this an excellent treatment for sensitive skin.

Figure 18.3
An audio sound machine

Physiological effects of audio sonic

* Massage occurs at a cellular level deep within the tissue.
* There is an immediate tightening of cell wall membranes.
* Cellular activity is increased and metabolism is improved.
* Warmth is produced in the tissues.
* The increase in circulation supplies nourishment to the area.
* The lymphatic system is stimulated, therefore waste products are removed more efficiently.
* Tension nodules are relaxed.

Contraindications to audio sonic treatment

* Skin diseases.
* Sunburn.
* Bruises.
* Recent scar tissue.
* Highly vascular skin.
* Undiagnosed pain.
* In the chest area of a client with a cardiac pacemaker.
* In areas with a metal plate or pin.
* Back and abdomen during pregnancy.

Vacuum massage

The main purpose of this treatment is to increase the body's circulation and lymphatic flow to aid in the removal of waste products and excess fluid. It may be used on any area of the body which has sufficient fatty tissue to allow for comfortable treatment. It is normally used as part of a course of treatments combined with manual massage and diet. This treatment can be used for spot reduction on legs, back, arms, thighs and buttocks.

A thorough knowledge of the body's lymphatic system is essential as the movements used in this treatment are all related to the position of the lymph nodes in the body. The lymphatic vessels are closely connected to the larger veins and are responsible for the interchange of tissue fluids. The lymph carries waste products along the lymph vessels towards the lymph nodes which act as filters.

The machine

Most manufacturers produce body units only and combined body and facial units.

The body unit can be either a basic unit which works with a single cup that glides manually over the skin, or a multi-cup unit that can operate up to six cups at a time. The application for each method is different but the effects are the same.

Figure 18.4
Vacuum suction

The combined unit has a fine intensity control so that it is easily adjusted for use, from the delicate tissues of the face to the more dense adipose tissues of the body. The unit has a combination of small ventouses for use on small facial areas and a set of cups of varying size which are suitable for the body. The ventouses are usually made from clear perspex or plexiglass which is very tough and hard to break.

How the machine works

Whichever type of machine is chosen they both work in the same way.

They contain a vacuum pump connected by a long flexible plastic tube to a cup which is placed on the area being treated. The vacuum pump is driven by an electric motor and the amount of suction, or 'reduced pressure', is controlled by a regulating switch. There is also a vacuum gauge which indicates the amount of pressure being exerted on the tissues during treatment.

The air pressure in the cup is reduced which causes the skin tissue to be lifted up into the cup and then, with care, the cup is guided in a gliding movement over the tissues in the direction of the lymph glands. Several cups may be placed on the area to be treated statically with the multi-cup unit.

With the single-cup unit, the therapist glides the cup over the area, releasing the pressure by uncovering a hole in the cup or using a finger to release the vacuum at the end of each movement.

With the multi-cup unit, the cups are applied statically to a localised area and the vacuum suction is pulsed, that is, it alternates between a high level of suction and a low level of suction, just enough to keep the cup in place. This is achieved by an automatic pulsation control in the machine itself. The higher degree of suction must not be so high that it causes discomfort or bruising to the skin.

Treatment initially should have longer periods of the low-level and shorter periods of the higher level of suction. These periods can be adjusted as the client becomes used to the treatment and the therapist has assessed the skin reaction. When using static multi-cup vacuum suction it is normally preceded by the gliding method.

Effects of vacuum suction

* Increase in circulation dilates blood vessels and causes a hyperaemia.
* Increase in circulation nourishes skin and muscle.
* Stimulates the lymphatic system moving tissue fluids.
* Reduces puffiness caused by fluid retention when it is not caused by a medical condition.

* Helps in the breakdown and removal of fatty cells particularly when used in conjunction with a diet.
* Aids in desquamation.
* Stimulates the metabolism.

Contraindications to vacuum suction

* Varicose veins.
* Bruised skin.
* Skin diseases.
* Recent scar tissue.
* An area heavily stretch marked.
* Sunburn.
* Very thin or hypersensitive skin.

Mechanical lymphatic massage treatment

The lymphatic system rids the body of toxic materials and waste products before they can damage the cells, tissues and organs of the body. However, the system sometimes finds it difficult to cope with the increased demands put upon it because of an overload of toxins due to:

* exposure to industrial waste
* exposure to chemicals and pesticides
* highly processed foods
* medication/drugs
* alcohol
* nicotine
* stress.

These are just a few examples and when the waste products and toxins start to build up, they may require some help in their removal. This can be achieved by changing to a healthy diet, body brushing, manual massage, aromatherapy, exercise and manual or mechanical lymphatic drainage.

Manual treatment aids lymphatic drainage to improve blood circulation, skin tone and body shape. Lymphatic drainage is essential to ensure a healthy body free from toxins, and mechanical methods imitate the body's muscular pumping action to move the lymph fluid around the body while at the same time giving a pleasant and relaxing massage to the legs and improving the general blood circulation.

Manual or mechanical treatment is often combined with the use of essential oils for maximum effect. The mechanical method uses boots to cover the legs and a pumping action is exerted on the legs, starting from the toes and moving rhythmically up the leg to the hips. Pure essential oils are dispersed in water to make a compress. Bandages or support stockings are then immersed to soak up the compress liquid, the excess liquid is squeezed out and they are then applied to the legs from the ankle to the knees. The oils used have different effects:

* stimulating
* toning
* relaxing
* decongesting.

The legs are then encased in the massage boots which are inflated and a sequential, flowing, regulated pressure massage is applied simultaneously to both legs, starting from the feet and moving rhythmically upwards towards the inguinal lymph nodes.

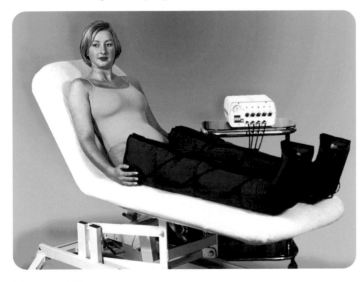

Figure 18.5 *Vacuum massage boots*

Effects of mechanical lymphatic massage
* Increases blood circulation.
* Increases lymphatic flow.
* Helps with the removal of excess fluids.
* Speeds up the removal of toxins.
* Provides a feeling a well-being.
* Relaxes the client.

Benefits of mechanical lymphatic massage
* Detoxification leads to better toned skin.
* Helps improve a cellulite condition by removing excess fluids and waste products.
* Helps in the prevention and relief of varicose veins.
* Relaxing and soothing.
* Warms the tissues.
* Eases aches and pains.

Contraindications to mechanical lymphatic massage
* Client with a pacemaker.
* Acute thrombophlebitis.
* History of deep vein thrombosis.
* History of pulmonary embolism.
* Congestive cardiac failure.
* Pitting oedema.
* High blood pressure.
* Open cuts or wounds.
* New scar tissue.
* Client under medical supervision/undergoing medical treatment.
* Sunburn.
* Acute infections.

A healthy lymphatic system is necessary because it assists with the absorption of nutrients required for health. It carries immune cells around the body to help protect it from damage. It is also the body's metabolic waste disposal system and removes toxins, by-products of fatigue, stress, bacteria, dead cells and viruses.

High frequency

As in facial therapy, this treatment may be applied to the body either directly or indirectly. The high frequency current is a rapidly alternating (oscillating) current and does not have a stimulating effect on the nerve endings in the skin.

Direct method

This treatment is most appropriate to sufferers of acne as the condition often affects the upper back and the chest. With this method, ozone is produced when the glass electrode is applied to the skin and this has a germicidal effect, helping to dry and cleanse the area being treated.

Talcum powder must be applied to the skin to allow the electrode ease of movement and to absorb excess sebum on the skin.

The lighter the movements over the skin, the stronger the germicidal effect will be. The high frequency current mixing with oxygen produces the ozone. Therefore, the firmer the contact with the skin, the less high frequency current is released through the electrodes into the air so reducing the amount of ozone produced.

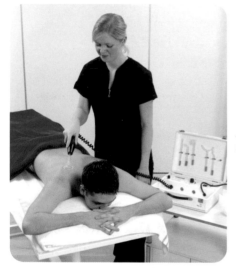

Figure 18.6
Direct high frequency treatment to the back

Effects of direct method

* Increases circulation causing an erythema and warmth in the area being treated.
* Stimulates a sluggish skin.
* Improves the lymphatic flow and the removal of waste products.
* Desquamates the skin, improving texture.
* Cleanses the skin, healing pustules.

Indirect method

One of the main benefits of indirect high frequency is the feeling of relaxation. Therefore, when used with manual body massage it will increase the relaxation effect of the treatment.

It is applied in the same way as for facial therapy, with the client holding a saturator and the therapist performing the massage, remembering to maintain contact with the client at all times to keep the circuit complete and ensuring client comfort.

Effects of indirect method

* Increases circulation, warming the tissues and improving the interchange of tissue fluids and skin function.
* Sedative – relieves tension.
* The warm tissues absorb the nourishing products applied to the skin more easily.
* Helps those clients who suffer from poor circulation which may cause other problems such as chilblains.
* The massage will be more relaxing, the deeper the movements are performed and more stimulating when the hands are in light contact.

Contraindications to high frequency

* Pregnancy.
* Epilepsy.
* Metal plates or pins in the body.
* High blood pressure.

Body galvanism

This is a very popular and successful treatment to aid in the removal of cellulite, which can occur on different parts of the body. It is applied locally on the specific areas that require treatment to help in stimulating the area and helping to reshape the body contours.

Galvanism

The two methods of galvanism have been discussed in detail in Chapter 11 Facial electrical treatments. For body treatment, the method used is **iontophoresis**. This method is used to allow active substances into the skin, in this case anti-cellulite substances, on a galvanic charge. **Electrophoresis** describes the use of the current only. In this case, saline solution would be used on the pads to aid the flow of current – 1 per cent saline solution on the active pad and 2 per cent saline solution on the dispersive pad (1 per cent saline = 1 teaspoon of salt to 1 pint of water).

Aim of treatment

The aim of galvanic treatment is to soften stubborn areas of fat and disperse the fluid retained in the area, thus removing the lumps and bumps associated with a cellulite condition. This is achieved by using active substances specifically to stimulate a sluggish circulation and improve the interchange of tissue fluids in the area of cellulite, combined with the specific effect of the polarity chosen.

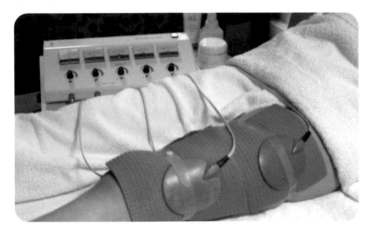

Figure 18.7 *Body galvanic treatment*

The substance introduced into the skin is the therapeutic part of the treatment. The galvanic current provides the transport into the skin of the therapeutic product and the polarity chosen provides the physiological response required for the breakdown and removal of cellulite. Anti-cellulite products used with the galvanic current are based on natural substances which have a diuretic effect on the body allowing fluid to be removed naturally.

Precautions

Medical history must be checked very carefully for any disorder of the nervous system which may contraindicate treatment and, if necessary, ask the client to seek medical advice.

Clients who suffer from kidney or urinary tract infections must ask their doctor for permission before having this treatment. The effects of the treatment will cause the client to pass more water as urine, because of the diuretic qualities of the active substances.

Clients will pass water far more often after treatment and it would be advisable to ask clients to pass water just before a full body treatment commences. The therapist should explain to clients why they must continue to drink a normal amount of fluid but preferably in the form of water, fruit juice or other healthy drinks, rather than tea, coffee and sugary soft drinks.

The galvanic machine

There are many different models on the market. They can be for body use only, providing eight pairs of electrodes, which allow the therapist to treat large areas of the body. They can also be a combined body and facial unit with two to four pairs of pads which allows only a small area of the body to be treated.

The controls on the machine include:

* an on/off switch
* outlets for the electrodes
* a milliamp meter for each outlet (some models only)
* a polarity change-over switch for each outlet
* an intensity control for each outlet.

The polarity

The most effective polarity for body iontophoresis is the negative pole and this is because of its specific effects which will help in the removal of cellulite. The effects of the negative pole include:

* stimulation of the circulation
* stimulation of the nerve endings in the skin
* softening of the tissues
* opening of the pores
* production of an alkaline effect on the skin
* fluid movement towards the negative pole.

These stimulating effects produced by the negative pole are ideal for this treatment, and the movement of tissue fluid in the area will help in diluting the toxins and removing them when the polarity is reversed for the final part of treatment.

Treatment

The electrodes used are in pairs. The working electrode (negative) is placed over the area to be treated and the second electrode, which will be the indifferent or non-working electrode (positive) that will complete the circuit, is placed opposite, for example on opposite sides of the thigh when this area is being treated.

The active electrode, which is negatively charged, will have a stimulating effect on the area of cellulite, helping to increase circulation and move the fluid which is retained and causing the lumps and bumps associated with cellulite.

The anti-cellulite products, which are also negatively charged, are applied to the skin under the negative electrode and the negative charge will repel the negatively charged product into the skin.

Treatment time

Fifteen minutes on the negative pole and then reverse the polarity to positive for the last five minutes. This will remove the tissue fluid away from the area carrying toxins and the positive pole will soothe the treated area, as the effects are to reduce circulation, soothe nerve endings, harden the skin, close the pores and produce an acid effect on the skin.

Safety

Make sure the machine is in good working order with no loose wires or connections. Follow the manufacturers' instructions when using equipment. There are many different models available which are different in the way in which they work, for example some have colour-coded leads, red for positive and black for negative.

Clients must be checked for contraindications to ensure that the treatment can be carried out safely. Give clients a thermal skin test (see Chapter 13 Spa and heat therapies, page 198) and also a test for skin sensitivity (see Chapter 11 Facial electrical treatment, page 155).

Each electrode must be placed inside a thick viscose sponge pocket or a thick viscose sponge pad slightly larger than the electrode placed underneath it, to protect the skin from the current. The viscose sponge must be evenly damp to aid the flow of current and must also be in firm contact with the skin. Ensure that the viscose sponges do not dry out as this will concentrate the current on a small area and may lead to a galvanic burn.

Any scratch or abrasion on the skin must be covered as the current would be concentrated in the area causing discomfort to the client and a possible galvanic burn. The electrodes and sponge must be firmly attached to the area being treated with non-conductive straps.

Make sure that all intensity controls are at zero at the beginning of treatment. The current must be turned up slowly, keeping the intensity low to begin with until the milliamp meter registers a breakdown in the skin's resistance. This will be shown by a sudden movement of the indicator. Treatment must not exceed 2–3 milliamps per square inch of electrode. Some models have an in-built safety feature preventing the milliamperage chosen from increasing when the skin's resistance breaks down. This helps to prevent a galvanic burn.

During treatment maintain visual and verbal contact with clients to make sure that they are comfortable. Follow the manufacturer's advice when timing the treatment. When the pads are removed at the conclusion of treatment the skin should be thoroughly cleansed with warm water.

Improving the effectiveness of treatment

The more the skin is prepared for galvanic treatment, the more effective it will be in the removal of the cellulite condition, thereby improving the body shape and the skin texture. The skin should be cleansed and if necessary a gentle peeling medium may be used. The effects are to cleanse the area of grease and desquamate the skin cells, increase the circulation and warm the tissues. This allows more efficient penetration of the products used.

Gentle heat such as infrared or massage may be applied. This will increase circulation and the interchange of tissue fluids, removing waste and at the same time relaxing the client. The therapist could perform a massage to the area while applying the heat.

If the cellulite problem is exacerbated by weak flabby muscles, then faradism could be applied after the heat. The muscles will be warm and receptive to the flow of current which will exert a pumping action on the area, stimulating the interchange of tissue fluids and encouraging the elimination of waste. Vacuum suction may also be incorporated to stimulate the flow of lymph.

Finish the whole treatment routine with the galvanic iontophoresis, which causes the penetration of the anti-cellulite products into the skin, increasing the circulation, speeding up the interchange of tissue fluids and improving elimination.

The client should be advised to have a course of ten or twelve treatments and, depending on the skin's reaction, at least twice a week. However, it is important to define the client's particular problem before planning any programme of treatment. All of the above treatments may be used in various combinations according to the client's needs.

Contraindications to galvanism

* Any skin disease.
* Metal pins or plates.
* Poor skin sensitivity.
* Diabetics – impaired skin sensitivity.
* Defective circulation.
* Sunburn or skin inflammation.
* Cuts or abrasions.
* Varicose veins.
* Oedema.
* Hypersensitive skin.
* Over the abdominal area in the first few days of menstruation.
* Areas *never* to be treated are:
  – kidney area
  – bony area
  – breasts
  – sciatic nerve.

Ultrasound

Ultrasound is the most up-to-date treatment for the removal of cellulite. It has been found that over time cellulite becomes very difficult to remove because cell permeability is reduced, circulation becomes less efficient and the toxins are trapped within the tissues, forming hardened deposits around individual fat cells,

so making them more difficult to remove or be utilised by the body. The treatment is sensation-free, relaxing and comfortable for the client.

Ultrasound breaks down and disperses the hardened deposits in the cellulite. The treatment is very safe to use as it is based on the same technology as medical ultrasound scans.

For the treatment of cellulite, it only penetrates a few millimetres below the skin surface to reach the adipose tissue where the cellulite is trapped. It works in the following way:

* The ultrasound is emitted at a very high frequency. This sets up vibrations in the cells and breaks down the hardened fatty deposits (the same way an opera singer's high-pitched voice may shatter a glass).
* The ultrasound waves pass into the tissues, creating a micromassaging effect.
* Localised heat is produced, helping to disperse the rigid structures formed by the hardened deposits. This stimulates the release of toxins and waste products out of the cells and transfers them to the lymphatic system.
* Lymphatic massage is performed to remove the toxins towards the nearest drainage point for natural elimination.

A good home care routine should be recommended to the client to help maintain the improved condition after treatment.

The latest systems incorporate thermographic diagnosis to help assess the areas requiring treatment. Thermographic (heat sensitive) plates display heat and cold as a series of colours and when microcirculation is reduced areas, of cellulite will show up as 'cold'. This enables therapists to determine the precise location and density of the cellulite. Because of this they will be able to tailor their treatment to the specific requirements of the client and assess the correct length of treatment required to treat the condition successfully.

The consultation

This is important for the usual reasons of recording details, assessing the client for treatment and checking for contraindications, but also lifestyle plays an important part in the recognition and treatment of cellulite. Therefore, it is important to ask the client the following questions:

Do you exercise regularly?

Do you smoke?

Do you use anti-cellulite products?

Do you have a healthy diet?

Do you eat lots of spicy foods?

Do you drink, tea, coffee, alcohol or carbonated drinks including sparkling water?

Do you have a sedentary or active lifestyle.

Do you take any medication and if so, for what?

Do you have a hereditary history of circulatory related problems?

Have you had any previous anti-cellulite treatment?

Preparation

After the consultation, treatment may begin, but it is important to prepare the area to be treated by brushing the skin for about five minutes. Alternatively, a G5 with the prickly head can be used. The purpose of this is to gently exfoliate the skin and stimulate the circulation. The skin should have a healthy pink glow by this time and a special gel may be applied using lymphatic massage movements. This will allow the ultrasound head to glide smoothly over the treated area and ensure an even contact with the skin.

Figure 18.9 *Body brushing*

A full treatment would include:

* client preparation and assessment/body brush or G5 – 10 minutes
* lymph massage and application of ultrasound gel – 5–10 minutes
* ultrasound treatment – 25 minutes
* lymph massage to aid absorption and elimination – 15 minutes.

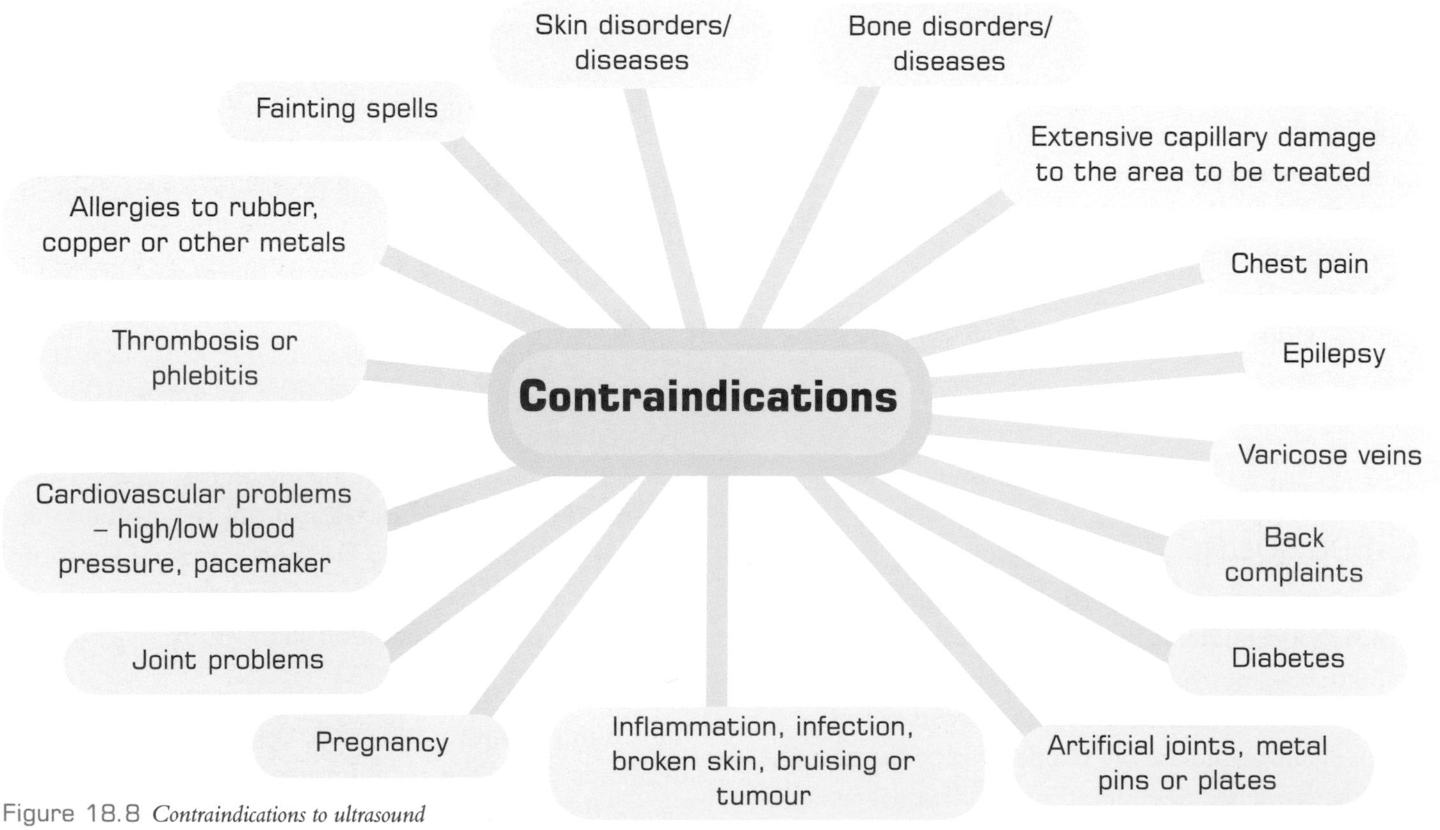

Skin disorders/ diseases

Bone disorders/ diseases

Fainting spells

Extensive capillary damage to the area to be treated

Allergies to rubber, copper or other metals

Chest pain

Thrombosis or phlebitis

Contraindications

Epilepsy

Varicose veins

Cardiovascular problems – high/low blood pressure, pacemaker

Back complaints

Joint problems

Diabetes

Pregnancy

Inflammation, infection, broken skin, bruising or tumour

Artificial joints, metal pins or plates

Figure 18.8 *Contraindications to ultrasound*

Safety

* Do not use ultrasound over areas which contain underlying organs, that is, the abdominal cavity.
* Do not use on bony areas of the body, that is, elbows, knees, spinal column, shoulder blades, face and head.
* There should be no sense of electrical stimulation, vibration or pain and if this should occur, treatment must stop.
* If the hand-piece becomes overheated due to a long working period, application must be interrupted for a few minutes.

Treatment recommendation

A course of ten treatments is advisable for the best results – dispersing the hardened deposits and eliminating the orange peel effect of cellulite.

Treatments should be as close together as possible. The recommended number of treatments a week is a minimum of two or three with 24 hours in between. One hour should be allocated for treatment to include preparation with body brushing and massage. Application of ultrasound for 25 minutes and lymph drainage massage at the end.

The intensity of treatment varies, being set according to the relative thickness of the adipose tissue. As a guide, increase the intensity as the adipose tissue increases in density:

* Thin fatty layer or delicate area – lower setting.
* Average thickness – medium setting.
* Thick layers of adipose tissue – highest setting.

Always follow the manufacturer's instructions when applying the treatment.

Home care

This plays an important part in the treatment of cellulite and clients should be advised to do the following:

* Drink plenty of water, but not carbonated water as this helps the formation of cellulite. Add lemon to the water as this helps rid the body of toxins.
* Try not to drink while eating as this dilutes the enzymes required for efficient digestion.
* Sip water slowly as this will help bathe the cells and take waste with it.
* Use a body brush or loofah every day before bathing, brushing for five minutes until the skin feels warm and glowing.
* Use a good cream or oil to massage in morning and evening directly after bathing.

Electrical muscle stimulation

Commonly known as faradism, this treatment is very popular for toning slack muscles and improving figure shapes. The client does not have to participate in this treatment, although it does closely resemble natural exercise in the effect it has on the muscles. Therefore, it may be classified as passive exercise. It is also isometric exercise as there is no movement of the joints.

It is only effective, however, if a course of treatment is undertaken, so the client must attend regularly for a specified length of time. The nature of the treatment is such that clients will lose inches without losing weight, so they may follow a diet while having the treatment, and it may be included in a course of several different body treatments.

Most modern machines use a faradic-type current, which is an interrupted or surged direct current and which, when applied, produces a contraction in the muscle. The surged current is one which causes a gradual contraction of the muscle, increasing in strength and then gradually decreasing in strength. This surging is controlled by a timing device within the machine. The interrupted current is when the current flow stops and starts again and the contraction is only maintained while the current is flowing.

Figure 18.10 *Electrical muscle stimulation*

The faradic machine

The large faradic machine used for body work normally has ten outlets, with an intensity control for each outlet, and ten pairs of pads or electrodes made from carbon-impregnated plastic in the more modern machines. The machine has an on/off switch and a timer to regulate the length of the contraction and the relaxation period. There is an indicator light to show that the machine is switched on and an indicator light to show the pulse or contraction period.

Depending on the treatment, there is a frequency control and an intensity control. The frequency control indicates the impulses per second. This varies from 60 to 120 on most units. Frequency set at 60 will help to achieve comfortable contractions on large untoned muscles, areas of dense subcutaneous fat or areas with a high resistance. A frequency of 120 will stimulate superficial fascia and muscle and may be used on areas with little or no fat or well-toned muscles.

The intensity control will increase the level of contraction which is chosen to suit each individual client. There is an intensity control for each set of pads, so that each muscle or muscle group can be set to an intensity that is comfortable for the client. The intensity is turned up slowly as the current is flowing and the muscle is contracting. These controls must be at zero at the beginning of treatment and returned to zero at the conclusion of treatment.

There is a phase control which can be set on monophasic or biphasic. Monophasic is when the current flows in one direction only, from the negative to the positive. The negative pad will have the stronger contraction. Biphasic is when the current flows in one direction and then reverses to travel in the opposite direction. It produces strong even contractions and this setting is the one most generally used. Each pad of a pair can be regarded, therefore, as having the same polarity.

There is often a gain control which is useful when the client has become accustomed to the contractions and the intensity of all the pads can be turned up at the same time. A special safety feature in most modern machines is a reset button which prevents the machine from working until all the outlet intensity controls are at

zero. A variable switch allows the frequency of the contractions to be altered for those clients who are used to the treatment.

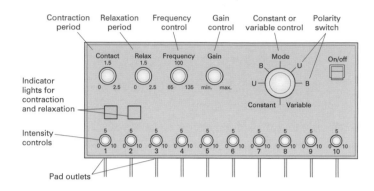

Figure 18.11 *Faradic body machine (EMS treatment)*

Effects of the current

* **The current stimulates the nerves**. When the current is applied there is a slight tingling sensation caused by stimulation of the sensory nerve endings in the skin. The current is then intensified and the motor nerves respond by contracting the muscle that is being treated.
* **Blood circulation is increased**. Blood flow is stimulated because of the muscle contracting and this also helps the lymphatic flow. The muscles are supplied with more oxygen and nutrients, and waste products are more efficiently removed.
* **An erythema is produced**. As a result of the increased blood supply, there is a reddening of the skin.
* **The muscle contracts**. The motor point of the muscle is where the motor nerve enters the muscle and when this point is stimulated accurately, a good contraction is obtained with the least amount of current necessary. The muscles are firmed and toned helping to reshape body contours and retain the new shape because of an increase in strength.

Client consultation

It is important for the therapist to establish whether electrical muscle stimulation is the correct form of treatment for the client. Some clients may be overweight, others may simply have loose flabby muscles in poor tone. The therapist should take the measurements of clients and if they are also on a diet, their weight. The measurements need only be recorded in the area being treated and they need to be taken at regular intervals during the course.

This is the time to ensure that clients are medically fit to have this treatment and a record card with all the necessary information should be completed. Information required from clients includes the number of children they have, their medical history, how much exercise they take and their family history since any problem they might have could be hereditary.

Muscle contraction treatment

This treatment works by placing the electrodes in pairs, with the polarity constantly changing between them, on the muscle or muscle groups to be treated. The contraction of the muscle caused by the application of the current should resemble natural muscle movements. The results achieved are similar to periods of active exercise.

Muscles can work **isotonically** when the contractions of the muscles cause movement of the joints and **isometrically** when the muscle contractions do not cause the joints to move. The electrical muscle stimulation treatment is generally isometric. Giving the client some form of heat treatment first will prepare the muscles so that they are warm and more responsive to treatment. Reassure clients before and during treatment and explain to them what is happening. If they are tense, then the treatment will feel more uncomfortable.

In the case of a client being allergic to the pads, small pieces of sponge or lint cut to fit and evenly soaked in saline solution may be placed under the pad. This allows the treatment to be carried out by protecting the client's skin from any irritation.

Padding layouts

Split padding is when the pair of pads are split and placed on corresponding muscles on either side of the body. This is normally used for very small muscles, for example the pectorals.

Dual padding is when the pair of pads are placed on the same muscle or muscle group on either side of the body. Each side of the body is dealt with separately and different intensities of current may be used. This will compensate for differences in muscle size, shape and bulk as well as natural strength in either the right or left side.

The pads may be placed longitudinally down the length of the muscle to take greatest advantage of the muscle shortening effect of the contraction, for example on the rectus abdominis when it has been stretched after childbirth. They may also be placed diagonally, either following the natural contour of the muscle or for general toning of muscle groups.

Caution!

Accurate placement of the pad over the motor point is essential if it is to be effective, particularly in clients who are overweight and have slack muscles.

Antagonistic muscles, that is, those that are working eccentrically and concentrically at the same time, must not be padded up together. These movements would not occur naturally and therefore should not be applied artificially.

Pads must never be placed directly over the heart.

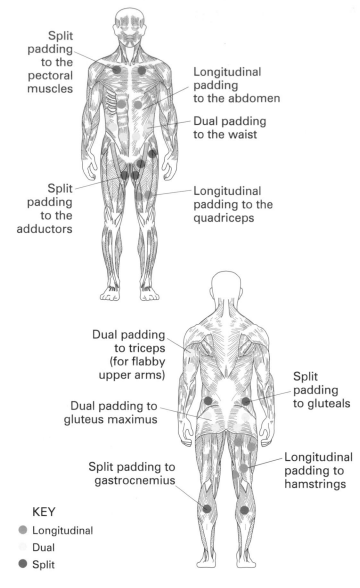

Split padding to the pectoral muscles

Longitudinal padding to the abdomen

Dual padding to the waist

Split padding to the adductors

Longitudinal padding to the quadriceps

Dual padding to triceps (for flabby upper arms)

Split padding to gluteals

Dual padding to gluteus maximus

Longitudinal padding to hamstrings

Split padding to gastrocnemius

KEY
● Longitudinal
○ Dual
● Split

Figure 18.12 *Suggested padding layouts for common problem areas*

Before placing the pads, consider carefully the effects to be achieved and the reason for using electrical muscle stimulation. Look at the way in which the muscles work naturally to help in placing the pads. The pads should be moistened with saline solution to help the current flow.

The area of treatment must be cleansed first with warm soapy water, particularly if there has been no pre-heating treatment such as sauna or steam. This will remove any oil on the skin's surface which may form a barrier to the current. The pads should be in firm contact with the skin to provide a good contraction.

Reasons for poor muscle contractions

✳ When the skin has not been sufficiently cleansed and there are oils on the skin to form a barrier.

✳ A faulty machine. All connections should be checked before use.

✳ Insufficient moisture in the form of saline solution on the pads or if the pads have dried out during the treatment.

✳ When the pads have been positioned badly and are not directly stimulating the motor point of the muscle.

✳ When the pads are strapped too lightly to the body.

✳ When the intensity of the current is not sufficient to stimulate the muscle to contract.

✳ When the subcutaneous fat in an obese client creates a barrier to the flow of current.

✳ Fatigue in the muscle, possibly by being overworked.

Uses of electrical muscle stimulation

✳ General toning treatment incorporated into a course of combined treatments, which could include diet, massage and galvanic treatments.

✳ For strengthening weak muscles.

✳ After childbirth, but only with the doctor's permission – usually after the six-week check-up.

✳ Reshaping specific areas, e.g. the buttocks, inside thighs or the top of the arms.

✳ To improve posture by exercising and strengthening muscles which are little used.

✳ After losing a lot of weight.

✳ Body maintenance.

Contraindications to electrical muscle stimulation

✳ Any muscular disorder.

✳ Any disorder of the nervous system.

✳ Cuts or abrasions in the skin.

✳ Metal plates, pins or piercings in the area or an IUD coil.

✳ Skin disease.

✳ After an operation, unless medical permission has been given.

* Loss of skin sensation.
* Epilepsy.
* Heart conditions, thrombosis or phlebitis.

Microcurrent

Microcurrent treatment has been used for many years for the treatment of sports injury to speed up recovery (see Chapter 11 Facial electrical treatments). It is now one of the most popular treatments used in salons for tightening and firming muscles and skin tissue. The microcurrent is of low intensity – a modified direct current which produces low frequency pulses with different wave forms. Its effects on the body include the following:

* It increases energy in the muscles.
* It increases the production of collagen in the skin.
* It increases protein synthesis in muscle and skin.
* It stimulates healing on a cellular level. All the above effects are helpful in the treatment of stretch marks and scar tissue.
* Cell permeability is increased, allowing nutrients an easy passage into cells and waste products an easy passage out.
* Lymphatic drainage is improved. This helps in the treatment of cellulite as lymph fluid is stimulated, toxins are removed and the appearance of 'orange peel dimpled skin' is diminished.
* Muscles are re-educated, lifted and toned when the microcurrent and particular wave form transmit a series of electrical signals to the area to be treated.

Areas for lifting treatment are the buttocks, thighs, stomach and bust. The current is applied through roller bar probes that lift the muscle or special gloves that the therapist wears to massage the area to be treated. The gloves are attached to the machine via a pair of leads. Some manufacturers recommend that small pads are applied to the therapist's arms and the hands then deliver the current directly into the area being treated using a Swedish massage technique. Some microcurrent machines have an electro-cellulite massager that tackles cellulite, fluid retention and stubborn fatty areas such as thighs and buttocks.

New developments

Over the past few years, there has been a gradual move away from the normal electrical muscle stimulation (EMS) systems used in body toning and slimming and several manufacturers have produced a variety of equipment which is said to have a much improved action of inch reduction. However, the principles of operation of these pieces of equipment should be very carefully considered.

From the information provided by these companies, it would seem that we now have something totally new in the concepts of total body therapy. However, upon closer investigation, the majority of these systems are simply modifications of normal EMS treatments. To produce the results of inch loss in the short periods of time that are claimed, the manufacturers are relying on modifications to the normal padding layout systems that are used in conventional body therapy practice. The conventional padding systems being taught in beauty therapy are those which the profession borrowed many years ago from medical practice. The current trends are to follow the new developments in isotonic and isometric methods of EMS.

New wave forms

There are advanced machines which use a different wave form, causing the muscles to react in a different way and providing a general inch and weight loss. As well as the usual effects of EMS:

* the new wave actually increases metabolism so utilising fat deposits
* it also increases lymphatic drainage helping to eliminate waste products.

The maximum time required for each treatment is 15 minutes and a course of ten treatments, two or three a week, is recommended for the best results. However, there should be no repeat treatment within 48 hours because of the build-up of lactic acid in the muscles. Once the required inch loss has been achieved, a maintenance programme of one treatment every ten days is all that is needed.

Interferential treatment

An interferential current is a combination of two similar or dissimilar currents. It is used to combine the effects of low-level muscular stimulation with the benefits of polar and interpolar effects of a galvanic current. Forms of interferential currents are used in certain body therapy systems where they are promoting the effects of ionisation and thermal increase in circulation. The interferential treatment is soothing and warming and is an enhanced form of body galvanism.

Unlike the faradic-type current used for electrical muscle stimulation treatment, interferential treatment causes very little sensation in the skin and is therefore more pleasant for the client. Frequencies up to and not much more than 100 Hertz will stimulate the muscles to produce a contraction.

The interferential current

Two currents of medium frequency are applied, one of 3900 Hertz and the other 4000 Hertz. When they cross in the area being treated another frequency is produced, as a result of the first two frequencies interfering with one another. This is why it is called an interferential current. This resultant frequency, therefore, is the equivalent of the difference between the original two frequencies, for example:

First frequency = 4000 hertz
Second frequency = 3900 hertz

The resultant frequency = 100 hertz

The low frequency current is generated in the tissues by the crossing of the two medium frequency currents through the body. The resultant frequency, although stimulating muscular tissue, is low enough to have a soothing effect on the otherwise highly stimulated nerve endings. It will stimulate muscle contraction, but because it does not have to pass directly through the skin to achieve this effect, it causes no painful sensation in the skin, normally a characteristic of a faradic treatment.

Effects of an interferential current

* Stimulates muscle to contract.
* Increases the flow of blood.
* Increases lymphatic flow.
* Increases the metabolic processes.

Application

It is necessary to use four electrodes for large areas of the body or four small electrodes incorporated into one viscose pad for small areas to ensure that the frequencies cross. The two currents are applied independently of each other, with the electrode pairs placed diagonally opposite each other to ensure the crossing of the two medium frequency currents to produce a natural smooth body treatment.

19 Ultraviolet, infrared and radiant heat treatments

Ultraviolet and infrared ray treatments

The infrared and ultraviolet (UV) ray treatments are available in most health and beauty establishments and are used for both therapeutic and cosmetic purposes. There are now many specialist tanning establishments that provide the opportunity to maintain a tan all year round.

There is continuing debate within the beauty profession, about the effects of UV radiation on the skin and, in particular, the use of sun beds. Sun overexposure is known to damage the skin, cause premature ageing and may contribute to the appearance of skin cancer. The dilemma for the beauty therapist is that there is a demand for this treatment in spite of the negative press that it often receives. It is important, therefore, to understand the dangers of UV exposure, its safe use and to provide clients with a clear picture of the effects, benefits and disadvantages of treatment so that they make an informed decision about using such equipment

Infrared ray treatment is used by many therapists as a pre-heat treatment, to soothe aching muscles and joints or to reinforce the effects of other treatments such as a specialised face mask.

The different pieces of equipment available are many and varied and the application of these treatments must be carried out safely, carefully following the manufacturers' instructions, otherwise there is a risk of over treatment and burning if carelessly applied.

The rays used are UV visible light and infrared which form part of the electromagnetic spectrum.

The electromagnetic spectrum

Energy is transmitted from the sun as radiation of different **wavelengths** through space. This radiation consists of an enormous range of wavelengths and collectively they are known as the electromagnetic spectrum which includes:

* x-rays
* gamma rays
* radio waves
* microwave radiation
* ultraviolet (UV) radiation
* visible light
* infrared radiation.

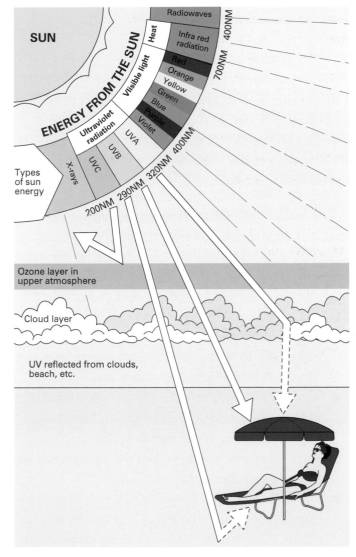

Figure 19.1 *The electromagnetic spectrum*

They are all electromagnetic rays/waves which transfer energy from one point to another and they consist of varying electric and magnetic fields, which vibrate at a given **frequency**. Each type of ray has a particular wavelength and frequency, but they all travel at the same speed. These wavelengths are like the wave in a rope when it is shaken across the floor.

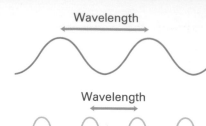

Figure 19.2 *Infrared and UV ray wavelengths*

The wavelength is an important characteristic of any type of radiation. It is the distance travelled by the wave in one complete cycle – the distance from the point on one wave to the same point on the next wave. The frequency is the number of cycles that occur in a unit of time and is measured in cycles per second or Hertz. As the wavelength increases, the frequency decreases, and as wavelength decreases, the frequency increases.

UV rays have shorter wavelengths and infrared rays have longer wavelengths than visible light. The UV ray, therefore, requires more cycles to cover the same distance as infrared rays and has a higher frequency and more energy.

Radiation waves used in beauty therapy include:

* UV rays are used to produce a tan, but they are not visible to the naked eye and cannot be felt, so some light from the visible spectrum and infrared range is added to give blue warm rays.
* Visible light is white light split up into a band of colours – red, orange, yellow, green, blue, indigo and violet. It lies in the middle of the electromagnetic spectrum and the wavelengths are longer than those of UV.
* Infrared rays have a longer wavelength than visible light and can be felt as heat but are not visible. They can be made visible by the addition of some visible light to give radiant heat.

Measuring wavelength

The **nanometre** is the unit of measurement of the wavelength of rays and is equal to one-millionth of a millimetre.

* UV rays are between 200 and 390 nanometres.
* Visible light is between 400 and 700 nanometres, with 400 being the blue end and 700 being the red end of the spectrum of light.

* Infrared rays are between 700 and 4000 nanometres.

Ultraviolet

UV rays are situated at the violet end of the light spectrum and although they produce little heat they do have a strong reaction on the skin, causing erythema and tanning. There are three bands of UV rays:

* ultraviolet A (UVA) rays
* ultraviolet B (UVB) rays
* ultraviolet C (UVC) rays.

UVA rays

These are lower energy UV rays which penetrate deep into the dermis. They are responsible for ageing as they cause fragmentation of the collagen and elastin fibres, which provide the skin with support, thus causing lines and wrinkles. They are the same intensity all year round in all weather conditions, even on a cloudy day.

Many sun bed manufacturers claim that tanning occurs without burning because the output is almost entirely UVA with minute amounts of UVB added. The absence of UVB means that the normal protective response of thickening of the epidermis does not occur, thus allowing excessive amounts of UVA to penetrate into the dermis and eventually causing ageing of the skin.

UVA rays produce a tan in a skin which tans easily by stimulating the existing melanin in the skin, but it is not a long-lasting tan. They alone do not cause cancer but have a predisposition to the effects of UVB in causing skin cancers.

The wavelength is 315–400 nanometres.

UVB rays

UVB rays penetrate only into the epidermis and they are the rays responsible for sunburn. These rays stimulate the **melanocytes** (pigment forming cells) in the basal layer of the epidermis to produce **melanin** (a colour molecule), resulting in a longer lasting tan. They are the rays chiefly responsible for skin cancers.

The wavelength is 280–315 nanometres.

UVC rays

None of these rays reaches the earth's surface as they are absorbed by the atmosphere. These rays are lethal to living cells.

The wavelength is 200–280 nanometres.

Effects of UV radiation

The radiation from natural sunshine is beneficial to most people in small doses. The skin's physiological response to the application of UV light is a protective one, to prevent more harm coming to the skin and the body. It has certain beneficial effects:

* It warms the body.
* It stimulates chemical activity in the skin increasing cellular regeneration and desquamation.
* It kills some bacteria on the skin.
* It stimulates the production of vitamin D in the skin, which is important in the development and maintenance of healthy bones, and is also involved in normal cell growth and maturation. Vitamin D ensures the functioning of healthy nerves and muscles by regulating calcium levels in the blood, vital for nerve impulse transmission and muscle contraction.
* It promotes a feeling of well-being giving a psychological boost. In fact, there are many sufferers of a condition called SAD, or seasonal affective disorder. It is caused by a biochemical imbalance in the hypothalamus due to the shortening of daylight hours and the lack of sunlight in winter.
* It is cosmetic in effect as it produces a tan giving the appearance of good health.
* It has a beneficial effect on some skin disorders, e.g. psoriasis and acne.

Figure 19.3 *UV is beneficial in small doses and with protection*

The amount of UV exposure that we receive depends upon several factors:

* The part of the world in which we live.
* The season of the year.
* The thickness of the ozone layer, which prevents a large proportion of rays from reaching the earth.

UV radiation also has certain damaging effects:

* It thickens the stratum corneum, when the UV rays stimulate the cells in the basal layer of the epidermis to produce more rapidly. This creates additional protection for the skin against UV radiation, but the skin appears coarse in texture and is sometimes described as 'leathery'.
* It can cause sunburn, which is painful and may damage the skin.
* In the long-term, overexposure to UVA will cause ageing of the skin and UVB may cause skin cancer.
* Skin may be more sensitive to artificial light or sunlight if a person is taking certain medications, e.g. antihistamines, tranquillisers or birth control pills.

The physiological process involved in the production of a tan

The technical term for tanning is **melanogenesis**. As the UV rays are absorbed by the skin, they stimulate into action the enzyme **tyrosinase**, which is present in the melanocytes, the pigment forming cells in the basal layer of the epidermis. This chemical process causes the transformation of **tyrosin**, a colourless amino acid, into melanin, a colourful molecule which migrates upwards to the surface of the skin. Melanin gives skin its characteristic golden or bronze tan and helps to filter out the harmful UV rays protecting the skin from further radiation.

Exposure to UV light should be limited to times when the sun is not high in the sky. It is at its strongest between the hours of 11 am and 3 pm. The rays also increase in strength if they are reflected off another surface, for example sand, snow or water. On winter skiing holidays there is a high incidence of sunburn on the fairly sensitive and usually unexposed area underneath the chin from UV radiation which is reflected off the snow.

Many people will burn when exposed to UV radiation before they tan and some people burn without producing a tan. The skin's reaction will normally depend upon the skin type. There are many different skin types, which have developed to suit different climatic conditions. Black African skin is heavily pigmented and usually thicker and more greasy. This skin, however, will still become darker when exposed to UV light and lighter if protected from it. In northern European countries the skin type is normally thin, fair and dry and would require maximum protection.

No matter which skin type a person has, the skin will burn if there is overexposure. Sensitive skins will only be safe for a very short time without some form of protection and darker skins are safe only if they are not overexposed.

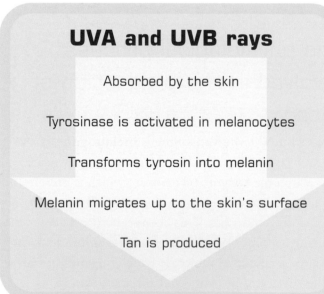

UVA and UVB rays

Absorbed by the skin

Tyrosinase is activated in melanocytes

Transforms tyrosin into melanin

Melanin migrates up to the skin's surface

Tan is produced

Figure 19.4 *Action of UVA and UVB rays on the skin*

Skin types

Skin types may be divided into five groups:

1 Sensitive skin which burns easily and does not develop a tan.
2 Sensitive skin which burns but tans slightly.
3 Normal skin which burns slightly and tans slowly.
4 Skin which easily tans and rarely burns.
5 Skin that is deeply pigmented and never burns.

Figure 19.5 *Examples of a sensitive skin which burns easily and a deeply pigmented skin which never burns*

Sunburn

Several hours after exposure, the skin will become red and this reddening is called an **erythema**. There are four degrees of erythema:

* **First-degree erythema** – a slight reddening which appears several hours after exposure and disappears within 24 hours without causing any irritation.
* **Second-degree erythema** – a marked redness with slight itching which lasts for two to three days.
* **Third-degree erythema** – extremely red, hot, swollen and sore skin which lasts for a week.
* **Fourth-degree erythema** – the same as third-degree erythema but the swelling leads to blistering and peeling. The skin is very hot and painful.

Physiological response to sunburn

Sunburn is an injury to the skin and the body responds by releasing histamine from the skin cells, which in turn cause the blood vessels to dilate allowing more blood to reach them. Fluid leaks from the widened blood vessels so that the infected area becomes red from the increased

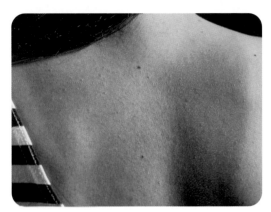

Figure 19.6
Sunburned skin

blood supply and swollen from the increased fluid. This swelling causes pain and tenderness in the area.

The skin begins the normal healing process, which is very efficient and exactly the same whether the injury is caused by infection, a wound or sunburn. The cells in the skin divide quickly to form new tissue but if the sunburn is severe, then scarring may occur.

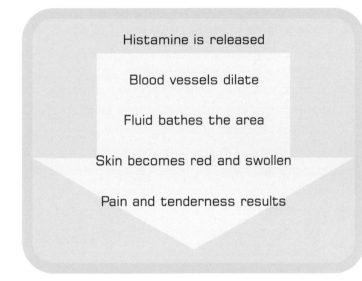

Histamine is released

Blood vessels dilate

Fluid bathes the area

Skin becomes red and swollen

Pain and tenderness results

Figure 19.7 *The skin's response to sunburn*

Sunscreens

There are two types of sunscreens – physical and chemical.

Physical

This type of sunscreen is an opaque film used on the skin to reflect the UV radiation. The most common example is zinc oxide cream used by winter holiday enthusiasts when skiing. It forms a dense barrier but actually blocks perspiration, so its use is limited to small exposed areas such as the bridge of the nose and the cheekbones.

Chemical

This type of sunscreen can be a water- or oil-soluble chemical which absorbs UV radiation reducing its intensity. It comes in the form of cream, oil, lotion or milk and some brands are waterproof. Sunscreens are now being included in skin care products and make-up.

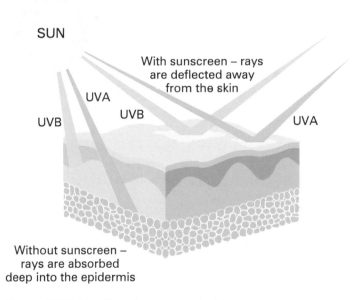

SUN

With sunscreen – rays are deflected away from the skin

UVA

UVB   UVB   UVA

Without sunscreen – rays are absorbed deep into the epidermis

Figure 19.8 *The effects of sunscreen on the skin*

The best type of sunscreen product is a **broad-spectrum** sunscreen which will filter out both the UVA and UVB rays. These sunscreens are graded by their **sun protection factor (SPF)**.

The SPF is determined by the amount of time the sunscreen can extend the time that a person can spend in the sun without burning. For example, a person who could stay in the sun for 10 minutes before burning could extend that period of time to 60 minutes without burning by using a sunscreen with an SPF of 6.

SPF numbers vary, but some manufacturers produce them as high as 30 as well as total sun blocks. The most sensitive skin types, that is, fair skins, babies and anyone who has not previously been exposed to UV radiation, should use the highest factor available.

One of the most common constituents of sunscreens, which filters out UVB rays, is **para aminobenzoic acid**. New sunscreens have been developed to absorb the A and B rays, the broad spectrum absorbers, **dioxybenzone** and **oxybenzophenone**.

> For maximum benefit:
> * Apply before going into the sun.
> * Reapply regularly during the day.
> * Water-resistant sunscreens should be reapplied approximately 30 minutes before going into the water.

Ultraviolet lamp treatment

The application of UV by artificial means has become very popular in recent years with specialist salons opening and many beauty salons and health clubs promoting their use.

Sun beds to be used at home are advertised extensively in the press, unfortunately allowing untrained people to apply UV radiation without knowing the rules of safe use, which they should apply. The association of Sun Tanning Operators has agreed to a code of practice based on guidelines from the Health & Safety Executive. If a salon is a member of the association, then it will have a badge prominently displayed on the premises. The Sunbed Association's (TSA) primary aim is to promote consistent good practice in the use of sun beds and it requires its members to adhere to its strict code of practise.

Reasons for the use of UV lamps

* For tanning purposes, to produce or maintain a tan.
* To promote healing and increase desquamation in an acne skin condition.
* To stimulate a sluggish skin.
* To improve some skin conditions, e.g. psoriasis, if the client is not on medication for the condition.

Figure 19.9
Client using a tan cab

Ultraviolet lamps

Modern UV lamps are mercury vapour, which can be either high or low pressure, and are designed to produce UVA only. They use fluorescent tubes similar to fluorescent lighting tubes, but they emit UV rays as well as visible blue light.

The lamps come in various forms:
* A small sun lamp, which is portable and easily packed away but only used to treat small areas and is not as efficient for general treatment.
* A sun bench, which is a modified couch with a transparent, concave surface on which the client lies, receiving the treatment from below.
* A solarium which is a combination of a sun bench and a canopy above, allowing the whole body to be treated at once.
* Tan cabs in which the client stands, surrounded by tubes emitting UV light, allowing an all-over tan even around the sides.
* Spa solarium, combining a hydrobath with an in-built solarium. This allows the client to lie in a whirlpool bath absorbing important minerals, essential oils or herbal bath salts and at the same time benefit from the warmth and tanning effects from the solarium canopy above.

The glass used in sun beds and solaria is made of a special type, which allows the penetration of UV rays. The heat produced from the lamps is caused by a small amount of infrared being added.

19 Ultraviolet, infrared and radiant heat treatments

Safety

Patch test

Before applying any UV treatment, the client's skin must be assessed first using a patch test, which shows how long it will take to cause a minimal erythema.

An area of skin not previously exposed to UV rays must be chosen, for example inside of the arm. The area must be clean and grease-free so the skin is not sensitised by anything which has been applied and there is no barrier to the rays.

Use a sheet of opaque paper and cut out three different shapes and position them securely over the area to be treated. The surrounding area must be protected with towels, the lamp carefully positioned and the distance recorded.

The three shapes should then be exposed to the UV for one minute. The first shape should then be covered with a towel and the two remaining shapes exposed for a second minute. The second shape should then be covered with a towel and the last shape exposed for another minute. A record of each shape and the time it was exposed to the UV rays should be kept. The client must then return after 24 hours to have the patches checked for any signs of reaction.

If the results of the test are negative, then the client should have another test and the time exposed to the UV rays should be increased. The time it took to produce a minimal erythema is the time the therapist will use for the first treatment, using the distance recorded from the patch test.

Inverse square law of radiation

UV rays cannot be felt, so it is vitally important that a free-standing lamp is not placed too close to the client. The closer the rays are to the body, the higher the intensity of radiation and the more likely they are to burn the skin. The rays travelling from a lamp actually spread out, so the further away they are from the point of contact, the weaker they will become. By increasing the distance away from the point of contact, the rays will spread over a larger area and become weaker in effect.

The inverse square law of radiation states:

The intensity of rays from a point source varies inversely with the square of the distance from the source.

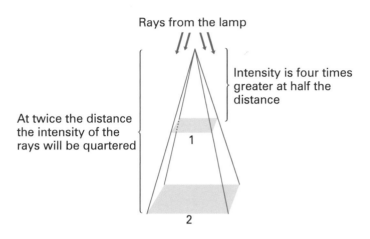

Figure 19.10 *Inverse square law of radiation*

This means that if the distance from the lamp to the area treated is doubled, the intensity of the rays is quartered. For example, if UV treatment is given for one minute, at a distance of 30 cm and the lamp is then moved to 60 cm away (doubling the distance), the time of treatment would be increased to four minutes because the intensity of the rays has quartered. Therefore, at half the distance, the intensity is four times *greater* and at *twice* the distance, the intensity is four times *weaker*.

To work out the distance and the time to obtain the same intensity:

Halve the distance – divide the time by 4.

Double the distance – multiply the time by 4.

Client consultation

Client consultation is important because it provides the opportunity to discuss with clients anything which may affect the treatment they are undertaking. A record card should be filled in with all the details of the client and, in particular, any form of medication he or she is taking. Many drugs are photosensitisers, which make the body extra sensitive to UV.

Check with clients if they have recently been in the sun and if there have been any adverse reactions. Assess the sensitivity of the skin and carry out a patch test. Check for contraindications.

Contraindications to UV lamp treatment

* Extra sensitive skin.
* Photosensitive skin.
* Vitiligo – skin with a total absence of melanin.
* Sun allergy.
* If the client is taking medication, that might cause an adverse reaction when exposed to UV.
* History of skin cancer.
* Immediately after heat treatment.
* Skin disease.

During treatment

Therapists and clients must wear goggles when exposed to UV rays and the importance of this procedure must be stressed to clients so that when left unattended they will not be tempted to remove the goggles and leave eyes open to damage. For health and safety reasons disposable eye protectors should be used.

The distance of the lamp from the client must be measured accurately. The UV rays must strike the body at an angle of 90° for maximum effect and the treatment must be accurately timed.

Those clients who hope to maintain an all-year-round tan should be informed of the dangers and if they still wish to have the treatment, then exposure should be carefully monitored to prevent any burning or peeling.

Records must be kept of the:

* date of treatment
* lamp used
* area treated
* distance of the lamp from the body
* time of treatment
* general effects
* erythema reaction
* therapist's name
* any other relevant information.

Health and Safety at Work Act (1974)

This law states that the owner of a business is legally responsible for the safety of his or her employees and clients. Therefore, the following points must be considered:

* Understand the equipment being used.
* Train all members of staff in their safe use.

* Follow the manufacturers' instructions to the letter.
* Have the equipment serviced once a year and make sure it is mechanically safe.
* Always ensure client safety.
* There should be ease of access to the sun bed.
* There should be adequate ventilation particularly with 'high pressure' solaria because UV produces ozone and in excess can be irritating.
* There should be a notice in the sun bed room stating the correct procedures, safety factors and hygiene precautions to be followed.
* There should be a notice prominently displayed which warns the clients of the effects of UV radiation.
* There must be some means by which a client can summon help, e.g. a bell.
* There must be a timer fitted to the machine for accuracy.
* The overhead canopies must be made of a suitable material so that lamps will not fall out or explode.
* When new lamps have been fitted to an existing solarium a notice to this effect must be prominently displayed to inform clients, as the general effect is more marked with new lamps.

Effects of overexposure to UV radiation

Wrinkling

The name given to the changes that occur in the skin due to exposure to UV radiation is **solar elastosis**. The skin loses its normal strength and elasticity. The collagen and elastin fibres in the dermis are affected causing the breakdown of the support in the skin as well as a loss of fluid as the skin becomes much drier with constant exposure.

Areas of pigmentation

Brown patches occur on exposed areas of skin (chloasma), which are larger and more irregular in shape than the smaller freckles or lentigo.

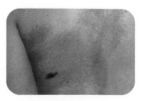

Figure 19.11 *Areas of pigmentation from sun damage*

Broken veins

Tissue affected by UV radiation is not as tough as normal connective tissue. The blood vessels widen and become more visible on the surface of the skin. These are known as **telangiectasia**.

Reduction of skin immunity

The **langerhans cells** in the skin are part of the immune system. They locate dangerous substances in the skin and initiate an immune response. Exposure to UVB rays reduces the numbers and function of these cells, adversely affecting the body's immune system by preventing it from recognising and dealing with foreign bodies. Therefore, rogue cells that appear may be allowed to flourish.

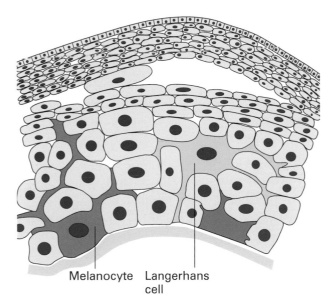

Melanocyte   Langerhans
cell

Figure 19.12 *Langerhans cells in the skin*

Infrared and radiant heat treatment

There are two types of heat radiation:

* infrared
* radiant heat.

Infrared is divided into near infrared, which is nearest to the visible part of the electromagnetic spectrum, and far infrared, which is further away from the visible light. Radiant heat is near infrared mixed with red light. They both produce infrared radiation and are similar in effect, producing heat in the part of the body being treated. Infrared rays are, however, longer than radiant heat rays.

Skin penetration

Infrared rays penetrate the superficial epidermis only and heat is produced, warming and soothing the skin.

Radiant heat rays are more intense and penetrate deep into the dermis, producing heat, affecting the nerve endings of pain. This irritant effect makes this a more stimulating form of heat treatment.

Heat lamps

The lamps available are many and varied, but the principles of application are the same. There are two types of heat lamp available to the beauty therapist:

* The infrared or non-luminous lamp provides no visible light but produces heat. It can be used for a longer period of time as it is less irritating.
* The radiant heat or luminous lamp combines near infrared rays and visible light to produce heat.

When giving treatment with heat lamps the characteristics of each lamp need to be considered before choosing which one to use. Table 19.1 lists the characteristics of each type of lamp.

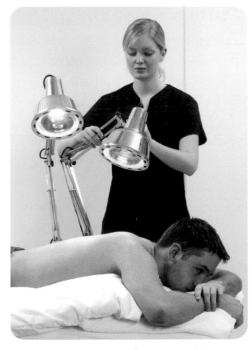

Figure 19.13 *Infrared lamp*

Infrared

The infrared lamp has to be switched on at least 10–15 minutes before it is required to reach its maximum intensity
The infrared generator should be mounted in a reflector, which is perfectly designed without any dents that may cause the tissues to be heated unevenly
A defective reflector would cause the rays to concentrate in certain areas and create a 'hot spot'
The radiation is of a longer wavelength and is less irritating, so may be used for longer periods

Radiant heat

The radiant heat lamp does not need time to warm up as it reaches its peak 30 seconds after being switched on.
The heat is also more evenly dispersed as it has its own built-in reflector system
A red glow is given out and this has a psychologically soothing effect on clients as they lie bathed in the warm red light
This treatment is ideal when treating muscular aches and pains
The radiation from this lamp is of shorter wavelengths and the heat is quite deep, so treatment time has to be kept shorter

Table 19.1 *Characteristics of lamps*

Effects of heat lamps

Increase in circulation

An increase in circulation is caused by the application of heat. The blood vessels dilate and the increased blood flow brings nourishment to the area being heated and increases the lymph flow, thus removing waste products.

A hyperaemia or reddening of the skin is produced due to the increased circulation and it begins to fade soon after the conclusion of treatment.

Pain relief

With mild heating, the rays have an analgesic effect on the superficial sensory nerve endings in the skin. More intense heating actually irritates the superficial sensory nerve endings and pain is relieved due to counter irritation.

Mild heating is helpful in easing pain caused by an accumulation of waste products in the tissues. The increased flow of lymph helps in the speedier removal of these waste products.

Increase in body temperature

The increase in temperature usually occurs locally, just in the area being treated. This stimulates the sweat glands to produce more sweat, aiding the elimination of waste products and deep cleansing the skin. The warmth produced also allows creams to be absorbed more readily into the skin.

Relaxation

Muscles relax making them more responsive to further treatment. The soothing effect on the nerve endings relieves pain, so relieving tension in the body, helping the muscles to relax.

Uses of heat lamp treatment

* As a preparatory treatment, it will relax the muscles before electrical muscle stimulation or body massage and allow easier penetration of creams and oils into the epidermis.
* To relax a tense, nervous client.
* To relieve muscular pain or tension.
* To relieve pain in the joints.
* To replace other forms of heat treatment such as sauna or steam.
* To promote healing.

Contraindications to heat lamp treatment

* Heart or circulatory problems.
* Hypersensitive skin.
* Skin disorders.
* Diabetes because of the inefficient circulation and poor skin sensitivity.
* Any loss of skin sensation.
* High or low blood pressure.
* Sunburn.
* Metal pins or plates.

Hazards when using infrared radiation

* Burning of the skin caused by overheating or contact with the lamp.
* Fainting, particularly if the client rises quickly from a lying position.

* Headache may follow treatment, particularly in hot weather. The back of the head should be protected if it is exposed during treatment.
* Injury to the eyes.

Reducing the risk

The client

When applying any form of heat to the skin a thermal skin test must be carried out prior to treatment to avoid burning the skin and to ensure that the client's skin sensitivity is not impaired. (For details of how to carry out a thermal skin test, see Chapter 13 Spa and heat therapies, page 198.)

Check the client has no contraindications and has removed all jewellery.

The skin must be free from grease so the client should take a shower before treatment. Alternatively, the skin can be wiped over with witch hazel or skin tonic.

The client's eyes must be protected if these are likely to be exposed to the rays. Damp cotton wool pads can be used to protect them – the water will absorb the rays.

Always maintain contact with the client during treatment.

The heat lamp

* Always follow the manufacturer's instructions. The heat lamp must be checked before treatment to see that it is in good working order.
* The plug should not have any loose connections. The flex should not be frayed and it should be positioned so that nobody can trip over it. The switches should be in good working order.
* Bulbs should be screwed firmly in place. All reflective surfaces should be clean and free from dents.
* The joints in a free-standing model should be tightened sufficiently to prevent any movement once the lamp has been correctly positioned.
* The lamp should be warmed up away from clients to prevent accidents.
* The lamp must be positioned at the correct distance and angle from the client. This may be between 45 cm and 60 cm according to the output from the generator. At the end of the treatment the lamp should be positioned safely away from the client to cool down.

The cosine law for radiation

This compares the intensity of the rays with the angle at which the rays contact the skin. The lamp should be placed perpendicular to the area being treated so that the rays are at right angles to the body for maximum intensity. If the angle is reduced, then the rays cover a larger area and the intensity will be lowered.

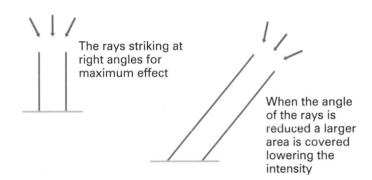

The rays striking at right angles for maximum effect

When the angle of the rays is reduced a larger area is covered lowering the intensity

Figure 19.14 *The cosine law for radiation*

Timing of treatment

Normal treatment time varies from 10 to 30 minutes depending on the size of the area to be treated and the distance the lamp is placed from the client. The more sensitive the client is to the heat, the further away the lamp must be positioned and the longer the treatment time should be to compensate for the lower intensity of the rays.

The effects of extreme heat and overexposure to UV radiation

Exhaustion

Anything which causes the body to produce excessive perspiration will deplete the body of necessary minerals and salt. Low levels of potassium and calcium will result in fatigue and cramps. There will be a feeling of lethargy accompanied by headaches and dizziness and in severe cases a feeling of nausea and collapse.

To counteract these symptoms, the sufferer should lie down quietly and drink plenty of fluids, preferably water. Eating foods high in the mineral such as bananas, nuts and avocados can increase levels of potassium.

Sunstroke

This is a dangerous condition and occurs when the body's normal protection against overheating fails. The body is unable to cope with the excessive heat and its temperature rises to unacceptable levels. The symptoms are rapid rise in temperature, severe headaches, vomiting, collapse and in extreme cases, unconsciousness. This condition requires medical help and immediate cooling of the body with cold water. When the body begins to return to normal, rest and plenty of fluids are required.

Miliaria

This is a condition which affects the sweat glands and it comes in two forms:

* **Miliaria crystallina (sudamina)** occurs when the skin around the sweat ducts becomes swollen resulting in a blockage of the sweat gland. As the sweat gland continues to work, the end of the duct becomes distended causing a clear fluid-filled vesicle. There may be an accompanying itchiness of the skin, but the condition soon subsides if the body is kept cool.

* **Miliaria rubra (prickly heat)** is a reaction to heat and, in particular, exposure to UV radiation. It is also a blockage of the sweat ducts but, in this case, the duct ruptures, allowing the sweat to escape into the epidermis. This causes the formation of itchy red pimples on inflamed skin. Loose clothing must be worn in natural fabrics to allow the skin to perspire freely. Cool the body by taking cool showers and if infection occurs consult a doctor.

Swelling

This normally occurs in the lower limbs because the blood vessels dilate as a response to heat and the walls of the superficial blood vessels become stretched and fluid leaks into the surrounding tissue. To treat this problem, it is advisable to lie down and rest with the legs slightly elevated and to take cool showers.

It is no longer necessary to spend weeks lying on a beach to develop a tan. This is now an all-year-round option for clients and is achieved in just a short time in the salon using their choice of application. The application of a false tan is also a popular salon treatment for those who are photosensitive. There are a growing number of people who prefer not to expose themselves to the effects of ultraviolet radiation but still want a tan and this is an ideal solution.

The self-tanning creams are made from dihydroxy acetone (DHA) and rich moisturising creams which when applied to the skin can produce a golden tan. A chemical reaction occurs when the cream is applied to the skin causing superficial staining of the top layer of the epidermis. Some manufacturers have added ingredients to mask the smell of traditional creams and to improve the condition of the skin with ingredients such as alpha hydroxy acids, aloe vera, carrot seed oil, allantoin and vitamin E.

Table 20.1 lists the advantages and disadvantages of false tan treatment.

Precautions

* Use the correct product for face and body as the facial creams contain more moisturiser and less of the tanning ingredient to produce a more natural tan.
* An exfoliation treatment must be applied first – brush, massage or special exfoliating creams may be used. This will prevent the self-tan over staining areas of dry skin.
* Moisturise the skin well to provide a good base for application of the cream, to give a perfect finish with no streaking.
* A small patch test may be applied prior to treatment to ensure that the client is not allergic to the product and the colour is compatible with the client's own skin.

New self-tan treatments

In the past, the application of false tans has been a lengthy treatment with much preparation before treatment, buffing after treatment and special care required throughout to achieve an even result. The latest methods used in many salons are the automatic tanning cubicles or the manual airbrush systems, which may take anything from six seconds to 20 minutes. Advances in new technology mean that the products are clean, effective and streak resistant.

The features, advantages and disadvantages and potential cost of the automated tanning cubicle and the manual airbrush system are described in Table 20.2.

Advantages	Disadvantages
The client may have an all-year-round tan	The colours of different self-tanning creams can vary greatly
It can help to prolong the life of an existing tan	It may leave a streaky effect on the skin
It can be used for special occasions when a low-cut or backless dress is worn	The dry areas of skin tend to absorb more colour, so may produce a blotchy effect, in particular on the elbows, knees and ankles
Those who are allergic to natural sunlight can achieve a tanned look	It has to be re-applied regularly to maintain the colour
It produces a tan without ageing the skin	
It provides colour to the face and removes the need for foundation	

Table 20.1 *Advantages and disadvantages of false tan treatment*

Body treatments

Treatment	Automated tanning cubicle	Manual airbrush system
Features	Automated voice instruction system Static or moving spray nozzles (vary in number depending on manufacturer) Extractor fan or ventilation system Automated self-cleaning system	Uses a hand-held air gun Used with or without a protective cubicle
Advantages	No client preparation Client activates equipment Quick to apply – approximately 60 seconds Instant colour Even tan achieved No buffing required Equipment is self-cleaning	No client preparation required Application is controlled by the therapist Instant colour Application is evenly applied No buffing required
Disadvantages	The system requires plumbing and electrical connection The client is required to exfoliate and moisturise the night before treatment The client may inhale the vapour The client has to move around to tan the inside of the arms and thighs Application may be uneven Hair protection, disposable foot protectors and knickers are advisable	Messy if a protective cubicle is not used as the mist produced is fine and settles on all surfaces The client is required to exfoliate and moisturise the night before treatment Takes longer than automated system Face mask must be worn by the client Operator must wear a face mask Airbrush requires regular cleaning
Potential cost	£20 000–£30 000	£650 for the airbrush alone; £10 500 with the cubicle

Table 20.2 *Comparison of automated tanning cubicle and manual airbrush system*

Hair removal

* Temporary hair removal

* Electrical epilation

Introduction

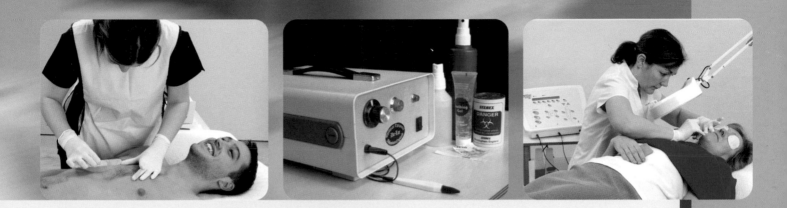

Whatever the vision or image of the beauty salon or spa, whether the specialist treatments include massage therapies, spa therapies, anti-ageing treatments or body conditioning, there will always be hair removal! There is an increasing demand for all methods of hair removal, and waxing or sugaring are probably one of the most requested treatments. Having hair-free legs is an essential for many women and there is no part of the female body that cannot be waxed, particularly now with the rise in popularity of the Brazilian.

Hair removal for men is catching up fast and the chest and back wax have become popular options with the male market. Swimmers and cyclists have been having wax treatments for the last 30 years, but now they do not have to slip in the back door pretending to be the man who has come to fix the plumbing!

Most salons offer electrolysis as a more permanent method of hair removal and the NHS in some authorities will employ therapists to work with endocrinologists and dermatologists to help treat patients with severe cases of excess hair conditions. Some therapists will also work with male to female transsexual clients. Electrolysis is a treatment that some therapists specialise in, devoting all of their working time to the one therapy, becoming extremely proficient and offering advanced treatment in the removal of skin tags, red veins and other skin blemishes.

Modern technology for the beauty therapist has advanced to such a degree that laser and pulsed light therapy is now used for the removal of excess hair. Many salons are providing this as a treatment option and there are many specialist salons and clinics specialising only in hair removal.

21 Temporary hair removal

Having a hair-free body is becoming an essential for many women and now also for many men! Summer means less clothing, bikini-clad bodies and ultra-smooth limbs, so the demand for waxing treatments in the summer months is very high. Fashion also dictates the type of hair removal treatment and client. Currently, men are eager to have a smooth, hair-free chest and back; many women are opting for the fashionable Brazilian, which removes all hair, or landing strip styles of bikini wax.

Depilation

Depilation is any method of temporary hair removal and includes:

* waxing
* sugaring
* tweezing and plucking
* shaving
* depilatory creams.

Waxing

The most commonly used method in the beauty salon is depilatory waxing. There are two methods of waxing:

* hot wax
* cool wax.

The hot wax method of depilation is long established but has been superseded by the cool wax method, which is now used more extensively, and there are many different waxing systems available to provide this service for your clients.

Hot wax

The basic ingredients in hot wax are beeswax and resins plus a soothing agent such as azulene. Beeswax is a true wax from the honeycomb and is solid in appearance. Resin is added to the beeswax to give it some flexibility and other soothing ingredients such as azulene or anti-bacterial such as tea tree oil. Depending upon the manufacturer, the wax varies in colour. It may be pale yellow, deep brown, rusty brown or green.

The melting point of hot wax is approximately 50°C and the working temperature is approximately 55°C.

Always follow the individual manufacturer's instructions when using a hot wax machine as manufacturers' instructions vary.

The modern hot wax machine has enclosed heating elements and is thermostatically controlled to prevent overheating. Because of stringent hygiene regulations, the hot wax should not be re-used. Therefore, it is not as necessary to have the larger wax machines with two pots, one in use and the other for filtering the used wax. However, they are still readily available and those salons that use them will use both sides for heating wax for the treatment and then discard it immediately after use.

Modern machines are much smaller and easier to keep clean and should comply with British Standard regulations.

Ingredients

Resins come mainly from Spain, Brazil, Portugal and China. Soothing ingredients such as azulene, chamomile, aloe vera and rose are used extensively and these come from many different countries. A popular ingredient used by many companies is tea tree for its antiseptic and bactericide properties. It is an ingredient used in the wax as well as being incorporated into a pre-wax skin wash and soothing after-wax lotion.

Cool wax

The ingredients in cool waxes vary and they are not always a wax. They can be a mixture of rubber latex solution and solvents or organic substances such as honey.

Some of these mixtures need warming and others may be applied cold. They never set hard on the skin, making it far easier to treat larger areas quickly.

The working temperature of cool wax is approximately 43°C. However, more and more companies are offering wax systems that work very well at lower temperatures, so you must always follow the manufacturer's instructions. The wax is heated in a compact, thermostatically controlled unit to a fairly low temperature. The cool wax is thrown away once it has been used and is therefore very hygienic.

The most recent cool wax machine comes in the form of a cartridge with a roller applicator head, which attaches to a handle. All parts are disposable, except the handle, making this method totally hygienic to the client.

New waxing system

One of the major problems with waxing is that it must be totally hygienic in application and treatment. The industry requires very high standards and new systems have been developed which are said to be the most hygienic methods of depilation available. These new methods use disposable applicator heads for applying the wax and this means that clients have their own applicator which is not inserted into the wax, but is screwed on to a tube instead. It is then discarded after use and this minimises the risk of cross-infection during waxing treatments.

The system consists of the following:

* A compact unit, which has a compartment for all the items required, a double-heater for the wax and a booster for use when required.
* Pre-depilatory cleansing gel containing aloe vera and witch hazel for their soothing and antiseptic properties.
* Wax which comes in tubes.
* Pre-sealed, disposable applicator heads to be attached to the tubes for each treatment.
* Wax removal strips.
* Post-depilatory lotion for hydrating and conditioning the skin. It contains witch hazel and allantoin for their antiseptic and healing properties and lemongrass oil for its refreshing smell.
* The special applicator dispenses the wax evenly, cleanly and quickly. The wax does not smell as strongly in the tubes as it does in a wax heater.

A comparison of hot and cool wax

Preparation of the client

Whichever method is employed a thermal skin test should be carried out to test the client's sensitivity to heat so that there is no risk of burning the skin,

particularly with the hot method. (For details of how to carry out a thermal skin test, see Chapter 13 Spa and heat therapies, page 198.) Contraindications to waxing should also be checked.

Equipment required for hot wax treatment

* Hot wax machine.
* Witch hazel to cleanse the skin.
* Talcum powder to ensure the skin is dry and to lift the hairs away from the skin to ensure the wax surrounds the hair providing a good grip.
* Cotton wool.
* Disposable spatulas, gloves and apron
* Soothing after-wax lotion.
* Waste bowl.

Preparation for hot wax treatment

The area to be treated must first be wiped over with witch hazel to remove any grease. Talcum powder should then be applied against the hair growth. This will lift the hairs away from the surface of the skin ensuring good adherence to the wax.

The temperature of the wax must then be tested on the inside of the therapist's wrist and then tested on a small patch of the client's skin.

Application and removal for hot wax treatment

Wax is applied with a spatula against the hair growth so that as the wax hardens it grips and contracts around the hair. The strips should be approximately 7.5 cm wide by any length, which may be easily removed by the therapist, usually between 10 cm and 15 cm, and several layers are built up until the strip is quite thick.

On a large area, such as the leg, as many strips as possible should be applied leaving a similarly sized gap between each strip. A second set of strips may then be applied to the gaps after

Figure 21.1 *Application pattern and removal of hot wax*

removal of the first, being very careful not to overlap the previously treated area with the hot wax, as this will be painful to the client.

As the wax is beginning to set and is still flexible, the edge of the strip should be very quickly flicked up. When it is set sufficiently the raised edge allows the therapist to grip the wax and pull the strip off decisively, following through with a soothing rub to the area to relieve the stinging sensation.

Aftercare for hot wax treatment

Cotton wool saturated with witch hazel may be applied over the treated area to remove any traces of wax and to soothe the skin. A special lotion may be applied if there is a strong reaction and to hydrate and soothe the skin.

Equipment required for cool wax treatment

* Cool wax machine.
* Witch hazel for cleansing the skin.
* Disposable spatulas, gloves and apron.
* Muslin or paper strips to remove the wax.
* Cotton wool.
* After-wax soothing lotion.
* Waste bowl.

Preparation for cool wax treatment

Once again, the area to be treated should be wiped over with witch hazel to remove surface grease. Nothing else should be applied, as this will form a barrier between the cool wax and the skin and could prevent the wax adhering, causing the treatment to be ineffective, unless the manufacturer recommends it.

The temperature of the wax is tested in the same way as hot wax by applying a small test strip to the therapist's wrist and then on the client.

Application and removal for cool wax treatment

When the wax is at the correct working temperature it is applied with a spatula to the whole area to be treated. The wax should be applied with the direction of hair growth and as thinly as possible, using the spatula at an angle of 90°.

A muslin strip is then placed on to the wax, smoothed down to bond firmly with the wax and then

pulled back against the hair growth, almost parallel to the skin, to remove the hairs cleanly and efficiently.

There is less reaction on the skin to this method and wax may be re-applied over areas already treated as long as there is no reaction. However, a skilled therapist will complete the treatment efficiently without the need to re-apply the wax.

Figure 21.2
Application of cool wax

Figure 21.3
Removal of cool wax

Aftercare for cool wax treatment

Any remaining traces of wax may be removed by applying an after-wax oil or lotion.

Sugaring

This is one of the oldest forms of hair removal which has been passed down through generations in many Middle Eastern homes. Originally, a mixture of sugar, water and lemon juice was boiled in a pan to form a sticky paste. Manufacturers have now developed products that are similar and far safer to use than boiling sugar! This pliable sugar paste is thought to be gentler on the skin than other waxing methods because it may be used at such a low temperature and the natural ingredients do not irritate a sensitive skin. It is also water soluble making it easier to clean from any surface including the client's skin.

The paste may be very soft and pliable or slightly firmer requiring warmth to bring it to the correct working consistency. The paste clings to the hair and not the skin and may be reapplied over areas already treated. Some manufacturers produce a sugar paste, which may also be used with strips in the same manner as warm wax providing the benefits of sugaring and the ease of application associated with strip waxing.

Figure 21.4 shows the contraindications to waxing.

Preparation of work area and client

The wax machine should be placed on a stable surface, which is not made of glass as it could shatter, and it should be placed in such a position to allow ease of movement during treatment. All other equipment and materials should be placed within easy reach.

The couch should be protected with a plastic sheet and a towel placed on the area where the client will be sitting. All clothing should be removed from the area to be treated and the client's clothing should be protected with towels, paper roll or tissues.

The client should be positioned comfortably on the couch.

Precautions for safe use

* All wax machines must be wired correctly. The heating elements must be enclosed and all machines should comply with the British Standard of safety.
* The wax must be left to heat up in a safe position away from anything inflammable. The wax machine must not be moved while hot.
* The wax should not be overheated and the temperature should be regularly checked, even on thermostatically controlled units.
* The machine must be cleaned immediately after use to prevent drips of wax burning and to maintain high professional standards. Special equipment cleaner or surgical spirit should be used.
* The covers provided with the machine must be left in place while it is not in use.
* Always check the client for contraindications.
* Use the correct techniques for each method.
* The therapist must wear latex gloves, as body fluids may be present on the client's skin after waxing.

Advantages and disadvantages of hot wax

Advantages

* The higher working temperature of this wax allows strong hair growth such as underarm or bikini line to be removed more easily. It also removes shorter hair more efficiently.

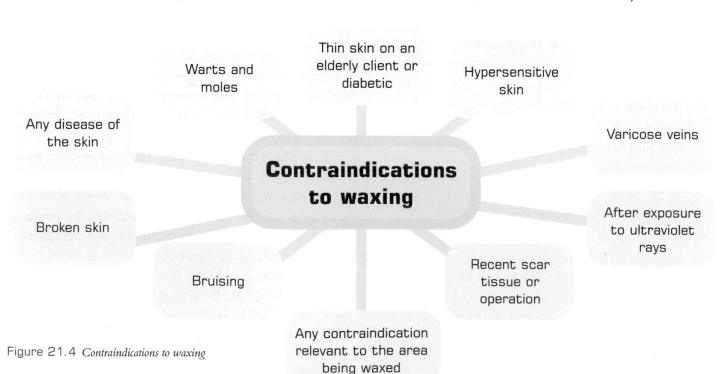

Figure 21.4 *Contraindications to waxing*

* Hair regrowth is tapered and soft and takes up to six weeks to grow back.

Disadvantages

* The wax takes longer to heat up.
* Application and removal takes longer. A half leg wax will take approximately 30 minutes.
* The wax may not be re-applied if all the hairs do not come out.
* The reaction of the skin to this wax is more severe. An increased reddening and blotchy effect can take several hours to subside.
* The wax often becomes brittle with overuse or overheating.
* This method is not permanent.
* Hairs must be at least 2 cm long to be effectively removed.
* It can be painful.
* It can be messy to use if the therapist is not proficient.
* More of the product is required in application.

Advantages and disadvantages of cool wax

Advantages

* The lower working temperature makes this wax suitable for more sensitive skins.
* The application and removal procedure is very quick. A half leg wax should take approximately 15 minutes.
* Regrowth is tapered and soft, taking up to six weeks to grow back.
* It is clean and easy to use.
* Less wax is required in application, therefore it is more economical to use.

Disadvantages

* It is not as efficient in the removal of coarse dark hair as the hot method.
* If the therapist is not proficient in its use, removal can be very sticky.
* It can be painful.
* This method is not permanent.
* It may cause ingrowing hairs.

Areas to be treated

Legs

The treatment can be either half leg or full. The fronts of the legs should be completed before turning the client over and treating the backs of the legs. The knee must always be in a bent position when applying and removing the wax on the front of the leg. When removing hair from the back of the leg be extra careful if there are hairs on the back of the knee. The hair growth on the backs of the legs and the thighs can vary in direction and it is important to bear this in mind when applying and removing the wax. It is also important when removing the wax from the thigh area to support and tighten the skin to make the treatment more comfortable.

Bikini line

The bikini line is normally a separate treatment and the price of this area should be in addition to the full leg treatment. Client consultation is important to ascertain how much of the area is to be waxed. The Brazilian wax, the complete removal of all hair in the pubic area, is a very popular treatment. This will probably depend upon the sportswear or swimwear to be worn. The client's leg should be bent in a figure of four position and supported by a cushion to make the treatment more comfortable and the muscles less tense. The skin around the area being treated must be held firmly when removing the strips to prevent too much discomfort. The hair growth pattern in this area is quite erratic, so small strips should be applied.

Skin may react more to waxing of this sensitive area and tiny blood spots may occur. This is due to the fact that the hair in this area is often much stronger than other areas and the skin more sensitive. Regular waxing should be advised to prevent this problem, as less hair will be present at each treatment and hot wax is more effective in removing bikini line hair.

The client should be advised to avoid friction from tight fitting underwear after treatment and to use a soothing, antiseptic lotion if necessary.

Chest and back

Waxing is no longer a treatment for women only. There is a current trend for men to have their chests and backs waxed, as the fashion is for smooth, hair-free, tanned skin. The hair may grow in different directions, but the same principles apply when applying and removing the wax. Smaller strips are advisable and special care must be taken around the nipple area.

It is also important to stress the necessity for aftercare, in particular the use of perfumed body products and tight fitting clothing must be avoided to prevent any irritation.

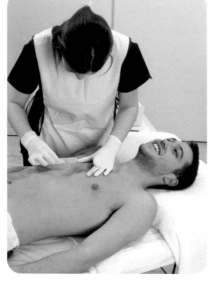

Figure 21.5
Male chest wax

Underarm

This is a popular salon treatment because, once depilated, the hairs do not regrow very quickly and there is rarely a shadow left, even in very dark-haired clients, as there is with some of the other methods used.

The client must again be positioned comfortably, with her hand behind her head in such a position that the area is flat and easier to treat, with the back of the couch slightly elevated for client comfort.

Perspiration, which may be present, could affect the efficient application of the wax. Therefore, the area needs to be cleansed first and then dried before applying the wax.

The hair growth pattern is again erratic in this area. Small strips must be used and the direction of growth must be carefully followed – cool wax application *with* the growth and hot wax application *against* the growth. Hot wax is more effective used on this area, particularly if the hair is coarse or short.

The client should be advised not to wear antiperspirant or deodorant for 24 hours after treatment and to avoid friction from clothing.

Arms

This is a relatively easy area to treat as the hairs grow in the same direction. This is particularly effective on clients who have a very dark hair growth even if it is not particularly thick. Cool wax is probably the best method to employ and because of the size of the area, the muslin strips should be cut into smaller pieces to aid removal.

Lip and chin waxing

The area must be thoroughly cleansed first, particularly if make-up is worn. Either type of wax may be used, although there is often less reaction on sensitive skin from the hot wax method.

The lip area, although small, should be treated in three sections (either side of the upper lip and then a small section in the middle). If cool wax is used, small strips must be cut to size to fit the area.

Soothing lotion must be applied immediately after removal and if the area reacts and becomes very red or even slightly swollen, a cold compress should be applied.

Eyebrow waxing

Always use an orange wood stick to apply the wax, protect the hairs of the brow not to be waxed with petroleum jelly and use small strips for removal. Take extra care when applying the wax so that the eye is protected.

Advice to the client

After a wax depilatory treatment, it is necessary to advise the client how to prevent an adverse reaction on the skin:

* Wash or shower in lukewarm water.
* Do not use soap as this could irritate the skin.
* Do not use any perfumed body lotions.
* Do not expose the area to ultraviolet light.
* Do not wear tight fitting clothing.
* Do not have a heat treatment after waxing.
* Do not have any stimulating treatment on the area waxed.

Other methods of depilation

There are several methods of hair removal which may be used, but these methods are not usually performed in the salon.

Plucking

This method is used in a salon but only for shaping the eyebrows. The hair is completely removed from the follicle. There is a depilation machine, which is available to the general public, which allows mass plucking of the hairs. It can be used on the legs and arms.

Shaving

With this method, an electrical shaver or a wet razor used with soap or cream may be used. The hair itself is cut off at skin level and the hair then grows with a coarse blunt-ended tip and regrowth is usually apparent 24–48 hours afterwards.

Depilatory creams

Although these creams are not in general use in beauty salons, they are, however, an alternative treatment which can be provided in cases of varicose veins when leg waxing would be contraindicated over an area.

Due to the chemical constituents in depilatory creams, it is important to test first on a small area of skin to see that the client is not allergic to the product. The active ingredient in a depilatory cream is a **keratolytic**, which is a keratin dissolving substance. Therefore, it will cause the skin to become very sensitive if used regularly as it will attack the skin as well as the hair, because it also contains the protein keratin.

Before applying the cream, the area to be treated must be thoroughly cleansed. It is then applied using a spatula and left on for the required amount of time. The removal of the depilatory cream should be completed with a spatula before rinsing the area with lukewarm water. Removing all the cream first before applying water should reduce the nasty smell which often occurs with the use of these products. Soap or deodorant must not be used for several hours afterwards.

The hair is only removed from the surface of the skin and blunt regrowth is apparent after only a few days.

Composition of depilatory creams

Manufacturers are careful with the composition of these creams so that they do not irritate the skin. They should also be pleasant smelling, clean and easy to apply, and remove the hair quickly. There are two chemical compounds which are effective in this type of preparation:

* **Strontium sulphide** is very effective in removing hair in three to five minutes. The strength, however, may irritate certain skins. The main fault is the strong smell when it is washed away. Removing most of the cream with a spatula before applying water can lessen this. Severe reaction on the skin will occur if all traces are not removed.

* **Calcium thioglycollate** takes longer to act, but the action is far more gentle and this may be used on facial hair. The other advantage is the smell, which is barcly noticeable.

Formulations

Strontium sulphide

Strontium sulphide: 20 per cent – depilatory
Talc: 20 per cent – harmless powder in which the depilatory is dispersed
Methyl cellulose: 3 per cent – forms the mixture into a paste
Water: 42 per cent
Glycerine: 15 per cent – preservative

Calcium thioglycollate

Calcium thioglycollate: 7 per cent – depilatory
Calcium hydroxide: 7 per cent – alkali to help the depilatory
Calcium carbonate: 20 per cent – chalk in which the depilatory is dispersed
Cetyl alcohol: 5 per cent – makes a smooth cream
Sodium lauryl sulphate: 1 per cent – soapless detergent
Sodium silicate: 2.5 per cent – abrasive
Water and perfume: 55 per cent – provides the liquid base

Bleaching

There are some extremely effective cream bleaches available for clients to use at home if for some reason they prefer not to wax or use other forms of depilation. They may be used to:

* lighten dark hair
* fade areas of pigmentation
* lighten discoloured areas such as elbows and knees
* remove nicotine stains.

Advise the client to follow the manufacturer's instructions carefully, carry out a patch test in an inconspicuous place and discontinue use if there is any irritation.

When bleaching the skin the effect is only evident on the top superficial layers of the epidermis and when these layers are shed the hyperpigmentation returns.

22 Electrical epilation

Hair removal methods

Electrolysis is a common term used to describe the permanent removal of unwanted hair. There are several treatments currently available.

The **electrolysis method** of hair removal uses a direct galvanic current (negatively charged) to produce a chemical action, which destroys the hair follicle. The chemical process occurs when the galvanic current is applied to tissue salts and moisture contained inside the hair follicle and skin tissue, causing a chemical reaction resulting in the root of the hair being destroyed. This is a slower method as the chemical reaction takes time to develop and continues working after the needle is removed.

Short-wave diathermy, or thermolysis, is a method of epilation which has largely superseded the electrolysis method of hair removal. The principle of this method is the application of heat produced by a high frequency short-wave diathermy current to the active hair-producing part of the follicle. This heat is the destructive force used to cauterise or coagulate the cell producing part of the follicle, inhibiting or preventing the growth of a new hair. Cauterisation occurs when a high intensity of high frequency is applied, the heat vaporises any moisture in the tissues making it dry. Coagulation occurs when a lower intensity of high frequency current is applied to congeal protein in the tissue.

The **blend method** is more commonly used because it combines the more thorough galvanic current with the speed of the short-wave diathermy to produce a most effective method of epilation.

The aim of treatment

Whichever method is employed, the aim of the treatment is to permanently remove unwanted, superfluous hair without causing damage to the surrounding tissue while maintaining normal skin texture and appearance.

It is important to explain to the client that these results will not be achieved immediately but, with regular treatment, the growth of the superfluous hair can be greatly reduced and hopefully eliminated, depending on the cause of the problem.

Most of the cases, that the therapist has to treat are normal or cosmetic problems, which may have only occurred during those times in a woman's life when her body is changing physiologically and these are:

* puberty
* pregnancy
* menopause.

Types of hair

The hair itself is a dead structure composed of a hard durable protein called **keratin**. There are two types of hair:

* **Vellus** is very soft downy type hair, which is hardly visible because it is normally non-pigmented and it is found on most areas of the body. The vellus hair comes from a lobe of the sebaceous gland, which is situated at a shallow depth.
* **Terminal** is more deep rooted and is coarse, visible hair with well-developed roots, found on such areas as the scalp, the axillae and pubic region. During puberty terminal hairs develop because of the hormonal changes in the body. In males this will include beard and chest hair as well as hair growth in the axillae and pubic areas. In females this occurs in the axillae and pubic area.

Lanugo hair

This hair is formed on the foetus and then shed soon after birth. The growth rate is very slow, having quite an ineffective papilla and matrix and only if it is stimulated by a topical or systemic condition will it develop into a terminal hair.

The hair growing on the body is classified as:

* capilli – the head
* barba – the face
* supercilia – the eyebrows
* cilia – the eyelashes

* vibrissae – the nostrils
* tragi – the ears
* hirci – the armpit
* pubes – pubic region.

Areas most commonly treated include the eyebrows, upper lip, chin, face, underarms, chest/breast, abdomen, bikini line, as well as the neck or nape, fingers and toes.

Superfluous hair

Superfluous hair is an excess of hair, which is not abnormal for the age, sex and ethnic group of the person involved.

Hypertrichosis

This is a condition when the growth of terminal hair is abnormal and excessive on any area of the body for the age, sex and ethnic group of the person involved.

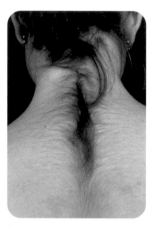

Figure 22.1 *Hypertrichosis*

Hirsutism

This is when the growth of excessive terminal hair appears in the 'adult male sexual pattern', upper lip, chin, chest and abdomen, normally caused by the androgens (male hormones) when there is a hormonal imbalance. When this is associated with recession of the hairline, deepening of the voice and loss of female body shape it is called **virilism**.

The target areas

There are certain areas on the body known as target areas where there will be a growth of hair when stimulated by the androgens, which are male hormones. As a woman's body produces these hormones in much smaller quantities, under normal circumstances, she does not develop hair in all the target areas, unlike the male. There are occasions, however, during puberty, pregnancy and menopause, when there may be an increase in androgens, which will result in the production of excess hair in these target areas.

The hair development in each individual will vary according to the hereditary sensitivity of the hair germ cells to the androgens.

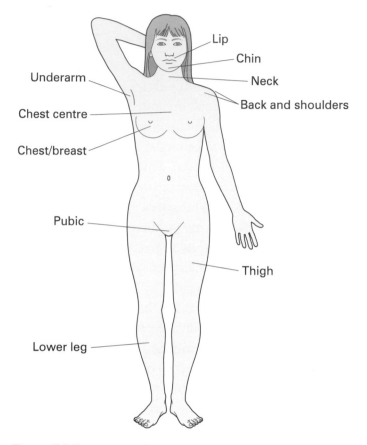

Figure 22.2 *Target areas for androgen-stimulated hair growth*

Causes of superfluous hair

An increase in blood supply to the existing hair will provide nourishment and encourage growth of the already established hair, turning a vellus hair into a terminal hair. Hormones also have the capacity to stimulate existing hair growth and also to create new growth, depending on the sensitivity of the hair germ cells in a particular area.

Normal congenital

The type and amount of hair growth could be hereditary as superfluous hair can be passed genetically from generation to generation. Some ethnic groups tend to be naturally more hairy than others, for example Italians,

Spaniards, Greeks and Syrians tend to be more hairy than Scandinavians, and people of Chinese origin and American Indians are the least hairy of all.

Abnormal congenital

Congenital hypertrichosis is rare and results from an abnormality in the genes. It may be present at birth or appear later in life. The excess hair can sometimes cover the person from head to toe.

Oestrogen

Oestrogen can accelerate mitosis, producing new cells in the skin. This is often why a woman on HRT regains a youthful bloom to her skin. The hair may be similarly affected and the increase in cell production can also increase the production of fine vellus hair.

Endocrine disorders which cause excessive hair growth

There are occasions when an endocrine imbalance resulting from a disease or disorder, which will require medical treatment, produces hypertrichosis. Once the problem has been medically diagnosed and treatment has begun to remove the underlying cause, the therapist may begin to treat the hair problem with the permission of the doctor.

An endocrine disorder usually is the result of:

* a defect of the endocrine system inherited from either parent
* a disease or an infection
* a tumour
* an injury.

Cushing's syndrome

The word syndrome refers to a combination of several symptoms or characteristics of a disease. Cushing's syndrome is a collection of symptoms caused by adrenal overactivity as a response to:

* excessive cell development of the adrenal cortex
* a tumour of the adrenal cortex
* a tumour of the anterior pituitary
* the steroids cortisone or hydrocortisone.

If the adrenal cortex is overactive, it will produce excessive amounts of hormones, including androgens:

* An excessive amount of mineralocorticoids, in particular aldosterone, results in water retention.
* An excessive amount of glucocorticoids, cortisol, can result in obesity in the face, neck and trunk, thin slender limbs which fracture easily, muscle weakness and thin easily bruised skin with purple striae (stretch marks) over the abdomen and thighs.
* An excessive amount of sex hormones, in particular androgens, causes cessation of menstruation and hair growth on the face.

Adrenogenital syndrome

This condition arises from the overproduction of androgens by the adrenal cortex. It may be congenital, appearing from birth, or it may occur in childhood or in adult life. Congenital characteristics include enlargement of the external genitalia; in girls the genitalia is outwardly masculine, but the internal sex organs are female. This condition may be treated successfully with plastic surgery. Girls in early childhood may develop beard and moustache growth, a deep voice and other male secondary sexual characteristics. In boys premature puberty may occur.

The characteristics of the female at puberty are delayed or absent menstruation, delayed breast development, an enlargement of external genitalia and hirsutism. The characteristics of the female adult are:

* virilism
* hirsutism
* breast atrophy
* enlargement of external genitalia
* deepening of the voice
* masculine appearance in build
* infertility
* frontal hair loss.

Acromegaly

A tumour on the pituitary gland, which causes an excessive secretion of growth hormone, usually causes this condition. When this occurs in an adult and the bones have stopped growing, the excess of growth hormone produced causes a thickening of the bones, an enlargement of the feet, hands, jaw and front of the skull. Goitre and menstrual abnormalities often accompany this condition.

If this condition occurs before the bones are fully formed, the condition is termed **gigantism** because an individual grows to excessively large proportions due to the overgrowth of the long bones in the body.

Adrenocorticotrophic hormone (ACTH) may also be produced in excess and this affects the adrenal cortex, stimulating the production of androgens in excess which may lead to hirsutism.

Topical causes

Sustained irritation to the epidermis is seen as a potential threat because it will cause a defensive reaction by the body. The blood supply to the area is increased, and the hairs growing in the follicles will receive increased nourishment, accelerating their growth. The hairs in the area of irritation will be stimulated to grow coarser and deeper, creating a protective covering on the skin, against further irritation.

Plucking the hairs with tweezers removes the hair from the follicle and regrowth takes longer than with other methods of removal, such as shaving or depilatory creams. However, blood supply is stimulated, which will eventually cause accelerated growth of the plucked hair.

Medication

Hair growth can be stimulated when a client is taking steroids for treatment of a medical condition.

Systemic causes

The endocrine system produces hormones, which control the growth, development and the metabolic functions of the body. An excess of certain hormones may result in the production of superfluous hair. During puberty, pregnancy and menopause, normal systemic changes take place, which may result in the production of superfluous hair, but there are also abnormal causes.

Normal systemic causes of superfluous hair

Puberty

When puberty is reached – this varies greatly from person to person – large amounts of hormones are secreted into the bloodstream. The hypothalamus sends a releasing factor to the anterior lobe of the pituitary gland. The pituitary gland responds by:

* secreting gonadotrophic hormones which stimulate the ovaries to produce oestrogen
* secreting adrenocorticotrophic hormones which stimulate the adrenal cortex to produce androgens.

The oestrogens and androgens are balanced and the secondary sexual characteristics develop. The androgens are responsible for the production of hair in the target areas. If there is an excess of androgens and a hereditary sensitivity to the androgens, then excess hair may develop. If the correct balance of oestrogens and androgens is restored after puberty, then the superfluous hair will probably disappear.

Pregnancy

The ovaries secrete large amounts of oestrogen during pregnancy and there will be an increase in androgens to maintain the balance. Any excessive hair growth usually affects the upper lip, chin and sides of the face and it is only accelerated vellus hair, which if it is not tampered with will probably disappear after childbirth.

Menopause

This is when menstruation ceases completely, but there are several years leading up to this when the functions of the ovaries slow down. The fall in oestrogen secretion can cause many physiological changes.

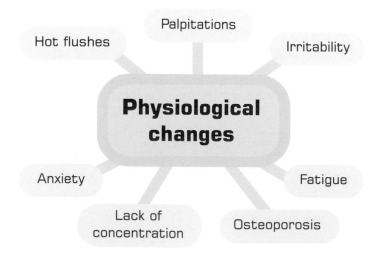

Figure 22.3 *Physiological changes during the menopause*

Some women may find superfluous hair appearing mainly in the area of the upper chin and lip. This occurs when functions of the ovaries slow down and they are less responsive to the gonadotrophic hormone, resulting in a decrease in the amount of oestrogens being secreted. The drop in oestrogen causes the hypothalamus to respond by secreting the releasing factor to the anterior lobe of the pituitary gland.

The pituitary gland then secretes the gonadotrophic hormones, which stimulate the ovaries to produce more oestrogen, but there is a reduced response from the ovaries because of the slowing down of the functions.

The pituitary gland also secretes the adrenocorticotrophic hormone which, in turn, stimulates the adrenal cortex to secrete more androgens. The normal balance has been lost and there is the possibility of excessive hair growth depending on the amount of androgens that are produced and the hereditary sensitivity of the hair germ cells.

Abnormal systemic causes of superfluous hair

Hysterectomy

One or both of the ovaries are removed during this operation, which results in a drop in oestrogen level. This causes an artificial menopause producing exactly the same symptoms that occur with the natural onset of the menopause. One of these symptoms can be the appearance of superfluous hair.

Polycystic ovaries (Stein Leventhal syndrome)

This is a condition where there are multiple cysts in the ovaries producing symptoms which include lack of menstruation, abnormal uterine bleeding, weight gain, aggravation of acne and, sometimes, infertility and hirsutism. Although the cause is not fully understood, there are several theories that problems with oestrogen production and hypothalmic-ovarian feedback may be responsible, or there is an increase in luteinising hormone (LH) from the brain and this elevated LH promotes secretion of androgens from the ovaries. Treatment for this condition is a surgical operation and drug therapy.

Anorexia nervosa

This condition usually affects younger women when they starve themselves of food because of a desire to lose weight. This results in a hormonal imbalance. The symptoms include cessation of periods and hirsutism, mainly of the downy type although some coarse hairs may appear on the face.

Stress

A severe nervous breakdown may cause the body to be suffering extreme stress. During times of crisis the adrenal glands produce large amounts of adrenalin from the adrenal medulla. This increase in activity has an effect on the adrenal cortex which then produces large amounts of androgens which will give rise to an excessive hair growth in target areas.

The structure of the hair follicle and the hair

The hair follicle

The follicle is an indentation of the epidermis into the dermis. It consists of layers relative to those of the epidermis, except for the stratum corneum which is constantly desquamating. The base of the follicle is shaped like a bulb and it contains the loose connective tissue of the dermal papilla, which also contains blood vessels, nerve endings and melanocytes.

The stratum germinativum cells of the epidermis cover the dermal papilla and all the cells in this area are mitotically active. As these cells reproduce and move further up into the area of keratinisation, they are invaded by the protein keratin and the hair becomes a horny dead structure.

Each hair follicle has a sebaceous gland, opening into the follicle to form a pilosebaceous unit. The sebum secreted from the sebaceous gland keeps the hair in the follicle supple.

A bundle of smooth muscle fibres, called the arrector pilorum, is inserted into the wall of the follicle below the sebaceous gland. When it is stimulated by nerve fibres, the muscle contracts causing the hair to stand on end.

The follicle consists of:

* the inner root sheath
* the outer root sheath
* a connective tissue sheath.

Inner root sheath

This has three layers of cells:

* Henle's layer, which is one cell thick.
* Huxley's layer, which is two or more cells thick.
* The cuticle layer on the inside which points downwards and interlocks with the cuticle of the hair which points upwards.

The inner root sheath grows from the dermal papilla, growing upwards with the hair until it reaches the level of the sebaceous gland, where it dissipates leaving the hair to continue growing upwards.

The outer root sheath

The thickness of the outer root sheath, which surrounds the inner root sheath, varies depending on the size of the follicle. It is normally thicker in the follicles of larger hairs. This thickness is uneven causing the hair to be slightly off centre (eccentric) in the follicle.

Just above the bulb, the outer sheath changes from two to three layers and is at its thickest about a third of the way up the follicle. It is a static structure which does not grow up with the hair.

Above the sebaceous gland the outer sheath is indistinguishable from the surface epidermis. This upper part of the outer sheath forms a keratinised surface layer which is constantly being desquamated.

New follicles are formed from the outer root sheath as it is a source of new 'hair germ cells'.

Connective tissue sheath

The connective tissue sheath is a continuous extension of the papillary layer and the dermal papilla. This layer covers the follicle and the sebaceous gland providing the same function that the papillary layer provides for the epidermis, that is, providing nerve endings and blood supply.

Vitreous membrane

This separates the connective tissue sheath from the outer root sheath and varies in thickness.

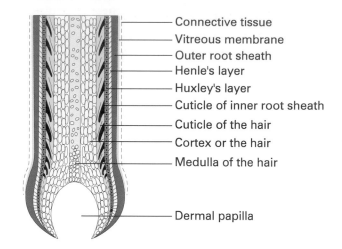

- Connective tissue
- Vitreous membrane
- Outer root sheath
- Henle's layer
- Huxley's layer
- Cuticle of inner root sheath
- Cuticle of the hair
- Cortex or the hair
- Medulla of the hair
- Dermal papilla

Figure 22.4 *Cross-section of the hair in the follicle*

The blood supply to the follicle

The follicle receives the nourishment required for growth from the blood supplied via the network of vessels, in the dermis, known as the **hypodermal plexus**. This network of blood vessels supplies the dermal papilla, the follicle and sebaceous gland with all its necessary nutrients.

The nerve supply

There are many nerve endings in the skin and surrounding the follicle. Some converge to form a meshwork of nerves called a **nerve plexus**. The nerves encircle and enter the connective tissue sheath just below the sebaceous gland. This is important to therapists when probing, as the base of the follicle is below the nerve plexus. Therefore, you may have to apply more current before the sensory nerves respond.

The nerve endings in the skin are dealt with in Chapter 11 Facial electrical treatments.

The hair

The hair grows out of the follicle at an angle to the surface of the skin, following the natural contours of the body. A terminal hair consists of two main portions:

* the root
* the shaft.

The root

The root is below the surface of the skin at the base of the follicle. It includes the bulb and the dermal papilla, an area of active cells which multiply and move forward to form a column of tightly packed cells, which will form the shaft. At its base, the hair root expands into a bulbous shape, the dermal papilla. This papilla is the crucial source of nourishment for the entire follicle structure and it obtains its blood supply from the capillary loop adjacent to it and this determines the growth and health of the hair.

The lower part of the bulb is called the matrix. Here the cells are mitotically active and undifferentiated. There is a point – the **critical level** – at which the cells differentiate. This is a process where they undergo change in growth and development, to become either the inner root sheath or the hair.

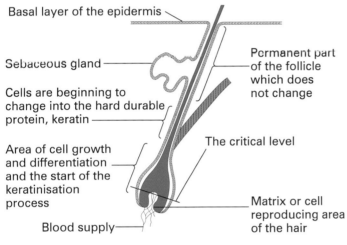

Figure 22.5 *Different areas of cell growth and keratinisation*

The shaft

The shaft is the part which extends above the skin surface and is made of dead keratinised cells. It is made up of three parts:

* the cuticle
* the cortex
* the medulla.

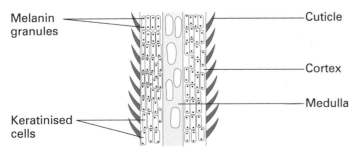

Figure 22.6 *Cross-section of a hair*

The cuticle

This is the outer layer of the shaft comprising cells which are overlapping, rather like roof tiles. These scale-like cells lie very tightly over each other. Heat and chemicals can damage the hair however, causing the scales to open and the hair becomes more porous. The cells are translucent and contain no pigment, thus reflecting the light and giving the hair its shine. The scaly cells of the cuticle point upwards and interlock with those of the inner root sheath and this anchors the hair firmly in the follicle.

The cortex

This layer makes up the largest portion of the hair and consists of elongated keratinised cells. There are granules of melanin found in pigmented hairs. There are air spaces between the cells in the cortex.

The medulla

This is the centre of the hair, but it may be absent in fine vellus hair. The cells are large, loosely connected and keratinised. There are large air spaces in and between the cells which help to reflect the light and give the hair its sheen.

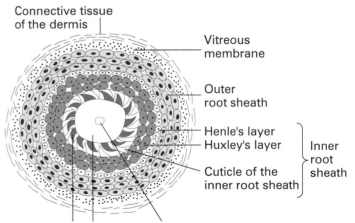

Figure 22.7 *Cross-section of a hair and follicle*

Stages of hair growth

Hair growth is divided into three stages:

* Anagen – the growing stage.
* Catagen – the transitory stage between anagen and telogen.
* Telogen – the resting stage.

The hair's normal lifetime is different from one area of the body to another. It also varies from one person to another. For example, eyelashes and brows last four to five months. Hair on the scalp lasts two to four years and, in some cases, can last up to seven years.

Each follicle has its own life cycle and at a particular point in this cycle, the terminal hair separates from the papilla and moves upward while remaining attached to the follicle wall. It is called a **club hair** at this stage. The lower half of the follicle degenerates and shrinks upwards and the club hair continues to rise until it falls out, after becoming detached from the follicle wall. The lower half of the follicle, therefore, changes with the hair growth cycle, but the upper half remains stable.

A collection of hair germ cells from the outer root sheath and the dormant dermal papilla cells is all that remains attached to the base of the shrunken follicle. It is from these cells that a new follicle will eventually form and this may be regarded as the beginning of the hair growth cycle.

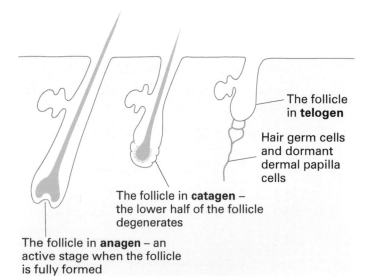

The follicle in **telogen**

Hair germ cells and dormant dermal papilla cells

The follicle in **catagen** – the lower half of the follicle degenerates

The follicle in **anagen** – an active stage when the follicle is fully formed

Figure 22.8 *The stages of follicle development*

Anagen

This starts with the total rebuilding of the lower follicle. The cells which remain attached to the base of the follicle are known as the **dermal cord** and these begin to multiply by mitosis, increasing in width and depth and moving down to form the new follicle.

The papilla cells develop into the life-giving papilla. The lower part of the dermal cord develops into the bulb, which surrounds the dermal papilla. Before the new follicle has reached its final depth, the mitotic cells in the matrix or lower part of the bulb move upwards, differentiating into hair and inner root sheath in the upper part of the bulb and for some short distance beyond.

The cells increase in size and elongate in the upper bulb past the critical level and keratinisation occurs. These keratinised cells push their way through the dermal cord in the form of the inner root sheath. The keratinised hair then follows, breaking through the inner root sheath approximately two-thirds of the way up the follicle to enter the permanent upper part producing the hair visible above the skin's surface.

Meanwhile, the follicle has continued growing down into the dermis. This downward growth stops when the hair has grown approximately 1.25 cm above the skin's surface.

A hair treated in the early anagen stage produces the best results.

Catagen

The hair grows constantly for a certain period and then the catagen stage begins. The papilla separates and withdraws from the matrix. The hair rises up and is still attached to the follicle wall, receiving nourishment to a small degree. The papilla collapses and the follicle degenerates in the lower half. Undifferentiated cells present in the lower half of the follicle form the dermal cord. The inner root sheath disintegrates. The hair becomes detached from the surrounding tissue. It has lost the bulb-like root and is now a club hair.

This stage of the cycle is very short and sometimes a new hair emerges before the club hair is shed.

Telogen

This is the resting stage for the upper half of the follicle until it is stimulated to begin a new cycle. The length of this stage varies and, in some cases, it does not occur as a new hair grows immediately.

Contraindications to treatment

There are specific reasons why treatment must not be carried out, but there are also conditions which will prevent treatment only in the affected area. There are also occasions when the therapist may feel that treatment is contraindicated and consultation with the client's doctor is necessary to ascertain whether treatment may be carried out.

* Any diseases of the skin which may be infectious as there will be a high risk of cross-infection.
* Acne vulgaris is a condition which affects adolescents and is caused by a hormonal imbalance. This may also cause the growth of superfluous hair. If the infected area is treated, the infection would spread and further aggravate an already inflamed skin.
* Herpes simplex is contraindicated in the immediate area because the virus may be spread to other areas.
* Sunburned skin is normally inflamed and sensitive and there will be a risk of hyperpigmentation with treatment.
* A heart condition or the presence of a pacemaker in the heart. Doctor's permission must be sought in the case of some heart conditions. In the case of high blood pressure, anxiety about the treatment may cause problems.
* Epilepsy can vary in severity so doctor's permission must be sought. The stress of the treatment could bring on an attack.
* Diabetes requires doctor's permission as this condition affects the skin's ability to heal itself. Once permission has been given, the treatment itself must be modified, by making treatment time shorter, spacing out the needle insertions and having longer periods between treatments.
* During pregnancy the stomach and breasts should not be treated, as the breasts become tender and swollen and the stomach stretches, causing the skin to become taut.
* The hairs in moles should not be treated without doctor's permission as moles are potentially pre-malignant.
* With girls under the age of sixteen, unwanted superfluous hair may be hereditary or related to their ethnic grouping, and after puberty may not go away. This can be treated easily, but before treatment it is advisable to seek the opinion of a doctor in case there is a hormonal abnormality which is causing the problem.

There are certain conditions, although not contraindicating treatment, where special care and consideration may be required:

* Black skin is prone to keloid scarring, which is an overgrowth of scar tissue, and pitted scarring may form more easily due to sensitivity. The follicles are curved causing a curly hair. Therefore, insertion of the needle has to be adapted. There is also a greater risk of ingrowing hairs and hyper-pigmentation as a result of treatment.
* Asian skin is prone to hyperpigmentation.
* Hairs in scar tissue may be treated if the scar is more than 12 months old.
* Mucous membranes should not be treated, e.g. the nose and ears because of the high moisture content in the area.
* Skin infections or any areas of inflammation.
* Bruising of the skin.

In view of the seriousness of the hepatitis B and the AIDS (Acquired Immune Deficiency Syndrome) virus, treatment may be at the discretion of the therapist.

Hepatitis B

Hepatitis B is caused by a virus and is an infection of the liver with an incubation period of two to six months. It is transmitted by means of body fluid and may be passed on through treatments administered with a needle, injections, acupuncture, tattooing, or electrolysis. Contaminated blood or tissue fluid on the electrolysis needle is sufficient to transmit the disease.

A vaccine against the hepatitis virus is available for all those practising electrolysis.

AIDS

This disease is caused by the Human Immunodeficiency Virus (HIV). It is a condition which develops when the body's immune system is not functioning normally. This leaves the body susceptible to illness and infection which may prove fatal.

The virus may be transmitted via body fluids. Therefore, special care must be taken when using any device that punctures the skin. This will include electrolysis needles and ear-piercing equipment. The most efficient method for the therapist of preventing the spread of AIDS is to use disposable needles and an autoclave to sterilise metal implements such as tweezers.

Client consultation

Because of the nature of the condition, a great many clients who come for treatment will feel embarrassed and a little apprehensive. Care and consideration therefore are of vital importance. A sympathetic approach will help to put clients at ease.

There will be occasions when you treat male clients who may feel uneasy or unsure about the treatment. It is important, particularly when the client is a male to female transsexual hoping to reduce beard growth before surgery, to put the client at ease and explain the procedure and time it will take to achieve the expected results. You can expect to treat the client for two to three years and it is advisable to start at least two years before surgery, if possible.

The initial consultation, not necessarily at the time of the first treatment, is important to gain the client's confidence and to obtain all the necessary information, which will help to plan the course of treatment.

Caution!

It is advisable when speaking to the client to refer to the hair problem as a 'hair condition' – it is less negative.

During consultation it is now becoming common practice to take a photograph of the areas to be treated and for client records a post-treatment photograph should also be taken. This provides an ideal record of treatment progress and results.

Points to consider

* The therapist's appearance must be professional to inspire confidence in the client.
* Professional badges should be worn as this is an indication to the client of the therapist's standard of training.
* The client should be greeted in a friendly, but assured manner.
* The client should be taken to a private room or cubicle where he or she may speak in confidence.

Points to discuss with the client

Encourage clients to talk about their condition, as this will have the beneficial effect of a problem shared. It may also indicate the cause of the superfluous hair without having to question them closely and allow them

Gender dysphoria

Gender dysphoria is a medical term used to describe anxiety or confusion about gender identity. A transexual believes that he or she is trapped in the wrong body – the individual thinks and feels like the opposite sex and has a strong desire to change his or her body in order to live as a member of the opposite sex. Some transexual men may have gender reassignment surgery once they meet all the criteria after being carefully assessed by two independent psychiatrists. Initially, they will be offered counselling and provided with information about support networks such as the Beaumont Trust and Gendys Network. They will then be required to live as a member of the opposite sex for at least 12 months. The Harry Benjamin International Gender Dysphoric Association (HBIGDA) has laid down minimum standards of care for those applying for hormonal or surgical gender reassignment.

to point out the area requiring treatment. Never assume from their appearance or they may be offended.

The benefits of electrolysis as a permanent method of hair removal must be explained as well as the expected results and limitations of treatment. Information regarding frequency and duration of treatment as well as the procedure can be given to the client at this stage.

Ascertain which methods of temporary hair removal, if any, have been used previously and the bearing this may have on the progress of the treatment and the effect it will have on regrowth. These methods may have caused certain problems, for example:

* Waxing or plucking is thought to distort the follicle and influence growth, so results may be far slower on hairs that have been regularly waxed or plucked.
* Depilatory creams work by dissolving the hair, but at the same time they attack the skin and this makes it more sensitive and possibly slow to heal.

It should be explained to clients that if they feel the need to use a temporary method of hair removal in between treatments, then cutting is the best alternative.

Hair growth will diminish with each successive treatment, depending on the stage of hair growth, until it is permanently removed with complete destruction of the follicle. The treatment will probably be long term as the follicle is not usually destroyed at the first treatment and a weakened hair will regrow.

There can also be hair which is lying below the surface of the skin and this may become visible after treatment. This may cause the client to become despondent, so it is important to explain that these are not the hairs that have been treated, but new hairs.

The client will also need to know that initially the visits for treatment must be quite frequent – to assess the hair growth rate, to allow time for the skin to heal and until the initial growth has been treated. Then appointments to treat the regrowth will be less often, so becoming less expensive. The cost of the treatment should be discussed to allow the client to budget for the visits.

How the equipment works, what the treatment entails, the sensations they will feel and the appearance of the skin after treatment, should be explained in a language that will not alarm the clients.

The opportunity to try out the treatment by removing one or two hairs from the affected area should be taken. This would be an ideal time to explain the aftercare instructions for clients to carry out at home.

The record card

During this initial consultation a record card must be filled in to provide necessary information that will help to determine the course of treatment. An effective record system will inspire confidence in the client and promote efficiency in the salon by providing all the necessary information for another member of staff to take over treatment of the client should the need arise.

Details to be recorded

These should include personal and medical history details, and the treatment record.

Name, address and telephone number

* Useful for filing record cards in alphabetical order.
* The client may be contacted in case of a change in appointment.
* It will provide a ready-made mailing list and allow the therapist to contact clients to inform them of new treatments or special offers.
* A note should be made of how the client was recommended to the salon as this will help to assess a salon's future advertising.

Doctor's name and address and telephone number

It may be necessary to contact the client's doctor, with his or her permission, to ask about the client's medical history, current medication and treatment or to clarify any other point before epilation treatment may begin. Additionally, if clients are taken ill during treatment it may be necessary to call their doctor.

Date of birth

This information helps the therapist determine the client's suitability for treatment and indicates whether the client is suffering from superfluous hair because of the menopause, pregnancy or puberty. The hormonal imbalance at these times is a common cause of superfluous hair.

Medical history

Recording details of the client's medical history may help determine the cause of the problem and whether epilation is contraindicated. Pregnancies or miscarriages and recent operations must be recorded and if the appearance of the superfluous hair coincided with any of these occurrences. It is important to record any medical conditions clients may suffer from and are receiving medication for as some medicines cause superfluous hair. The contraceptive pill or steroids may also be the cause of superfluous hair. Menstrual problems may also indicate an underlying hormonal imbalance. A client with hepatitis will require stringent hygiene precautions.

Hair and skin condition

The position of superfluous hair and how strong the growth is should be noted to help in establishing the intensity of the current to be used and to establish approximately how long it will take to clear.

Skin sensitivity will indicate how treatment must be adapted to suit the skin type. Skin blemishes and disorders which may contraindicate treatment should be checked. It is important to note any scarring to the skin or discoloration, as this could be the result of previous treatment. It should be noted to protect the therapist's professional reputation.

Details of each treatment

This section of the record card will be filled in after each treatment session and should include:

* date and time of treatment
* area treated
* current intensity used
* machine used, as intensity can vary on different machines
* spacing of the probes
* signature of the therapist.

The purpose of recording these details is to:

* provide a case history, which allows another therapist to take over
* evaluate the progress of treatment
* locate the therapist who has performed the treatment in case of complaint
* ensure the details of the treatment are readily available

* record problems, which may require future treatment to be adapted or modified
* verify the details recorded are accurate – you must obtain the client's signature.

Skin types

Each client treated has a skin type, which is specific to that individual, with different degrees of skin sensitivity and powers of healing. Treatment needs to be adapted for different skin types and it is important, therefore, to analyse the skin before beginning treatment. This will help the therapist determine what course of treatment will be most suitable for the client, the most suitable method of epilation to be used and the frequency of treatment.

The reaction of the skin to treatment is unique to each client and can, in fact, change from one treatment to the next, depending on the general state of health and well-being of the client or it may react differently on different parts of the body. It is important, therefore, to understand the factors present in the skin which will affect treatment.

Sensitive skin

Some clients are highly sensitive to pain while others have a high pain threshold. This means that they will be able to tolerate a higher intensity of current for longer periods of time without feeling too much discomfort. The advantage of this is that the superfluous hair can be successfully removed over a shorter period of time. The disadvantage is that the area may be over treated because of the client's tolerance to pain. The skill of therapists is important as they can determine with each treatment, and by keeping accurate records, exactly how long and at what intensity treatments may be given.

The degree of sensitivity will determine the amount of hair which can be treated in one session. There are varying degrees of sensitivity on different areas of the body.

The face

* Highly sensitive – the centre of the face to include the centre of the lip, under the nose and the centre of the forehead and the eyebrow area.
* Less sensitive – the sides of the lip, the sides of the face under the chin and the neck.
* Least sensitive – the chin itself.

Other parts of the body

* Most sensitive – the area surrounding the nipple.
* Less sensitive – the centre line, spine, chest and inside of the thigh and the axilla.
* Least sensitive – the lower legs and the arms.

Sensitivity depends on:

* the location of the nerves
* the depth of the follicle.

The skin has an abundance of sensory nerves, which pass messages to the brain. These nerves have sensory receptors or fibrils in the lower layers of the epidermis which respond to cold, heat, touch, pressure and pain. The more sensitive areas are caused because these nerve fibrils are close together or in some cases overlapping, causing an intense response to a stimulant such as epilation.

The accuracy of the probe at the lowest point in the follicle is important in reducing pain. This is because the pain receptors are situated in the epidermis, so the deeper the follicle and the further from the surface of the skin the therapist works, the more current may be applied before response from the sensory receptors in the nerves.

Soft skin

When the skin is very soft or loose it will be more difficult to insert the needle into the hair follicle. On the face, the firm areas of skin are found on the forehead and chin while the under-chin area and the neck are areas of soft or loose skin of varying degrees.

Thin and thick skin

If the epidermis is very thin and translucent, as in fine sensitive skin types, the area will become red very quickly as the blood can be seen quite easily.

If the epidermis is thick, then the follicles are probably deeper, therefore insertions will be deeper. The skin reaction is not so marked on this skin type.

Moist skin

Both short-wave diathermy and galvanic electrolysis rely on the moisture level in the tissues for their effectiveness, as the diathermy heats the moisture content and the galvanic method produces a chemical reaction when combined with the salty body fluids.

There is more water content in the lower, more active layers of the epidermis and dermis. A natural part of keratinisation (the change of living cells with a nucleus, to dead flat horny cells with no nucleus) is loss of fluid in the skin cells, so the moisture content of the skin decreases towards the surface layers.

The skin becomes less moist with age as the epidermal cells are much flatter and without water. On the face, there are varying degrees of moisture and the therapist will have to adapt treatment by changing the intensity of the current. The area at the corners of the mouth is moist in most people and the chin area is normally less moist.

Oily skin

This is a skin which has a shiny surface due to the activity of the sebaceous glands. The layer of oil on the skin acts as an insulating layer preventing loss of moisture from the skin. Naturally oily skins are usually moist skins also, unless clients have been using harsh products on their skin to combat the oil production and have a drying effect on the skin.

The moisture gradient of the skin

The moisture in the epidermis decreases as the cells reach the surface of the skin and this is known as the moisture gradient. The gradient varies in different people, but in everyone there is a difference in the amount of moisture at the base of the follicle compared to the epidermal tissue on the surface of the skin.

Water is an effective conductor of electricity and as a current flow takes the path of least resistance, it will be at its most destructive in the moist area of the follicle, which is the dermal papilla.

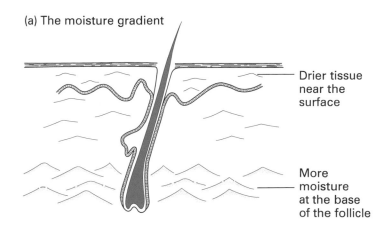

(a) The moisture gradient

Drier tissue near the surface

More moisture at the base of the follicle

Figure 22.9a *The moisture gradient*

Sebum insulation

The sebum coats the hair from the point where the sebaceous gland opens into the follicle, up and on to the surface of the skin. This coating of sebum insulates the epidermis from the action of the high frequency or galvanic current.

(b) Sebum insulation

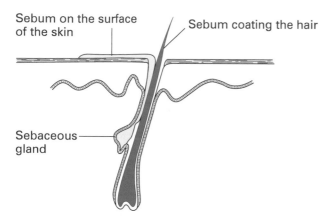

Figure 22.9b *Sebum insulation*

Short-wave diathermy

Short-wave diathermy, or **thermolysis** (meaning heat destruction), is the most commonly used method of permanent hair removal in salons today. It uses a **high frequency, short-wave alternating current** to produce heat as its destructive force. The current is applied through a fine metal needle inserted into the hair follicle and discharged for a very short time, producing heat in the tissues to cauterise and coagulate the papilla.

The heat is produced because a high frequency current is an oscillating current, 3 million to 30 million cycles per second, with high voltage and low amperage. In simpler terms, it is a rapidly alternating current of high pressure and low power. This continuous electrostatic attraction and repulsion (oscillation) produces friction which results in heat.

A high frequency current has an influence on the area around the conductor (the needle) and this is referred to as the high frequency field. Therefore heat is produced in the area of the follicle, which is affected by the high frequency field, in this case the area around the

papilla, cauterising this mitotically active area and retarding growth of a new hair.

Accurate placement of the needle is essential for the treatment to be effective.

Figure 22.10 *Short-wave diathermy machine*

The equipment

The epilation machine

There are many different types of epilation machines available, but the majority use short-wave diathermy and offer the following:

* an on/off switch
* an intensity control which is normally graduated from 1 to 10 and indicates the intensity of the current flow
* some machines have a milliamp metre which displays how much current is flowing
* a connection point for the needle holder
* a needle holder with a finger button to control the application of the current or without the button to be used in connection with the foot switch
* a foot switch connection
* a foot switch with lead to control the application of the current
* some have an automatic timing device for applying the current.

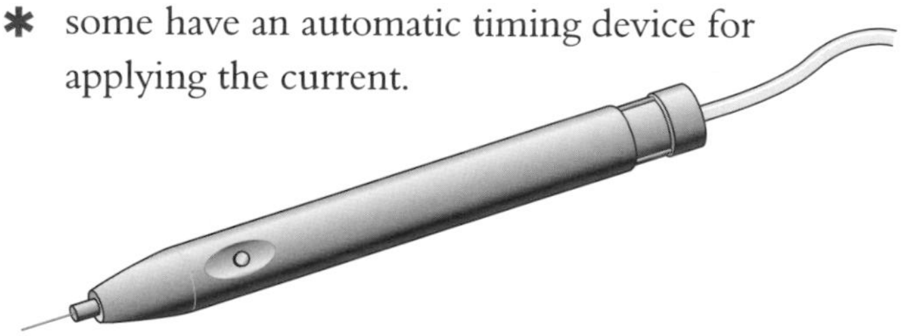

Figure 22.11 *Needle holder*

The epilation machine should be:

* well constructed and long lasting
* reliable in use and performance

* a simple design with easy-to-use controls
* small in size and clinical in appearance.

Needles

A selection of needles of various sizes and types is required. The most economical needle to use is made from stainless steel and is ideal for clients with strong healthy skin who respond well to epilation treatments. There is a 24-carat gold-plated needle available, for use on clients who suffer from allergies and sensitive skin and who may react negatively to standard stainless steel probes. An insulated needle has a special coating, to protect the most sensitive skin and reduce discomfort. It is ideal for use on a client who may perspire and also for diabetics, the main disadvantage is that it limits the action on the hair.

Needles can be classified as one-piece or two-piece. The one-piece is the earliest type of needle ground from a single piece of stainless steel making it strong but less flexible. The two-piece straight needle is the most flexible type in use. Each needle is divided into the shank, the part inserted into the needle holder and the shaft, the part that is inserted into the follicle – this must be smooth and highly polished to conduct the current and insert easily into the follicle.

Other equipment

A comfortable adjustable couch is essential to ensure client comfort throughout the treatment and allow all areas to be treated without causing tension in clients because they are seated uncomfortably.

The therapist will also need an adjustable stool to allow her to work effectively in the most comfortable position, reaching all areas of the client which require treatment, without causing backache as a result of bad positioning.

An illuminated magnifying lamp will allow the therapist to inspect the area to be worked upon more closely and provide a good source of light. The use of a magnifier allows more accurate work for longer, without causing eye strain and is an excellent substitute for good natural daylight, which is not consistent enough to be relied upon. It may be free-standing, wall-mounted or attached to the trolley.

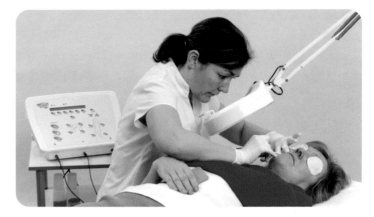

Figure 22.12 *The therapist using a magnifier and needle*

The therapist will also require a trolley, preferably with storage space such as drawers and shelves to hold equipment which should include the following:

* tweezers or forceps which should be used only for the purpose of epilation
* cotton wool and tissues in suitable containers
* appropriate cleansing preparations for areas to be treated
* a sterilising solution and medicated swabs
* a covered container for the disposal of used needles
* a small sterilising unit
* aftercare preparations
* a bin with a lid for waste material.

Hygiene precautions

Stringent precautions must be taken to maintain an environment free from bacteria. The therapist is bound by law to take any steps necessary in preventing the spread of disease.

It is important to contact the local environmental health officer (EHO) to obtain information about local by-laws relating to the setting up of an electrolysis clinic, or when adding this treatment to the list of services offered in an established salon. The EHO will also provide advice on matters of hygiene and safety in the salon that are necessary to protect both the clients attending for treatment and the therapists themselves.

Insufficient or incorrect hygiene measures may adversely affect the health of the therapist and client, in particular the risk of contracting hepatitis B (viral hepatitis) and from coming into contact with AIDS.

To avoid cross-infection the points outlined below should be considered.

Workplace

* The clinic or treatment room must be well maintained and scrupulously clean. The walls should be easy to clean, therefore it is inadvisable to use wallpaper unless it is durable and washable.
* The floor surface should be smooth, washable and impenetrable.
* The surfaces of all table tops and work surfaces should be smooth and impenetrable. They should be kept clean and wiped over with a suitable disinfectant before each treatment.
* The store cupboards and shelves must be used only for equipment and materials required for electrolysis.
* Chairs and treatment couches should be in good repair and kept clean by washing regularly with detergent. The covering should be in an easy-to-clean material and protected with bed-roll for each client.
* There must be adequate ventilation and good lighting.
* There must be a sink unit with hot and cold running water, which is connected to the drainage system, in the therapist's treatment room or cubicle.

The therapist (also called electrologist or electrolysist)

The personal hygiene of the therapist must be of the highest standards, because the nature of the work is such that she will be working in close proximity to clients most of the time. A therapist should not treat a client when suffering from an infectious illness or disease as this may be easily transmitted during treatment.

It is important for the therapist to protect herself from cross-infection by wearing latex gloves during treatment.

Equipment and materials

* Disposable needles must be used so that individual clients have their own needle which is then discarded after each use.
* Disposable paper tissues and towels should be used and changed for each client, then placed in a lidded bin, lined with a leak-proof sealable plastic bag.
* Stainless steel bowls are needed in which to place small items and cotton wool.
* Stainless steel tweezers are easy to sterilise.
* Pre-packed swabs impregnated with alcohol.
* A sharps disposable box for used needles clearly marked with the words 'DANGER CONTAMINATED SHARPS ONLY' which, when required, may be disposed of on the advice of the environmental health officer.
* Appropriate disinfectants should be used such as hypochlorite and glutaraldehyde which will neutralise most viruses, especially the hepatitis ones. Therapists providing electrical epilation must comply with the provisions laid down in the Health and Safety at Work etc Act (1974) (see Chapter 4 Health and Safety, page 43).

Autoclave moist heat is used for sterilising small metal instruments. Once the required temperature has been reached, the items will be sterilised after 15 minutes at 120°C, after 10 minutes at 126°C and after 3 minutes at 134°C.

Figure 22.13 *A sharps box*

Care and comfort of the client

* The client must always be lying or sitting in a comfortable position, which also allows the therapist to work efficiently and comfortably.
* The client's clothing in the area to be worked upon must be protected with clean towels. This helps to prevent possible cross-infection and also protects the client's clothing during treatment.
* The client's eyes should be covered with dry cotton wool or goggles if he or she is irritated by bright light.

* The client should be talked to in a reassuring and professional manner during treatment to put him or her at ease.
* If the therapist has a cold, then a surgical mask should be worn.
* The therapist should work as quickly and efficiently as possible.

Preparation of the client's skin for treatment

Even the removal of make-up prior to epilation can stimulate the skin and cause increased skin reaction during treatment. It is advisable to ask the client whenever possible not to wear make-up when attending for treatment.

A soothing cooling lotion such as witch hazel is applied to the skin to gently cleanse and soothe during treatment.

Probing

Skilled therapists will have a highly developed sense of touch enabling them to probe to the correct depth on each insertion and will also be able to manipulate the needle holder and the tweezers with great dexterity. Resistance will be felt in most cases when the base of the follicle has been reached. This does take a lot of practice and perseverance is required to be successful.

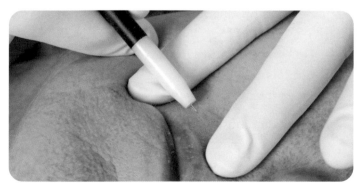

Figure 22.14 *Epilation probing*

The effectiveness of treatment is determined by the heating pattern created by the application of the high frequency current. The heating pattern is affected by:

* the intensity of the current applied
* the length of time the current is applied
* the depth of the follicle
* the diameter of the needle
* the moisture gradient.

A needle of the same diameter as the hair being treated will be the ideal size to use as it will slide easily into the follicle. Needles vary in size and the most commonly used are 004 and 005. Needle size 006 can be used on very coarse hair and 003 on very fine hair. The finer the needle, the less heat will rise up towards the surface.

The skin should be held taut around the base to allow the opening of the follicle to be seen more easily. The needle should then enter the follicle at the same angle as the hair leaves it. This is different on particular areas:

* Front of the chin – 60° angle.
* Most body hair and the side of the face – 45° angle.
* Front of the neck and throat – 30° angle.

The needle must then be held steady in the follicle and sufficient current applied to cauterise the papilla and allow the removal of the epilated hair.

Not being positive or precise when pressing the button on the needle holder or when pressing the foot switch to apply the current results in no current being applied and therefore the hair resists being removed by the tweezers.

Hair depth

When a hair is in the anagen or active stage of growth it is at its strongest and deepest, therefore the insertion will have to be deep. The epilated hair will have a fully formed root structure and tissue sheath.

The hair in the catagen stage is shorter in the follicle and the tissue sheath and root structure are not so well defined, therefore probing should be slightly more superficial.

Hairs in the telogen stage require very little current, but special care must be taken to avoid burning the surface of the skin as the hairs are quite high in the follicle. The hair will have no root sheath and will have a club-like end because of the disintegration of the hair bulb.

Current used

Current intensity should be chosen to suit the strength of the hair being treated, the skin sensitivity, the area to be epilated and the client's tolerance to pain. There should be the minimum amount of current used to remove the hair successfully. The timing of the application of the current can be altered to suit the requirements of each client.

Different machines use different levels of high frequency currents and it is up to the therapist to decide the way in which to work: a low current for a longer application time; or a high current for a short application time.

Both methods achieve the same results, but greater accuracy and competence are required when using the high current for a short length of time to prevent skin damage. It is advisable, therefore, while perfecting the skills required for epilation, that the lower current for a longer application time is used to produce the required results without causing too much discomfort to the client. A highly skilled therapist will be able to use the high current with short application. This will allow her to treat more of the superfluous hair in the time allocated for treatment while minimising pain and the adverse skin reaction which can occur.

The expected appearance of the skin after treatment

As a result of treatment and the heat produced, there is an increase in blood supply to the area and this will cause an erythema. This reddening of the skin will vary in intensity depending on the client's skin sensitivity and the intensity of the current which has been used.

The flow of lymph to the area is also stimulated because of the increase in blood supply and this will cause a slight swelling because of the excess fluid. In areas of extreme sensitivity such as the bikini line, breasts and abdomen as well as extremely sensitive skins, this effect can be more marked.

Care of the skin after treatment

To reduce the redness and the heat in the skin tissues, it is important to apply a soothing lotion immediately after treatment. When treating several areas at once a very fine piece of cotton wool soaked in the appropriate lotion can be applied to a previously treated area while treatment is performed elsewhere. This allows the healing process to begin and skin appearance to improve. Any lotion or cream applied to the skin after treatment must have the following properties:

* antibacterial
* protective
* soothing
* camouflaging, if required.

Some aftercare preparations have an antihistamine and when applied to the skin it helps to reduce the inflammation.

Galvanism may be used on the skin after treatment, utilising the soothing effects of the positive pole, which will reduce erythema, soothe the nerve endings, produce an acid reaction on the skin and promote healing.

After each treatment a small amount of epidermal tissue will be destroyed, therefore the area around the treated follicle will be susceptible to infection until the skin heals itself. It is important to advise clients on the care they must give their own skin at home and stress the importance of adhering to the following instructions strictly:

* Follow the aftercare instructions for 48 hours after treatment.
* Avoid the use of soap, make-up or any perfumed products which could cause an irritation.
* Cleanse twice a day with either witch hazel, which is also soothing, mild unscented toning lotion or a product recommended by the therapist.
* Apply a medicated soothing lotion after cleansing.
* If there is any soreness in the area treated after 48 hours, then the aftercare instructions must be continued until the skin is clear.

* After 48 hours use only unperfumed cleanser and toning lotion.
* Tiny scabs may form as these are part of the skin's natural healing process and must be left untouched to prevent secondary infection or scarring.
* Contact the therapist if there are any problems.
* Avoid heat treatment or exposure to ultraviolet radiation.
* Avoid using other methods of hair removal between treatments apart from cutting if necessary.

Appearance of the skin when damaged by incorrect techniques

Raised bumps

These may appear because of an excessive amount of lymph fluid in the area caused by an application of current which was too high, or had been applied for too long or in too small an area.

Blisters

Blisters or tiny lymph vesicles may form on the surface of the skin, again caused by over treatment and these will normally crust over and heal naturally if not touched by the client and all aftercare instructions are followed.

Burning of the skin

This shows up as small white marks on the skin's surface which can be flat or raised and do not fade away. They normally take two to four weeks to disappear and the skin's natural healing process provides a lymph or blood crust over the lesion to aid in healing. If this is knocked off or removed, a pitted scar or small depression in the skin may result.

The causes are:

* application of current which is too high or for too long
* passing the current when insertion or removal of the needle has not been completed
* moving the needle while it is in the follicle and the current is being applied
* incorrect insertion.

Blue-black mark

A blue-black mark or lump may appear, caused by an incorrect insertion or using a needle which is too large. It may appear immediately as a well-defined blue mark because the tiny blood capillaries have been ruptured or later as a widespread area of discoloration. Immediate pressure to the area and the application of cold compresses will help reduce the effect.

Permanent scars

These may be a result of persistently poor techniques causing severe burning or picked crusts over healing lesions. They are tiny indentations in the skin which have the appearance of orange peel when there are many situated in a small area.

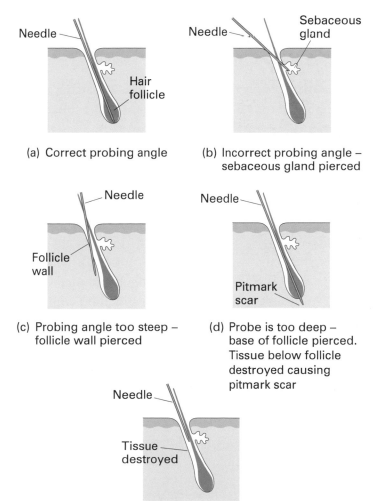

(a) Correct probing angle

(b) Incorrect probing angle – sebaceous gland pierced

(c) Probing angle too steep – follicle wall pierced

(d) Probe is too deep – base of follicle pierced. Tissue below follicle destroyed causing pitmark scar

(e) Probe is too shallow – current application too close to surface. Tissue close to skin's surface destroyed

Figure 22.15 *Correct and incorrect probing techniques*

Hair removal

Conditions which may result from epilation

Infection

This is characterised by the formation of pustules and occurs when either the therapist's hygiene methods are poor or home care advice given to the client has not been adhered to.

Ingrowing hair

This is a hair which grows horizontally along and just under the surface of the skin when it emerges from the follicle. Sometimes it will turn back on itself into the follicle opening and become compacted. Occasionally, infection will set in, but an ingrowing hair can be easily removed using a sterile needle to release the trapped hair and then left to heal.

Absence of root sheath

This sometimes occurs when the hair is epilated quite easily, but the root sheath is left behind in the follicle. The root sheath has been skimmed off before reaching the mouth of the follicle and this ball of tissue could become a breeding ground for bacteria and cause the formation of pustules.

Galvanic electrolysis

Although this method of epilation is not in common use on its own, it is an essential part of the blend method which utilises the effectiveness of this method with the speed of diathermy.

Electrolysis is the term used to describe the electrolytic action of the galvanic current for the removal of superfluous hair. When a direct current is applied to a salt water solution it causes the salt and the water to break up into their chemical elements, which then rearrange themselves to form entirely new substances. Acids form at the positive pole and alkalis form at the negative pole.

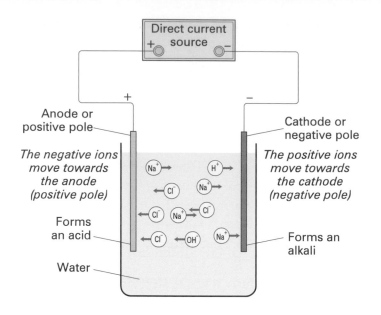

Figure 22.16 *Effects of a direct current passing through a salt solution*

This process is called electrolysis and the new substances that are formed are sodium hydroxide or lye, hydrogen and chlorine gas.

> Sodium chloride and water (salt) + direct current = sodium hydroxide, hydrogen gas and chlorine gas
>
> $NaCl + H_2O$ + direct current = $NaOH + H + Cl$

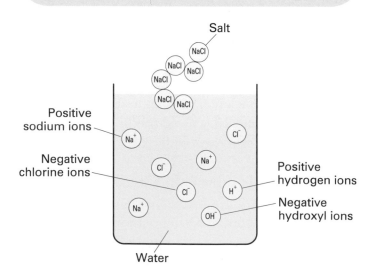

Figure 22.17 *Ionisation of sodium chloride*

An electrolyte is a solution which has the ability to conduct electricity and can be ionised. The tissues of the body are made up of a strong salt solution, therefore making it an efficient electrolyte.

Galvanic electrolysis is a chemical process which produces the caustic lye that is used as the destructive force in this method of superfluous hair removal. A galvanic current is a constant direct current and, as in facial treatment, the client must hold an indifferent electrode to complete the circuit. The active electrode in galvanic epilation is the needle and it will be used on the negative pole only. The indifferent electrode will be positively charged.

The needle is inserted into the follicle and the direct current is applied. When using a galvanic current it has to be applied for approximately 10–15 seconds so that enough lye is formed to decompose the tissue.

The area around the base of the follicle is moist with tissue fluid containing body salts (moisture gradient). The current only affects the tissue where it encounters moisture, therefore the galvanic current converts tissue moisture and body salts in the follicle into lye, causing hydrogen and chlorine gas to escape from the follicle mouth.

There are two factors which aid in the effectiveness of this treatment, as well as protecting the epidermis, particularly as the current has to be applied for a fairly long period:

* The moisture gradient of the skin ensures the largest amount of galvanic action is concentrated on the moist area of the lower follicle, causing decomposition of this vital active area without causing damage to the surface of the skin.
* The sebum secreted by the sebaceous gland attached to the follicle forms a layer over the part of the hair above the sebaceous gland and the surface of the skin, insulating it from the galvanic current.

The polarity

The alkali effects of the negative pole and the acid effect of the positive pole both destroy tissue. However, the positive pole must never be used as the hydrochloric acid produced also causes most metals to disintegrate.

In the case of the positive pole being used accidentally, a hard lump and scar will result that is slow to heal. It is very important, therefore, to only use the *negative pole* in galvanic electrolysis.

The blend method

This method of superfluous hair removal incorporates both the galvanic current used in electrolysis and the high frequency current used in short-wave diathermy.

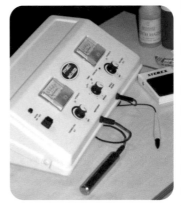

Figure 22.18 *A blend machine*

Most machines allow the currents to be used separately or together.

The combination of the speed of diathermy and the efficiency of the galvanic method is utilised for maximum effect. The high frequency current uses heat as its destructive force and the galvanic current produces lye, which is used as its destructive force. Together the heat from the high frequency current increases the caustic effect of the lye, which destroys the hair papilla.

Professional associations

There are two associations especially for therapists who specialise in electrical epilation – the Institute of Electrolysis and the British Association of Electrolysis (for details, see the Glossary of professional associations and organisations at the end of this book). It is a good idea to join one to make sure that you are kept up to date with the industry and you have a support network and can obtain advice from other professionals. To become a member you must first sit an examination, which helps the association to maintain standards. This is essential as, once a member, the association will recommend you to the medical profession as well as the general public.

Laser and pulsed light for hair removal

These treatments are becoming increasingly popular with clients, particularly for their efficiency in reducing the growth rate of superfluous hair and producing finer and softer regrowth compared to other methods of hair removal. All areas can be treated on a suitable skin type. However, areas close to the eyes or mucous membranes such as ears and nose, should not be treated.

The equipment delivers pulses of light energy into the skin, which are then absorbed by the pigment in the hair follicle and, to a much lesser degree, by the surrounding skin tissue. This light energy converts to heat and when it reaches a temperature of 70°C for the correct length of time, the follicle will be damaged to such an extent that new growth is reduced significantly. Treatment will be most successful when the hair is in the anagen stage of growth as it contains more melanin to absorb the light energy. Clients should be given as much information as possible during the consultation so that their expectations about the results of treatment are realistic and they know that a course of treatment is recommended.

Hair and skin colour

The best results are achieved on clients who have the most appropriate hair and skin type, when the hair colour is darker than the skin. The more contrast in colour, the more effective the treatment. Clients with dark skins have a higher risk of burns or hyperpigmentation as the skin colour may absorb too much light energy. When a client has a natural or false tan it would be advisable to postpone treatment until it has faded, for the same reason.

The contraindications are shown in Figure 22.19.

You may need to refer the client to his or her doctor if in doubt about any condition or medication.

Aftercare advice

* Avoid exposure to ultraviolet light (sun and sun beds) and false tan products.
* Avoid touching the treated area and wearing tight fitting clothes.
* Avoid heat treatments and using perfumed or chemical-based products.
* Use recommended aftercare products and a high factor sunscreen.
* Avoid waxing, plucking or bleaching the hair in between treatments.

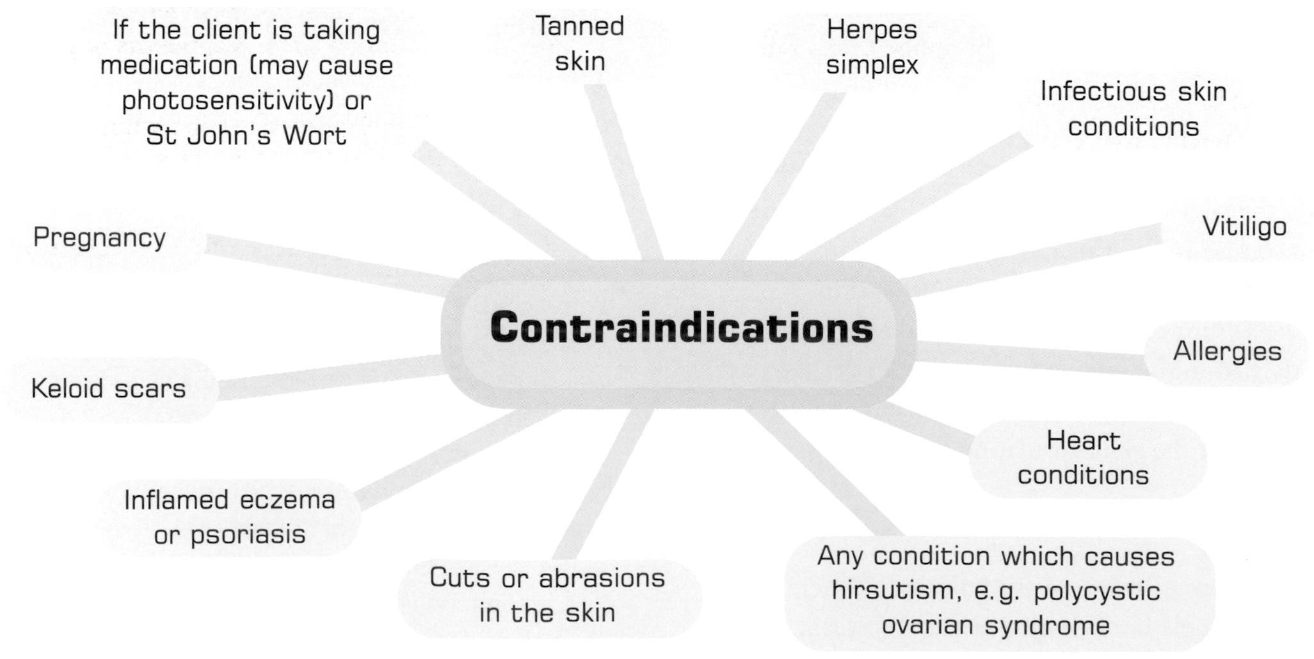

If the client is taking medication (may cause photosensitivity) or St John's Wort

Tanned skin

Herpes simplex

Infectious skin conditions

Pregnancy

Vitiligo

Contraindications

Allergies

Keloid scars

Heart conditions

Inflamed eczema or psoriasis

Cuts or abrasions in the skin

Any condition which causes hirsutism, e.g. polycystic ovarian syndrome

Figure 22.19 *Contraindications to laser and pulsed light hair removal*

Legal requirements

Every salon offering this service must register with the National Care Standards Commission (NCSC), a legal requirement under the Care Standards Act (2000) (For further information, see the Glossary of professional associations and organisations at the end of this book.) The salon has to be formally approved and registered to provide the service and will be inspected to ensure that all staff are 'fit to practice', the business is financially secure and it complies with all health and safety requirements, meeting the new minimum standards. The salon must then set out a formal written statement, or detailed plan – a **protocol** (see below) – that is strictly followed by all operatives undertaking treatment. This should include:

* pre-treatment checks
* the procedure
* acceptable limits for adapting treatment
* occasions when treatment is stopped.

All the health and safety Acts and regulations discussed in Chapter 4 Health and safety are relevant and, in particular, the Personal Protective Equipment at Work Regulations (1992). The therapist and the client must wear goggles, provided free of charge. These must fit properly and provide adequate protection. They should be stored correctly and well maintained to keep them in good condition and working effectively.

A risk assessment must be carried out and control measures put in place to ensure the health and safety of all those involved in the treatment.

Protocol

A trained and experienced medical practitioner or dentist should draw up this protocol in accordance with the treatment provided. It should show that you are using a protocol developed by the most skilled person with appropriate knowledge.

Many of the equipment manufacturers provide the training and instruction manuals that include treatment limits and protocols usually developed through clinical trials and studies when the equipment is being designed and tested under strict supervision.

Records

Your client records must be available for the NCSC inspectors and they should include:

* client details and records which must be kept for up to eight years
* a record of all laser or pulsed light treatments with details of the client, date, treatment area, the therapist who provided the treatment and any other relevant details such as accidents or contra-actions
* a record of all those providing treatment
* a record of the shifts worked and the working hours of each employee.

All records must be kept safely and in accordance with the Data Protection Act (1998).

Hand and foot treatments

* Hand and foot treatments

* Artificial nail treatments

Introduction

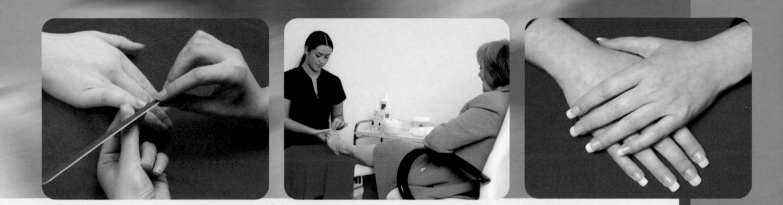

One of the largest growth areas in beauty therapy over the past five years has been the nail industry. From the humble manicure, a huge empire has grown. Quite often the first treatment a client will have is a manicure and this provides the therapist with the opportunity to talk to her while she is having the treatment and discuss all her other beauty requirements.

Initially, the changes that occurred were in manicure techniques with natural nail care becoming the trend. Then false nail systems came to the fore and they developed into the thriving business that it is today offering an array of special products designed to provide the client with any type of nail she desires. The natural progression was into nail adornment, and nail art has become a specialist service in its own right.

The nail treatments offered have been adapted to suit the image of many establishments. The holistic spas have introduced the special spa manicures and pedicures incorporating natural minerals, essential oils, mud and clay packs and specialised treatments. The nail bars have provided the speedy manicure for the busy client, while the new salons catering for the male market are providing a service with good grooming in mind.

Manicure

The word manicure means care of the hands, and the purpose of this treatment is to improve the appearance of the hands and nails by cleansing, nourishing and beautifying them. A manicure is also an ideal opportunity for the therapist to gain the client's confidence by giving a professional treatment and talking about any beauty needs and explaining what other treatments are available in the salon.

There are many very common nail disorders such as flaking, brittle and bitten nails which may be improved with regular manicures. Professional advice may also be given to the client regarding the care of hands and nails.

A manicure involves:

* shaping and moisturising the nails
* care of the cuticles
* hand and arm massage
* enamelling or buffing.

Once the therapist has become proficient, the manicure should take no longer than 30 minutes.

The manicure trolley should always be prepared well in advance, with all equipment positioned in a convenient order to save time and to allow the therapist to work comfortably. All working areas should be clean and new towels used for each client.

The full manicure consists of several different techniques, which must be carried out quickly and efficiently to produce a polished end result. The manicure routine will vary as different therapists have their own method of working, depending on the products used and the treatment procedure recommended by the company from which they purchase their products.

Filing

When filing the nails, the finger must always be supported and the emery board should be used carefully, filing from the outside inwards along the free edge, working each side alternately and quickly. It is important not to use a sawing action as this will disturb the layers of the nail plate causing split nails and may cause possible damage to the matrix due to the rocking movement. It will also produce heat in the nail plate which will dry out the natural oils causing flakiness. The nails should not be filed down into the sides as this, causes a weak point in the nail which will easily break.

The shape of the nail is chosen for various reasons:

* The client's preference.
* Fashion.
* The shape of the hands.
* The state of the nail.
* The ideal shape is oval, the strongest shape is square and the weakest shape is pointed.

Figure 23.1 *Filing the nail*

Buffing

This is often used instead of enamelling the nails for the following reasons:

* The client may be allergic to the enamel.
* The occupation of the client may not allow her to wear enamel.
* For a manicure on a male client.
* For a client who bites his or her nails, to stimulate circulation and improve the appearance.
* To remove superficial ridges on the nail plate.
* To remove stains from the nail plate.

Only the tiniest amount of buffing paste should be applied to each nail because it spreads very easily and this will prevent it spreading to the skin tissue at the sides of the nail. Buffing should be performed in one direction only, from the matrix to the free edge until the nail appears shiny. This will prevent damage to the matrix, which would be caused if the nails were buffed from side to side. The movements should be of a moderate speed and in one direction to prevent heat building up in the nail, thus drying it out.

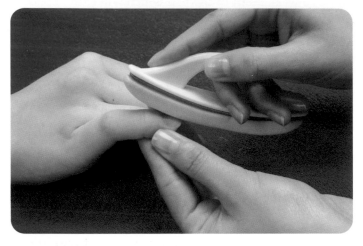

Figure 23.2 *Buffing the nail*

Cuticle work

Cuticle remover is slightly caustic, so it should be left on the nails for the shortest length of time necessary to complete the work and then it should be removed either with a nail brush or damp cotton wool.

Cuticle or orange sticks must always be tipped with cotton wool and when pushing the cuticle back, the stick should be used in small circular movements to prevent causing damage to the matrix.

The cuticle knife must only be used to remove excess cuticle adhering to the nail plate. The blade must be wet at all times as this provides a protective cushion to the nail plate and it should be held at an angle of 45° to prevent scratching the surface of the nail plate.

Figure 23.3 *A cuticle knife*

Cuticle nippers must only be used to remove hangnails and they must be held firmly, cutting the hangnail cleanly, without pulling and tearing the tissue. Always follow the natural curve of the nail fold or cuticle.

Figure 23.4 *Cuticle nippers*

Hand and arm massage

There are several reasons why massage is incorporated into the manicure, in some cases after the cuticle work and immediately prior to the enamelling. However, some therapists use the hydrating products with the massage nearer the beginning of the manicure as the oils used will have soaked into the nails long before enamelling, providing an oil-free surface to work on. The effects of massage include the following:

* It is relaxing to the client and if performed well, it may encourage the client to book further treatments such as facial or body massage.
* It also relaxes tense, tired and aching muscles.
* The blood circulation to the area is stimulated bringing essential nutrients to the area and removing waste products as well as improving skin colour.
* It helps with joint mobility and keeps the hands supple.
* As rich creams may be used, the skin's natural moisture content is replenished and the skin is softened. Dry and flaky nails are also nourished.
* It aids desquamation – the removal of dead skin cells from the surface of the skin – leaving it brighter looking.

To ensure comfort throughout:

* the client's arm must be well supported to ensure that the muscles are totally relaxed and the massage strokes should flow smoothly and continuously
* the hand cream should be warmed in the palm of the hands before applying it to the skin, as it can sometimes feel cold on application
* a fast-absorbing cream should be used which does not leave a sticky feeling on the skin
* the cream used must have a pleasant smell
* the client's clothing must be protected from the cream used.

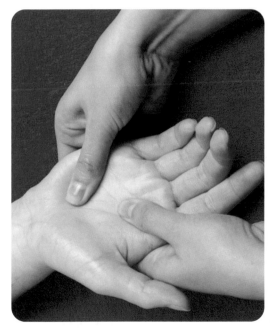

Figure 23.5
Hand and arm massage

Massage manipulations

Effleurage

The massage movements should begin and end with light stroking effleurage, a soothing, relaxing movement always performed in an upward direction, following the blood and lymph flow.

Petrissage

Finger and palmar kneading are both relaxing and soothing to the muscles. Slight pressure is added on each movement and these movements also follow the blood and lymph flow.

Rotations

Circular movements to the joints to aid joint mobility.

Contraindications

All contraindications which apply to manicure (see page 338) also apply to massage of the hand and arm, but there are also some reasons for omitting the massage from the manicure and these are:

* extremely hairy arms as the massage movements would be uncomfortable
* recent sunburn to the arms
* recent scar tissue
* overstretched, very thin skin.

Nail enamelling

Before the nails are enamelled, it is important to ensure that there is no grease left on the nail plate to create a barrier and prevent the enamel adhering to the nail. This is most easily achieved by wiping over the nail with a piece of cotton wool soaked in nail enamel remover, but this will dehydrate the nail. An alternative is to use warm water as this is less harsh.

A base coat must be applied first:

* to prevent pigments in the nail enamel from staining the nail plate
* to fill in any grooves and ridges which may be on the nail plate
* to provide a smooth base for the enamel, making the application easier
* to help in prolonging the life of the enamel
* to protect the nail plate by hardening it.

Figure 23.6 *Nail enamelling*

Hand and foot treatments

There are two different types of enamel:

* cream
* frosted.

When using the cream variety two applications should be used. When using a frosted enamel three coats should be applied.

A top coat is then applied to the cream enamel only; a frosted enamel does not require the added lustre of the top coat. The top coat is applied:

* to protect the enamel from chipping
* to prolong the life of the cream enamel
* to add a high gloss to cream enamel.

A quick-dry liquid may then be applied to speed up the process, but the best way to ensure the nails dry quickly is to have a pause in between the application of each coat of enamel. However, this is not always practical in a busy salon so clients must sit for a short period after the manicure to allow their nails to dry.

Certain problems may occur if the enamelling technique is less than perfect.

Enamel will peel away if:

* an oily residue is left on the nail plate
* the enamel is applied too thickly
* inferior enamel is used.

Enamel will chip if:

* there is a flaking nail condition present
* the enamel is forced dried
* there are ridges present on the nail plate
* the enamel has been thinned with too much solvent.

The French polish

This is a natural looking finish to a manicure using enamel. A white or cream colour is applied to the free edge, over a base coat and then a transparent colour in a natural shade is placed over this to achieve a healthy natural looking nail. The top coat is then applied to prolong the life of the enamel. It is very popular for brides and in the summer months, it also provides an excellent base for nail art. Some therapists will use the airbrush system of applying the colour to ensure a perfect finish.

The structure of the nail

The technical term for a nail is **onyx** and it consists of three main parts:

* the nail root or matrix
* the nail plate
* the free edge.

The nail is an appendage of the skin, which forms a protective covering for the ends of the fingers.

The chemical composition of the nail is:

* carbon
* hydrogen
* oxygen
* sulphur
* nitrogen.

A healthy nail is pink in colour with a smooth, slightly curved surface and clear of any mark or defect. A new nail will always grow in place of an injured or lost nail. However, if the matrix is damaged, a deformed nail may grow in its place.

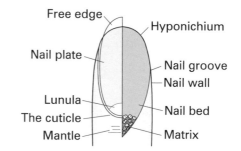

Figure 23.7 *The structure of the nail*

The matrix

This is situated immediately below the cuticle and is the only living reproducing part of the nail. It contains nerves and blood vessels and cell reproduction occurs here. When the new cells are formed they are continually pushing forward to form the nail plate. A healthy matrix will produce a healthy nail, but if injury occurs in this area, the nail may grow with a deformity which may be temporary or permanent. The cells receive their nourishment from the blood supply.

The lunula

This is the point where the matrix and the nail bed meet. It is crescent shaped and pearly in colour because the new cells are pushed so closely together that the blood capillaries in the nail bed, which provide the pink glow, cannot be seen.

Cell reproduction

Mitosis is the name given to cell division in which one cell produces two identical new cells. It is the way in which new body cells are produced for growth and repair.

The nail bed

This is a continuation of the matrix and is abundantly supplied with nerves, lymph and blood vessels. It is the part of the finger upon which the nail plate rests. It has numerous parallel ridges that dovetail exactly with ridges on the under surface of the nail plate.

The nail plate

This is the visible portion of the nail, which rests upon the nail bed and terminates at the free edge. It consists of many layers of dead cells held together with a minimum amount of moisture and it is semi-transparent, allowing the colour of the blood supply of the dermis to show through.

The mantle

This is the deep fold of skin over the matrix and around the base of the nail plate.

The free edge

This is an extension of the nail plate which overlaps the hyponichium and is the part of the nail filed to form its shape.

The hyponichium

This is the portion of skin at the end of the finger underneath the free edge.

The cuticle

This is the overlapping epidermis surrounding the nail, the function of which is to protect the matrix from invading bacteria and physical damage.

* The **eponychium** is the cuticle at the base of the nail.

* The **peronychium** is the cuticle at the sides of the nail.

The nail walls

These are the folds of the skin overlapping the sides of the nails.

The nail grooves

These are the grooves or furrows at the sides of the nail upon which the nail moves and acts as a guideline for the nail to follow.

Keratinisation of the nail

Keratinisation is the change of living cells containing a nucleus into flat, dead, horny cells with no nucleus. The process starts in the basal layer of the epidermis and ends in the horny layer.

The nail plate lies on the nail bed (the dermis) which contains nerves and blood vessels. It is made up of cells which are pushed forwards from the matrix and they go through a process of keratinisation causing the nail plate to grow in thickness and length. New cells are formed in the matrix – **stratum germinativum**. These cells divide to produce new cells in the matrix – **stratum spinosum**.

Partly keratinised cells, which are losing fluid and contain a nucleus, that is, beginning to disintegrate form the nail in the area of the lunula – **stratum granulosum**. Dead, horny keratinised cells make up the nail plate – **stratum lucidum** and **stratum corneum**.

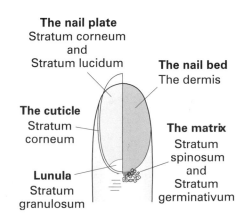

The nail plate
Stratum corneum and Stratum lucidum

The nail bed
The dermis

The cuticle
Stratum corneum

The matrix
Stratum spinosum and Stratum germinativum

Lunula
Stratum granulosum

Figure 23.8 *Structure of the nail in relation to the layers of the skin*

Growth of the nail

Age, ill health, crash dieting, malnutrition, medication, alcohol, anaemia, hormonal disorders and damage to the matrix can affect the growth of the nail. On average, it takes between five and six months to grow from the matrix to the free edge. The nail grows more quickly:

* in the summer than in the winter
* in younger people than in older
* on hands rather than feet
* on the dominant hand
* on men than women
* during pregnancy.

Manicure equipment

* A manicure table.
* A product stand, tray or small trolley with compartments for all manicure preparations.
* A container in which to place client's jewellery.
* A finger bowl for warm water, in which clients immerse their hands during the manicure.
* Two bowls, one for clean cotton wool and one for waste.
* Nail clippers or scissors for reducing the length of the nail.
* Emery boards for filing and shaping the nails.
* Orange sticks for treating the cuticles and removing some preparations, e.g. cuticle massage cream, from their containers.
* A cuticle knife to remove traces of cuticle adhering to the nail plate.
* Cuticle nippers to trim torn or ragged cuticle.
* A nail brush for removing any grease or debris on the nail plate.

Figure 23.9
The manicure trolley

* A nail buffer to buff and polish the nail.
* A spatula for removing hand cream from the container.

Manicure preparations

Nail enamel remover

Nail enamel remover is used to remove the enamel gently but effectively. It contains acetone or ethyl acetate, which is a solvent necessary to dissolve the enamel, and oil such as glycerol to counteract the drying effect of the solvent.

Cuticle cream

Cuticle massage cream is used to soften and nourish the cuticle, allowing it to be pushed back with ease and replacing natural oils lost due to exposure to drying elements. It is a mixture of fats and waxes such as:

* beeswax
* cocoa butter
* white soft paraffin.

Cuticle remover

Cuticle remover is an alkaline lotion applied to the cuticles to help in their removal from the nail plate. It does have an irritating effect on the skin because of its alkalinity and may dry out the nail plate. Therefore, it must be applied and removed quickly.

Its constituents are:

* potassium hydroxide which is alkaline
* glycerol to counteract the drying effect of the potassium hydroxide
* oleic acid to make it into a milky lotion.
* water.

Hand creams

Hand creams or lotions are used to supplement the natural moisture of the skin without leaving a greasy film and should be rich and creamy and easily absorbed by the skin. They may contain such ingredients as:

* lanolin, oils
* mineral oil or cetyl alcohol
* perfume
* preservatives
* water.

Paste polish

Paste polish is used when buffing the nails, as opposed to enamelling them. Powdered silica or powdered pumice may be combined with a wax polish, made from a base of mineral oil, soft paraffin and paraffin wax mixed together to form a smooth paste.

Nail enamels

Nail enamels include:

* base coat
* top coat
* coloured cream or frosted enamels.

    They are all made from:
* a plastic film such as nitrocellulose
* a plasticiser to provide flexibility
* a solvent to allow the enamel to dry
* a plastic resin to create a gloss
* pigments to provide colour.

    Pearl or frosted enamels contain guanine or bismuth oxychloride.

    An ideal coloured enamel should have a good consistency, not too thick or thin and be easy to apply. It should also be long lasting and protective.

    Allergy to nail enamel does occasionally occur and the ingredient which often causes this is formaldehyde. However, many enamels are now produced formaldehyde free to combat this problem.

Nail disorders and diseases

There are many disorders of the nail which are irregularities in growth or blemishes. These can be treated by the beauty therapist and in some cases can be improved with professional treatment in the salon and through professional advice on care.

    Nail diseases are normally characterised by the presence of infection, soreness or irritation but can also be caused by a health disorder.

Corrugations (pronounced cor-oo-ga-shuns)

These are superficial ridges in the nails which are caused by uneven growth and may be the result of an illness. Buffing should be included in regular manicures to eliminate this problem.

Furrows

These are deep ridges in the nail which may be caused by a nutritional problem, injury to the matrix or illness. Constant rubbing of the cuticle can cause friction in the area of the matrix and cause a deep ridge which will continue up the nail plate until it reaches the free edge. If, however, this nervous habit is removed, the problem will not recur.

Leuconychia (pronounced lu-co-nic-ee-ah)

This is a common condition of the nails and is usually referred to as white spots. It arises from injury to the base of the nail whereby a tiny air pocket forms between the nail bed and nail plate. To prevent this problem, injury to the nails must be avoided by treating them gently.

Pterygium (pronounced te-rij-ee-um)

This is a thick hardened growth of dry cuticle, which sticks to the nail plate as it grows. The treatment for this problem is to soften the cuticle by using oil or paraffin wax, then the cuticle may be gently pushed back and any remaining cuticle gently removed with cuticle nippers. The nails should be regularly manicured to prevent the problem recurring.

Hangnail

This is caused when the cuticle splits and can be as a result of pterygium, when the cuticle has stretched so much it begins to split or because the cuticle is very dry. Moisturising treatments are advisable and any torn or ragged cuticle should be removed with cuticle nippers. It is important to improve this condition as the torn cuticle could become infected.

Onychauxis (pronounced on-ee-cork-sis)

This is an excessive thickening of the nail plate and it may also change colour. The thickening may occur in response to a constant irritation, for example a badly fitting shoe rubbing on the nail. Internal disorders, infection or neglect may also cause it. This condition is sometimes referred to as hypertrophy and may only be treated by filing the nails smooth and buffing if there is no infection present.

Hand and foot treatments

Onychatrophia (pronounced on-ee-cat-row-fee-ah)

This condition is when the nail becomes smaller and smaller and in some cases wastes away completely. The nail loses its lustre, becoming opaque and ridged. It may be caused by injury to the matrix, nervous disorder or disease and should be treated very gently. Manicures would be inadvisable until the problem has been solved, but the nails must be protected from harsh products such as household detergents.

Onychophagy (pronounced on-ee-co-fa-jee)

This is the technical term for bitten nails and in some cases the cuticle around the nail. Nail biting is a nervous habit, which results in exposure of the hyponichium, and can cause very weak or even deformed nails. Regular manicures with oil treatments to soften the cuticles will help, but the best cure is to stop the nail biting.

Onychorrhexis (pronounced on-ee-co-rex-is)

This is a very common condition, when the nails become brittle and split. It is caused by overexposure to harsh detergents or overuse of nail cosmetics, in fact anything which dries out the nail plate. A bout of illness can leave the nails as well as the hair and skin in a very dry condition. Regular manicures, moisturising treatments and a good diet should be recommended.

Onychosis (pronounced on-ee-co-sis)

This is the technical term for a nail disease.

Onychomycosis (pronounced on-ee-com-ee-co-sis)

This is a fungal infection of the nails. (See Chapter 3 Contraindications page 26.)

Paronychia (pronounced pa-ro-nic-ee-ah)

This is an inflamed swelling of the nail folds. (See Chapter 3 Contraindications page 26.)

Onychocryptosis (pronounced on-ee-co-crip-toe-sis)

This condition affects the fingers or toes but is most common on the big toe. It is commonly known as ingrowing nail where the side of the nail plate actually grows into the flesh of the nail wall. The cause can be incorrect cutting or filing too far down the sides, pressure from ill-fitting shoes or just neglect. It can become very red, sore and painful. If the condition becomes uncomfortable, a chiropodist should be consulted, and if the nail becomes infected, it should be treated by a doctor.

Onychoptosis (pronounced on-ee-cop-toe-sis)

This can affect one or several nails and is the periodic shedding of either the whole nail or part of it.

Onycholisis (pronounced on-ee-co-li-sis)

This is a gradual separation of the nail plate from the nail bed whereby the nail loosens without coming away completely. There are several possible causes such as an internal disorder, psoriasis, eczema or rough treatment of the nails, for example cleaning too far down the nail under the free edge, particularly with a pointed object.

Onychophyma (pronounced on-ee-co-fee-mah)

This is a swelling of the nails.

Onychogryphosis (pronounced on-ee-co-gri-fo-sis)

This is an enlarged nail with an increased curve. The enlargement is caused by an increase in the production of the horny cells of the nail plate and this leads to a curvature of the nail resembling a ram's horn. It is more common in older people and the big toe is most frequently affected. The most common causes are age, neglect or ill-fitting shoes. This condition must be treated by a chiropodist or removed surgically if it causes pain.

Koilonychia (pronounced coy-lo-nic-ee-ah)

This condition may be caused by an accumulation of horny cells at the sides of the nail plate, under the nail wall or an abnormal growth stemming from the matrix. This abnormal growth gives the nail a spoon shape. The condition can be temporary or permanent depending upon the cause, which can be an inherited abnormality, a side effect of a certain type of anaemia or an overactive thyroid condition.

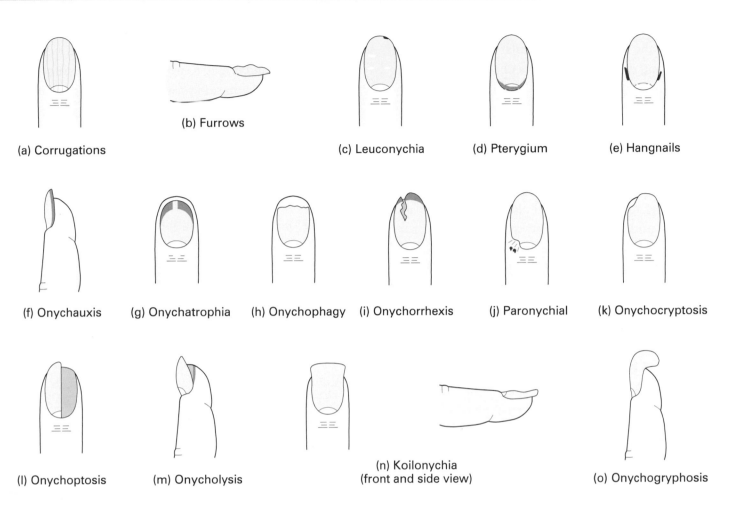

(a) Corrugations   **(b) Furrows**   **(c) Leuconychia**   **(d) Pterygium**   **(e) Hangnails**

(f) Onychauxis   **(g) Onychatrophia**   **(h) Onychophagy**   **(i) Onychorrhexis**   **(j) Paronychial**   **(k) Onychocryptosis**

(l) Onychoptosis   **(m) Onycholysis**   **(n) Koilonychia (front and side view)**   **(o) Onychogryphosis**

Figure 23.10 *Nail disorders*

Psoriasis

Although not an infectious condition, psoriasis has different degrees of severity and, as well as affecting the skin, it can affect the nails. The mildest form it takes is when it just causes a pitting of the nail plate. The next stage is when it causes a separation of the nail from the nail bed and there is a noticeable discoloration in the area. The most severe form causes thickening of the nail plate which at first becomes opaque and then turns yellowish brown in colour and the surface can become rough and atrophied.

Lamella dystrophy

This is a very common nail disorder with many causes. It is characterised by flaking, peeling and breaking of the nail plate and it can affect one or all of the nails. The causes are:

* nail disease
* exposure to harsh detergents or chemicals
* dietary deficiency
* overuse of caustic nail products, e.g. nail enamel remover and cuticle remover
* overuse of false or acrylic nails
* general ill health
* having the hands immersed in water for long periods
* incorrect filing
* incorrect buffing – produces heat and dries out the nail plate
* a hereditary factor
* the habit of nail biting
* wearing nail enamel for long periods of time
* using the nails as a tool
* poor circulation
* neglect.

In the majority of cases this condition is easily treated by the therapist with regular manicures, moisturising treatments and providing the client with good home care advice.

Blue nails

This is a characteristic of poor circulation, but in some cases may be attributed to a heart disorder.

Black/blue spots

These spots appear on the nail plate and are normally caused by injury to the nail bed which produces bleeding. The mark will disappear as the nail grows. Treatment should be gentle, avoiding pressure. When the nail suffers a severe blow from a heavy object it may turn completely blue and usually falls off. It will be replaced by a new nail in due course, unless the matrix has been damaged.

Splinter haemorrhages are caused by a disruption of blood vessels in the nail bed causing fine splinter-like vertical lines to appear under the nail plate. They are usually caused by injury to the nail, certain drugs and some types of heart disease. They usually get better of their own accord.

Contraindications to manicure

It is highly unlikely that clients will request a manicure if they have any condition that would contraindicate treatment. However, they may be unaware that a problem exists so it is left to the therapist to recognise any possible contraindication. In the case of a client wearing nail enamel, it may not be evident that there is a nail disorder until the nail enamel has been removed.

Any skin disease which affects the hands or nails would be a contraindication to manicure (see Chapter 3 Contraindications).

Tinea unguium, or ringworm, of the nail is highly contagious. It usually spreads from the free edge (the top of the nail) to the matrix (the root of the nail) and is caused by a fungus which can be of human or animal origin. The nail plate becomes discoloured and opaque with a rough horny appearance.

Scabies, bruising, new scar tissue, undiagnosed lumps and bumps would also contraindicate treatment.

Skin disorders such as eczema, psoriasis or dermatitis are contraindicated only when the condition is at its worst and it may cause the client discomfort. Mild cases of eczema and psoriasis generally benefit from manicures, especially if they include a special moisturising treatment.

Natural nail cultivation

There has been a revolution in nail care in recent years, with many therapists questioning the practices employed in caring for their clients' nails. Many of their clients were having regular manicures, quite often once a week, and yet a common complaint was that their nails did not appear to be growing. In response, many therapists are now employing different methods, following different procedures and eliminating harmful products to ensure the client is satisfied and the end result of regular manicures is strong, healthy nails.

Manicure has now become more of a treatment and more thought has gone into the development of products used, the practical procedures followed and in treating each client individually.

Principles of natural nail cultivation

* Treat clients as individuals and analyse their nail type accurately.
* Assess the condition of their hands and nails and devise a treatment plan.
* Choose the most appropriate products for the nail type.
* Use techniques which are not damaging to the nail.
* Advise clients on a good home care routine.
* Regularly review the nail condition.

Nail types

The nails are made up of the protein keratin, just as the skin and hair are. Therapists are accustomed to analysing skin types and using the appropriate treatment products and hairdressers are accustomed to analysing their clients' hair type and recommending the appropriate treatment products. It is a natural step, therefore, for therapists to analyse clients' nail type before carrying out any treatment.

There are five different nail types:

* dry
* brittle
* dehydrated/ageing
* normal
* damaged.

Characteristics of nail types

Dry nails

Figure 23.11 *Characteristics of dry nails*

The dry nail type is one of the most common and a large proportion of clients will have this condition. The causes are many:

* The hands may be exposed to detergents and chemicals. These may include washing and cleaning products, some of which are very harsh, hair treatment products, chlorine in the swimming pool or products which have to be used in a normal day at work or home.
* Cold weather conditions which will dehydrate the skin and nails if they are not well protected.
* Dietary deficiency, in particular a lack of fats, contributes to dry nails. Many clients will be

following a no-fat or low-fat diet to help them lose weight. Low levels of fat in the diet cause a dry skin condition and the nails will also be affected as they require a certain amount of fat for the layers of the nail plate to bond together. The small amount of fat which is obtained from natural sources will be required by the body for the essential functions, e.g. the uptake of fat-soluble vitamins.

* Illness from a common cold through to more serious conditions will affect the nails and cause a dry flaky condition.
* Overusing nail enamel remover, particularly one which contains acetone will dry out the nail plate, causing it to flake and peel.
* Excessive or over zealous buffing will contribute to a dry nail condition as the friction which occurs when buffing produces heat, which will dehydrate the nail and cause it to flake even more and the nail plate to become thinner and weaker.
* The client's occupation may mean that he or she has to perform some sort of task which will cause the nails to dry out or use products which will have the same effect.

Brittle nails

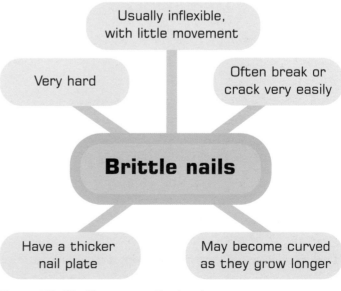

Figure 23.12 *Characteristics of brittle nails*

The causes of this nail type include the following:

* Age, because of the natural moisture loss which occurs as we get older causing the nails to become inflexible.
* Overuse of nail enamel remover which strips the nail plate of natural moisture affecting flexibility.
* Overuse of nail strengtheners. A nail strengthener is a product which contains ingredients to make the nails hard. Therefore, when used regularly it will achieve this result. However, once this has been achieved, if the strengthener is used continuously, the nails will become so hard that they become brittle.
* Poor diet, particularly a lack of fats which are necessary to maintain flexibility and to prevent breakage.

Dehydrated nails

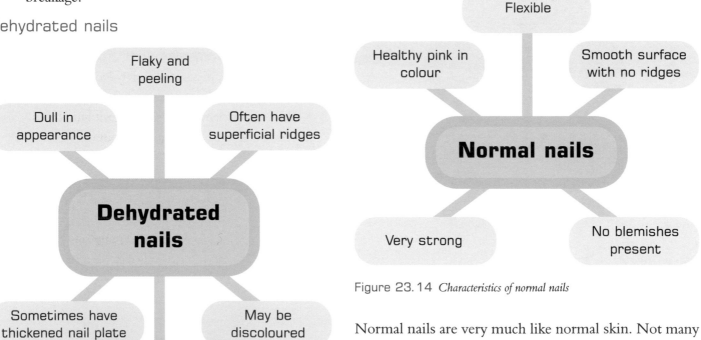

Figure 23.13 *Characteristics of dehydrated nails*

These nails are often a combination of dry and brittle, but the condition is more extreme. The external causes will be similar to those of the dry and brittle nail types, but there are other causes which are more age-related,

so this nail type is more common to the older, more mature client:

* Cell renewal slows down as we age and old cells are not shed so rapidly, causing a thickening of the nail and a dull finish.
* Circulation slows down as we age so nutrients and oxygen will not be so readily available to feed and generate the new cells.
* The menopause will often have an adverse effect on the nails because of the fluctuation in hormone levels and stress.
* Causes of the dry and brittle nail types will also apply.

Normal nails

Figure 23.14 *Characteristics of normal nails*

Normal nails are very much like normal skin. Not many people have normal nails as there are many external factors which act to prevent nails remaining in a normal condition. If a client has normal nails, it is often pure luck, hereditary or because the client works very hard to maintain them. The reasons for normal nails are as follows:

* The client has inherited good healthy nails.
* The client is probably eating a very healthy and well-balanced diet with all the necessary vitamins, minerals, nutrients and fat required for healthy nail growth.

* The nails are very well cared for, well-moisturised and manicured.
* The client may be in an occupation which requires constant movement of the hands, stimulating circulation and promoting healthy growth.

Damaged nails

Figure 23.15 *Characteristics of damaged nails*

One of the reasons why the popularity of natural nail cultivation has increased in the last few years is because of the rise in the number of clients with damaged nails.

There are several causes:

* The poor techniques used in the application of nail extensions.
* Over zealous buffing.
* Consistent nail biting over a long period of time.
* Systemic illness.
* After a major operation.
* Prolonged medication.

Quite often, the last three causes are inextricably linked because someone who has a serious illness will probably be taking some form of medication and may require an operation. The body will use all its resources to aid recovery and the nails will be the last to receive all the necessary nourishment required for healthy growth.

Treating nail types

Table 23.1 identifies the aims of treating the various nail types.

Manicure techniques

Nails are prepared in the usual way by removing existing nail enamel and checking for contraindications. The order of work for the rest of the manicure is different for the reasons outlined below.

The hands and nails are moisturised at the beginning of the manicure to hydrate and nourish the nails, bonding the layers of the nail plate together. This will prevent flaking of the free edge when it is filed later. The cream used will have time to penetrate into the nail plate before enamelling, so removing the need to 'squeak' clean with nail enamel remover if the cream is used at the end of the manicure.

Oil and cream are used to help soften and shrink back the cuticle naturally. This removes the need to use

Table 23.1 *Aims of treating nail types*

Dry	Dehydrated	Brittle	Normal	Damaged
To replace lost moisture To bond the layers together To prevent flaking	To replace lost moisture To bond the layers together To prevent flaking	To replace lost moisture To promote flexibility To prevent breakage	To maintain healthy condition and pH balance	To provide strength To improve condition To replace lost moisture To promote growth

caustic cuticle removers which are harmful to the nails because of their bleaching and drying effects. The oil contains ingredients such as jojoba and vitamin E which have healing properties.

Cuticle knives and orange sticks are replaced by a cuticle care machine, which is far more gentle in effect and helps to remove dead skin adhering to the nail plate which will become hard, thickened cuticle if left unattended.

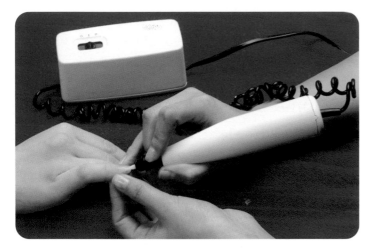

Figure 23.16 *A cuticle care machine*

Nails are degreased by using a wet brush or towel and not nail enamel remover which will strip the nails of oil and moisture.

Base coats, top coats and enamels are painted over and under the free edge to build up a protective covering on the whole nail.

Hand and nail treatments

There are occasions when the client will benefit from incorporating a special treatment into the manicure routine at the appropriate time. The most common treatments are:

* paraffin wax
* oil
* salt rub
* thermal mittens.

Paraffin wax

The aims of this treatment are:

* to nourish and moisturise the skin
* to improve a flaking nail condition
* to improve the skin colour
* to increase joint mobility.

The manicure should be performed in the usual manner and a rich nourishing cream applied after the cuticle work has been completed. The hand and arm should then be completely covered in the wax, heated to 48°C, either by immersing it in the wax or by painting the wax directly on to the hand and arm, building up several layers until the coating is quite thick. The whole area treated must then be wrapped in foil before being covered by towels. This maintains the heat for a short period allowing the treatment to take effect.

Encased in the warm paraffin wax the following actions occur:

* The circulation increases.
* Skin temperature rises.
* The pores open.
* Sebaceous gland activity increases.
* The activity of the sudoriferous glands also increases.

These actions result in:

* the absorption of the nourishing cream which has been applied
* an improvement in skin colour due to the increase in circulation
* a softening of the skin texture from the application of the cream and paraffin wax
* an increase in sebaceous gland activity
* a soothing effect on the joints due to the increased warmth in the area.

Oil

The aims of this treatment are:

* to moisturise dry cuticles
* to return lost moisture to flaking nails
* to soothe and moisturise a dry skin condition.

This treatment should also be carried out after the cuticle work has been completed and before the hand and arm massage. The oil used should be heated to a comfortable temperature and the nails or whole hands, depending upon the reason for the treatment, should be immersed in the warmed oil. They should be left to soak for 10–15 minutes and then the oil on the hands may be used to perform the massage. This treatment may be performed as often as required. The client may also be advised to follow the same routine at home until the condition has improved.

Figure 23.17
Thermal mittens

Salt rub

The aims of this treatment are:

* to improve skin colour
* to desquamate the dead skin cells
* to improve circulation
* to even out a fading suntan.

Once again, this treatment should be carried out after cuticle work and before the hand massage. The salt should be moistened with a small amount of water, the massage cream to be used or a moisturising lotion, and then rubbed well into the hands until there is a noticeable improvement in skin colour. This improvement is due to the increase in circulation.

The salt must then be rinsed off and after the therapist's hands have been dried, more hand cream should be applied and massaged well in. The actions on the skin are:

* stimulating
* nourishing
* refining.

Thermal mitten treatment

This special nourishing treatment combines heat and moisture to:

* nourish and hydrate the skin
* improve skin texture and colour
* add moisture to the nail plate, bonding the layers
* increase the circulation, bringing fresh nutrients
* increase lymph flow, removing waste products
* soothe aching joints and improve mobility.

The moisturising products are applied generously to the hands and nails that are wrapped in cling film and placed in a pair of lined thermal mittens. The mittens are thermostatically controlled so the temperature may be adjusted to suit the client.

Home care advice

To maintain healthy nails, clients must be responsible for their own nail care when they are not attending the salon for treatment. The condition of their nails will not improve if they do not attempt to remove the cause of their problems, so the advice given is very important.

* A well-balanced diet should be followed.
* The hands should be protected from detergents and household chemicals.
* Hand cream should be applied after immersing the hands in water, and last thing at night.
* The nails should not be used as tools.
* Metal files must never be used because they cause the nails to flake.
* An oily enamel remover should always be used to prevent too much moisture loss from the nail.
* A base coat should always be used to protect the nail.
* Nail hardeners should be used when the nails are weak.
* The nails should not be bitten and the cuticles should not be picked.
* Gloves should be worn in the winter to prevent chapping.

Pedicure

The feet take a lot of stress and strain every day and although they are not on show like the hands, the client will benefit greatly from pedicure treatment. Many clients will book a pedicure during the summer months because their feet are on display. However, feet need to be looked after all year round as most of the time they are enclosed in shoes and socks or tights, often becoming very hot and swollen because of the pressure put upon them. Although a pedicure is basically a manicure of the feet, it usually requires more time as there are a few differences in procedure.

It should be explained to the client that the therapist is not going to treat the feet in the same way as a chiropodist and such problems as ingrowing nails, corns, bunions and callouses should be treated by a chiropodist.

Equipment

The equipment used for a manicure is also required for a pedicure with the following additional pieces of equipment:

* a large bowl or foot spa in which to soak the feet
* a refreshing and cleansing foot soak
* nail clippers
* hoof stick
* an implement or cream for removing hard skin
* foot powder
* extra towels
* toe separators.

Preparation of the work area

The client should be seated in a comfortable position with the back well supported. Easily adjustable multi-position beauty couches are ideal, but if there is not one available or pedicures are carried out in a small area away from treatment cubicles, a comfortable chair with a back support must be used.

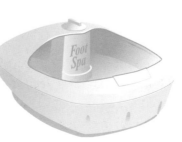

Figure 23.18 *A foot spa*

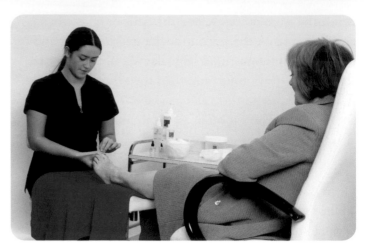

Figure 23.19 *Pedicure treatment*

A towel should be placed under the foot bowl in case of spillage and spare towels must be easily accessible to cover the client's foot which is not being worked upon, to keep it warm.

Pedicure techniques

Most clients who have a pedicure will come to the salon already having washed their feet, but the pedicure should begin by soaking the feet in warm water to which you have added an antiseptic or a refreshing foot soak such as peppermint.

Contraindications should be looked for before starting the treatment and if there are any signs of infection or abnormality, then the client should be advised to seek the advice of a doctor or a chiropodist.

Work should begin on one foot, keeping the other one well wrapped and warm.

Filing

After removing any enamel, the nails should be cut first with clippers to reduce the length and then filed straight across. The toe nails must not be shaped into the sides as this could cause ingrowing toe nails, a condition which can be very painful.

Hard skin removal

Hard skin tends to build up on the foot in those areas which receive the greatest pressure – the balls of the feet and the heels. The hard skin may be removed after the filing has been completed using the implement for hard skin removal. Alternatively, a cream specially formulated for hard skin removal can be massaged well into the problem areas. After applying cuticle massage cream to the cuticles, the foot may then be soaked in the warm water.

Cuticle work

The cuticles on the toes are often quite hard and thick unless the client has been having regular pedicures. The hoof stick, which is a rubber-tipped orange stick, is used to gently push back the cuticles and any tissue adhering to the nail plate can be removed with the cuticle knife and nippers. Care should be taken not to tear the cuticle leaving it open to infection.

Leg massage

It is very soothing and relaxing for the client to have a leg massage to the knee, as well as massage to the foot. The leg must be well supported making sure the knee joint is not hypo-extended.

Oil, body lotion or massage cream may be used as appropriate. Foot or talcum powder could be applied after the massage to absorb any excess cream or oil and allow the client to feel comfortable in shoes after the pedicure. Talcum powder will also keep the client's feet fresh and dry in the summer.

Enamelling

The foot must be flat when enamelling the toe nails or the enamel tends to run down towards the cuticles giving an uneven application. Toe separators must be used so that the wet enamel on the toe does not touch the next one and smudge.

Contraindications

Any infectious diseases of the skin or nails would contraindicate pedicure treatment. One of the most common conditions found on the feet is tinea pedis, commonly known as athlete's foot. For information on this condition, see Chapter 3 Contraindications, page 23.

There are several conditions of the feet which do not contraindicate pedicure treatment by a beauty therapist, but for specific treatment of the condition itself, a chiropodist or doctor should be consulted.

Corns

These are thickened, dense areas of skin, forming a raised appearance and situated on pressure areas such as the toes. They are most commonly caused by ill-fitting shoes and if they become sore or painful, it is advisable to consult a chiropodist. Seed corns are usually found on the heel or under the arch of the foot and are given their name because they have a small nucleus, which resembles a millet seed. This type of corn is not usually painful.

Callus

This is a patch of hard, thickened skin which accumulates as a result of pressure on the foot and the most common sites are the heel and the ball of the foot.

Bunions

This is another condition which can be caused by wearing badly fitted shoes and is the result of displacing the toe joint. The toe may be forced into an unnatural position by pressure from ill-fitting shoes over a period of time. A lump then forms on the inside of the foot at the base of the big toe. At first the lump will be sore and tender but will begin to harden as the bone itself begins to grow into the deformed shape. Bunions are permanent and may only be removed surgically.

Chilblains

These are painful itchy areas on the feet, varying in colour from dull blue to red. The cause is an inadequate blood supply, but the condition is aggravated by cold and damp. Those more susceptible to the condition are the elderly and anyone who works in hot, cold or damp conditions. To cure the problem, the affected parts must be kept warm and dry and an ointment may be applied, which will act as a vasodilator, dilating the blood vessels and improving circulation.

Onychogryphosis/Onychocryptosis
See page 336.

Flat feet

This condition is due to partial or total collapse of one or both arches of the feet. It can be hereditary or may be caused by:

* weak muscles

* injury
* being very overweight
* ill-fitting shoes.

Correcting flat feet

* Keep the feet mobile by exercising them. A good strengthening exercise is to pick up a pencil or a marble with the toes and pass it from one foot to the other.
* One of the best exercises for the feet generally is to walk barefoot in the sand as this will tone every muscle and ligament.
* Walk around the home barefoot as often as possible.
* Lose weight if this is a contributory factor.
* Make sure that shoes fit correctly.

Hyperhidrosis

This term refers to the over activity of the sweat glands. This is a common foot problem and can lead to other conditions of the feet.

Nail art

This is an additional service that you can offer clients after they have had a manicure or even pedicure. Many salons are now offering some wonderful designs, which complement a tanned foot very well, and because the feet are usually exposed when we are on holiday it is the ideal opportunity to be adventurous.

The paint used is a water-based acrylic that comes in a variety of colours and the brushes are extremely fine in several shapes to create different effects. They can be made from bristle or nylon. Bristle is longer lasting but more expensive. In addition to colour, there are tiny coloured stones, rhinestones and glitter dust, a dense sparkly powder to help create the brighter designs. Transfers may also be used but have to be covered with a top coat, to seal them in place.

Nail jewellery can also be used as part of this service in the form of a small diamond or a charm. The charm has to be placed into a hole that is drilled in the nail, therefore it is used more extensively with false nail systems.

The airbrushing technique used to apply make-up and spray tan is also used to apply colour as part of the nail art service. Because air brushing cuts down the drying time of the polish, it is proving popular with clients who like a French manicure but do not like the length of time it takes to dry.

These methods are also employed in the world of fashion and for photographic work as well as for special occasions. Many different images can be created by a talented therapist from a perfect French to an avant-garde wacky design.

General foot care

* Because tight-fitting shoes are the cause of many foot problems, shoes should be purchased later in the day when the feet are at their largest as feet tend to swell slightly when they become warm.
* High heels are very bad for the posture as they throw the body out of alignment, so if they are worn often they will eventually contribute to a bad back.
* The same pair of shoes must not be worn constantly. It is better to alternate between different pairs.
* A stock of products specially for the feet should be kept, e.g. foot powders, anti-perspirant or foot refreshing spray, all designed to keep the foot healthy.
* Foot salts are a useful antidote to swollen and aching feet as they draw out moisture. Epsom salts or sea salt in lukewarm water can be used to soak the feet.
* Massage the feet often as this is very therapeutic, not just for the feet but for the whole body.

The application of different types of nail extension has become a popular treatment. There are many specialist therapists practising this art and there is a great demand for these skills in several areas – as part of an existing beauty or hair salon, in a spa or hotel, on a cruise ship, as a mobile technician, ownership of a specialist nail care business, working in the fashion and photographic industry, as a sales representative for a nail company or providing training in a particular nail system, either privately or in training establishments. The client may want this service for several reasons:

* to conceal broken or damaged nails
* to improve the appearance of very short nails
* to help overcome the habit of nail biting
* for special occasions
* to repair a single broken nail to match the others.

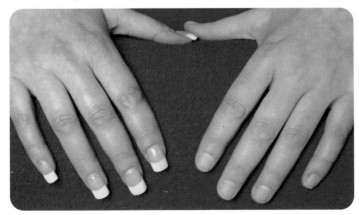

Figure 24.1 *Before and after nail extension treatment*

There are three different systems currently in use – acrylic, gel and fibreglass, and silk wrap. The system used will depend on the state of the client's nail plate and her occupation.

It may also be the personal choice of the therapist who may use one of the following categories:

* Sculptured – the use of liquid and powder or gel to create a tip over a nail form and then the application of an overlay.
* Tips and overlays – the use of tips and then overlaying them with acrylic, gel or fibreglass.
* Strengthening overlays – this is also known as a natural nail mend and is used to strengthen a weak nail or repair a split or broken nail.

A client with a good healthy nail plate could wear any system, but if she had a job that involved lots of manual work, for example working with horses, she would need a heavy-duty system such as acrylic overlay.

For a hairdresser, who often has her hands in water, or a professional swimmer, who is constantly immersed in water, it would be better to use fibreglass as this expands and contracts with wear.

Chemistry of artificial nails

The chemical process, which occurs when acrylic components (liquid and powder) cross link (mix and activate), is called **polymerisation**. This is when many small molecules, or **monomers**, join together to form large molecules, or **polymers**. The way in which this occurs is different in each particular system, but they all require an **initiator** to start the process by providing energy and a **catalyst** to control the subsequent speed of the cross linking process.

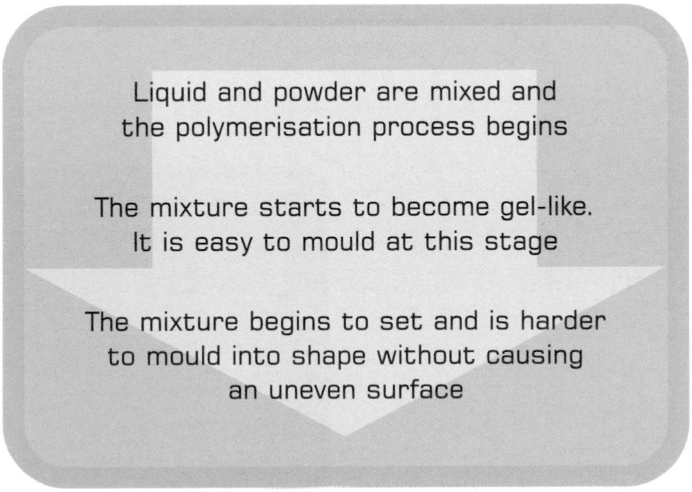

Liquid and powder are mixed and the polymerisation process begins

The mixture starts to become gel-like. It is easy to mould at this stage

The mixture begins to set and is harder to mould into shape without causing an uneven surface

Figure 24.2 *The polymerisation process*

Sculptured (liquid and powder)

This acrylic nail system is particularly strong and consists of a polymer powder (initiator) mixed with a monomer liquid (catalyst) to form a solid mass. The ratio of one to the other must be carefully controlled as too much liquid will result in the formation of a soft weak paste and too much powder will result in a very hard paste that may become brittle. This is why it is extremely important to follow the manufacturer's instructions. It is also important never to mix products from different brands as they may not be compatible.

Figure 24.3
Components of the sculptured acrylic system

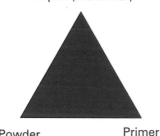

Liquid (Monomer)

Powder (Polymer)   Primer

The process works best at normal room temperature as too much heat speeds up the process and may cause a brittle nail with areas of weakness. Low temperatures slow down the process, causing the monomer, which is volatile, to evaporate leaving traces of the powder on the nail. This has the appearance of tiny crystal particles on the nail (crystalisation). The powders used come in different shades allowing the therapist to provide different effects such as a French manicure or to match the client's natural colouring. It provides a flexible and natural looking nail extension and is easy to use when correcting irregular shaped nails.

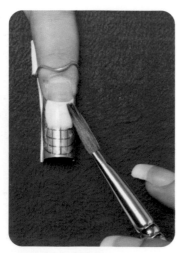

Figure 24.4 *Sculpting*

Sculptured (gel)

This acrylic nail system consists of a pre-mixed gel (initiator), which has to be 'cured' (set) by an ultraviolet (UV) lamp (catalyst). These lamps emit only UVA in very small quantities and this provides the energy required to start the polymerisation process and turn the semi-liquid gel into a solid. The gels that are available are normally of a thick **viscosity** (consistency) but do vary in their consistency and colour depending on the manufacturer. They are made from **oligomers** (short pre-joined chains of molecules, not long enough to be termed a polymer). Because UV gel is more sensitive to oxygen than other systems, polymerisation is completed and this leaves a slightly sticky residue on the surface which requires removal after curing.

Figure 24.5
Components of the sculptured gel system

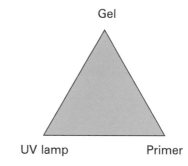

Gel

UV lamp   Primer

Tips

Tips are artificial nails made from plastic, nylon or acetate and are used to provide extra length to the natural nail. They come in many different shapes and sizes and are flexible and durable. Originally, tips were used to cover the whole nail, but they did not last very long and they had certain disadvantages in particular, becoming easily detached. The latest more natural looking tips are combined with a sculptured overlay or wrap which provides added strength and makes them an invaluable part of an effective false nail system.

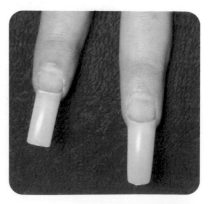

Figure 24.6 *A tip*

It is important to have a good selection of tips so that you can choose the most suitable shape and size for your client to create the most natural effect.

Strengthening overlays

These overlays, or wraps, are made from silk or fibreglass. Silk is strong, light in weight and made from a thin tightly woven natural material that becomes transparent when adhesive is applied, providing a smooth finish. Fibreglass, which is durable and stronger than silk, is also thin but loosely woven allowing adhesive to penetrate easily. Once the wrap is applied, it will be sprayed or brushed with an activator or accelerator (initiator), which quickly completes the hardening process. The wrap process consists of applying a resin to the nail and overlaying this with a mesh and then reapplying the resin in layers (approximately three). The activator must be used after the last application to tighten the chemical bonding and create a stronger nail.

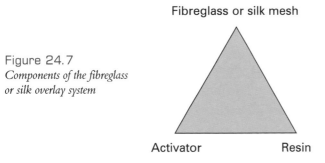

Figure 24.7
Components of the fibreglass or silk overlay system

Fibreglass or silk mesh

Activator **Resin**

Tools and equipment

Sculpting brush

The most important piece of equipment for the therapist is her sculpting brush. A sable brush is best when working with liquid and powder, but a synthetic nylon brush may be used with gel. The shape is dependent on personal choice – pointed, tapered or flat. You should choose the one most suited to your own technique.

The sable brush must be cleaned by using a monomer and then wiping carefully on a paper towel before storing in its own container to keep it clean and in good condition.

Sculpting forms

These are placed at the free edge to lengthen the natural nail and then removed when the application is complete. They come in different types of material such as metal, plastic and Teflon-coated reusable forms and paper disposable forms. The metal forms may be reused as they can be sterilised between treatments but are not suitable when using sculpting gel and UV light as the metal will become hot. Plastic forms are also reusable and come in different shapes and sizes. The Teflon-coated forms are the most expensive, but they grip the sides of the finger well staying securely in place. Paper forms are most commonly used. They can be cut to fit the individual nail size and they are the easiest to use on toe nails. They have a sticky back, which adheres well to the finger.

Tip cutters and cuticle nippers

Tip cutters are specially adapted to cut the nail tip. They have a curved hole through which the tip fits for cutting; the blade is fitted to the top side to prevent cutting the client's finger.

Cuticle nippers are used for removing hangnails and frayed cuticle only. They will become blunt if used for any other purpose.

Cuticle pushers, files and buffers

Cuticle pushers may come in the form of a wooden cuticle stick that should be disposed of after each use, a plastic hoof stick or metal pusher, both of which may be reused after sterilising correctly.

Files are abrasive and used to shape the nail. Ideally, they should be disposable to prevent cross infection. A high grit nail file is much gentler in effect than a low grit nail file, so a 100 grit file will be used for shaping artificial nails. A 240 grit file will be used for removing the surface shine of the natural nail in preparation for the application of the artificial nail.

Buffers are used to gently smooth the area between the natural nail plate and the tip so there is no visible line and also to remove glue residue. Block buffers may be used with cuticle oil to create a shine on the new nail extension. Graduated buffers have several working sides with varying degrees of abrasion.

Covered dappen dishes

These may be used to decant small amounts of monomer required for each treatment. They are small, flat-bottomed dishes with a lid that provide a stable container and reduce the evaporation of the volatile liquid.

Consumables and disposables

These are products that are used only once for each client and they include cotton wool, tissues, paper towels, lint-free pads and wooden orange sticks.

UV lamp

This emits UVA light through small tubes that vary between 5 and 9 watts. The emission is not harmful to the skin and is used to cure the gel used in the gel system of false nail application. Care must be taken by the therapist to apply only the required amount of gel and ensure that the nails are exposed for the recommended amount of time in order to make sure that the polymerisation process is complete. In the case of sculptured gel nails, the hands must be turned during this process to ensure that the underside of the nails are cured.

Scissors

Scissors may be used to cut and shape the tips to suit the client. They may also be used to trim silk and fibreglass to the required size in which case they must be kept specifically for this purpose or they may become blunt and ineffective.

Clean towels

These are required for each client and must be washed at 60°C to remove all accumulated dust attracted by the deep pile and ensure they are sterilised.

Personal protective equipment (PPE)

PPE may be required to prevent inhalation and absorption of products that will cause irritation, sensitivity or allergic response.

When filing, particularly when using a drill, dust is caused which may be inhaled. To prevent this, a dust mask may be worn.

Use sterile coverings for any cuts or abrasions in the client's or therapist's skin before treatment is carried out to prevent products from entering the skin and causing irritation.

The therapist may wear rubber or latex gloves to prevent absorption and sensitisation when applying nail extensions or when decanting chemicals. Safety glasses should also be worn when decanting to prevent splashing chemicals into the eye and during treatment to prevent vapours irritating the eyes.

Health and safety

It is important to ensure the health and safety of the client, the therapist and any other person who may be near the working area. The working environment can in some cases be quite small and the products used can cause sensitisation or allergy if not used correctly. The main risks from the products are:

* inhaling vapours and dust through the nose and mouth
* absorbing chemicals through the skin and eyes
* ingesting chemicals through the mouth.

The environment

Because many of the products used produce vapours (molecules of the chemicals used), they will accumulate in the working area and need to be removed through adequate ventilation so that they are not inhaled by anyone nearby. The local Health & Safety Executive will advise on the necessary requirements for the size of the business and the number of nail work stations in use.

All employees should follow a safe system of work, which should be devised by an expert after analysing the hazards and risks involved in using false nail systems. There are certain rules to follow that will reduce the amount of vapour produced:

* Follow manufacturers' instructions regarding the safe use, handling and storing of products.
* Replace the tops and lids of products in use.
* Use covers on bowls that contain volatile products.
* When using sprays use sparingly and at the correct angle to prevent inhalation.
* Place all waste immediately into a metal, covered waste bin.
* Chemical spillage must be wiped up immediately with absorbent paper and discarded in a large covered bin outside the salon.

* Any product left over must be discarded by soaking in absorbent paper and disposing of safely.
* Large quantities of any hazardous substance should be disposed of by the local authority or private waste disposal company.
* Ensure that the ventilation system is working effectively.

Figure 24.8
Nail treatment in progress

The salon should be maintained at a reasonable temperature. Extreme heat will have an evaporating effect on volatile products causing a higher concentration of them in the working environment. It may also affect the products used making them difficult to work with.

The work station

A comfortable nail workstation should be chosen to allow sufficient room for the therapist to work without stretching too far or having to bend her neck in an unnatural position. It should have several drawers with the capacity to hold all the equipment and products required and an easy-to-clean work top. Desks are available with built-in extractor fans to remove vapours from the area.

The therapist's chair must be at the correct height and with sufficient back support to provide a comfortable working position. The client will be sitting in one position for some time so it is important to ensure that she is also comfortable. Supply her with a padded seat with back support at the correct height to allow her to place her arms in a relaxed position on the work surface during treatment. The position of the client's chair should be straight in front of (immediately opposite) the therapist and not at an angle as this could lead to problems with applying the false nail in the correct place and cause discomfort.

The lighting should ideally be natural daylight, but an additional magnifying lamp may be used as this will help to provide additional light and enable the therapist to identify irregularities in the nails before and after treatment.

Contra-actions

Allergic reactions

Allergic reactions may occur to the therapist or client, particularly when they are overexposed to certain chemicals or other irritating substances. An allergic response may be evident when there is an itching or reddening of the area or if the skin, nails or cuticles feel very sore or sensitive. The only course to take is to discontinue using the product which is responsible or to have a break from wearing nail extensions until the problem subsides. The therapist will need to wear protective gloves and ensure that all health and safety procedures are followed and the techniques used reduce the risk of overexposure.

Overexposure through inhalation

Overexposure through inhalation may cause headaches, dizziness, nausea and an irritating cough. It is important, therefore, to provide efficient ventilation. If the person affected needs fresh air, then move her to a comfortable position elsewhere to recover.

Bacterial infection

This may occur either between the natural nail plate and the artificial nail or between the nail plate and nail bed. It may look like a dark stain often with a green hue and it is a by-product of an infection such as that caused by the pseudomonas bacteria, which thrive in moist places where there is dead tissue to feed on. The discoloration becomes darker and penetrates deeper the longer the infection has been present and it can lead to lifting of the natural nail plate away from the nail bed.

Bacterial infection may be caused when there is a gap between the two surfaces or a break in the nail extension or if an air bubble has been created when the loose nail is glued back creating an environment, which is warm, dark and damp. By following the correct health and safety procedures, offering aftercare advice and using the utmost care when applying and maintaining nail extensions, the therapist can prevent bacterial infection occurring. (See Fungal infections below for advice.)

Fungal infections

Fungal infections thrive in an atmosphere of warmth, moisture and darkness. When the artificial nail is applied the natural moisture in the nail bed can no longer evaporate through the natural nail plate, and if the body temperature is sufficiently high and fungal spores are present, then the environment is ideal for their growth.

Fungal infection often starts at the hyponychium (the area which attaches the nail plate to the nail bed) if it is damaged, so allowing entry to fungal spores. Fungus may cause damage to the nail plate, nail bed and matrix if it is left untreated and in some cases can lift the nail plate completely away from the nail bed. To avoid infection:

* make sure equipment and tools are sterilised before each client
* sterilise the nail plate before, during and after application
* make sure that the extension is tapered and at the cuticle area and at the nail groove
* ask the client to return for infills every two weeks
* ask the client to inform you immediately if she notices any discoloration.

Do not diagnose the condition but always advise the client to consult her doctor for treatment if you suspect there is a bacterial or fungal infection present.

Onycholysis

This occurs when the nail plate begins to separate from the nail bed. It appears as a larger white area at the free edge. This may be caused by bacterial or fungal infection or an allergic reaction to a particular product, in some cases trauma to the hyponychium. Nail extensions should be removed and nails trimmed to prevent them catching.

Premature loss of the nail extension

Premature loss of the extension may occur because the preparation of the natural nail was insufficient and oil or water was left on the nail plate, the nail extension was too long or the products used to make the artificial nail were not compatible and therefore ineffective.

Breaking, splitting and thinning of the natural nail

These may be caused by over buffing when preparing the natural nail, over blending the tip to the natural nail or the client removing the extensions incorrectly. A split right across the nail plate could be a result of an unbalanced nail caused by the client failing to return for an infill appointment.

Softening of the natural nail

Softening may be caused by the nail plate being over filed, over primed, not dehydrated sufficiently before the product is applied or moisture trapped between the natural nail and nail extension.

Breaking or splitting of the nail extension

If there is a vertical split in the nail tip, this may be caused by the therapist using inferior tips, over filing a tip or using a tip shape that is not compatible with the client's own nail shape. The product applied over the tip may be insufficient or the client may have been biting the extension. When this occurs it cannot be repaired and the tip should be removed and replaced.

If the nail extension is splitting and coming away from the side walls, it may be caused by insufficient product being used or too much product which has seeped on to the surrounding skin. It may be a result of the area of the nail not being prepared in the correct manner, either not dehydrated or buffed to remove surface shine.

Yellowing of natural nail or nail extension

Yellowing may occur if the client is a regular user of sun beds, particularly with the acrylic system. If the nail looks yellow on application, then it may indicate that the product has been contaminated.

Contraindications

* Nail separation.
* Skin conditions such as eczema and psoriasis.
* Severely bitten nails.
* Severely damaged nails.
* Nail disease.
* Skin disease.
* Broken bones.
* Cuts or abrasions.

It may be necessary to refer the client to her doctor if you suspect a contraindication is present that she may not be aware of. Explain tactfully that treatment may not be carried out without making a diagnosis. Do not alarm the client but explain that it is in her best interest to seek medical advice.

If the client's hands and nails are in a poor condition – dry skin, split cuticles, weak, brittle or ridged nails – offer her advice and a manicure to improve the condition of her natural nails before you apply the artificial nails.

To keep the nails in good condition and to prevent problems occurring, you will need to provide the client with good advice on care and maintenance:

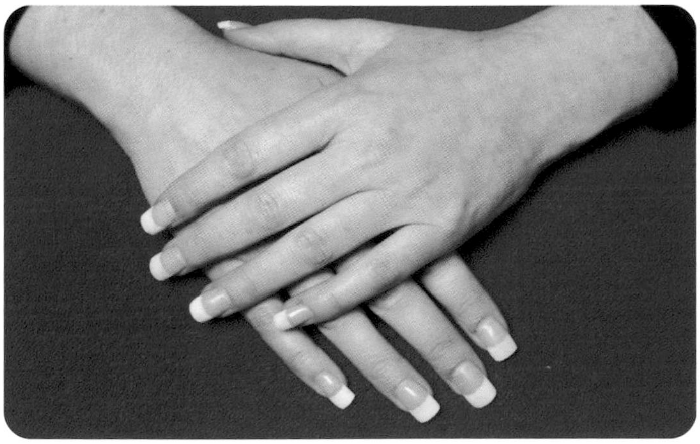

Aftercare advice

* Contact the therapist immediately if there are any problems with the artificial nails.
* When removing or changing nail enamel use an acetone-free product.
* Always use a base coat under the coloured enamel to prevent staining.
* Always apply a top coat over the coloured enamel to maintain the finished result.
* Avoid using bleach or strong detergents and household cleaners.
* Use cotton-lined rubber gloves when gardening or doing housework.
* Have regular appointments for infills and corrections.
* Apply hand and cuticle cream daily.

Figure 24.9 *The finished result*

Anatomy and physiology

* Cell tissues and the skin
* The skeletal system
* The muscular system
* The cardiovascular system
* The lymphatic system
* The respiratory system
* The digestive system
* The urinary system
* The nervous system
* The endocrine system
* The reproductive system
* The special senses

Introduction

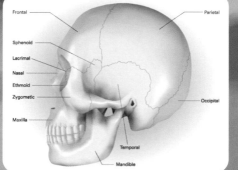

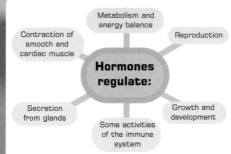

A thorough understanding of the anatomy and physiology of the body is essential to the beauty therapist no matter what course you are undertaking. It is important to understand the different systems and how they work with each other to maintain a healthy body. When applying treatments you must be aware of the body structure, the functions of each system and the problems that can occur. The therapeutic treatments all have an effect on the client's health and well-being and these effects are related to the anatomy and physiology of the body.

The effects may be:

* **physical** – those that you can see on the surface of the body and also what the client can feel during treatment

* **physiological** – those that occur inside the body when any of the systems are stimulated

* **psychological** – those that affect the mind and emotions of the client.

Understanding anatomy and physiology will also assist

you in preparing effective treatment plans to suit each individual client and help you to recognise how and when treatment must be adapted for particular physiological conditions. The more you learn about the human body, the more in tune you can become with your client so providing a highly professional service.

This section covers all systems of the body.

What are anatomy and physiology?

Anatomy is the science of the structure of the body. **Physiology** is the science of the normal function of the body. It is essential to have a thorough knowledge of anatomy and physiology for all face and body beauty treatments when analysis of the skin and body is so important in planning the correct treatments for your client.

Homeostasis

Homeostasis is the condition in which the body's internal environment remains relatively constant, within certain limits. In simple terms, the body is balanced and all systems are working effectively.

Homeo means same.

Stasis means standing still.

Homeostasis is disturbed by stress which creates an imbalance in the internal environment of the body. Stress comes from different sources:

* External, e.g. excessive heat or cold, lack of oxygen or persistent loud noise.
* Internal, e.g. high blood pressure, pain, anxiety, fear or bereavement.

Severe stress may be caused by such things as surgical operations, systemic illness, poisoning, accidents or prolonged overworking, fear and anxiety. The body is normally able to cope with these problems and helps itself to re-balance internally. These coping mechanisms are called homeostatic functions, keeping the internal environment of the body within normal limits.

Below are examples of homeostatic functions:

* The cardiovascular system keeps fluids constantly moving, changing pace to cope with activity and bringing the increased amounts of nutrients required for the body to cope with the increase in activity.
* The respiratory system works faster during increased activity to prevent oxygen falling below normal limits and to prevent excessive amounts of carbon dioxide from accumulating.
* The nervous system regulates homeostasis by detecting when the body is moving away from its balanced state. It then sends messages to the organs concerned to counteract the problem.

Homeostasis of blood pressure

If the heartbeat speeds up due to physical or mental stress, the following occurs:

More blood is pushed into the arteries.

Blood pressure is increased.

Nerve cells in the walls of some arteries detect the change.

Nerve impulses are sent to the brain.

The brain responds by sending messages to the heart to slow down.

Blood pressure is decreased. Homeostasis is maintained.

Homeostasis of blood sugar

Hormones are responsible for maintaining homeostasis of blood sugar levels:

Glucose, a principal source of energy, is found in blood.

Sugar levels are maintained by insulin and glucagon secreted by the pancreas.

After eating food high in sugar, it is digested and enters the blood.

Stress is caused because the blood sugar level is raised above normal.

In response the pancreas secretes insulin.

In the blood insulin increases sugar uptake by cells.

Blood sugar levels are lowered.

Insulin also accelerates the process by which sugar is stored in the liver and muscles.

More sugar is removed from the blood. Homeostasis is maintained.

Cells

A cell may be defined as 'the basic, living, structural and functional unit of the body and all other organisms'. The human body is composed of millions of cells that differ in size, shape, structure and function. Each cell is made up of many parts, which are called organelles (small organs). It is in these parts that chemical reactions take place contributing to the living processes in the cell.

Despite their differences, all body cells have some common characteristics:

* They have the ability to absorb nutrients, which may then be used for growth and repair.
* They have the ability to utilise oxygen and nutrients to release heat and energy and, as a result, produce carbon dioxide and water.
* They have the ability to increase in size and multiply in number.
* They have the ability to respond to environmental change such as light and temperature.

Cell structure

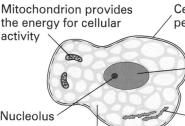

Mitochondrion provides the energy for cellular activity

Cell membrane – a selectively permeable barrier

Nucleus contains genetic material DNA in chromosomes. It controls the cell's functions

Nucleolus

Ribosomes make proteins for the cell

Cytoplasm contains nutrients necessary for growth, reproduction and repair.

Figure 25.1 *The structure of a cell*

Cells contain protoplasm, a colourless jelly-like substance, enclosed by a cell membrane, which is semi-permeable, allowing soluble substances to enter or leave the cell. Each cell contains a nucleus or dense mass of protoplasm in the centre, which is important for cell reproduction, and is surrounded by its own nuclear membrane. The nucleus is surrounded by cytoplasm, which contains the nutrients necessary for growth and repair.

The mitochondria in the cell provides the energy required by the cell for its activities. Cellular respiration takes place. This is when the cell takes up oxygen that we breathe in and glucose (produced by the digestion of the food we have eaten) which are then converted to carbon dioxide and water in a chemical reaction that gives off energy, that is:

> Glucose + oxygen → carbon dioxide + water + energy

Mitosis

Mitosis is the process of cell division or reproduction which, after a series of changes within the cell, produces two new identical cells. This occurs in human tissue, including the hair and skin. Groups of similar cells form body tissues, which have specific functions and they may be classified as:

* epithelial
* connective
* nerve
* muscular
* blood.

> When cells in some areas of the body duplicate without control, the excess tissue that develops is called a tumour. Tumours may be harmless (benign) but in some cases can be fatal (malignant).

Epithelial tissue

This tissue provides a protective covering for surfaces inside and outside the body. The skin, the lining of the heart, blood and lymphatic vessels and the digestive and respiratory organs are all made up of epithelial tissue. The skin is made up of stratified epithelium, which means it has many layers.

Epithelial tissue may be:

* **simple** – single layer of cells
* **compound** – several layers of cells.

Classification of simple epithelium

Squamous

These cells fit closely together like flat stones and provide a smooth lining for the heart, blood and lymph vessels and the alveoli in the lungs. They are found in areas of the body which have little wear and tear.

Cuboidal

These cube-shaped cells lying on a basement membrane are actively involved in secretion and absorption. They are found in the tubules of the kidney and some glands.

Columnar

Rectangular in shape on a basement membrane with a nucleus near its base, columnar cells are found lining the ducts of glands, the gall bladder, and the organs of the alimentary tract, where some cells secrete mucus and others absorb the products of digestion.

Ciliated

These are columnar cells with fine hair-like processes on their free surface. They are found on wet surfaces. The hairs are called cilia and their function is to move the contents of the tubes they line in one direction only. They are found in respiratory passages and uterine tubes.

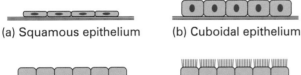

(a) Squamous epithelium   (b) Cuboidal epithelium

(c) Columnar epithelium   (d) Ciliated columnar epithelium

Figure 25.2 *Simple epithelium tissue*

Classification of compound epithelium

Stratified

Composed of at least two layers of cells, stratified epithelium is durable and protects underlying structures. In the more superficial layers the cells are flat, but in the deeper layers the cells are cuboidal or columnar. The basal cells are continually multiplying, producing new cells which flatten the cells above, pushing them outwards. These cells may be:

* **keratinised** – found on dry surfaces such as skin, nails and hair, providing protection to and preventing drying out of the underlying cells
* **non-keratinised** – found on wet surfaces that may be subjected to wear and tear such as the lining of the mouth, the oesophagus and the conjunctiva of the eyes.

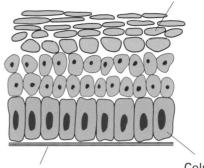

Squamous cells

Basement membrane

Columnar basal cells

(a) Stratified epithelium

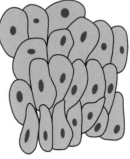

(b) Transitional epithelium

Figure 25.3 *Stratified and transitional epithelium*

Transitional

Transitional epithelium is similar to non-keratinised epithelium, but the cells in the outer layer tend to be large and rounded rather than flat. This type of epithelium lines hollow structures that are subjected to expansion from within, for example the urinary bladder. The function of these cells is to prevent rupture of the organ.

Connective tissue

Connective tissue takes various forms and provides support for, and protects and binds together, other body tissues. It includes bone, cartilage and adipose tissue.

Collagen is a fibrous connective tissue which is non-elastic and found in bundles throughout many organs and other structures. It is important in the subcutaneous layer of the skin as it provides support which, when broken down, contributes to the wrinkling which occurs, particularly after exposure to ultraviolet radiation.

Also present in the subcutaneous layer of the skin is **elastic fibrous connective tissue**. These fibres help to maintain the elasticity of the skin and provide support helping to maintain a youthful skin. With age and exposure to the environment, these fibres become less effective so contributing to the formation of wrinkles.

Cells of connective tissue are:

* **fibroblasts** – large flat cells which form collagen and elastin and help with tissue repair
* **macrophages** – irregular in shape, they engulf bacteria by the process of phagocytosis, thus defending the body from bacterial invasion
* **plasma** – developed from B lymphocytes, they give rise to antibodies providing a defence mechanism in the blood
* **mast** – similar to basophil leucocytes, they are found in abundance along the blood vessels; they produce heparin, an anticoagulant which helps the passage of protective substances from the blood to the affected tissues and histamine, released when cells are damaged
* **melanocytes and fat cells** – also present in loose connective tissue.

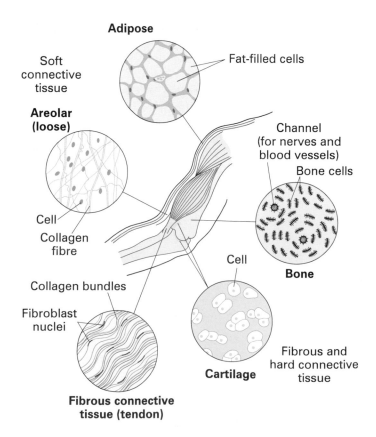

Figure 25.4 *Connective tissue*

Cartilage

This is much firmer tissue capable of enduring a lot more stress than other connective tissue. It has no blood vessels or nerves and it is a dense network of collagen and elastin fibres surrounded by the perichondrium. There are three kinds of cartilage:

* Hyaline cartilage has a bluish white tinge and is found at joints or over the end of long bones and forming the nose, larynx, trachea, bronchi and bronchial tubes. It provides support and flexibility.
* White fibrocartilage is found in the discs between the vertebrae (intervertebral discs). It provides strength and rigidity. It is also found between the articulating surfaces of the bones that form the knee joint and the sockets of the hip and shoulder joints.
* Elastic cartilage consists of yellow elastic fibres. It provides strength and maintains the shape of certain organs, the pinna (the earlobe), the larynx and the auditory tubes connecting the middle ear and the upper throat.

Membranes

A membrane is a thin flexible sheet of tissue composed of an epithelial layer and an underlying connective tissue layer. Membranes cover or line organs and cavities of the body and may be classified as mucous, serous and synovial.

Mucous membrane

Mucous membrane lines body cavities that open directly to the exterior, the entire digestive, respiratory, excretory and reproductive tracts. The epithelial layer secretes mucus that prevents the cavities from drying out, it traps dust in repiratory passageways, lubricates food as it moves throught the digestive tract and secretes digestive enzymes. The connective tissue layer binds the epithelium to the underlying structures while still allowing flexibility. It also holds blood vessels in place and protects underlying muscles and enables the epithelium tissue to receive nourishment and remove waste.

Serous membrane,

This membrane lines a body cavity that does not open to the exterior and covers the organs that lie within the cavity. Three important serous membranes are:

* the pleura which lines the thoracic cavity and covers the lungs
* the pericardium which covers the heart and lines the heart cavity
* the peritoneum which lines the abdominal cavity and covers the abdominal organs.

Synovial membranes

These membranes are composed of loose connective tissue with elastic fibres and they line the cavities of joints. They secrete synovial fluid, lubricating the ends of the bones as they articulate and nourishing the hyaline cartilage which covers the articular surfaces of the bones.

Nerve tissue

Nerve tissue is sensitive to stimulation, initiating a response to stimuli and carrying messages to and from the brain.

Muscular tissue

Muscular tissue provides the body with the power of movement as it is contractile tissue. There are three main types of muscle tissue:

* **Skeletal** – muscles under our conscious control.
* **Visceral** – involuntary muscle not under our conscious control.
* **Cardiac** – not under our conscious control. The heart muscle is responsible for the constant pumping action of the heart.

Blood

Blood is fluid connective tissue. Its cells circulate in blood vessels carrying food, waste products and hormones around the body.

Red blood cells – erythrocytes

These contain millions of molecules of a substance called haemoglobin. In the lungs oxygen breathed in combines with the haemoglobin and this gives the cells their bright red colour. This oxygenated blood is carried in the arteries to the tissues. Carbon dioxide and water, waste products of cellular activity, are carried from the tissues by the red blood cells to the lungs via the veins.

Red blood cells are manufactured in bone marrow and the body needs iron for their production. The body has the ability to control the number of red cells according to its needs, for example when there is a large blood loss the bone marrow immediately begins to increase red cell production.

White blood cells – leucocytes

These are larger than the red cells and they are irregular in shape. White blood cells are involved in the body's defence against disease. Some white blood cells are manufactured in the bone marrow and lymphocytes are formed in the spleen, tonsils and lymph glands. They are classified as polymorphs, lymphocytes and monocytes.

Polymorphs

There are three types of polymorphs:

* Neutrophils engulf and destroy bacteria.
* Eosinophils combat bacterial invasion and reduce the effects of histamine released into the tissue when antigens or foreign substances enter the body.
* Basophils are essential to life because they release a substance called heparin that works to stop the blood from clotting inside the vessels.

Lymphocytes

Lymphocytes make up about 25 per cent of the blood's white cells and they provide the body with its natural immunity to disease. They make antitoxins to combat the toxins or chemicals produced by some bacteria and antibodies to destroy antigens.

Monocytes

Monocytes form up to 8 per cent of the white cells. The larger monocytes engulf bacteria and also remove cell debris, which results from bacterial invasion.

* The activities of polymorphs and monocytes is called an inflammatory response.
* The activities of the lymphocytes is called an immune response.

Both these responses may be activated at the same time.

Inflammation is the body's response to injury or invasion at a local level.

Platelets or thrombocytes

Platelets are made in the bone marrow. They are the tiniest cells in the body (one millilitre of blood contains about 250 million platelets), disc-shaped and without a nucleus. Their function is to make blood clot when bleeding has to be stopped. When platelets come into contact with the damaged blood vessel they begin to enlarge, their shape becomes irregular and they become sticky, causing them to adhere to the collagen fibres. More platelets are produced and these stick to the existing platelets. This accumulation of platelets makes a **platelet plug** which will prevent blood loss from small wounds. The plug tightens and becomes more secure as it is reinforced by **fibrin** threads which are formed during the coagulation process.

The skin

The skin is the largest organ of the body. It provides a protective outer covering to the underlying structures and prevents the invasion of bacteria.

The structure of the skin

The skin has three main layers:

* the **epidermis** – the surface of the skin
* the **dermis** – supports the epidermis and provides contour and elasticity
* the **hypodermis**, also referred to as the **subcutaneous layer** – consists of adipose tissue containing fat cells, muscles and veins.

The epidermis

This is the most superficial layer of the skin, composed of stratified epithelium (layered cells). The thickness varies from one part of the body to another, the thinnest being on the eyelids and the thickest on the soles of the feet and the palms of the hands. This layer is free from nerve endings of pain but is extremely sensitive to touch. There are two distinct regions, which consist of five different layers:

The upper area where cells are changing from living to dead	} Stratum corneum Stratum lucidum Stratum granulosum
The active area of cell renewal	} Stratum spinosum Stratum germinativum

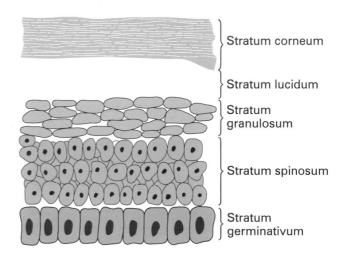

Figure 25.5 *The epidermis*

Cell renewal is the change of living cells containing a nucleus (the vital body in a cell, essential for its growth and reproduction) into dead, horny flat cells with no nucleus which are constantly shed from the surface of the skin.

Stratum germinativum – basal layer

This is the deepest layer of the epidermis. Its lower surface is attached to the dermis, from which it receives nutrient fluid from the blood vessels. It is in this layer that the development of new cells (mitosis) occurs. This leads to a gradual displacement of the older cells towards the surface.

Melanin-forming cells called **melanocytes** are formed in this layer. Melanin is the skin's natural protection against the harmful effects of ultraviolet light and is responsible for the change in skin colour when exposed to the sun.

Stratum spinosum – prickle cell layer

This consists of the cells immediately above the basal layer and includes langerhans cells, which set up an immune response to foreign bodies. Each cell connects with the next by means of fine threads or filaments through which they receive nourishment from the tissue fluid or protoplasm.

Towards the upper part of this layer, chemical changes take place and the keratinisation process begins.

> Keratinisation is the change of living cells containing a nucleus into layers of flat cells composed of the hard durable protein keratin.

Stratum granulosum – granular layer

The final stages of keratinisation take place in this layer. The cells become flattened and the nucleus begins to disintegrate. There is a loss of fluids which contributes to the transformation of cells into keratin, a tough fibrous protein.

Stratum lucidum – transparent layer

This is made up of small, tightly packed transparent cells with no nucleus. This layer is thought to be the barrier zone controlling the transmission of water through the skin. It lies between the outer horny layer and the inner granular layer. It is more evident in the thickest areas of skin, the soles of the feet and the palms of the hands.

Stratum corneum – horny layer

This consists of several layers of keratinised epithelial cells tightly packed together. As they contain the protein keratin they are very tough and horny and they have no nucleus. The superficial layers are constantly being shed and the cells beneath contain an epidermal fatty substance resembling bees' wax which keeps them waterproof and helps prevent the skin from cracking and becoming open to bacterial infection.

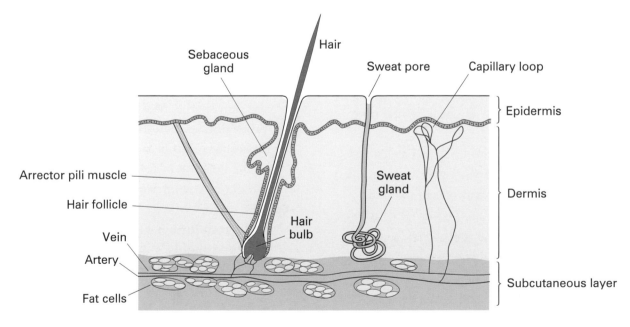

Figure 25.6 *The structure of skin*

The dermis

This is the chief supportive section of the visible surface skin or epidermis. It is composed of dense connective tissue which is tough, highly elastic and flexible, and it creates the strength, contour, elasticity and smoothness of the skin. The tissue is highly sensitive and fibrous, and comprises:

* **collagen** – provides support to the skin
* **elastin** – gives the skin its elasticity and resilience
* **fibroblast cells** – responsible for the manufacture of collagen and to a lesser degree elastin.

The dermis also contains:

* blood and lymph vessels
* nerve endings
* hair follicles
* sweat and sebaceous glands
* papillary muscles.

The dermis has a higher water content than any other region of the skin and it provides nourishment to the epidermis. It has two layers: the superficial papillary layer and the deep reticular layer.

The superficial papillary layer

This is irregular in shape with protrusions into the epidermis called papillae. There are several nerve endings in this layer including touch, which end in rounded bodies, and pain, cold and heat, which have delicate branched nerve endings.

Fine capillaries are found here, bringing oxygen and nourishment to the skin and carrying away waste products. This is a highly active and important area of the skin.

The deep reticular layer

This layer is situated below the papillary layer. The tough and elastic collagen fibres, interwoven with elastic fibres in this layer, are responsible for the elasticity and general tone of the skin. Sweat and sebaceous glands are present as well as the arrector pili muscles, small bundles of involuntary muscle fibres which are attached to the hair follicles and nerve endings of pressure.

There are many fine veins and arteries passing through this area which link up with the papillary capillaries. The lymph vessels also form a network through the dermis allowing the removal of waste from the skin.

The hypodermis – subcutaneous layer

This layer is an area for the formation and storage of fat. It is composed of the following:

* **Adipose tissue** – fibrous connective tissue containing fat cells. This is a major energy reserve and it supports and protects certain organs. Excess food is converted to fats and stored in these cells.
* **Areolar tissue** – loose connective tissue containing collagen, elastic and reticular fibres, which makes this layer elastic and flexible, binding the skin to underlying muscles. It is thicker in women than men, thus giving a more rounded appearance to their contours.

As fat is a poor conductor of heat, the hypodermis helps to reduce the loss of heat through the skin and so keep the body warm.

Functions of the skin

Protection

The skin performs many protective functions:

* It provides a protective cover for the underlying internal organs. The stratum corneum, as long as it remains intact, acts as a barrier against bacterial invasion. The sebum produced by the sebaceous glands has slight antiseptic properties and keeps the skin supple. Melanin is the skin's natural protection against ultraviolet light and the langerhans cells help the immune system respond to the invasion of foreign bodies by alerting the lymphocytes to neutralise the invaders.
* The sensory nerve endings in the skin prevent the body from further injury by reflex action to a painful stimulus.
* It is waterproof and prevents the absorption of water and the loss of essential body fluids.

Temperature control

Blood carries heat and the normal body temperature is 36.8°C. The centre for the regulation of heat and sweating is in the brain (the hypothalamus). The blood supply and the sweat glands of the skin mainly control loss of body heat.

A great deal of the body's heat is distributed by the circulatory system around the body. When the body temperature rises, the capillaries in the skin dilate and heat from the extra blood, which has been brought to the surface, is lost by:

* **radiation** (heat moves away from the body)
* **conduction** (clothing absorbs the heat)
* **convection** (cool air touches the body, heats and rises, and is replaced by more cool air).

When the body temperature lowers, the capillaries in the skin constrict and keep the heat within the body.

Evaporation of sweat from the skin's surface helps to regulate body temperature, because when the temperature rises, the sweat glands are sent a message by the brain and are stimulated to produce sweat which then evaporates on the skin's surface and cools the body.

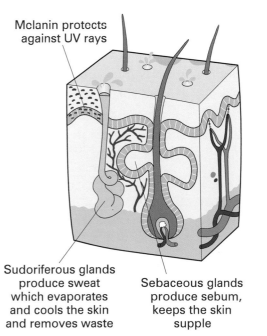

Figure 25.7 *Functions of the skin*

Sensation

The skin contains sensory nerve endings that when stimulated by external stimuli send messages to the brain which, in turn, responds via the motor nerves.

The nerve receptors are located at different levels in the skin and some messages are interpreted before

reaching the brain when reflex action occurs. The sensory nerve endings in the skin react to heat, cold, touch, pressure and pain.

Motor nerves supply the arrector pili muscle which is attached to the hair follicle and causes it to stand on end, and secretory nerve fibres innervate the sweat and oil glands of the skin.

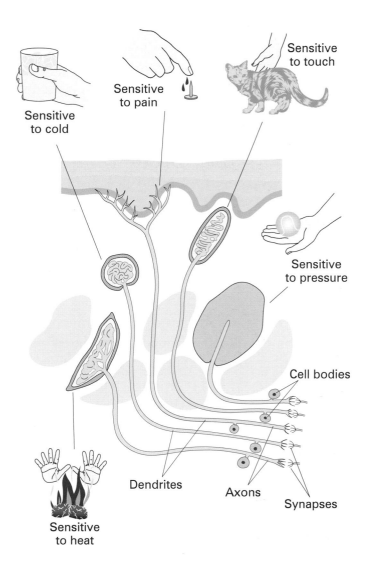

Figure 25.8 *Nerve receptors in the skin*

Absorption

Since the skin acts as a waterproof barrier, very little absorption takes place. The very superficial layers of the stratum corneum absorb small amounts of special conditioning creams used to improve very dry skin conditions. There is a passage via the hair follicles to some fatty substances and minute amounts of water may be absorbed over a large surface area.

Excretion and secretion

Perspiration is excreted by the sweat glands removing waste from the skin. Secretion is the production of sebum from the sebaceous glands and this is the skin's natural moisturiser which helps to keep it soft, supple and intact.

Vitamin production

Ultraviolet rays convert 7-dehydro-cholesterol found in sebum into vitamin D which is necessary for the absorption of calcium and phosphorous required by the body for healthy teeth and bones.

Appendages to the skin

The sebaceous glands

The sebaceous glands are situated in the dermis opening into the hair follicle and are found all over the body apart from the palms and soles. They are more numerous in the scalp and on the face particularly around the forehead, nose, cheeks and chin and they secrete sebum, which forms a protective oily film on the skin.

Sebum is the skin's natural moisturiser. It prevents hair from drying out, it also prevents excessive evaporation of water from the skin and inhibits the growth of certain bacteria. It can, however, attract dirt, trapping it on the skin and causing blackheads, papules and pustules to form.

In cases when too little sebum is produced, dry patches and irritation may occur. This condition is called **asteatosis**. When there is an overproduction of sebum and the skin takes on a very oily appearance, this condition is called **seborrhoea**.

The sebaceous glands are affected by the endocrine system and during puberty can become overactive. The male sex hormone **testosterone** causes the gland to enlarge. The female sex hormone **oestrogen** decreases the size of the gland.

The sudoriferous or sweat glands

These glands consist of a coiled base emanating from the deeper layers of the dermis, a tube-like duct which rises through the epidermis ending at the skin's surface to form a sweat pore.

There are two kinds of sweat glands:

* The **eccrine glands** are found all over the body except on the margins of the lip, the nail bed and the eardrum. They have a duct and a pore through which secretions are brought to the skin's surface and are most numerous on the palms of the hands and the soles of the feet.
* The **apocrine glands** are connected with hair follicles and are found chiefly in the underarm, breast and genital areas of the body. As well as water and salt, fatty substances are secreted from these glands and react with the air to cause body odour.

Disorders of the sudoriferous glands

* **Anhidrosis** – lack of perspiration, partially or complete.
* **Hyperhidrosis** – over secretion of perspiration, localised or general. Most affected are the axillae, palms of the hand and soles of the feet.
* **Bromhidrosis** – foul smelling perspiration caused by decomposition of retained sweat in covered areas of the body, an intake of strong smelling foods or a chronic bacterial infection of the sweat glands.
* **Miliaria rubra** – a prickly rash characterised by itching, small raised spots. It is caused by a blockage of the sweat ducts after exposure to a hot atmosphere and excessive sweating.

Anatomical positions and body movements

The technical terms used in anatomy describe **anatomical positions** and body movements. The anatomical position is 'erect' with the head facing forward, arms by the sides with the palms of the hands facing forward.

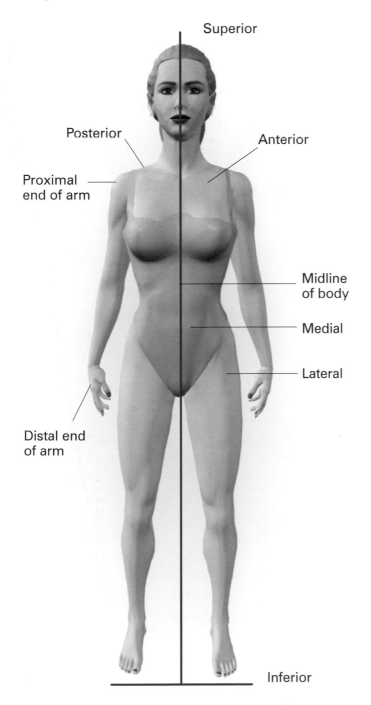

Superior
Posterior
Anterior
Proximal end of arm
Midline of body
Medial
Lateral
Distal end of arm
Inferior

Useful anatomical terms

Anterior/ventral – front of the body

Posterior/dorsal – back of the body

Superior – above

Inferior – below

Median line – an imaginary line through the centre of the body from head to toe

Proximal – nearest to the point of attachment of a limb

Distal – furthest away from the point of attachment of a limb

Medial – towards the mid line of the body

Lateral – away from the mid line of the body

Supine – lying face upwards

Prone – lying face down

Plantar – front surface, sole of the foot

Dorsal – back surface or top of the foot

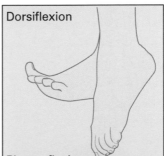

Dorsiflexion

Plantar flexion

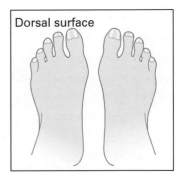

Dorsal surface

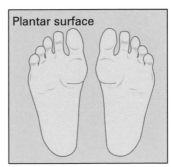

Plantar surface

Figure 26.1
Anatomical positions

Movements

Abduction – a movement away from the median line

Adduction – movement towards the median line

Flexion – decreasing of an angle between two bones at a joint as in bending

Extension – increasing of an angle between two bones at a joint as in straightening

Circumduction – a combined movement incorporating, flexion, extension, abduction and adduction

Depression – a downward movement

Elevation – an upward movement

Lateral flexion – a sideways bending movement of the vertebral column as a whole or any part of it

Pronation – movement of the palm of the hand downwards

Supination – movement of the palm of the hand upwards

Rotation – movement of a bone around its long axis

Eversion – when the plantar surface of the foot is turned laterally or outwards

Inversion – when the plantar surface of the foot is turned medially or inwards

Plantar flexion – when the foot is stretched downwards

Dorsiflexion – when the dorsum of the foot is brought upwards

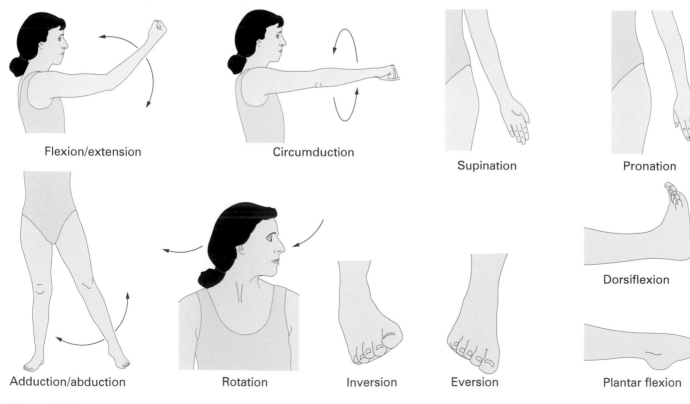

Flexion/extension   Circumduction   Supination   Pronation

Adduction/abduction   Rotation   Inversion   Eversion   Dorsiflexion   Plantar flexion

Figure 26.2 *Body movements*

Functions of bone

The skeletal system provides the framework for the body. It consists of bones and the cartilage, ligaments and tendons that hold them together.

Bones provide support, shape and movement to the body and they provide attachment for muscles and tendons. They protect vital organs, for example the brain is protected by the cranial bones and the heart and lungs are protected by the rib cage. Blood cells develop in the red bone marrow and bone also acts as a reservoir for minerals, in particular calcium and phosphordus which can be distributed to other parts of the body on demand.

Figure 26.3 *The skeleton*

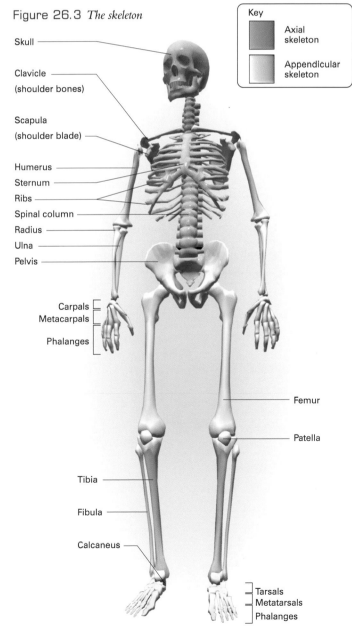

Skull

Clavicle
(shoulder bones)

Scapula
(shoulder blade)

Humerus

Sternum

Ribs

Spinal column

Radius

Ulna

Pelvis

Carpals
Metacarpals

Phalanges

Femur

Patella

Tibia

Fibula

Calcaneus

Tarsals
Metatarsals
Phalanges

Key

Axial skeleton

Appendicular skeleton

Classification of bones

The bones of the skeleton are classified as:

* **long** – these form the limbs
* **short** – these are found in the wrists and ankles
* **flat** – these are for protection, e.g. the skull, or for attachment of certain muscles; they are made from a sandwich of hard bone with a spongy layer in between
* **irregular** – these are irregular in shape to cope with the job they do, e.g. the vertebrae
* **sesamoid** – these are small bones which develop in the tendons around certain joints, e.g. the patella in the knee.

The skeleton

The **axial skeleton** forms the centre axis of the body and is made up of the skull (cranium face and lower jaw), the vertebral column, the ribs and the sternum.

The **appendicular skeleton**, or the parts which are appended (joined to) the axial skeleton, is made up of the shoulder girdle and arms and the pelvic girdle and legs.

The skeleton has about 200 bones, which vary in shape, size and function.

The bones of the skeleton

The skull

The skull is divided into:

* the **cranium**, which consists of:
  – one frontal   – one ethmoid
  – two parietal   – one sphenoid
  – two temporal   – one occipital
* the **face**, which consists of:
  – two maxillae
  – two zygomatic
  – two nasal
  – two lacrimal
  – one mandible
  – two palatine part of the hard palate
  – two inferior turbinate in the nasal cavities
  – one vomer lower and back of nasal septum.

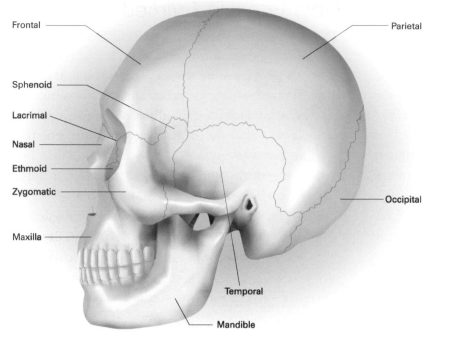

Figure 26.4
The bones of the skull

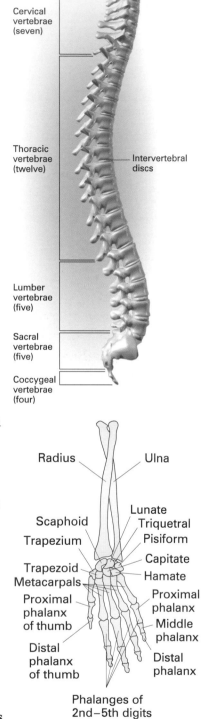

Figure 26.5
The vertebral column

The trunk

The trunk comprises:

* the sternum or breast bone
* twelve ribs
* the spinal column, which consists of:
  - seven cervical vertebrae
  - twelve thoracic vertebrae
  - five lumbar vertebrae
  - five sacral vertebrae fused together to form the sacrum
  - four coccygeal vertebrae fused together to form the coccyx.

The spinal column provides flexibility and strength to the body. The arms are joined to the spinal column by the shoulder girdle and the legs are joined by the pelvic girdle.

The shoulder girdle and arms

The clavicles (collar bones) and scapulae (shoulder blades) form the bones of the shoulder girdle. The humerus is the long bone of the upper arm and the radius and ulna are the long bones of the forearm. The radius is on the outer side when the palm of the hand is facing forward. The bones of the hand consist of five metacarpals and fourteen phalanges and the bones of the wrist consist of eight irregularly shaped carpal bones, arranged in two rows of four.

The pelvic girdle and legs

The pelvic girdle comprises two innominate bones, each consisting of three individual bones fused together. The **ilium** is the upper part, the **pubis** is the anterior part and the **ischium** is the posterior part.

The leg consists of:

* the femur (thigh bone) – the largest and strongest bone in the body

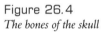

Figure 26.6
The bones of the hand and wrist

* the patella – a small flat bone protecting the knee joint
* the tibia and fibula – the bones of the lower leg beneath the knee.

The foot consists of seven tarsals, five metatarsals and fourteen phalanges.

The arches of the feet

The bones are arranged in two flexible arches, supported by muscles and ligaments. These allow the weight of the body to be supported and they provide leverage when walking. They are the longitudinal arch and the transverse arch.

The **longitudinal arch** has two parts: the medial longitudinal arch and the lateral longitudinal arch. The medial longitudinal arch, which is the higher of the two, originates at the calcaneus, ascends to the talus, descends through the navicular, the three cuneiform and the three medial metatarsals. The lateral longitudinal arch also begins at the calcaneus; it rises at the cuboid and descends to the two lateral metatarsals. The talus is the key part of the medial arch and the cuboid is the key part of the lateral arch.

The **transverse arch** runs across the foot and is formed by the calcaneus, navicular, cuboid and the posterior part of the five metatarsals.

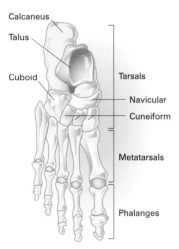

Figure 26.7
The bones of the foot

Figure 26.8 *The arches of the foot*

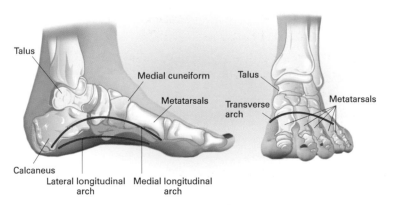

How bone is formed

The process by which bones are formed is called **ossification**. Osteoblasts are bone forming cells which, when calcified, become **osteocytes** and where there is a cluster of osteoblasts, it is called a centre of ossification.

The osteoblasts secrete substances composed of collagenous fibres, forming a framework into which calcium salts are deposited. This process is called **calcification**. When the osteoblasts are surrounded by this calcification they are known as **trabecula**.

The bone develops hollow centres that contain marrow in which the manufacture of blood cells takes place. **Periosteum** is a tough fibrous sheet covering the surface of bones, except where the bone forms a joint and is covered by **hyaline cartilage**. The blood supply to the bones is received via the periosteum on its surface and via an artery in the nutrient foramen (a hole in the bone) in the shaft of the bone.

Most of the bones of the skeleton have protuberances and ridges for the attachment of muscles and tendons.

The joints

Bones are rigid structures and any movement that takes place occurs at the joints. A joint is the point at which two or more bones meet. There are three main types of joint in the body and these are:

* **fibrous** – fixed or immovable joints, which have fibrous tissue between the bones
* **cartilaginous** – slightly movable with cartilage between the ends of the bones
* **synovial** – freely movable joints which have particular characteristics:
    - The articulating surfaces of the bones are covered with hyaline cartilage.
    - A fibrous capsule supported by ligaments surrounds the joint to provide protection while allowing freedom of movement.

– A synovial membrane lines the capsule of the joint.
– The capsule of the joint contains synovial fluid, which is a lubricant and provides nutrients for the living cells.

Synovial joints are classified depending on their range of movement and structure, as shown in Table 26.1.

The main synovial joints of the limbs are:

* shoulder joint – ball and socket
* elbow joint – hinge
* wrist joint – condyloid
* hip joint – ball and socket
* knee joint – hinge
* ankle joint – hinge.

Joint classification	Range of movement
Plane (gliding)	Short gliding movements
Hinge	In one plane only, it will flex and extend
Ball and socket	The widest range of movement – flexion, extension, abduction, adduction, circumduction, rotation
Pivot	Rotation only
Condyloid	Movement in two planes, flexion and extension, abduction and adduction, limited circumduction
Saddle	Movement in two planes, flexion and extension, abduction and adduction and circumduction

Table 26.1 *Classification of joints by range of movement*

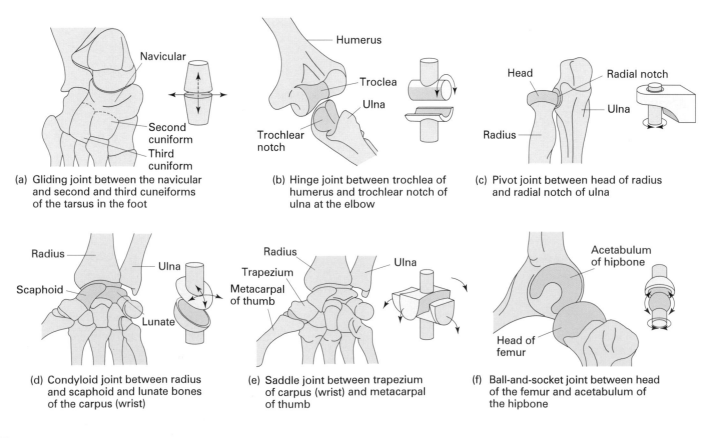

(a) Gliding joint between the navicular and second and third cuneiforms of the tarsus in the foot

(b) Hinge joint between trochlea of humerus and trochlear notch of ulna at the elbow

(c) Pivot joint between head of radius and radial notch of ulna

(d) Condyloid joint between radius and scaphoid and lunate bones of the carpus (wrist)

(e) Saddle joint between trapezium of carpus (wrist) and metacarpal of thumb

(f) Ball-and-socket joint between head of the femur and acetabulum of the hipbone

Figure 26.9 *Joint classifcations*

Bones and joints form the framework of the body, but they require help to produce movement, which is an essential body function, and this is achieved by the contraction and relaxation of the muscles.

Muscle tissue is composed of highly specialised cells and makes up about 40 per cent of the body's total weight. Its characteristics are important in maintaining homeostasis, the condition in which the body's internal environment remains relatively constant within limits, under ever-changing conditions.

Characteristics of muscle tissue

* **Excitability** – the ability of muscle tissue to receive messages and respond to stimuli.
* **Contractability** – the ability to shorten and thicken (contract) in response to a stimulus.
* **Extensibility** – the ability of muscle tissue to stretch.
* **Elasticity** – the ability of the muscle to return to its original shape after contraction or extension.

Types of muscle

There are three different kinds of muscle in the body:

* **Skeletal muscle** is attached to bones and is **striated** (ribbed) **voluntary** (under our control) muscle tissue.
* **Visceral muscle** is smooth, or **non striated involuntary** muscle located in the walls of hollow internal structures, e.g. the blood vessels.
* **Cardiac muscle** forms the walls of the heart and it is **striated involuntary**.

Skeletal muscle

Skeletal muscle is protected by **fascia**, a layer of connective tissue. Deep fascia holds muscles together, separating them into functioning groups, allowing free movement of the muscles and carrying nerves and blood vessels. The **epimysium** is an extension of deep fascia and covers the entire muscle.

This type of muscle tissue looks like a series of parallel fibre bundles, the smallest of which are called

actin and **myosin filaments**. Made of protein, they are sometimes known as the contractile proteins. These filaments are gathered into bundles called **myofibrils**, which are gathered into further bundles called **muscle fibres** surrounded by **endomysium** and then gathered into further bundles called **fasciculi** which are surrounded by **perimysium**.

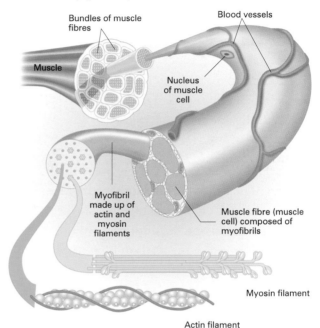

Figure 27.1 *Structure of voluntary muscle*

Actin and myosin filaments gathered into bundles make

Myofibrils gathered into bundles make

Muscle fibres or cells containing nucleii, nerve fibres and blood supply

Muscle fibres are surrounded by a membrane called endomysium

Muscle fibres gathered into bundles are called fasiculi

Fasciculi are surrounded by perimysium

Muscle is made up of bundles of fasiculi wrapped in epimysium, an extension of deep fascia

Figure 27.2 *Voluntary muscle*

Tendons attach the muscles to bones and they vary in length and size. Some tendons are broad and flat and are called an aponeurosis, for example the epicranial aponeurosis, which joins the occipitalis and frontalis muscles of the scalp.

Ligaments are bands of strong fibrous tissue which run between the ends of bones forming the joint. They hold the surface of the joint together and prevent it from moving excessively

Cartilage provides stability in the joints, reducing friction and absorbing shock.

Skeletal muscles, in general, are attached to bones, although some facial muscles are attached to soft tissue in the face or ligaments and cartilage.

Visceral muscle

This muscle is smooth, non striated and usually involuntary. The cells are spindle shaped with one central nucleus and are bound together in sheets by areolar connective tissue. It is not under our conscious control and is found in the walls of blood and lymph vessels, the stomach, the alimentary canal, the respiratory tract, the bladder and the uterus. Visceral muscle does not become fatigued.

Cardiac muscle

This muscle is only found in the heart and is striated in appearance like skeletal muscle with fibres that are short and thick, forming a dense mass, but it is involuntary muscle tissue, not under our conscious control. The cardiac muscle cells have one nucleus and very little connective tissue. Cardiac muscle contracts rhythmically even without nervous stimulation and it does not tire easily but could if the heartbeat was raised considerably for a long period of time without enough rest between contractions.

Nerve and blood supply

Muscles are well supplied with nerves and blood vessels as this is important for contraction to take place. For a muscle to contract it must first be stimulated by an impulse from a nerve. It also requires energy in the form of nutrients and oxygen and the waste products produced as a result of exercise must be removed. Therefore, muscle movement is reliant on a healthy blood supply.

Muscle condition

Muscle tone

This is when the muscle is in a state of partial contraction with some of the muscle fibres contracted and some relaxed. Partial contraction will tighten a muscle without actually moving it. Tone is an essential in maintaining posture; if tone is lost, this may cause physical problems.

Muscle strength

This may be defined as 'the maximum force exerted by a muscle or muscle groups at a specific rate of motion' or, more simply, the maximum contraction achieved against a resistance.

Muscular endurance

This describes the capacity of skeletal muscles to sustain repeated contractions.

Muscle fatigue

This occurs when skeletal muscle has been contracted for a long period of time. It becomes tired and weaker in response until it stops responding altogether. This is usually as a result of inadequate blood supply and lack of oxygen, together with a build-up of lactic acid and carbon dioxide which accumulate in the muscle during exercise.

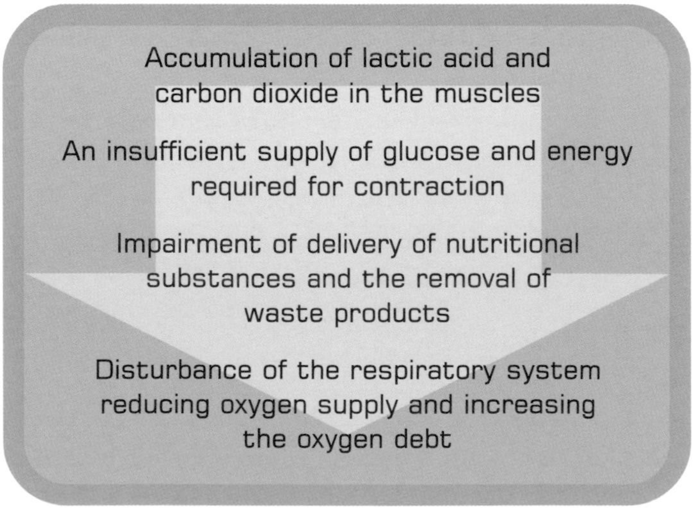

Accumulation of lactic acid and carbon dioxide in the muscles

An insufficient supply of glucose and energy required for contraction

Impairment of delivery of nutritional substances and the removal of waste products

Disturbance of the respiratory system reducing oxygen supply and increasing the oxygen debt

Figure 27.3 *Over-activity of skeletal muscle*

When muscle contracts, its ends are pulled towards each other, so that it exerts a force on the bones to which it is attached and produces movement at the joint that it crosses. One end of a muscle tends to be fixed so that the other, free end moves towards it. The **origin** of a muscle is the end which usually remains fixed during contraction. The **insertion** of a muscle is the end which moves during a contraction.

Table 27.1 shows the classification of the muscle groups. (See also Figure 26.2 on page 370.)

Muscle group classification	Movement produced
Flexors	Bend the limb at a joint (flex)
Extensors	Straighten the limb at a joint (extend)
Adductors	Move a limb towards the midline of the body
Abductors	Move a limb away from the midline of the body
Supinators	Turn the palm of the hand upwards
Pronators	Turn the palm of the hand downwards

Table 27.1 *Classification of muscle groups by range of movement produced*

Functions of muscle tissue

* **Motion** involves the usual movements of the whole body such as walking, running, swimming and localised movements such as nodding the head, waving a hand or drawing a picture. The less obvious types of motion are the beating of the heart, peristalsis (the movement of food along the digestive tract) and the contraction of the bladder.

* **Maintaining posture**, the contraction of the skeletal muscles, enables the body to sit and stand.

* **Heat production**. When skeletal muscles contract heat is produced and this helps to maintain normal body temperature. When the body is cold shivering occurs. This is an involuntary muscle action causing the muscle to work and produce more heat and when the body is exposed to cold air there is an increase in muscle tone. When the body is exposed to extreme heat the muscles relax.

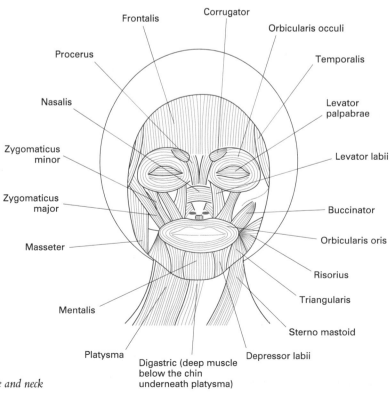

Figure 27.4 *Muscles of the face and neck*

Muscle	Position	Action
Occipitalis	Covers the occipital bone, back of the scalp	Draws scalp backwards
Frontalis	Covers the frontal bone, front of the scalp and over the forehead	Draws scalp forwards, raises the eyebrows and wrinkles the forehead horizontally
Corrugator	The inside corner of each eyebrow	Draws eyebrows together causing vertical furrows
Procerus	Top of the nose between the eyes	Depresses the eyebrow and causes wrinkles across the bridge of the nose
Orbicularis occuli	Around the eye	Closes eyes tightly
Levator palpabrae	The eyelid	Opens the upper lid
Nasalis	Immediately below procerus, across the bridge of the nose	Compresses the nasal openings
Levator labii	From outer edge of the mouth up and over the maxilla	Raises the upper lip
Zygomaticus – major and minor	Skin and fascia at the angle of the mouth to the zygomatic bone	Raises the lips as in laughing
Risorius	From the corner of the mouth across the cheek	Draws the corners of the mouth out and back as in grinning
Buccinator	From the corner of the mouth, outwards and upwards across the cheek	Compresses the cheeks and aids in mastication
Orbicularis oris	Around the mouth	Closes the mouth and causes the lips to wrinkle. Also puckers the lips as in kissing
Triangularis	The corner of the lower lip to the chin	Pulls down the corner of the mouth
Depressor labii	The lower lip down to the chin	Pulls the lower lip down and to one side
Mentalis	Over the chin	Pushes up the lower lip, wrinkling the chin
Temporalis	From the temple down to the jaw	Raises the lower jaw and draws it backwards; helps with chewing
Masseter	From the cheekbone down to the jaw	Raises the jaw; helps with chewing
Platysma	Covers the front of the neck	Helps draw down the mandible and lower lip and wrinkles the skin of the neck
Sterno mastoid	Side of the neck from the ear to the clavicle and sternum	Both sides together flex the neck. One side alone bends the head sideways
Digastric	Deep muscle under the chin attached to the mandible, temporal and hyoid bones	Helps in moving the tongue and swallowing

Table 27.2 *Position and action of the muscles of the face and neck*

Muscles of the face and neck

The muscles of the face are made up of voluntary muscle tissue, which is under our control, and consists of cells that are capable of contraction. Over the years, lines and wrinkles will form as a result of the constant use of the muscles of facial expression. Table 27.2 describes the muscles of the face and neck.

The muscles of the face are in constant use all our lives and, with age, wrinkles and dropped contours occur. Wrinkles form because the muscles are constantly contracting during normal facial movements and, with age, the skin loses its elasticity and the natural moisture in the skin slows down.

Dropped contours happen when certain muscles lose their tone by overstretching and lengthening or with age.

Common problems include:

✱ frontalis – causes horizontal lines across the forehead
✱ corrugator – causes deep vertical lines to develop between the eyebrows
✱ orbicularis occuli – causes overhanging lids and bags under the eyes when it loses tone and fine lines under the eyes
✱ procerus – causes horizontal lines on the bridge of the nose
✱ levator labii and zygomaticus – causes naso labial folds when they lose tone

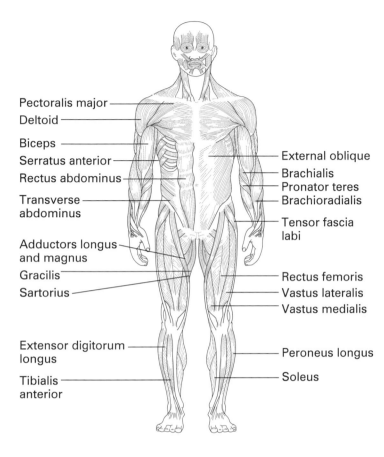

Figure 27.5 *Muscles of the body (anterior view)*

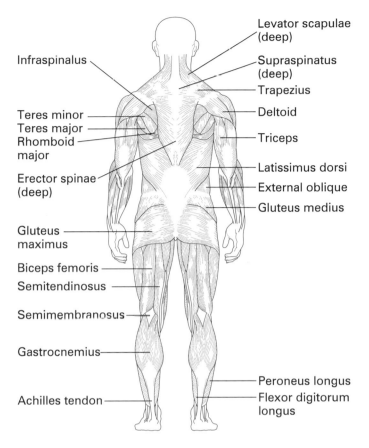

Figure 27.6 *Muscles of the body (posterior view)*

* orbicularis oris – fine vertical lines around the mouth caused through constant puckering, e.g. through smoking
* triangularis/masseter – causes jowls to form when tone is lost
* platysma – causes a crepey neck and dropped contour of the chin
* digastric – this is deeply situated under platysma and when it loses tone causes a double chin.

Muscles of the shoulder and back

These muscles are described in Table 27.3.

Muscles of the chest and abdomen

These muscles are described in Table 27.4.

Muscles of the buttocks and legs

These muscles are described in Table 27.5.

Table 27.3 *Muscles of the shoulder and back*

Muscle	Position	Action
Trapezius	The top of the back attached to the occipital bone and all thoracic vertebrae, tapering toward the shoulder	Elevates and braces the shoulder and rotates the scapula
Deltoid	The shoulder from the clavicle and scapula to the upper part of the humerus	Front – draws arm forwards. Back – draws arm back. Middle – abducts the arm
Latissimus dorsi	Thoracic and lumbar region of the back outwards and upwards to the humerus	Draws the arm backwards and inwards
Erector spinae	Three groups of muscles, each group consisting of overlapping muscles stretching from the pelvis up to the neck	Extends and flexes the trunk and maintains the erect position of the spine
Rhomboids	Thoracic area of the spine to the vertebral side of scapula	Braces the shoulder and rotates scapula
Levator scapulae	Upper cervical vertebrae and upper part of the vertebral border of scapula	Elevates scapula
Supraspinatus	From the scapula to the humerus	Abducts the arm
Infraspinatus	From the scapula to the humerus	Rotates arm outwards
Teres major	Scapula to humerus	Adducts and inwardly rotates the arm
Teres minor	Scapula to humerus	Rotates the arm outwards

Table 27.4 *Muscles of the chest and abdomen*

Muscle	Position	Action
Pectoralis major	Upper chest from ribs to the humerus	Adducts and rotates arm inwards
Serratus anterior	From upper nine ribs to vertebral border of scapula	Draws shoulder forwards and rotates scapula
Rectus abdominus	Front of the abdomen from the pubic bone up to the sternum and lower ribs	Flexes the vertebral column
External oblique	At the waist, at an angle from the lower eight ribs to iliac crest and linea alba	Both together compress the abdomen. Contraction of one side bends the trunk laterally
Internal oblique	Deeper muscle below external oblique from the iliac crest upwards to the lower ribs	
Transversus abdominus	Deepest abdominal muscle from the iliac crest across the abdominal wall to the linea alba	Compresses the abdomen

Muscle	Position	Action
Gluteus maximus	Large superficial muscle forming the buttocks	Extends the hip and laterally rotates the thigh and hip joint
Gluteus medius	Deeper muscle forming the buttocks	Abducts femur and medially rotates the thigh
Psoas	Crosses front of hip joint to femur	Flexes and rotates the thigh laterally and flexes the vertebral column
Iliacus	Crosses front of hip joint to femur	Flexes and rotates the thigh laterally
Tensor fasciae latae	From the hip down the lateral side of the thigh	Flexes and abducts the thigh

Muscle	Position	Action
Quadriceps	Muscles on the anterior aspect of the thigh	
Rectus femoris		Extends knee and flexes thigh
Vastus medialis		Extension of knee joint
Vastus lateralis		Extension of knee joint
Sartorius	Medial aspect of thigh	Flexes the leg and rotates thigh laterally
Adductors	Muscles on the medial aspect of the thigh	
Adductor longus		Adducts rotates and flexes the thigh
Adductor magnus		Adducts the thigh
Gracilis		Flexes the leg and adducts the thigh
Hamstrings	Muscles on the posterior aspect of the thigh	
Biceps femoris		Extends the thigh and flexes the leg
Semitendinosus		Extends the thigh and flexes the leg
Semimembranosus		Extends the thigh and flexes the leg
Gastrocnemius	Below the knee	Flexes the knee and plantar flexes the foot and flexes the leg
Soleus	Below gastrocnemius	Plantar flexes the foot
Tibialis anterior	Crosses the front of the lower leg from tibia to first metatarsal and cuneiform	Inverts and dorsiflexes the foot
Extensor digitorum longus	Lateral anterior aspect of lower leg	Extends the toes and and dorsiflexes the foot
Peroneus longus	Lateral aspect of lower leg	Plantar flexes the foot
Flexor digitorum longus	From tibia down to phalanges of four lateral toes	Plantar flexes and inverts foot. Flexes the toes
Achilles tendon	Attached to soleus and gastrocnemius down to the calcaneum	Raises the foot

Table 27.5 *Muscles of the buttocks and leg*

Muscles of the arm and hand

The muscles of the arm and hand are described in Table 27.6.

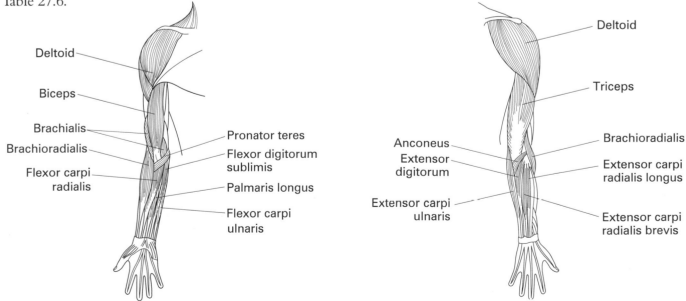

Figure 27.7 *Muscles of the arm (anterior view)*

Figure 27.8 *Muscles of the arm (posterior view)*

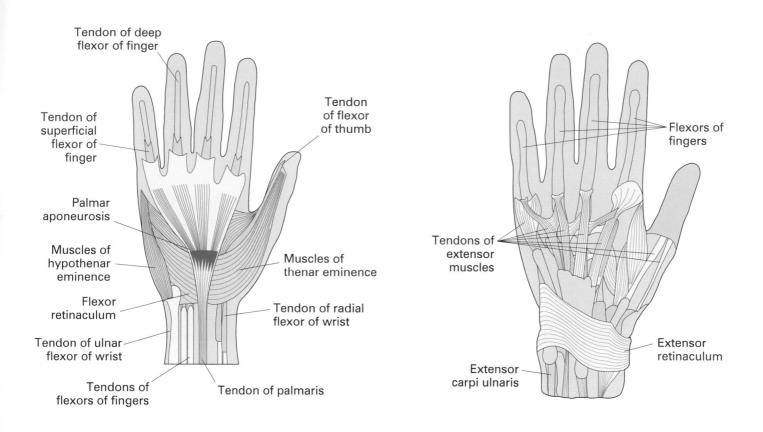

Figure 27.9 *Muscles of the hand (anterior view)*

Figure 27.10 *Muscles of the hand (posterior view)*

Table 27.6 *Muscles of the arm and hand*

Muscle	Position	Action
Biceps	Anterior arm to radius	Flexes elbow and supinates forearm and hand
Triceps	Posterior arm to ulna	Extends the forearm
Brachialis	Anterior elbow	Flexes the forearm
Brachioradialis	From humerus to radius	Flexes the forearm
Pronator teres	From humerus, inside of elbow to radius and ulna	Pronates the forearm so the palm faces downward
Palmaris longus	Anterior aspect of forearm	Flexes the wrist
Flexors	Anterior aspect of forearm	
Carpi radialis		Flex the wrist, abduct the hand
Carpi ulnaris		Flex the wrist and adduct the hand
Digitorum sublimis		Flexes the fingers
Extensors	Posterior aspect of forearm	
Carpi radialis longus		Extend and abduct the wrist
Carpi radialis brevis		Extend and abduct the hand
Digitorum		Extends the fingers

Most treatments performed by the beauty therapist will improve the flow of blood around the body. This is an important effect, as it will help to provide the essential nutrients required for growth and repair and to maintain a healthy skin. It is also beneficial to those clients who suffer from poor or sluggish circulation as it will stimulate and improve skin colour and texture, re-energise and aid relaxation because of the increased warmth produced in the tissues.

The cardiovascular system consists of:

* the heart
* blood
* blood vessels.

The heart provides the power to pump the blood around the body through the blood vessels. The blood is the vehicle by which the circulatory system carries oxygen, nutrients, hormones and other substances to the tissues, carbon dioxide to the lungs and other waste products to the kidneys.

The heart

The heart is the centre of the cardiovascular system. It is a large muscular organ and it beats over 100 000 times a day to pump the blood through the blood vessels. The blood vessels are a network of tubes that transport blood from the heart to the tissues and then back to the heart again.

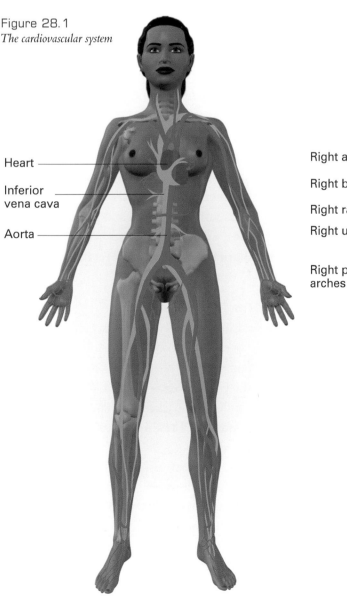

Figure 28.1
The cardiovascular system

Heart

Inferior
vena cava

Aorta

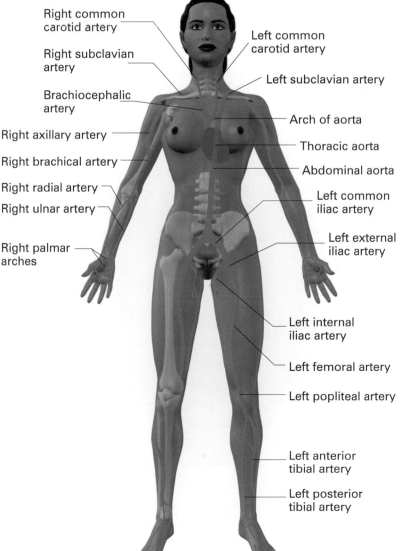

Right common
carotid artery

Right subclavian
artery

Brachiocephalic
artery

Right axillary artery

Right brachical artery

Right radial artery

Right ulnar artery

Right palmar
arches

Left common
carotid artery

Left subclavian artery

Arch of aorta

Thoracic aorta

Abdominal aorta

Left common
iliac artery

Left external
iliac artery

Left internal
iliac artery

Left femoral artery

Left popliteal artery

Left anterior
tibial artery

Left posterior
tibial artery

It is located between the lungs in the thoracic cavity with about two-thirds lying to the left of the body's midline. It is enclosed in a loose fitting serous membrane called the **pericardial sac**.

The wall of the heart is divided into:

* the **epicardium**, or external layer, which is thin and transparent
* the **myocardium**, or middle layer, composed of specialised cardiac muscle which makes up the bulk of the heart and is responsible for the heart contraction
* the **endocardium**, or inner layer, which lines the inside of the myocardium and covers the valves of the heart and tendons that hold them open. It is made up of a thin layer of endothelium which lies over a thin layer of connective tissue.

The heart is divided into four chambers, or cavities, and each chamber is a muscular bag with walls that contract and push the blood through:

* the two upper chambers – the **atria**
* the two lower chambers – the **ventricles**.

Each atrium has an appendage called an auricle which increases its surface area. The right and left sides of the heart are separated by the **septum**, a solid wall which prevents venous blood from the right side coming into contact with the arterial blood from the left side of the heart.

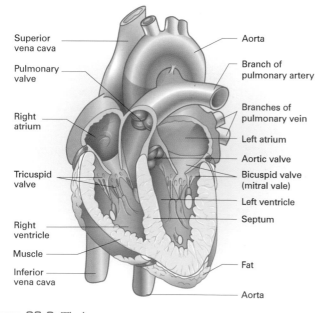

Superior vena cava
Pulmonary valve
Right atrium
Tricuspid valve
Right ventricle
Muscle
Inferior vena cava

Aorta
Branch of pulmonary artery
Branches of pulmonary vein
Left atrium
Aortic valve
Bicuspid valve (mitral vale)
Left ventricle
Septum
Fat
Aorta

Figure 28.2 *The heart*

The passage of blood through the heart

Blood circulates from the heart, through the organs and tissues, delivering food and oxygen. The blood then returns to the heart in the veins having had all the oxygen absorbed from it. The heart then pumps blood on its second circuit to the lungs to replace oxygen, returning with its oxygen supply renewed.

The heart receives blood via the right atrium from all parts of the body except the lungs through three veins:

* the **superior vena cava**, which transports blood from parts of the body that are superior to the heart
* the **inferior vena cava**, which transports blood from parts of the body that are inferior to the heart
* the **coronary sinus**, which drains blood from most of the vessels which supply the walls of the heart.

The blood from the right atrium is delivered to the **right ventricle** through the **tricuspid valve**.

Blood is then pumped into the **right and left pulmonary arteries** and transported to the lungs, where it has its oxygen renewed and releases carbon dioxide. It returns to the heart via four **pulmonary veins** which empty into the **left atrium** and then pass through to the **left ventricle**. The blood is then pumped into the **ascending aorta** and passed into the **coronary arteries**, **arch of the aorta**, **thoracic aorta** and **abdominal aorta**, which transports the blood to all parts of the body but the lungs.

Valves of the heart

The heart depends on a series of valves to function efficiently. They open and close automatically to receive and send out blood to and from the four chambers of the heart, ensuring the blood flow is in one direction only and preventing it from flowing backwards. These valves are:

* the **pulmonary** and **tricuspid** valves on the right-hand side
* the **aortic** and **mitral** valves on the left-hand side.

The pulmonary semilunar valve lies where the pulmonary trunk leaves the right ventricle. It consists of three semilunar (half moon-shaped) cusps.

The tricuspid valve is situated between the right atrium and the right ventricle and consists of three cusps or flaps.

The aortic semi-lunar valve lies at the opening between the left ventricle and the aorta. This is also made up of three semi-lunar cusps.

The mitral or bicuspid valve is situated between the left atrium and the left ventricle and it consists of two cusps or flaps.

Blood

Blood is a viscous fluid which circulates through the heart and blood vessels and constitutes about 8 per cent of total body weight. It has a number of functions:

* It transports oxygen from the lungs to the cells of the body.
* It transports carbon dioxide from the cells to the lungs.
* It transports nutrients from the digestive tract to the cells of the body.
* It transports waste products from the cells to kidneys, lungs and sweat glands for excretion.
* It transports hormones from the endocrine glands to the cells.
* It transports enzymes to the appropriate cells.
* It helps in the regulation of body temperature.
* It transports white corpuscles to the source of infection helping to protect the body against foreign substances.
* It regulates the water content of cells.
* It prevents fluid loss because of the clotting mechanism.

Blood consists of plasma and corpuscles. Plasma is the liquid portion and accounts for about 55 per cent of the volume. Figure 28.3 shows the contents of plasma.

The corpuscles in the blood account for about 45 per cent of the volume and they are:

* **erythrocytes**, or red blood cells, which contain haemoglobin and transport oxygen around the body
* **leucocytes**, or white blood cells, which provide the body with protection
* **platelets**, or **thrombocytes**, necessary for blood clotting.

The white blood cells are divided into two groups:

* Granular – developed from red bone marrow; known as **neutrophils**, **eosinophils** and **basophils**.
* Agranular – developed from lymphoid and myeloid tissue; known as **lymphocytes** and **monocytes**.

Neutrophils and monocytes are phagocytic – they ingest bacteria and dead matter.

Eosinophils produce **antihistamine**, which helps to fight an allergic reaction caused by an irritant. Basophils are also involved in fighting irritants releasing histamine to aid vasodilation and increase permeability of blood vessels, **heparin**, a quick acting anticoagulant, which helps to prevent clotting, and **serotonin**, which also aids vasodilation.

Lymphocytes help to produce antibodies, which will deactivate antigens.

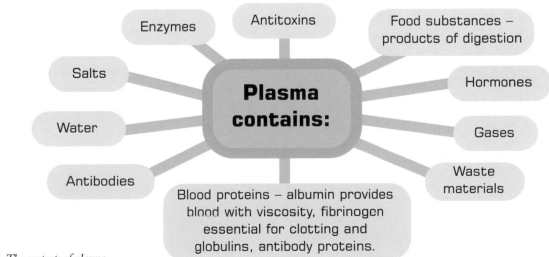

Figure 28.3 *The contents of plasma*

Anatomy and physiology

Blood vessels

These are the channels along which the blood flows.

Arteries

These are thick-walled blood vessels which carry blood from the heart to the capillaries. They help to maintain blood pressure. The thick elastic walls are important in that most of the force of each heartbeat is taken up in the elastic walls of the large arteries, which continue pushing the blood forward in the pause between each heartbeat.

Arterioles

These are small arteries, which carry blood to the capillaries.

Capillaries

These are microscopic blood vessels composed of a single layer of cells, which connect arterioles and venules. Their main function is to allow the passage of nutrients and waste products between the blood cells and the tissue cells.

In addition to the change of substances, they have an important function in helping to regulate body temperature. The capillaries widen when the body heats up and this allows more blood to reach the surface of the skin where it is cooled.

Veins

These have much thinner walls than the arteries and they convey blood back to the heart from the capillaries. They contain valves to prevent back flow allowing blood to move towards the heart.

The arteries and veins are similarly distributed throughout the body and those associated with a particular organ or tissue often run together.

Venules

These are found when groups of capillaries join together. They collect blood from the capillaries and drain it into veins.

Nervous control of the blood vessels

Most arteries in the body are under the control of the autonomic nervous system and the centres of control are in the hypothalamus and medulla oblongata. There are two sets of nerves – vasoconstrictor and vasodilator.

Vasoconstrictor nerves

These narrow the blood vessels reducing the amount of blood to the area of the body they supply. When impulses are sent from all the vasoconstrictor nerves, then the blood vessels of the whole of the arterial system will become narrower, so raising the blood pressure.

Vasodilator nerves

The action of these nerves is to dilate the blood vessels, allowing a greater amount of blood to reach the area. For example, during very strenuous exercise, the blood vessels which supply the muscles dilate allowing more blood to reach the area.

Circulation of blood around the body

Arteries carry blood from the heart to all parts of the body. They branch out and become smaller arterioles, which in turn carry blood to the capillaries, the microscopic blood vessels in the tissues.

Interchange of tissue fluids (interstitial fluid) takes place. This is when oxygen and nutrients are received by the tissues and carbon dioxide and other waste products (the result of cell metabolism) are removed.

The capillaries then drain into venules, which form veins to carry the deoxygenated blood back to the heart.

Arteries supplying the head and neck

External carotid artery

This artery supplies the superficial tissues of the head and neck. The branches are:

* thyroid artery – supplies the thyroid gland and adjacent muscles
* lingual artery – supplies the tongue, mouth and throat
* facial artery – supplies the muscles of facial expression and the mouth
* maxillary artery – supplies the jaw area and interior of the skull
* occipital artery – supplies the occipital part of the scalp
* temporal artery – supplies the frontal, parietal and temporal areas of the scalp.

Internal carotid artery

This artery supplies the brain, the eyes, forehead and nose.

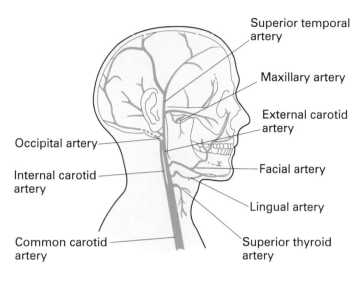

Superior temporal artery

Maxillary artery

External carotid artery

Occipital artery

Facial artery

Internal carotid artery

Lingual artery

Common carotid artery

Superior thyroid artery

Figure 28.4 *The main arteries of the head and neck*

Venous return from the head and neck

Venous blood is returned from the face and scalp by means of the superficial and deep veins. The superficial veins have the same names as the branches of the external carotid artery and they unite to form the **external jugular vein**. Venous blood from the brain is collected in the **venous sinuses**.

Deep sinuses

These empty into the internal jugular vein and include:

* superior sagittal sinus
* inferior sagittal sinus
* straight sagittal sinus
* transverse sagittal sinus.

This is a subsidiary circulatory system and is composed of lymph, lymph vessels, nodes and ducts as well as highly specialised lymphoid organs and tissues including the thymus, spleen and tonsils. Lymph vessels are found in all parts of the body except the central nervous system, bone, cartilage and teeth.

The primary functions of the lymphatic system are to protect the body from disease, clean it of waste and toxins and maintain fluid balance.

The lymphatic system is important to the therapist as it provides an internal cleansing system to complement the treatments provided. Many skin conditions are improved by helping the lymphatic system remove waste products, so

reinforcing the deep cleansing effect of manual and electrical treatment. Anti-cellulite treatments are greatly enhanced by stimulating this system and encouraging it to work more efficiently. Using certain manual and mechanical methods of lymph drainage are also beneficial to many clients who suffer from fluid retention, but only if it is not caused by a medical condition.

Lymph

Blood itself does not flow into the tissues but remains inside the blood vessels. Certain parts of the blood, however, permeate through the capillary walls and into the tissue spaces. This is called interstitial fluid. When this interstitial fluid enters the lymphatic vessels it is then called lymph. It consists mainly of water and important substances found in blood plasma such as fibrinogen, a protein which when converted to fibrin by the action of thrombin is essential in blood clotting, and serum albumin, which helps to regulate the osmotic pressure of plasma.

Figure 29.1 *The lymphatic system of the body*

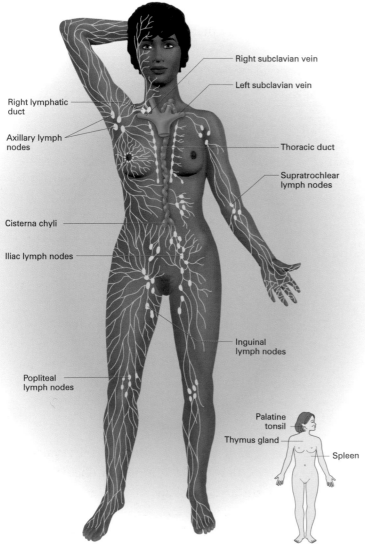

- Right subclavian vein
- Left subclavian vein
- Right lymphatic duct
- Axillary lymph nodes
- Thoracic duct
- Supratrochlear lymph nodes
- Cisterna chyli
- Iliac lymph nodes
- Inguinal lymph nodes
- Popliteal lymph nodes
- Palatine tonsil
- Thymus gland
- Spleen

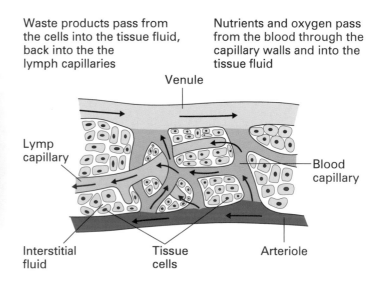

Waste products pass from the cells into the tissue fluid, back into the the lymph capillaries

Nutrients and oxygen pass from the blood through the capillary walls and into the tissue fluid

- Venule
- Lymp capillary
- Blood capillary
- Interstitial fluid
- Tissue cells
- Arteriole

Figure 29.2 *The exchange of tissue fluid*

Lymph vessels

Lymph vessels transport excess fluid, foreign particles and waste materials from the tissues and cells of the body. There are lymph capillaries into which tissue fluid passes from the tissue spaces running alongside the body's arteries and veins. Their walls are thin and permeable, allowing larger molecules including bacteria, which cannot enter the blood capillaries, to be carried away. There are larger vessels known as lymphatics, which are the size of small veins, and are provided with valves to prevent back flow. The larger vessels eventually converge into two large ducts – the thoracic duct and the right lymphatic duct – which drain into the innominate veins, returning the lymph into the blood. So there is a constant circulation of lymph into the tissues, via the capillaries and back again into the bloodstream.

Lymph nodes

These are situated around the body. They are usually small groups of oval or bean-shaped structures found around major arteries, for example the groin, armpits and neck. The groups are arranged in two sets: superficial and deep. Their main functions are:

* to filter the lymph, so preventing bacteria and other foreign substances from entering the blood stream
* to produce white corpuscles, a defence against bacteria
* to filter and destroy bacteria, which may be present in the lymph, in the lymph glands. For this reason these glands may become inflamed, swollen and painful.

Lymph nodes are small round structures. The outer region of the lymph node (cortex) contains densely packed lymphocytes, which are arranged in masses called lymph nodules separated by trabeculae (partitions). The inner region (medulla) contains lymphocytes arranged in strands and are called medullary cords.

The lymphatic vessels carry lymph to the node in afferent (convey towards a centre) vessels and once the lymph has been filtered, it is taken from the node in efferent (convey away from a centre) vessels.

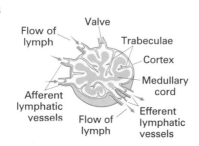

Flow of lymph
Valve
Trabeculae
Cortex
Medullary cord
Afferent lymphatic vessels
Flow of lymph
Efferent lymphatic vessels

Figure 29.3 *A lymph node*

Lymph ducts

From the lymph nodes the lymphatic vessels combine to form lymph trunks which empty into two main ducts:

* the thoracic duct, which is the main collecting duct of the lymphatic system beginning as a dilation called the cisterna chylli and receiving lymph from the left side of the head, neck, chest, the left upper extremity and the entire body below the ribs
* the right lymphatic duct, which receives lymph from the right side of the head and neck, the thorax and the right arm.

From these two ducts the lymph returns to the blood circulation via the subclavian veins and the cycle repeats itself continuously.

Lymph organs

The lymph organs are the:

* tonsils
* thymus gland
* spleen.

Tonsils

The tonsils are part of a ring of lymphoid tissue which encircles the entrance to the food and air passages in the throat. They include the adenoid or pharyngeal tonsil, the palatine tonsil and the lingual tonsil.

They play a part in the body's defence against disease, reacting to ingested material that poses a threat to health. This immunity is provided by the lymphocytes that are processed in the tonsils and the production of antibodies in the tonsils, which deal with local infection. Infected tonsils are enlarged and inflamed with spots of pus exuding from the surface.

The adenoid is situated at the back of the nose and any infection breathed in is filtered and destroyed. Adenoids are present at birth but usually disappear by puberty.

Thymus gland

This is a mass of lymphatic tissue situated in the upper thoracic cavity. Its function is to produce antibodies to destroy foreign particles. It is large in children and by puberty it reaches maximum size, becoming involuted and most of it being replaced by fat and connective tissue.

Spleen

This is the largest mass of lymphatic tissue in the body and is situated between the fundus of the stomach and diaphragm. It is one of the main filters of blood, removing worn out red blood cells and abnormal cells, with white cells and platelets filtered selectively. It makes antibodies, which immobilise foreign particles, stores blood and releases it into the circulatory system in times of need, for example when there is a heavy blood loss during haemorrhage.

Functions of the lymphatic system

The lymphatic system carries excess fluid, foreign particles and other materials from the body's tissues and cells (see Figure 29.4). It also transports fats from the digestive tract to the blood. Lymphocytes are produced which deal with waste products and toxins that build up in the tissues. The development of antibodies occurs in the lymphatic system and this helps to protect the body against disease and provide immunity against further attack .

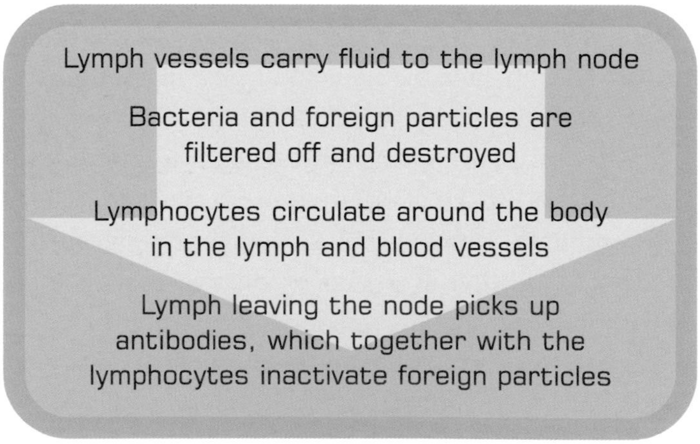

Lymph vessels carry fluid to the lymph node

Bacteria and foreign particles are filtered off and destroyed

Lymphocytes circulate around the body in the lymph and blood vessels

Lymph leaving the node picks up antibodies, which together with the lymphocytes inactivate foreign particles

Figure 29.4 *The role of the lymphatic system*

Immunity is a specific resistance to disease and it requires the production by the body of a specific antibody to destroy a specific antigen. We receive immunity to certain serious illnesses by being vaccinated against disease (artificially acquired active immunity) and our bodies provide their own immunity (naturally acquired active immunity), having been exposed at some time to a specific disease or illness.

Useful terms

Immunity is when the body is resistant to injury, particularly by poison, foreign bodies and parasites, due to the presence of antibodies.

An **antigen** is any substance which, when introduced into the body, brings about an immune response through the production of specific antibodies to neutralise the effects.

An **antibody** provides protection against invasion by antigens which may prove dangerous or irritating. It is a protein the body produces in response to the exposure to a specific antigen that has entered the body.

Oedema

This is an excessive build-up of fluid in the tissues. It may be caused by:

* an excessive amount of lymph being formed and an increase in the permeability of the capillary walls
* a blockage in the system between the lymph capillaries and the subclavian veins
* an increase in blood pressure.

Oedema may be localised in the area of an injury or it may be general as a result of heart or kidney conditions. Subcutaneous oedema commonly occurs in the legs and ankles due to the influence of gravity and in women it may occur before menstruation.

The beauty therapist must *never* treat any client who suffers from oedema caused by a medical condition. Always advise the client to seek medical advice or approval before treatment may be carried out.

The respiratory system consists of organs that exchange gases between the blood and the atmosphere. Oxygen (O_2) is essential for cells to survive. It is brought into the body every time we breath in (inhale) and carbon dioxide (CO_2) is released when we breath out (exhale). This process is called respiration. The cardiovascular system and the respiratory system together are responsible for supplying oxygen to the tissues and removing carbon dioxide, but the nervous system helps control respiration automatically to meet the body's demands.

Useful terms

Respiration is the process by which oxygen is taken into the body and used for the oxidation of food materials, to release the energy necessary to support life, and carbon dioxide and water are released as waste.

External respiration is the physical means by which the oxygen is obtained and the carbon dioxide is removed from the body.

Internal respiration is a chain of chemical processes which take place in every living cell to release the energy required for its vital activities.

The respiratory system consists of:
* the nose
* pharynx
* larynx
* trachea
* lungs
* bronchi
* bronchioles
* intercostal muscles
* diaphragm.

The nose

The nose is the natural pathway of air entering the body and it also acts as protection against irritants such as dust, which the nose expels by sneezing so that foreign bodies do not enter the lungs.

Breathing

We breathe on average 12 times per minute. This rate increases considerably during physical exercise – up to 80 times per minute. In a 24-hour period we breathe in and breathe out more than 8000 litres of air. Oxygen is carried to the body's tissues to produce the energy required for life via the lungs, the heart and the blood vessels.

Oxygen enters through the mouth, nose and trachea into the lungs where it travels to the alveoli, via the bronchioles, and the exchange of oxygen and carbon dioxide takes place. Oxygen is taken up by the haemoglobin in the blood and the red blood cells discharge carbon dioxide back into the lungs to be exhaled.

The nose is divided into two narrow cavities – nasal fossae – by the nasal septum, which is made up of bone and cartilage and covered with a soft delicate membrane called a mucous membrane that is continuous with the lining of the nostrils.

The nostrils are lined with coarse hairs, which protect the entrance to the nose. Air entering the nose is warmed to body temperature and moistened by contact with the mucous membrane and then filtered by the tiny hairs, or cilia, and mucus from the mucous membrane. The cilia then move the mucus gradually into the pharynx where it is swallowed. In the upper part of the nasal cavities the olfactory nerve endings detect smells.

The pharynx and larynx

The throat is the area which leads into the respiratory and digestive tracts from the oral and nasal cavities to the oesophagus and trachea. It is made up of the pharynx which, together with the trachea, nose and mouth, form the **upper respiratory tract**. The pharynx (throat) and larynx (voice box) have two main functions:
* to channel food and liquid into the digestive tract

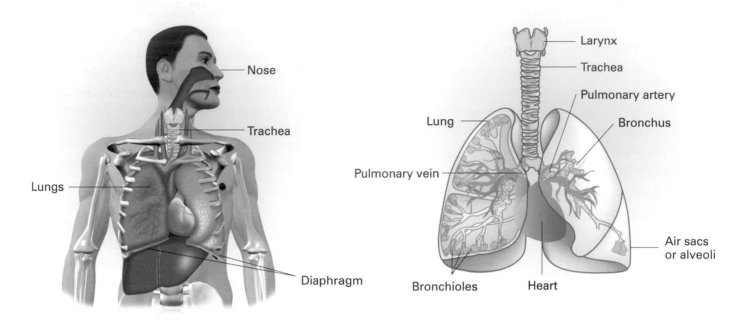

Figure 30.1 *The respiratory system*

* to transport air into the lungs
  The pharynx is made up of:
* the **nasopharynx** which lies above the soft palate and forms the back of the nose
* the **oropharynx** at the back of the mouth which is part of the airway between the mouth and the lungs
* the **laryngopharynx** – the lowest part of the pharynx which is involved entirely with swallowing.

The movements of the pharynx are carefully coordinated to ensure that respiratory gases end up in the lungs and food ends up in the oesophagus.

The larynx is situated between the pharynx and the trachea. It contains the vocal cords which vibrate to produce speech. The function of the larynx in respiration is its secondary function. The opening from the pharynx into the larynx is called the glottis and is closed by the epiglottis. When we breathe in or out the epiglottis is opened to allow air into the lungs.

The trachea

The trachea, or windpipe as it is more commonly known, is a tubular passageway for air approximately 12 cm in length and 2.5 cm in diameter. It extends from the larynx to the right and left bronchi. The wall of the trachea is made up of smooth muscle and elastic connective tissue with hoops of cartilage that hold open the elastic tissue. It is lined with mucous membrane and cilia, which waft invading germs and foreign particles back up into the throat to be swallowed.

The lungs

The two lungs fill most of the thorax and each one is divided into lobes containing a dense network of tubes. The right lung is larger and is divided into three lobes – the upper, middle and lower lobes. The left lung is slightly smaller, as the heart takes up more room on the left side of the thorax, and it is divided into two lobes – the upper and lower.

The largest of the tubes in the lungs are the bronchi and the smallest are the bronchioles, which terminate in air sacs called alveoli where the exchange of oxygen and carbon dioxide takes place. The second system of tubes is formed by the pulmonary arteries, which enter the lungs alongside the right and left bronchi. These tubes branch into smaller blood vessels running alongside the bronchioles and at the alveoli they form small capillaries.

The pleural membrane encloses and protects each lung and they are held open by the surface tension created by the fluid produced by the pleural membrane.

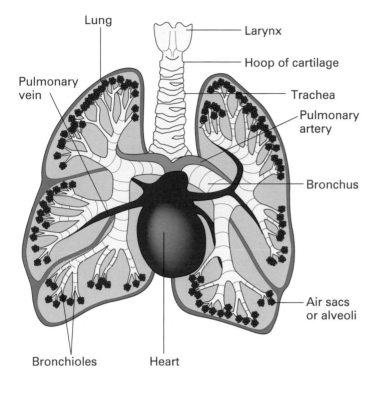

Figure 30.2 *The lungs*

The bronchi and bronchioles

Where the trachea terminates in the chest, it divides into the right bronchus which enters the right lung and the left bronchus which enters the left lung. Inside the lungs the bronchi further divide into secondary and tertiary (third) bronchi which become smaller tubes called bronchioles.

The intercostal muscles

The internal and external intercostal muscles are situated between the ribs. When the external muscles are contracted they move the ribcage upwards helping to increase lung volume during inspiration (breathing in). When the internal muscles are contracted they force air out of the lungs during expiration (breathing out).

The diaphragm

This is a sheet of muscle which forms the floor of the thoracic cavity. When it contracts it flattens increasing the vertical space in the thoracic cavity and allowing the lungs to expand and fill with air during inspiration. When this muscle is relaxed it increases in size, becoming dome-shaped, which reduces the space in the thoracic cavity and this helps to squeeze air out of the lungs during expiration.

Food is vital to life as it provides the body with the energy required for essential activities such as muscle contraction, nerve functioning and cell activity and renewal. The food we eat is too large to pass through to the cells that require it, so it has to be broken down for use by the body's cells during **digestion**. The organs which perform this function make up the **digestive system**.

The digestive system depends on a number of different organs, glands and the enzymes they produce working together to change the food we eat into a digestible form that is absorbed from the small intestine and carried by the blood for immediate use or storage.

Digestion

Digestion is the process by which the food is broken down into molecules small enough to be absorbed by the cells and used by the body for energy, growth and repair. Digestion occurs in the alimentary canal and this consists of:

* the mouth
* the pharynx
* the oesophagus
* the stomach
* the small intestine
* the large intestine
* the rectum and anal canal.

The organs and glands which assist the digestive system are the liver, the gall bladder, the pancreas.

The stages of digestion

Digestion occurs in several stages.

1 Ingestion

Ingestion is the taking in of food through the mouth.

2 Digestion

Digestion is the breakdown of food by chemical and mechanical means.

Chemical digestion occurs when enzymes present in the secretions from the glands of the digestive system react with the food swallowed, breaking it up into small

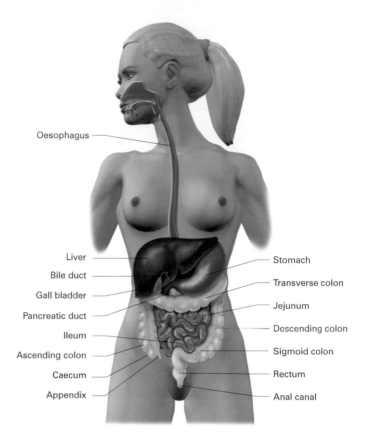

Oesophagus

Liver
Bile duct
Gall bladder
Pancreatic duct
Ileum
Ascending colon
Caecum
Appendix

Stomach
Transverse colon
Jejunum
Descending colon
Sigmoid colon
Rectum
Anal canal

Figure 31.1 *The digestive system*

molecules which may pass through the walls of the digestive organs to be utilised by the body's cells.

Mechanical digestion is a combination of voluntary and involuntary movements that aid the chemical process. Digestion starts in the mouth but takes place mainly in the stomach and small intestine.

The secretions from the glands of the digestive system are:

* saliva from the salivary glands
* gastric juice from the stomach
* intestinal juice from the small intestine
* pancreatic juice from the pancreas.
* bile from the liver.

Teeth are an essential part of digestion as they help to cut, shred, crush and grind the food we eat.

3 Absorption

Absorption is the uptake of fluids or other substances by the tissues of the body. Digested food is absorbed into the blood and lymph from the alimentary canal and transported to the cells to provide energy. The stomach also plays a very small part in absorption as it does allow some water, electrolytes, certain drugs and alcohol to permeate through the walls into the bloodstream.

4 Excretion

Excretion is the final stage of digestion when the indigestible food substances or those which have no value to the body are passed out of the body.

The process of digestion

Digestion begins in the mouth where the food is mechanically broken down by the teeth and chemically broken down when mixed with saliva produced by the salivary glands. The saliva contains the enzyme ptyalin, which starts breaking down some of the carbohydrates into smaller molecules known as maltose and glucose. The food becomes easier to swallow as it is formed into a rounded mass of food called a **bolus**.

After swallowing the food, by contraction of the muscles in the walls of the pharynx, digestion occurs automatically as there is now no control over its movement. The food is carried down the oesophagus by involuntary muscular contractions by the process of **peristalsis**.

When the food reaches the stomach it is acted upon chemically by the digestive juices secreted from the glands of the mucous membrane and mechanically by the muscles of the stomach wall. Mucus, hydrochloric acid and the enzyme pepsin are poured on to the food and a new series of chemical reactions begins. Nerve impulses, the presence of food and the secretion of hormones govern the amount of stomach juices that are released. The hormone gastrin stimulates the stomach cells to release hydrochloric acid and the pepsin breaks the food down into peptones. The mucus secretion prevents the stomach lining from becoming damaged by acid and the gastrin production ceases when the acidity reaches a certain point.

The food is broken down into a semi-fluid called **chyme**, which then passes into the **duodenum**, the first and smallest part of the small intestine, via the **pyloric sphincter** muscle, which relaxes to allow the chyme to pass through.

Pancreatic juice from the pancreas and **bile** from the liver neutralise the acid chyme. The enzymes from the pancreas process the proteins, carbohydrates and fats further and bile helps in the emulsification of fats. The bile is stored in the gall bladder until it is required in the small intestine. The digested food then travels along the **jejunum** where the useful nutrients from the food are absorbed.

The **ileum**, which is the final part of the small intestine, absorbs any remaining nutrients into the bloodstream and material that is of no use to the body enters the large intestine through the **ileocaecal valve** to be removed.

The remaining food material accumulates in the ascending colon and then by means of peristalsis moves through the transverse and descending colon to the rectum via the **sigmoid colon**. These solid faeces are stored in the rectum before being released through the anus.

Figure 31.2 *The large intestine*

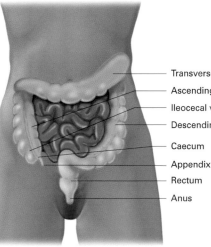

- Transverse colon
- Ascending colon
- Ileocecal valve
- Descending colon
- Caecum
- Appendix
- Rectum
- Anus

The body is continuously producing by-products and waste as a result of the metabolism of nutrients, which must be removed to prevent the body poisoning itself. It has several methods of ridding itself of these waste products through the excretory systems in the body. **Excretion** is the process by which the body eliminates waste.

The urinary system is one of the main systems responsible for excretion and it consists of:

* two kidneys
* two ureters
* the bladder
* the urethra.

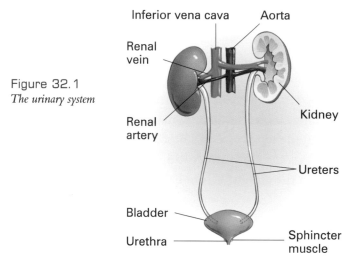

Figure 32.1
The urinary system

The kidneys

The kidneys are found just above the waist on the back wall of the abdomen. They contain thousands of tiny filtering units – **nephrons** – and each nephron is divided into two parts:

* the **glomerulus**, or filtering part
* the **tubule**, where water and essential nutrients are extracted from the blood.

The glomerulus contains a knot of tiny blood capillaries which have very thin walls. Water and waste pass easily across these walls into the collecting system of tubules on the other side. The tubules run between the glomeruli to a collecting system which drains into the bladder. Each glomerulus is surrounded by a **Bowman's capsule** and it is here that most of the filtered water and salt is reabsorbed.

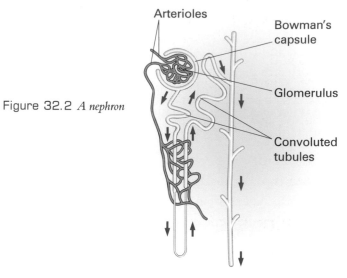

Figure 32.2 *A nephron*

The kidneys are responsible for filtering nitrogen containing waste, the most common compound of which is urea, out of the blood stream and regulating the amount of water passed out of the body maintaining the correct balance of salt in the body.

The kidneys receive about one litre of blood every minute through a renal artery. This is then filtered, separating the watery element (plasma) of blood, which passes into the tubule, from the rest – water, salt and other valuable substances (glucose, amino acids, minerals and vitamins) which are then absorbed back into the bloodstream. Some water, urea and other waste substances are then passed in the form of urine down two tubes (ureters) to the bladder for excretion.

The ureters and urethra

These are two tubes through which urine passes from the kidneys to the bladder. They have one-way valves in the opening to the bladder to prevent urine from flowing back to the kidneys when the bladder is full. The urine passes out of the bladder through the urethra which is situated at the lowest point in the bladder, the opening of which is kept closed by a sphincter, a circular muscle which contracts to seal the passageway. During urination this sphincter muscle relaxes at the same time as the bladder wall contracts to expel the urine.

The bladder

This is a hollow, thick-walled, muscular organ lying in the lower part of the pelvic basin between the pubic bones and the rectum and it is a reservoir for urine. The bladder walls are composed of a number of muscular layers, which stretch when the bladder is filling and then contract when it is emptying. There is an almost continuous trickle of urine from the kidneys to the bladder and when the bladder starts to resist, the need to pass urine is felt.

Functions of the urinary system

The main function is to help keep the body in homeostasis (the body's internal environment remaining balanced) by controlling the composition and volume of blood. It achieves this by removing and restoring selected amounts of water and solutes. Waste is filtered from the blood and excreted from the body in the form of liquid urine. There are three processes involved in the formation of urine: **filtration**, **reabsorption** and **secretion**. This system also helps to control the pH of the blood and regulate blood pressure (renal autoregulation).

The kidneys also help in synthesising glucose by secreting a hormone (erythropoietin) that stimulates the production of red blood cells and help in the synthesis of vitamin D.

This is the control centre and communication network of the body and it works in conjunction with the endocrine system. The functions of the nervous system are:

* to sense change within the body
* to sense change in the environment outside the body
* to interpret and respond to the changes to maintain homeostasis.

These responses are in the form of muscular contraction or glandular secretion. The response from the nervous system is much faster than the response from the endocrine system, but they are equally effective in their roles.

Figure 33.1 *The nervous system*

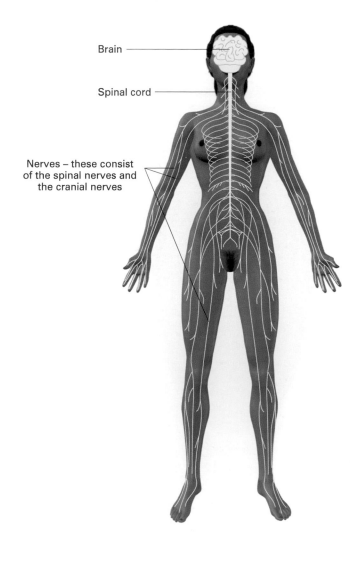

Brain

Spinal cord

Nerves – these consist of the spinal nerves and the cranial nerves

The central and peripheral nervous systems

The nervous system is divided into the **central nervous system** (CNS), consisting of the brain and spinal cord, and the **peripheral nervous system** (PNS), consisting of the **spinal** and **cranial nerves**. The cranial nerves originate from nuclei in the brain and there are 12 pairs. Spinal nerves are connected to the spinal cord and there are 31 pairs.

The brain and the spinal cord receive messages via the sensory fibres from the body's sense organs and receptors. They then filter and analyse them and send signals along the motor fibres which produce an appropriate response in the muscles and glands. **Sensory nerves** carry messages into the brain. **Motor nerves** carry messages from the brain.

The PNS is divided into the afferent system, which carries information from sense organs and receptors to the central nervous system, and the efferent system, which carries information from the central nervous system to muscles and glands. The efferent system is further subdivided into the autonomic and somatic nervous systems and the autonomic is subdivided into the sympathetic and parasympathetic nervous systems (see Figure 33.2).

Figure 33.2 *Organisation of the nervous system*

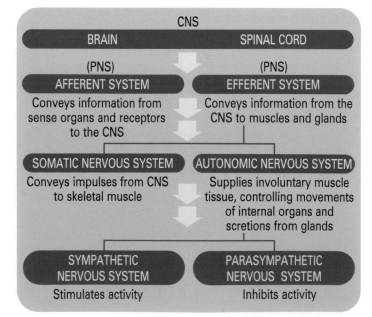

CNS	
BRAIN	SPINAL CORD
(PNS)	(PNS)
AFFERENT SYSTEM	EFFERENT SYSTEM
Conveys information from sense organs and receptors to the CNS	Conveys information from the CNS to muscles and glands
SOMATIC NERVOUS SYSTEM	AUTONOMIC NERVOUS SYSTEM
Conveys impulses from CNS to skeletal muscle	Supplies involuntary muscle tissue, controlling movements of internal organs and scretions from glands
SYMPATHETIC NERVOUS SYSTEM	PARASYMPATHETIC NERVOUS SYSTEM
Stimulates activity	Inhibits activity

The cells, which make up the nervous system are called **neurones** and they come in various shapes and sizes. Each neurone is a nerve cell of grey matter with projections called **dendrites** and **axons**. The long fibrous axon has a delicate covering called a **neurilemma** and most axons have a **myelin sheath** which acts as an insulator protecting the axon from injury and speeding the flow of nerve impulses along its length. These impulses are then carried to the nerve cell via the dendrites.

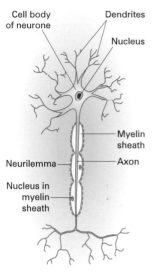

Figure 33.3 *A neurone*

Neurones or nerve cells

Neurones conduct impulses (messages) from one part of the body to another. They process information for the nervous system. The ability to respond to stimuli and convert them to impulses is called excitability.

The autonomic nervous system

This is the part of the nervous system that supplies involuntary muscle tissue in the body controlling movements of internal organs and secretions from glands. It is divided into:

* the sympathetic nervous system
* the parasympathetic nervous system.

The two parts have opposing effects on the body in stressful situations. The sympathetic nerves speed up body activity; the parasympathetic nerves slow down body activity. The sympathetic impulses become stronger as a reaction to stress. The heart beats faster, blood vessels dilate, the liver produces more glucose, the pupils of the eyes dilate, hair stands on end, sweat glands produce more sweat and blood pressure rises due to the constriction of small arterioles in the skin. All this prepares the body to cope with the stress.

When the stressful situation passes the parasympathetic nerves take over and help the function of the organs to return to normal.

The brain

The brain is one of the largest organs in the body. It consists of:

* the brain stem, which comprises the medulla oblongata, pons varolii and the midbrain
* the cerebrum, which makes up about seven-eighths of the weight of the brain and occupies most of the cranium
* the thalamus and hypothalamus above the brain stem
* the cerebellum, which lies below the cerebrum and behind the brain stem.

The brain is protected by the cranial bones and the cranial meninges which is composed of dense fibrous connective tissue. The cerebrospinal fluid also acts as a protection against injury circulating around the brain and through the ventricles in the brain serving as a shock absorber for the central nervous system. It has good supply of blood vessels, which provide oxygen and nutrients.

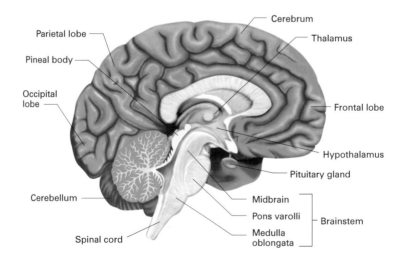

Figure 33.4 *The brain*

The brain stem

The medulla oblongata

This is a continuation of the upper part of the spinal cord and is the lowest part of the brain stem. It contains centres which help to control the heart rate, the depth and rate of breathing and other non-vital autonomic reflexes such as swallowing, sneezing and coughing.

The pons varolii

This is situated just above the medulla oblongata and in front of the cerebellum. It is a bridge connecting the spinal cord with the brain and parts of the brain with each other.

The midbrain

This is the highest part of the brain stem and is situated centrally under the cerebrum just below the hypothalamus.

The thalamus and hypothalamus

The thalamus is the main relay station for the sensory impulses sent to the cerebral cortex from the spinal cord, brain stem, cerebellum and parts of the cerebrum and it interprets sensory messages to the brain. It is also concerned with memory and certain emotions. It is situated above the midbrain and is approximately 3 cm in length.

The hypothalamus is a small but important area under the thalamus and just above the pituitary gland, and is responsible for controlling many body activities, most of them related to homeostasis:

* It helps to control the autonomic nervous system, regulating the heartbeat, controlling the secretion of many glands, the movement of food through the digestive tract and contraction of the urinary bladder.
* It receives sensory impulses.
* It is the principal intermediary between the nervous system and the endocrine system. When it detects certain changes occurring in the body it releases chemicals that stimulate or inhibit the anterior pituitary gland.
* It produces two hormones – ADH and oxytocin – which are transported and stored in the posterior pituitary gland.
* It controls normal body temperature.
* It stimulates hunger and inhibits food intake when full.
* It produces a sensation of thirst when fluid is reduced in the body.
* It helps to maintain sleeping and waking patterns.

The cerebrum

Often referred to as the cerebral cortex, the cerebrum forms a large part of the brain and is divided into four

lobes, each of which takes its name from the bone under which it lies. These are:

* the frontal lobe
* the parietal lobe
* the occipital lobe
* the temporal lobe.

The functions of the cerebrum include:

* mental activities involving memory, intelligence, sense of responsibility, thinking and reasoning
* sensory perceptions of pain, temperature, touch, sight, hearing, taste and smell
* initiation and control of voluntary muscle contraction.

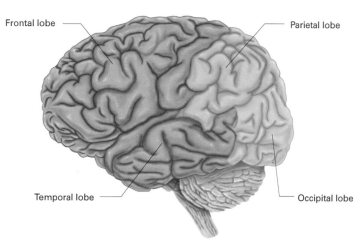

Frontal lobe

Parietal lobe

Temporal lobe

Occipital lobe

Figure 33.5 *The cerebrum*

Emotions

Emotion involves the entire nervous system, in particular the limbic system and the autonomic nervous system.

The limbic system

This system is a complex set of structures that lies above and around the thalamus and just under the cerebrum. Some of the structures are:

* the hypothalamus, which controls the autonomic nervous system and is connected to the pituitary gland and thus regulates the endocrine system
* the hippocampus, which is involved in the formation of long-term memory

* the amygdala, which is involved in aggression and fear.

The limbic system is primarily responsible for emotions such as aggression, fear and pleasure. It also controls appetite and sleep cycles, promotes bonding, processes the sense of smell and modulates libido (see Chapter 16 Aromatherapy, page 231).

Cerebellum

This is the second largest area in the brain occupying the posterior, inferior aspect of the cranial cavity. It is a motor area of the brain controlling subconscious movements of the skeletal muscles, movements required for posture, coordination, balance and delicate movements such as playing the piano or typing a letter. Messages are transmitted from the inner ear to the cerebellum, which responds by sending impulses to the muscles necessary for maintaining balance.

The cranial nerves

There are twelve pairs of cranial nerves, ten of which originate from the brain stem. Each pair has a number representing the order in which they arise from the brain and a name indicating their distribution or function. Some cranial nerves are sensory only, others have both functions and are referred to as 'mixed'.

1 Olfactory – sensory (smell).

2 Optic – sensory (vision).

3 Oculomotor – mixed: motor (movement of the eyelid and eyeball, constriction of pupil); sensory (muscle sense).

4 Trochlear – mixed: motor (movement of the eyeball); sensory (muscle sense).

5 Trigeminal – mixed: motor (chewing); sensory (touch, pain, temperature from the upper eyelid down to the jaw).

6 Abducent – mixed: motor (movement of the eyeball); sensory (muscle sense).

7 Facial – mixed: motor (facial expressions, secretion of saliva and tears); sensory (taste, muscle sense).

8 Vestibulocochlear – sensory (conveys impulses associated with hearing and equilibrium).

9 Glossopharyngeal – mixed: motor (swallowing and secretion of saliva); sensory (taste, regulation of blood pressure, muscle sense).

10 Vagus – mixed: motor (swallowing, visceral muscle movement); sensory (sensations from pharynx, larynx, respiratory passageways, lungs, oesophagus, heart, stomach, small intestine, part of large intestine and gall bladder).

11 Accessory – mixed: motor (swallowing, movement of the head); sensory (muscle sense).

12 Hypoglossal – mixed: motor (movement of tongue during speech and swallowing); sensory (muscle sense).

The spinal cord

The spinal cord begins as a continuation of the medulla oblongata extending down the vertebral column. Its main function is to carry impulses to and from the brain and the peripheral nervous system. Its second function is to provide reflexes, which are fast responses to internal or external stimuli, helping to maintain the body's internal balance or homeostasis.

There are 31 spinal nerves, which are named according to the region from which they emerge. They are:

* eight pairs of cervical nerves
* twelve pairs of thoracic nerves
* five pairs of lumbar nerves
* five pairs of sacral nerves
* one pair of coccygeal nerves.

Each spinal nerve splits into branches that, in turn, split into smaller branches to form a network which radiates all over the body.

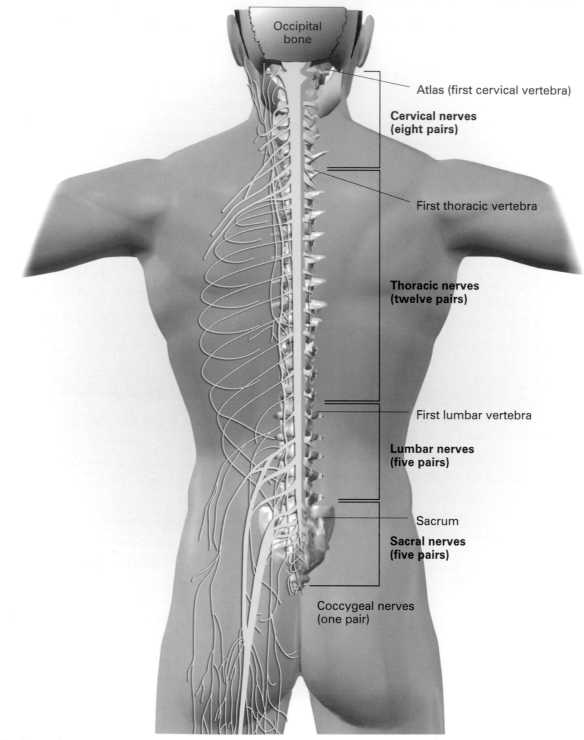

Occipital bone

Atlas (first cervical vertebra)

**Cervical nerves
(eight pairs)**

First thoracic vertebra

**Thoracic nerves
(twelve pairs)**

First lumbar vertebra

**Lumbar nerves
(five pairs)**

Sacrum

**Sacral nerves
(five pairs)**

Coccygeal nerves
(one pair)

Figure 33.6 *The spinal nerves*

34 The endocrine system

The endocrine system is responsible for controlling many of the body's functions, providing the driving force behind mental and physical activity, growth and reproduction of humans. It works in conjunction with the nervous system – the nervous system controls muscular contraction and secretion from glands while the endocrine system initiates changes in the metabolic activities of tissues. It consists of endocrine or ductless glands, which are also referred to as organs of internal secretion as they secrete chemical substances called hormones directly into the bloodstream.

The endocrine glands are composed of millions of cells, each of which makes hormones or chemical messengers that are then transported by the blood to the target cells in the body.

Hormones

Some hormones affect most parts of the body and increase the rate of chemical reaction in all of the body's cells, for example growth hormone.

Some hormones only affect certain tissues called 'target' tissues and only these tissues respond to the hormone. This is because these tissues have specific receptors which receive a hormone and so initiate a response.

The endocrine system consists of:
* the hypothalamus
* one pineal gland
* one pituitary gland
* one thyroid gland
* four parathyroid glands
* one thymus gland
* two adrenal glands
* islets of langerhans in the pancreas
* two ovaries in the female
* two testes in the male.

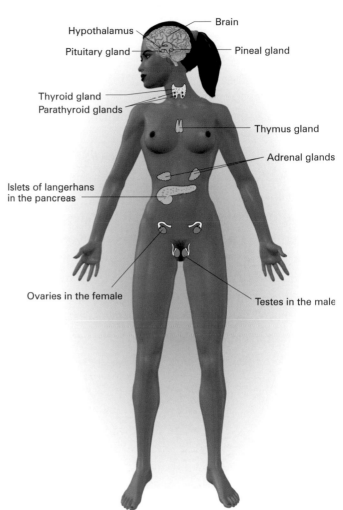

Figure 34.1 *The endocrine system*

The endocrine glands

The pineal gland
This is situated in front of the cerebellum and is thought to produce a hormone melatonin, which informs the brain when it is day and night. It inhibits the growth and maturation of the gonads or sex glands until puberty.

The pituitary gland
Also known as the **hypophisis**, this gland is situated at the base of the brain and is often called the master gland because its hormones help to control so many of the other endocrine glands in the body. However, it is known that the hypothalamus produces secretions, which regulate the pituitary gland.

The gland has two parts, the anterior and the posterior lobes.

The anterior lobe produces the following hormones:

* The thyroid stimulating hormone (TSH) controls the thyroid gland.
* The adrenocorticotrophic hormone (ACTH) stimulates the adrenal cortex.
* The somatotrophin or growth hormone (GH) controls general body growth.
* The follicle stimulating hormone (FSH) stimulates the production of eggs in the ovaries and sperm in the testes.
* The luteinising hormone (LH) prepares the uterus for implantation of the egg and prepares the mammary glands for milk production in the female. In the male, it stimulates the testes to develop and secrete testosterone.
* Prolactin (PRL) initiates and maintains milk secretion.

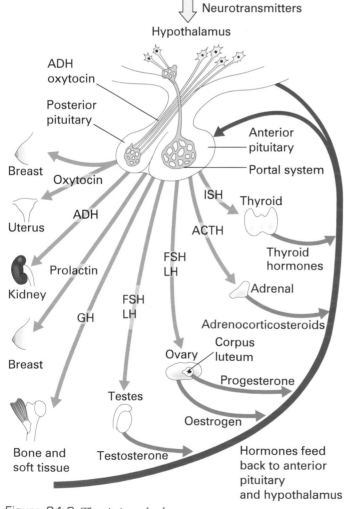

Figure 34.2 *The pituitary gland*

* The melanocyte-stimulating hormone (MSH) stimulates the dispersal of melanin in the melanocytes.

The posterior lobe stores the following hormones produced by the hypothalamus:

* The vasopressin antidiuretic hormone (ADH) decreases urine volume.
* Oxytocin stimulates the uterus to contract and the mammary glands to produce milk.

The hypothalamus

This is an area of the brain near the pituitary gland and is the link between the nervous system and the endocrine glands. It has special nerve cells, which make releasing factors that act on cells of the anterior pituitary before they can send out their hormones.

The thyroid gland

The thyroid gland has two lobes situated on either side of the trachea and by a narrow strip of tissue. The thyroid gland is responsible for regulating the body's metabolic rate and influencing the growth of the body. It secretes thyroxine which if over secreted (hypersecretion) causes **hyperthyroidism** or **exophthalmic goitre**. This causes an enlarged thyroid, bulging eyes, rapid pulse, excessive sweating and restlessness.

If there is an under secretion (hyposecretion) it causes cretinism, poor mental and physical development in children or **myxoedema** in middle age. The characteristics of the latter condition are a slowing down of metabolism, puffy tissues and a slowness of speech and movement.

The parathyroid glands

There are two pairs situated on the posterior surface of the thyroid gland. These glands together with the thyroid gland regulate the levels of calcium in the blood. The thyroid lowers the amount of calcium and the parathyroid controls calcium metabolism.

When blood calcium levels are high calcitonin is released by the thyroid gland and excess calcium is then deposited in the bones. When blood calcium levels become too low, parathormone is released by the parathyroids and calcium is reabsorbed.

Thymus gland

This is a lymph organ which lies behind the sternum in front of the heart. It is thought to be important in helping the process of cellular immunity by processing T cells and B cells, lymphocytes that help with cellular immunity.

The adrenal glands (suprarenals)

These glands are situated immediately above the kidneys and each gland consists of two distinct parts, the outer part or **cortex** and the inner core or **medulla**.

The adrenal cortex

The adrenal cortex secretes hormones called **steroids**. The most important divide into three main groups:

* **Mineralocorticoids**. The most important of these is aldosterone and its functions are sodium and chloride retention and potassium excretion. The water and electrolyte balance in the body are maintained by these functions.
* **Glucocorticoids**. Cortisone and hydrocortisone (cortisol) assist in the conversion of carbohydrate into glycogen. They increase the blood sugar level, help utilise fat and suppress the natural reaction to inflammation. A deficiency in cortisone production can cause the pituitary to stimulate an over production of adrenal androgens, thereby creating hypertrichosis.
* **Sex hormones**. A small number of both androgens (male hormones) and oestrogens (female hormones) are secreted. They are influential in sexual development and growth but are not as important as the sex hormones produced by the gonads. In females, however, the adrenals are the principal sources of androgens, which are capable of stimulating facial and body hair. Under secretion of adrenal cortex hormones causes Addison disease, the characteristics of which are low blood pressure, an excessive loss of salt, dehydration, muscle weakness, increased pigmentation of the skin, menstrual disturbances and loss of body hair.

The adrenal medulla

The adrenal medulla secretes **adrenalin** and **noradrenalin**. These are known as the 'fight or flight' hormones because they prepare the body to cope with danger or stress. A surge of adrenalin when the body faces danger or excitement causes the heart to beat faster and more strongly, which then raises the blood pressure. At the same time, the blood vessels constrict and blood is diverted to the muscles and heart where it is most needed. The liver is stimulated to convert glycogen into glucose supplying the muscles with the necessary fuel to provide extra energy.

The pancreas

This gland is situated in the abdomen and is attached to the duodenum by the pancreatic duct. It is an endocrine gland secreting **insulin** and also an exocrine gland (secreting on to a free surface or into ducts) as the pancreatic juice is secreted directly into the intestine to aid digestion and not into the bloodstream. The islets of langerhans are cells in the pancreas which secrete insulin necessary for controlling the sugar level in the body. A deficiency of insulin results in diabetes mellitus.

The ovaries and testes (gonads)

The male gonads or testes secrete androgens, the most important one being testosterone and oestrogen in small amounts. Testosterone is the hormone responsible for the development of the secondary sexual characteristics of the male such as the distribution of hair, deepening of the voice and enlargement of the genitalia.

The female gonads or ovaries produce ova and secrete the hormones oestrogen and progesterone and small amounts of androgens. They regulate menstruation and play an important part in the development of secondary sexual characteristics. Progesterone's principal function is to initiate changes in the endometrium, the lining of the womb, in preparation for pregnancy. The ovaries also produce a hormone called relaxin, which helps dilate the cervix towards the end of pregnancy.

Hormones

Hormones are secretions of endocrine glands that alter the physiological activity of cells in the body helping to maintain homeostasis (see Figure 34.3).

When this balance is upset and hormone levels become either excessive or deficient, disorders will occur. Some hormones affect most parts of the body and increase the rate of chemical reaction in all of the body's cells, while others only affect certain tissues called 'target tissues'. Table 34.1 shows the actions of hormones.

Hormones	Actions
Pituitary gland (AL)	
Thyroid stimulating hormone (TSH)	Controls the growth of the thyroid gland and stimulates hormones including the secretion of thyroxine. Secretion is controlled by the hypothalamus and it affects the body's metabolism
Adrenocorticotrophic hormone (ACTH)	Stimulates the adrenal gland to produce cortisol, provides negative feedback to the hypothalamus when hormone levels drop, stimulates the production of other steroids, excess causes over production of androgens
Somatotrophin or growth hormone (GH)	Causes cells to grow and multiply, increases the rate of protein synthesis and fat and carbohydrate metabolism
Follicle stimulating hormone (FSH)	Initiates the development of the ova in the female and stimulates the secretion of female sex hormones. In the male, it stimulates the testes to produce sperm
Luteinising hormone (LH)	Stimulates the ovary to release the ovum in the female and prepares the uterus to receive the fertilised egg, stimulates formation of the corpus luteum in the ovary and secretion of oestrogen and progesterone. In the male, it stimulates the testes to produce testosterone
Prolactin (PRL)	Initiates and maintains milk production in the mammary glands
Melanocyte stimulating hormone (MSH)	Stimulates the dispersal of melanin in the melanocytes
Pituitary gland (PL)	
Oxytocin	Stimulates the contraction of the uterus and milk flow after birth
Vasopressin (ADH)	An antidiuretic hormone which decreases urine volume
Thyroid gland	
Thyroxine	Regulates metabolism, growth and development and activity of the nervous system
Triiodothyronine	Regulates metabolism, growth and development and activity of the nervous system
Calcitonin	Lowers levels of calcium in the blood by accelerating the absorption of calcium by the bones
Parathyroid	
Parathormone	Controls the balance of calcium and phosphate in the blood, increases the rate of calcium absorption into the blood from the gastro-intestinal tract and activates vitamin D

Hormones	Actions
Adrenal cortex	
Mineralocorticoids (aldosterone)	Increases the levels of sodium and water in the blood and decreases the levels of potassium, maintaining water balance in the body
Glucocorticoids (cortisol)	Help promote normal metabolism, resistance to stress and counter inflammatory response
Sex hormones	Influential in sexual development, insignificant in the adult, only small quantities of oestrogens and androgens are produced
Adrenal medulla	
Adrenalin (epinephrine)	Helps the body resist stress, increases blood pressure by increasing heart rate and constricting blood vessels, accelerates respiration, decreases the rate of digestion, increases blood sugar level and makes the muscles work more efficiently
Noradrenalin (norepinephrine)	Less potent in action than adrenalin but effects are the same
Pancreas	
Insulin	Lowers blood sugar levels by transporting glucose (sugar) into the body cells converting it into glycogen. Stimulates protein synthesis and inhibits the breakdown of fats
Glucagon	Raises blood sugar levels, converts glycogen in the liver into glucose which is then released into the bloodstream
The ovaries	
Oestrogen	Develops and maintains female sexual characteristics and fat distribution. Regulates the menstrual cycle, maintains pregnancy and prepares the mammary glands for lactation
Progesterone	Prepares the lining of the uterus for pregnancy, develops the placenta and prepares mammary glands for lactation
The testes	
Testosterone	Stimulates the development and maintenance of the male sexual characteristics, hair growth on the body, enlargement of the larynx, production of sperm, etc.

Table 34.1 *Hormones and their actions*

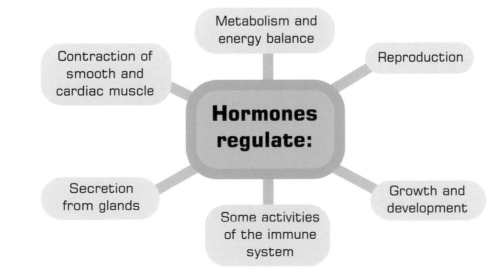

Figure 34.3 *The function of hormones*

Reproduction is the means by which life is sustained and genetic material is passed from generation to generation maintaining the continuation of human life.

The reproductive organs of the male and female are different both anatomically and physiologically. The function of the male reproductive system is to produce numerous, minute spermatazoa (reproductive cells), store them and transfer them to the female reproductive system. The functions of the female reproductive system are to produce ova (reproductive cells), provide a place for the fertilised ovum to grow, nourishment to sustain it and provide milk to feed it after birth.

The male reproductive system

The organs of the male reproductive system are:
* the testes which produce sperm
* ducts and glands that store or transport sperm
* accessory glands to add secretions (semen)
* the penis to introduce spermatozoa into the vagina.

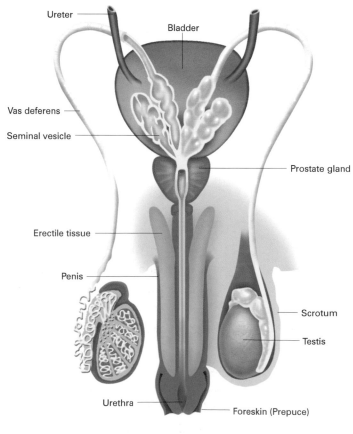

Ureter
Bladder
Vas deferens
Seminal vesicle
Prostate gland
Erectile tissue
Penis
Scrotum
Testis
Urethra
Foreskin (Prepuce)

Figure 35.1 *The male reproductive system*

The testes

The testes or male gonads are a pair of oval glands, which are supported by the scrotum. They produce spermatozoa and the male hormone testosterone. Spermatozoa are produced at the rate of about 300 million per day and have a life expectancy of 48 hours within the female reproductive system. Testosterone controls the development, growth and maintenance of the male sex organs. It stimulates bone growth, sexual behaviour, final maturation of sperm and the development of male sexual characteristics.

Ducts and accessory glands

There are numerous fine ducts leading from the testes (vas efferentia) which join the epididymis in which spermatozoa are stored. A single duct, the vas deferens, runs from the epididymis through the inguinal canal to the abdomen where it is joined by the seminal vesicles and together they form the ejaculatory ducts which open into the urethra. The prostate and bulbo-urethral glands open directly into the urethra and they produce secretions which contain seminal fluid to aid the motility and viability of the spermatozoa.

The penis

The penis is erectile tissue, which dilates with blood under the influence of sexual stimulation ejaculating the spermatozoa into the vagina of the female.

The female reproductive system

The organs of the female reproductive system are:
* the ovaries which produce ova
* the fallopian tubes which transport the ova to the uterus
* the uterus or womb
* the vagina
* the mammary glands.

The ovaries

The ovaries, or female gonads, are a pair of glands positioned in the upper pelvic cavity on each side of the

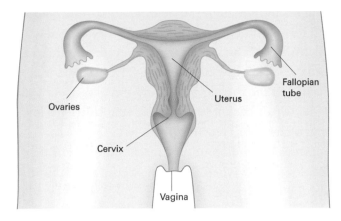

Figure 35.2 *The female reproductive system*

uterus. They produce and discharge the ova and secrete the female sex hormones, progesterone, oestrogens and relaxin.

The fallopian tubes

There are two fallopian or uterine tubes which extend laterally from the uterus transporting the ova from the ovaries to the uterus. About once a month an ovum ruptures from the ovary, a process known as ovulation, and is swept into the fallopian tube and moved along to be fertilised by the spermatozoa. If it is fertilised, it descends into the uterus and develops into an embryo; an unfertilised ovum disintegrates and is removed during menstruation.

The uterus

This is a hollow muscular organ lying in the pelvic cavity between the urinary bladder and the rectum. It is the site of menstruation after puberty and the environment for the developing embryo during the 40-week gestation period.

The vagina

This is a fibromuscular tube connecting the internal and external organs of reproduction. It is a passageway for the menstrual flow and is the tube into which the penis is inserted during sexual intercourse and the lower part of the birth canal through which the baby is delivered.

The mammary glands

The breasts, or mammary glands, are accessory glands of the female reproductive system. Each gland consists of 15–20 lobes separated by adipose tissue. The size of the

female breasts is determined by the amount of adipose tissue present. Each lobe is separated into compartments called lobules, which contain milk secreting cells called alveoli. The alveoli carry the milk into a series of secondary tubules and from there they pass into the mammary ducts. Close to the nipple, these ducts form ampullae where milk is stored and they become lactiferous ducts that terminate at the nipple.

The female breasts start to develop at the onset of puberty and their main function is the secretion and ejection of milk, commonly called lactation. The secretion of milk is largely controlled by the hormone prolactin with some help from progesterone and oestrogens. Oxytocin stimulates the release of the milk in response to the stimulation of the nipple by the baby sucking.

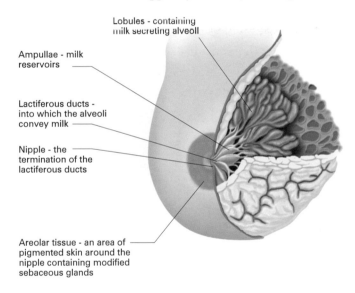

Lobules - containing milk secreting alveoli

Ampullae - milk reservoirs

Lactiferous ducts - into which the alveoli convey milk

Nipple - the termination of the lactiferous ducts

Areolar tissue - an area of pigmented skin around the nipple containing modified sebaceous glands

Figure 35.3 *The mammary gland*

The menstrual cycle

This occurs regularly in females throughout their childbearing years, which last approximately 35 years. It is a series of changes in the endometrium, the mucous membrane lining of the uterus, of a non-pregnant female and these changes are controlled by the hypothalamus which acts as a menstrual clock.

An egg is released from an ovary and travels to the womb. If it is fertilised, it will be nourished by secretions from the cells lining the womb until it burrows into the wall itself and receives nourishment from the mother's own blood supply. When the egg is not fertilised, the lining of the womb breaks up and is shed during the menstrual flow, a new lining then forms for the next egg to be released.

Reproduction

Fertilisation takes place when the spermatozoa penetrate the surface of the egg and they fuse together to form a single nucleus which then begins to divide. Within 72 hours, the nucleus travels into the uterus where it burrows into the lining to be nourished. The placenta then forms and by the twelfth week it is a separate organ which allows substances to pass from the mother to the foetus ensuring its development. The placenta is attached to the foetus via the umbilical cord and waste products pass back to the mother after nutrients and oxygen have been received from her. The foetus continues to develop until it reaches the end of the gestation period when the mother goes into labour and the baby is delivered.

The special senses include smell, taste, sight, hearing and balance and they allow us to detect changes in the environment.

The sense of smell

The nose has two functions – respiration (see Chapter 30 The respiratory system) and sense of smell, which has a connection with the part of the brain that has grown to be the sorting house for emotional responses. Our sense of smell provides us with a warning system giving us valuable information about the environment and it is closely linked with our sense of taste.

Structure and function of the olfactory system

The sensory receptors for smell are found in the roof of the nasal cavity just below the frontal lobes of the brain. This is known as the **olfactory area** and it contains millions of **olfactory cells**. Each of these cells has

about a dozen fine hairs called cilia which are surrounded by mucus to keep the cilia moist and trap odorous substances and these cilia help to increase our sensitivity to smell.

Most substances that have a smell are chemically complex and particles of these chemicals are given off into the air and then inhaled into the nostrils and to the mucus which surrounds the cilia. These chemicals must then dissolve in the mucus before they can be detected. In order that a substance can be smelled, it must be volatile, that is, capable of giving off a gas which can enter the nostrils. The chemicals in gas form are far more efficient as high concentrations will reach the olfactory cells through the air. Wetness also heightens smell because when the water evaporates from a substance it will carry particles with it into the air. A good example is perfume which is chemically complex and gives off gas easily.

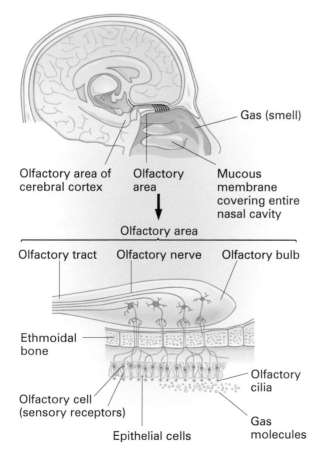

Figure 36.1 *The olfactory system*

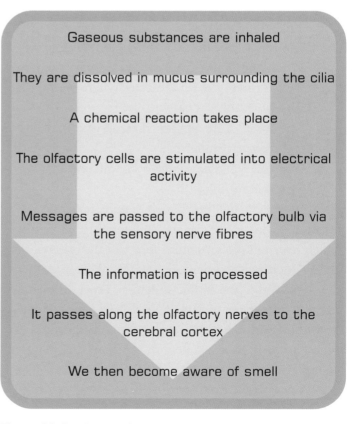

Figure 36.2 *The sense of smell*

Sniffing concentrates particles very quickly in the roof of the nose, increasing the number of cells stimulated and therefore the perception of smell. When the nasal mucosa become inflamed through illness or sensitivity it will prevent odorous substances from reaching the olfactory area, causing a loss or a reduction in the sense of smell.

When an individual is continuously exposed to a particular odour, his or her perception of that particular smell will decrease and eventually cease.

The limbic system

This is the part of the brain which deals with emotions, moods, our motivation, memory and creativity. It is sometimes referred to as the primitive brain. It is closely connected with the part of the brain which receives the messages from the olfactory cells in the nose.

This connection explains why smells bring to mind particular memories and feelings and smells are richly endowed with emotional significance. For example:

* The smell of a mother's scent can provide instant comfort to a child. A perfume may remind us instantly of a loved one whom we may not have seen for many years or a place where we may have first worn the fragrance.
* The smell of freshly baked bread may make us feel instantly hungry.
* The smell of a new-born baby can stimulate maternal feelings.

Some smells will bring back memories of special occasions. This is because we remember those things which have emotional significance and the areas of the brain which process memories and recall events are closely linked to the limbic system and this, in turn, is linked to the centres in the brain for the sense of smell.

Odour stimulates the release of neurotransmitters which, in turn, have a beneficial effect on the body, for example:

* **encephaline** and **endorphins** help to reduce pain and create a feeling of well-being
* **serotonin** helps to relax and have a calming effect
* **noradrenalin** will stimulate and help us to wake up.

The sense of taste

The sense of taste provides us with less information than the other senses. Its chief role is to select and appreciate food and drink, but much of our sense of taste is, in fact, linked with our sense of smell. The receptors for sensations of taste are located in our taste buds, which are most numerous on the tongue, but also located on the soft palate and in the throat. We have four primary taste sensations – sour, salt, bitter and sweet. Most tastes are combinations of these four and modified by the sense of smell. Sweet and salty tastes stimulate taste buds at the tip of the tongue, sour at the sides and bitter at the back. In order to taste the substances, the chemicals must be dissolved in liquid form, so the saliva plays an important part in dissolving the substances to be tasted. The nerve cells then pass messages to the brain and together with the sense of smell, taste occurs.

Sight

The eye is the organ of the sense of sight. It is situated in the orbital cavity and is supplied by the optic nerve.

Light is reflected into the eyes on to the retina by objects within the field of vision. Clear vision depends on the coordination of two processes – the refraction of the light rays and the accommodation of the eyes to the light (pupils of the eyes dilate in poor light and constrict in bright light). The size of the pupil is controlled by the autonomic nervous system. The movement of the eyes to view an object is caused by the muscular activity of six muscles and the oculomotor, trochlear and abducent, cranial nerves.

The eyebrows protect the eyes from the sun, sweat, dust and foreign bodies, which may cause them harm. The skin of the eyebrows has a great many sebaceous glands and the hairs are usually coarse. The eyelids provide a protective covering for the eyes when closed protecting them from strong light and foreign objects as well as spreading lubrication over the eyeballs. The eyelashes filter out particles and foreign bodies which may enter and irritate the eye. The lacrimal glands secrete tears, composed of water, salts and lysozyme, a protective bactericidal enzyme, that wash away irritating materials and prevent microbial infection and also help to prevent drying out of the conjunctiva, the membrane lining the eyelids.

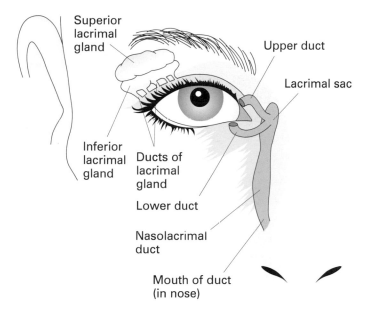

Figure 36.3 *The eye*

Hearing and balance

The ear is the organ of hearing and is supplied by the vestibulocochlear cranial nerve. It contains receptors for sound waves and receptors for balance and is divided into three parts – the external, middle and inner ears.

The external ear collects the sound waves and directs them inwards to the middle ear or tympanic cavity, which is a small air-filled cavity separated from the external ear by the eardrum. There is an auditory tube in this part of the ear, which is responsible for equalising air pressure. The inner ear contains the organs of hearing and balance. Sound waves pass from the middle to the inner ear in a series of vibrations, which ultimately lead to the generation of nerve impulses that reach the brain and sound is heard.

The ear is also responsible for the monitoring of the position of the body and movements of the head. The inner ear, in particular, contains a maze of tubes filled with fluid, all at different levels and angles, working together to maintain balance. Together with the brain, eyes and muscles, the body remains balanced and in an upright position as long as nothing disturbs the equilibrium.

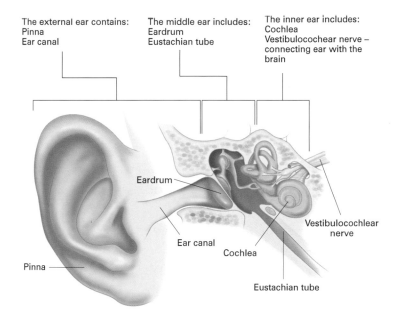

Figure 36.4 *The ear*

Business management

* Setting up a business

* Aspects of a profitable business

* Marketing and promotion

* Increasing sales

* Consumer protection

Introduction

There are many wonderful opportunities available to the therapist with management skills. The demand is great because of the rapid growth of the beauty industry. Many new spas have opened worldwide as well as many more therapists opening their own small business. Developing these skills is important because employers expect the therapist to contribute to the growth of the business and are offering incentives in the form of commission, profit sharing and promotion.

This section deals with the practicalities of setting up and running a business.

Many therapists intend to open their own business at some time in their career, particularly after they have had the experience of working for others and developed their technical and professional skills. Having your own business provides job satisfaction and independence but means working longer hours, fewer holidays and initially, lower earnings. Commitment is essential and those who produce a good business plan are more likely to succeed.

There are several options:

* Buying an existing business.
* Establishing a business at home.
* Mobile beauty business.
* Franchising.

Figure 37.1 *Setting up your own business involves commitment*

Buying an existing business

It is important to find out exactly why a business is up for sale. There are many reasons why businesses are sold, but the owner of the business you are interested in may feel that it is under threat or no longer a viable business and is cutting his or her losses and selling out. When you are completely satisfied that this is not the case, then it is time to examine all aspects of the business.

A thriving beauty business relies on the continuing patronage of the existing clientele. Therefore, it is important to obtain an undertaking from the present owner that he or she will not be opening up elsewhere in competition with you and the clients will be

remaining with the salon. The sale price may include equipment which will only be of use to you if it is in good working order and has a long working life ahead of it. It would be worthwhile, therefore, to have everything checked by an expert. Retail stock must be up to date and preferably of products which will be easy to sell.

It is advisable to have the accounts for the last few years checked by an accountant to ensure the business is profitable.

Establishing a business at home

The idea of working from home is very appealing as there would be no travelling to and from work and the hours worked could fit in with your normal daily routine.

Such a business is only viable if there is the room available to use for the salon. Space such as a loft, spare bedroom or an integral garage could be converted, but first it is necessary to decide what equipment and furniture you will require and this will indicate how much space will be needed. Since many beauty therapy equipment manufacturers now make combined self-standing units, it is possible to offer a variety of different face and body treatments in a limited space.

Before making any decisions it is important to ascertain if you are legally entitled to use your home for a business. Planning permission must be sought if the business will materially change the use of your home. This is open to interpretation by different local authorities.

Check the deeds of the house to ensure there are no clauses to prevent part of the house being used for business purposes. If your home is mortgaged, it is important to check the documents to ensure there is no breach of contract.

The insurance cover may need to be changed on your home when using it for a business so check with your insurance company for advice.

Figure 37.2 *A beauty therapist working from home*

Mobile beauty business

A mobile business is an increasingly popular option for the many fully trained beauty therapists who want to specialise in one particular treatment or offer services for those people who find it difficult to travel due to work or family commitments, disability or personal choice. There are also many more therapists who are training in just one specialised subject. These specialisms may include:

* aromatherapy
* Indian head massage
* body massage
* anti-ageing treatments
* hair removal
* make-up artist
* nail technician.

Table 37.1 lists the advantages and disadvantages of running a mobile beauty business.

Before setting up a mobile business, you will need to consider the following:

* The local authority by-laws should be checked before offering a mobile service to ensure that all regulations are complied with.
* Registration will be required for electrolysis and ear piercing.
* Many suppliers of equipment will supply special mobile units in a protective carrying case, which will reduce the risk of damage occurring in transit.
* Some product suppliers also provide cushioned carrying cases to prevent accidents.
* Lightweight sturdy equipment is a must for mobile businesses to prevent therapists suffering from back strain or injury when loading or unloading.
* Team up with a mobile hairdresser, holistic therapist or reflexologist and share client lists. It will help to increase business and ensure clients are recommended.

Franchising

The basic principle involved in franchising is when a successful company that manufactures, retails products or provides a service decides to expand its business by becoming a franchiser instead of opening up other branches which are owned by its parent company.

The company is selling its already established reputation and valuable expertise to a franchisee. In effect, the franchisee is buying a complete business system or way of trading. The franchisee enters into a contract to sell the product or provide the service under the franchiser's name, following strict guidelines laid down by the franchiser.

Table **37.1** *Advantages and disadvantages of running a mobile beauty business*

Advantages	Disadvantages
There is a captive market as there are many prospective clients who cannot leave home because they are disabled or elderly, are a carer looking after a relative, are without transport, or even agoraphobic. In rural areas there may not be a beauty salon and travelling to the nearest large town or city may be time-consuming, inconvenient and expensive and some clients just like to have the treatment in the comfort of their own home	A limited number of treatments may be achieved in a day because of the time needed to travel. Planning of appointments will be essential to prevent unnecessary time wasted
There is a relatively small capital outlay particularly when offering only one specialist treatment, as the mode of transport is the largest expense	It is necessary to carry all equipment and products required to ensure an efficient service, so good planning and organisation are essential
Overheads are low as the location for business is the client's own premises which could be a home or workplace	Equipment may get damaged
	Repetitive strain or back injury may occur lifting heavy items in and out of the car
It is easier to offer a specialised service, e.g. aromatherapy	Setting up equipment may be difficult depending on the location to be used for the treatment
A choice of working hours and flexibility is available to the mobile therapist allowing other commitments to be accommodated without having to consult with colleagues or superiors	Business expansion is difficult
The service is more personal and a good client-therapist relationship is easily established and maintained	There are risks involved when attending new clients. It is important, therefore, to vet any prospective clients or rely on personal recommendation
There are increased benefits to clients because they will not have to travel and treatments will be far more relaxing	

The legal form the franchise will take will be the same as any other business, that is, sole trader, partnership or limited company.

The advantages and disadvantages of running a franchise are shown in Table 37.2.

Steps to take before buying a franchise

* An accountant should examine the forecasts given by the franchiser.
* A solicitor should go through any contract before it is signed to see how the franchiser is making money and to analyse the restrictions the contract might impose.
* The franchisee should find out how many franchises have already been sold and how long they have been trading.
* The franchisee should talk to existing franchisees.

Useful franchising terms

A **franchise** is a licence to operate a business in a particular area, given by a business with an established name and reputation.

The **franchisee** is the person who buys the franchise.

The **franchiser** is the person or company who sells the franchise.

Researching the business

To establish the viability of the proposed business, you may find it helpful to produce a research plan. This should include:

* assessing the potential market and competition
* establishing client requirements

Table 37.2 *Advantages and disadvantages of running a franchise*

Advantages	Disadvantages
The chief advantage of starting a business by buying a franchise is that there are reduced risks as all the problems normally encountered when running a business from scratch will already have been analysed and solved and, with a reputable franchiser, there is a greater chance of success The business is your own There is continuing support provided by the franchiser which is particularly important for those inexperienced in business The product or service bought has a recognisable name with an established reputation The business will benefit from the advertising and promotion carried out by the franchiser Previous experience is not necessary in most cases, e.g. retail sales, as training is normally given by the franchiser	There will be restrictions on how the business is run, as all business transactions must be in the best interest of the franchiser and the other franchisees There is usually a large initial fee to be paid for the franchise Subsequent payments must then be paid each year, usually as a percentage of turnover The franchiser has the right to come to the business premises to inspect records, and sales statistics have to be sent regularly to the franchiser Operating methods laid down by the franchiser have to be strictly adhered to, which may prevent franchisees using their own initiative and expertise All stock may have to be purchased from the franchiser, not allowing the franchisee freedom to seek competitive alternatives If the franchisee wants to sell the business before the end of the contract, the franchiser has to agree The franchise runs for a set number of years with an option to renew 'if the franchisee's performance is satisfactory'. This may mean a commitment to spending on refurbishment If the franchisee cannot renew, there may be little to sell as the franchisee cannot sell the name and goodwill

* finding premises
* finding equipment and product suppliers
* establishing legal requirements
* obtaining specialist advice
* methods of obtaining finance.

Assessing the potential market and competition

Market research involves collecting, collating and analysing data relevant to the business to help establish its viability. You will need to assess how many people are likely to want your service and if the numbers will be sufficient to make your business viable. For example, is it a growing or static market and what share in that market do you think you might achieve? Look at your competitors, how well established they are and how your services or prices compare with theirs and what

you will provide that they do not. One of the easiest ways in which to achieve this is to visit your competitor(s) as a client and gain reliable first-hand knowledge.

Market research allows you to establish if there is a **market segment** on which to concentrate. Market segmentation involves dividing an existing market into a number of smaller submarkets, identifying groups of customers with similar requirements, for example the house bound, the busy professional, health and fitness fans, male clients, ethnic groups, those who prefer the holistic approach or pregnant mums! Look for a gap in the market that you could fill. The more information you acquire about potential clients and the current market, the better the chance of minimising risk and maximising success.

Establishing client requirements

Your clients will come from all walks of life and different age groups; they will have varying lifestyles and may have particular beauty problems or requirements. It is important to be able to cater for the clients' individual requirements and these could include some or all of the following:

* Specialising in specific therapies such as spa, anti-ageing, or hair removal.
* Providing a mobile service for those people who are house bound or find it difficult to travel.
* Providing flexible opening hours for those people who work nine to five, Monday to Friday. Many clients appreciate an evening or weekend appointment.
* Providing your services in situ, possibly working from a room within another business or large building servicing many businesses. These businesses could be high powered and stressful and may appreciate the services of a beauty therapist to be available as an antidote to the stresses and strains of the job. Some large organisations provide hair, beauty and massage services for their staff as a perk of the job.

* Providing additional services, which complement beauty therapy.
* Working with other professionals in a combined business.
* Providing easy access to your premises for disabled clients.
* Providing a professional and relaxing environment in which to have the treatment, using quality equipment and products.

Market research is again a useful tool for collecting the information that you require to establish what your potential clients will need. Once you have an established clientele, it is easier to collect information as you may already be aware of their requirements, you can question them about their needs, or ask them to fill in questionnaires to obtain specific information.

Finding premises

Premises should be in the right area and at the right price, centrally situated in a well-populated area. If it is close to other businesses which have a brisk trade you can benefit from passing trade, for example post offices, banks, building societies or pharmacies. Situated near other businesses such as a hairdressing salon, popular restaurant or near a medical health centre could also bring in new clients.

The more central the position in a town, the more expensive the cost of buying, renting or leasing premises. You will need to consider the space required for your business. One or two treatment rooms, a toilet and small reception area is all that is required for a small business, but you may need more space and this will add to the cost. Ensure that the fixtures and fittings are adequate. These may include lighting, heating, electricity and water supplies, telephone and sanitary facilities. If it is necessary to install some or all of these facilities, it may add considerably to your start-up costs.

One important consideration to be taken into account is the expansion of the business. If you intend to employ staff or take on other therapists, it is best to plan for this initially and buy or lease somewhere of a suitable size, as it may prove costly to move to larger premises as you grow.

Playing music in your salon

If you intend to play background music in the reception area or the treatment room, which will be heard by members of the public (a public performance), you may need to obtain a licence. The **Copyright Designs and Patents Act** provides protection for composers whose music is played for public performance. A licence may be obtained from Phonographic Performance Ltd which, together with the Performing Rights Society, collects licence payments for distribution in the form of royalties to performers and record companies who are members of those bodies. (For further details, see the Glossary of professional associations and organisations at the end of this book.)

Once you have found the right premises, there are four options – to rent, lease or buy, or to use a room in your own home.

Renting

A short-term rental agreement is an option for a new business as the financial outlay will not be so great while establishing the business. However, the shorter the term of the agreement, the higher the rental cost. Opting for a long-term agreement will lower the rent, but it will commit you to the agreement for several years. A good way to start is to find a room to rent within another business such as a hairdressing salon, holistic centre or with a health care professional. You have the advantage of sharing costs, gaining clients from an already established clientele, the use of the available resources, such as telephone, computer, fax machine, etc. and possibly the services of a receptionist.

It is important before signing any agreement to make sure there are no clauses making you liable for the upkeep of the property, unless you have agreed a reasonable rent to reflect this.

Leasing

This is when the business buys the leasehold rights to the premises for a period of time, perhaps 25 or 50 years, and then pays an annual ground rent. The main advantage is that existing capital will be available for the business, rather than being tied up in buying a property with high mortgagee repayments that could be a burden, and you will have a capital asset for balance sheet purposes with less expenditure than when buying.

When negotiating the lease it may be advisable to go for as short a lease as possible with the option to renew the lease for a longer period of time when you feel sure the business will be a success. The main disadvantage is that over a long period of time the lease will cost as much if not more than buying a property. You must also seek permission from the landlord before carrying out any alterations. When the lease expires you have the right to agree new terms, but the landlord may refuse if you have not been a good tenant or if he or she requires the premises for their own occupation.

Figure 37.3 *Beauty treatment room*

The Landlord and Tenant Act (1954)

The purpose of this Act is to give the tenant some security in remaining in the premises after the lease has expired and to be compensated for improvements which have added to the value of business premises. The landlord has to give six months' notice if the lease is to be terminated. This will give the tenant the opportunity to apply to the court to have the lease renewed. The court may refuse the application if the landlord can show the following:

* The rent is in arrears.
* The property has been allowed to fall into disrepair.
* The landlord has found alternative premises for the tenant.
* The premises are to be demolished or reconstructed.
* The landlord needs the premises for his or her own occupation.

It is advisable to seek the advice of a solicitor before signing a lease and always check the following:

* Can the premises be used for the purpose you require?
* Will you be able to make any alterations that you need for your business?
* Who is responsible for the repair and maintenance of the premises?
* What is the length of the lease?
* Is subletting part of the premises permitted?
* How often is the rent reviewed?

Buying

A small business may buy freehold premises along with the business in them. Normally, when purchasing a business property you will have to provide 20–25 per cent of the total purchase price and then arrange a commercial mortgage, which may be difficult to obtain for a new business.

The advantages are that it is a good long-term investment, particularly if a good quality property is bought at the right price and then sold at a profit some years later. You will have no rent to pay and tax relief can be claimed on interest payments and capital allowance claimed against the purchase price. The disadvantages include finding the high deposit required, tying up available finance in the property, which could be used to invest in the business itself, and the cost of maintaining and improving the property.

It is essential to seek professional help and advice when buying a freehold property and check that there are no undeclared mortgages or charges existing against the premises. It is also advisable to check that there are no proposed building plans or changes to the area which may adversely affect your business.

Business from home

The final option is using a room in your own home for your business. If you build a separate structure to accommodate the business, then you will require Building Regulations approval and an inspector will regularly check that foundations are sufficient and that the builder is complying with the approved details of the building plan.

Finding equipment and product suppliers

Make a detailed list of all your requirements and research as many companies as you can. Ask them for estimates, minimum order requirements and terms of payment. It is essential that they can deliver quickly so that you can maintain a healthy stock level without tying up too much capital.

Electrical equipment should be bought from a reputable supplier who will provide you with efficient after-sales service and replace faulty machines when they are being repaired. It is advisable to enter into a contract with an electrician to regularly service the equipment.

Establishing legal requirements

There are many Acts of Parliament, European Directives and local by-laws that may affect the small business. In recent years, there has been a rapid increase in legislation, particularly in the area of health and safety (see Chapter 4 Health and safety).

The **Local Government Miscellaneous Act (1982)** gives the local authority power to grant a licence to provide certain services such as epilation, ear piercing, massage and tattooing. Establishments are inspected to ensure that strict hygiene methods are in place. As local councils vary, it is advisable to check with your local authority if you think your business may be offering a service or treatment that requires a licence.

Obtaining specialist advice and obtaining finance

When starting any business you must consider how much money you will need to survive while you are establishing yourself and remember to include this in your cash flow forecast and budgets. Find out as much as you can from specialists. For example, contact your local authority, as it will have information on local funding for small businesses. It will also know of local training and enterprise agencies who will provide advice on all matters related to setting up a new business and have lists of experts such as solicitors, accountants, insurance companies, bank managers and book keepers, who will provide valuable advice and support when starting up a new venture.

Government departments and local authorities will provide you with impartial advice when setting up a business. The Department of Trade and Industry (DTI) publishes, 'A guide to help for small businesses' which contains details of government and other schemes specifically to help small businesses (see Glossary of professional associations and organisations at the end of this book).

Business Link is an organisation that provides practical and financial help in setting up a new business (see Glossary of professional associations and organisations). There may be a small charge or an initial free review and then a subsidised consultancy charge.

An insurance broker will be able to find you the best insurance policies for your requirements. Under the Financial Services Act, a broker is required to give you the best impartial advice and not recommend a particular company if it is not appropriate. A free booklet entitled 'Insurance advice for small businesses' is available from the Association of British Insurers (see Glossary of professional associations and organisations).

Business insurance may also be obtained from a professional body such as the Federation of Holistic Therapists, the Guild of Professional Beauty Therapists, BABTAC and VTCT (see Glossary of professional associations and organisations).

The business plan

It is important for anyone hoping to start a business to produce a comprehensive business plan as this provides a concise document which details the business you wish to establish and the expectations you have for its continuing growth and success. This will then help you decide on the viability of your ideas and give you something to measure the progress you are making once established, as well as allowing you to maintain the course you have set by following the plan and achieving your objectives.

If you need to raise funds when starting a new business or for expansion of an already established business, a thorough and impressive business plan will be essential in convincing potential backers that they should invest their money with you. If a business plan is well written and presented, it will show that you have a professional and business-like approach and also shows the effort you are making and your determination to succeed.

Setting objectives

Your objectives are the goals you wish to achieve in your business. Your main or primary objectives are often known as your **mission statement** and will state the purpose of your business and the market it will cater for.

Once you have stated your primary objectives, you must then decide how you will achieve them, what you will require to finance your plans, put them into operation, market the business and monitor the outcomes. This will necessitate defining objectives in much more detail, forming the body of your business plan.

There are many standard formats available from banks or other financial institutions that you may use when writing your business plan. However, to be successful a great deal of thought and preparation needs to go into producing a *high quality* business plan. When raising finance it may be essential to use the format laid down by the institution that you wish to borrow money from, as it will have certain requirements. In some circumstances, the standard format may not be quite the right approach for your business, so use it simply as a guide, selecting those parts of it which are most appropriate to your business.

Mission statement

'Our aim is to be the premier salon in the area. We will provide efficient and effective service of the highest quality to our clients, in a relaxing environment, making the best use of resources and striving to offer the latest and most up-to-date treatments and techniques while providing challenging and interesting work for our employees.'

Content of a business plan

Business details

* The name and type of business, e.g. spa, clinic, health and beauty salon, mobile therapist, holistic therapist, nail technician or make-up artist.
* The services you will be offering, e.g. facial and body treatments, laser therapy, advanced nail techniques, aromatherapy, massage therapy or spa therapies.
* Why you have chosen this business – should include your experience in your chosen field, your qualifications and continuing professional development.
* Your legal status – sole trader, partnership, limited company.
* Any previous business experience or courses you may have attended to provide you with skills for running your own business.

These details will serve as a simple but informative introduction to the business plan providing a brief overview for the reader.

The location

Explain where you will be based. This may be in your own home, in a room you have converted or an extension to provide you with a separate treatment area. You may decide to offer mobile services and visit clients in their own homes or work within another practice, either medical, beauty or complementary, renting a room from another professional. You may even have bought or are leasing your own premises. Whatever the location, you will need to provide details of the catchment area from where you will be drawing clients.

The market

To have a successful business and to convince backers of your future success, it is important to demonstrate that there is a market for the services you offer. You will need to consider the following points and record them in your plan:

* Where is your market and how large is it?
* Does it have the potential for growth?
* Identify the potential clients.

* Identify your competitors, the prices they charge and assess their strengths and weaknesses.
* State the possibility of tailoring services to meet the demands of other sectors within the market.

Operating the business

The information required here would include premises, transport, staff, equipment and suppliers.

Premises

For existing premises, you should provide details of location, size and type of premises and if there are any plans for expansion, future development or change. If the premises are leasehold, state the term of the lease, what period is outstanding and if there is an option to renew, the present rent, when it is paid and date of next review. It is also important to establish who is responsible for the repair and upkeep of the premises. If you are liable, you will need to know the extent of this liability, for example is it simply general painting, decorating and repairs, or will you be responsible for the roof, foundations or load bearing walls? This could prove costly!

Transport

A mobile business will rely heavily on the means of transport you choose and as this will be an expensive outlay, it must be reliable and appropriate for your requirements. State the reasons why you need a particular vehicle. For example, an estate car with five doors would be ideal when lifting equipment in and out and the capacity will allow you room to store items safely without causing damage in transit.

Equipment and suppliers

State how much equipment will be needed, the cost, the name of suppliers and what the alternatives are if they fail to supply. Retail and consumable suppliers may be separate from equipment suppliers. It is important to shop around and find a reliable company who will deliver promptly, offer quality products and not expect you to invest huge sums of money on an initial order. The type of equipment you buy for a mobile service will need to be durable, packed away easily and light to carry. Many equipment suppliers provide specially boxed equipment which is well protected in transit.

Services

This will provide details of the services you offer emphasising anything that is different or special about the various treatments and why it will be successful. List the prices for the treatments and a breakdown of how the cost was established. State whether you are researching new areas or learning new skills, which may be added to your treatment list in the near future.

Selling retail products is an important service to the client and an essential in maximising profit, so you will need to itemise the lines you have chosen, explain their relevance to the business, and state the selling price and original cost.

Staffing

As a sole trader, you will need to provide a curriculum vitae (CV), detailing your personal information, qualifications, professional memberships, career history and any other activities and interests which may be relevant. List all the skills you have which are relevant and all the experience you have had which will contribute to the success of the business. Most people sell themselves short when listing previous experience. For example, if you have worked in a retail environment, you will have been involved in handling cash, customer care, stock control and marketing, all skills relevant to a beauty salon or spa. In addition, you should provide a personal profile to include a description of yourself, your ambitions, reasons and motivation for your proposed business, and your long-term objectives.

In the case of a partnership, details will be required of all concerned and an outline of the roles and responsibilities of all those involved.

If you will be employing staff, you must provide details to include their name, address, qualifications, relevant work experience and their position in the business. There may be other skills you will require to help establish and operate the business within the next year. If so, state what they are and the staff you will be hoping to employ. You may wish to employ a cleaner, a receptionist, a trainee, a book-keeper, other therapists or

Figure 37.4 *You may need to employ a full team of staff*

even a business manager.

Estimate the cost of employing staff and buying in the required skills. These costs should include your own salary and other partners in the business, and may be shown as monthly or annual costs.

Financial details

This provides the information required by a bank manager or investor when you wish to borrow money. There is a risk involved when lending money, therefore it is important to show what assets you have available, as insurance against anything going wrong. These may include:

* capital you have available
* other sources of funds, e.g. savings, stocks and shares, redundancy money, inheritance, a loan from a member of the family, and so on
* another investor
* enterprise fund – help given by the government to encourage small businesses
* local enterprise agencies which are a partnership between industry and local central government – they will provide advice or recommend experts to help with financial matters as well as marketing, finding premises and planning
* the Prince's Trust which helps young people aged 18–30 to set up and run their own business.

You must state how much you wish to borrow, for how long and how you propose to pay it back. You will be required to supply a budget and cash flow forecast for 12 months. This will demonstrate your ability to repay the loan after all your business expenses have been met.

CASHFLOW FORECAST FOR: MONTH TO															
	Month		Month		Month		Month		Month		Month		TOTALS	
	Budget	Actual	Budget	Actual	Budget	Actual	Budget	Actual	Budget	Actual	Budget	Actual	Budget	Actual
RECEIPTS														
Cash sales														
Cash from Debtors														
Capital introduced														
TOTAL RECEIPTS (a)														
PAYMENTS														
Payments to Creditors														
Salaries/Wages														
Rent/Rates/Water														
Insurance														
Repairs/Renewals														
Heat/Light/Power														
Advertising														
Printing/Stationery/Postage														
Cash Purchases														
Telephone														
Professional Fees														
Capital Payments														
Interest Charges														
Other														
VAT Payable (refund)														
TOTAL PAYMENTS (b)														
NET CASHFLOW (a–b)														
OPENING BANK BALANCE														
CLOSING BANK BALANCE														

Figure 37.5 *A cash flow forecast*

It analyses your expenditure and receipts for that period. An example of a cash flow forecast is given in Figure 37.5.

Expenditure may include such things as :

* capital expenditure
* rent, rates and water
* services such as power, heat, light and telephone
* insurance
* leasing repayments
* payment to suppliers for equipment and products
* other purchases
* staff wages
* loan repayments, interest and bank charges
* advertising and marketing
* professional fees and subscriptions
* any other.

Receipts or money coming into the business will include:

* the capital you have invested
* loans received initially and at a later date
* cash from treatments, services and retail sales
* other sources of income such as rent from other therapists sharing your premises.

The cash flow forecast is based on assumptions which form a vital part of the financial forecast. It is important, therefore, to be realistic as it will then be evident when your need for cash is greatest and what your funding requirements may be.

Essential content for a business plan is shown on page 429.

Business status

One of the most important decisions to make when opening a business is the legal form the business will take. There are four options:

* Sole trader.
* Partnership.
* Limited company.
* Co-operative.

Each one of these options has its advantages and disadvantages.

Sole trader

To start up as a sole trader, all you have to do is inform your local tax inspector and Department of Social Security office, then open a business bank account. Being a sole trader means that you are solely responsible for the business and liable for all the money the business owes. When there is not enough money in the business, all personal possessions, including your home, could be taken to settle debts. All the profits, however, belong solely to you. Accounts do not have to be submitted to Companies House, but annual accounts must be

Essential content for a business plan

Introduction to the business
Name
Address
Telephone numbers, email address, fax number
Business status
Business type
Date began trading
Business objectives
Business activities

Personal details
Name, contact details (address, telephone numbers, email, etc.)
Qualifications
Relevant work experience
Business experience
Professional development

Personnel details
Names of all personnel
Position held
Qualifications gained
Work experience
Professional development
Current salary
Estimated cost:

Additional skills you may need to buy in during the first two years
Receptionist
Specialists
Book-keeper
Consultant
Estimated cost:

Premises, equipment, products and treatments
Premises and equipment costs

Treatment descriptions
Cost – materials, labour, overheads
Treatment price charged
Estimated number of treatments in a given period
Estimated profit:

Product details
Cost price
Retail price
Estimated turnover:
Estimated profit:

Market
Description – general, particular segments or niches
Location
Possibilities for future growth and development
Competition treatments, products, prices, strengths, weaknesses

Differentiation
How is your business different from the competition?
Advantages of your products/treatments
Strengths

Sales forecast
Months 1–3
Months 4–6
Months 7–9
Months 10–12

Marketing strategy
Results of market research
Methods of promotion
Types of advertising

Finance
Own funds available
Business assets
Creditors
Grants
Security available to secure a loan

Other
Accountant
Solicitor
VAT registration if turnover will exceed £56,000 (2003)
Insurance details

submitted to the Inland Revenue. As a sole trader, income tax is paid at the normal rate and is paid on a preceding year basis. This means that tax may be paid on profits up to two years afterwards and this helps a small business with cash flow.

You are not answerable to anyone else for the decisions you make regarding the business, changes can be implemented at your own pace and you can offer a personal service to clients.

When using a trade name you must put your own name and address as proprietor on all business stationery and on a notice displayed in the business premises.

Partnership

This is where there are a minimum of two people or a maximum of 20 people who will provide the start-up cash and share the workload in a business. In a business partnership there may be either a full partner who will participate fully in the business sharing both the profits and losses. Alternatively, you could have a sleeping partner who takes no active part in the running of the business but who provides working capital and takes responsibility for any debts, but only up to the amount he or she has put into the business.

As each partner is responsible for the debts of the others, it is advisable for a partnership agreement to be drawn up by a solicitor so that each partner has some protection. The partners should agree on:

* the name of the business
* the date the partnership will start and how long it will last
* the amount of capital to be provided by each partner
* who is authorised to operate bank accounts
* how the business will be managed and what each partner's responsibilities will be
* how the profits will be divided
* what provision will be made for holidays and other time off
* what will happen in the event of a partner withdrawing from the partnership for whatever reason, e.g. retirement
* what provision will be made in the event of the death of a partner

* arrangements for admitting new partners
* the conditions under which the partnership may be terminated in case of a dispute
* the arrangements to be made for dissolving the partnership.

If there is no agreement, then any of the partners can pull out of the partnership at any time, leaving the other partners to find the money to buy out their share of the business. If a dispute arises and no partnership agreement exists, then the Partnership Act (1980) will apply.

Case study: partnership

Marianne and Tracey have recently combined their particular skills and formed a partnership in a day spa. Marianne is a qualified beauty therapist providing the practical expertise in spa therapies and beauty treatments. Tracey has a business management background, having worked for Marks & Spencer for five years, and she looks after the running of the spa. They travelled for six months before putting a business plan together to gain inspiration and ideas for their perfect spa.

Figure 37.6
Business partners

Limited company

Forming a limited company is more complicated than a partnership and advice must be sought from a solicitor.

When a limited company is set up a new legal entity is being created. A company must have at least two shareholders, one director and a company secretary who may also be a director. The company must be registered with the Registrar of Companies and the following should be provided:

* memorandum of association
* articles of association
* various forms
* a registration fee.

The Certificate of Incorporation should be on public display. There is also certain information, which must be displayed on all stationery and letterheads:

* the registered name and address of the company in full
* the place of registration
* the registration number
* either all or none of the directors' names.

Table 37.3 lists the advantages and disadvantages of a limited company.

Co-operative

A co-operative is an alternative business structure to consider if you and a group of other people wish to work together on a democratic basis, sharing all control and profits of the business. A minimum of two people is required to set up a co-operative.

Co-operatives are governed by different legislation from companies and are registered under the Industrial and Provident Societies Act (1965) or the Companies Act and have the benefit of limited liability.

Characteristics of co-operatives

* Each member has equal say; decisions are taken on a one person one vote basis.
* Members decide how to share profits generated by the business.
* Members have collective responsibility for management and financial control.
* Interest payments on capital which members have introduced will be limited in a specified way.

Naming the business

A sole trader is not obliged to register the name of the business if it is not his or her own name, but it must not be too much like a name already in existence as this may be misleading to the public. However, the sole trader's own name must be displayed prominently on:

* business letters
* written orders for goods
* invoices
* written demands for payment of debts.

When a limited company is formed the name must be registered with Companies House and it must not be identical to any other company's name. The name must not be considered illegal or offensive and it must not contain the word 'limited' anywhere in the name but at the end. Information may be obtained from Companies House. The name for your business must conform to the Companies Name Act (1985) and the Business Names Act (1985).

Table 37.3 *Advantages and disadvantages of a limited company*

Advantages	Disadvantages
The main advantage of a limited company is that the shareholders have a limited liability for debts. They are not personally responsible for the company's debts and creditors may only claim on the assets of the company and not on personal assets A limited company may lend credibility to your business and investors and creditors may have greater confidence Directors are required to pay income tax, but the company pays corporation tax on company profits, which is one rate of tax only and averages out at much less than if income tax were paid on the profits	Annual accounts have to be submitted to Companies House The details of the company are open to public scrutiny An annual meeting of members is compulsory The directors are subject to company law and have responsibilities to act in the best interests of the company and its shareholders, answering personally for failure to do so

38 Aspects of a profitable business

It is the aim of any business to be financially effective and make a profit and it is the responsibility of each individual – from the owner to the most junior member of staff – to make their contribution. If the business does not make a profit, then overheads cannot be met, jobs may be lost and the business might even have to close. When profits increase and the business is able to grow, then every member of staff will benefit in some way, through promotion, receiving an increase in wages and commission, bonuses and other incentives.

Communication

The most successful beauty therapists are those who establish an enduring relationship with their clients. As the therapist provides a personal service and works very closely with clients, communication is a vital part of this process.

Communication may be defined as the process of creating, transmitting and interpreting ideas, opinions and facts. Excellent communication skills are an essential requirement for anyone wishing to work in a salon, clinic or spa environment. It is particularly important for the management as they will need to keep staff informed about the business, how it will develop and what part each member of the team has to play in this development. Employees also need to know how well they are doing and regular feedback will be useful in providing motivation as well as highlighting areas of weakness. The link with suppliers is an important one and effective communication will ensure that a successful relationship is established.

There are many aspects of communication which will help to increase efficiency in the work environment. In order to contribute, each employee must:

* offer support and help to colleagues willingly
* treat all clients with respect
* accept help and advice in the spirit in which it is offered
* provide only relevant information
* be open and honest with colleagues, management and clients
* be sensitive to the feelings of others
* always use positive body language
* accept positive and negative feedback and use it to improve service.

Communication can be :

* one-way and two-way
* formal and informal
* open and closed
* vertical and horizontal.

One-way and two-way communication

One-way communication is when the sender transmits a message to the receiver. It is quick and a reply is not required, for example an information memo or written record of a telephone message. One-way communication provides no feedback, however, so the accuracy cannot be checked.

A two-way communication will allow the receiver to comment on the message and receive clarification, making this a more accurate form of communication. For example, when in consultation with a new client you will be asking many questions, providing information and advice and planning treatments. The client will, in turn, be asking you many questions as well as providing you with specific information. In two-way communication you can make sure that the client understands everything that has been discussed and the feedback that he or she gives will allow you to recommend the most appropriate treatments.

Formal and informal communication

Formal methods of communication have to be used, for example, when employing staff at interview, when providing essential information to staff such as health and safety issues and in discussion with a bank manager or investor when raising finance. Most businesses will have a formal method of answering the telephone and records follow a set format.

Informal methods of communication may involve providing information in an unofficial capacity (leaked) and the reaction to it can be assessed before any final official information is given. When people chat in an informal capacity issues and problems are often highlighted and good ideas shared which may not be the case at a formal meeting. The only problem with the 'grapevine' is that information may become distorted and can cause misunderstanding. It is probably true that the 'grapevine' carries more bad news than good and provides a vehicle for dissatisfied employees.

Open and closed communication

Open communication refers to the language used when transmitting the message. It should be easily understood by the receiver and should be used when communicating with clients. Closed communication refers to terminology that is only understood by those who have particular skills and understanding. This type of language will be used between therapists when discussing technical issues or during training sessions – it is not suitable when discussing treatments with clients.

Vertical and horizontal communication

Communication through vertical channels exists in large organisations and information is passed from senior management down and from the employees up to the top. This two-way communication between the levels of management encourages discussion and involvement. It is a motivating factor and increases job satisfaction.

Horizontal communication occurs when two or more employees at the same level exchange information for mutual benefit. For example, the senior therapists responsible for body treatments, facial treatments, holistic therapies and hairdressing in a hotel spa will be responsible for their own team but will have common issues and problems. Together they can help each other by sharing good practice and benefit the business as a whole.

Methods of communication

Good communication is vital for the success of any business. Problems will soon arise if the methods used are not effective or the channels of communication are not working efficiently. Communication is effective when a message is sent, received and understood. Some of the methods available to a business are shown in Figure 38.1.

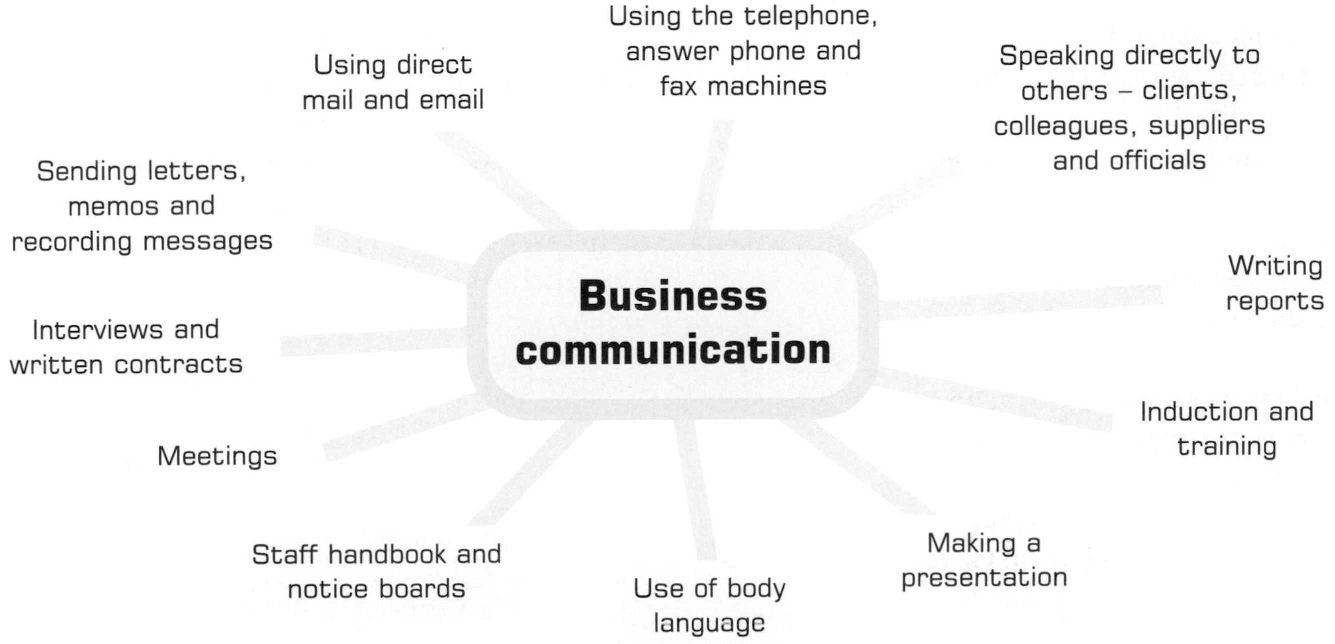

Figure 38.1 *Methods of business communication*

Horizontal communication

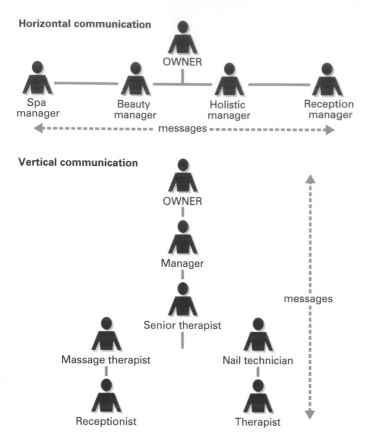

Vertical communication

Figure 38.2 *Vertical and horizontal channels of communication*

Figure 38.3 *The therapist must develop good communication skills*

Choosing the method of communication

How you communicate will depend on the nature of the information to be sent:

* It may require confidentiality.
* It may have to reach a large audience.
* Consultation may be necessary.
* Feedback may be required.
* It may involve a disciplinary or grievance issue.
* It may be to provide specific information to a particular person.

A disciplinary letter to a particular employee who has acted unprofessionally in the course of his or her duties will require confidentiality or when personal information about a client is discussed with another professional, for example the client's doctor.

The news that the management is offering the incentive of a foreign holiday to the employee who achieves the highest sales target in a given period will probably be announced in a team meeting, placed on the staff notice board and staff email.

Decisions about introducing new treatments or business expansion can be made at a brainstorming meeting with the staff involved so that feedback is instant and all those affected are given the opportunity to voice their opinion.

Speed may be a priority if important information is required, so email or verbal communication will be most appropriate.

It may be necessary to communicate information using more than one method, for example the rules and regulations laid down by the management may be provided verbally at induction and also in a staff manual to be kept or accessed by the employee.

The cost involved may be an issue. Clients may need to be informed about new opening times. Costs may be kept to a minimum by putting up notices in the salon or sending an email or text message to as many clients as you can.

It is important to maintain interest by using a variety of methods as employees sometimes stop reading messages left on notice boards, particularly when there are too many and they may be out of date or irrelevant. Clients become immune to posters and leaflets, so change to a company video playing discreetly in the background at reception or send them a regular newsletter.

When the message is long and detailed, written information is best as it can be accessed later; if information is given verbally, then some of it may be forgotten. When a simple yes or no is required, then verbal communication is ideal, either face to face or over the telephone. When a record is required, written communication is more effective than verbal as there will be evidence available particularly when using email.

Table 38.1 *Methods of communication, their advantages and disadvantages*

Method	Advantages	Disadvantages
Verbal or oral communication – speaking directly to another person or group of people	Instant communication Personalised May be reinforced with non-verbal Quick Provides instant feedback Provides opportunity for clarification Does not have to be face to face, e.g. telephone	Some of the information will be forgotten There is no point of reference later Lacks the considered nature of written communications
Non-verbal, the use of body language, gestures and facial expressions	Conveys a silent message and can be used when silence is required Quick	Open to misinterpretation
Written, includes letters, memos, reports, manuals, forms, notices, faxes and email	Permanent Less liable to misinterpretation Information may be absorbed at the reader's own pace Provides evidence that a message has been sent Ideal for important, detailed or complicated information May be referred to at a later date Can be used for communication outside the business as well as internally Email is fast There are no geographical boundaries, information can be transmitted in text and image format anywhere in the world Can reach a large number of people	Takes time to produce Impersonal No opportunity for discussion or immediate feedback Possibility that it may not be received Not necessarily secure Email may be lost when technical problems arise Notice boards can become out of date, untidy and irrelevant if not updated regularly

Figure 38.4 *Keep your clients informed of new developments with a regular, lively presented newsletter*

There are occasions when only one-way communication is required, for example information is being sent which does not require feedback, and this could be in the form of a memo, a telephone message or placed on the notice board.

Each method of communication used can be categorised as **verbal**, **non-verbal** and **written** and each method has advantages and disadvantages, as shown in Table 38.1.

Barriers to communication

It may not always be easy to communicate the information you wish because there are sometimes barriers which prevent it. Recognise any barriers that exist and do your best to overcome them and make sure any information communicated is accurate, relevant, complete and easily understood. Barriers may include:

* The sender may not have the skill to send the message effectively, e.g. trying to use a telephone switchboard, send an email or fax when no training has been given.
* The sender does not want to send the message. It may be that the therapist has to deal with a difficult client and feels that she does not have the authority to do so.
* The receiver does not understand what is being said, e.g. a client who has English as an additional language.
* The information given may be too complicated for the receiver to understand. When speaking to clients always describe treatments and procedures in non-technical language. They will only be interested in the benefits to them. When placing orders be specific about products, quantities required, delivery dates and special requirements, or orders may be received that are incorrect.
* The receiver is hostile to the sender or lacks interest in what is being said. An employee who is being disciplined may feel hostile towards the manager or others involved in the procedure or a client who has been caught out making a false complaint to obtain a free treatment.
* The client is not concentrating. Never try to give important information about times and dates of future treatments or special requirements to a client who is leaving the salon in a hurry to get somewhere else. The client will not be interested and is unlikely to remember the information because his or her mind will be elsewhere.
* The means of communication are temporarily unavailable, e.g. a computer system may crash, the telephone line may be affected after a storm or there could be a power cut.

Stock

Stock is a valuable resource and most salons will have invested a large amount of capital in products to be used for treatments as well as retail lines and other complementary products.

The control of stock is a very important function. For a salon that sells retail products as well as providing treatments, a large amount of stock will be required to cope with the demand. An efficient stock control system will ensure that the business holds goods only in the quantities required, to meet the demands of the clients. The benefits of an efficient system are:

* to ensure that the correct stock will always be available for clients, thus avoiding disappointment or causing them to go elsewhere to buy an item they particularly need
* to maintain the correct stock level required for the smooth running of the business, allowing therapists to carry out their treatments in the full knowledge that they will have everything that they need
* to ensure that over stocking does not occur and working capital is not tied up in excess stock
* to prevent stock from deteriorating, becoming out of date, or out of fashion because it is sitting in a stock room.

Requirements of an effective stock control system

One member of staff should be put in charge of stock control, as the more people there are involved, the more chance there is of mistakes being made. In larger salons, the person responsible for stock control may delegate responsibility to other responsible members of staff. In a spa, for example, an employee from each area such as reception, body therapies, facial therapies and holistic therapies could be responsible for the stock each will require. Each of these members of staff will then be responsible to the stock controller or manager. The duties of the stock controller will be:

* to set minimum and maximum stock levels
* to order stock
* to check stock deliveries
* to maintain records
* to distribute stock
* to carry out regular stock checks
* to delegate responsibility to others
* to train other members of staff.

There should be a stock room or a large stock cupboard in which to store a large percentage of stock. The shelving should be adjustable to accommodate different sized containers, particularly when buying in bulk. Everything in the room should be easy to clean for hygiene purposes and to keep stock in good condition. The shelves should be clearly labelled to show exactly where each item is to be stored.

Stock being used in treatment rooms or salons should be the responsibility of the individual therapist. Therapists should keep the stock in good order, use it economically and replace it when necessary. Trolleys with drawers, or small cupboards with shelves are ideal to store small quantities of treatment products so that the therapist has sufficient stock to hand and it is kept clean and secure.

Figure 38.5
A trolley stocked with products

Electrical equipment should be stored safely when not in use, covered to protect it from dust and with all leads and wires securely attached.

Stock control procedures

Choose a supplier

It is important to choose a manufacturer or supplier that is competitively priced. Shop around before making any decisions and speak to as many company representatives as you can before making a final decision. Check that the company will deliver stock quickly when required, and will offer you terms of credit that allow you sufficient time to settle your account to maintain a healthy cash flow. Dealing with one or two main suppliers has the benefit of building a professional relationship, receiving discounts, support in product training and promotional events and help and advice when required. When a supplier provides attractive discounts this enables you to cut costs and increase profits. There are many companies now with their own Internet website and special trade beauty suppliers allow orders to be placed 24 hours a day saving time for the therapist during the working day. Refer to a directory such as *Professional Beauty* for a comprehensive list of suppliers (See Glossary of professional associations and organisations at the end of this book).

Purchasing mail order is very easy over the phone or via the Internet and stock is delivered to your door, saving you time visiting cash and carry warehouses. It is advisable to check if the company is a member of the Mail Order Traders' Association, as it will have to abide by an agreed set of regulations. Member companies must:

* provide a full and accurate description of goods in their catalogues
* meet quoted delivery dates
* inform the consumer of any delays or restricted availability
* make prompt refunds on unwanted goods.

When you are a direct mail purchaser you have rights under the Consumer Protection (Distance Selling) Regulations. You are allowed a cooling-off period, during which if you change your mind you can cancel without any reason and receive a full refund. If your order does not arrive within the specified time, or within 30 days, you are entitled to a full refund and your statutory rights are not affected.

Complete paperwork

When purchasing stock use an official numbered order form on which the date is clearly written, with a duplicate copy for future reference. Retain the advice or despatch note if sent by the supplier to inform you the order is being processed. When the goods arrive check the delivery note, which will itemise the products that have been delivered, and check them against the original order. If the order is complete, unpack the stock and store it safely, record all the items received in the appropriate format.

Store stock

When correctly stored the stock will not be damaged or deteriorate. Try to get large boxes full of stock delivered to a point where they do not have to be moved again. If they do, make sure the staff involved use the correct lifting and handling techniques to prevent injury (see Chapter 4 Health and safety). When unpacking stock ensure everything is intact. If there are any breakages, dispose of them in a sharps box and handle carefully to avoid injury.

Stock must then be put away in the correct place following health and safety procedures. Liquids should be stored in plastic bottles to prevent breakage and large or heavy items should be stored at the bottom or on the lower shelves. Dangerous or hazardous chemicals should be stored in a locked metal cupboard away from heat and direct sunlight. Both containers and cupboard must be appropriately marked with a symbol denoting the hazard contained.

The most frequently used stock should be placed at eye level or slightly below. This will prevent unnecessary bending and stretching. New stock should be placed behind existing stock to ensure that it is used in strict rotation (use the FIFO principle – first in, first out – when using stock). Any stock reaching its sell-by date should be used immediately, sold at a reduced price or given away with a treatment to avoid wastage.

Check stock

Stock must be checked regularly. The higher the turnover, the more often it will require checking. As soon as the minimum number for any one product is reached, an order must be placed. Always allow sufficient time for products to be delivered. Knowing your supplier well will allow you to calculate how long it will take. In exceptional circumstances or for an additional fee suppliers will provide a next-day delivery. A computerised stock control system will be helpful with retail stock, particularly when it is linked to the point of sale.

Figure 38.6 *A therapist checks the stock*

Display stock

A large profit can be made on products, so care should be taken to display retail stock in the most eye-catching way to attract the attention of clients in the salon or passers-by. Displays should always be placed in a prominent position, as identified in Figure 38.7.

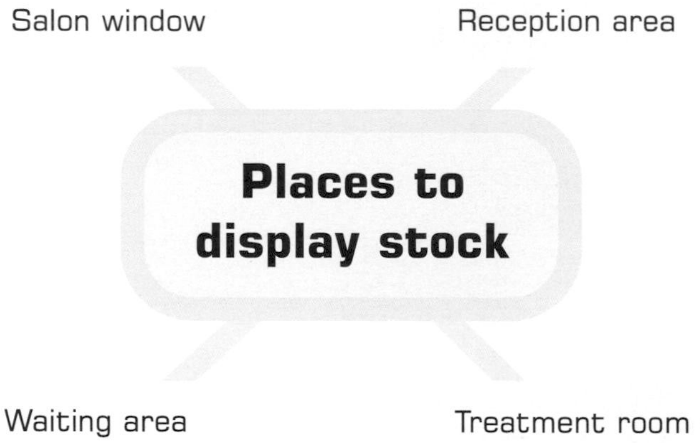

Salon window   Reception area

Places to display stock

Waiting area   Treatment room

Figure 38.7 *Where to display stock*

Whatever the position of the display, it is essential that it is well maintained, clean and colourful.

A salon at street level can use its shop window to promote the business by using posters, products or different props and materials to promote an image. The type of display will depend upon the amount of window space available and if it is open with the interior of the salon clearly visible or completely closed in. The disadvantage of a window display is that it will deteriorate when exposed to sunlight, the colours will begin to fade, liquids will evaporate and some products will change in consistency because of the increase in temperature. This problem may be overcome by using dummy products and empty boxes with posters and changing the display regularly. Some larger companies will provide display materials and equipment as well as practical advice, particularly when the business has a large account with them.

The reception and waiting area is an ideal place to display retail stock as the client starts and finishes a visit here. Sometimes clients or guests will be sitting in the reception area for a period of time, allowing the opportunity to browse. The attention of passers-by may also be attracted by goods displayed in reception when it can be viewed from outside. Stock may be displayed on freestanding units, on shelves or in glass-fronted cabinets. There may be other communal waiting areas such as a rest room or sitting area for clients between treatments, and these may also have interesting displays and cabinets.

Figure 38.8 *Products on display in a reception area*

It is often during the course of treatment that retail sales are made and having a display of goods in treatment rooms may encourage the process. Also, being able to give the product to the client to take out to the reception when paying the bill is more likely to ensure a sale than giving the client the opportunity to change his or her mind or forget when he or she has left the treatment room. The main disadvantage is that it will make stock control slightly more difficult and clients may forget to pay if the therapist does not accompany them to reception or inform the receptionist of the purchase.

Information and communication systems

Nowadays, no business can be truly competitive without the use of computers. They are fast becoming an essential part of any business, whatever the size. There is no doubt that a specialised computer software system can improve the efficiency of all business practice, from booking appointments to maintaining stock levels. This resource will help in the day-to-day running of a business, saving valuable time for the manager to use elsewhere and contributing to the financial effectiveness of the business. It may be expensive to install, but a business will soon recoup its investment due to the efficient working practices that result from its use.

A computer may be used to:

* keep accounts and financial records
* process payments
* store client records and data
* make appointments
* manage staff and payroll
* control stock
* contact clients
* advertise and promote the business.

Keeping accounts and financial records can be made easier by using a system to process wages, commission, daily purchase and sales accounts and VAT. Processing payment using a computerised till will help with the cashing up at the end of each day and will provide immediate information about the number of clients, daily turnover, product sales and retail sales.

Figure 38.9 *Therapists using a computer system*

Business management

Maintaining detailed records is useful for any organisation as it provides instant access to a bank of information and helps to monitor business activities on a daily/weekly/monthly/yearly basis, thus recognising potential problems and allowing management to correct them in order to maintain high standards.

The computer is an efficient method of keeping personnel records, organising staff rotas and wages, monitoring staff holidays and sickness, and also to record staff appraisals. It will also collect data on the amount and type of work that each employee is doing over a set period, identifying strengths and weaknesses, analysing the treatments that are being performed and if there are any which are being avoided. You can also find out who is the best at turning new clients into regular clients.

Stock control is simplified by using your computer. All new stock can be recorded and linked to the point of sale. Product sales are automatically deducted as they occur and the computer will indicate when stock is running low and re-ordering is required. Many companies include bar codes on their products, and when the client purchases the product the bar code is scanned and the computer registers the item taken from stock. Some systems will even generate a purchase order based on the minimum and maximum product requirements of the salon.

Email provides a quick and easy method of communication. It allows you to contact clients to confirm appointments, provide information, send special offers, newsletters and home care advice.

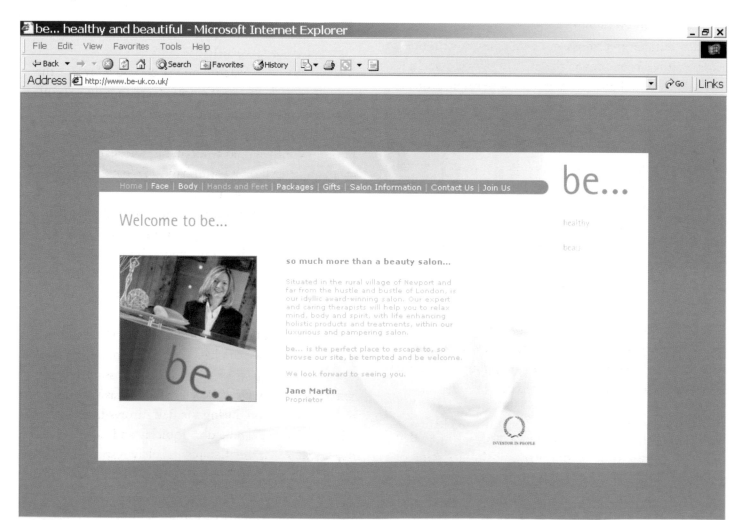

Figure 38.10 *A business website*

Products can be purchased via the Internet. This can increase retail sales considerably as it offers clients a convenient way to purchase products. This extra service will also enhance customer satisfaction. Advertising and promoting the business can now also be done via the Internet. Many businesses have their own website which allows them to communicate information about the treatments offered, display price lists and advertise special offers and promotional events. You will be able to establish a mailing list from the people who access your website and this will enable you to promote your business to a target audience at minimal cost.

For further information on maintaining salon records using a computer, see Chapter 1 pages 9–10.

Time

Inefficient methods of work and poor time management are often difficult to change, but with commitment this is possible. It has been proved that it only takes six weeks for new behaviour to become habit, therefore improvements can be seen and results achieved very quickly.

It is important to evaluate your personal time management and focus on the areas you can improve. This will help to reduce stress at work, improve your efficiency and allow you to enjoy your work more. No matter how busy you are, you must always have time for the client, so good time management is an essential to business success.

One of the simplest methods of time management is having a 'Things to do' list. This provides you with a daily schedule and should contain a list of jobs, appointments and tasks you hope to achieve that day. This is something that individual members of staff could use daily to help them utilise their time more effectively. It could be similar to a shopping list and each item can be ticked off as it is completed.

Organising your day

Make sure you have several changes of uniform so that you do not waste time before work, washing, drying or ironing clean clothing. Plan your route to work and avoid traffic and other problems that may delay you. Check your appointments the night before and make a mental note of any potential problems, Deal with these problems as soon as you arrive at work. Try and arrive early to allow you to prepare yourself for the busy day ahead, liaise with the reception coordinator and make any necessary phone calls to clients. Check your room, equipment and products and collect any leaflets, brochures and samples you may require for the day.

Organising your work space

Organising the room or area in which you work will help you to maximise your time as you will not spend time searching for items of importance because they are tucked away in a pile or have been moved somewhere else. Make sure all essential items are within easy reach and that your trolleys and work surfaces are well organised, with products and equipment placed in a logical order so that you can see at a glance where everything is. Product information should be kept in files and stored neatly in order, for quick reference.

Organising appointments

The appointment system you use should allow for the best use of each therapist's time. Certain points should be highlighted such as booking appointments in an orderly fashion throughout the day, filling earlier appointments first and re-booking cancellations as they occur – always have a list to hand of clients to ring who are waiting for an appointment.

Therapists will require training in dealing with clients who arrive late for appointments and still expect their treatments to be completed as booked. Company policy should be followed in such cases so the therapist knows that any decisions she makes are fully supported by the management.

Throughout the day, the receptionist should keep all therapists informed of changes to their appointments so that they can adapt their plans when necessary. Late cancellations may mean that a therapist has nothing to do for a certain period during the day. Always have a list of tasks or jobs that can be done quickly and easily. These may be ones that the therapist is solely responsible for or it may be a communal task that anyone can do given the time to do it. Consider charging clients a cancellation fee when they give less than 24 hours' notice – this may discourage them from doing so again.

The market

The market may be defined as a group of existing clients and potential new clients who will use your services and products. A very important function in any business is to increase turnover and profits and this may be achieved through promotion. Marketing is an ongoing process or business philosophy, which helps to provide what the client needs and wants and allows a business to be prepared to respond to change when necessary. The importance of marketing has increased over the past 50 years for several reasons:

* **Economic growth**. There has been an increase in the disposable income of many consumers and this has resulted in a growth in demand for products and services with a far wider range of choice.
* **Fashion**. There has been a considerable change in fashion, tastes and lifestyles of consumers. Many more women consider a visit to the beauty therapist a necessity rather than a luxury and men are becoming increasingly more aware of the benefits of the therapeutic treatments that are available and the need to have a well-groomed and healthy appearance.
* **Technology**. Firms are constantly inventing, designing and launching new or more advanced products on to the market, offering increased benefits to the consumer.
* **Competition**. The number of businesses competing for consumers' attention is increasing.

Marketing therefore is essential, particularly in a business which is so highly client orientated. It is necessary to:

* assess clients' needs and wants accurately
* monitor changes taking place in the market place
* anticipate future trends
* promote the business to maintain and improve its market position.

Offering treatments that appeal to existing clients will require you to assess their current requirements and anticipate future needs through market research This may be informal chatting to clients and asking them for feedback and suggestions, or listening to their requests and acting upon them. A more formal method is through a questionnaire that the client will complete, useful when you want to introduce a new treatment or service. Offering treatments or services that will encourage new clients may require you to invest in new products, employ therapists with particular skills or to retrain existing staff. You must then use promotion to bring them to the attention of the clients. Anticipating trends in the industry is often the key to a successful business and allows you to stay one step ahead of your competitor. Therapists are encouraged to attend trade shows and exhibitions and keep abreast of current trends. This is also important for their own continuing professional development.

Differentiation

When you are competing with other businesses you must be able to show how you are different from your competitors and make it clear which **segment**, or part, of the market you are appealing to (see Chapter 37 Setting up a business, page 418). To do this you will need to consider:

* employing therapists with excellent practical skills
* offering treatments that are not available elsewhere
* providing a high quality service
* providing additional services that will complement the business
* developing a particular philosophy or image.

Figure 39.1
Creating the right image is an important aspect of marketing

Promoting your business once established is necessary to ensure that you continue to provide what your existing clients want and need and to introduce treatments and products that will attract new clients and increase business.

Client categories

Clients (consumers, purchasers) all differ in terms of attitude, income and preferences. They all have different priorities and may be categorised according to their socio-economic group based on the head of each household's income:

A – chief executives of large companies, barristers, judges, etc.

B – head teachers, solicitors, accountants, doctors, etc.

C1 – skilled workers, supervisors, junior managers, teachers, etc.

C2 – skilled manual workers such as plumbers, electricians

D – semi skilled and unskilled manual workers such as road sweepers, refuse collectors, window cleaners

E – pensioners, casual workers and students.

Consumers may also be categorised using the 'family tree' method. This is where market segmentation is based on the stage in the consumer's life:

* young single
* young married
* full nest (children at home)
* empty nest (children left home)
* retired.

Each of these groups will have different amounts of disposable income and different priorities. Some may be restricted by their working hours, looking after children or have a lack of mobility whereas others may have plenty of free time and disposable income with no restrictions or responsibilities. They will all require different services, treatments and products and will therefore respond to different marketing methods.

The marketing mix

Marketing activities will include carrying out market research, creating the right image, advertising the business, selling and promotions. For a business to achieve its marketing objectives it must consider the **marketing mix**.

> To meet the needs of the consumer, the business must have the right **product** at the right **price**, make it available in the right **place** and inform consumers through **promotion**. These are the **4Ps** of the marketing mix.

Your products are the treatments you offer and the retail lines you have established. You will have set the price for treatments and retail products based on your overheads, the competition and the area in which you are working. The place will be either your own premises, within another organisation, working from home or a mobile service, covering a specified area. The final part of the marketing mix, promotion, is vitally important to help maintain the market share you already have and increase it further by attracting new business. Clients will buy the product which provides the greatest benefit to them. Therefore, when promoting the business, you will need to emphasise what the end result will be in having a particular treatment or buying a particular product.

You will need to manage your product mix as the business grows and develops, phasing out old products and introducing new products as you respond to the needs of your clients. It is also important to understand the life of a product and know when it has come to a profitable end. There is no point clinging on to old treatments or products if they are not popular, unprofitable or have been superseded by something more effective or attractive to the consumer.

Product life cycle

Trends in treatments and services have changed greatly in the health and beauty industry over the past ten years. Emphasis has changed often from one aspect to another, highlighting the life cycle of a product. For example, several years ago there was a boom in the use of sun beds and solaria to produce an all-year-round golden tan. Recent research has shown that exposure to any form of ultraviolet radiation is harmful to the skin in that it may increase the chance of skin cancer and cause premature ageing. These facts have been constantly reinforced through the media, as well as by the medical profession. The increased awareness of the general public to these dangers and their insistence on using different, safer methods to produce a tan has provided the opportunity for therapists to offer false tan treatments, which are becoming ever more sophisticated and natural looking. This service is now growing rapidly to satisfy the demand and the use of sun beds is declining.

There may be many other factors that will contribute to the growth or decline in a particular product or treatment, as shown in Table 39.1.

You must be aware of problems which may arise at each stage in the life cycle of a product and take the necessary action.

Table 39.1 *Factors influencing the growth or decline of a product*

Growth of a product	Decline of a product
It is fashionable	It is unfashionable
It is well promoted creating a demand	There is saturation in the market place
It is a high quality product	It has been proved ineffective
It improves the quality of life for the user	It does not live up to expectations
It promotes good health	It is too expensive
It has noticeable benefits	It is not environmentally friendly
It is environmentally friendly	
It fulfils a need	
It is therapeutic	

Stages of the product life cycle

1 **Introduction**. When introducing a new treatment the initial cost is high and sales are low, so steps must be taken to promote the product and recoup the cost quickly. Offering discount on courses of new treatments booked and paid for in advance will bring in capital and ease the financial burden. The manufacturer may allow payment in instalments over a period, but this may increase the overall cost of the product.

2 **Growth**. The treatment is well established and sales rise rapidly increasing profits. Capitalise on this by ensuring that there are sufficient numbers of staff to cope with the demand and opening hours are flexible to accommodate all clients.

3 **Maturity**. Sales will continue to rise, but competition in the market place may cause a reduction in price of the treatment resulting in a fall in profits.

4 **Saturation**. The competition is extensive, prices will fall and profits will be less. Consider changes or upgrading the current treatment.

5 **Decline**. Sales are poor and profits are low or non-existent. It is advisable to consider introducing a new treatment to replace the ailing one or to discontinue using it altogether.

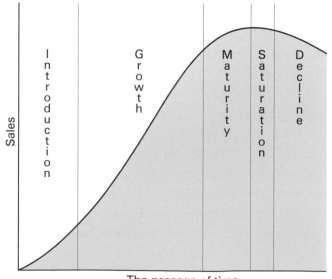

Figure 39.2 *The product life cycle*

Promotion

Promotion is a form of indirect advertising. It provides incentives to stimulate sales and is used:

* to draw the client's attention to a new business, treatment or product
* to stimulate sales
* to encourage bookings in off-peak times
* to increase turnover.

Types of promotion

* Introducing a new treatment at a special introductory price for a limited period.
* Booking a course of treatments at a discount.
* Providing a free gift with purchase.
* Including a discount voucher in a newspaper advertisement or article.
* Introduce a friend and receive a free treatment.
* Open evenings with demonstrations and refreshments.
* Birthday cards with treatment vouchers sent to existing clients.
* Special offer of the month.
* Give each new client a free treatment voucher after his or her first visit to the salon as a thank you to encourage the client to return.

Figure 39.3 *A promotional Christmas card*

The first promotion you are likely to have is the launch of the business and this can be an enjoyable social occasion for clients. Contact all the relevant people and send invitations to as many prospective clients as possible. Friends and relatives should also be invited as they are potential clients and they may know at least one other person who might be interested. If you provide refreshments and have a special opening offer, you will persuade more people to attend and, hopefully, establish some new clients. Make sure that all those people involved in the business are on hand to discuss any issues, provide information and book appointments.

Advertising the business

All businesses will benefit to some extent from advertising at some time. The aims of advertising are to inform potential clients about the nature and availability of treatments and products and to persuade clients to buy treatments and products. There are two main types of advertising:

* informative advertising
* persuasive advertising (see Figures 39.4 and 39.5).

Elements Beauty Salon

Manchester Road, Altrincham, Cheshire WA14 5SQ

Will be offering Laser Hair Removal
on
Thursday, Friday and Saturday 10.00–15.00
from
Monday 10 April 2004

Appointments now being taken
Tel: 202 4275

Figure 39.4 *Informative advertising*

Choosing advertising for your business

Advertising is successful when it achieves an increase in sales or in the number of clients. There are many types of advertising and it is important to select the best method for your business, so that the money spent is

Elements Beauty Salon

Manchester Road, Altrincham, Cheshire WA14 5SQ

Look ten years younger with our new anti-ageing facial using a combination of alpha hydroxy acids, essential oils and light therapy.

For one day only we are offering a free treatment to the first five people to present this advertisement at our reception.

Figure 39.5 *Persuasive advertising*

Figure 39.6 *A salon advertisement*

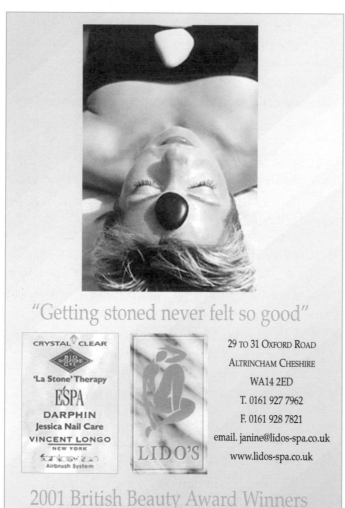

"Getting stoned never felt so good"

CRYSTAL CLEAR
'La Stone' Therapy
ESPA
DARPHIN
Jessica Nail Care
VINCENT LONGO
NEW YORK
fantasy tan
Airbrush System

29 TO 31 OXFORD ROAD
ALTRINCHAM CHESHIRE
WA14 2ED
T. 0161 927 7962
F. 0161 928 7821
email. janine@lidos-spa.co.uk
www.lidos-spa.co.uk

LIDO'S

2001 British Beauty Award Winners

used to the best advantage. The method you choose will depend upon the budget you have for advertising, the market you are aiming at and the likelihood that you will reach the target audience. Some options are:

* newspapers
* local radio
* magazines
* specialist brochures
* leaflets and posters
* mail shots
* word of mouth
* demonstrations
* directory
* website
* packaging and giveaways.

Newspapers

Local free papers are delivered to all households in a particular catchment area, so an advertisement or insert (printed leaflet, card or brochure) included will reach a large audience. Advertisements may be classified or display. Classified are grouped together under a particular heading consisting of text only and display are specially designed. Newspapers have the facility to design an advertisement for you, but this is more costly.

You can contribute an editorial (sometimes called an advertorial), a specialist feature or write an advice column to obtain free advertising and this will often ensure a prominent position in the newspaper. You may wish to highlight a new or innovative treatment or product, famous people visiting the salon, special anniversaries, winning special awards or providing sponsorship. National newspapers are not the right media to advertise a hair or beauty treatment package but would be ideal if you had a product to sell through mail order.

There are several points to consider when sending a suggestion for a story to a newspaper:

* Let the headline speak for itself – it should be factual and easily understood. The first paragraph should contain a summary of the story – sometimes if space is limited, this will be the only part that will be printed.

✱ Any claims you make should be backed up with facts and the least important facts placed near the end of the copy.

✱ Make the layout easy to read with short paragraphs highlighting specific points.

✱ The page layout should be double spaced to allow the editor room to make amendments and add printing instructions.

Local radio

Local radio is an expensive advertising medium but sometimes may be helpful in reaching a niche market. Take the opportunity of providing advisory services on phone-in programmes or take part in discussions when an expert is required. The exposure could prove to be an invaluable source of free advertising.

Magazines

Specialist magazines will allow you to reach your target audience. However, there will be many similar adverts, so yours will need to stand out from the others. An effective advertisement will follow the AIDA formula:

Attention – it must be well designed and attract the attention of the reader.

Interest – the text must be interesting and produce a reaction.

Desire – must be created in the reader by explaining the benefits.

Action – include an incentive or information to encourage the reader to act.

Specialist brochures

This particular advertising medium will reach its target audience. For example, a bridal brochure (produced by a hotel) detailing the services that it offers to couples planning a wedding will invite other related businesses to place advertisements in the brochure. The wedding make-up or pre-wedding package could receive an excellent response when advertised in this type of publication. Many brides who do not normally have beauty treatments will often do so on such a special occasion and this provides you with the potential opportunity of gaining new business on a permanent basis.

Leaflets and posters

Advertising leaflets can look like a second-rate form of advertising unless they are of a high quality. They can be used in several ways.

Figure 39.7 *Uses of advertising leaflets*

Posters can be placed prominently in the salon or in other businesses.

Mail shots

Start to record the names and addresses of any enquirers and clients who are interested and compile a mailing list of people to contact with information, special offers or new treatments. A regular newsletter for clients will keep them informed and is a gentle reminder if they have not attended for a while.

Word of mouth

Word of mouth is the most valuable form of advertising because it is free, and once you have established a reputation for quality, professionalism, excellent client care and the treatments you offer are competitively priced, clients will automatically recommend you to friends, relatives and colleagues.

Demonstrations

Demonstrations are an ideal way to bring a new concept or technique to the notice of the general public or to provide a means of raising money for charity, which will, in turn, provide your business with publicity. It is an interesting way to educate the public about beauty therapy, the many different treatments and new techniques available and their benefits. For a successful demonstration:

* Find out the type of audience and the general age group that will attend.
* Be sure of the numbers attending so that you can provide everybody with the necessary samples, advertising literature, price lists and obligatory goody bag.
* Have a basic format to follow and time the demonstration well – not too long or the audience may lose interest.
* Prepare a set of cards with key points to ensure everything of importance is covered.
* Use interesting anecdotes and case histories to add interest and reinforce the benefits of the treatments or products you are demonstrating.
* Know your subject well and prepare answers to questions that you think may arise.
* Involve the audience whenever possible, in particular encourage them to ask questions and use them as demonstration models.
* Use other members of staff, one to carry out any practical procedure, one to provide the commentary and answer questions and one to ensure everything runs smoothly.
* Use good judgement when choosing a model from the audience. For a make-up, choose someone who will enhance your products – an unmade-up face will show a greater difference after the application of make-up and time will not be wasted cleansing.
* Use your own model, if necessary, to ensure unknown factors do not interfere with the demonstration, for example a very sensitive skin or skin blemishes.

* Know the retail prices of treatments and products and the advantage they have over your competitors.
* Practise the demonstration in advance if it is your first or the particular technique being demonstrated is a new one.

Directory

Entering the name, address and telephone number in a directory such as Yellow Pages is a useful form of advertising. Many people who are looking for a service may automatically refer to a directory. It is important, therefore, when choosing a name for the business to consider choosing one which begins with one of the first letters in the alphabet so that your name is one of the first that they call. You may, however, be competing with many other similar businesses, so you must make sure that your advertisement stands out from the rest and emphasises the difference and value you offer.

The Internet

This is a valuable method of reaching your customers. If you provide an interesting and easy-to-use website, you may attract many new clients as more and more people are using the Internet as a research method. You can provide up-to-the minute information about treatments, costs and special offers. You may also have a newsletter that is changed regularly to maintain interest and have links to other useful websites.

Packaging and giveaways

Many salons now have their name and logo on bags and boxes which are used to hold retail goods. Giveaways are becoming increasingly more popular and they may include items such as diaries, calendars, pens, key rings, tissues and candles.

The business image

The image the business portrays will be an important part of marketing as it provides an instant picture to prospective clients. Image may be expressed in various ways, as shown in Figure 39.8.

The image varies depending on the market it is aimed at, the type of clientele it already has, fashion or even a reflection of the owner's personality or taste.

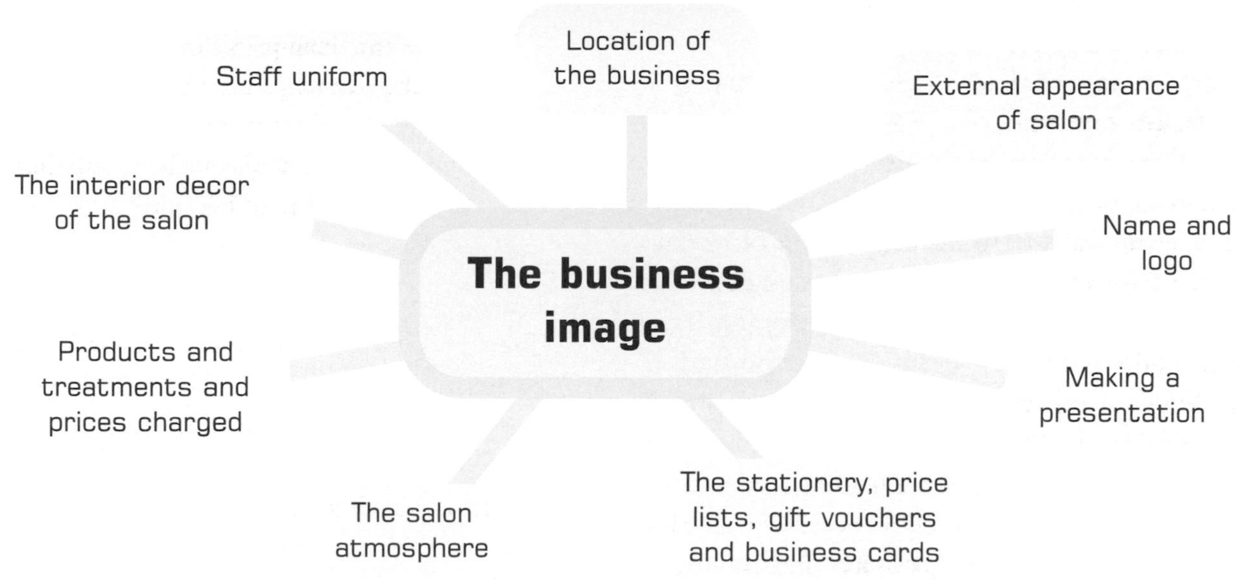

The interior decor of the salon

Staff uniform

Location of the business

External appearance of salon

The business image

Name and logo

Products and treatments and prices charged

Making a presentation

The salon atmosphere

The stationery, price lists, gift vouchers and business cards

Figure 39.8 *Establishing a business image*

Salons often choose an image which may be glamorous, high tech and ultra modern, minimalist, with an eastern influence or fantasy – it will depend on the vision of the salon owner. The image may also be influenced by the location, particularly if it is part of another business or practice.

Figure 39.9 *Luxurious image of Spa Illuminata in london*

Spas are often based on a particular theme such as spiritual, fitness or well-being or designed with many water features to reinforce the spa theme. The decor may often be designed in such a way that it reflects the types of treatment on offer. A specialised nail salon, for example, may have a nail bar so that all the clients are

situated together in one area, there is often lively music playing in the background and plenty of interaction between clients and therapists. A holistic therapy centre, on the other hand, may be a quiet oasis of calm with private treatment rooms, relaxing music playing quietly in the background and a water feature situated prominently in reception.

The business logo is a useful marketing tool as it is a visual message that identifies you to your clients. It is a trademark that is unique to you and can be a symbol, words or a picture and it is the first stage in creating a business image. It may then be used on all stationery, appointment cards, treatment lists, staff uniforms, gowns for clients and packaging.

The reception will provide the client with the first impression of the business once inside so it should be attractive, relaxing and inviting.

Figure 39.10 *A business logo*

The changing market

The male market

The need to look good applies as much to senior executives as it does to young people wanting to present the right image and fit in with the crowd. Nowadays, many men are trying beauty treatments to groom, polish and revitalise as well as slow down skin ageing. There is an increasing trend in the beauty industry towards salons and spas for men, specially designed treatment lists, particular days or evenings devoted to the male client, and most product manufacturers are producing lines specifically for men.

The hectic lifestyles and constant pressure mean an increasing number of men are suffering from the negative effects of stress and are therefore looking for the relaxing facial and body treatments to counteract these problems. The media are also promoting the well-groomed image, raising awareness and writing about celebrities who have manicures, anti-ageing facials, waxing, laser and IPL, false tan treatments and enjoy hot stone therapy.

To make sure that you capture a good slice of this male market you should do the following:

✳ Use advertising to reach the male market, e.g. in golf clubs, health clubs, in sports fixture brochures, men's magazines, male hairdressing salons and any other male-dominated environment.

✳ Make sure that the salon is male friendly. Create an image to appeal to men – a neutral decor, natural materials and a relaxing environment will all help to put them at ease, something which is unlikely to happen in a pink and feminine salon. Make sure that the salon furniture is big enough to accommodate even the largest male client. There are massage couches available that are wider and longer than average, and leather sofas in reception will provide a masculine edge. Supply motor, sport and lifestyle magazines for the men to read and make sure that male product displays are as prominent as the female displays.

✳ Make sure the products you sell are meeting men's needs, treating their specific skin problems and packaged with the right image.

✳ Devise a treatment menu and product list that you can give to the male client and your female clients to pass on to their partners, relatives and male friends. The treatments offered should be described in such a way that they do not sound feminine, e.g. hand grooming instead of manicure, an energising or revitalising massage or skin refining treatment instead of facial.

✳ Hold men-only promotional events and offer incentives to female clients when they introduce their partner to the salon or have a special event when fathers and sons can attend together.

Selling more

Figure 40.1 *Products for sale*

Selling retail products to clients is essential for business growth and should account for at least 40 per cent of turnover. There is a limit to the profit made on treatments carried out in the salon as there are set prices for each treatment to be performed in a particular time. You do, however, have a captive audience and every opportunity to sell clients products and materials for their benefit. A specialised facial may take an hour and a half and earn £45, but spend ten minutes selling a client a set of skin care products and earn £100! The potential for increasing sales of retail products is enormous. There are many things that may benefit your client and they may include:

* face care products to complement professional treatments and improve skin condition
* body care products to reinforce effects of professional treatments
* books relating to topics of interest such as self-help, aromatherapy, diet and nutrition, etc.
* music CDs and cassettes
* candles
* essential oils and burners
* gifts
* herbal teas.

Methods of increasing sales

To help in selling retail products, all staff should be trained in sales techniques and encouraged to sell products to complement the range used during beauty treatments. Commission should be given to all therapists on their sales to encourage them to sell more and they should be encouraged to use the products they are selling so that they will sell the products from personal experience.

All members of staff should receive the relevant training from the manufacturers or distributors of all products sold as they have a thorough knowledge of their particular ranges and their unique selling points. Being able to provide up-to-date, accurate information and explaining the features and benefits of products will inspire confidence in the client. The features describe the product and the benefits explain to the client what effects the features will achieve. Table 40.1 gives an example of the features and benefits of a special foot cream used as a moisturiser and exfoliant.

Table 40.1 *Features and benefits of a special foot cream*

Features	Benefits
A rich cream	Moisturises and softens dry flaking skin, helps to reduce hard skin on the feet
Contains lavender essential oil	Soothing and antiseptic, beneficial for treating aches and pains, eczema and athlete's foot and has a lovely fragrance
Contains glycolic acid, a naturally occurring fruit acid	Gently exfoliates, preventing a build up of hard skin, corns and calluses
Has a pump dispenser	Easy to use, economical as it prevents waste
Comes in three sizes	Choice of size and price – small size ideal for carrying in a handbag, the large sizes are more economical

Most companies provide up-to-date information through newsletters or offer a telephone helpline which salons may call for assistance. Ensure that all the staff have a good technical knowledge of all treatments so

451

that they may sell with confidence. Make sure that all the selling aids therapists need such as testers, free samples and product leaflets are readily available When employing new staff, sales experience could be an important point to include in the job specification.

Make sure the products you are selling are in stock to avoid disappointing the client. Record all sales on the client's record card as this will be helpful to other therapists when they are treating that client and it will allow you to contact the right people when there are special offers that they may be interested in.

Place an attractive display of retail products in the salon window to catch the attention of the passer-by. This could also create new business. When a prospective new client comes in to buy something on offer this will give you the opportunity to sell beauty treatments. The reception area is an ideal place for a retail display as the clients can browse when entering or leaving the salon or if they are waiting for treatment. Most companies provide display stands, which show products to their best advantage. When making your own displays they will need to be changed regularly to maintain client interest and also to change with the season. Each working area could have a small display of relevant products, for example skin care in a facial treatment room, aromatherapy oils in a body treatment room and sun care products in a sun bed room.

If the reception is left unattended, it would be advisable to store retail products in a glass-front cabinet where the goods can be on permanent display but which can be locked when unattended. Using a cabinet also ensures that the goods remain in good condition and do not become dusty and dirty. When products are displayed on open shelves or unattended it is a good idea to use dummy products which will be provided by some companies. This cuts down on the risk of theft as the actual products could be stored in a locked cupboard.

Leaflets and information booklets should be available for clients to read, particularly when you are selling products which require advice on their use. Give free samples to clients if the company provides them. If they are available, it is a good idea to allow the client to try the product before buying. This will be particularly

Figure 40.2 *A product display should attract the clients' attention*

important if the product is very expensive or the client suspects a reaction to the product. Some companies provide 'trial size' products at a greatly reduced price for the client to buy.

Use positive body language, be helpful and smile when making a sale, but do not stare directly at the clients and intimidate them into a sale. Do not rush the sale or be too persistent in your approach as this can also be very intimidating. Concentrate solely on the client you are selling to, answering any questions and asking your own. Open questions should be used (see Chapter 2 Client Consultation, page 15). These are questions which may not be answered with a yes or no; they should include words such as why, how, when, what and which, to obtain information which may help to make the sale. Involve the clients by allowing them to smell, feel, touch and test the products.

Figure 40.3 *Making a sale. A therapist advising a client about a skin care product*

It may be worth investing money in advertising or changing the advertising methods you already use. Other ideas include selling gift vouchers for clients to give as presents as this will bring in new business as well as providing revenue and promoting specific treatments or products at the appropriate time of the year:

* The month leading up to Christmas is an ideal time for promoting gift sets of skin-care products and make-up.
* In the summer months you can promote the sun protection products, false tans and treatments such as waxing, eyelash tinting, pedicures and figure correction.
* When you know that business will be quiet, have special offers on treatments, a free gift with each booking or a reduction on the price of a treatment if the client brings along a friend at the time specified.

It is important to be professional at all times, listen to clients and ensure that you do not miss an opportunity to sell a product, in particular when they are telling you about a problem they may have, sympathise with them and then assure them that you have just the product for them.

You must, however, be honest and sell clients something that will be effective. Once you have built a good client-therapist relationship, the client will always ask for your advice. You should also introduce clients to products you know will benefit them even when they have not asked. They will be relying on your expert opinion. Try using the link selling technique. When the client asks for a product always link it to another product which complements the one asked for, for example a toning lotion with a cleanser or a quick-dry top coat nail polish with an enamel.

Closing the sale

This is when you feel that the time has come to complete the transaction and the client in your opinion is convinced that he or she wants one or more of the products which are on offer. There are several ways to close a sale:

* **The alternative close**. This is when you ask clients questions such as 'Would you like the large or small size?' or 'Would you like the red or pink?'. Clients will then make a decision.
* **The professional recommendation**. This is when you use your professional judgement to advise clients, so you would say, 'I would strongly recommend that you use the primer for your brittle nails to give them flexibility and stop them from breaking'. This is a most effective method as a regular client with whom you have a good relationship would not hesitate to buy what you recommend.
* **The 'yes' technique**. This is when you ask clients a series of questions to which they will answer 'yes', so the final question completing the sale will be answered with a 'yes'.
* **The elimination technique**. Many clients like to feel in control of the sale, so you must allow them to eliminate a number of products you are offering but make sure that you are left with an alternative.

The key to successful selling is to be honest with clients and ensure that the products you are selling to them are appropriate, will be effective in their use and value for money.

Case study: recognising buying signals

Mrs Simpson arrives late and flustered for her facial appointment. Her young son is ill and she thought she would have to cancel the appointment until a neighbour offered to look after him. There was an accident on the motorway that held her up and then she had trouble finding a parking space. In her rush, she snagged her last pair of designer body sculpting tights on a broken finger nail.

On entering the treatment room she notices a display of your new range of anti-ageing skin care products and she stops to browse. You hurry her along politely and ask her to undress. She gives you her handbag to put away safely and you notice a large paper wallet with the words 'Elegant Resorts' emblazoned across the front, protruding from the open bag.

As soon as you begin treatment, Mrs Simpson brings you up to date with the details of her busy life, her current problems and the latest news of her children. As the newly elected chairperson of a local charity, she is wondering what gift to buy to present to the retiring chairperson at a meeting later in the day. Her daughter has recently become engaged and Mrs Simpson is hosting a dinner party for the future-in-laws, whom she has never met but wishes to impress. Her best friend is having liposuction and Mrs Simpson asks your opinion about the cellulite she has on her hips and stomach and if you feel she also needs to consider cosmetic surgery.

By the time you have completed the facial massage, she informs you that she is feeling very relaxed and comments on the wonderful smell of the essential oils you have used and the soothing music that has been playing in the background. Once you have applied her face mask, you review and complete the latest details of her treatment on the record card. You take a relaxed and revitalised Mrs Simpson to the reception area to process payment and book future appointments with the receptionist who is busy designing a new window display, to include a new range of sun protection products, designer stockings and gifts.

Buying signals

* Client arrives flustered – suggest booking relaxing body massage, aromatherapy or heat treatments.
* She has laddered her tights – suggest she buys a pair of designer stockings from your selection.
* She has a broken finger nail – suggest a nail repair, manicure or false nails.
* She shows an interest in the anti-ageing products – ask if she would like her facial using the new products, give her samples and suggest the correct home care.
* Client is going on holiday – suggest buying sun care products, waxing treatments, eyelash tinting or a false tan treatment before she goes away.
* She needs a gift for the retiring chairperson – suggest she buys a gift voucher, the chairperson will then be able to buy a gift of her choice and you will have a potential new client.
* Dinner party for in-laws – suggest a make-up and manicure on the day; therapist could make a home visit as she will be busy preparing for the party.
* Does she need liposuction? Suggest anti-cellulite treatments and home care products to buy.
* She likes the oils you have used and the music – offer the oils to buy for use in a burner or in her bath and a copy of the CD.

As a salon owner or therapist, you will need to be aware of the clients' rights regarding the services and products they buy from you. The consumer (client) is any person who buys goods and services for money. Consumers are well protected by law and voluntary associations of traders and manufacturers. These bodies include:

* the Consumers Association – a non-profit making organisation that publishes *Which?* magazine and runs a personal advice service
* the Department of Trade and Industry (DTI)
* the local Trading Standards Department of your local authority – administers the legislation involving criminal offences in the consumer field
* the National Association of Citizens Advice Bureaux – a voluntary organisation providing impartial, confidential advice on almost any problem.

(For details of these organisations, see the Glossary of professional associations and organisations at the end of this book.)

Legislation

The greatest protection for consumers is provided by legislation which gives them statutory rights.

The Sale of Goods Act (1979) (amended by the Sale of Goods Act (1994)

The main points of the Act are as follows:

* **The goods bought must be of satisfactory quality** and free from fault, so if you buy a new wax machine, for example, and discover that the heater is dented and badly scratched, you would be entitled to a replacement.
* **The goods must be fit for the purpose**. For example, the wax machine is thermostatically controlled, but the first time it is used, it overheats and burns the wax when set at a low temperature. In this case, you would be entitled to a full refund as the machine was not fit for the purpose.
* **The goods must correspond with the description**, which may be verbal, in a picture, in words, on the packaging, in an advert or on a sign.

If, for example, the model of wax machine delivered by the suppliers was not the model agreed upon, the goods were not as described, then you would be entitled to a refund.

Faulty goods should be returned immediately if one of the above conditions has been broken. If the supplier thinks the manufacturer is to blame, then the supplier must claim for them.

This Act only applies to a sale between a business and the public and does not apply to sales made through classified advertisements or private transactions.

The Trade Descriptions Act (1968)

This Act provides protection for the consumer who has been misled or given inaccurate descriptions of goods or services offered. False descriptions given by word of mouth, written contract, advertisement or labelling are all covered.

The Consumer Safety Act (1978)

This Act lays down legal safety standards to minimise risks to the consumer from potentially harmful or dangerous products.

Consumer Protection Act (1987)

This Act implements European Union (EU) directives by providing a safeguard from products used or sold that are not safe.

The Supply of Goods and Services Act (1982)

This Act was introduced to improve the rights of the consumer in relation to poor service or workmanship. It was intended to make up for the shortcomings of the Sale of Goods Act (1979), which applied only to the transfer of goods to the buyer from the seller and not to a situation where goods were being provided as part of a service. The conditions are the same in that goods must be of merchantable quality, fit for purpose and fit the description, but it applies to:

* contracts for work and materials
* free gifts – applicable to many health and beauty establishments
* part exchange – a method used to update equipment

* contracts for hire of goods – many companies provide equipment in this way for use by the therapist.

The Act also requires the person providing a service to:

* act with reasonable care and skill
* work within a reasonable time
* charge a reasonable price.

The Prices Act (1974)

Prices must be displayed in such a way that they do not give a false impression.

The Resale Prices Act (1976)

Manufacturers are not allowed to enforce a price at which their goods must be sold. Many companies have a recommended retail price which they suggest a supplier should use.

The Consumer Credit Act (1974)

This Act regulates consumer credit and consumer hire agreement for amounts up to £25 000. It provides certain safeguards to consumers who purchase goods and services on credit.

Cosmetic Products (Safety) Regulations (1996)

The EU has agreed to the use of a common system for the ingredient labelling of cosmetic products. One of the many benefits of the full ingredient labelling system is that consumers with an allergy to a particular chemical can examine the ingredient list on the product to establish whether or not the formulation contains the material causing the allergy.

These regulations require all cosmetics to be marked with:

* a list of ingredients
* the name and address of manufacturer or supplier
* date of minimum durability
* warning statements
* precautionary information
* batch number or lot code
* product function, when appropriate.

Additionally:

* the declared quantity of contents is required under the Weights and Measures Act (1985) and related legislation (advice on weights and measures can be obtained from local Trading Standards Officers)
* all lettering must be visible, indelible and easily legible
* warning statements, precautionary information and best-before date and product function must be in English.

For the purpose of the regulations, the definition of cosmetics sets out six functions for substances or preparations which may be cosmetic products:

* to clean
* to perfume
* to change the appearance
* to protect
* to keep in good condition
* to correct body odours.

The field of application of cosmetics is shown in Figure 41.1.

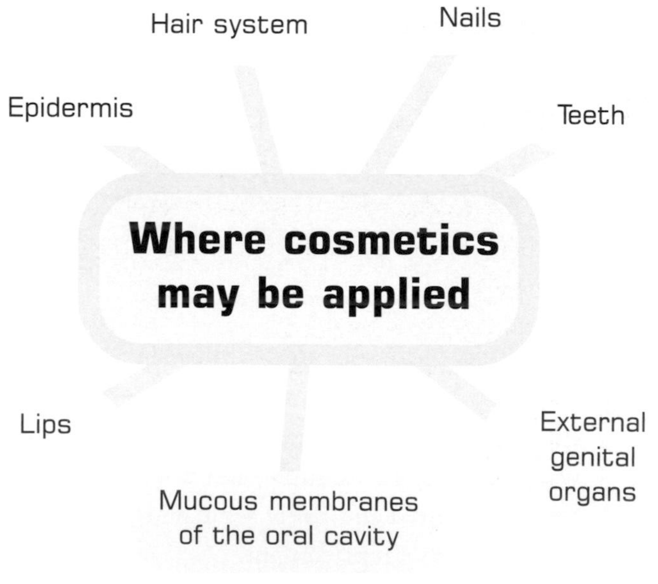

Hair system   Nails

Epidermis   Teeth

Where cosmetics may be applied

Lips   External genital organs

Mucous membranes of the oral cavity

Figure 41.1 *The field of application of cosmetics*

British Standards Institution

The British Standards Institution (BSI) is an independent body which establishes voluntary standards of quality and reliability. Its now famous Kitemark indicates that goods conform to the high standards set by the institution. Its main objectives are:

* the promotion of health and safety
* the protection of the environment
* the establishment of quality standards.

It provides specifications on such things as:

* strength
* safety
* quality
* ingredients.

Figure 41.2 *The BSI Kitemark*

Manufacturers may submit products voluntarily for testing. If they pass, they will carry a Kitemark which provides the consumer with a guarantee that they are at least of reasonable quality.

Returned goods

Any business which provides retail products will, on occasion, have to deal with a customer returning goods that have been found to be unsuitable. This could be for several reasons:

* The product is damaged.
* The product does not work.
* The colour was wrong.
* The product was inappropriate.

* The stock was out of date.
* An incorrect product was originally given.

Whatever the reason, the therapist must be courteous as more often than not the complaint will be genuine. Even if it is not, the situation will be resolved much more quickly and effectively if the therapist adopts a professional and concerned attitude.

It is important to follow rules laid down by the management when dealing with returned goods or complaints. Listen to what the client has to say, inspect the goods, ask the client relevant questions and decide on a course of action. When the complaint is, in your opinion, genuine, either exchange the goods or offer an alternative. When the required goods are not in stock, provide the client with a credit note, offer a refund or order a replacement which will be given to the client as soon as it becomes available.

When in doubt about the validity of the complaint, the best course of action is to refer the problem to your immediate superior, supervisor or manager.

Always keep a record of returned goods and refunds given for stock control and accounting purposes.

Contact the suppliers or manufacturers of defective goods, which have been returned to you and then follow their set procedure for customer complaint. There are occasions when you may feel that the returned goods are defective through no fault of your own or your supplier. It may be in the best interest of the business to accept the returned goods and lose a small amount of money rather than lose regular income and the goodwill of a client. This is a decision which must be made by the management and is often a company policy.

Index of essential oils with botanical names

Essential oil	Botanical name	Essential oil	Botanical name
Angelica	Angelica archangelica	Mimosa	Acacia dealbata
Basil	Ocimum basilium	Myrrh	Commiphora myrrha
Bergamot	Citrus bergamia	Neroli	Citrus aurantium
Birch	Betula alba	Niaouli	Melaleuca viridiflora
Black pepper	Piper nigrum	Orange	Citrus sinesis
Cajeput	Melaleuca leucodendron	Patchouli	Pogostemom cablin
Calendula (marigold)	Calendula officinalis	Peppermint	Mentha piperita
Camphor	Cinnamomum camphora	Petitgrain	Citrus aurantium
Cedar wood atlas	Cedrus atlantica	Pine	Pinus sylvestris
Chamomile (Roman)	Anthemis nobilis	Rose	Rosa damascena *and* centifolia
Cypress	Cypressa sempervirens		
Eucalyptus	Eucalyptus globulus	Rosemary	Rosmarinus officinalis
Fennel	Foeniculum vulgare	Rosewood	Aniba rosadora
Frankincense	Boswellia thurifera	Sage	Salvia officinalis
Geranium	Pelargonium graveolens	Sage (clary)	Salvia sclarea
Ginger	Zingiber officinale	Sandalwood	Santalum album
Hyssop	Hyssopus officinalis	Spruce	Tsuga canadensis
Jasmine	Jasminum officinale	Tarragon	Artemisia dracunculus
Juniper	Juniperus communis	Tea tree	Melaleuca alternifolia
Laurel	Laurus nobilis	Thyme	Thymus vulgaris
Lavender	Lavendula augustifolia *or* officinalis	Valerian	Valeriana fauriei
		Vetiver	Vetivera zizanoides
Lemon	Citrus limonum	Violet	Viola odorata
Lemongrass	Cymbopogon citratus	Yarrow	Achillea millefolium
Lime	Citrus limetta	Ylang ylang	Cananga odorata
Mandarin	Citrus reticulata		
Marjoram	Origanum marjorana		

Glossary of professional associations and organisations

Professional associations

Association of Nail Technicians, Alexander House, Forehill, Ely, Cambridgeshire CB7 4AF
Tel. 01353 665577

British Association of Beauty Therapy and Cosmetology, BABTAC House, 70 Eastgate Street, Gloucester GL1 1QN
Tel: 01452 421114; www.babtac.com

British Association of Electrolysis, 40 Parkfield Road, Ickenham, Middlesex UB10 8LW
Tel. 0870 1280477, Helpline 01474 325574; www.electrolysis-bae-ltd.co.uk

British Association of Skin Camouflage, c/o Resources for Business, South Park Road, Macclesfield SK11 6FP
Tel: 01625 267880; www.skin-camouflage.net

British Massage Therapy Council, 7 Rymers Lane, Oxon OX4 3JU
Tel: 01865 774123; www.bmtc.co.uk

Federation of Holistic Therapists, 3rd Floor, Eastleigh House, Upper Market Street, Eastleigh, Hampshire SO50 9FD
Tel: 023 8048 8900; www.fht.org.uk

Floatation Tank Association, 7a Clapham Common Southside, London SW4 7AA
Tel: 020 7627 4962; www.floatationtankassociation.net
Provides full training in floatation tank therapy including a client care, equipment care, marketing and day-to-day running of a floatation tank centre

Guild of Professional Beauty Therapists, Guild House, 320 Burton Road, Derby DE23 6AF
Tel: 0870 000 4242; www.beauty-guild.com

Guild Press, (the trade publication of the Guild)
Tel: 0870 000 4242; www.beautyserve.net

Hair and Beauty Industry Authority (HABIA), Fraser House, Nether Hall Road, Doncaster, South Yorkshire DN1 2PII
Tel: 01302 380000; www.habia.org.uk

Institute of Electrolysis, PO Box 5187, Milton Keynes MK4 2ZF
Tel: 01908 521511; www.electrolysis.co.uk

International Federation of Aromatherapists, 182 Chiswick High Road, London W4 1PP
Tel: 020 8742 2605; www.ifparoma.org

International Nail Association, Guild House, 320 Burton Road, Derby DE23 6AF
Tel: 0870 000 4242

Independent Professional Therapists International, PO Box 106, Retford, Nottinghamshire DN22 7WN
Tel: 01777 700383; www.iptiuk.com

Institute of Indian Head Massage, PO Box 1, Windsor, Berkshire SL4 4UZ
Tel: 01753 831 841; www.indianheadmassage.org

Association of Professional Aestheticians of Australia (APAA), PO Box 96, Robina, Queensland 4226, Australia
Tel: +07 5575 9364; www.apaa.com.au

South African Association of Health and Skin Care Professionals (SAAHSP),
www.cosmeticweb.co.za; www.saahsp.co.uk

Awarding bodies

City and Guilds of London Institute (CGLI), 1 Giltspur Street, London EC1A 9DD
Tel: 020 7294 2800; www.city-and-guilds.co.uk

BTEC, Edexcel, Stewart House, 32 Russell Square, London WC1B 5DN
Tel: 0870 240 9800; www.edexcel.org.uk

Confederation of International Beauty Therapy and Cosmetology (CIBTAC), 70 Eastgate Street, Gloucester GL1 1QN
Tel: 01452 421114; www.cibtac.com

International Therapy Examination Council (ITEC), 4 Heathfield Terrace, Chiswick, London W4 4JE
Tel: 020 8994 4141; www.itecworld.co.uk

Vocational Training Charitable Trust (VTCT), Unit11, Brickfield Trading Estate, Brickfield Lane, Chandlers Ford, Dorset SO53 4DR
www.vtct.org.uk

Australia Council for Private Education and Training (ACPET), Box Q1076, QVB PO, New South Wales 1230, Australia
Tel: +61 29299 4555; www.acpet.edu.au

Comité International d'Esthétique et de Cosmétologie (CIDESCO), Secretariat, Witikonerstrasse 365, 8053 Zurich, Switzerland
Tel: +41 1380 0075; www.cidesco.com

Vocational Education and Training Accreditation Board (VETAB), Level 14, 1 Oxford Street, Darlinghurst, New South Wales 2010, Australia
Tel: +02 9244 5335; www.vetab.nsw.gov.au

Business organisations

Association of British Insurers, 51 Gresham Street, London EC2V 7HQ
Tel: 020 7600 3333; www.abi.org.uk
Contact the association for a free booklet 'Insurance advice for small businesses'

ACAS, Brandon House, 180 Borough High Street, London SE1 1LW
Tel: 020 7210 3680; www.acas.co.uk

Business Link
To contact your local business link, Tel: 0845 600 9006 or visit www.businesslink.gov.uk

Centre for Accessible Environments, Nutmeg House, 60 Gainsford Street, London SE1 2NY
Tel: 020 7357 8182; www.cae.org.uk
Contact the centre for an access audit, a checklist for appraising the accessibility of your premises for people with disabilities

Consumers' Association, 2 Marylebone Road, London NW1 4DF
www.which.net – the Consumers' Association website
www.which.co.uk – the *Which?* magazine website

Data Protection Commissioner, Wycliffe House, Water Lane, Wilmslow, Cheshire SK9 5AF
Tel: 01625 545 745; www.dataprotection.gov.uk

Department of Trade and Industry (DTI), 1 Victoria Street, London SW1H OET
Tel: 020 7215 6740; www.dti.gov.uk
'A guide to help for small businesses' may be ordered from the DTI Publications orderline 0870 150 2500

Health & Safety Executive (HSE), HSE Information Centre, Broad Lane, Sheffield S3 7HQ
Tel: 08701 545500; www.hse.gov.uk
Contact the HSE for a free leaflet 'Basic advice on first aid at work' (IND(G)215L 1997, published by HSE Books)

The **Incident Contact Centre (ICC)** holds records on all incidents currently reportable under RIDDOR (see Chapter 4 Health and safety):
ICC, Caerphilly Business Park, Caerphilly CF83 3GG
Tel: 0845 3009923; Fax: 0845 3009924;
www.riddor.gov.uk

National Association of Citizens Advice Bureaux, Myddelton House, 115–123 Pentonville Road, London N1 9LZ
Tel: 020 7833 2181; www.carestandards.org.uk
A voluntary organisation providing impartial, confidential advice on almost any problem

National Care Standards Commission (NCSC) (England only), St Nicholas Building, St Nicholas Street, Newcastle-upon-Tyne NE1 1NB
Tel: 0191 233 3600; www.carestandards.org.uk;
In **Scotland**, contact the **Scottish Commision for the Regulation of Care** www.carecommission.com
In **Wales**, contact the **Care Standards Inspectorate for Wales**
www.wales.gov.uk/subisocialpolicycarestandards/index. htm/sponsorship;
You must apply for registration with the relevant body if your business offers Class 4 laser treatment and IPL (intensive pulsed light) for non-invasive cosmetic surgery administered by non-medically qualified staff

The Prince's Trust, Head Office, 18 Park Square East, London NW1 4LH
Tel: 0800 842 842 (this will put you through to the Prince's Trust office in your area);
www.princes-trust.org.uk
Helps young people aged 18–30 to set up businesses

Trading Standards Central

For a local office, visit www.tradingstandards.gov.uk and type in your post code

Phonographic Performance Ltd, 1 Upper James Street, London W1F 9DE

Tel: 020 7534 1000; www.ppluck.com

Other useful information

* Refer to a directory such as *Professional Beauty* for a comprehensive list of suppliers: www.professionalbeauty.co.uk

* For information on naming a limited company, visit www.companies-house.gov.uk

* When looking for investors in your business a possibility might be National Business Angels Network, 3rd Floor, 40/42 Cannon Street, London EC4N 6JJ: Tel. 020 7329 2929; www.nationalbusangels.co.uk

* For more information on the Disability Discrimination Act 1995, contact the Department for Education and Employment for a series of free booklets, 'Bringing the DDA to life for small shops', the first of which is a hairdressing salon. Tel: 0845 762 2633; www.disability.gov.uk. You can also contact the Disability Rights Commission for advice: www.drc-gb-org

* For advice on fire safety, visit www.firesafe.org.uk

* For cruise liner work, Tel. 020 8909 5074; www.steinerleisure.com

* For a national recruitment agency specialising in placing beauty therapists in a retail environment working for prestigious cosmetic and perfume houses, contact Retail Solutions Recruitment Ltd, 34/35 Eastcastle Street, London W1 8DW, Tel. 020 7436 8484; www.rsr-solutions.co.uk

* For information on gender dysphoria, visit www.beaumontsociety.org.uk (Beaumont Trust) and www.gender.org.uk/gendys (Gendys Network) (see Chapter 22 Electrical epilation)

Useful websites

www.susan-cressy.com

www.elemis.com

www.pevonia.com

www.findershealth.com

Index